Freedom

Ian Carter is Associate Professor of Political Philosophy at the University of Pavia, Italy. He is the author of *A Measure of Freedom* (1999) and *La libertà eguale* (2005), and the editor, with Mario Ricciardi, of *Freedom, Power and Political Morality* (2001). He is also the author of the entry on "Positive and Negative Liberty" in the *Stanford Encyclopedia of Philosophy*.

Matthew H. Kramer is Professor of Legal and Political Philosophy at Cambridge University; Fellow of Churchill College, Cambridge; and Director of the Cambridge Forum for Legal and Political Philosophy. The two most recent of his ten books are *The Quality of Freedom* (2003) and *Where Law and Morality Meet* (2004).

Hillel Steiner is Professor of Political Philosophy at the University of Manchester. Among his many books and articles are *An Essay on Rights* (Blackwell, 1994) and, with Matthew H. Kramer and N. E. Simmonds, *A Debate over Rights* (1998). A Fellow of the British Academy, he is co-editor with Peter Vallentyne of a two-volume anthology on left-libertarianism (2000).

Freedom

A Philosophical Anthology

Edited by
Ian Carter, Matthew H. Kramer, and
Hillel Steiner

Blackwell
Publishing

Editorial material and organization © 2007 by Blackwell Publishing Ltd

BLACKWELL PUBLISHING
350 Main Street, Malden, MA 02148-5020, USA
9600 Garsington Road, Oxford OX4 2DQ, UK
550 Swanston Street, Carlton, Victoria 3053, Australia

The right of Ian Carter, Matthew H. Kramer, and Hillel Steiner to be identified as the Authors
of the Editorial Material in this Work has been asserted in accordance with the UK Copyright,
Designs, and Patents Act 1988.

First published 2007 by Blackwell Publishing Ltd

1 2007

Library of Congress Cataloging-in-Publication Data

Freedom : a philosophical anthology / edited by Ian Carter,
Matthew H. Kramer, and Hillel Steiner.
    p. cm.
  Includes bibliographical references and index.
  ISBN-13: 978-1-4051-4503-9 (hardback : alk. paper)
  ISBN-10: 1-4051-4503-X (hardback : alk. paper)
  ISBN-13: 978-1-4051-4504-6 (pbk. : alk. paper)
  ISBN-10: 1-4051-4504-8 (pbk. : alk. paper)
  1. Liberty. I. Carter, Ian, 1964– II. Kramer, Matthew H., 1959–
III. Steiner, Hillel.

  B105.L45F72 2006
  320.01′1—dc22

                                                2006009503

A catalogue record for this title is available from the British Library.

Set in 10.5 on 13 pt Galliard
by SNP Best-set Typesetter Ltd, Hong Kong
Printed and bound in Singapore
by COS Printers Pte Ltd

The publisher's policy is to use permanent paper from mills that operate a sustainable forestry
policy, and which has been manufactured from pulp processed using acid-free and elementary
chlorine-free practices. Furthermore, the publisher ensures that the text paper and cover board
used have met acceptable environmental accreditation standards.

For further information on
Blackwell Publishing, visit our website:
www.blackwellpublishing.com

Contents

You're a philosophy student. Come on now.

Contents

Preface

This anthology offers a wide range of philosophical selections on social and political freedom (including economic freedom). It does not deal, except in passing, with metaphysical issues of free will and determinism. All the same, because of the expansiveness of the topics that it does cover, we have had to make many difficult choices. Although we have assembled extracts from numerous works, and although we have striven to present a diversity of philosophical points of view on each topic, we have inevitably had to omit a host of important writings from our collection. We trust that the omissions are offset by the breadth and quality of the excerpts that have been included.

We have designed this anthology especially for use in undergraduate and postgraduate courses, but it should also serve as a handy point of departure for anyone engaging in research on social and political freedom. Given that the philosophical literature on freedom is sprawlingly huge, a broad guide to that literature should be useful for advanced researchers as well as for novices. The extracts themselves are supplemented by a Further Reading list at the end of the introduction to each section of the anthology, and the list of Additional Writings at the close of the volume provides still further citations. (Only works that are neither excerpted in any of the sections nor cited in any of the Further Reading lists are included in the list of Additional Writings.)

We offer a measured apology, though only a measured apology, for the brevity of some of the extracts. Our scholarly instincts lead us to be wary of isolating passages from the larger works in which they appear, but our pedagogical experience impels us to recognize that students best grasp the issues in debates over freedom if their attention is squarely directed to germane lines of argument. Moreover, in most cases – such as those of Jeremy Bentham and James Harrington – our especially short extracts are the only portions of the respective texts that directly bear on the topics under which they have been subsumed. Hence, the inclusion of any further passages from those texts would have unhelpfully blurred the thematic foci of the sections that cover the afore-mentioned topics. (While the ease of excerpting is what chiefly accounts for the brevity of some selections, the difficulty of excerpting is what chiefly accounts for the relative lengthiness of one or two of the other selections. For instance, we could not find any satisfactory way to abridge the first selection from the work of J. P. Day.)

In any event, we have not been aiming to provide a detailed compilation of the ideas of any single author. Our objective, rather, has been to set each author within the context of some anfractuous controversies concerning the nature of freedom or the nature of a closely related property such as auto-nomy. For that purpose, the presentation of many different viewpoints – at some expense to the depth of the presentation of any particular viewpoint – has been the optimal way of proceeding. In an anthology that is not unman-ageably huge, we cannot convey to students the complexity and richness of debates over freedom unless we quite sharply limit the voluminousness of our extract(s) from each contributor to those debates.

Within some of the selections, we have silently deleted or shortened many of the footnotes. We have, however, retained footnotes that make substantive or clarificatory points. Whenever portions of an extract have been put together from discontinuous places, we have indicated the gap(s) with ellipses.

We wish to thank our editors, Nick Bellorini and Kelvin Matthews, and their colleagues at Blackwell for their labors and their supportiveness. We are immensely grateful as well to the many scholars whom Blackwell recruited to read the initial proposal and the detailed table of contents. Their suggestions have influenced a number of our selections. We owe particular thanks to Thom Brooks for answering some subsequent questions about Hegel, to Thomas Hurka for supplying us with a copy of his fine article on autonomy, and to James Nickel, Mark Reiff, and Serena Olsaretti for their encouragement.

Given that this volume is intended primarily for students in political and legal and moral philosophy, we wish to dedicate this anthology to our respec-tive students at Pavia, Cambridge, and Manchester. We are grateful to them for their lively interest in the topics explored herein.

Ian Carter   Matthew H. Kramer   Hillel Steiner
Pavia, Italy   *Cambridge, England*   *Manchester, England*

Acknowledgments

The editors and publisher gratefully acknowledge the permission granted to reproduce the copyright material in this book:

Chapter 3: Jean-Jacques Rousseau, *The Social Contract*, I, ch. 6, pp. 190–3; II, ch. 3, pp. 203–4; IV, ch. 2, pp. 276–9 from G. D. H. Cole (ed.), *The Social Contract*. London: Everyman, 1973. Reprinted with the kind permission of Everyman's Library London.

Chapter 4: Immanuel Kant, "Introduction to the Theory of Right," in *The Metaphysics of Morals*, pp. 132–5 from H. Reiss (ed.), *Kant's Political Writings*. Cambridge: Cambridge University Press, 1970. © Cambridge University Press, translated and reprinted with permission of Cambridge University Press and the author.

Chapter 5: Benjamin Constant, "The Liberty of the Ancients Compared with That of the Moderns," pp. 309–17 from B. Fontana (ed.), *Political Writings*. Cambridge: Cambridge University Press, 1988. © Cambridge University Press, translated and reprinted with permission of Cambridge University Press and the author.

Chapter 6: G. W. F. Hegel, paras. 4–7 and 15 from T. M. Knox (ed.), *The Philosophy of Right*. Oxford: Clarendon Press, 1942. Reprinted by permission of Oxford University Press.

Chapters 7 and 61: Karl Marx, "On the Jewish Question" and "The German Ideology," pp. 51–3 and p. 169 from D. McLellan (ed.), *Karl Marx: Selected Writings*. Oxford: Oxford University Press, 1977. Reprinted by permission of Blackwell Publishing Ltd.

Chapter 9: Guido De Ruggiero, "Negative Freedom and Positive Freedom," pp. 350–7 from R. G. Collingwood (ed.), *The History of European Liberalism*. Boston, MA: Beacon Press, 1969. Reprinted with permission of Oxford University Press.

Chapters 10, 19, and 73: Isaiah Berlin, "Two Concepts of Liberty," pp. 168–200, 200–12, 212–17 from *Liberty*. Oxford: Oxford University Press, 2002. Reprinted with permission of Curtis Brown Ltd.

Chapters 11 and 26: J. P. Day, "On Liberty and the Real Will," pp. 1–17 from *Liberty and Justice*. London: Croom Helm, 1987. Reprinted with permission of Taylor & Francis.

Chapters 13 and 65: John Rawls, "The Concept of Liberty," pp. 176–8, 178 from *A Theory of Justice*. Cambridge, MA: Harvard University Press, 1971. Copyright © 1971, 1999 by The President and Fellows of Harvard College.

Chapter 14: Nicolò Machiavelli, "The Transition from Servitude to Freedom," pp. 252–8 from L. J. Walker (ed.), *The Discourses of Nicolò Machiavelli*. London: Routledge and Kegan Paul, 1950. Reprinted with permission of Taylor & Francis.

Chapter 18: Charles de Secondat, Baron de Montesquieu, Book 11, chs. 3–4; Book 12, ch. 2, pp. 155–6, 188 from Anne Cohler et al. (eds.), *The Spirit of the Laws*. Cambridge: Cambridge University Press, 1989. © Cambridge University Press. Reprinted with permission of Cambridge University Press.

Chapters 20, 47, 62, and 72: F. A. Hayek, pp. 11–16, 16–19, 18–21, 22–5, 29–32, 40–4, 44, 133–43 from *The Constitution of Liberty*. London: Routledge & Kegan Paul, 1960. Reprinted with permission of Taylor & Francis, the author and The University of Chicago Press.

Chapter 21: Philip Pettit, "Liberty as Non-domination," pp. 51–66 from *Republicanism*. Oxford: Oxford University Press, 1997. Reprinted by permission of Oxford University Press.

Chapter 22: Quentin Skinner, pp. 77–86 from *Liberty before Liberalism*. Cambridge: Cambridge University Press, 1998). © Cambridge University Press 1997. Reprinted with permission of Cambridge University Press.

Chapter 25: Isaiah Berlin, "Introduction," pp. xxxviii–xl from *Four Essays on Liberty*. Oxford: Oxford University Press, 1969. Reprinted with permission of Curtis Brown Ltd.

Chapter 27: John Gray, "On Negative and Positive Liberty," pp. 57–60 from *Liberalisms* (London: Routledge, 1989). Reprinted by permission of Taylor & Francis.

Chapter 28: Richard J. Arneson, "Freedom and Desire," pp. 425–40 from *Canadian Journal of Philosophy* 15 (1985). Reprinted by permission of University of Calgary.

Chapter 29: John Christman, "Liberalism and Individual Positive Freedom," pp. 344–7, 351–4, 359 from *Ethics* 101 (1991). Reprinted with permission of The University of Chicago Press.

Chapter 30: Charles Taylor, "What's Wrong with Negative Liberty," pp. 177–93 from A. Ryan (ed.), *The Idea of Freedom*. London: Oxford University Press, 1979. Reprinted by permission of the author.

Chapter 31: Christopher Megone, "One Concept of Liberty," pp. 611, 620–2 from *Political Studies* 35 (1987). Reprinted by permission of Blackwell Publishing Ltd.

Chapters 32 and 44: Richard E. Flathman, *The Philosophy and Politics of Freedom*, pp. 91–107, 322. Chicago: Chicago University Press, 1987. Reprinted with permission of The University of Chicago Press.

Chapters 33 and 46: Matthew H. Kramer, *The Quality of Freedom*, pp. 59–65, 255–71. Oxford: Oxford University Press, 2003. Reprinted by permission of Oxford University Press.

Chapter 35: Felix E. Oppenheim, pp. 53–9, 150, 153–4, 158–60 from *Political Concepts*. Oxford: Basil Blackwell, 1981. Reprinted with permission of the University of Chicago Press.

Chapter 36: William E. Connolly, "Freedom as a Contested Concept," pp. 139–43 from *The Terms of Political Discourse*, 3rd edn. Oxford: Blackwell, 1993. Reprinted by permission of Blackwell Publishing Ltd.

Chapters 37 and 49: Robert Nozick, pp. 160–4, 262–5 from *Anarchy, State, and Utopia*. New York: Basic Books/Oxford: Basil Blackwell, 1974. © 1974 by Basic Books. Reprinted with permission of the Perseus Books Group.

Chapter 38: G. A. Cohen, "Illusions about Private Property and Freedom," pp. 225–8, in J. Mepham and D. H. Ruben (eds.), *Issues in Marxist Philosophy*, vol. 4. Brighton: Harvester, 1981.

Chapter 39: S. I. Benn and W. L. Weinstein, "Being Free to Act, and Being a Free Man," pp. 194–7, 200–8 from *Mind* 80 (1971). Reprinted by permission of Oxford University Press Journals.

Chapter 40: David Miller, "Constraints on Freedom," pp. 66–75, 81–5 from *Ethics* 94 (1983). Reprinted with permission of the University of Chicago Press.

Chapter 41: Felix E. Oppenheim, " 'Constraints on Freedom' as a Descriptive Concept," pp. 305–9 from *Ethics* 95 (1985). Reprinted with permission of the University of Chicago Press.

Chapter 42: David Miller, "Reply to Oppenheim," pp. 310–14 from *Ethics* 95 (1985). Reprinted with permission of the University of Chicago Press.

Chapter 43: Kristján Kristjánsson, pp. 32–3, 70–9 from *Social Freedom*. Cambridge: Cambridge University Press, 1996. © Cambridge University Press 1996. Reprinted with permission of Cambridge University Press.

Chapters 45 and 51: Hillel Steiner, pp. 6–11, 12–15, 22–30 from *An Essay on Rights*. Oxford: Blackwell, 1994. Reprinted with permission of Blackwell Publishing Ltd.

Chapter 48: Robert Nozick, "Coercion," pp. 102–9, 112–20, 127–35 from P. Laslett et al. (eds.), *Philosophy, Politics, and Society*, 4th series. Oxford: Blackwell, 1994. Reprinted with permission of Blackwell Publishing Ltd.

Chapters 50 and 67: G. A. Cohen, pp. 34–7, 53–61 from *Self-ownership, Freedom, and Equality*. Cambridge: Cambridge University Press, 1995. © Maison des Sciences de l'Homme and Cambridge University Press 1995. Reprinted with permission of Cambridge University Press.

Chapter 52: David Zimmerman, "Coercive Wage Offers," pp. 121–4, 131–4, 137–8, 144–5 from *Philosophy and Public Affairs* 10 (1981). Reprinted with permission of Blackwell Publishing Ltd.

Chapter 53: Christine Swanton, pp. 104–13 from *Freedom: A Coherence Theory*. Indianapolis: Hackett, 1992. Reprinted by permission of Hackett Publishing Company, Inc. All rights reserved.

Chapter 54: Michael J. Gorr, pp. 20–1, 24–7, 29–34 from *Coercion, Freedom, and Exploitation*. New York: Peter Lang, 1989. © Peter Lang Publishing Inc. 1989. Reprinted by permission of Peter Lang Publishing Inc.

Chapter 55: Alan Wertheimer, pp. 184–91, 255–8 from *Coercion*. Princeton, NJ: Princeton University Press, 1987. © 1988 Princeton University Press, 1990, paperback edition. Reprinted with permission of Princeton University Press.

Chapter 56: Serena Olsaretti, pp. 138–43, 148–50 from *Liberty, Desert, and the Market*. Cambridge: Cambridge University Press, 2004. © Serena Olsaretti 2004. Reprinted with permission of Cambridge University Press.

Chapter 57: Stanley I. Benn, pp. 152–7, 176–7, 179–80, 181–2 from *A Theory of Freedom*. Cambridge: Cambridge University Press, 1988. © Cambridge University Press 1988. Reprinted with permission of Cambridge University Press.

Chapter 58: Gerald Dworkin, pp. 12–20 from *The Theory and Practice of Autonomy*. Cambridge: Cambridge University Press, 1988. © Cambridge University Press 1997. Reprinted with permission of Cambridge University Press.

Chapter 59: Onora O'Neill, "Autonomy, Coherence, and Independence," pp. 205–8, 212–21 from D. Milligan et al. (eds.), *Liberalism, Citizenship, and Autonomy*. Aldershot: Avebury, 1992. Reprinted with the kind permission of the author.

Chapter 60: Janice Moulton and Francine Rainone, "Women's Work and Sex Roles," pp. 189–96 from Carol Gould (ed.), *Beyond Domination: New Perspectives on Women and Philosophy*. Totowa, NJ: Rowman & Allanheld, 1984. Reprinted with permission of Francine Rainone, DO, PhD, MS, Clinical Associate Professor, Albert Einstein College of Medicine, Bronx NY, and Janice Moulton, PhD, Department of Philosophy, Smith College, Northampton, MA.

Chapter 63: Bruno Leoni, pp. 52–8 from *Freedom and the Law*. Los Angeles, CA: Nash, 1961. Reprinted with the kind permission of the Institute for Humane Studies.

Chapter 64: Murray N. Rothbard, pp. 215–18 from *The Ethics of Liberty*. Atlantic Highlands, NJ: Humanities Press, 1982. Reprinted with permission of New York University Press.

Chapter 66: Philippe Van Parijs, pp. 20–4 from *Real Freedom for All*. Oxford: Oxford University Press, 1995. Reprinted with permission of Oxford University Press.

Chapters 68 and 76: Amartya Sen, pp. 12–16, 21–3, 39–42, 44–6 from *Inequality Reexamined*. Oxford: Oxford University Press, 1992. Reprinted with permission of Oxford University Press.

Chapter 71: Karl R. Popper, pp. 152–9 from *The Poverty of Historicism*. New York: Harper and Row, 1964. Reprinted with permission of Melitta Mew, the Estate of Karl R. Popper.

Chapter 74: John Rawls, pp. 21–4, 42–6, 112–14 from *Justice as Fairness: A Restatement*. Cambridge, MA: Harvard University Press, 2001. Copyright © 2001 by the President and Fellows of Harvard College.

Chapter 75: Joseph Raz, pp. 407–12 from *The Morality of Freedom*. Oxford: Clarendon Press, 1986. Reprinted with permission of Oxford University Press.

Chapter 77: Thomas Hurka, "Why Value Autonomy?," pp. 362–8, 370 from *Social Theory and Practice* 13 (1987). Reprinted with permission of Social Theory and Practice.

Chapter 78: Joel Feinberg, "The Interest in Liberty on the Scales," pp. 27–34 from A. I. Goldman et al. (eds.), *Values and Morals*. Dordrecht: Reidel, 1978. Reprinted with permission of Springer Verlag.

Chapter 79: Ronald Dworkin, pp. 266, 268–74 from *Taking Rights Seriously*. London: Duckworth, 1977. Copyright © 1977, 1978 Ronald Dworkin. Reprinted with permission of Gerald Duckworth Publishers and Harvard University Press.

Chapters 80 and 82: Ian Carter, pp. 11, 18–20, 32–4, 44, 45–7, 50–2, 171–2, 174–6, 180–6, 188, 226–8 from *A Measure of Freedom*. Oxford: Oxford University Press, 1999. Reprinted with permission of Oxford University Press.

Chapter 81: Hillel Steiner, "How Free: Computing Personal Liberty," pp. 73–83 from A. Phillips-Griffiths (ed.), *Of Liberty, Royal Institute of Philosophy Lecture Series: 15 Supplement to Philosophy*. Cambridge: Cambridge University Press, 1983. © The Royal Institute of Philosophy, published by Cambridge University Press, reproduced with permission.

Chapter 83: Prasanta K. Pattanaik and Yongsheng Xu, "On Ranking Opportunity Sets in Terms of Freedom of Choice," pp. 383–90 from *Recherches Economiques de Louvain* 54 (1990). Reprinted with permission of Recherches Economiques de Louvain.

Chapter 84: Amartya Sen, "Welfare, Freedom, and Social Choice: a Reply," pp. 469–72 from *Recherches Economiques de Louvain*, 54 (1990). Reprinted with permission of Recherches Economiques de Louvain.

Chapter 85: Robert Sugden, "The Metric of Opportunity," pp. 311–12, 316–29, in *Economics and Philosophy*, 14 (1998). © Cambridge University Press. Reprinted with permission of Cambridge University Press.

Chapter 86: Martin van Hees, pp. 134–7, 141–50 from *Legal Reductionism and Freedom*. Dordrecht: Kluwer, 2000. Reprinted with kind permission of Springer Science and Business Media.

Every effort has been made to trace copyright holders and to obtain their permission for the use of copyright material. The publisher apologizes for any errors or omissions in the above list and would be grateful if notified of any corrections that should be incorporated in future reprints or editions of this book.

General Introduction

You see – you see, boys forget what their country means by just reading "the land of the free" in history books. When they get to be men, they forget even more. Liberty is too precious a thing to be buried in books, Miss Saunders. Men should hold it up in front of them every single day of their lives and say, "I'm free – to think and to speak. My ancestors couldn't. I can. And my children will."

(Frank Capra's film *Mr. Smith Goes to Washington*)

No one in love is free – or wants to be.
(Richard Brooks's film *Sweet Bird of Youth*)

Freedom often figures in political discussions as though it were an idea with a single and transparently clear meaning. If only it were so! Even a cursory perusal of the writings collected in this volume will suffice to convince the reader that the matter is very far from being so straightforward. Nonetheless, entertaining that wishful thought – that the term "freedom" speaks to us univocally – is understandable enough. For, notwithstanding the second quotation above, virtually everyone cares passionately about freedom. And when we fiercely argue with others over such issues as whether the sacrifice of some freedom is really worth the gain in security that it promises, or whether the respective demands of justice and liberty are mutually incompatible, or whether the repeal of some law will increase or decrease individuals' freedom, we quite naturally assume that the persons with whom we are debating mean the same thing as we do in using that word. Regrettably, and as we dishearteningly come to realize only on subsequent reflection, they often do not. Such reflection all too frequently reveals that our heated debate amounted, in fact, to little more than "ships passing in the night."

This book explains why. The underlying reason is not all that elusive. Like other ideas that figure saliently in our political thinking – democracy, authority, and equality are good examples – the idea of freedom is complex, not simple. For freedom is a concept that comprises many aspects or dimensions, each of which is at least somewhat open to rival interpretations. And what adds significantly to this complexity is the fact that these various constituent dimensions do not readily lend themselves to the sort of clear demarcation that would hermetically seal them off from one another, and thereby ensure that an interpretation of one is logically independent of any interpretation of another. Any particular conception of freedom consists in some permutation of these rival dimensional interpretations. But that permutation – unlike a standard café meal – is not completely *à la carte*: that is to say, its components, though sometimes mutually independent, often imply one another.

Confronted with this web of complexity, we have sought to identify topics that each form the focus of important contributions to the vast literature on freedom, and have selected nine of these that tend to figure more prominently than others in philosophical discussions. Each of our sections is devoted to one of these topics, and the excerpts anthologized in each of them address a number of closely related issues, which are outlined in the section's editorial introduction. It should not, however, be assumed that all the excerpts in each section address exactly the same set of issues, much less that they are directly responding to one another.

What would be convenient, of course, is to have had all the anthologized authors assembled at one and the same set of colloquia or academic conferences, and to have required them to respond to the claims of one another in just such a manner. Alas, no such colloquia or conferences could have been held without the benefit of time travel, for many of these excerpts are taken from works by authors who are separated by several centuries. This inclusion of passages from classic texts as well as contemporary ones does, indeed, serve a vital purpose: it enables the reader to see how the works of many later authors are not only informed by those of their earlier counterparts, but are also seeking to address important problems overlooked or left unresolved by those predecessors.

Why is the philosophical interest in freedom so extensive and of such long standing? The answer is, again, not hard to find. From earliest times, human societies have concerned themselves with the serious difficulties of coordinating the activities of their members, who pursue their obligations and preferences in ways that can – and frequently do – obstruct one another's pursuits. Laws and many other types of social rules are imposed on this conduct through mechanisms of enforcement in an effort to ensure that such activities do not exceed certain bounds, and sometimes in an effort to ensure that they achieve certain outcomes. Precisely what those bounds are, or should be, has varied considerably from one time and place to another.

What virtually all restrictions have in common, however, is that their presence forecloses some possibilities of acting and opens up others. So, for example, when the pneumatic drilling outside an office building is stopped, the people inside are thereby enabled to conduct interviews. There are a number of questions that could be asked about this elementary example. Some theorists would see all of those questions as having a direct bearing on whether (and to what extent) freedoms are at stake here, whereas other theorists would strongly disagree and would deem some of those questions irrelevant (though these latter theorists disagree strongly among themselves when they seek to identify which questions are the irrelevant ones). Among these questions are:

(a) What is the value of continuing the drilling in comparison with the value of conducting the interviews?
(b) Are the persons respectively engaged in these activities motivated to perform them by a rationally considered conviction that their doing so is justified?
(c) Does either of these activities violate someone's rights? Is preventing either of them a means of giving effect to someone's rights?
(d) Are the persons engaged in these activities doing so under threat of a penalty for failing to do them? Do they perform them on the promise of a considerable reward for doing so?
(e) Are these activities ones that would be undertaken in a politically and/or economically just society?
(f) Is the value of *not* preventing either of these activities entirely dependent on the value of that activity itself?
(g) How *much* of a reduction, in their respective overall sets of action-possibilities, would be entailed by preventing the parties from engaging in these activities?

As suggested above, it seems highly unlikely that readers who reflect carefully upon these questions, and on many others that could be asked about this example, would each come to one and the same set of conclusions concerning their relevance to the matter of whether (and to what extent) freedoms are at stake here. Philosophers certainly haven't.

So what is to be done? One reaction might be simply to resign ourselves to the prospect that political debates about freedom will forever be beset by ineliminable confusion, by persons invariably talking at cross-purposes with one another. Such a counsel of despair, however, would be hasty because it is seriously overdrawn. At the very least, it is possible to distinguish between different conceptions of freedom, and to assign them different designations in order to bring some greater clarity into our conversations: "I now realize that, when we've argued about whether policy X reduces our freedom, I've been talking about Freedom One, whereas what you've meant is Freedom Two. So perhaps we haven't really been disagreeing."

Of course, those who have written about the concept of freedom have long engaged in just such clarificatory practices: for instance, and as this volume indicates, conceptions of freedom have frequently been classified as being negative, positive, or republican. But it is generally agreed that there is much more work to be done along these lines. For one thing, not all writers accept that this threefold taxonomy – or any other that has been proffered – exhaustively captures or perspicuously groups together all the conceptions of freedom that find some basis in everyday ways of speaking. Even writers who accept the neg-ative/positive/republican taxonomy would nonetheless insist that these clas-sifications represent, at best, families of conceptions of freedom: the taxonomy takes account neither of the many significant differences that lie between conceptions sharing the same classification, nor, conversely, of the many sig-nificant affinities that lie between conceptions in different classifications. In the absence of a finer-grained understanding, our political debates concerning freedom would thereby remain in serious danger of quickly descending into uninstructive confusion. Supplying that understanding is a job for philosophers.

But there is another, and stronger, reason why that aforementioned counsel of despair is unwarranted. Philosophers have aimed to do more than perform the highly useful task of isolating and classifying distinct conceptions of freedom: they have frequently argued that some of those conceptions are mis-taken, and they further contend that the jumbling together of disparate con-ceptions in ordinary discourse leads to logical inconsistencies. How can they do this? After all, philosophers are not linguistic legislators. They utterly lack the authority – and, usually, the inclination – to tell people what they are not entitled to mean when they use the term "freedom." Surely we all have at least the same rights of free speech as Humpty Dumpty, who, in *Through the Looking-Glass*, famously retorts to Alice: "When *I* use a word, it means just what I choose it to mean – neither more nor less."

To which Alice might have rejoined, philosophically, "Yes, Humpty, but what you choose it to mean might not make sense." Why not? The answer lies in that earlier-mentioned complexity of the concept of freedom. Our judg-ments whether a person is free or unfree – or more or less free than another person – rest on reasons of various types, which differ from one conception to another. These reasons state the several conditions deemed necessary and sufficient for warranting such judgments. The domain of reasons is, of course, the philosopher's home ground. While certainly lacking the authority to deter-mine what Humpty Dumpty is permitted to say about freedom, philosophers are well placed to determine whether his reasons for saying it are mutually consistent or generate logical contradictions and paradoxes. They are some-times also well placed to assess how closely or loosely those reasons reflect fea-tures of everyday thought and discourse about freedom, and sometimes, too, to assess the significance of those features themselves. It perhaps hardly needs remarking that some things that are said about freedom are less likely to survive this sort of assessment than others. Failing it, they suffer the fate predicted for them by Alice, of not making sense.

This book should thus be seen as posing an engaging challenge to the reader. It invites you to impose some critical distance between yourself and the polit-ical arguments you observe or participate in or read about, whether in the public media or in academic literature. And it challenges you to employ your analytical capacities, first to identify the reasons for and against a particular understanding of freedom, and then to assess their cogency. Though the writings anthologized here will certainly aid you in this enterprise, it is you who must do the work.

Part I

Negative and Positive Freedom

Introduction to Part I

Although the division between negative and positive liberty has for centuries played a major formative role in Western thinking about freedom, and although this section consequently offers a wider range of selections from the writings of pre-twentieth-century philosophers than any of the other sections in this anthology, the salience of that division in recent decades is due above all to the publication of Isaiah Berlin's famous essay "The Two Concepts of Liberty" (which is excerpted below). Roughly, negative liberty consists in opportunities and combinations of opportunities – that is, it consists in an absence of obstacles or constraints – whereas positive liberty resides in certain accomplishments that amount to a person's or group's self-determination. A positive-liberty theorist believes that one's exercise of some worthy faculties or one's achievement of some commendable aims or one's performance of some valuable activities or one's basing of one's projects and decisions on autonomously formed objectives is essential for the free realization of one's potential as a human being and the free expression of one's self. In other words, when such a theorist seeks to determine whether people are free, the focus is on what they have done or how they have done it. For a negative-liberty theorist, the focus of any such enquiry is very different. In order to ascertain whether people are free in some respect, a proponent of negative liberty asks not what they have done but whether they are unprevented from doing something. A negative-liberty theorist is interested primarily in whether various courses of action are open to people, and only secondarily in whether those courses of action have been taken; the latter question is relevant insofar, but only insofar, as it bears on the former.

Other differences between the two types of liberty follow from the principal difference just outlined. For example, although most theorists in either camp believe that the imposition and enforcement of wisely chosen legal obligations can be freedom-enhancing on the whole, they part ways over the question whether such wisely chosen obligations are also freedom-restricting. Since a key effect of the regular enforcement of legal obligations is to close down certain options or combinations of options (even while opening up other options or combinations of options), negative-liberty theorists maintain that the processes of enforcement inevitably remove various freedoms. By contrast, most positive-liberty theorists argue that the eliminated options would not have been genuine instances of liberty at all. Instead, they submit, those options would have been instances of license to perform actions that thwart the realization of true freedom.

Of course, the divide between negative-liberty theorists and positive-liberty theorists should not obscure the disagreements within each of those camps. For example, although Thomas Hobbes is plainly a seminal figure in the negative-liberty tradition, his ideas about freedom are certainly not endorsed wholeheartedly by most contemporary exponents of negative liberty. Among his theses that would be rejected by most such exponents is the notion that, so long as impediments attributable to some person do not prevent some other person X from acting in accordance with her desires, X is not rendered unfree in any respect by those impediments. Likewise objectionable is Hobbes's wholesale failure to distinguish between normative freedom – such as moral and legal freedom – and physical freedom. (These issues are explored in some of the excerpts in this anthology's sections on "Freedom and the Mind" and "Freedom and Morality.") Contemporary positive-liberty theorists, too, frequently repudiate the positions of their luminous predecessors. Writing in the aftermath of a long period during which the ideal of positive liberty was persistently invoked by many Marxists in support of ruthless tyrannies, most present-day champions of positive liberty strive to distance themselves from totalitarian versions of their doctrine. Many of them, for example, now focus on the processes by which goals are pursued rather than on the actual realization of goals. (This issue is explored in some of the excerpts in this anthology's sections on "Freedom and the Mind" and "Autonomy.")

Disputes occur as well among the contemporary philosophers in each of the two main camps, of course. For instance, modern negative-liberty theorists disagree with one another about the sufficient conditions for the existence of any liberties. Some of those theorists, including Berlin and J. P. Day and Hillel Steiner, contend that someone is free to do X if he or she is not prevented from doing X by any external constraints or obstacles. Other such theorists, including G. A. Cohen and Matthew Kramer, maintain that the existence of the freedom-to-do-X requires not only the absence of external constraints or obstacles but also the presence of internal capacities. These disputes are as fiercely fought as the disputes that are waged across the negative/positive divide.

Thirty to forty years ago, some philosophers believed that the controversies between negative-liberty theorists and positive-liberty theorists could be cleared up through a search for linguistic errors. Very few contemporary philosophers believe as much. Neither side in the negative/positive controversies is guilty of linguistic impropriety; the language of "freedom" is sufficiently expansive to cover both the unrestrictedness of opportunities and the achievement of self-expression. Virtually everybody now recognizes that the relevant considerations for one's choice between negative-liberty doctrines and positive-liberty doctrines are moral and political values and theoretical-explanatory values (such as clarity, precision, and parsimony). By reference to those values, the positions espoused and the arguments advanced in this section – or anywhere else in this anthology – should be judged.

Further Reading

Baldwin, Tom, "MacCallum and the Two Concepts of Freedom," *Ratio* 26, no. 125 (1984) ⟨measured defense of positive-liberty theories⟩.

Carter, Ian, *A Measure of Freedom* (Oxford University Press, 1999), pp. 148–65 ⟨critique of an influential conception of positive liberty⟩.

Flathman, Richard, *The Philosophy and Politics of Freedom* (University of Chicago Press, 1987) ⟨balanced assessment of many negative and positive conceptions of liberty⟩.

Kramer, Matthew H., *The Quality of Freedom* (Oxford University Press, 2003), pp. 92–104 ⟨several objections to positive-liberty theories⟩.

Macpherson, C. B., *Democratic Theory* (Oxford University Press, 1973), pp. 95–119 ⟨criticism of Berlin's understanding of the negative/positive distinction⟩.

Chapter 1

Thomas Hobbes, from *Leviathan* (1651)

Chapter XIV
Of the First and Second Natural Laws, and of Contracts

2.   By LIBERTY, is understood, according to the proper signification of the word, the absence of external impediments: which impediments, may oft take away part of a man's power to do what he would; but cannot hinder him from using the power left him, according as his judgment, and reason shall dictate to him.

Chapter XXI
Of the Liberty of Subjects

1.   LIBERTY, or FREEDOM, signifieth (properly) the absence of opposition; (by opposition, I mean external impediments of motion;) and may be applied no less to irrational, and inanimate creatures, than to rational. For whatsoever is so tied, or environed, as it cannot move, but within a certain space, which space is determined by the opposition of some external body, we say it hath not liberty to go further. And so of all living creatures, whilst they are imprisoned, or restrained, with walls, or chains; and of the water whilst it is kept in by banks, or vessels, that otherwise would spread itself into a larger space, we use to say, they are not at liberty, to move in such manner, as without those external impediments they would. But when the impediment of motion, is in the constitution of the thing itself, we use not to say, it wants the liberty; but the power to move; as when a stone lieth still, or a man is fastened to his bed by sickness.

   [. . .]

5.   But as men, for the attaining of peace, and conservation of themselves thereby, have made an artificial man, which we call a commonwealth; so also have they made artificial chains, called *civil laws*, which they themselves, by mutual covenants, have fastened at one end, to the lips of that man, or assembly, to whom they have given the sovereign power; and at the other end to their own ears. These bonds in their own nature but weak, may nevertheless be made to hold, by the danger, though not by the difficulty of breaking them.

6.   In relation to these bonds only it is, that I am to speak now, of the *liberty of subjects*. For seeing there is no commonwealth in the world, wherein there be rules enough set down, for the regulating of all the actions, and words of men; (as being a thing impossible:) it followeth necessarily, that in all kinds of actions, by the laws praetermitted [passed over], men have the liberty, of doing what their own reasons shall suggest, for the most profitable to themselves. For if we take liberty in the proper sense, for corporal liberty; that is to say, freedom from chains, and prison, it were very absurd for men to clamour as they do, for the liberty they so manifestly enjoy.

Again, if we take liberty, for an exemption from laws, it is no less absurd, for men to demand as they do, that liberty, by which all other men may be masters of their lives. And yet as absurd as it is, this is it they demand; not knowing that the laws are of no power to protect them, without a sword in the hands of a man, or men, to cause those laws to be put in execution. The liberty of a subject, lieth therefore only in those things, which in regulating their actions, the sovereign hath praetermitted: such as is the liberty to buy, and sell, and otherwise contract with one another; to choose their own abode, their own diet, their own trade of life, and institute their children as they themselves think fit: and the like.

Thomas Hobbes, chs. XIV, XXI, from J. C. A. Gaskin (ed.), *Leviathan* (Oxford: Oxford University Press, 1996).

Chapter 2

Jeremy Bentham, from *Of Laws in General* (1782)

Appendix B
Part I

3. As yet there is no law in the land. The legislator hath not yet entered upon his office. As yet he hath neither commanded nor prohibited any act. As yet all acts therefore are free: all persons as against the law are at liberty. Restraint, constraint, compulsion, coercion, duty, obligation (those species I mean of each which issue from the law) are things unknown. As against the law all persons possess as great a measure of this great blessing of liberty as it is possible for persons to possess: and in a greater measure than it is possible for men to possess it in any other state of things. This is the first day of the political creation: the state is without form and void. As yet then you and I and everyone are at liberty. Understand always, as against the law: for as against one another this may be far from being the case. Legal restraint, legal constraint and so forth are indeed unknown: but legal protection is unknown also. You and your neighbour, suppose, are at variance: he has bound you hand and foot, or has fastened you to a tree: in this case you are certainly not at liberty as against him: on the contrary he has deprived you of your liberty: and it is on account of what you have been made suffer by the operation which deprives you of it that the legislator steps in and takes an active part in your behalf. Since the legislator then takes an active part, how is it that he must demean himself? He must either command or prohibit: for there is nothing else that he can do: he therefore cuts off on the one side or the other a portion of the subject's liberty. Liberty then is of two or even more sorts, according to the number of quarters from whence coercion, which it is the absence of, may come: liberty as against the law, and liberty as against those who first in consideration of the effect of their conduct upon the happiness of society, and afterwards in consideration of the course taken against them by the law, may be styled *wrong-doers*. These two sorts of liberty are directly opposed to one another: and in as far as it is in favour of an individual, that the law exercises its authority over another, the generation of the one sort is, as far as it extends, the destruction of the other. In the same proportion and by the same cause by which the one is increased, the other is diminished.

Jeremy Bentham, from H. L. A. Hart (ed.), *Of Laws in General* (Oxford: Oxford University Press, 1970), pp. 253–4.

Chapter 3

Jean-Jacques Rousseau, from
The Social Contract (1762)

Book I

Chapter 6
The Social Compact

I suppose men to have reached the point at which the obstacles in the way of their preservation in the state of nature show their power of resistance to be greater than the resources at the disposal of each individual for his maintenance in that state. That primitive condition can then subsist no longer; and the human race would perish unless it changed its manner of existence.

But, as men cannot engender new forces, but only unite and direct existing ones, they have no other means of preserving themselves than the formation, by aggregation, of a sum of forces great enough to overcome the resistance. These they have to bring into play by means of a single motive power, and cause to act in concert.

This sum of forces can arise only where several persons come together: but, as the force and liberty of each man are the chief instruments of his self-preservation, how can he pledge them without harming his own interests, and neglecting the care he owes to himself? This difficulty, in its bearing on my present subject, may be stated in the following terms:

'The problem is to find a form of association which will defend and protect with the whole common force the person and goods of each associate, and in which each, while uniting himself with all, may still obey himself alone, and remain as free as before.' This is the fundamental problem of which the social contract provides the solution.

The clauses of this contract are so determined by the nature of the act that the slightest modification would make them vain and ineffective; so that, although they have perhaps never been formally set forth, they are everywhere the same and everywhere tacitly admitted and recognized, until, on the violation of the social compact, each regains his original rights and resumes his natural liberty, while losing the conventional liberty in favour of which he renounced it.

These clauses, properly understood, may be reduced to one – the total alienation of each associate, together with all his rights, to the whole community; for, in the first place, as each gives himself absolutely, the conditions are the same for all; and, this being so, no one has any interest in making them burdensome to others.

Moreover, the alienation being without reserve, the union is as perfect as it can be, and no associate has anything more to demand: for, if the individuals retained certain rights, as there would be no common superior to decide between them and the public, each, being on one point his own judge, would ask to be so on all; the state of nature would thus continue, and the association would necessarily become inoperative or tyrannical.

Finally, each man, in giving himself to all, gives himself to nobody; and as there is no associate over which he does not acquire the same right as he yields others over himself, he gains an equivalent for everything he loses, and an increase of force for the preservation of what he has.

If then we discard from the social compact what is not of its essence, we shall find that it reduces itself to the following terms:

'Each of us puts his person and all his power in common under the supreme direction of the general will, and, in our corporate capacity, we receive each member as an indivisible part of the whole.'

At once, in place of the individual personality of each contracting party, this act of association creates a corporate and collective body, composed of as many members as the assembly contains voters, and receiving from this act its unity, its common identity, its life, and its will. This public person, so formed by the union of all other persons, formerly took the name of *city*, and now takes that of *Republic* or *body politic*; it is called by its members *State* when passive, *Sovereign* when active, and *Power* when compared with others like itself. Those who associated in it take collectively the name of *people*, and severally are called *citizens*, as sharing in the sovereign authority, and *subjects*, as being under the laws of the State. But these terms are often confused and taken one for another: it is enough to know how to distinguish them when they are being used with precision.

[. . .]

Book II

Chapter 3
Whether the General Will Is Fallible

It follows from what has gone before that the general will is always upright and always tends to the public advantage; but it does not follow that the deliberations of the people always have the same rectitude. Our will is always for our own good, but we do not always see what

that is; the people is never corrupted, but it is often deceived, and on such occasions only does it seem to will what is bad.

There is often a great deal of difference between the will of all and the general will; the latter considers only the common interest, while the former takes private interest into account, and is no more than a sum of particular wills: but take away from these same wills the pluses and minuses that cancel one another, and the general will remains as the sum of the differences.

If, when the people, being furnished with adequate information, held its deliberations, the citizens had no communication one with another, the grand total of the small differences would always give the general will, and the decision would always be good. But when intrigues arise, and partial associations are formed at the expense of the great association, the will of each of these associations becomes general in relation to its members, while it remains particular in relation to the State: it may then be said that there are no longer as many votes as there are men, but only as many as there are associations. The differences become less numerous and give a less general result. Lastly, when one of these associations is so great as to prevail over all the rest, the result is no longer a sum of small differences, but a single difference; in this case there is no longer a general will, and the opinion which prevails is purely particular.

It is therefore essential, if the general will is to be able to make itself known, that there should be no partial society in the state and that each citizen should express only his own opinion: which was indeed the sublime and unique system established by the Great Lycurgus. But if there are partial societies, it is best to have as many as possible and to prevent them from being unequal, as was done by Solon, Numa, and Servius. These precautions are the only ones that can guarantee that the general will shall be always enlightened, and that the people shall in no way deceive itself.

[. . .]

Book IV

Chapter 2
Voting

If then there are opponents when the social compact is made, their opposition does not invalidate the contract, but merely prevents them from being included in it. They are foreigners among citizens. When the State is instituted, residence constitutes consent; to dwell within its territory is to submit to the Sovereign.[1]

Apart from this primitive contract, the vote of the majority always binds all the rest. This follows from the contract itself. But it is asked how a man can be both free and forced to conform to wills that are not his own. How are the opponents at once free and subject to laws they have not agreed to?

I retort that the question is wrongly put. The citizen gives his consent to all the laws, including those which are passed in spite of his opposition, and even those which punish him when he dares to break any of them. The constant will of all the members of the State is the general will; by virtue of it they are citizens and free. When in the popular assembly a law is proposed, what the people is asked is not exactly whether it approves or rejects the proposal, but whether it is in conformity with the general will, which is their will. Each man, in giving his vote, states his opinion on that point; and the general will is found by counting votes. When therefore the opinion that is contrary to my own prevails, this proves neither more nor less than that I was mistaken, and that what I thought to be the general will was not so. If my particular opinion had carried the day I should have achieved the opposite of what was my will; and it is in that case that I should not have been free.

This presupposes, indeed, that all the qualities of the general will still reside in the majority: when they cease to do so, whatever side a man may take, liberty is no longer possible.

Note

1   This should of course be understood as applying to a free State; for elsewhere family, goods, lack of a refuge, necessity, or violence may detain a man in a country against his will; and then his dwelling there no longer by itself implies his consent to the contract or to its violation.

Jean-Jacques Rousseau, I, ch. 6; II, ch. 3; IV, ch. 2 in G. D. H. Cole (ed.), *The Social Contract* (London: Everyman, 1973). pp. 190–3, 203–4, 276–9.

Chapter 4

Immanuel Kant, from *The Metaphysics of Morals* (1797)

Introduction to the Theory of Right

§A
Definition of the Theory of Right

The sum total of those laws which can be incorporated in external legislation is termed the *theory of right* (*Ius*). If legislation of this kind actually exists, the theory is one of *positive right*. If a person who is conversant with it or has studied it (*Iuriconsultus*) is acquainted with the external laws in their external function, i.e. in their application to instances encountered in experience, he is said to be *experienced in matters of right* (*Iurisperitus*). This body of theory may amount to the same as *jurisprudence* (*Iurisprudentia*), but it will remain only the *science of right* (*Iuriscientia*) unless both its elements are present. The latter designation applies to a *systematic* knowledge of the theory of natural right (*Ius naturae*), although it is the student of natural right who has to supply the immutable principles on which all positive legislation must rest.

§B
What Is Right?

The *jurist*, if he does not wish to lapse into tautology or to base his answer on the laws of a particular country at a particular time instead of offering a comprehensive solution, may well be just as perplexed on being asked this as the logician is by the notorious question: '*What is truth?*' He will certainly be able to tell us what is legally right (*quid sit iuris*) within a given context, i.e. what the laws say or have said in a particular place and at a particular time: but whether their provisions are also in keeping with right, and whether they constitute a universal criterion by which we may recognise in general what is right and what is unjust (*iustum et iniustum*), are questions whose answers will remain concealed from him unless he abandons such empirical principles for a time and looks for the sources of these judgements in the realm of pure reason. This will enable him to lay the foundations of all possible positive legislations. And while empirical laws may give him valuable guidance, a purely empirical theory of right, like the wooden head in Phaedrus' fable, may have a fine appearance, but will unfortunately contain no brain.

The concept of right, in so far as it is connected with a corresponding obligation (i.e. the moral concept of right), applies within the following conditions. *Firstly*, it applies only to those relationships between one person and another which are both external and practical, that is, in so far as their actions can in fact influence each other either directly or indirectly. But *secondly*, it does not concern the relationship between the will of one person and the *desires* of another (and hence only the latter's needs, as in acts of benevolence or hardheartedness); it concerns only the relationship between the will of the first and the *will* of the second. And *thirdly*, the will's *material* aspect, i.e. the end which each party intends to accomplish by means of the object of his will, is completely irrelevant in this mutual relationship; for example, we need not ask whether someone who buys goods from me for his own commercial use will gain anything in the process. For we are interested only in the *form* of the relationship between the two wills, in so far as they are regarded as *free*, and in whether the action of one of the two parties can be reconciled with the freedom of the other in accordance with a universal law.

Right is therefore the sum total of those conditions within which the will of one person can be reconciled with the will of another in accordance with a universal law of freedom.

indifference to me or although I may wish in my heart to deprive him of it. That I should make it my maxim to *act* in accordance with right is a requirement laid down for me by ethics.

Thus the universal law of right is as follows: let your external actions be such that the free application of your will can co-exist with the freedom of everyone in accordance with a universal law. And although this law imposes an obligation on me, it does not mean that I am in any way expected, far less required, to restrict my freedom *myself* to these conditions purely for the sake of this obligation. On the contrary, reason merely says that individual freedom *is* restricted in this way by virtue of the idea behind it, and that it may also be actively restricted by others; and it states this as a postulate which does not admit of any further proof.

If it is not our intention to teach virtue, but only to state what is *right*, we may not and should not ourselves represent this law of right as a possible motive for actions.

§C
The Universal Principle of Right

'Every action which by itself or by its maxim enables the freedom of each individual's will to co-exist with the freedom of everyone else in accordance with a universal law is *right*.'

Thus if my action or my situation in general can co-exist with the freedom of everyone in accordance with a universal law, anyone who hinders me in either does me an injustice; for this hindrance or resistance cannot co-exist with freedom in accordance with universal laws.

It also follows from this that I cannot be required to make this principle of all maxims my own maxim, i.e. *to make it the maxim of my own actions*, for each individual can be free so long as I do not interfere with his freedom by my *external actions*, even although his freedom may be a matter of total

§D
Right Entails the Authority to Use Coercion

Any resistance which counteracts the hindrance of an effect helps to promote this effect and is consonant with it. Now everything that is contrary to right is a hindrance to freedom based on universal laws, while coercion is a hindrance or resistance to freedom. Consequently, if a certain use to which freedom is put is itself a hindrance to freedom in accordance with universal laws (i.e. if it is contrary to right), any coercion which is used against it will be a *hindrance* to a *hindrance of freedom*, and will thus be consonant with freedom in accordance with universal laws – that is, it will be right. It thus follows by the law of contradiction that right entails the authority to apply coercion to anyone who infringes it.

§E
In its 'Strict' Sense, Right Can also Be Envisaged as the Possibility of a General and Reciprocal Coercion Consonant with the Freedom of Everyone in Accordance with Universal Laws

This proposition implies that we should not conceive of right as being composed of two elements, namely the obligation imposed by a law, and the authority which someone who obligates another party through his will possesses to coerce the latter into carrying out the obligation in question. Instead, the concept of right should be seen as consisting immediately of the possibility of universal reciprocal coercion being combined with the freedom of everyone. For just as the only object of right in general is the external aspect of actions, right in its strict sense, i.e. right unmixed with any ethical considerations, requires no determinants of the will apart from purely external ones; for it will then be pure and will not be confounded with any precepts of virtue. Thus only a completely external right can be called right in the *strict* (or narrow) sense. This right is certainly based on each individual's awareness of his obligations within the law; but if it is to remain pure, it may not and cannot appeal to this awareness as a motive which might determine the will to act in accordance with it, and it therefore depends rather on the principle of the possibility of an external coercion which can coexist with the freedom of everyone in accordance with universal laws.

Thus when it is said that a creditor has a right to require the debtor to pay his debt, it does not mean that he can make the latter feel that his reason itself obliges him to act in this way. It means instead that the use of coercion to compel everyone to do this can very well be reconciled with everyone's freedom, hence also with the debtor's freedom, in accordance with a universal external law: thus right and the authority to apply coercion mean one and the same thing.

The law of reciprocal coercion, which is necessarily consonant with the freedom of everyone within the principle of universal freedom, is in a sense the *construction* of the concept of right: that is, it represents this concept in pure *a priori* intuition by analogy with the possibility of free movement of bodies within the law of the *equality of action and reaction*. Just as the qualities of an object of pure mathematics cannot be directly deduced from the concept but can only be discovered from its construction, it is not so much the *concept* of right but rather a general, reciprocal and uniform coercion, subject to universal laws and harmonising with the concept itself, which makes any representation of the concept possible. But while this concept of dynamics (i.e. that of the equality of action and reaction) is based upon a purely formal concept of pure mathematics (e.g. of geometry), reason has taken care that the understanding is likewise as fully equipped as possible with *a priori* intuitions for the construction of the concept of right.

Immanuel Kant, *The Metaphysics of Morals*, from H. Reiss (ed.), *Kant's Political Writings* (Cambridge: Cambridge University Press, 1970), pp. 132–5.

Chapter 5

Benjamin Constant, from "The Liberty of the Ancients Compared with That of the Moderns" (1819)

Speech Given at the Athénée Royal in Paris

Gentlemen,

I wish to submit for your attention a few distinctions, still rather new, between two kinds of liberty: these differences have thus far remained unnoticed, or at least insufficiently remarked. The first is the liberty the exercise of which was so dear to the ancient peoples; the second the one the enjoyment of which is especially precious to the modern nations. If I am right, this investigation will prove interesting from two different angles.

Firstly, the confusion of these two kinds of liberty has been amongst us, in the all too famous days of our revolution, the cause of many an evil. France was exhausted by useless experiments, the authors of which, irritated by their poor success, sought to force her to enjoy the good she did not want, and denied her the good which she did want.

Secondly, called as we are by our happy revolution (I call it happy, despite its excesses, because I concentrate my attention on its results) to enjoy the benefits of representative government, it is curious and interesting to discover why this form of government, the only one in the shelter of which we could find some freedom and peace today, was totally unknown to the free nations of antiquity.

I know that there are writers who have claimed to distinguish traces of it among some ancient peoples, in the Lacedaemonian republic for example, or amongst our ancestors the Gauls; but they are mistaken.

The Lacedaemonian government was a monastic aristocracy, and in no way a representative government. The power of the kings was limited, but it was limited by the ephors, and not by men invested with a mission similar to that which election confers today on the defenders of our liberties. The ephors, no doubt, though originally created by the kings, were elected by the people. But there were only five of them. Their authority was as much religious as political; they even shared in the administration of government, that is, in the executive power. Thus their prerogative, like that of almost all popular magistrates in the ancient republics, far from being simply a barrier against tyranny, became sometimes itself an insufferable tyranny.

The regime of the Gauls, which quite resembled the one that a certain party would like to restore to us, was at the same time theocratic and warlike. The priests enjoyed unlimited power. The military class or nobility had markedly insolent and oppressive privileges; the people had no rights and no safeguards.

In Rome the tribunes had, up to a point, a representative mission. They were the organs of those plebeians whom the oligarchy – which is the same in all ages – had submitted, in overthrowing the kings, to so harsh a slavery. The people, however, exercised a large part of the political rights directly. They met to vote on the laws and to judge the patricians against whom charges had been levelled: thus there were, in Rome, only feeble traces of a representative system.

This system is a discovery of the moderns, and you will see, Gentlemen, that the condition of the human race in antiquity did not allow for the introduction or establishment of an institution of this nature. The ancient people could neither feel the need for it, nor appreciate its advantages. Their social organization led them to desire an entirely different freedom from the one which this system grants to us.

Tonight's lecture will be devoted to demonstrating this truth to you.

First ask yourselves, Gentlemen, what an Englishman, a Frenchman, and a citizen of the United States of America understand today by the word 'liberty'.

For each of them it is the right to be subjected only to the laws, and to be neither arrested, detained, put to death or maltreated in any way by the arbitrary will of one or more individuals. It is the right of everyone to express their opinion, choose a profession and practise it, to dispose of property, and even to abuse it; to come and go without permission, and without having to account for their motives or undertakings. It is everyone's right to associate with other individuals, either to discuss their interests, or to profess the religion which they and their associates prefer, or even simply to occupy their days or hours in a way which is most compatible with their inclinations or whims. Finally it is everyone's right to exercise some influence on the administration of the government, either by electing all or particular officials, or through representations, petitions, demands to which the authorities are

more or less compelled to pay heed. Now compare this liberty with that of the ancients.

The latter consisted in exercising collectively, but directly, several parts of the complete sovereignty; in deliberating, in the public square, over war and peace; in forming alliances with foreign governments; in voting laws, in pronouncing judgements; in examining the accounts, the acts, the stewardship of the magistrates; in calling them to appear in front of the assembled people, in accusing, condemning or absolving them. But if this was what the ancients called liberty, they admitted as compatible with this collective freedom the complete subjection of the individual to the authority of the community. You find among them almost none of the enjoyments which we have just seen form part of the liberty of the moderns. All private actions were submitted to a severe surveillance. No importance was given to individual independence, neither in relation to opinions, nor to labour, nor, above all, to religion. The right to choose one's own religious affiliation, a right which we regard as one of the most precious, would have seemed to the ancients a crime and a sacrilege. In the domains which seem to us the most useful, the authority of the social body interposed itself and obstructed the will of individuals. Among the Spartans, Therpandrus could not add a string to his lyre without causing offence to the ephors. In the most domestic of relations the public authority again intervened. The young Lacedaemonian could not visit his new bride freely. In Rome, the censors cast a searching eye over family life. The laws regulated customs, and as customs touch on everything, there was hardly anything that the laws did not regulate.

Thus among the ancients the individual, almost always sovereign in public affairs, was a slave in all his private relations. As a citizen, he decided on peace and war; as private individual, he was constrained, watched and repressed in all his movements; as a member of the collective body, he interrogated, dismissed, condemned, beggared, exiled, or sentenced to death his magistrates and superiors;

as a subject of the collective body he could himself be deprived of his status, stripped of his privileges, banished, put to death, by the discretionary will of the whole to which he belonged. Among the moderns, on the contrary, the individual, independent in his private life, is, even in the freest of states, sovereign only in appearance. His sovereignty is restricted and almost always suspended. If, at fixed and rare intervals, in which he is again surrounded by precautions and obstacles, he exercises this sovereignty, it is always only to renounce it.

I must at this point, Gentlemen, pause for a moment to anticipate an objection which may be addressed to me. There was in antiquity a republic where the enslavement of individual existence to the collective body was not as complete as I have described it. This republic was the most famous of all: you will guess that I am speaking of Athens. I shall return to it later, and in subscribing to the truth of this fact, I shall also indicate its cause. We shall see why, of all the ancient states, Athens was the one which most resembles the modern ones. Everywhere else social jurisdiction was unlimited. The ancients, as Condorcet says, had no notion of individual rights. Men were, so to speak, merely machines, whose gears and cogwheels were regulated by the law. The same subjection characterized the golden centuries of the Roman republic; the individual was in some way lost in the nation, the citizen in the city.

We shall now trace this essential difference between the ancients and ourselves back to its source.

All ancient republics were restricted to a narrow territory. The most populous, the most powerful, the most substantial among them, was not equal in extension to the smallest of modern states. As an inevitable consequence of their narrow territory, the spirit of these republics was bellicose; each people incessantly attacked their neighbours or was attacked by them. Thus driven by necessity against one another, they fought or threatened each other constantly. Those who had no ambition to be conquerors, could still not lay down their weapons, lest they should themselves be conquered. All had to buy their security, their independence, their whole existence at the price of war. This was the constant interest, the almost habitual occupation of the free states of antiquity. Finally, by an equally necessary result of this way of being, all these states had slaves. The mechanical professions and even, among some nations, the industrial ones, were committed to people in chains.

The modern world offers us a completely opposing view. The smallest states of our day are incomparably larger than Sparta or than Rome was over five centuries. Even the division of Europe into several states is, thanks to the progress of enlightenment, more apparent than real. While each people, in the past, formed an isolated family, the born enemy of other families, a mass of human beings now exists, that under different names and under different forms of social organization are essentially homogeneous in their nature. This mass is strong enough to have nothing to fear from barbarian hordes. It is sufficiently civilized to find war a burden. Its uniform tendency is towards peace.

This difference leads to another one. War precedes commerce. War and commerce are only two different means of achieving the same end, that of getting what one wants. Commerce is simply a tribute paid to the strength of the possessor by the aspirant to possession. It is an attempt to conquer, by mutual agreement, what one can no longer hope to obtain through violence. A man who was always the stronger would never conceive the idea of commerce. It is experience, by proving to him that war, that is the use of his strength against the strength of others, exposes him to a variety of obstacles and defeats, that leads him to resort to commerce, that is to a milder and surer means of engaging the interest of others to agree to what suits his own. War is all impulse, commerce, calculation. Hence it follows that an age must come in which commerce replaces war. We have reached this age.

I do not mean that amongst the ancients there were no trading peoples. But these peoples were to some degree an exception to the general rule. The limits of this lecture do not allow me to illustrate all the obstacles which then opposed the progress of commerce; you know them as well as I do; I shall only mention one of them.

Their ignorance of the compass meant that the sailors of antiquity always had to keep close to the coast. To pass through the pillars of Hercules, that is, the straits of Gibraltar, was considered the most daring of enterprises. The Phoenicians and the Carthaginians, the most able of navigators, did not risk it until very late, and their example for long remained without imitators. In Athens, of which we shall talk soon, the interest on maritime enterprises was around 60 percent, while current interest was only 12 percent: that was how dangerous the idea of distant navigation seemed.

Moreover, if I could permit myself a digression which would unfortunately prove too long, I would show you, Gentlemen, through the details of the customs, habits, way of trading with others of the trading peoples of antiquity, that their commerce was itself impregnated by the spirit of the age, by the atmosphere of war and hostility which surrounded it. Commerce then was a lucky accident, today it is the normal state of things, the only aim, the universal tendency, the true life of nations. They want repose, and with repose comfort, and as a source of comfort, industry. Every day war becomes a more ineffective means of satisfying their wishes. Its hazards no longer offer to individuals benefits that match the results of peaceful work and regular exchanges. Among the ancients, a successful war increased both private and public wealth in slaves, tributes and lands shared out. For the moderns, even a successful war costs infallibly more than it is worth.

Finally, thanks to commerce, to religion, to the moral and intellectual progress of the human race, there are no longer slaves among the European nations. Free men must exercise all professions, provide for all the needs of society.

It is easy to see, Gentlemen, the inevitable outcome of these differences.

Firstly, the size of a country causes a corresponding decrease of the political importance allotted to each individual. The most obscure republican of Sparta or Rome had power. The same is not true of the simple citizen of Britain or of the United States. His personal influence is an imperceptible part of the social will which impresses on the governments its direction.

Secondly, the abolition of slavery has deprived the free population of all the leisure which resulted from the fact that slaves took care of most of the work. Without the slave population of Athens, 20,000 Athenians could never have spent every day at the public square in discussions.

Thirdly, commerce does not, like war, leave in men's lives intervals of inactivity. The constant exercise of political rights, the daily discussion of the affairs of the state, disagreements, confabulations, the whole entourage and movement of factions, necessary agitations, the compulsory filling, if I may use the term, of the life of the peoples of antiquity, who, without this resource would have languished under the weight of painful inaction, would only cause trouble and fatigue to modern nations, where each individual, occupied with his speculations, his enterprises, the pleasures he obtains or hopes for, does not wish to be distracted from them other than momentarily, and as little as possible.

Finally, commerce inspires in men a vivid love of individual independence. Commerce supplies their needs, satisfies their desires, without the intervention of the authorities. This intervention is almost always – and I do not know why I say almost – this intervention is indeed always a trouble and an embarrassment. Every time collective power wishes to meddle with private speculations, it harasses the speculators. Every time governments pretend to do our own business, they do it more incompetently and expensively than we would.

I said, Gentlemen, that I would return to Athens, whose example might be opposed to some of my assertions, but which will in fact confirm all of them.

Athens, as I have already pointed out, was of all the Greek republics the most closely engaged in trade: thus it allowed to its citizens an infinitely greater individual liberty than Sparta or Rome. If I could enter into historical details, I would show you that, among the Athenians, commerce had removed several of the differences which distinguished the ancient from the modern peoples. The spirit of the Athenian merchants was similar to that of the merchants of our days. Xenophon tells us that during the Peloponnesian war, they moved their capitals from the continent of Attica to place them on the islands of the archipelago. Commerce had created among them the circulation of money. In Isocrates there are signs that bills of exchange were used. Observe how their customs resemble our own. In their relations with women, you will see, again I cite Xenophon, husbands, satisfied when peace and a decorous friendship reigned in their households, make allowances for the wife who is too vulnerable before the tyranny of nature, close their eyes to the irresistible power of passions, forgive the first weakness and forget the second. In their relations with strangers, we shall see them extending the rights of citizenship to whoever would, by moving among them with his family, establish some trade or industry. Finally, we shall be struck by their excessive love of individual independence. In Sparta, says a philosopher, the citizens quicken their step when they are called by a magistrate; but an Athenian would be desperate if he were thought to be dependent on a magistrate.

However, as several of the other circumstances which determined the character of ancient nations existed in Athens as well; as there was a slave population and the territory was very restricted; we find there too the traces of the liberty proper to the ancients. The people made the laws, examined the behaviour of the magistrates, called Pericles to account for his conduct, sentenced to death the generals who had commanded the battle of the Arginusae. Similarly ostracism, that legal arbitrariness, extolled by all the legislators of the age; ostracism, which appears to us, and rightly so, a revolting iniquity, proves that the individual was much more subservient to the supremacy of the social body in Athens, than he is in any of the free states of Europe today.

It follows from what I have just indicated that we can no longer enjoy the liberty of the ancients, which consisted in an active and constant participation in collective power. Our freedom must consist of peaceful enjoyment and private independence. The share which in antiquity everyone held in national sovereignty was by no means an abstract presumption as it is in our own day. The will of each individual had real influence: the exercise of this will was a vivid and repeated pleasure. Consequently the ancients were ready to make many a sacrifice to preserve their political rights and their share in the administration of the state. Everybody, feeling with pride all that his suffrage was worth, found in this awareness of his personal importance a great compensation.

This compensation no longer exists for us today. Lost in the multitude, the individual can almost never perceive the influence he exercises. Never does his will impress itself upon the whole; nothing confirms in his eyes his own cooperation.

The exercise of political rights, therefore, offers us but a part of the pleasures that the ancients found in it, while at the same time the progress of civilization, the commercial tendency of the age, the communication amongst peoples, have infinitely multiplied and varied the means of personal happiness.

It follows that we must be far more attached than the ancients to our individual independence. For the ancients when they sacrificed that independence to their political rights, sacrificed less to obtain more; while in making the same sacrifice, we would give more to obtain less.

The aim of the ancients was the sharing of social power among the citizens of the same fatherland: this is what they called liberty. The aim of the moderns is the enjoyment of security in private pleasures; and they call liberty the guarantees accorded by institutions to these pleasures.

Benjamin Constant, "The Liberty of the Ancients Compared with That of the Moderns," from B. Fontana (ed.), *Political Writings* (Cambridge: Cambridge University Press, 1988), pp. 309–17.

Chapter 6

G. W. F. Hegel, from *The Philosophy of Right* (1821)

4. The basis of right is, in general, mind; its precise place and point of origin is the will. The will is free, so that freedom is both the substance of right and its goal, while the system of right is the realm of freedom made actual, the world of mind brought forth out of itself like a second nature. [. . .]

5. The will contains (α) the element of pure indeterminacy or that pure reflection of the ego into itself which involves the dissipation of every restriction and every content either immediately presented by nature, by needs, desires, and impulses, or given and determined by any means whatever. This is the unrestricted infinity of absolute abstraction or universality, the pure thought of oneself.

Those who regard thinking as one special faculty, distinct from the will as another special faculty, and who even proceed to contend that thinking is prejudicial to the will, especially the good will, reveal at the very outset their complete ignorance of the nature of the will – a remark we shall have to make rather often when dealing with this same subject.

In Paragraph 5, it is only one side of the will which is described, namely this unrestricted possibility of abstraction from every determinate state of mind which I may find in myself or which I may have set up in myself, my flight from every content as from a restriction. When the will's self-determination consists in this alone, or when representative thinking regards this side by itself as freedom and clings fast to it, then we have negative freedom, or freedom

as the Understanding conceives it. This is the freedom of the void which rises to a passion and takes shape in the world; while still remaining theoretical, it takes shape in religion as the Hindu fanaticism of pure contemplation, but when it turns to actual practice, it takes shape in religion and politics alike as the fanaticism of destruction – the destruction of the whole subsisting social order – as the elimination of individuals who are objects of suspicion to any social order, and the annihilation of any organization which tries to rise anew from the ruins. Only in destroying something does this negative will possess the feeling of itself as existent. Of course it imagines that it is willing some positive state of affairs, such as universal equality or universal religious life, but in fact it does not will that this shall be positively actualized, and for this reason: such actuality leads at once to some sort of order, to a particularization of organizations and individuals alike; while it is precisely out of the annihilation of particularity and objective characterization that the self-consciousness of this negative freedom proceeds. Consequently, what negative freedom intends to will can never be anything in itself but an abstract idea, and giving effect to this idea can only be the fury of destruction.

6. (β) At the same time, the ego is also the transition from undifferentiated indeterminacy to the differentiation, determination, and positing of a determinacy as a content and object. Now further, this content may either be given by nature or engendered by the concept of mind. Through this positing of itself as something determinate, the ego steps in principle into determinate existence. This is the absolute moment, the finitude or particularization of the ego. [. . .]

7. (γ) The will is the unity of both these moments. It is particularity reflected into itself and so brought back to universality, i.e. it is individuality. It is the *self*-determination of the ego, which means that at one and the same time the ego posits itself as its own negative, i.e. as restricted and determinate, and yet remains by itself, i.e. in its self-identity and universality. It determines itself and yet at the same time binds itself together with itself. The ego determines itself in so far as it is the relating of negativity to itself. As this self-relation, it is indifferent to this determinacy; it knows it as something which is its own, something which is only ideal, a mere possibility by which it is not constrained and in which it is confined only because it has put itself in it. – This is the freedom of the will and it constitutes the concept or substantiality of the will, its weight, so to speak, just as weight constitutes the substantiality of a body.

Every self-consciousness knows itself (i) as universal, as the potentiality of abstracting from everything determinate, and (ii) as particular, with a determinate object, content, and aim. Still, both these moments are only abstractions; what is concrete and true (and everything true is concrete) is the universality which has the particular as its opposite, but the particular which by its reflection into itself has been equalized with the universal. This unity is individuality, not individuality in its immediacy as a unit, our first idea of individuality, but individuality in accordance with its concept; indeed, individuality in this sense is just precisely the concept itself. The first two moments – (i) that the will can abstract from everything, and (ii) that it is also determined in some specific way either by itself or by something else – are readily admitted and grasped because, taken independently, they are false and moments of the Understanding. But

the third moment, which is true and speculative (and everything true must be thought speculatively if it is to be comprehended) is the one into which the Understanding declines to advance, for it is precisely the concept which it persists in calling the inconceivable. It is the task of logic as purely speculative philosophy to prove and explain further this innermost secret of speculation, of infinity as negativity relating itself to itself, this ultimate spring of all activity, life, and consciousness. Here attention can only be drawn to the fact that if you say 'the will is universal, the will determines itself', the words you use to describe the will presuppose it to be a subject or substratum from the start. But the will is not something complete and universal prior to its determining itself and prior to its superseding and idealizing this determination. The will is not a will until it is this self-mediating activity, this return into itself.

[. . .]

15. At this stage, the freedom of the will is arbitrariness (*Willkür*) and this involves two factors: (*a*) free reflection, abstracting from everything, and (*b*) dependence on a content and material given either from within or from without. Because this content, implicitly necessary as purpose, is at the same time qualified in the face of free reflection as possible, it follows that arbitrariness is contingency manifesting itself as will.

The idea which people most commonly have of freedom is that it is arbitrariness – the mean, chosen by abstract reflection, between the will wholly determined by natural impulses, and the will free absolutely. If we hear it said that the definition of freedom is ability to do what we please, such an idea can only be taken to reveal an utter immaturity of thought, for it contains not even an inkling of the absolutely free will, of right, ethical life, and so forth. Reflection, the formal universality and unity of self-consciousness, is the will's abstract certainty of its freedom, but it is not yet the truth of freedom, because it has not yet got *itself* as its content and aim, and consequently the subjective side is still other than the objective; the content of this self-determination, therefore, also remains purely and simply finite. Instead of being the will in its truth, arbitrariness is more like the will as contradiction.

Additions

4. *Paragraph 4*
The freedom of the will is best explained by a reference to the physical world. Freedom, I mean, is just as fundamental a character of the will as weight is of bodies. If we say: matter is 'heavy', we might mean that this predicate is only contingent; but it is nothing of the kind, for nothing in matter is without weight. Matter is rather weight itself. Heaviness constitutes the body and is the body. The same is the case with freedom and the will, since the free entity is the will. Will without freedom is an empty word, while freedom is actual only as will, as subject.

The following points should be noted about the connexion between the will and thought. Mind is in principle thinking, and man is distinguished from beast in virtue of thinking. But it must not be imagined that man is half thought and half will, and that he keeps thought in one pocket and will in another, for this would be a foolish idea. The distinction between thought and will is only that between the theoretical attitude and the practical. These, however, are surely not two faculties; the will is rather a special way of thinking, thinking translating itself into existence, thinking as the urge to give itself existence.

This distinction between thought and will may be described as follows. In thinking an object, I make it into thought and deprive it of its sensuous aspect; I make it into something which is directly and essentially mine. Since it is in thought that I am first by myself, I do not penetrate an object until I understand it; it then ceases to stand over against me and I have taken from it the character of its own which it had in opposition to me. Just as Adam said to Eve: 'Thou art flesh of my flesh and

bone of my bone', so mind says: 'This is mind of my mind and its foreign character has disappeared.' An idea is always a generalization, and generalization is a property of thinking. To generalize means to think. The ego is thought and so the universal. When I say 'I', I *eo ipso* abandon all my particular characteristics, my disposition, natural endowment, knowledge, and age. The ego is quite empty, a mere point, simple, yet active in this simplicity. The variegated canvas of the world is before me; I stand over against it; by my theoretical attitude to it I overcome its opposition to me and make its content my own. I am at home in the world when I know it, still more so when I have understood it. So much for the theoretical attitude.

The practical attitude, on the other hand, begins in thinking, in the ego itself, and it appears first as though opposed to thinking because, I mean, it sets up a sort of diremption. In so far as I am practical or active, i.e. in so far as I do something, I determine myself, and to determine myself simply means to posit a difference. But these differences which I posit are still mine all the same; the determinate volitions are mine and the aims which I struggle to realize belong to me. If I now let these determinations and differences go, i.e. if I posit them in the so-called external world, they none the less still remain mine. They are what I have done, what I have made; they bear the trace of my mind.

Such is the distinction between the theorical attitude and the practical, but now the tie between them must be described. The theoretical is essentially contained in the practical; we must decide against the idea that the two are separate, because we cannot have a will without intelligence. On the contrary, the will contains the theoretical in itself. The will determines itself and this determination is in the first place something inward, because what I will I hold before my mind as an idea; it is the object of my thought. An animal acts on instinct, is driven by an inner impulse and so it too is practical, but it has no will, since it does not bring before its mind the object of its desire. A man, however, can just as little be theoretical or think without a will, because in thinking he is of necessity being active. The content of something thought has the form of being; but this being is something mediated, something established through our activity. Thus these distinct attitudes cannot be divorced; they are one and the same; and in any activity, whether of <u>thinking</u> or <u>willing</u>, both moments are present.

5.   *Paragraph 5*
In this element of the will is rooted my ability to free myself from everything, abandon every aim, abstract from everything. Man alone can sacrifice everything, his life included; he can commit suicide. An animal cannot; it always remains merely negative, in an alien destiny to which it merely accustoms itself. Man is the pure thought of himself, and only in thinking is he this power to give himself universality, i.e. to extinguish all particularity, all determinacy. <u>This negative freedom, or freedom as the Understanding conceives it, is one-sided;</u> but a one-sided view always contains one essential factor and therefore is not to be discarded. But the Understanding is defective in exalting a single one-sided factor to be the sole and the supreme one.

In history this form of freedom is a frequent phenomenon. Amongst the Hindus, for instance, the highest life is held to be persistence in the bare knowledge of one's simple identity with oneself, fixation in this empty space of one's inner life, as light remains colourless in pure vision, and the sacrifice of every activity in life, every aim, and every project. In this way man becomes Brahma; there is no longer any distinction between the finite man and Brahma. In fact in this universality every difference has disappeared.

This form of freedom appears more concretely in the active fanaticism of both political and religious life. For instance, during the Terror in the French Revolution all differences of talent and authority were supposed to have been superseded. This period was an upheaval, an agitation, an irreconcilable hatred of everything particular. Since fanaticism wills an abstraction only, nothing articulated, it follows that, when distinctions appear, it finds them antagonistic to its own indeterminacy and annuls them. For this reason, the French Revolutionaries destroyed once more the institutions which they had made themselves, since any institution whatever is antagonistic to the abstract self-consciousness of equality.

6.   *Paragraph 6*
This second moment appears as the moment opposed to the first; it is to be grasped in its general character; it is intrinsic to freedom, although it does not constitute the whole of freedom. Here the ego leaves undifferentiated indeterminacy and proceeds to differentiate itself, to posit a content or object and so to give itself determinacy. My willing is not pure willing but the willing of something. A will which, like that expounded in Paragraph 5, wills only the abstract universal, wills nothing and is therefore no will at all. The particular volition is a restriction, since the will, in order to be a will, must restrict itself in some way or other. The fact that the will wills *something* is restriction, negation. Thus particularization is what as a rule is called finitude. Reflective thinking usually takes the first moment, i.e. indeterminacy, as the higher and absolute moment, while it regards restriction as a mere negation of this indeterminacy.[1] But this indeterminacy is itself only a negation in contrast with the determinate, with finitude; the ego is this solitude and absolute negation.[2] The indeterminate will is to this extent just as one-sided as the will rooted in sheer determinacy.

7.   *Paragraph 7*
What is properly called the will includes in itself both the preceding moments. The ego as such is in the first place pure activity, the universal which is by itself. But this universal determines itself and to that extent is no longer by itself but posits itself as an other and ceases to be the universal. Now the third moment is that, in its restriction, in this other, the will is by itself; in determining itself it still

remains by itself and does not cease to keep hold of the universal. This moment, then, is the concrete concept of freedom, while the two previous moments have been found to be through and through abstract and one-sided.

Freedom in this sense, however, we already possess in the form of feeling – in friendship and love, for instance. Here we are not inherently one-sided; we restrict ourselves gladly in relating ourselves to another, but in this restriction know ourselves as ourselves. In this determinacy a man should not feel himself determined; on the contrary, since he treats the other as other, it is there that he first arrives at the feeling of his own self-hood. Thus freedom lies neither in indeterminacy nor in determinacy; it is both of these at once. The will which restricts itself simply to a *this* is the will of the capricious man who supposes that he is not free unless he has *this* will. But the will is not tied to something restricted; it must go beyond the restriction, since the nature of the will is other than this one-sidedness and constraint. Freedom is to will something determinate, yet in this determinacy to be by oneself and to revert once more to the universal.

[. . .]

12.   *Paragraph 15*

Since it is possible for me to determine myself in this way or that, or in other words since I can choose, I possess the arbitrary will, and to possess this is what is usually called freedom. The choice which I have is grounded in the universality of the will, in the fact that I can make this or that mine. This thing that is mine is particular in content and therefore not adequate to me and so is separate from me; it is only potentially mine, while I am the potentiality of linking myself to it. Choice, therefore, is grounded in the indeterminacy of the ego and the determinacy of a content. Thus the will, on account of this content, is not free, although it has an infinite aspect in virtue of its form. No single content is adequate to it

and in no single content is it really at grips with itself. Arbitrariness implies that the content is made mine not by the nature of my will but by chance. Thus I am dependent on this content, and this is the contradiction lying in arbitrariness. The man in the street thinks he is free if it is open to him to act as he pleases but his very arbitrariness implies that he is not free. When I will what is rational, then I am acting not as a particular individual but in accordance with the concepts of ethics in general. In an ethical action, what I vindicate is not myself but the thing. But in doing a perverse action, it is my singularity that I bring on to the centre of the stage. The rational is the high road where everyone travels, where no one is conspicuous. When great artists complete a masterpiece, we may speak of its inevitability, which means that the artist's idiosyncrasy has completely disappeared and no mannerism is detectable in it. Pheidias has no mannerisms; his figures themselves live and declare themselves. But the worse the artist is, the more we see in his work the artist, his singularity, his arbitrariness. If you stop at the consideration that, having an arbitrary will, a man can will this or that, then of course his freedom consists in that ability. But if you keep firmly in view that the content of his willing is a given one, then he is determined thereby and in that respect at all events is free no longer.

Notes

1   [Hegel is thinking e.g. of Spinoza's view that all determination is negation and that only the indeterminate, or the infinite, is real.]

2   [i.e. the pure ego of Paragraph 5. It is 'alone' and negative because it is the renunciation of everything determinate and is simply turned in upon itself.]

G. W. F. Hegel, paras. 4–7 and 15 from T. M. Knox (ed.), *The Philosophy of Right* (Oxford: Clarendon Press, 1942), pp. 20–4, 27, 225–31.

Chapter 7

Karl Marx, from "On the Jewish Question" (1844)

According to Bauer man must sacrifice the 'privilege of belief' in order to be able to receive general human rights. Let us discuss for moment the so-called human rights, human rights in their authentic form, the form they have in the writings of their discoverers, the North Americans and French! These human rights are partly political rights that are only exercised in community with other men. Their content is formed by participation in the common essence, the political essence, the essence of the state. They fall under the category of political freedom, under the category of civil rights, which, as we have seen, in no way presuppose the consistent and positive abolition of religion, nor, consequently, of Judaism. It remains to discuss the other part of human rights, the rights of man, in so far as they differ from the rights of the citizen.

Among them are freedom of conscience, the right to exercise a chosen religion. The privilege of belief is expressly recognized either as a human right, or as a consequence of one of the human rights, freedom.

Declaration of the Rights of Man and of the Citizen, 1791, Article 10: 'No one should be molested because of his opinions, not even religious ones'. In the first section of the constitution of 1791 'the liberty of every man to practise the religion to which he adheres' is guaranteed as human right. *The Declaration of the Rights of Man . . . 1793* counts among human rights, in Article 7, 'the free exercise of religious practice'. Indeed, concerning the right to publish one's thoughts and opinions,

to hold assemblies and practise one's religion, it goes as far as to say: 'the necessity of announcing these rights supposes either the present or the recent memory of despotism'. Compare the constitution of 1795, Section 14, Article 354.

Constitution of Pennsylvania, Article 9, Paragraph 3: 'All men have a natural and indefeasible right to worship Almighty God according to the dictates of their own consciences: no man can of right be compelled to attend, erect or support a place of worship, or to maintain any ministry, against his consent; no human authority can, in any case whatever, control or interfere with the rights of conscience.'

Constitution of New Hampshire, Articles 5 & 6: 'Among the natural rights, some are in their very nature unalienable. . . . Of this kind are rights of conscience' [. . .].

The incompatibility of religion with the rights of man is so far from being evident in the concept of the rights of man, that the right to be religious, to be religious in one's own chosen way, to practise one's chosen religion is expressly counted as one of the rights of man. The privilege of faith is a universal right of man.

The rights of man are as such differentiated from the right of the citizen. Who is the 'man' who is different from the 'citizen?' No one but the member of civil society. Why is the member of civil society called 'man', simply man, and why are his rights called the rights of man? How do we explain this fact? From the relationship of the political state to civil society, from the nature of political emancipation.

Above all we notice the fact that the so-called rights of man, the rights of man as different from the rights of the citizen are nothing but the rights of the member of civil society, i.e. egoistic man, man separated from other men and the community. The most radical constitution, the constitution of 1793, can say:

Declaration of the Rights of Man..., Article 2. These rights etc. (natural and impre-scriptable rights) are: equality, liberty, security, property.

What does liberty consist of?

Article 6: 'Liberty is the power that belongs to man to do anything that does not infringe on the right of someone else' or according to the declaration of the rights of man of 1791 'liberty consists in the power of doing anything that does not harm others'.

Thus freedom is the right to do and perform what does not harm others. The limits within which each person can move without harming others is defined by the law, just as the boundary between two fields is defined by the fence. The freedom in question is that of a man treated as an isolated monad and withdrawn into himself. Why is the Jew, according to Bauer, incapable of receiving the rights of man? 'So long as he is a Jew the limited nature that makes him a Jew will get the upper hand over the human nature that

should unite him as a man to other men and will separate him from the non-Jew.' But the right of man to freedom is not based on the union of man with man, but on the separation of man from man. It is the right to this sepa-ration, the rights of the limited individual who is limited to himself.

The practical application of the rights of man to freedom is the right of man to private property.

What does the right of man to property consist in?

Article 16 (Constitution of 1793): 'The right of property is the right which belongs to all citizens to enjoy and dispose at will of their goods and revenues, the fruit of their work and industry.'

Thus the right of man to property is the right to enjoy his possessions and dispose of the same arbitrarily, without regard for other men, independently from society, the right of selfishness. It is the former individual freedom together with its latter application that forms the basis of civil society. It leads man to see in other men not the realization but the limita-tion of his own freedom. Above all it proclaims the right of man 'to enjoy and dispose at will of his goods, his revenues and fruits of his work and industry'.

Karl Marx, "On the Jewish Question," from D. McLellan (ed.), *Karl Marx: Selected Writings* (Oxford: Oxford University Press, 1977), pp. 51–3.

Chapter 8

Thomas Hill Green, from *On the Different Senses of 'Freedom' as Applied to Will and to the Moral Progress of Man* and *Lectures on the Principles of Political Obligation* (1882)

[. . .] Hegel holds that freedom, as the condition in which the will is determined by an object adequate to itself, or by an object which itself as reason constitutes, is realised in the state. He thinks of the state in a way not familiar to Englishmen, a way not unlike that in which Greek philosophers thought of the πόλις, as a society governed by laws and institutions and established customs which secure the common good of the members of the society – enable them to make the best of themselves – and are recognised as doing so. Such a state is 'objective freedom'; freedom is realised in it because in it the reason, the self-determining principle operating in man as his will, has found a perfect expression for itself (as an artist may be considered to express himself in a perfect work of art); and the man who is determined by the objects which the well-ordered state presents to him is determined by that which is the perfect expression of his reason, and is thus free.

5. There is, no doubt, truth in this view. I have already tried to show how the self-distinguishing and self-seeking consciousness of man, acting in and upon those human wants and ties and affections which in their proper human character have as little reality apart from it as it apart from them, gives rise to a system of social relations, with laws, customs, and institutions corresponding; and how in this system the individual's consciousness of the absolutely desirable, of something that should be, of an ideal to be realised in his life, finds a content or object which has been constituted or brought into being by that consciousness itself as working through generations of men; how interests are thus supplied to the man of a more concrete kind than the interest in fulfilment of a universally binding law because universally binding, but which yet are the product of reason, and in satisfying which he is conscious of attaining a true good, a good contributory to the perfection of himself and his kind. There is thus something in all forms of society that tends to the freedom at least of some favoured individuals, because it tends to actualise in them the possibility of that determination by objects conceived as desirable in distinction from

objects momentarily desired, which is determination by reason. To put it otherwise, the effect of his social relations on a man thus favoured is that, whereas in all willing the individual seeks to satisfy himself, this man seeks to satisfy himself, not as one who feels this or that desire, but as one who conceives, whose nature demands, a permanent good. So far as it is thus in respect of his rational nature that he makes himself an object to himself, his will is autonomous. This was the good which the ideal πόλις, as conceived by the Greek philosophers, secured for the true πολίτης, the man who, entering into the idea of the πόλις, was equally qualified ἄρχειν καὶ ἄρχεσθαι. No doubt in the actual Greek πόλις there was some tendency in this direction, some tendency to rationalise and moralise the citizen. Without the real tendency the ideal possibility would not have suggested itself. And in more primitive forms of society, so far as they were based on family or tribal relations, we can see that the same tendency must have been at work, just as in modern life the consciousness of his position as member or head of a family, wherever it exists, necessarily does something to moralise a man. In modern Christendom, with the extension of citizenship, the security of family life to all men (so far as law and police can secure it), the establishment in various forms of Christian fellowship of which the moralising functions grow as those of the magistrate diminish, the number of individuals whom society awakens to interests in objects contributory to human perfection tends to increase. So far the modern state, in that full sense in which Hegel uses the term (as including all the agencies for common good of a law-abiding people), does contribute to the realisation of freedom, if by freedom we understand the autonomy of the will or its determination by rational objects, objects which help to satisfy the demand of reason, the effort after self-perfection.

6. On the other hand, it would seem that we cannot significantly speak of freedom except with reference to individual persons; that only in them can freedom be realised; that therefore the realisation of freedom in the state can only mean the attainment of freedom by individuals through influences which the state (in the wide sense spoken of) supplies, – 'freedom' here, as before, meaning not the mere self-determination which renders us responsible, but determination by reason, 'autonomy of the will'; and that under the best conditions of any society that has ever been such realisation of freedom is most imperfect. To an Athenian slave, who might be used to gratify a master's lust, it would have been a mockery to speak of the state as a realisation of freedom; and perhaps it would not be much less so to speak of it as such to an untaught and under-fed denizen of a London yard with gin-shops on the right hand and on the left. What Hegel says of the state in this respect seems as hard to square with facts as what St. Paul says of the Christian whom the manifestation of Christ has transferred from bondage into 'the glorious liberty of the sons of God.' In both cases the difference between the ideal and the actual seems to be ignored, and tendencies seem to be spoken of as if they were accomplished facts. It is noticeable that by uncritical readers of St. Paul the account of himself as under the law (in *Romans* vii.), with the 'law of sin in his members warring against the law of his reason,' is taken as applicable to the regenerate Christian, though evidently St. Paul meant it as a description of the state from which the Gospel, the 'manifestation of the Son of God in the likeness of sinful flesh,' set him free. They are driven to this interpretation because, though they can understand St. Paul's account of his deliverance as an account of a deliverance achieved for them but not in them, or as an assurance of what is to be, they cannot adjust it to the actual experience of the Christian life. In the same way Hegel's account of freedom as realised in the state does not seem to correspond to the facts of society as it is, or even as, under the unalterable conditions of human nature, it ever could be; though undoubtedly there is a work of moral liberation, which society, through its

various agencies, is constantly carrying on for the individual.

7.   Meanwhile it must be borne in mind that in all these different views as to the manner and degree in which freedom is to be attained, 'freedom' does not mean that the man or will is undetermined, nor yet does it mean mere self-determination, which (unless denied altogether, as by those who take the strictly naturalistic view of human action) must be ascribed equally to the man whose will is heteronomous or vicious, and to him whose will is autonomous; equally to the man who recognises the authority of law in what St. Paul would count the condition of a bondman, and to him who fulfils the righteousness of the law in the spirit of adoption. It means a particular kind of self-determination; the state of the man who lives indeed for himself, but for the fulfilment of himself as a 'giver of law universal' (Kant); who lives for himself, but only according to the true idea of himself, according to the law of his being, 'according to nature' (the Stoics); who is so taken up into God, to whom God so gives the spirit, that there is no constraint in his obedience to the divine will (St. Paul); whose interests, as a loyal citizen, are those of a well-ordered state in which practical reason expresses itself (Hegel). Now none of these modes of self-determination is at all implied in 'freedom' according to the primary meaning of the term, as expressing that relation between one man and others in which he is secured from compulsion. All that is so implied is that a man should have power to do what he wills or prefers. No reference is made to the nature of the will or preference, of the object willed or preferred; whereas according to the usage of 'freedom' in the doctrines we have just been considering, it is not constituted by the mere fact of acting upon preference, but depends wholly on the nature of the preference, upon the kind of object willed or preferred.

"Lectures on the Principles of Political Obligation"

[. . .]

M. The Right of the State to Promote Morality

207.   THE right of the individual man as such to free life is constantly gaining on its negative side more general recognition. It is the basis of the growing scrupulosity in regard to punishments which are not reformatory, which put rights finally out of the reach of a criminal instead of qualifying him for their renewed exercise. But the only rational foundation for the ascription of this right is the ascription of capacity for free contribution to social good. We treat this capacity in the man whose crime has given proof of its having been overcome by anti-social tendencies, as yet giving him a title to a further chance of its development; on the other hand, we act as if it conferred no title on its possessors, before a crime has been committed, to be placed under conditions in which its realisation would be possible. Is this reasonable? Yet are not all modern states so acting? Are they not allowing their ostensible members to grow up under conditions which render the development of social capacity practically impossible? Was it not more reasonable, as in the ancient states, to deny the right to life in the human subject as such, than to admit it under conditions which prevent the realisation of the capacity that forms the ground of its admission? This brings us to the fourth of the questions that arose out of the assertion of the individual's right to free life. What is the nature and extent of the individual's claim to be enabled positively to realise that capacity for freely contributing to social good which is the foundation of his right to free life?

208.   In dealing with this question, it is important to bear in mind that the capacity we are considering is essentially a free or (what is the same) a moral capacity. It is a capacity, not

for action determined by relation to a certain end, but for action determined by a conception of the end to which it is relative. Only thus is it a foundation of rights. The action of an animal or plant may be made contributory to social good, but it is not therefore a foundation of rights on the part of an animal or plant, because they are not affected by the conception of the good to which they contribute. A right is a power of acting for his own ends, – for what he conceives to be his good, – secured to an individual by the community, on the supposition that its exercise contributes to the good of the community. But the exercise of such a power cannot be so contributory, unless the individual, in acting for his own ends, is at least affected by the conception of a good as common to himself with others. The condition of making the animal contributory to human good is that we do not leave him free to determine the exercise of his powers; that we determine them for him; that we use him merely as an instrument; and this means that we do not, because we cannot, endow him with rights. We cannot endow him with rights because there is no conception of a good common to him with us which we can treat as a motive to him to do to us as he would have us do to him. It is not indeed necessary to a capacity for rights, as it is to true moral goodness, that interest in a good conceived as common to himself with others should be a man's dominant motive. It is enough if that which he presents to himself from time to time as his good, and which accordingly determines his action, is so far affected by consideration of the position in which he stands to others, – of the way in which this or that possible action of his would affect them, and of what he would have to expect from them in return, – as to result habitually, without force or fear of force, in action not incompatible with conditions necessary to the pursuit of a common good on the part of others. In other words, it is the presumption that a man in his general course of conduct will of his own motion have respect to the common good, which entitles him to

rights at the hands of the community. The question of the moral value of the motive which may induce this respect – whether an unselfish interest in common good or the wish for personal pleasure and fear of personal pain – does not come into the account at all. An agent, indeed, who could only be induced by fear of death or bodily harm to behave conformably to the requirements of the community, would not be a subject of rights, because this influence could never be brought to bear on him so constantly, if he were free to regulate his own life, as to secure the public safety. But a man's desire for pleasure to himself and aversion from pain to himself, though dissociated from any desire for a higher object, for any object that is desired because good for others, may constitute a capacity for rights, if his imagination of pleasure and pain is so far affected by sympathy with the feeling of others about him as to make him, independently of force or fear of punishment, observant of established rights. In such a case the fear of punishment may be needed to neutralise antisocial impulses under circumstances of special temptation, but by itself it could never be a sufficiently uniform motive to qualify a man, in the absence of more spontaneously social feelings, for the life of a free citizen. The qualification for such a life is a spontaneous habit of acting with reference to a common good, whether that habit be founded on an imagination of pleasures and pains or on a conception of what ought to be. In either case the habit implies at least an understanding that there is such a thing as a common good, and a regulation of egoistic hopes and fears, if not an inducing of more 'disinterested' motives, in consequence of that understanding.

209.   The capacity for rights, then, being a capacity for spontaneous action regulated by a conception of a common good, either so regulated through an interest which flows directly from that conception, or through hopes and fears which are affected by it through more complex channels of habit and association, is a capacity which cannot be generated – which on the contrary is neutralised

– by any influences that interfere with the spontaneous action of social interests. Now any direct enforcement of the outward conduct, which ought to flow from social interests, by means of threatened penalties – and a law requiring such conduct necessarily implies penalties for disobedience to it – does interfere with the spontaneous action of those interests, and consequently checks the growth of the capacity which is the condition of the beneficial exercise of rights. For this reason the effectual action of the state, i.e. the community as acting through law, for the promotion of habits of true citizenship, seems necessarily to be confined to the removal of obstacles. Under this head, however, there may and should be included much that most states have hitherto neglected, and much that at first sight may have the appearance of an enforcement of moral duties, e.g. the requirement that parents have their children taught the elementary arts. To educate one's children is no doubt a moral duty, and it is not one of those duties, like that of paying debts, of which the neglect directly interferes with the rights of someone else. It might seem, therefore, to be a duty with which positive law should have nothing to do, any more than with the duty of striving after a noble life. On the other hand, the neglect of it does tend to prevent the growth of the capacity for beneficially exercising rights on the part of those whose education is neglected, and it is on this account, not as a purely moral duty on the part of a parent, but as the prevention of a hindrance to the capacity for rights on the part of children, that education should be enforced by the state. It may be objected indeed, that in enforcing it we are departing in regard to the parents from the principle above laid down; that we are interfering with the spontaneous action of social interests, though we are doing so with a view to promoting this spontaneous action in another generation. But the answer to this objection is, that a law of compulsory education, if the preferences, ecclesiastical or otherwise, of those parents who show any practical sense of their responsibility are duly respected, is from the beginning only felt as compulsion by those in whom, so far as this social function is concerned, there is no spontaneity to be interfered with; and that in the second generation, though the law with its penal sanctions still continues, it is not felt as a law, as an enforcement of action by penalties, at all.

210.   On the same principle the freedom of contract ought probably to be more restricted in certain directions than is at present the case. The freedom to do as they like on the part of one set of men may involve the ultimate disqualification of many others, or of a succeeding generation, for the exercise of rights. This applies most obviously to such kinds of contract or traffic as affect the health and housing of the people, the growth of population relatively to the means of subsistence, and the accumulation or distribution of landed property. In the hurry of removing those restraints on free dealing between man and man, which have arisen partly perhaps from some confused idea of maintaining morality, but much more from the power of class-interests, we have been apt to take too narrow a view of the range of persons – not one generation merely, but succeeding generations – whose freedom ought to be taken into account, and of the conditions necessary to their freedom ('freedom' here meaning their qualification for the exercise of rights). Hence the massing of population without regard to conditions of health; unrestrained traffic in deleterious commodities; unlimited upgrowth of the class of hired labourers in particular industries which circumstances have suddenly stimulated, without any provision against the danger of an impoverished proletariate in following generations. Meanwhile, under pretence of allowing freedom of bequest and settlement, a system has grown up which prevents the landlords of each generation from being free either in the government of their families or in the disposal of their land, and aggravates the tendency to crowd into towns, as well as the difficulties of providing healthy house-room, by keeping land in a few hands. It would be out of place here to consider in

detail the remedies for these evils, or to discuss the question how far it is well to trust to the initiative of the state or of individuals in dealing with them. It is enough to point out the directions in which the state may remove obstacles to the realisation of the *capacity* for beneficial exercise of rights, without defeating its own object by vitiating the spontaneous character of that capacity.

Thomas Hill Green, *Lectures on the Principles of Political Obligation* (London: Longmans, 1941), pp. 6–9, 206–10.

Chapter 9

Guido De Ruggiero, from *The History of European Liberalism* (1925)

§2. Negative Freedom and Positive Freedom

We have spoken of individual and social freedom, civil and political freedom, freedom *from* the State and freedom *through* the State; but in all these inquiries we have in some sense presupposed a freedom unqualified by any adjectives, lying at the root of these various specific forms. We must now undertake a more fundamental inquiry, which alone can justify these others, into the essence of human freedom itself.

History presents us with two conceptions, one inspiring the political systems of the eighteenth century, the other those of the nineteenth and twentieth. According to the first, freedom is the ability to do what one likes, a liberty of choice implying the individual's right not to be hampered by others in the development of his own activity. Considered in itself, in its strict essence, this liberty is all but a nonentity, precisely because it is devoid of content, and exhausts itself in the formal assertion of an abstract capacity, wholly arbitrary in its indifference to any particular determination. It therefore acquires coherence and character only in its historical or polemical expression, which reveals it as liberty *from* something, as the rejection of some external impediment which hampers the free expansion of the individual will. The extreme vitality of eighteenth-century Liberalism is due entirely to its polemical tone, to the critical energy with which it attacks and dissolves the rigid world of custom and authority, and liberates in this dissolution a myriad of new-born individuals living for the first time a life of their own.

In this way abstract liberty begins to acquire a content, produced by its conflict with the historical environment forming the object of its criticism. It is no longer the indifferent caprice which it appears to be in its inadequate theoretical formulae, but the affirmation of a definite *something*, namely the modern individual with his beliefs, opinions, needs, and activities; no mere ultimate natural fact, purged of all the accretions of historical life, but the product of modern history, the outcome of education, culture, and work. If resistance to oppression asserts itself in the name of an abstract universal faculty, that is only because concrete particular faculties are already at work, capable of generalizing from their own experience.

Thus the negative or polemical notion of liberty leads to a positive or constructive notion, systematically developed during the nineteenth century. According to this, freedom is not indeterminate caprice, but man's ability to determine himself, and thus by the spontaneous act of his own consciousness to rise above the necessities and the bonds in which practical life imprisons him. Thus it is not a natural fact, but the result of an unremitting education of character, and the mark of civil maturity. The really free man is not the man who can choose any line of conduct indifferently – this being rather a frivolous and weak-willed man – but the man who has the energy to choose that which is most conformable to his moral destiny; to realize, in his own act, his universally human nature. The absence of external compulsion is the merely outward aspect of this freedom; its inner value lies in the concentrated strength of the personality which dominates and controls all the factors and elements of its spiritual life. To be free is to be *sui iuris*, independent of others in the sense that all natural and coercive dependence is abolished and replaced by a dependence spontaneously affirmed in the consciousness of duty towards oneself and others. This notion develops by opposing, point by point, the notion that preceded it. Negative freedom consisted in denying all authority and all law; the new positive freedom consists in transferring the source of authority and law to the intimacy of one's own mind. To be a law to one's self, or in other words autonomous; to obey an authority recognized by conscience, because springing from its own law, is to be truly free. The eternal glory of Kant is to have demonstrated that obedience to the moral law is freedom.

Freedom thus coincides with the reality of the mind. It is not a faculty, an adventitious mode of being which might be withdrawn, leaving the substantial structure of mind unmodified and unimpaired. It is the spiritual energy which presides over, nourishes, and regulates all the activities of man. To act and to act freely are the same; without freedom there is not action, but passion, mechanism, habit. This is why ability in any art, creative vigour in any science, initiative in any enterprise, progress in any branch of human activity, are rooted in freedom, because freedom is nothing but the creative 'spontaneity of the mind and at the same time the law which controls its development.

As such, it is not restricted or atomically isolated within the narrow sphere of the individual life. This would be the result of a merely negative freedom, tending to exclude all interferences from without, and to justify caprice. In the higher conception of which we are speaking, the individual is more than a mere individual, because his conscience represents for him a law, an authority, in which are already expressed the universal elements of his nature, and from which arises the demand for an organization of human life transcending the demands of mere selfishness. The man who acts according to duty is no longer alone in the world; he stands face to face with an *other*, in whom his original *self* is duplicated; and this fundamental relation is the source of all human relations.

It was the great merit of Hegel to have extracted from the Kantian identification of freedom with mind the idea of an organic development of freedom, coinciding with the organization of human society in its progressively higher and more spiritual forms. The historical experience of the nineteenth century had vindicated Hegel's view, by showing that freedom has the force of a bond capable of holding men together in associations the more lasting and fertile according as they are more spontaneous in their origin and autonomous in their choice of ends. The destruction of outward bonds, which the timid conservatives of the early nineteenth century believed would bring about a ruinous anarchy, proved on the contrary the best means of effecting, without undue violence, a redistribution of social forces and of facilitating their expansion. The generations that followed the Revolution, still trained in the sensationalism and naturalism of illuminist philosophy, were unable to recognize that ideal bonds are far more effective than material facts in uniting men, and that consent is the real force of modern Society.

Thus freedom not only created a rich variety of subordinate associations, replacing by degrees the historical organizations which the Revolution in its first onset destroyed, but found a further expression in the highest and most complex human association, the State; and here provided the most irrefragable proof of its own constructive power. We are to-day so much accustomed to the idea of the Liberal State that we do not notice its paradoxical character, which was plain enough to its first inexperienced observers. The State, the organ of coercion *par excellence*, has become the highest expression of liberty; the traditional enemy of the individual has reconstructed itself after the pattern of the individual consciousness.

These experiences have emphatically disproved the opinion of despots and their partisans, that liberty can destroy but cannot construct, and can at most add ornamental features to a fabric constructed by servile labour. Of these two opinions the first applies only to the freedom of revolted slaves, the second to that of slaves liberated by grace of their masters; in both cases the freedom in question is a servile freedom, the creature of despotism. True freedom, the freedom of a man *sui iuris*, can both destroy and reconstruct; it only adorns the fabric which itself has built. To a free man nothing can be more repulsive than the opinion entertained by courtiers, that freedom is an ornament and a luxury: he knows that it is something far more serious than that, a discipline, a responsibility, a sacrifice. A free action is by no means synonymous with an easy action: freedom deprives a man of the comfortable support of ready-made decisions imposed from without, which save him the pains of an inner struggle; it leaves him naked in the sight of his conscience, burdened with the unshared responsibility for the consequences of his own actions, which no kindly authority can conceal or disguise. The joy of being the sole author of his actions is inseparable from the torment which preceded it: both alike are equally elements in his spiritual progress.

This explains the great difference between the eighteenth-century notion of liberty as a natural fact and what we may now call our own notion, which treats it as a development, a becoming. To say that man is born free

involves admitting that he becomes a slave; because every bond that connects him with his fellows, every relation in the life of the family, Society, and the State, implies a surrender of this original and fundamental freedom. A strange freedom this, which man possesses only when he is not human, and which begins to vanish as soon as he is born! Everything which we regard as a spiritual development, an enlargement of our sphere of action, the acquisition of a wider experience, is on such a view a diminution of the freedom of the will, a restriction of human personality.

We, on the contrary, are profoundly convinced that men are not born free but become free. This applies both to the life of the individual and to the historical life of humanity. The child is not free, dominated as he is by impulses, by transitory and changing passions; we place him on the contrary under watchful control. Childish peoples like those which are not controlled by stable laws and organic government are not free, though they may seem to be; among them we find only caprice above, among the dominant strong, and servitude beneath, in the dominated weak.

Liberty does not exist at the origin of human development, but comes into being as it proceeds. As the action of man widens its field, it becomes more free, because focused in a more complex personality. As children we are dominated by the senses and the passions; in our youth we begin to dominate them; adult, we possess them more completely in the calm of our reflection. The isolated individual is less free than the man who lives in the family, in Society, and in the State; because family, Society, and the State offer him an increasingly wide sphere of activity in which to strengthen and enrich his personality. If freedom were an abstract individual faculty, the faculty to do whatever one pleases, it would disappear as the individual began to live more genuinely in the world; but that faculty is what we call caprice, the opposite of the freedom which men feel to be their social and moral mission.

Freedom exists so far as it is exercised, so far as it faces the increasingly complex demands of life. What is the freedom of an outlaw, a savage, or an exile? Slavery to his own passions or caprices, slavery to nature and necessity; in either case the motive of a brutal and deadening existence. The true freedom is that of the man who lives in civil Society, with all its bonds and all its burdens, from whose servitude he is continually liberating himself by the very fact of finding in it the necessary means to the development of his own moral personality.

Are the two notions of freedom, here sketched in outline, merely two historical systems of thought, one of which follows the other in an irreversible order, the first wholly vanishing when superseded by the second? Or are they also two ideal elements in our present life, the one subordinated to the other, yet incapable of being entirely suppressed, and reappearing with an insistent claim to survival whenever we think we have destroyed it? To deny the second alternative would be to discredit the direct experience of our psychological and social life, and – more serious – to deny the genetic character of freedom. However we try to confine the freedom of caprice and selfishness to the lowest stage of social evolution, we can never deny that it contains a spark of spiritual and spontaneous life, that is, of true freedom. The negation of custom and social mechanism, however lawless and arbitrary, marks the first liberation of the mind from that which burdened and paralysed it; the first act of faith in itself, the first movement of its creative energy. The experience of error and evil, necessarily acquired in its long pilgrimage, is a vital element in its growth, without which truth and goodness could not be its achievement, its joy, and its pride. And even in its highest stages of spiritual progress, when freedom is a sure possession that has already borne fruit, the work of negation and criticism must still be renewed if the mind is not to lose itself in a passive stagnation.

The simultaneous presence in the same social world and the same individual life of different stages in the development of freedom creates the first political problem of Liberalism. Ought we to recognize freedom only in its most mature and highly developed form? Ought we, for example, to make the State an assembly of free men, separated from the servile mass which must be governed by authority? This would amount to recognizing as the only form of freedom the freedom to do right, a doctrine consistently taught by the Catholic Church and all but embraced by some professedly Liberal politicians. But clearly such a policy destroys even that freedom which it would preserve, whose existence is inseparable from the entire spiritual process that has produced it. Without an inferior freedom, an elementary school of character, no truly free personality can ever emerge into the light. And if these experiments demand a great expenditure of energy, it is not wasted, for all the energy that is used returns multiplied to its source.

Yet this solution, however straightforward in outline, becomes more difficult and complicated in the rich variety of circumstances perpetually presented by historical reality. There is a freedom which, in the shape of caprice or licence, while promoting the activity of one person, impairs that of others; to permit this would be to destroy civil life, and with it the very root of human freedom. Here then is the first Liberal limitation of freedom, which consists in guaranteeing the coexistence of different free wills in the same society. Together with liberty comes into existence law, equality of rights. Again, individual caprice may injure not the rights of others, but the growth of new beings emerging into a free spiritual life; and here again public interest demands another and an even stricter limitation. For example, a person who employs a child in work that is too severe for it is smothering a nascent personality: the veto of Society on such employment is therefore just and liberal. Further, there are cases in which the caprice of individuals hurts nobody but themselves, squandering their chances of a higher and worthier freedom; so that here again Society is right to intervene. For example,

Society may prescribe compulsory elementary education, may limit the purchase of unwholesome beverages, and so forth.

The innumerable cases presented by everyday experience cannot be dealt with by deduction from a general notion of liberty. The main thing is a liberal spirit, able to pierce the often deceptive appearances of formal liberty, and to grasp its more substantial and genuine content.

Guido De Ruggiero, "Negative Freedom and Positive Freedom," from R. G. Collingwood (ed.), *The History of European Liberalism* (Boston, MA: Beacon Press, 1969), pp. 350–7.

Chapter 10

Isaiah Berlin, from "Two Concepts of Liberty" (1969)

I

To coerce a man is to deprive him of freedom – freedom from what? Almost every moralist in human history has praised freedom. Like happiness and goodness, like nature and reality, it is a term whose meaning is so porous that there is little interpretation that it seems able to resist. I do not propose to discuss either the history of this protean word or the more than two hundred senses of it recorded by historians of ideas. I propose to examine no more than two of these senses – but they are central ones, with a great deal of human history behind them, and, I dare say, still to come. The first of these political senses of freedom or liberty (I shall use both words to mean the same), which (following much precedent) I shall call the 'negative' sense, is involved in the answer to the question 'What is the area within which the subject – a person or group of persons – is or should be left to do or be what he is able to do or be, without interference by other persons?' The second, which I shall call the 'positive' sense, is involved in the answer to the question 'What, or who, is the source of control or interference that can determine someone to do, or be, this rather than that?' The two questions are clearly different, even though the answers to them may overlap.

The notion of negative freedom

I am normally said to be free to the degree to which no man or body of men interferes with my activity. Political liberty in this sense is simply the area within which a man can act unobstructed by others. If I am prevented by others from doing what I could otherwise do, I am to that degree unfree; and if this area is contracted by other men beyond a certain minimum, I can be described as being coerced, or, it may be, enslaved. Coercion is not, however, a term that covers every form of inability. If I say that I am unable to jump more than ten feet in the air, or cannot read because I am blind, or cannot understand the darker pages of Hegel, it would be eccentric to say that I am to that degree enslaved or coerced. Coercion implies the deliberate interference of other human beings within the area in which I could otherwise act. You lack political liberty or freedom only if you are prevented from attaining a goal by human beings.[1] Mere incapacity to attain a goal is not lack of political freedom.[2] This is brought out by the use of such modern expressions as 'economic freedom' and its counterpart, 'economic slavery'. It is argued, very plausibly, that if a man is too poor to afford something on which there is no legal ban – a loaf of bread, a journey round the world, recourse to the law courts – he is as little free to have it as he would be if it were forbidden him by law. If my poverty were a kind of disease which prevented me from buying bread, or paying for the journey round the world or getting my case heard, as lameness prevents me from running, this inability would not naturally be described as a lack of freedom, least of all political freedom. It is only because I believe that my inability to get a given thing is due to the fact that other human beings have made arrangements whereby I am, whereas others are not, prevented from having enough money with which to pay for it, that I think myself a victim of coercion or slavery. In other words, this use of the term depends on a particular social and economic theory about the causes of my poverty or weakness. If my lack of material means is due to my lack of mental or physical capacity, then I begin to speak of being deprived of freedom (and not simply about poverty) only if I accept the theory.[3] If, in addition, I believe that I am being kept in want by a specific arrangement which I consider unjust or unfair, I speak of economic slavery or oppression. The nature of things does not madden us, only ill will does, said Rousseau.[4] The criterion of oppression is the part that I believe to be played by other human beings, directly or indirectly, with or without the intention of doing so, in frustrating my wishes. By being free in this sense I mean not being interfered with by others. The wider the area of non-interference the wider my freedom.

This is what the classical English political philosophers meant when they used this word.[5] They disagreed about how wide the area could or should be. They supposed that it could not, as things were, be unlimited, because if it were, it would entail a state in which all men could boundlessly interfere with all other men; and this kind of 'natural' freedom would lead to social chaos in which men's minimum needs would not be satisfied; or else the liberties of the weak would be suppressed by the strong. Because they perceived that human purposes and activities do not automatically harmonise with one another, and because (whatever their official doctrines) they put high value on other goals, such as justice, or happiness, or culture, or security, or varying degrees of equality, they were prepared to curtail freedom in the interests of other values and, indeed, of freedom itself. For, without this, it was impossible to create

the kind of association that they thought desirable. Consequently, it is assumed by these thinkers that the area of men's free action must be limited by law. But equally it is assumed, especially by such libertarians as Locke and Mill in England, and Constant and Tocqueville in France, that there ought to exist a certain minimum area of personal freedom which must on no account be violated; for if it is overstepped, the individual will find himself in an area too narrow for even that minimum development of his natural faculties which alone makes it possible to pursue, and even to conceive, the various ends which men hold good or right or sacred. It follows that a frontier must be drawn between the area of private life and that of public authority. Where it is to be drawn is a matter of argument, indeed of haggling. Men are largely interdependent, and no man's activity is so completely private as never to obstruct the lives of others in any way. 'Freedom for the pike is death for the minnows';[6] the liberty of some must depend on the restraint of others. Freedom for an Oxford don, others have been known to add, is a very different thing from freedom for an Egyptian peasant.

This proposition derives its force from something that is both true and important, but the phrase itself remains a piece of political claptrap. It is true that to offer political rights, or safeguards against intervention by the State, to men who are half-naked, illiterate, underfed and diseased is to mock their condition; they need medical help or education before they can understand, or make use of, an increase in their freedom. What is freedom to those who cannot make use of it? Without adequate conditions for the use of freedom, what is the value of freedom? First things come first: there are situations in which – to use a saying satirically attributed to the nihilists by Dostoevsky – boots are superior to Pushkin; individual freedom is not everyone's primary need. For freedom is not the mere absence of frustration of whatever kind; this would inflate the meaning of the word until it meant too much or too little. The Egyptian peasant needs clothes or medicine before, and more than, personal liberty, but the minimum freedom that he needs today, and the greater degree of freedom that he may need tomorrow, is not some species of freedom peculiar to him, but identical with that of professors, artists and millionaires.

What troubles the consciences of Western liberals is, I think, the belief, not that the freedom that men seek differs according to their social or economic conditions, but that the minority who possess it have gained it by exploiting, or, at least, averting their gaze from, the vast majority who do not. They believe, with good reason, that if individual liberty is an ultimate end for human beings, none should be deprived of it by others; least of all that some should enjoy it at the expense of others. Equality of liberty; not to treat others as I should not wish them to treat me; repayment of my debt to those who alone have made possible my liberty or prosperity or enlightenment; justice, in its simplest and most universal sense – these are the foundations of liberal morality. Liberty is not the only goal of men. I can, like the Russian critic Belinsky, say that if others are to be deprived of it – if my brothers are to remain in poverty, squalor and chains – then I do not want it for myself, I reject it with both hands and infinitely prefer to share their fate. But nothing is gained by a confusion of terms. To avoid glaring inequality or widespread misery I am ready to sacrifice some, or all, of my freedom: I may do so willingly and freely; but it is freedom that I am giving up for the sake of justice or equality or the love of my fellow men. I should be guilt-stricken, and rightly so, if I were not, in some circumstances, ready to make this sacrifice. But a sacrifice is not an increase in what is being sacrificed, namely freedom, however great the moral need or the compensation for it. Everything is what it is: liberty is liberty, not equality or fairness or justice or culture, or human happiness or a quiet conscience. If the liberty of myself or my class or nation depends on the misery of a number of other human beings, the system

which promotes this is unjust and immoral. But if I curtail or lose my freedom in order to lessen the shame of such inequality, and do not thereby materially increase the individual liberty of others, an absolute loss of liberty occurs. This may be compensated for by a gain in justice or in happiness or in peace, but the loss remains, and it is a confusion of values to say that although my 'liberal', individual freedom may go by the board, some other kind of freedom – 'social' or 'economic' – is increased. Yet it remains true that the freedom of some must at times be curtailed to secure the freedom of others. Upon what principle should this be done? If freedom is a sacred, untouchable value, there can be no such principle. One or other of these conflicting rules or principles must, at any rate in practice, yield: not always for reasons which can be clearly stated, let alone generalised into rules or universal maxims. Still, a practical compromise has to be found.

Philosophers with an optimistic view of human nature and a belief in the possibility of harmonising human interests, such as Locke or Adam Smith or, in some moods, Mill, believed that social harmony and progress were compatible with reserving a large area for private life over which neither the State nor any other authority must be allowed to trespass. Hobbes, and those who agreed with him, especially conservative or reactionary thinkers, argued that if men were to be prevented from destroying one another and making social life a jungle or a wilderness, greater safeguards must be instituted to keep them in their places; he wished correspondingly to increase the area of centralised control and decrease that of the individual. But both sides agreed that some portion of human existence must remain independent of the sphere of social control. To invade that preserve, however small, would be despotism. The most eloquent of all defenders of freedom and privacy, Benjamin Constant, who had not forgotten the Jacobin dictatorship, declared that at the very least the liberty of religion, opinion, expression, property must be guaranteed against arbitrary invasion. Jefferson, Burke, Paine, Mill compiled different catalogues of individual liberties, but the argument for keeping authority at bay is always substantially the same. We must preserve a minimum area of personal freedom if we are not to 'degrade or deny our nature'. We cannot remain absolutely free, and must give up some of our liberty to preserve the rest. But total self-surrender is self-defeating. What then must the minimum be? That which a man cannot give up without offending against the essence of his human nature. What is this essence? What are the standards which it entails? This has been, and perhaps always will be, a matter of infinite debate. But whatever the principle in terms of which the area of non-interference is to be drawn, whether it is that of natural law or natural rights, or of utility, or the pronouncements of a categorical imperative, or the sanctity of the social contract, or any other concept with which men have sought to clarify and justify their convictions, liberty in this sense means liberty *from*; absence of interference beyond the shifting, but always recognisable, frontier. 'The only freedom which deserves the name, is that of pursuing our own good in our own way,' said the most celebrated of its champions.[7] If this is so, is compulsion ever justified? Mill had no doubt that it was. Since justice demands that all individuals be entitled to a minimum of freedom, all other individuals were of necessity to be restrained, if need be by force, from depriving anyone of it. Indeed, the whole function of law was the prevention of just such collisions: the State was reduced to what Lassalle contemptuously described as the functions of a night-watchman or traffic policeman.

What made the protection of individual liberty so sacred to Mill? In his famous essay he declares that, unless the individual is left to live as he wishes in 'the part [of his conduct] which merely concerns himself', civilisation cannot advance; the truth will not, for lack of a free market in ideas, come to light; there will be no scope for spontaneity, originality, genius, for mental energy, for moral courage. Society will

be crushed by the weight of 'collective mediocrity'. Whatever is rich and diversified will be crushed by the weight of custom, by men's constant tendency to conformity, which breeds only 'withered' capacities, 'pinched and hidebound', 'cramped and dwarfed' human beings. 'Pagan self-assertion' is as worthy as 'Christian self-denial'. 'All errors which [a man] is likely to commit against advice and warning, are far outweighed by the evil of allowing others to constrain him to what they deem his good.' The defence of liberty consists in the 'negative' goal of warding off interference. To threaten a man with persecution unless he submits to a life in which he exercises no choices of his goals; to block before him every door but one, no matter how noble the prospect upon which it opens, or how benevolent the motives of those who arrange this, is to sin against the truth that he is a man, a being with a life of his own to live. This is liberty as it has been conceived by liberals in the modern world from the days of Erasmus (some would say of Occam) to our own. Every plea for civil liberties and individual rights, every protest against exploitation and humiliation, against the encroachment of public authority, or the mass hypnosis of custom or organised propaganda, springs from this individualistic, and much disputed, conception of man.

Three facts about this position may be noted. In the first place Mill confuses two distinct notions. One is that all coercion is, in so far as it frustrates human desires, bad as such, although it may have to be applied to prevent other, greater evils; while non-interference, which is the opposite of coercion, is good as such, although it is not the only good. This is the 'negative' conception of liberty in its classical form. The other is that men should seek to discover the truth, or to develop a certain type of character of which Mill approved – critical, original, imaginative, independent, non-conforming to the point of eccentricity, and so on – and that truth can be found, and such character can be bred, only in conditions of freedom. Both these are liberal views, but they are not identical, and the connection between them is, at best, empirical. No one would argue that truth or freedom of self-expression could flourish where dogma crushes all thought. But the evidence of history tends to show (as, indeed, was argued by James Stephen in his formidable attack on Mill in his *Liberty, Equality, Fraternity*) that integrity, love of truth and fiery individualism grow at least as often in severely disciplined communities, among, for example, the puritan Calvinists of Scotland or New England, or under military discipline, as in more tolerant or indifferent societies; and if this is so, Mill's argument for liberty as a necessary condition for the growth of human genius falls to the ground. If his two goals proved incompatible, Mill would be faced with a cruel dilemma, quite apart from the further difficulties created by the inconsistency of his doctrines with strict utilitarianism, even in his own humane version of it.[8]

In the second place, the doctrine is comparatively modern. There seems to be scarcely any discussion of individual liberty as a conscious political ideal (as opposed to its actual existence) in the ancient world. Condorcet had already remarked that the notion of individual rights was absent from the legal conceptions of the Romans and Greeks; this seems to hold equally of the Jewish, Chinese and all other ancient civilisations that have since come to light. The domination of this ideal has been the exception rather than the rule, even in the recent history of the West. Nor has liberty in this sense often formed a rallying cry for the great masses of mankind. The desire not to be impinged upon, to be left to oneself, has been a mark of high civilisation on the part of both individuals and communities. The sense of privacy itself, of the area of personal relationships as something sacred in its own right, derives from a conception of freedom which, for all its religious roots, is scarcely older, in its developed state, than the Renaissance or the Reformation.[9] Yet its decline would mark the death of a civilisation, of an entire moral outlook.

The third characteristic of this notion of liberty is of greater importance. It is that liberty in this sense is not incompatible with some kinds of autocracy, or at any rate with the absence of self-government. Liberty in this sense is principally concerned with the area of control, not with its source. Just as a democracy may, in fact, deprive the individual citizen of a great many liberties which he might have in some other form of society, so it is perfectly conceivable that a liberal-minded despot would allow his subjects a large measure of personal freedom. The despot who leaves his subjects a wide area of liberty may be unjust, or encourage the wildest inequalities, care little for order, or virtue, or knowledge; but provided he does not curb their liberty, or at least curbs it less than many other regimes, he meets with Mill's specification.[10]

Freedom in this sense is not, at any rate logically, connected with democracy or self-government. Self-government may, on the whole, provide a better guarantee of the preservation of civil liberties than other regimes, and has been defended as such by libertarians. But there is no necessary connection between individual liberty and democratic rule. The answer to the question 'Who governs me?' is logically distinct from the question 'How far does government interfere with me?' It is in this difference that the great contrast between the two concepts of negative and positive liberty, in the end, consists.[11] For the 'positive' sense of liberty comes to light if we try to answer the question, not 'What am I free to do or be?', but 'By whom am I ruled?' or 'Who is to say what I am, and what I am not, to be or do?' The connection between democracy and individual liberty is a good deal more tenuous than it seemed to many advocates of both. The desire to be governed by myself, or at any rate to participate in the process by which my life is to be controlled, may be as deep a wish as that for a free area for action, and perhaps historically older. But it is not a desire for the same thing. So different is it, indeed, as to have led in the end to the great clash of ideologies that dominates our world. For it is this, the 'positive' conception of liberty, not freedom from, but freedom to – to lead one prescribed form of life – which the adherents of the 'negative' notion represent as being, at times, no better than a specious disguise for brutal tyranny.

II
The notion of positive freedom

The 'positive' sense of the word 'liberty' derives from the wish on the part of the individual to be his own master. I wish my life and decisions to depend on myself, not on external forces of whatever kind. I wish to be the instrument of my own, not of other men's, acts of will. I wish to be a subject, not an object; to be moved by reasons, by conscious purposes, which are my own, not by causes which affect me, as it were, from outside. I wish to be somebody, not nobody; a doer – deciding, not being decided for, self-directed and not acted upon by external nature or by other men as if I were a thing, or an animal, or a slave incapable of playing a human role, that is, of conceiving goals and policies of my own and realising them. This is at least part of what I mean when I say that I am rational, and that it is my reason that distinguishes me as a human being from the rest of the world. I wish, above all, to be conscious of myself as a thinking, willing, active being, bearing responsibility for my choices and able to explain them by reference to my own ideas and purposes. I feel free to the degree that I believe this to be true, and enslaved to the degree that I am made to realise that it is not.

The freedom which consists in being one's own master, and the freedom which consists in not being prevented from choosing as I do by other men, may, on the face of it, seem concepts at no great logical distance from each other – no more than negative and positive ways of saying much the same thing. Yet the 'positive' and 'negative' notions of freedom historically developed in divergent directions, not always by logically reputable steps, until, in the end, they came into direct conflict with each other.

One way of making this clear is in terms of the independent momentum which the, initially perhaps quite harmless, metaphor of self-mastery acquired. 'I am my own master'; 'I am slave to no man'; but may I not (as Platonists or Hegelians tend to say) be a slave to nature? Or to my own 'unbridled' passions? Are these not so many species of the identical genus 'slave' – some political or legal, others moral or spiritual? Have not men had the experience of liberating themselves from spiritual slavery, or slavery to nature, and do they not in the course of it become aware, on the one hand, of a self which dominates, and, on the other, of something in them which is brought to heel? This dominant self is then variously identified with reason, with my 'higher nature', with the self which calculates and aims at what will satisfy it in the long run, with my 'real', or 'ideal', or 'autonomous' self, or with my self 'at its best'; which is then contrasted with irrational impulse, uncontrolled desires, my 'lower' nature, the pursuit of immediate pleasures, my 'empirical' or 'heteronomous' self, swept by every gust of desire and passion, needing to be rigidly disciplined if it is ever to rise to the full height of its 'real' nature. Presently the two selves may be represented as divided by an even larger gap; the real self may be conceived as something wider than the individual (as the term is normally understood), as a social 'whole' of which the individual is an element or aspect: a tribe, a race, a Church, a State, the great society of the living and the dead and the yet unborn. This entity is then identified as being the 'true' self which, by imposing its collective, or 'organic', single will upon its recalcitrant 'members', achieves its own, and therefore their, 'higher' freedom. The perils of using organic metaphors to justify the coercion of some men by others in order to raise them to a 'higher' level of freedom have often been pointed out. But what gives such plausibility as it has to this kind of language is that we recognise that it is possible, and at times justifiable, to coerce men in the name of some goal (let us say, justice or public health) which they would, if they were more enlightened, themselves pursue, but do not, because they are blind or ignorant or corrupt. This renders it easy for me to conceive of myself as coercing others for their own sake, in their, not my, interest. I am then claiming that I know what they truly need better than they know it themselves. What, at most, this entails is that they would not resist me if they were rational and as wise as I and understood their interests as I do. But I may go on to claim a good deal more than this. I may declare that they are actually aiming at what in their benighted state they consciously resist, because there exists within them an occult entity – their latent rational will, or their 'true' purpose – and that this entity, although it is belied by all that they overtly feel and do and say, is their 'real' self, of which the poor empirical self in space and time may know nothing or little; and that this inner spirit is the only self that deserves to have its wishes taken into account.[12] Once I take this view, I am in a position to ignore the actual wishes of men or societies, to bully, oppress, torture them in the name, and on behalf, of their 'real' selves, in the secure knowledge that whatever is the true goal of man (happiness, performance of duty, wisdom, a just society, self-fulfilment) must be identical with his freedom – the free choice of his 'true', albeit often submerged and inarticulate, self.

This paradox has been often exposed. It is one thing to say that I know what is good for X, while he himself does not; and even to ignore his wishes for its – and his – sake; and a very different one to say that he has *eo ipso* chosen it, not indeed consciously, not as he seems in everyday life, but in his role as a rational self which his empirical self may not know – the 'real' self which discerns the good, and cannot help choosing it once it is revealed. This monstrous impersonation, which consists in equating what X would choose if he were something he is not, or at least not yet, with

what X actually seeks and chooses, is at the heart of all political theories of self-realisation. It is one thing to say that I may be coerced for my own good, which I am too blind to see: this may, on occasion, be for my benefit; indeed it may enlarge the scope of my liberty. It is another to say that if it is my good, then I am not being coerced, for I have willed it, whether I know this or not, and am free (or 'truly' free) even while my poor earthly body and foolish mind bitterly reject it, and struggle with the greatest desperation against those who seek, however benevolently, to impose it.

This magical transformation, or sleight of hand (for which William James so justly mocked the Hegelians), can no doubt be perpetrated just as easily with the 'negative' concept of freedom, where the self that should not be interfered with is no longer the individual with his actual wishes and needs as they are normally conceived, but the 'real' man within, identified with the pursuit of some ideal purpose not dreamed of by his empirical self. And, as in the case of the 'positively' free self, this entity may be inflated into some super-personal entity – a State, a class, a nation, or the march of history itself, regarded as a more 'real' subject of attributes than the empirical self. But the 'positive' conception of freedom as self-mastery, with its suggestion of a man divided against himself, has in fact, and as a matter of history, of doctrine and of practice, lent itself more easily to this splitting of personality into two: the transcendent, dominant controller, and the empirical bundle of desires and passions to be disciplined and brought to heel. It is this historical fact that has been influential. This demonstrates (if demonstration of so obvious a truth is needed) that conceptions of freedom directly derive from views of what constitutes a self, a person, a man. Enough manipulation of the definition of man, and freedom can be made to mean whatever the manipulator wishes. Recent history has made it only too clear that the issue is not merely academic.

The consequences of distinguishing between two selves will become even clearer if one considers the two major forms which the desire to be self-directed – directed by one's 'true' self – has historically taken: the first, that of self-abnegation in order to attain independence; the second, that of self-realisation, or total self-identification with a specific principle or ideal in order to attain the selfsame end.

III

The retreat to the inner citadel

I am the possessor of reason and will; I conceive ends and I desire to pursue them; but if I am prevented from attaining them I no longer feel master of the situation. I may be prevented by the laws of nature, or by accidents, or the activities of men, or the effect, often undesigned, of human institutions. These forces may be too much for me. What am I to do to avoid being crushed by them? I must liberate myself from desires that I know I cannot realise. I wish to be master of my kingdom, but my frontiers are long and insecure, therefore I contract them in order to reduce or eliminate the vulnerable area. I begin by desiring happiness, or power, or knowledge, or the attainment of some specific object. But I cannot command them. I choose to avoid defeat and waste, and therefore decide to strive for nothing that I cannot be sure to obtain. I determine myself not to desire what is unattainable. The tyrant threatens me with the destruction of my property, with imprisonment, with the exile or death of those I love. But if I no longer feel attached to property, no longer care whether or not I am in prison, if I have killed within myself my natural affections, then he cannot bend me to his will, for all that is left of myself is no longer subject to empirical fears or desires. It is as if I had performed a strategic retreat into an inner citadel – my reason, my soul, my 'noumenal' self – which, do what they may, neither external blind force, nor human malice, can touch. I have withdrawn into myself; there, and there alone, I am secure. It is as if I were to say: 'I have a wound in my leg. There are two methods of freeing myself from pain. One is to heal the wound. But if the cure is too difficult or uncertain, there is another method. I can get rid of the wound by cutting off my leg. If I train myself to want nothing to which the possession of my leg is indispensable, I shall not feel the lack of it.' This is the traditional self-emancipation of ascetics and quietists, of stoics or Buddhist sages, men of various religions or of none, who have fled the world, and escaped the yoke of society or public opinion, by some process of deliberate self-transformation that enables them to care no longer for any of its values, to remain, isolated and independent, on its edges, no longer vulnerable to its weapons. All political isolationism, all economic autarky, every form of autonomy, has in it some element of this attitude. I eliminate the obstacles in my path by abandoning the path; I retreat into my own sect, my own planned economy, my own deliberately insulated territory, where no voices from outside need be listened to, and no external forces can have effect. This is a form of the search for security; but it has also been called the search for personal or national freedom or independence.

From this doctrine, as it applies to individuals, it is no very great distance to the conceptions of those who, like Kant, identify freedom not indeed with the elimination of desires, but with resistance to them, and control over them. I identify myself with the controller and escape the slavery of the controlled. I am free because, and in so far as, I am autonomous. I obey laws, but I have imposed them on, or found them in, my own uncoerced self. Freedom is obedience, but, in Rousseau's words, 'obedience to a law which we prescribe to ourselves', and no man can enslave himself. Heteronomy is dependence on outside factors, liability to be a plaything of the external world that I cannot myself fully control, and which *pro tanto* controls and 'enslaves' me. I am free only to the degree to which my person is 'fettered' by nothing that obeys forces over which I have no control; I cannot control the laws of nature; my free activity must therefore, *ex hypothesi*, be lifted above the empirical world of causality. This is not the place in which to discuss the validity of this ancient and famous doctrine; I only wish to remark that the related notions of freedom as resistance to (or escape from) unrealisable desire, and as independence of the sphere of causality, have played a central role in politics no less than in ethics.

For if the essence of men is that they are autonomous beings – authors of values, of ends in themselves, the ultimate authority of which consists precisely in the fact that they are willed freely – then nothing is worse than to treat them as if they were not autonomous, but natural objects, played on by causal influences, creatures at the mercy of external stimuli, whose choices can be manipulated by their rulers, whether by threats of force or offers of rewards. To treat men in this way is to treat them as if they were not self-determined. 'Nobody may compel me to be happy in his own way,' said Kant. Paternalism is 'the greatest despotism imaginable'. This is so because it is to treat men as if they were not free, but human material for me, the benevolent reformer, to mould in accordance with my own, not their, freely adopted purpose. This is, of course, precisely the policy that the early utilitarians recommended. Helvétius (and Bentham) believed not in resisting, but in using, men's tendency to be slaves to their passions; they wished to dangle rewards and punishments before men – the acutest possible form of heteronomy – if by this means the 'slaves' might be made happier. But to manipulate men, to propel them towards goals which you – the social reformer – see, but they may not, is to deny their human essence, to treat them as objects without wills of their own, and therefore to degrade them. That is why to lie to men, or to deceive them, that is, to use them as means for my, not their own, independently conceived ends, even if it is for their own benefit, is, in effect, to treat them as subhuman, to behave as if their ends are less ultimate and sacred than my own. In the name

of what can I ever be justified in forcing men to do what they have not willed or consented to? Only in the name of some value higher than themselves. But if, as Kant held, all values are made so by the free acts of men, and called values only so far as they are this, there is no value higher than the individual. Therefore to do this is to coerce men in the name of something less ultimate than themselves – to bend them to my will, or to someone else's particular craving for (his or their) happiness or expediency or security or convenience. I am aiming at something desired (from whatever motive, no matter how noble) by me or my group, to which I am using other men as means. But this is a contradiction of what I know men to be, namely ends in themselves. All forms of tampering with human beings, getting at them, shaping them against their will to your own pattern, all thought-control and conditioning,[13] is, therefore, a denial of that in men which makes them men and their values ultimate.

Kant's free individual is a transcendent being, beyond the realm of natural causality. But in its empirical form – in which the notion of man is that of ordinary life – this doctrine was the heart of liberal humanism, both moral and political, that was deeply influenced both by Kant and by Rousseau in the eighteenth century. In its a priori version it is a form of secularised Protestant individualism, in which the place of God is taken by the conception of the rational life, and the place of the individual soul which strains towards union with him is replaced by the conception of the individual, endowed with reason, straining to be governed by reason and reason alone, and to depend upon nothing that might deflect or delude him by engaging his irrational nature. Autonomy, not heteronomy: to act and not to be acted upon. The notion of slavery to the passions is – for those who think in these terms – more than a metaphor. To rid myself of fear, or love, or the desire to conform is to liberate myself from the despotism of something which I cannot control. Sophocles, whom Plato reports as saying that old age alone has liberated him from the passion of love – the yoke of a cruel master – is reporting an experience as real as that of liberation from a human tyrant or slave owner. The psychological experience of observing myself yielding to some 'lower' impulse, acting from a motive that I dislike, or of doing something which at the very moment of doing I may detest, and reflecting later that I was 'not myself', or 'not in control of myself', when I did it, belongs to this way of thinking and speaking. I identify myself with my critical and rational moments. The consequences of my acts cannot matter, for they are not in my control; only my motives are. This is the creed of the solitary thinker who has defied the world and emancipated himself from the chains of men and things. In this form the doctrine may seem primarily an ethical creed, and scarcely political at all; nevertheless its political implications are clear, and it enters into the tradition of liberal individualism at least as deeply as the 'negative' concept of freedom.

It is perhaps worth remarking that in its individualistic form the concept of the rational sage who has escaped into the inner fortress of his true self seems to arise when the external world has proved exceptionally arid, cruel or unjust. 'He is truly free', said Rousseau, 'who desires what he can perform, and does what he desires.' In a world where a man seeking happiness or justice or freedom (in whatever sense) can do little, because he finds too many avenues of action blocked to him, the temptation to withdraw into himself may become irresistible. It may have been so in Greece, where the Stoic ideal cannot be wholly unconnected with the fall of the independent democracies before centralised Macedonian autocracy. It was so in Rome, for analogous reasons, after the end of the Republic.[14] It arose in Germany in the seventeenth century, during the period of the deepest national degradation of the German States that followed the Thirty Years War, when the character of public life, particularly in the small principalities, forced those who prized the dignity of human life, not for the first or last

time, into a kind of inner emigration. The doctrine that maintains that what I cannot have I must teach myself not to desire, that a desire eliminated, or successfully resisted, is as good as a desire satisfied, is a sublime, but, it seems to me, unmistakable, form of the doctrine of sour grapes: what I cannot be sure of, I cannot truly want.

This makes it clear why the definition of negative liberty as the ability to do what one wishes – which is, in effect, the definition adopted by Mill – will not do. If I find that I am able to do little or nothing of what I wish, I need only contract or extinguish my wishes, and I am made free. If the tyrant (or 'hidden persuader') manages to condition his subjects (or customers) into losing their original wishes and embracing ('internalising') the form of life he has invented for them, he will, on this definition, have succeeded in liberating them. He will, no doubt, have made them *feel* free – as Epictetus feels freer than his master (and the proverbial good man is said to feel happy on the rack). But what he has created is the very antithesis of political freedom.

Ascetic self-denial may be a source of integrity or serenity and spiritual strength, but it is difficult to see how it can be called an enlargement of liberty. If I save myself from an adversary by retreating indoors and locking every entrance and exit, I may remain freer than if I had been captured by him, but am I freer than if I had defeated or captured him? If I go too far, contract myself into too small a space, I shall suffocate and die. The logical culmination of the process of destroying everything through which I can possibly be wounded is suicide. While I exist in the natural world, I can never be wholly secure. Total liberation in this sense (as Schopenhauer correctly perceived) is conferred only by death.[15]

I find myself in a world in which I meet with obstacles to my will. Those who are wedded to the 'negative' concept of freedom may perhaps be forgiven if they think that self-abnegation is not the only method of overcoming obstacles; that it is also possible to do so by removing them: in the case of nonhuman objects, by physical action; in the case of human resistance, by force or persuasion, as when I induce somebody to make room for me in his carriage, or conquer a country which threatens the interests of my own. Such acts may be unjust, they may involve violence, cruelty, the enslavement of others, but it can scarcely be denied that thereby the agent is able in the most literal sense to increase his own freedom. It is an irony of history that this truth is repudiated by some of those who practise it most forcibly, men who, even while they conquer power and freedom of action, reject the 'negative' concept of it in favour of its 'positive' counterpart. Their view rules over half our world; let us see upon what metaphysical foundation it rests.

IV

Self-realisation

The only true method of attaining freedom, we are told, is by the use of critical reason, the understanding of what is necessary and what is contingent. If I am a schoolboy, all but the simplest truths of mathematics obtrude themselves as obstacles to the free functioning of my mind, as theorems whose necessity I do not understand; they are pronounced to be true by some external authority, and present themselves to me as foreign bodies which I am expected mechanically to absorb into my system. But when I understand the functions of the symbols, the axioms, the formation and transformation rules – the logic whereby the conclusions are obtained – and grasp that these things cannot be otherwise, because they appear to follow from the laws that govern the processes of my own reason,[16] then mathematical truths no longer obtrude themselves as external entities forced upon me which I must receive whether I want to or not, but as something which I now freely will in the course of the natural functioning of my own rational activity. For the mathematician, the proof of these theorems is part of the free exercise of his natural reasoning capacity. For

the musician, after he has assimilated the pattern of the composer's score, and has made the composer's ends his own, the playing of the music is not obedience to external laws, a compulsion and a barrier to liberty, but a free, unimpeded exercise. The player is not bound to the score as an ox to the plough, or a factory worker to the machine. He has absorbed the score into his own system, has, by understanding it, identified it with himself, has changed it from an impediment to free activity into an element in that activity itself.

What applies to music or mathematics must, we are told, in principle apply to all other obstacles which present themselves as so many lumps of external stuff blocking free self-development. That is the programme of enlightened rationalism from Spinoza to the latest (at times unconscious) disciples of Hegel. *Sapere aude.* What you know, that of which you understand the necessity – the rational necessity – you cannot, while remaining rational, want to be otherwise. For to want something to be other than what it must be, is, given the premisses – the necessities that govern the world – to be *pro tanto* either ignorant or irrational. Passions, prejudices, fears, neuroses spring from ignorance, and take the form of myths and illusions. To be ruled by myths, whether they spring from the vivid imaginations of unscrupulous charlatans who deceive us in order to exploit us, or from psychological or sociological causes, is a form of heteronomy, of being dominated by outside factors in a direction not necessarily willed by the agent. The scientific determinists of the eighteenth century supposed that the study of the sciences of nature, and the creation of sciences of society on the same model, would make the operation of such causes transparently clear, and thus enable individuals to recognise their own part in the working of a rational world, frustrating only when misunderstood. Knowledge liberates, as Epicurus taught long ago, by automatically eliminating irrational fears and desires.

Herder, Hegel and Marx substituted their own vitalistic models of social life for the older, mechanical, ones, but believed, no less than their opponents, that to understand the world is to be freed. They merely differed from them in stressing the part played by change and growth in what made human beings human. Social life could not be understood by an analogy drawn from mathematics or physics. One must also understand history, that is, the peculiar laws of continuous growth, whether by 'dialectical' conflict or otherwise, that govern individuals and groups in their interplay with each other and with nature. Not to grasp this is, according to these thinkers, to fall into a particular kind of error, namely the belief that human nature is static, that its essential properties are the same everywhere and at all times, that it is governed by unvarying natural laws, whether they are conceived in theological or materialistic terms, which entails the fallacious corollary that a wise lawgiver can, in principle, create a perfectly harmonious society at any time by appropriate education and legislation, because rational men, in all ages and countries, must always demand the same unaltering satisfactions of the same unaltering basic needs. Hegel believed that his contemporaries (and indeed all his predecessors) misunderstood the nature of institutions because they did not understand the laws – the rationally intelligible laws, since they spring from the operation of reason – that create and alter institutions and transform human character and human action. Marx and his disciples maintained that the path of human beings was obstructed not only by natural forces, or the imperfections of their own characters, but, even more, by the workings of their own social institutions, which they had originally created (not always consciously) for certain purposes, but whose functioning they systematically came to misconceive, in practice even more than in theory, and which thereupon became obstacles to their creators' progress. Marx offered social and economic hypotheses to account for the inevitability of such misunderstanding, in particular of the illusion that such man-made arrangements were independent forces, as inescapable as the laws of nature. As instances

of such pseudo-objective forces, he pointed to the laws of supply and demand, or the institution of property, or the eternal division of society into rich and poor, or owners and workers, as so many unaltering human categories. Not until we had reached a stage at which the spells of these illusions could be broken, that is, until enough men reached a social stage that alone enabled them to understand that these laws and institutions were themselves the work of human minds and hands, historically needed in their day, and later mistaken for inexorable, objective powers, could the old world be destroyed, and more adequate and liberating social machinery substituted.

We are enslaved by despots – institutions or beliefs or neuroses – which can be removed only by being analysed and understood. We are imprisoned by evil spirits which we have ourselves – albeit not consciously – created, and can exorcise them only by becoming conscious and acting appropriately: indeed, for Marx understanding is appropriate action. I am free if, and only if, I plan my life in accordance with my own will; plans entail rules; a rule does not oppress me or enslave me if I impose it on myself consciously, or accept it freely, having understood it, whether it was invented by me or by others, provided that it is rational, that is to say, conforms to the necessities of things. To understand why things must be as they must be is to will them to be so. Knowledge liberates not by offering us more open possibilities amongst which we can make our choice, but by preserving us from the frustration of attempting the impossible. To want necessary laws to be other than they are is to be prey to an irrational desire – a desire that what must be X should also be not-X. To go further, and believe these laws to be other than what they necessarily are, is to be insane. That is the metaphysical heart of rationalism. The notion of liberty contained in it is not the 'negative' conception of a field (ideally) without obstacles, a vacuum in which nothing obstructs me, but the notion of self-direction or self-control. I can do what I will with my own. I am a rational being; whatever I can demonstrate to myself as being necessary, as incapable of being otherwise in a rational society – that is, in a society directed by rational minds, towards goals such as a rational being would have – I cannot, being rational, wish to sweep out of my way. I assimilate it into my substance as I do the laws of logic, of mathematics, of physics, the rules of art, the principles that govern everything of which I understand, and therefore will, the rational purpose, by which I can never be thwarted, since I cannot want it to be other than it is.

This is the positive doctrine of liberation by reason. Socialised forms of it, widely disparate and opposed to each other as they are, are at the heart of many of the nationalist, Communist, authoritarian, and totalitarian creeds of our day. It may, in the course of its evolution, have wandered far from its rationalist moorings. Nevertheless, it is this freedom that, in democracies and in dictatorships, is argued about, and fought for, in many parts of the earth today. Without attempting to trace the historical evolution of this idea, I should like to comment on some of its vicissitudes.

V

The Temple of Sarastro

Those who believed in freedom as rational self-direction were bound, sooner or later, to consider how this was to be applied not merely to a man's inner life, but to his relations with other members of his society. Even the most individualistic among them – and Rousseau, Kant and Fichte certainly began as individualists – came at some point to ask themselves whether a rational life not only for the individual, but also for society, was possible, and if so, how it was to be achieved. I wish to be free to live as my rational will (my 'real self') commands, but so must others be. How am I to avoid collisions with their wills? Where is the frontier that lies between my (rationally determined) rights and the identical rights of

others? For if I am rational, I cannot deny that what is right for me must, for the same reasons, be right for others who are rational like me. A rational (or free) State would be a State governed by such laws as all rational men would freely accept; that is to say, such laws as they would themselves have enacted had they been asked what, as rational beings, they demanded; hence the frontiers would be such as all rational men would consider to be the right frontiers for rational beings.

But who, in fact, was to determine what these frontiers were? Thinkers of this type argued that if moral and political problems were genuine – as surely they were – they must in principle be soluble; that is to say, there must exist one and only one true solution to any problem. All truths could in principle be discovered by any rational thinker, and demonstrated so clearly that all other rational men could not but accept them; indeed, this was already to a large extent the case in the new natural sciences. On this assumption the problem of political liberty was soluble by establishing a just order that would give to each man all the freedom to which a rational being was entitled. My claim to unfettered freedom can prima facie at times not be reconciled with your equally unqualified claim; but the rational solution of one problem cannot collide with the equally true solution of another, for two truths cannot logically be incompatible; therefore a just order must in principle be discoverable – an order of which the rules make possible correct solutions to all possible problems that could arise in it. This ideal, harmonious state of affairs was sometimes imagined as a Garden of Eden before the Fall of Man, an Eden from which we were expelled, but for which we were still filled with longing; or as a golden age still before us, in which men, having become rational, will no longer be 'other-directed', nor 'alienate' or frustrate one another. In existing societies justice and equality are ideals which still call for some measure of coercion, because the premature lifting of social controls might lead to the oppression of the weaker and the stupider by the stronger or abler or more energetic and unscrupulous. But it is only irrationality on the part of men (according to this doctrine) that leads them to wish to oppress or exploit or humiliate one another. Rational men will respect the principle of reason in each other, and lack all desire to fight or dominate one another. The desire to dominate is itself a symptom of irrationality, and can be explained and cured by rational methods. Spinoza offers one kind of explanation and remedy, Hegel another, Marx a third. Some of these theories may perhaps, to some degree, supplement each other, others are not combinable. But they all assume that in a society of perfectly rational beings the lust for domination over men will be absent or ineffective. The existence of, or cravings for, oppression will be the first symptom that the true solution to the problems of social life has not been reached.

This can be put in another way. Freedom is self-mastery, the elimination of obstacles to my will, whatever these obstacles may be – the resistance of nature, of my ungoverned passions, of irrational institutions, of the opposing wills or behaviour of others. Nature I can, at least in principle, always mould by technical means, and shape to my will. But how am I to treat recalcitrant human beings? I must, if I can, impose my will on them too, 'mould' them to my pattern, cast parts for them in my play. But will this not mean that I alone am free, while they are slaves? They will be so if my plan has nothing to do with their wishes or values, only with my own. But if my plan is fully rational, it will allow for the full development of their 'true' natures, the realisation of their capacities for rational decisions, for 'making the best of themselves' – as a part of the realisation of my own 'true' self. All true solutions to all genuine problems must be compatible: more than this, they must fit into a single whole; for this is what is meant by calling them all rational and the universe harmonious. Each man has his specific character, abilities, aspirations, ends. If I grasp both what these ends and natures are, and how they all relate to one another, I can, at least in princi-

ple, if I have the knowledge and the strength, satisfy them all, so long as the nature and the purposes in question are rational. Rationality is knowing things and people for what they are: I must not use stones to make violins, nor try to make born violin-players play flutes. If the universe is governed by reason, then there will be no need for coercion; a correctly planned life for all will coincide with full freedom – the freedom of rational self-direction – for all. This will be so if, and only if, the plan is the true plan – the one unique pattern which alone fulfils the claims of reason. Its laws will be the rules which reason prescribes: they will only seem irksome to those whose reason is dormant, who do not understand the true 'needs' of their own 'real' selves. So long as each player recognises and plays the part set him by reason – the faculty that understands his true nature and discerns his true ends – there can be no conflict. Each man will be a liberated, self-directed actor in the cosmic drama. Thus Spinoza tells us that children, although they are coerced, are not slaves, because they obey orders given in their own interests, and that the subject of a true commonwealth is no slave, because the common interests must include his own. Similarly, Locke says 'Where there is no law there is no freedom', because rational law is a direction to a man's 'proper interests' or 'general good'; and adds that since law of this kind is what 'hedges us in only from bogs and precipices' it 'ill deserves the name of confinement', and speaks of desires to escape from it as being irrational, forms of 'licence', as 'brutish', and so on. Montesquieu, forgetting his liberal moments, speaks of political liberty as being not permission to do what we want, or even what the law allows, but only 'the power of doing what we ought to will', which Kant virtually repeats. Burke proclaims the individual's 'right' to be restrained in his own interest, because 'the presumed consent of every rational creature is in unison with the predisposed order of things'.

The common assumption of these thinkers (and of many a schoolman before them and

Jacobin and Communist after them) is that the rational ends of our 'true' natures must coincide, or be made to coincide, however violently our poor, ignorant, desire-ridden, passionate, empirical selves may cry out against this process. Freedom is not freedom to do what is irrational, or stupid, or wrong. To force empirical selves into the right pattern is no tyranny, but liberation. Rousseau tells me that if I freely surrender all the parts of my life to society, I create an entity which, because it has been built by an equality of sacrifice of all its members, cannot wish to hurt any one of them; in such a society, we are informed, it can be in nobody's interest to damage anyone else. 'In giving myself to all, I give myself to none', and get back as much as I lose, with enough new force to preserve my new gains. Kant tells us that when 'the individual has entirely abandoned his wild, lawless freedom, to find it again, unimpaired, in a state of dependence according to law', that alone is true freedom, 'for this dependence is the work of my own will acting as a lawgiver'. Liberty, so far from being incompatible with authority, becomes virtually identical with it. This is the thought and language of all the declarations of the rights of man in the eighteenth century, and of all those who look upon society as a design constructed according to the rational laws of the wise lawgiver, or of nature, or of history, or of the Supreme Being. Bentham, almost alone, doggedly went on repeating that the business of laws was not to liberate but to restrain: every law is an infraction of liberty – even if such infraction leads to an increase of the sum of liberty.

If the underlying assumptions had been correct – if the method of solving social problems resembled the way in which solutions to the problems of the natural sciences are found, and if reason were what rationalists said that it was – all this would perhaps follow. In the ideal case, liberty coincides with law: autonomy with authority. A law which forbids me to do what I could not, as a sane being, conceivably wish to do is not a restraint of my freedom. In the ideal society, composed of wholly responsible beings, rules, because I should scarcely be conscious of them, would gradually wither away. Only one social movement was bold enough to render this assumption quite explicit and accept its consequences – that of the Anarchists. But all forms of liberalism founded on a rationalist metaphysics are less or more watered-down versions of this creed.

In due course, the thinkers who bent their energies to the solution of the problem on these lines came to be faced with the question of how in practice men were to be made rational in this way. Clearly they must be educated. For the uneducated are irrational, heteronomous, and need to be coerced, if only to make life tolerable for the rational if they are to live in the same society and not be compelled to withdraw to a desert or some Olympian height. But the uneducated cannot be expected to understand or co-operate with the purposes of their educators. Education, says Fichte, must inevitably work in such a way that 'you will later recognise the reasons for what I am doing now'. Children cannot be expected to understand why they are compelled to go to school, nor the ignorant – that is, for the moment, the majority of mankind – why they are made to obey the laws that will presently make them rational. 'Compulsion is also a kind of education.' You learn the great virtue of obedience to superior persons. If you cannot understand your own interests as a rational being, I cannot be expected to consult you, or abide by your wishes, in the course of making you rational. I must, in the end, force you to be protected against smallpox, even though you may not wish it. Even Mill is prepared to say that I may forcibly prevent a man from crossing a bridge if there is not time to warn him that it is about to collapse, for I know, or am justified in assuming, that he cannot wish to fall into the water. Fichte knows what the uneducated German of his time wishes to be or do better than he can possibly know this for himself. The sage knows you better than you know yourself, for you are the victim of your passion, a slave living a heteronomous life, purblind, unable to understand your true goals. You want to be a human being. It is the aim of the State to satisfy your wish. 'Compulsion is justified by education for future insight.' The reason within me, if it is to triumph, must eliminate and suppress my 'lower' instincts, my passions and desires, which render me a slave; similarly (the fatal transition from individual to social concepts is almost imperceptible) the higher elements in society – the better educated, the more rational, those who 'possess the highest insight of their time and people' – may exercise compulsion to ratoinalise the irrational section of society. For – so Hegel, Bradley, Bosanquet have often assured us – by obeying the rational man we obey ourselves: not indeed as we are, sunk in our ignorance and our passions, weak creatures afflicted by diseases that need a healer, wards who require a guardian, but as we could be if we were rational; as we could be even now, if only we would listen to the rational element which is, *ex hypothési*, within every human being who deserves the name.

The philosophers of 'Objective Reason', from the tough, rigidly centralised, 'organic' State of Fichte, to the mild and humane liberalism of T. H. Green, certainly supposed themselves to be fulfilling, and not resisting, the rational demands which, however inchoate, were to be found in the breast of every sentient being.

But I may reject such democratic optimism, and turning away from the teleological determinism of the Hegelians towards some more voluntarist philosophy, conceive the idea of imposing on my society – for its own betterment – a plan of my own, which in my rational wisdom I have elaborated; and which, unless I act on my own, perhaps against the permanent wishes of the vast majority of my fellow citizens, may never come to fruition at all. Or, abandoning the concept of reason altogether, I may conceive myself as an inspired artist, who moulds men into patterns in the light of his unique vision, as painters combine colours or composers sounds; humanity is the raw material upon which I impose my creative will; even though men suffer and die in the process,

they are lifted by it to a height to which they could never have risen without my coercive – but creative – violation of their lives. This is the argument used by every dictator, inquisitor and bully who seeks some moral, or even aesthetic, justification for his conduct. I must do for men (or with them) what they cannot do for themselves, and I cannot ask their permission or consent, because they are in no condition to know what is best for them; indeed, what they will permit and accept may mean a life of contemptible mediocrity, or perhaps even their ruin and suicide. Let me quote from the true progenitor of the heroic doctrine, Fichte, once again: 'No one has . . . rights against reason.' 'Man is afraid of subordinating his subjectivity to the laws of reason. He prefers tradition or arbitrariness.' Nevertheless, subordinated he must be. Fichte puts forward the claims of what he called reason; Napoleon, or Carlyle, or romantic authoritarians may worship other values, and see in their establishment by force the only path to 'true' freedom.

The same attitude was pointedly expressed by August Comte, who asked why, if we do not allow free thinking in chemistry or biology, we should allow it in morals or politics. Why indeed? If it makes sense to speak of political truths – assertions of social ends which all men, because they are men, must, once they are discovered, agree to be such; and if, as Comte believed, scientific method will in due course reveal them; then what case is there for freedom of opinion or action – at least as an end in itself, and not merely as a stimulating intellectual climate – either for individuals or for groups? Why should any conduct be tolerated that is not authorised by appropriate experts? Comte put bluntly what had been implicit in the rationalist theory of politics from its ancient Greek beginnings. There can, in principle, be only one correct way of life; the wise lead it spontaneously, that is why they are called wise. The unwise must be dragged towards it by all the social means in the power of the wise; for why should demonstrable error be suffered to survive and breed? The immature and untutored must be made to say to themselves: 'Only the truth liberates, and the only way in which I can learn the truth is by doing blindly today what you, who know it, order me, or coerce me, to do, in the certain knowledge that only thus will I arrive at your clear vision, and be free like you.'

We have wandered indeed from our liberal beginnings. This argument, employed by Fichte in his latest phase, and after him by other defenders of authority, from Victorian schoolmasters and colonial administrators to the latest nationalist or Communist dictator, is precisely what the Stoic and Kantian morality protests against most bitterly in the name of the reason of the free individual following his own inner light. In this way the rationalist argument, with its assumption of the single true solution, has led by steps which, if not logically valid, are historically and psychologically intelligible from an ethical doctrine of individual responsibility and individual self-perfection to an authoritarian State obedient to the directives of an élite of Platonic guardians.

What can have led to so strange a reversal – the transformation of Kant's severe individualism into something close to a pure totalitarian doctrine on the part of thinkers some of whom claimed to be his disciples? This question is not of merely historical interest, for not a few contemporary liberals have gone through the same peculiar evolution. It is true that Kant insisted, following Rousseau, that a capacity for rational self-direction belonged to all men; that there could be no experts in moral matters, since morality was a matter not of specialised knowledge (as the Utilitarians and *philosophes* had maintained), but of the correct use of a universal human faculty; and consequently that what made men free was not acting in certain self-improving ways, which they could be coerced to do, but knowing why they ought to do so, which nobody could do for, or on behalf of, anyone else. But even Kant, when he came to deal with political issues, conceded that no law, provided that it was such that I should, if I

were asked, approve it as a rational being, could possibly deprive me of any portion of my rational freedom. With this the door was opened wide to the rule of experts. I cannot consult all men about all enactments all the time. The government cannot be a continuous plebiscite. Moreover, some men are not as well attuned to the voice of their own reason as others: some seem singularly deaf. If I am a legislator or a ruler, I must assume that if the law I impose is rational (and I can consult only my own reason) it will automatically be approved by all the members of my society so far as they are rational beings. For if they disapprove, they must, *pro tanto*, be irrational; then they will need to be repressed by reason: whether their own or mine cannot matter, for the pronouncements of reason must be the same in all minds. I issue my orders and, if you resist, take it upon myself to repress the irrational element in you which opposes reason. My task would be easier if you repressed it in yourself; I try to educate you to do so. But I am responsible for public welfare, I cannot wait until all men are wholly rational. Kant may protest that the essence of the subject's freedom is that he, and he alone, has given himself the order to obey. But this is a counsel of perfection. If you fail to discipline yourself, I must do so for you; and you cannot complain of lack of freedom, for the fact that Kant's rational judge has sent you to prison is evidence that you have not listened to your own inner reason, that, like a child, a savage, an idiot, you are either not ripe for self-direction, or permanently incapable of it.[17]

If this leads to despotism, albeit by the best or the wisest – to Sarastro's temple in *The Magic Flute* – but still despotism, which turns out to be identical with freedom, can it be that there is something amiss in the premises of the argument? That the basic assumptions are themselves somewhere at fault? Let me state them once more: first, that all men have one true purpose, and one only, that of rational self-direction; second, that the ends of all rational beings must of necessity fit into a single universal, harmonious pattern, which some men may be able to discern more clearly than others; third, that all conflict, and consequently all tragedy, is due solely to the clash of reason with the irrational or the insufficiently rational – the immature and undeveloped elements in life, whether individual or communal – and that such clashes are, in principle, avoidable, and for wholly rational beings impossible; finally, that when all men have been made rational, they will obey the rational laws of their own natures, which are one and the same in them all, and so be at once wholly law-abiding and wholly free. Can it be that Socrates and the creators of the central Western tradition in ethics and politics who followed him have been mistaken, for more than two millennia, that virtue is not knowledge, nor freedom identical with either? That despite the fact that it rules the lives of more men than ever before in its long history, not one of the basic assumptions of this famous view is demonstrable, or, perhaps, even true?

Notes

1 I do not, of course, mean to imply the truth of the converse.

2 Helvétius made this point very clearly: 'The free man is the man who is not in irons, not imprisoned in a gaol, nor terrorised like a slave by the fear of punishment.' It is not lack of freedom not to fly like an eagle or swim like a whale. *De l'esprit*, first discourse, chapter 4.

3 The Marxist conception of social laws is, of course, the best-known version of this theory, but it forms a large element in some Christian and utilitarian, and all socialist, doctrines.

4 *Émile*, book 2: vol. 4, p. 320, in *Oeuvres complètes*, ed. Bernard Gagnebin and others (Paris, 1959–95).

5 'A free man', said Hobbes, 'is he that . . . is not hindered to do what he has a will to.' *Leviathan*, chapter 21: p. 146 in Richard Tuck's edition (Cambridge, 1991). Law is always a fetter, even if it protects you from being bound in chains that are heavier than those of the law, say some more repressive law or custom, or arbitrary despotism or chaos. Bentham says much the same.

6 R. H. Tawney, *Equality* (1931), 3rd ed. (London, 1938), chapter 5, section 2, 'Equality and Liberty', p. 208 (not in previous editions).

7 J. S. Mill, *On Liberty*, chapter 1: vol. 18, p. 226.

8 This is but another illustration of the natural tendency of all but a very few thinkers to believe that all the things they hold good must be intimately connected, or at least compatible, with one another. The history of thought, like the history of nations, is strewn with examples of inconsistent, or at least disparate, elements artificially yoked together in a despotic system, or held together by the danger of some common enemy. In due course the danger passes, and conflicts between the allies arise, which often disrupt the system, sometimes to the great benefit of mankind.

9 Christian (and Jewish or Muslim) belief in the absolute authority of divine or natural laws, or in the equality of all men in the sight of God, is very different from belief in freedom to live as one prefers.

10 Indeed, it is arguable that in the Prussia of Frederick the Great or in the Austria of Joseph II men of imagination, originality and creative genius, and, indeed, minorities of all kinds, were less persecuted and felt the pressure, both of institutions and custom, less heavy upon them than in many an earlier or later democracy.

11 'Negative liberty' is something the extent of which, in a given case, it is difficult to estimate. It might, prima facie, seem to depend simply on the power to choose between at any rate two alternatives. Nevertheless, not all choices are equally free, or free at all. If in a totalitarian State I betray my friend under threat of torture, perhaps even if I act from fear of losing my job, I can reasonably say that I did not act freely. Nevertheless, I did, of course, make a choice, and could, at any rate in theory, have chosen to be killed or tortured or imprisoned. The mere existence of alternatives is not, therefore, enough to make my action free (although it may be voluntary) in the normal sense of the word. The extent of my freedom seems to depend on (*a*) how many possibilities are open to me (although the method of counting these can never be more than impressionistic; possibilities of action are not discrete entities like apples, which can be exhaustively enumerated); (*b*) how easy or difficult each of these possibilities is to actualise; (*c*) how important in my

plan of life, given my character and circumstances, these possibilities are when compared with each other; (*d*) how far they are closed and opened by deliberate human acts; (*e*) what value not merely the agent, but the general sentiment of the society in which he lives, puts on the various possibilities. All these magnitudes must be 'integrated', and a conclusion, necessarily never precise, or indisputable, drawn from this process. It may well be that there are many incommensurable kinds and degrees of freedom, and that they cannot be drawn up on any single scale of magnitude. Moreover, in the case of societies, we are faced by such (logically absurd) questions as 'Would arrangement X increase the liberty of Mr A more than it would that of Messrs B, C and D between them, added together?' The same difficulties arise in applying utilitarian criteria. Nevertheless, provided we do not demand precise measurement, we can give valid reasons for saying that the average subject of the King of Sweden is, on the whole, a good deal freer today [1958] than the average citizen of Spain or Albania. Total patterns of life must be compared directly as wholes, although the method by which we make the comparison, and the truth of the conclusions, are difficult or impossible to demonstrate. But the vagueness of the concepts, and the multiplicity of the criteria involved, are attributes of the subject-matter itself, not of our imperfect methods of measurement, or of incapacity for precise thought.

12 '[T]he ideal of true freedom is the maximum of power for all members of human society alike to make the best of themselves', said T. H. Green in 1881. [. . .] Apart from the confusion of freedom with equality, this entails that if a man chose some immediate pleasure – which (in whose view?) would not enable him to make the best of himself (what self?) – what he was exercising was not 'true' freedom: and if deprived of it, he would not lose anything that mattered. Green was a genuine liberal: but many a tyrant could use this formula to justify his worst acts of oppression.

13 Kant's psychology, and that of the Stoics and Christians too, assumed that some element in man – the 'inner fastness of his mind' – could be made secure against conditioning. The development of the techniques of hypnosis, 'brain-washing', subliminal suggestion and the like has made this a priori assumption, at least as an empirical hypothesis, less plausible.

14 It is not perhaps far-fetched to assume that the quietism of the Eastern sages was, similarly, a response to the despotism of the great autocracies, and flourished at periods when individuals were apt to be humiliated, or at any rate ignored or ruthlessly managed, by those possessed of the instruments of physical coercion.

15 It is worth remarking that those who demanded – and fought for – liberty for the individual or for the nation in France during this period of German quietism did not fall into this attitude. Might this not be precisely because, despite the despotism of the French monarchy and the arrogance and arbitrary behaviour of privileged groups in the French State, France was a proud and powerful nation, where the reality of political power was not beyond the grasp of men of talent, so that withdrawal from battle into some untroubled heaven above it, whence it could be surveyed dispassionately by the self-sufficient philosopher, was not the only way out? The same holds for England in the nineteenth century and well after it, and for the United States today.

16 Or, as some modern theorists maintain, because I have, or could have, invented them for myself, since the rules are man-made.

17 Kant came nearest to asserting the 'negative' ideal of liberty when (in one of his political treatises) he declared that 'The greatest problem of the human race, to the solution of which it is compelled by nature, is the establishment of a civil society universally administering right according to law. It is only in a society which possesses the greatest liberty . . . – and also the most exact determination and guarantee of the limits of [the] liberty [of each individual] in order that it may co-exist with the liberty of others – that the highest purpose of nature, which is the development of all her capacities, can be attained in the case of mankind.' [. . .] Apart from the teleological implications, this formulation does not at first appear very different from orthodox liberalism. The crucial point, however, is how to determine the criterion for the 'exact determination and guarantee of the limits' of individual liberty. Most modern liberals, at their most consistent, want a situation in which as many individuals as possible can realise as many of their ends as possible, without assessment of the value of these ends as such, save in so far as they may frustrate the purposes of others. They wish the frontiers between individuals or groups of men to be drawn solely with a view to preventing collisions between human purposes, all of which must be considered to be equally ultimate,

uncriticisable ends in themselves. Kant, and the rationalists of his type, do not regard all ends as of equal value. For them the limits of liberty are determined by applying the rules of 'reason', which is much more than the mere generality of rules as such, and is a faculty that creates or reveals a purpose identical in, and for, all men. In the name of reason anything that is non-rational may be condemned, so that the various personal aims which their individual imaginations and idiosyncrasies lead men to pursue – for example, aesthetic and other non-rational kinds of self-fulfilment – may, at least in theory, be ruthlessly suppressed to make way for the demands of reason. The authority of reason and of the duties it lays upon men is identified with individual freedom, on the assumption that only rational ends can be the 'true' objects of a 'free' man's 'real' nature.

I have never, I must own, understood what 'reason' means in this context; and here merely wish to point out that the a priori assumptions of this philosophical psychology are not compatible with empiricism: that is to say, with any doctrine founded on knowledge derived from experience of what men are and seek.

Isaiah Berlin, "Two Concepts of Liberty," in *Liberty* (Oxford: Oxford University Press, 2002), pp. 168–200.

Chapter 11

J. P. Day, from "On Liberty and the Real Will" (1970)

1 Introduction

In the chapter which he devotes to the applications of his principle of individual liberty, Mill considers the question 'how far liberty may legitimately be invaded for the prevention of crime, or of accident'. On the latter topic, he writes: '. . . it is a proper office of public authority to guard against accidents. If either a public officer or anyone else saw a person attempting to cross a bridge which had been ascertained to be unsafe, and there were no time to warn him of his danger, they might seize him and turn him back, without any real infringement of his liberty; for liberty consists in doing what one desires, and he does not desire to fall into the river.' (Q1)

Bosanquet claims that here Mill admits the existence of a Real (or General) Will in Rousseau's and Hegel's sense. He writes: '. . . as has commonly been said, "What people demand is seldom what would satisfy them if they got it". We may recall the instances in which even Mill admitted that it is legitimate to infer . . . that people do not really "will" something which they desire to do at a given moment.' (Q2)

As a preliminary to a discussion of the notion of 'the public interest', Professor Barry defines 'interest' thus: 'an action or policy is in a man's interests if it increases his opportunities to get what he wants.' (Q3) But he chooses to leave 'want' and 'want-satisfaction', which are the leading concepts of his system, as primitive or undefined terms.

These three quotations (Q1–Q3) provide a convenient introduction to the theme of this essay, which is the concept of the Real Will, particularly as it figures in political arguments, and the closely related notion of Real Liberty.

2 Preliminary Analysis

The rule of the Thélémites in Rabelais' novel consists in the single article, FAY CE QUE VOULDRAS. It can be englished correctly as 'Do what you *will*, or *want*, or *wish*, or *like*, or *choose*'. But although these five verbs are mutually substitutable in this context, they are not so in all contexts, and so do not express the same concept. Thus, 'We really *will* not have State Socialism' does not mean the same thing as 'We do not really *want* (to have) State Socialism'. For whereas the former records our firm resolve, the latter reports either our desire or our need. [. . .] Again, 'I *wish* that I were you' makes sense, but 'I *want* to be you' does not. I.e. the impossible is a possible object of wishing, but not a possible object of wanting. Yet again, 'I *choose X*' presupposes the existence of some alternative, *Y*, which I could have chosen instead, whereas 'I *want X*' does not. Finally, there is nothing illogical, or even unusual, in saying that *A wants X* although he would not *like* it if he got (i.e. were to get) it. (See Q1, Sec. 1; Sec. 4.)

Which of these five concepts, then, are we to investigate? One might well think that, since our topic is the Real Will, it must be the first one listed, viz. '*A* really will *D*' (where *D* is a deed-variable). But this would be to make the mistake of *literalism* in philosophical analysis. Here, as elsewhere, it is the first step which counts, and to select the wrong concept for treatment is to start off on the wrong foot at the foot of the wrong ladder. Actually, it is the second concept in the list which needs attention: not what a man really will do must be our theme, but what he really wants to do. However, warnings are not wanting that the ground is likely to prove slippery underfoot. Thus, Mrs Jean Austin, in examining Pleasure and Happiness, unmasks as the 'real villain of the piece, the verb *to want*'.

Here, then, is an argument which might be deployed by an autocrat at the breakfast-table: 'My people do not really want democracy – they only think they do; for none of them has ever lifted a finger against my personal rule; so I am not really denying them political liberty by withholding a democratic constitution – I am only appearing to do so.' (A1) This argument brings out one of the many ambiguities in the word 'real'. For in its first appearance in A1, the function of 'really' is to contrast what actually is the case with what is mistakenly believed to be the case; whereas in its second appearance its function is to contrast what actually is the case with what misleadingly seems to be the case. (It is an error to suppose, as Idealists are prone to do, that the opposite of Reality is always and only Appearance.) This in turn discloses the meaning of 'Real Liberty'. To be really free is to be not really, but only apparently restrained by another person. A1 also raises a question about the objects of wanting, namely, are these things (or persons), or events, or propositions? In fact, it does not matter which one says, since one can speak equally well of people wanting *the* vote, or *to* vote, or *that* they should vote. But it is the verb form which brings out most clearly the putative connexion between desire and freedom, since freedom is freedom *to D*.

But is A1 convincing? It relies on the truth that, if *A* wants *X*, then he will try to get *X*. Nevertheless, it is not irrefutable. For instance,

the reason why the people have not lifted a finger against the autocrat's personal rule may be that he has made it very dangerous for them to do so. Moreover, there is another, more fundamental objection which applies to all the arguments A1–A6 that we shall criticise in this essay. Even if the people's outward passivity did show that they did not (really) want democracy, this would not prove that the autocrat was not (really) denying them political liberty by withholding a democratic constitution. All that it would show would be that they would not feel frustrated by his action. They would not *feel* constrained by it; but they would nevertheless *be* constrained by it. The mistake lies in thinking that *A* is unfree when he is restrained from doing something *which he wants to do*; whereas in fact he is unfree when he is restrained by *B* from doing anything that it is in his power to do, regardless of whether he wants to do it or not. If I am legally prohibited from importing cannabis, my freedom is to that extent restricted; and to urge that this is not so because, as it happens, I do not want to do so (or for that matter because I want not to do so, or do want to do so, or am indifferent as to whether I do so or not) is to argue beside the point.

This error is found in Mill's definition, 'liberty consists in doing what one desires' (Q1, Sec. 1). It is also found in Hobbes' definition: 'A free man is he that, in those things which . . . he is able to do, is not hindered to do what he has a will to do.' The following remarks by Mr Mabbott illustrate the corresponding confusion between feeling free and being free: 'It is only a genius for vicarious slavery that enables a man to develop the individualist case. I am compelled to send my children to school (not that I have any, and I should anyhow); I am unable to buy novocain (*not that I want to*) . . . in short, I suppose no session passes but Parliament adds a round dozen to these pseudo-interferences with a liberty I do not covet, and I remain in fact as free as ever.' (My italics) But the interferences in question are real interferences, not pseudo-interferences; and it is just not true that the effect of them is to leave Mabbott (and the rest of us) as free as ever. It is a point of great practical importance. Most collectivist legislation affects only relatively small sections of the population, such as importers, employers, and landowners. Consequently, the mass of the people do not feel frustrated by it, and are apt to conclude that it leaves the country as free as ever it was. But in this they are much mistaken.

It may be objected that it does not matter if people are unfree so long as they do not feel unfree. Mabbott's remarks perhaps suggest this. But the following example shows the falsity of this thesis. For political reasons, a tyranny suppresses all genetic theories except one, which it protects. Since the proportion of the population who want to propound genetic theories is minute, next to nobody will be made to feel unfree by this policy. However, the protected theory may be false and one of the suppressed theories true; and the practical application of the false, protected theory may lead to a disastrous agricultural policy which inflicts great hardship on all the citizens. The mistake inherent in the objection is the false belief that liberty is valuable only because, and insofar as, the lack of it makes people feel unfree. In this connexion, it is highly important that being free and feeling free by no means always go together. Not only can people feel free when they are unfree, as we have just seen, they can also feel unfree when they are free. E.g., I would feel unfree, but not be unfree, if I wanted to import cannabis and believed, mistakenly, that to do so was still illegal, when in fact the relevant statute had been repealed last week.

Hobbes' definition of 'freedom' (above) raises the question of the logical relation of Liberty to Ability. It is that the former *presupposes* the latter. I.e. the truth of '*A* can *D*' is a necessary condition not only of the truth, but also of the falsity of '*A* is free to *D*'. Or, in homelier terms, if *A* cannot *D*, then the question of whether or not he is free to *D* does not arise. Since *A* cannot square the circle, he cannot be restrained from doing so by *B*, nor consequently be not restrained from doing so by *B*, i.e. be free to do so. I believe that it is the opinion of Hobbes, Mill, Carritt, Mabbott and others that the logical relation of Liberty to Desire is also one of presupposition. That is, they think that, unless *A* wants to *D*, the question of whether or not he is free to *D* does not arise. On the other hand, the main thesis of this essay is that Desire (or Will) is *irrelevant* to Freedom; meaning by this that the truth or falsity of '*A is* free to *D*' is independent of the truth or falsity of '*A* wants to *D*'. But it is not disputed that '*A feels* free to *D*' presupposes '*A* wants to *D*'. On the contrary, it is suggested that the erroneous view that Liberty presupposes Desire arises precisely from the failure to distinguish between feeling free and being free.

Hobbes' definition of 'freedom' also raises the question of the nature of the 'hindrance' involved in liberty. Suppose that Mill's man is prevented from walking on the bridge by a tree lying horizontally across its entrance; is he unfree to do so? The answer depends on how the tree got there. If it had been blown down by the wind, it would be incorrect to say that the man's freedom had been curtailed by the wind which had caused the tree to be there. But if the tree had been placed there by another person with or without the intention of preventing him from walking on the bridge, then it would be correct to say that his freedom had been restricted by that other person.

Another argument which the autocrat might use is this one: 'My people do not really want . . . etc. (as in A1); for none of them has the faintest idea what democracy is; so I am not really denying . . . etc. (as in A1).' (A2) This argument relies on the fact that '*A* wants *X*' entails '*A* knows what *X* is'. But it is no more irrefutable than A1 is. Perhaps what the autocrat means by saying that none of his people know what democracy is, is that none of them can give a definition of 'democracy' which would satisfy a political scientist. Yet it is perfectly possible to know well enough what a thing is to be able to desire it without being able to give a correct definition of it. The autocrat might well say of his people in this case that they do not know what they want. However, the statement '*A* does not know what he wants' is ambiguous. Here, it is an ellipsis, the sense of which can be made plain by using brackets to show what it is an ellipsis of, thus: '*A* does not know what he (thinks he) wants (actually is).' But '*A* does not know what he wants' can also mean '*A* wants *X* but does not know that he wants *X*'. We shall touch on this use of the expression, together with yet another use, in due course. (Sec. 6)

As Bosanquet says, the Real Will is the same thing as the General Will. (Q2, Sec. 1) Nevertheless, the notion of a General Will raises problems different from those discussed so far, or to be discussed later in this essay. The principal question which arises is whether the generality of a General Will resides in its subject or in its object. Thus, suppose that *A* and *B* both want *X*. Have we here not only *A*'s desire for *X* and *B*'s desire for *X*, but also the pair's desire for *X*? Or again, have we here not *A*'s desire that he should have *X* and *B*'s desire that he should have *X*, but rather *A*'s desire that he and *B* should have a 'common good', namely *X*, and *B*'s desire that he and *A* should have the same common good? But we only mention these points in passing in the interests of a general clarification.

3   Acts, Consequences, and Liberty

The autocrat might also argue as follows: 'My people do not really want . . . etc.; for introducing democracy here would lead straight to anarchy, which is the last thing they want; so I am not really denying . . . etc.' (A3) This argument is of the same logical type as Mill's (Q1, Sec. 1), and the form of the implication corresponding to both inferences is: 'If *Y* is a consequence of *X* and *A* does not want *Y*, then *A* does not want *X*.' However, it is easy to show that the inference-pattern is invalid, and that the corresponding implication-formula is false, by the normal method of adducing an instance in which the antecedent is true but the consequent is false. Thus, it may be true that the result of Richard Roe's eating curried lobster will be a stomach-ache which he does not want, and yet be false that he does not want to eat curried lobster.

How could a thinker of Mill's distinction come to advance so plainly unsound an argument? The explanation probably lies in what Sir Isaiah Berlin calls 'the natural tendency of all but a very few thinkers to believe that all the things they hold good must be intimately connected, or at least compatible, with one another'. Indeed, this tendency proceeds to the actual *identification* of the things believed to be good. Yet this is clearly wrong. *Ceteris paribus*, it is a good thing that the man should be free to walk on the bridge; and, in the circumstances which Mill describes, it is another good – and indeed better – thing that he should be prevented from walking on the bridge and so drowning. But it does not follow that the second good thing is identical with the first good thing, so that when the man is restrained from walking on the bridge he is still (really) free to do so. The correct description of the situation is that a lesser good, namely, the man's freedom of movement is properly postponed to a different and greater good, namely, the preservation of his life.

The form of Mill's argument naturally invites consideration of the implication-formula 'If *Y* is a consequence of *X* and *A* wants *Y*, then *A* wants *X*'. This is commonly rendered 'He who wills the end wills the means' and regarded as a truism. But here again it is easy to show by the same method that arguments in the corresponding inference-pattern are not in fact valid. It may be perfectly true both that if John Doe kills his father he will inherit his father's fortune, and also that John Doe wants to inherit his father's fortune, and yet be quite false that John Doe wants to kill his father.

4   Desire, Pleasure, and Liberty

Alternatively, our autocrat might argue thus: 'My people do not really want . . . etc.; for they certainly would not like democracy if they got it; so I am not really denying . . . etc.' (A4) This is the argument which Bosanquet uses. (Q2, Sec. 1) However, it too is invalid. For it relies on the supposed fact that '*A* wants *X*' entails '*A* would like *X* if he got it'. But there is no such entailment: there is nothing illogical in '*A* wants *X*, but *X* will not make him *happy* if he gets it'. If '*A* wanted *X*' and '*A* likes *X*' are both true, that is a matter of fact, not of logic; and quite often the latter happens to be false when the former is true. As Jean Austin points out: '. . . though we may very much want . . . to bring about some specific state of affairs, we may not at all like it when we have done so. This is the moral of many legends: we may have to use the last of our three wishes to wish away the sausages that landed on our nose as the result of the granting of the first.'

The second step in A4 depends on the false conditional statement 'If *A* does not (really) want to *D* (e.g. vote), then he is not (really) unfree – i.e. is (really) free – when he is *restrained from D*ing.' Now, 'restrain' and 'constrain' are symmetrical verbs, since being restrained from *D*ing is identical with being constrained to not *D*, and being constrained to *D* is identical with being restrained from not *D*ing. Therefore, the preceding false conditional statement is equivalent to 'If *A* does not (really) want to *D*, then he is not (really) unfree – i.e. is (really) free – when he is *constrained to* not *D*.' Hence Rousseau's contention that one can be 'forced to be free', i.e. that one can be free to *D* even when he is compelled to not *D*. It is the falsity of the conditional statement which explains the paradox.

As with A3, the cause of the mistake in A4 probably lies in the tendency to identify things which are connected but different. The connexion between Desire and Pleasure is cer-

tainly close, since, as a general rule even if not always, men both want to get what they like and also like getting what they want. Moreover, although '*A* wants *X*' does not entail '*A* would like *X*', it does entail '*A* thinks he would like *X*', and it is easy to confuse the last two formulas. There is evident absurdity in saying 'I want cannabis although I believe (or know) that I shall not like it'. The philosopher's old friend, the masochist, provides no exception to this. For the masochist is not the man who wants a whipping although he believes (or thinks he knows) that he will not like it when he gets it. On the contrary, he is the man who wants a whipping because he believes (or thinks he knows) that he will like it when he gets it. The proclivity to identify wanting something with liking it is plainly revealed in common speech, since – as was noted earlier – we say indifferently 'Do as you want' and 'Do as you please.' (Sec. 2)

Finally, since '*A* wants *X*' entails '*A* thinks he would like *X*', it is natural to wonder whether the converse also holds. But the answer is clearly negative, because one can quite well say, e.g., 'I think I should like heroin if I tried it; nevertheless, I do not want to try it.' One would say this if, for instance, he feared that he would become addicted to heroin if he tried it.

5   Desire, Need, and Liberty

Yet another argument which the autocrat might employ goes like this: 'My people do not really want . . . etc.; for democracy is the last thing that they want at this time; so I am not really denying . . . etc.' (A5) It is invalid because it equivocates on two different senses of the word 'want', viz. 'desire' and 'need', which it will be convenient to distinguish as 'want(d)' and 'want(n)' respectively. For the autocrat infers from the premiss 'my people do not want(n) democracy at this time' the conclusion 'my people do not (really) want(d) democracy'.

That it is indeed 'want(n)' which appears in the premiss and 'want(d)' in the conclusion is clear from the context; and this is true generally. When it is said, e.g., that what Britain wants is another Cromwell, the chances are that the speaker is saying what, in his opinion, Britons want(n); though it is admittedly possible that he is reporting the findings of a poll on what Britons want(d) in this matter. Again, that 'War on Want' is a philanthropic slogan and not an ascetic one can be inferred from observing that those who act on it occupy themselves with distributing food etc. to those who want(n) it, and not in withholding food etc. from those who want(d) it. Yet again, when King Belshazzar was weighed in the balances and found wanting, he was discovered to be, not ravenous, but impious. He was found to be, not wanting(d) food, but wanting(n) in proper reverence for the Lord.

As Professor Peters points out, one main difference between 'want(d)' and 'want(n)' is that the latter is evaluative whereas the former is not. The analysis of 'want(d)' will be given later, when it will be shown to be partly descriptive and partly imperative, but not at all normative. (Sec. 6) But the normative force of 'want(n)' is easy to see. When the general of the division says of a subaltern 'That young man wants a hair-cut', he is most unlikely to mean that the subaltern wants(d) a haircut. In all probability he means that the subaltern wants(n) a haircut in order to reach the standard of smartness expected of an officer of the division. Another difference between 'want(d)' and 'want(n)' is that the possible subjects of the former verb are a smaller class than are the possible subjects of the latter verb. Both Jones and his car can want(n) water, but whereas Jones can also want(d) water, his car cannot. There is a third use of 'want', namely 'want(l)', in the sense of 'lacks'. 'It wants five minutes to ten' obviously does not ascribe a desire to 'it'; but neither, on the other hand, does it imply that the later time is in some way better than the earlier time.

As is often the case when one word is used for more than one concept, there are important connexions between 'want(d)' and 'want(n)'. When the normal, healthy man wants(n) X, then he also tends to want(d) X. This is obviously true of food, drink, sleep, etc. But of course the converse does not hold, because normal, healthy persons generally want(d) many more things than they want(n); though this point is complicated by the consideration that, since needs are indeterminate, a man's list of his wants(n) *can* be stretched to coincide with the list of his wants(d). The position of the abnormal, unhealthy man is, then, not that he wants(d) things that he does not want(n) to have. It is rather that he wants(d) things that he wants(n) not to have, i.e. things that are bad for him. This is the situation of the alcoholic, the chain-smoker, etc.

It would be wrong to think that the notion of 'want' can be completely elucidated simply by distinguishing between 'want(d)', 'want(l)', and 'want(n)'. For the meanings of 'want(d)' and 'want(n)' themselves need to be explained. As just said, an analysis of 'want(d)' will be advanced in the next Section. But the foregoing remarks on 'want(n)', though sufficient for present purposes, by no means exhaust the question. In fact, Peters finds that 'the concept of "need" is a very dangerous and ambiguous one'. To mention only one of his points by way of illustration: it is necessary to distinguish the non-technical uses of 'need' (or 'want(n)'), such as those considered above, from its technical use in psychological theory, where the concepts of 'need' and 'need-satisfaction' provide one familiar type of all-inclusive explanations in terms of 'end-states'. But it would not be relevant to pursue the analysis of 'want(n)' any further here.

The psychologists' concepts of 'need' and 'need-satisfaction' strongly recall Barry's concepts of 'want' and 'want-satisfaction', and we must now apply the distinction between 'want(d)' and 'want(n)' to his definition of 'interest'. (Q3, Sec. 1) Is his definition true or false? The question cannot be answered unless one knows whether the 'wants' which appears in it is 'wants(d)' or 'wants(n)'. If Barry means the former, his definition is false. For it involves, e.g., that if A wants(d) opium, then the policy of allowing the unrestricted import of opium into A's country is in his interest; which is untrue. But if Barry means the latter, his definition is true, since there is indeed a close connexion of meaning between 'interest', 'want(n)' and – be it added – 'good'. For 'Guinness is good for you', 'You need Guinness' and 'It is in your interest to drink Guinness' are all equivalent in meaning, if not in advertising-power. This link between 'need' and 'good' brings out the correctness of Peters' contention that 'want(n)' is a normative notion.

Finally, the distinction between 'want(d)' and 'want(n)' throws light on Rousseau's paradox about being 'forced to be free'. (See Sec. 4) Maybe he reached the conclusion that one can be forced to be free by reasoning thus: '(1) A can be forced to do what he wants; (2) If and only if A does what he wants, then he is free; therefore, (3) A can be forced to be free.' In appraising this argument, it is first necessary to become clear whether 'wants' in (1) and (2) means 'wants(d)' or 'wants(n)'. In (2), it is 'wants(d)', for (2) is equivalent to Mill's definition of 'liberty'. (Q1, Sec. 1) But in (1), 'wants' may mean either 'wants(d)' or 'wants(n)'. If it means 'wants(n)', then (1) is true, since A can certainly be compelled to act in his own interest. But the argument nevertheless fails to prove (3) true because it is invalid through equivocation, since 'wants' has different meanings in (1) and (2). If, on the other hand, 'wants' means 'wants(d)', (1) is again true, but the argument again fails to prove (3) true because, although it is valid, (2) is false. To explain these two points: (1) is true because, as we have seen earlier, A can be forced to do what he wants(d), since 'A wants(d) to D' is irrelevant to 'A is forced to D'. E.g. I can be compelled by law not to import cannabis when I want not to do so. Similarly, (2) is false because 'A wants(d) to D' is irrelevant to 'A is free to D'. (See Sec. 2)

The point of the criticism of the argument imputed to Rousseau in the preceding paragraph can also be put as follows. Since A can, logically, be forced to do what he wants(d),

but cannot, logically, be forced to be free, being free cannot consist in doing what one wants(d), as Mill avers. This Rousseau sometimes saw, as when he writes 'Liberty consists less in doing what we want than in not being subject to another's will.' However, this is not his main view of liberty, which is rather that 'obedience to a law which we prescribe to ourselves is liberty'. Hegel is equally critical of Mill's sort of definition: '. . . if we hear it said that the definition of freedom is the ability to do what we please, such an idea can only be taken to reveal an utter immaturity of thought, for it contains not even an inkling of right, ethical life, and so forth'. Yet the distinction between 'want(d)' and 'want(n)' may shed light on the Hegelian notion of freedom too. Perhaps Hegelians interpret the specious proposition (2), above, as meaning 'A is free if and only if he does what he wants(n)'. For, on this definition, to be free is to do what is *good* for one, or to behave *reasonably*, and to be liable to be *forced* to be free by another – since, as just said, one can be constrained to act in his own interest.

6   Knowledge, Command, and Liberty

We will consider now a final argument which the autocrat might use, namely this one: 'My people do not really want . . . etc.; for it is for me to say what they want, since I am the best judge of that, and I know that they do not want democracy; so I am not really denying . . . etc.' (A6) This argument is exposed to an objection which may be put in the form of the following dilemma: The 'want' in the premiss 'it is for me . . . not want democracy' is either 'want(d)' or 'want(n)'. If it is 'want(d)', then the premiss is false, so that the argument fails to prove the truth of the conclusion. If it is 'want(n)', then the argument is invalid because equivocal, and so again fails to prove the truth of the conclusion. Now to show this.

There are a number of arguments to show that, if 'want' is taken in the sense of 'want(d)', then the premiss in question is false.

Firstly, there is the argument that *B* never knows what *A* wants(d) better than *A* does because *A*'s wants(d) are inward occurrences which can only be discovered by the introspection of *A* himself. This is the Cartesian doctrine of Privileged Access, and it is criticised accordingly by Ryle, who maintains that '... "want" and "desire" do not denote pangs, itchings or gnawings ... desire and aversion are, then, not "internal" episodes which their owner witnesses, but his associates do not witness'.

Secondly, there is the argument that *B* never knows what *A* wants(d) better than *A* does, because *A* cannot want(d) *X* without knowing that he wants(d) it, so that *B* can at best know what *A* wants(d) equally as well as *A* knows it. The reason is that 'I know what I want(d)' is an analytic and *a priori* truth. This is McGuinness's thesis. He meets the obvious objection that there are cases where *B* can and does claim to know what *A* (really) wants(d) better than *A* himself does by saying that his thesis is true in the 'primary' sense of 'want(d)', and that all senses in which his thesis is false are 'secondary' senses. A familiar case of such a secondary use is 'unconscious wanting(d)', where the psychiatrist may not only claim correctly to know what his patient really wants(d) better than the patient himself does, but eventually get his patient to agree with him about what he really wants(d). (See A2, Sec. 2)

Thirdly, there is the argument that it is never for *B* to say what *A* wants(d), because this is a thing that only *A* can say. The reason is that 'I want(d) *X*' means 'I choose *X*', and only I can, logically, make my choices. On this view, to say 'I want(d) *X*' is to perform an 'executive', i.e. illocutionary, speech-act. This is Toulmin's position.

There is something to be learnt from all three of these theses. For, in my submission, 'I want(d) *X*' means 'I feel deprived, and I think (or I know) that *X* would satisfy me, so (please) give me *X*'. One can recognise the presence of all three constituents in the meaning by reflecting on the oddity of saying any of the following three things: (1) 'I want(d) *X*, but I do not feel in any way deprived'; (2) 'I want(d) *X*, but I think (or I know) that *X* would not satisfy me (or that I should not like *X* if I got it)'; and (3) 'I want(d) *X*, but (please) do not give it to me'. The paradoxical character of statement (2) was discussed earlier. (Sec. 4) Of these three constituents, (1) and (2) are descriptive, but (3) is not. However, (3) is not elective, as Toulmin maintains, but rather imperative, and expresses either an order or a request. For, as we saw earlier, although 'Do as you choose' is indeed equivalent to 'Do as you want', choosing presupposes the existence of alternatives, whereas wanting(d) does not. (Sec. 2) In the debate between Toulmin on the one hand and Abelson and Ezorsky on the other about whether 'I want(d) *X*' is descriptive or not, there is right on both sides. *Pace* Ryle, the Privileged Access thesis is also right in that it gives a true account of the first component of the meaning of 'I want(d) *X*'. The feelings of frustration and deprivation suffered by the man who has no voice in choosing his governors and who says 'I want(d) democracy' are genuine, private introspectibles; just as are the pangs suffered by the hungry man who says 'I want food'. Further, my analysis shows why '*A* wants(d) *X*' entails '*A* believes (or thinks he knows) that he would like *X*', but does not entail '*A* would like *X*'. (See Secs. 2, 4) For although *A* is not normally mistaken about his feeling dissatisfied, he may well be mistaken in his belief that what will allay this feeling is his getting *X*. It is quite possible that what is required in order to do that is his getting, not *X*, but *Y*. This explains in turn the third of the three senses of '*A* does not know what he wants(d)', which we distinguished earlier. (Sec. 2) In this sense, as Toulmin suggests, the man who knows what he wants(d), or who knows his own mind, is the man whose beliefs about what would relieve his feelings of deprivation tend to be right. In this sense, when *A* says of himself 'I do not know what I want(d)', he is saying that, to date, his beliefs about what would satisfy him have proved incorrect, and that he is now unable to imagine what would do so. And when *A* says of *B* 'He does not know what he wants(d)', his evidence for his assertion is likely to include his observations that *B* switches inexplicably from pursuing one goal to pursuing another, or pursues simultaneously goals which are in fact incompatible.

My analysis also makes it possible to decide whether it is for *A* or for *B* to say what *A* wants(d). It is for *A* to say, for the following reasons. Firstly, because *A* generally knows better than *B* whether or not he has a feeling of dissatisfaction – or, for that matter, any other feeling. Secondly, because only *A* can, logically, give his orders (or make his requests), such as '(Please) give me political liberty'. One may object to this that actually we do speak of *B* giving *A*'s orders. The reply is that we do indeed, but that this manner of speaking must not be allowed to trip us. When the waiter gives the diner's order to the cook, the verb 'gives' means 'transmits', not 'issues'. *B* can give (= transmit) *A*'s order to *C*, but he cannot, logically, give (= issue) *A*'s order to *C*, since if *B* issues the order it is necessarily his order and not *A*'s. So similarly with choice, a point which arises out of Toulmin's analysis of 'I want(d) *X*' as 'I choose *X*'. When, at *A*'s request, *B* chooses between *X* and *Y* for him, *B* is said to make *A*'s choice for him. But this locution must not be permitted to mislead us either. In this situation, the choice is in fact no less *B*'s than if he had made it on his own behalf and not on *A*'s. Finally, it is for *A* to say what he wants(d) because he tends to know best whether or not X would satisfy him, provided only that he is adult and sane. The last proposition is true because it is analytic, since being the best judge of whether or not he would like *X* if he got it forms an important part of what is *meant* by calling a person 'adult' and 'sane'. The upshot is, then, that if 'want' in the premiss of A6 means 'want(d)', then A6 fails to prove the truth of the conclusion because that premiss is false.

Taking now the other horn of the dilemma, the question is whether it can be true that it is for the autocrat to pronounce on what his people want(n), since he is the best judge of that. The question is as contentious as it is important, and the different answers to it reflect two great opposed traditions in social and political thought.

On the one hand, writers in the liberal and utilitarian tradition maintain that *A* tends to know best what he wants(n), and argue from this to *laisser-faire* in political economy and democracy in politics. E.g., Mill contends that '*laisser-faire* . . . should be the general practice' on the ground that, on the whole, 'individuals are the best judges of their own interest'. This last proposition is now generally known as the Principle of Rational Self-interest. But he admits that this non-interference rule is subject to large exceptions, the exceptions to the rule being in the main the exceptions to the Principle. Education is such an exception, since it is false that here 'the consumer is a competent judge of the commodity'. Furthermore, Mill tries to prove that 'democracy is the ideally best form of government' from the premiss that 'each person is the only safe guardian . . . of his own . . . interests'.

Mill's remarks invite the following comments. Firstly, it is an important point that the Principle is proportional (or statistical), and not universal; i.e., that it is claimed to be true only as a general rule. Secondly, one should not perhaps conclude too readily that, because the Principle is approximately true in economic matters, it is also approximately true in political matters. It is quite possibly true that each tends to be the best judge of his economic interests, but false that each tends to be the best judge of his political interests. E.g., the public is more liable to be deceived by the false promises of politicians than it is by the fraudulent prospectuses of confidence-men. Thirdly, there is a great deal of difference between saying, as Mill does in the economic context, that each is the best *judge* of his interests, and saying as he does in the political context that each is the best *guardian* of his interests. For, whereas to be a good judge of one's interests requires only intelligence and knowledge, to be a good guardian of them requires not only these but also power. A perfectly intelligent and completely informed pauper may be a very poor guardian of his interests when making a wage-contract with a rich employer because his bargaining-position is so weak. Mill himself recognises this fact when he argues for governmental interference with freedom of contract respecting hours of labour on the ground that 'there are matters in which the interference of law is required, not to overrule the judgement of individuals respecting their own interest, but to *give effect* to that judgement'. (My italics) Finally, it is well worth recording Plamenatz's conclusion on this liberal and utilitarian thesis: 'that every man is apt to be the best judge of his own needs is not enough to justify even *laisser-faire*, let alone democracy'. The reader is referred to his illuminating discussion for his reasons for this opinion. (The part played by the Principle of Rational Self-interest in Political Economy is indeed about interests and not about needs, as Plamenatz claims. Interests and needs are, of course, different. If *A* needs *X*, then it is in *A*'s interest that *A* should have *X*. But it may be in *A*'s interest that *A* should have *X* although *A* does not need *X*. For example, if *A* has 1 billion pounds, it is in *A*'s interest that *A* should have another 1 billion pounds, although *A* does not need it.)

On the other hand, writers in the paternalist and collectivist tradition have contended that, in political affairs, there not only can be, but ought to be, Another who always knows better what the citizens want(n) than they do themselves. This Other manifests himself in various guises. Now he appears as the Philosopher-King, who is the best judge of what his subjects want(n) just as, in one of Plato's favourite tropes, the physician knows best what is best for his patients. Then he appears as the Legislator, the desirability of whose existence Rousseau establishes as follows: 'How can a blind multitude, which often does not know what it wants, because it rarely knows what is good for it, carry out for itself so great and difficult an enterprise as a system of legislation? . . . This makes a legislator necessary'. Yet again he appears as the Hero, of whom Hegel is reported to have said: 'The great man of the age is the one who can . . . tell his age what its will is, and accomplish it.' Not least, he figures as the Leader of the 'Party of the Proletariat', whose infallible knowledge, and perfect devotion to the provision, of what the people want(n), is a truth by definition.

In fact, of course, whether rulers know better what the ruled want(n) than do the ruled themselves, depends on which rulers and which ruled one is speaking of. Enlightened despots over barbaric nations have certainly done so; but there have been many governors with a less sure grasp of their subjects' interests than their subjects have had. In Britain today, it is still probably true that the gentleman in Whitehall knows better what the citizens want(n) than do the majority of the citizens themselves; but this is likely to become progressively less true if the general level of education rises.

We may therefore grant our autocrat, for the sake of argument, that he knows better what his people want(n) than they themselves do. But the concession avails him nothing, since although the premiss in his argument A6 is allowed to be true, the argument is invalid. For the first step in it is the move from 'My people do not want(n) democracy' to 'My people do not (really) want(d) democracy', which is clearly equivocal. In conclusion, it must be remembered that, even if this first step in A6 were valid, the argument would still fail, because the second step is also invalid. This is the step from 'My people do not (really) want(d) democracy' to 'I am not (really) denying them political liberty by withholding a democratic constitution', which commits the fallacy of *ignoratio elenchi*. As was said earlier, arguments A1–A5 are also exposed to this basic criticism. (Sec. 2)

7 Conclusion

It is submitted that A1–A6 comprise all the important 'Real Will' arguments on liberty. We have found each of them to be defective on more than one count, the chief count being the fallacy of *ignoratio elenchi* just referred to, which is common to them all. So much for what Hobhouse correctly calls 'the most penetrating and subtle of all the intellectual influences which have sapped the rational humanitarianism of the eighteenth and nineteenth centuries'. For although Popper is undoubtedly right in finding one main putative justification of the tyrannies of our era in their supposed 'inevitability', I am sure that an at least equally important one is the doctrine that these *régimes* do not really diminish liberty, because they do not really prevent people from doing anything that they really want to do.

We have also found that this same fundamental fallacy vitiates the definitions of 'liberty' given by Hobbes, Mill and others. (Sec. 2) Nor is it a coincidence that the same fault occurs both in these definitions and also in arguments A1–A6. For the Empiricist and Positivist thesis, that *A cannot be free to D unless (among other things) he wants(d) to D*, has generated the Rationalist and Idealist antithesis, that *A cannot (really) be unfree to D if he does not (really) want(d) to D*. Perhaps the dialectical movement has now reached the point where this 'contradiction' is resolved in a higher synthesis, which consists in recognition of the fact that whether or not *A* wants(d) to *D* is irrelevant to whether or not he is free to *D*; i.e., that *there is no connexion between Freedom and the Will*.

J. P. Day, "On Liberty and the Real Will," from *Liberty and Justice* (London: Croom Helm, 1987), pp. 1–15.

Chapter 12

Gerald C. MacCallum, Jr., from "Negative and Positive Freedom" (1967)

This paper challenges the view that we may usefully distinguish between two kinds or concepts of political and social freedom – negative and positive. The argument is not that one of these is the only, the "truest," or the "most worthwhile" freedom, but rather that the distinction between them has never been made sufficiently clear, is based in part upon a serious confusion, and has drawn attention away from precisely what needs examining if the differences separating philosophers, ideologies, and social movements concerned with freedom are to be understood. The corrective advised is to regard freedom as always one and the same triadic relation, but recognize that various contending parties disagree with each other in what they understand to be the ranges of the term variables. To view the matter in this way is to release oneself from a prevalent but unrewarding concentration on "kinds" of freedom, and to turn attention toward the truly important issues in this area of social and political philosophy.

I

Controversies generated by appeals to the presence or absence of freedom in societies have been roughly of four closely related kinds – namely (1) about the nature of freedom itself, (2) about the relationships holding between the attainment of freedom and the attainment of other possible social benefits, (3) about the ranking of freedom among such benefits, and (4) about the consequences of this or that policy with respect to realizing or attaining freedom. Disputes of one kind have turned readily into disputes of the other kinds.

Of those who agree that freedom is a benefit, most would also agree that it is not the *only* benefit a society may secure its members. Other benefits might include, for example, economic and military security, technological efficiency, and exemplifications of various aesthetic and spiritual values. Once this is admitted, however, disputes of types (2) and (3) are possible. Questions can be raised as to the logical and causal relationships holding between the attainment of freedom and the attainment of these other benefits, and as to whether one could on some occasions reasonably prefer to cultivate or emphasize certain of the latter at the expense of the former. Thus, one may be led to ask: *can* anyone cultivate and emphasize freedom at the cost of realizing these other goals and values (or vice versa) and, secondly, *should* anyone ever do this? In practice, these issues are often masked by or confused with disputes about the consequences of this or that action with respect to realizing the various goals or values.

Further, any of the above disputes may stem from or turn into a dispute about what freedom *is*. The borderlines have never been easy to keep clear. But a reason for this especially worth noting at the start is that disputes about the nature of freedom are certainly historically best understood as a series of attempts by parties opposing each other on very many issues to capture for their own side the favorable attitudes attaching to the notion of freedom. It has commonly been advantageous for partisans to link the presence or absence of freedom as closely as possible to the presence or absence of those other social benefits believed to be secured or denied by the forms of social organization advocated or condemned. Each social benefit is, accordingly, treated as either a result of or a contribution to freedom, and each liability is connected somehow to the absence of freedom. This history of the matter goes far to explain how freedom came to be identified with so many different kinds of social and individual benefits, and why the status of freedom as simply one among a number of social benefits has remained unclear. The resulting flexibility of the notion of freedom, and the resulting enhancement of the value of freedom, have suited the purposes of the polemicist.

It is against this background that one should first see the issues surrounding the distinction between positive and negative freedom as two fundamentally different kinds of freedom. Nevertheless, the difficulties surrounding the distinction should not be attributed solely to the interplay of Machiavellian motives. The disputes, and indeed the distinction itself, have also been influenced by a genuine confusion concerning the concept of freedom. The confusion results from failure to understand fully the conditons under which use of the concept of freedom is intelligible.

II

Whenever the freedom of some agent or agents is in question, it is always freedom from some constraint or restriction on, interference with, or barrier to doing, not doing, becoming, or not becoming something. Such freedom is thus always *of* something (an agent or agents), *from* something, *to* do, not do,

become, or not become something; it is a triadic relation. Taking the format "*x* is (is not) free from *y* to do (not do, become, not become) *z*," *x* ranges over agents, *y* ranges over such "preventing conditions" as constraints, restrictions, interferences, and barriers, and *z* ranges over actions or conditions of character or circumstance. When reference to one of these three terms is missing in such a discussion of freedom, it should be only because the reference is thought to be understood from the context of the discussion.

Admittedly, the idioms of freedom are such that this is sometimes not obvious. The claim, however, is not about what we say, but rather about the conditions under which what we say is intelligible. And, of course, it is important to notice that the claim is only about what makes talk concerning the freedom of agents intelligible. This restriction excludes from consideration, for example, some uses of "free of" and "free from" – namely, those not concerned with the freedom of agents, and where, consequently, what is meant may be only "rid of" or "without." Thus, consideration of "The sky is now free of clouds" is excluded because this expression does not deal with agents at all; but consideration of "His record is free of blemish" and "She is free from any vice" is most probably also excluded. Doubt about these latter two hinges on whether these expressions might be thought claims about the freedom of agents; if so, then they are not excluded, but neither are they intelligible *as* claims about the freedom of agents until one is in a position to fill in the elements of the format offered above; if not, then although probably parasitic upon talk about the freedom of agents and thus perhaps viewable as figurative anyway, they fall outside the scope of this investigation.

The claim that freedom, subject to the restriction noted above, is a triadic relation can hardly be substantiated here by exhaustive examination of the idioms of freedom. But the most obviously troublesome cases – namely, those in which one's understanding of the context must in a relevant way carry past the limits of what is explicit in the idiom – may be classified roughly and illustrated as follows:

(a) *Cases where agents are not mentioned*: for example, consider any of the wide range of expressions having the form "free *x*" in which (*i*) the place of *x* is taken by an expression not clearly referring to an agent – as in "free society" or "free will" – or (*ii*) the place of *x* is taken by an expression clearly not referring to an agent – as in "free beer." All such cases can be understood to be concerned with the freedom of agents and, indeed, their intelligibility rests upon their being so understood; they are thus subject to the claims made above. This is fairly obvious in the cases of "free will" and "free society." The intelligibility of the free-will problem is generally and correctly thought to rest at least upon the problem's being concerned with the freedom of persons, even though the criteria for identification of the persons or "selves" whose freedom is in question have not often been made sufficiently clear.[1] And it is beyond question that the expression "free society," although of course subject to various conflicting analyses with respect to the identity of the agent(s) whose freedom is involved, is thought intelligible only because it is thought to concern the freedom of agents of some sort or other. The expression "free beer," on the other hand (to take only one of a rich class of cases some of which would have to be managed differently), is ordinarily thought intelligible because thought to refer to beer that *people* are free *from* the ordinary restrictions of the market place *to* drink without paying for it.

For an expression of another grammatical form, consider "The property is free of (or from) encumbrance." Although this involves a loose use of "property," suppose that the term refers to something like a piece of land; the claim then clearly means that *owners* of that land are free *from* certain well-known restrictions (for example, certain types of charges or liabilities consequent upon their ownership of the land) *to* use, enjoy, dispose of the land as they wish.

(b) *Cases where it is not clear what corresponds to the second term*: for example, "freedom of choice," "freedom to choose as I please." Here, the range of constraints, restrictions, and so forth, is generally clear from the context of the discussion. In political matters, legal constraints or restrictions are most often thought of; but one also sometimes finds, as in Mill's *On Liberty*, concern for constraints and interferences constituted by social pressures. It is sometimes difficult for persons to see social pressures as constraints or interferences; this will be discussed below. It is also notoriously difficult to see causal nexuses as implying constraints or restrictions on the "will" (the person?) in connection with the free-will problem. But the very fact that such difficulties are the focus of so much attention is witness to the importance of getting clear about this term of the relation before such discussions of freedom can be said to be intelligible.

One might think that references to a second term of this sort could always be eliminated by a device such as the following. Instead of saying, for example, (*i*) "Smith is free *from* legal restrictions on travel *to* leave the country," one could say (*ii*) "Smith is free *to* leave the country *because* there are no legal restrictions on his leaving." The latter would make freedom appear to be a dyadic, rather than a triadic, relation. But we would be best advised to regard the appearance illusory, and this may be seen if one thinks a bit about the suggestion or implication of the sentence that nothing hinders or prevents Smith from leaving the country. Difficulties about this might be settled by attaching a qualifier to "free" – namely, "*legally* free." Alternatively, one could consider which, of all the things that might still hinder or prevent Smith from leaving the country (for example, has he promised someone to remain? will the responsibilities of his job keep him here? has he enough money to buy passage and, if not, why not?), could count as limitations on his freedom to leave the country; one would then be in a position to determine whether the claim had been misleading or false. In either case, however, the devices adopted would reveal that our understanding of what has been said hinged upon our understanding of the range of obstacles or constraints from which Smith had been claimed to be free.

(*c*) *Cases where it is not clear what corresponds to the third term*: for example, "freedom from hunger" ("want," "fear," "disease," and so forth). One quick but not very satisfactory way of dealing with such expressions is to regard them as figurative, or at least not really concerned with anybody's freedom; thus, being free from hunger would be simply being rid of, or without, hunger – as a sky may be free of clouds (compare the discussion of this above). Alternatively, one might incline toward regarding hunger as a barrier of some sort, and claim that a person free *from* hunger is free *to* be well fed or to do or do well the various things he could not do or do well if hungry. Yet again, and more satisfactorily, one could turn to the context of the initial bit of Rooseveltian rhetoric and there find reason to treat the expression as follows. Suppose that hunger is a feeling and that someone *seeks* hunger; he is on a diet and the hunger feeling reassures him that he is losing weight. Alternatively, suppose that hunger is a bodily condition and that someone seeks it; he is on a Gandhi-style hunger strike. In either case, Roosevelt or his fellow orators might have wanted a world in which these people were free from hunger; but this surely does not mean that they wanted a world in which people were not hungry despite a wish to be so. They wanted, rather, a world in which people were not victims of hunger they did not seek; that is, they wanted a world without barriers keeping people hungry despite efforts to avoid hunger – a world in which people would be free *from* barriers constituted by various specifiable agricultural, economic, and political conditions *to* get enough food to prevent hunger. This view of "freedom from hunger" not only makes perfectly good and historically accurate sense out of the expression, but also conforms to the view that freedom is a triadic relation.

In other politically important idioms the *range* of the third term is not always utterly clear. For example, does freedom of religion include freedom *not* to worship? Does freedom of speech include *all* speech no matter what its content, manner of delivery, or the circumstances of its delivery? Such matters, however, raise largely historical questions or questions to be settled by political decision; they do not throw doubt on the need for a third term.

That the intelligibility of talk concerned with the freedom of agents rests in the end upon an understanding of freedom as a triadic relation is what many persons distinguishing between positive and negative freedom apparently fail to see or see clearly enough. Evidence of such failure or, alternatively, invitation to it is found in the simple but conventional characterization of the difference between the two kinds of freedom as the difference between "freedom from" and "freedom to" – a characterization suggesting that freedom could be either of two dyadic relations. This characterization, however, cannot distinguish two genuinely different kinds of freedom; it can serve only to emphasize one or the other of two features of *every* case of the freedom of agents. Consequently, anyone who argues that freedom *from* is the "only" freedom, or that freedom *to* is the "truest" freedom, or that one is "more important than" the other, cannot be taken as having said anything both straightforward and sensible about two distinct kinds of freedom. He can, at most, be said to be attending to, or emphasizing the importance of only one part of what is always present in any case of freedom.

Unfortunately, even if this basis of distinction between positive and negative freedom as two distinct kinds or concepts of freedom is shown to collapse, one has not gone very far in understanding the issues separating those philosophers or ideologies commonly said to utilize one or the other of them. One has, however, dissipated one of the main confusions blocking understanding of these issues. In recognizing that freedom is always *both* freedom from something and freedom to do or become something, one is provided with a means of making sense out of interminable and poorly defined controversies concerning, for example, when a person really is free, why freedom is important, and on what its importance depends. As these, in turn, are matters on which the distinction between positive and negative freedom has turned, one is given also a means of managing sensibly the writings appearing to accept or to be based upon that distinction.

III

The key to understanding lies in recognition of precisely how differing styles of answer to the question "When are persons free?" could survive agreement that freedom is a triadic relation. The differences would be rooted in differing views on the ranges of the term variables – that is, on the ("true") identities of the agents whose freedom is in question, on what counts as an obstacle to or interference with the freedom of such agents, or on the range of what such agents might or might not be free to do or become. Although perhaps not always obvious or dramatic, such differences could lead to vastly different accounts of when persons are free. Furthermore, differences on one of these matters might or might not be accompanied by differences on either of the others. There is thus a rich stock of ways in which such accounts might diverge, and a rich stock of possible foci of argument.

It is therefore crucial, when dealing with accounts of when persons are free, to insist on getting *quite* clear on what each writer considers to be the ranges of these term variables. Such insistence will reveal where the differences between writers are, and will provide a starting point for rewarding consideration of what might justify these differences.

The distinction between positive and negative freedom has, however, stood in the way of this approach. It has encouraged us to see differences in accounts of freedom as resulting from differences in concepts of freedom. This in turn has encouraged the wrong sorts of questions. We have been tempted to ask such questions as "Well, who *is* right? Whose concept of freedom *is* the correct one?" or "Which *kind* of freedom do we really want after all?" Such questions will not help reveal the fundamental issues separating major writers on freedom from each other, no matter *how* the writers are arranged into "camps." It would be far better to insist that the same concept of freedom is operating throughout, and that the differences, rather than being about what *freedom* is, are for example about what persons are, and about what can count as an obstacle to or interference with the freedom of persons so conceived.

The appropriateness of this insistence is easily seen when one examines prevailing characterizations of the differences between "positive" and "negative" freedom. Once the alleged difference between "freedom from" and "freedom to" has been disallowed (as it must be; see above), the most persuasive of the remaining characterizations appear to be as follows:

1. Writers adhering to the concept of "negative" freedom hold only the *presence* of something can render a person unfree; writers adhering to the concept of "positive" freedom hold that the *absence* of something may also render a person unfree.

2. The former hold that a person is free to do *x* just in case *nothing due to arrangements made by other persons* stops him from doing *x*; the latter adopt no such restriction.

3. The former hold that the agents whose freedom is in question (for example, "persons," "men") are, in effect, identifiable as Anglo-American law would identify "natural" (as opposed to "artificial") persons; the latter sometimes hold quite different views as to how these agents are to be identified (see below).

The most obvious thing to be said about these characterizations, of course, is that appeal to them provides at best an excessively crude justification of the conventional classification of writers into opposing camps. When one presses on the alleged points of difference, they have a tendency to break down, or at least to become less dramatic than they at first seemed.[2] As should not be surprising, the patterns of agreement and disagreement on these several points are in fact either too diverse or too indistinct to support any clearly justifiable arrangement of major writers into two camps. The trouble is not merely that some writers do not fit too well where they have been placed; it is rather that writers who are purportedly the very models of membership in one camp or the other (for example, Locke, the Marxists) do not fit very well where they have been placed – thus suggesting that the whole system of dichotomous classification is futile and, even worse, conducive to distortion of important views on freedom.

But, even supposing that there were something to the classification and to the justification for it in terms of the above three points of difference, what then? The differences are of two kinds. They concern (*a*) the ("true") identities of the agents whose freedom is in question, and (*b*) what is to count as an "obstacle" or "barrier" to, "restriction" on, or "interference" with the freedom of such agents. They are thus clearly about the ranges of two of the three term variables mentioned earlier. It would be a mistake to see them in any other way. We are likely to make this mistake, however, and obscure the path of rewarding argument, if we present them as differences concerning what "freedom" means.

Consider the following. Suppose that we have been raised in the so-called "libertarian" tradition (roughly characterized as that of "negative" freedom). There would be nothing unusual to us, and perhaps even nothing troubling, in conventional accounts of what the adherent of negative freedom treats as the ranges of these variables.

1. He is purported to count persons just as we do – to point to living human bodies and say of each (and only of each), "There's a person." Precisely what we ordinarily call persons. (And if he is troubled by nonviable fetuses, and so forth, so are we.)

2. He is purported to mean much what we mean by "obstacle," and so forth, though this changes with changes in our views of what can be attributed to arrangements made by human beings, and also with variations in the importance we attach to consenting to rules, practices, and so forth.[3]

3. He is purported to have quite "ordinary" views on what a person may or may not be free to do or become. The actions are sometimes suggested in fairly specific terms – for example, free to have a home, raise a family, "rise to the top." But, on the whole, he is purported to talk of persons being free or not free "to do what they want" or (perhaps) "to express themselves."[4] Furthermore, the criteria for determining what a person wants to do are those we customarily use, or perhaps even the most naïve and unsophisticated of them – for example, what a person wants to do is determined by what he *says* he wants to do, or by what he manifestly *tries* to do, or even *does* do.[5]

In contrast, much might trouble us in the accounts of the so-called adherents of "positive" freedom.

1. They sometimes do not count, as the agent whose freedom is being considered, what inheritors of our tradition would unhesitatingly consider to be a "person." Instead, they occasionally engage in what has been revealingly but pejoratively called "the retreat to the inner citadel"; the agent in whose freedom they are interested is identified as the "real" or the "rational" or the "moral" person who is somehow sometimes hidden within, or has his seed contained within, the living human body. Sometimes, however, rather than a retreat to such an "inner citadel," or sometimes in addition to such a retreat, there is an

expansion of the limits of "person" such that the institutions and members, the histories and futures of the communities in which the living human body is found are considered to be inextricable parts of the "person."

These expansions or contractions of the criteria for identification of persons may seem unwarranted to us. Whether they are so, however, depends upon the strength of the arguments offered in support of the helpfulness of regarding persons in these ways while discussing freedom. For example, the retreat to the "inner citadel" may be initiated simply by worries about which, of all the things we want, will give us lasting satisfaction – a view of our interests making it possible to see the surge of impulse or passion as an obstacle to the attainment of what we "really want." And the expansion of the limits of the "self" to include our families, cultures, nations, or races may be launched by awareness that our "self" is to some extent the product of these associations; by awareness that our identification of our interests may be influenced by our beliefs concerning ways in which our destinies are tied to the destinies of our families, nations, and so forth; by the way we see tugs and stresses upon those associations as tugs and stresses upon us; and by the ways we see ourselves and *identify* ourselves as officeholders in such associations with the rights and obligations of such offices. This expansion, in turn, makes it possible for us to see the infringement of the autonomy of our associations as infringement on our freedom.

Assessing the strengths of the various positions taken on these matters requires a painstaking investigation and evaluation of the arguments offered – something that can hardly be launched within the confines of this paper. But what should be observed is that this set of seemingly radical departures by adherents of positive freedom from the ways "we" ordinarily identify persons does not provide us with any reason whatever to claim that a different concept of *freedom* is involved (one might as well say that the shift from "The apple is to the left of the orange" to "The seeds of the apple

are to the left of the seeds of the orange" changes what "to the left of" means). Furthermore, that claim would draw attention away from precisely what we should focus on; it would lead us to focus on the wrong concept – namely, "freedom" instead of "person." Only by insisting at least provisionally that all the writers have the same concept of freedom can one see clearly and keep sharply focused the obvious and extremely important differences among them concerning the concept of "person."

2. Similarly, adherents of so-called "positive" freedom purportedly differ from "us" on what counts as an obstacle. Will *this* difference be revealed adequately if we focus on supposed differences in the concept of "freedom"? Not likely. Given differences on what a person is, differences in what counts as an obstacle or interference are not surprising, of course, since what could count as an obstacle to the activity of a person identified in one way might not possibly count as an obstacle to persons identified in other ways. But the differences concerning "obstacle" and so forth are probably not due solely to differences concerning "person." If, for example, we so-called adherents of negative freedom, in order to count something as a preventing condition, ordinarily require that it can be shown a result of arrangements made by human beings, and our "opponents" do not require this, why not? On the whole, perhaps, the latter are saying this: if one is concerned with social, political, and economic policies, and with how these policies can remove or increase human misery, it is quite irrelevant whether difficulties in the way of the policies are or are not *due to* arrangements made by human beings. The only question is whether the difficulties can be removed by human arrangements, and at what cost. This view, seen as an attack upon the "artificiality" of a borderline for distinguishing human freedom from other human values, does not seem inherently unreasonable; a close look at the positions and arguments seems called for. But again, the issues and arguments will be misfocused if we fail to see them as

about the range of a term variable of a single triadic relation (freedom). Admittedly, we *could* see some aspects of the matter (those where the differences do not follow merely from differences in what is thought to be the agent whose freedom is in question) as amounting to disagreements about what is meant by "freedom." But there is no decisive reason for doing so, and this move surely threatens to obscure the socially and politically significant issues raised by the argument suggested above.

3. Concerning treatment of the third term by purported adherents of positive freedom, perhaps enough has already been said to suggest that they tend to emphasize conditions of character rather than actions, and to suggest that, as with "us" too, the range of character conditions and actions focused on may influence or be influenced by what is thought to count as agent and by what is thought to count as preventing condition. Thus, though something more definite would have to be said about the matter eventually, at least some contact with the issues previously raised might be expected in arguments about the range of this variable.

It is important to observe here and throughout, however, that close agreement between two writers in their understanding of the range of one of the variables does not make *inevitable* like agreement on the ranges of the others. Indeed, we have gone far enough to see that the kinds of issues arising in determination of the ranges are sufficiently diverse to make such simple correlations unlikely. Precisely this renders attempts to arrange writers on freedom into two opposing camps so distorted and ultimately futile. There is too rich a stock of ways in which accounts of freedom diverge.

If we are to manage these divergences sensibly, we must focus our attention on each of these variables and on differences in views as to their ranges. Until we do this, we will not see clearly the issues which have in fact been raised, and thus will not see clearly what needs arguing. In view of this need, it is both clumsy

and misleading to try to sort out writers as adherents of this or that "kind" or "concept" of freedom. We would be far better off to insist that they all have the same concept of freedom (as a triadic relation) – thus putting ourselves in a position to notice how, and inquire fruitfully into why, they identify differently what can serve as agent, preventing condition, and action or state of character vis-à-vis issues of freedom.

Notes

1 Indeed, lack of clarity on just this point is probably one of the major sources of confusion in discussions of free will.

2 For example, consider No. 1. Perhaps there is something to it, but the following cautionary remarks should be made. (*a*) The so-called adherents of "negative" freedom might very well accept the *absence* of something as an obstacle to freedom. Consider a man who is not free because, although unguarded, he has been locked in chains. Is he unfree because of the *presence* of the locked chains, or is he unfree because he *lacks* a key? Are adherents of "negative" freedom prohibited from giving the latter answer? (*b*) Even purported adherents of "positive" freedom are not always straightforward in their acceptance of the lack of something as an obstacle to freedom. They sometimes swing toward attributing the absence of freedom to the presence of certain conditions causally connected with the lack, absence, or deprivation mentioned initially. For example, it may be said that a person who was unable to qualify for a position owing to lack of training (and thus not free to accept or "have" it) was prevented from accepting the position by a social, political, economic, or educational "system" the workings of which resulted in his being bereft of training.

Also, in so far as this swing is made, our view of the difference mentioned in No. 2 may become fuzzy; for adherents of "positive" freedom might be thought at bottom to regard those "preventing conditions" counting as infringements of freedom as most often if not always circumstances due to human arrangements. This might be true even when, as we shall see is sometimes the case, the focus is on the role of "irrational passions and appetites." The presence or undisciplined character of these may be treated as resulting from the operation of certain specifiable social, educational, or moral institutions or arrangements. [. . .] Thus one might in the end be able to say no more than this: that the adherents of "negative" freedom are on the whole more inclined to require that the *intention* of the arrangements in question have been to coerce, compel, or deprive persons of this or that. The difference here, however, is not very striking.

3   The point of "consent theories" of political obligation sometimes seems to be to hide from ourselves the fact that a rule of unanimity is an unworkable basis for a system of government and that government does involve coercion. We seem, however, not really to have made up our minds about this.

4   These last ways of putting it are appreciably different. When a person who would otherwise count as a libertarian speaks of persons as free or not free to express themselves, his position as a libertarian may muddy a bit. One may feel invited to wonder which of the multitudinous wants of a given individual *are* expressive of his nature – that is, which are such that their fulfillment is conducive to the expression of his "self."

5   The possibility of conflicts among these criteria has not been much considered by so-called libertarians.

Gerald C. MacCallum, Jr., "Negative and Positive Freedom," *Philosophical Review*, 76 (1967), pp. 312–34.

Chapter 13

John Rawls, from *A Theory of Justice* (1971)

The Concept of Liberty

In discussing the application of the first principle of justice I shall try to bypass the dispute about the meaning of liberty that has so often troubled this topic. The controversy between the proponents of negative and positive liberty as to how freedom should be defined is one I shall leave aside. I believe that for the most part this debate is not concerned with definitions at all, but rather with the relative values of the several liberties when they come into conflict. Thus one might want to maintain, as Constant did, that the so-called liberty of the moderns is of greater value than the liberty of the ancients. While both sorts of freedom are deeply rooted in human aspirations, freedom of thought and liberty of conscience, freedom of the person and the civil liberties, ought not to be sacrificed to political liberty, to the freedom to participate equally in political affairs.[1] This question is clearly one of substantive political philosophy, and a theory of right and justice is required to answer it. Questions of definition can have at best but an ancillary role.

Therefore I shall simply assume that any liberty can be explained by a reference to three items: the agents who are free, the restrictions or limitations which they are free from, and what it is that they are free to do or not to do. Complete explanations of liberty provide the relevant information about these three things.[2] Very often certain matters are clear from the context and a full explanation is unnecessary. The general description of a liberty, then, has the following form: this or that person (or persons) is free (or not free) from this or that constraint (or set of constraints) to do (or not to do) so and so. Associations as well as natural persons may be free or not free, and constraints may range from duties and prohibitions defined by law to the coercive influences arising from public opinion and social pressure. For the most part I shall discuss liberty in connection with constitutional and legal restrictions. In these cases liberty is a certain structure of institutions, a certain system of public rules defining rights and duties. Set in this background, persons are at liberty to do something when they are free from certain constraints either to do it or not to do it and when their doing it or not doing it is protected from interference by other persons. If, for example, we consider liberty of conscience as defined by law, then individuals have this basic liberty when they are free to pursue their moral, philosophical, or religious interests without legal restrictions requiring them to engage or not to engage in any particular form of religious or other practice, and when other men have a legal duty not to interfere. A rather intricate complex of rights and duties characterizes any particular basic liberty. Not only must it be permissible for individuals to do or not to do something, but government and other persons must have a legal duty not to obstruct. I shall not delineate these rights and duties in any detail, but shall suppose that we understand their nature well enough for our purposes.

Several brief clarifications. First of all, one must keep in mind that the basic liberties are to be assessed as a whole, as one system. The worth of one such liberty normally depends upon the specification of the other liberties. Second, I assume that under reasonably favorable conditions there is always a way of defining these liberties so that the most central applications of each can be simultaneously secured and the most fundamental interests protected. Or at least that this is possible provided the two principles and their associated priorities are consistently adhered to. Finally, given such a specification of the basic liberties, it is assumed to be clear for the most part whether an institution or law actually restricts a basic liberty or merely regulates it. For example, certain rules of order are necessary for regulating discussion; without the acceptance of reasonable procedures of inquiry and debate, freedom of speech loses its value. On the other hand, a prohibition against holding or arguing for certain religious, moral, or political views is a restriction of liberty and must be judged accordingly. Thus as delegates in a constitutional convention, or as members of a legislature, the parties must decide how the various liberties are to be specified so as to give the best total system of liberty. They must note the distinction between regulation and restriction, but at many points they will have to balance one basic liberty against another; for example, freedom of speech against the right to a fair trial. The best arrangement of the several liberties depends upon the totality of limitations to which they are subject.

Notes

1 See Constant's essay *Ancient and Modern Liberty* (1819). His ideas on this are discussed by Guido de Ruggiero, *The History of European Liberalism*, trans. R. G. Collingwood (Oxford, The Clarendon Press, 1927), pp. 159–64, 167–9. For a general discussion, see Isaiah Berlin, *Four Essays on Liberty* (London, Oxford University Press, 1969), esp. the third essay and pp. xxxvii–lxiii of the introduction; and G. G. MacCallum, "Negative and Positive Freedom," *Philosophical Review*, vol. 76 (1967).

2 Here I follow MacCallum, "Negative and Positive Freedom." See further Felix Oppenheim, *Dimensions of Freedom* (New York, St. Martin's Press, 1961), esp. pp. 109–18, 132–4, where a notion of social freedom is also triadically defined.

John Rawls, *A Theory of Justice* (Cambridge, MA: Harvard University Press, 1971), pp. 176–8.

Part II

Freedom, Government, and Arbitrary Power

Introduction to Part II

Like the preceding part, the present part includes several extracts from the works of pre-twentieth-century thinkers. The themes addressed herein are indeed of ancient lineage, and most modern discussions of them are still heavily influenced by those ancient roots. Focused especially on political institutions and relationships, the present topic concerns the conditions under which both individuals and nations are free. Of particular interest in this connection is a tradition of political thought usually known as "civic republicanism" (though Quentin Skinner, one of its foremost contemporary exponents, has recently designated it as "neo-romanism" in order to acknowledge that some of its advocates have been in favor of a constitutional monarchy). Civic republicans are to some degree avowedly within the tradition of negative liberty, but they purport to overcome the narrowness of the conception of freedom that they impute to most negative-liberty theorists.

Civic republicans are keenly alert to the role of public virtue and public service in bolstering the cause of freedom. They maintain that, in the absence of active civic participation on the part of all or most citizens, a government and its elite supporters will amass autocratic powers that extinguish many of the precious liberties which citizens have enjoyed. Individuals who wish to retain their freedoms must frequently put aside their private affairs to participate collaboratively in holding governmental leaders to account. Republican attentiveness to the crucial role of civic virtue in securing the enjoyment of freedoms is supposed to be in contrast with liberalism's putative emphasis on the sanctity of the private spheres of individuals. Whereas liberals are said to be primarily concerned with drawing clear limits past which the state may not intrude into people's lives, republicans are principally concerned to stimulate people to engage robustly with the institutions that govern them. The sustainability of this dichotomy between republicanism and liberalism has been contested by most of the works listed in the Further Reading for this section, but the dichotomy remains prominent in republican thought. (One can grasp just how doubtful that dichotomy is, when one notes that an extract from John Locke – a quintessentially liberal thinker – is included here as representative of the republican outlook. By contrast, an extract from Thomas Hobbes, whose status as a liberal is more problematic, is included as an expression of his wary hostility toward the republican understanding of freedom.)

Civic republicans believe further that their very conception of freedom is more capacious than what they take to be the standard conception within the negative-liberty tradition. Instead of concentrating on freedom as the absence of actual intervention or interference, republicans concentrate on freedom as the absence of domination. Domination occurs through actual intervention or interference (by the state or by some other powerful party), but it also occurs through the maintenance of background conditions of intimidating control that render any actual intervention or interference unnecessary. Unless we take due account of the full range of ways in which domination can be exercised, and unless we understand freedom as the negation of domination, we shall overlook the debilitatingly confining effects of social conditions that subordinate some people to others. So the civic republicans argue. They further argue that their position on this matter contrasts with that of liberals. Once again, however, the sustainability of this contrast between republicanism and liberalism is dubious. Most of the works listed in the Further Reading for this part have challenged the notion that the conception of freedom favored by liberals is any narrower than the conception upheld by republicans.

Just as there are disagreements within the camp of the negative-liberty theorists and within the camp of the positive-liberty theorists, so too the civic republicans diverge from one another in various respects. One principal point of contention among them is centered on the relationship between freedom and morality (to which a part of this anthology is devoted). Skinner asserts, in line with most contemporary negative-liberty theorists, that the existence of any particular instance of freedom or unfreedom is independent of the moral character of the conduct to which the freedom or unfreedom pertains. If some person P is unprevented from doing x, then P is free-to-do-x whether or not the act of doing x would be morally legitimate; and if P is prevented by somebody else from doing x, P is unfree-to-do-x whether or not the preventative steps by the other person are morally legitimate. So Skinner maintains, and so most of the modern proponents of negative liberty would agree. However, Philip Pettit – who is closely aligned with Skinner in most respects as a champion of civic republicanism – has taken quite a different view. He holds that freedom as the absence of domination consists only in the absence of arbitrary preventative measures, rather than in the absence of all preventative measures. If actions that prevent somebody from doing x are undertaken in accordance with proper moral principles, the prevention does not render the person unfree-to-do-x at all. By adopting such a stance (shared, at least to some degree, by Locke), Pettit has placed himself at odds not only with most present-day proponents of negative liberty but also with many of his fellow civic republicans. Like the tradition of negative liberty and the tradition of positive liberty, then, the tradition of civic-republican thinking about freedom is far from monolithic. Whether or not that civic-republican tradition is genuinely distinctive, it is fruitfully controversial.

Further Reading

Carter, Ian, *A Measure of Freedom* (Oxford University Press, 1999), pp. 237–45 ⟨critique of modern civic republicanism, with a focus on Pettit⟩.

Kramer, Matthew H., *The Quality of Freedom* (Oxford University Press, 2003), pp. 105–48 ⟨multifaceted critiques of civic republicanism, with sustained attention to both Skinner and Pettit⟩.

Patten, Alan, "The Republican Critique of Liberalism," *British Journal of Political Science* 26, no. 25 (1996) ⟨critique of modern civic republicanism, with a focus on Skinner⟩.

Pettit, Philip, *A Theory of Freedom* (Polity Press, 2002), chs. 6–7 ⟨elaboration of the republican theory of freedom⟩.

Skinner, Quentin, "A Third Concept of Liberty," *Proceedings of the British Academy* 117, no. 237 (2002) ⟨affirmation of the distinctiveness of the republican conception of freedom⟩.

Chapter 14

Nicolò Machiavelli, from *Discourses* (1531)

Discourses 16 and 17

16
A People Accustomed to Live under a Prince, Should They by Some Eventuality Become Free, Will with Difficulty Maintain their Freedom

How difficult it is for a people accustomed to live under a prince to preserve their liberty, should they by some accident acquire it as Rome did after the expulsion of the Tarquins, is shown by numerous examples which may be studied in the historical records of ancient times. That there should be such a difficulty is reasonable; for such a people differs in no wise from a wild animal which, though by nature fierce and accustomed to the woods, has been brought up in captivity and servitude and is then loosed to rove the countryside at will, where, being unaccustomed to seeking its own food and discovering no place in which it can find refuge, it becomes the prey of the first comer who seeks to chain it up again.

The same thing happens to a people which has been accustomed to live under foreign rulers and so has taken no thought for either public defence or offence and is acquainted with no princes nor yet are any acquainted with it; it forthwith returns to the yoke, and ofttimes to a heavier one than that which, a

while back, it threw off its neck. This difficulty may occur, no matter how free the material be from corruption. But, since a people which has become wholly corrupt, cannot even for a brief space, no, not even for a moment, enjoy its freedom, as we shall show later, we shall confine ourselves in the present discourse to peoples in whom corruption has not advanced too far, and in whom there is still more goodness than rottenness.

In addition to the difficulty already mentioned there is yet another. It is that the government of a state which has become free evokes factions which are hostile, not factions which are friendly. To such hostile factions will belong all those who held preferment under the tyrannical government and grew fat on the riches of its prince, since, now that they are deprived of these emoluments, they cannot live contented, but are compelled, each of them, to try to restore the tyranny in order to regain their authority. Nor, as I have said, will such a government acquire supporters who are friendly, because a self-governing state assigns honours and rewards only for honest and determinate reasons, and, apart from this, rewards and honours no one; and when one acquires honours or advantages which appear to have been deserved, one does not acknowledge any obligation towards those responsible for the remuneration. Furthermore, that common advantage which results from a self-governing state is not recognised by anybody so long as it is possessed – the possibility of enjoying what one has, freely and without incurring suspicion for instance, the assurance that one's wife and children will be respected, the absence of fear for oneself – for no one admits that he incurs an obligation to another merely because that other has done him no wrong.

It is, then, as I have said. The government of a state which is free and has been newly formed, will evoke hostile factions but not friendly factions. If then one desires to remedy these difficulties and to cure the disorders which the aforesaid difficulties bring about, there is no way more efficient, more sure, more safe, or more necessary, than to kill the sons of Brutus, who, as history shows would not together with other Roman youths have been induced to conspire against their country if it had not been that, under consuls, they could not attain to an outstanding position, as they could under the kings; so that the freedom of the people was, from their point of view, but servitude.

He then who sets out to govern the masses, whether in a free state or in a principality, and does not secure himself against those who are hostile to the new order, is setting up a form of government which will be but short-lived. True, I look upon those rulers as unhappy who, to make their government secure, have to adopt abnormal methods because they find the masses hostile; for he who has but the few as his enemies, can easily and without much scandal make himself secure, but he who has the public as a whole for his enemy can never make himself secure; and the greater his cruelty, the weaker does his regime become. In such a case the best remedy he can adopt is to make the populace his friend.

Though to speak now of a prince, now of a republic is to distort the plan of this discourse, I propose, none the less, to talk of princes that I may not have to return to this topic. If, then, a prince wants to make sure of a populace that might be hostile to him – I speak of such princes as have become tyrants in their own country – what I say is that he ought first to ask what it is that the people desire, and that he will always find that they desire two things:

(i) to avenge themselves against the persons who have been the cause of their servitude, and (ii) to regain their freedom. The first of these demands the prince can satisfy entirely, the second in part.

Of the first demand there is an example much to the point. When Clearchus, tyrant of Heraclea, was in exile, it happened that in Heraclea a controversy arose between its populace and the upper class who were in the weaker position, and so decided to support Clearchus and, despite the popular feeling, swore to bring him back and to deprive the populace of its freedom. It thus came about that Clearchus found himself between an arrogant upper class which he could in no way either satisfy or correct, and a raving populace who could not stand having lost its freedom. He decided therefore at one stroke to free himself from the vexations caused by the leading men and to win over the populace. So, choosing a suitable opportunity, he cut to pieces all the nobles to the immense satisfaction of the popular party, and in this way satisfied one of the demands of the populace, namely, the demand for vengeance.

As to the second popular demand – the restoration of freedom, since this the prince is unable to satisfy, he should enquire as to the grounds on which the demand for freedom is based. He will find that a small section of the populace desire to be free in order to obtain authority over others, but that the vast bulk of those who demand freedom, desire but to live in security. For in all states, whatever be their form of government, the real rulers do not amount to more than forty or fifty citizens and, since this is a small number, it is an easy thing to make yourself secure in their regard either by doing away with them or by granting them such a share of honours, according to their standing, as will for the most part satisfy them. As for the rest, who demand but to live in security, they can easily be satisfied by introducing such institutions and laws as shall, in conjunction with the power of the prince, make for the security of the public as a whole. When a prince does this, and the people see that on no occasion does he break such laws, in a short time they will begin to live in security and contentment.

This is exemplified by the kingdom of France, in which people live in security simply because its kings are pledged to observe numerous laws on which the security of all their people depends. It was the intention of the founder of this state that its kings should do as they thought fit in regard to the use of arms and to finance, but that in other respects they should act as the laws required. That prince, therefore, or that republic which has not made its government secure at the outset, must take the first opportunity of doing so, as the Romans did. He who fails to do this will repent too late of having omitted to do what he ought to have done.

Thus, since the Roman people were not as yet corrupt when they regained their freedom, they were able to maintain themselves when the sons of Brutus were dead and there was an end of the Tarquins, and to maintain also those methods of government and those institutions which are discussed elsewhere. On the other hand, had this people already become corrupt, neither in Rome nor anywhere else would remedies adequate for its maintenance have been found, as will be shown in the next chapter.

17
A Corrupted People, Having Acquired Liberty, Can Maintain It only with the Greatest Difficulty

In Rome it was inevitable, in my opinion, that either the kings should be removed or that in a very short time the state would have become weak and of no account; because, if one considers how corrupt the kings had become, it is clear that in the course of two or three generations the corruption inherent in the kingship would have begun to spread to the members, and, when the members had become corrupt, it would no longer have been possible to reform them. But, since the head was lost while the trunk remained whole it was easily possible to bring it back to a free and ordered mode of life. It should be assumed, then, as a basic and established principle that to a state which has been under a prince and has become corrupt, freedom cannot be restored even if the prince and the whole of his stock be wiped out. On the contrary, what will happen is that one prince will wipe out another, and without the creation of a new lord it will never settle down unless indeed the goodness of some one man, conjoined with virtue, should keep it free. Such freedom, however, will last only so long as he lives. This happened to Syracuse in the case of Dion and of Timoleon, whose virtue was such that on both occasions the city remained free so long as they lived, but when they were dead returned to its ancient tyranny.

Nor can any better example of this be found than in Rome, which, when the Tarquins were expelled, was able forthwith both to acquire and to maintain its liberty; yet, when Caesar was killed, and Gaius Caligula and Nero were killed, and the whole of Caesar's stock was exhausted, was not only unable ever to maintain liberty, but could not even make a start. Results so diverse in one and the same city are caused by nought else but that in the time of the Tarquins the Roman populace was not yet corrupt, but in the later period was extremely corrupt. For in the former case, in order to stiffen the people up and to keep them averse to a king, it sufficed to make them swear never to consent to any king ruling in Rome. But in the other period the authority and severity of Brutus, backed by all the legions of the East, did not suffice to keep them disposed to desire that liberty to be maintained which he, after the manner of the first Brutus, had introduced. This was due to the corruption with which the Marian faction had impregnated the populace. For, when Caesar became the head of this faction, he so successfully blinded the masses that they were unaware of the yoke which they themselves had placed on their necks.

Though the example of Rome is preferable to any other, yet I propose to add to it further examples with which those who live at the present time will be familiar. I assert, then, that nothing that befell Milan or Naples, however grave and however violent in character, could ever bring them freedom, since their members were wholly corrupt. This is apparent after the death of Filippo Visconti, for, though it was proposed to introduce freedom in Milan, it could not be done, nor could any means of maintaining it be devised. Rome, then, was extremely lucky in that its kings quickly became corrupt, with the result that they were expelled before their corruption had penetrated to the bowels of that city. This absence of corruption was, in fact, the reason why the numerous tumults which took place in Rome, instigated by men of good intentions, did no harm, but, on the contrary, were an advantage to that republic.

It is possible, then, to arrive at this conclusion: when the material is not corrupt, tumults and other scandals do no harm, but, when it is corrupt, good legislation is of no avail unless it be initiated by someone in so extremely strong a position that he can enforce obedience until such time as the material has become good. Whether this has ever happened or whether it is possible for it to happen I do not know. For, as I have just said, it is clear that, if in a state which is on the decline owing to the corruption of its material a renaissance is ever to be brought about, it will be by the virtue of some one person who is then living, not by the virtue of the public as a whole, that good institutions are kept up, and, as soon as such a person is dead, they will relapse into their former habits.

This happened at Thebes, which, thanks to the virtue of Epaminondas, successfully maintained a republican form of government as long as he lived, but, on his death, forthwith returned to its former disorderly state. The reason is that no individual can possibly live long enough for a state which has long had bad customs to acquire good ones. Even if such a man should live for a very long time, or one virtuous man should be succeeded by another, it could not be done, since on their passing away, as we have said, there would be a collapse, unless the renaissance had been brought about at considerable risk and with no small blood-shedding. For corruption of this kind and ineptitude for a free mode of life is due to the inequality one finds in a state, and, to restore equality it is necessary to take steps which are by no means normal; and this few people either know how to do or are ready to do, a point that will be dealt with in detail in another place.

Nicolò Machiavelli, Discourses 16 and 17 from excerpts from L. J. Walker (ed.), *The Discourses of Nicolò Machiavelli* (London: Routledge and Kegan Paul, 1950), pp. 252–8.

Chapter 15

Thomas Hobbes, from *Leviathan* (1651)

Chapter XXI
"Of the Liberty of Subjects"

8. The liberty, whereof there is so frequent, and honourable mention, in the histories, and philosophy of the ancient Greeks, and Romans, and in the writings, and discourse of those that from them have received all their learning in the politics, is not the liberty of particular men; but the liberty of the commonwealth: which is the same with that, which every man then should have, if there were no civil laws, nor commonwealth at all. And the effects of it also be the same. For as amongst masterless men, there is perpetual war, of every man against his neighbour; no inheritance, to transmit to the son, nor to expect from the father; no propriety of goods, or lands; no security; but a full and absolute liberty in every particular man: so in states, and commonwealths not dependent on one another, every commonwealth, (not every man) has an absolute liberty, to do what it shall judge (that is to say, what that man, or assembly that representeth it, shall judge) most conducing to their benefit. But withal, they live in the condition of a perpetual war, and upon the confines of battle, with their frontiers armed, and cannons planted against their neighbours round about. The Athenians, and Romans were free; that is, free commonwealths: not that any particular men had the liberty to resist their own representative; but that their representative had the liberty to resist, or invade other people. There is written on the turrets of the city of Lucca in great characters at this day, the word LIBERTAS; yet no man can thence infer, that a particular man has more liberty, or immunity from the service of the commonwealth there, than in Constantinople. Whether a commonwealth be monarchical, or popular, the freedom is still the same.

9. But it is an easy thing, for men to be deceived, by the specious name of liberty; and for want of judgment to distinguish, mistake that for their private inheritance, and birthright, which is the right of the public only. And when the same error is confirmed by the authority of men in reputation for their writings on this subject, it is no wonder if it produce sedition, and change of government. In these western parts of the world, we are made to receive our opinions concerning the institution, and rights of commonwealths, from Aristotle, Cicero, and other men, Greeks and Romans, that living under popular states, derived those rights, not from the principles of nature, but transcribed them into their books, out of the practice of their own commonwealths, which were popular; as the grammarians describe the rules of language, out of the practice of the time; or the rules of poetry, out of the poems of Homer and Virgil. And because the Athenians were taught, (to keep them from desire of changing their government,) that they were freemen, and all that lived under monarchy were slaves; therefore

Aristotle puts it down in his *Politics*, (*lib.* 6. *cap.* 2.) *In democracy*, LIBERTY *is to be supposed: for it is commonly held, that no man is* FREE *in any other government.* And as Aristotle; so Cicero, and other writers have grounded their civil doctrine, on the opinions of the Romans, who were taught to hate monarchy, at first, by them that having deposed their sovereign, shared amongst them the sovereignty of Rome; and afterwards by their successors. And by reading of these Greek, and Latin authors, men from their childhood have gotten a habit (under a false show of liberty,) of favouring tumults, and of licentious controlling the actions of their sovereigns; and again of controlling those controllers; with the effusion of so much blood; as I think I may truly say, there was never any thing so dearly bought, as these western parts have bought the learning of the Greek and Latin tongues.

Thomas Hobbes, ch. xxi, from J. C. A. Gaskin (ed.), *Leviathan* (Oxford: Oxford University Press, 1996), pp. 142–4.

Chapter 16

James Harrington, from *The Commonwealth of Oceana* (1656)

Again, if the liberty of a man consist in the empire of his reason, the absence whereof would betray him unto the bondage of his passions; then the liberty of a commonwealth consisteth in the empire of her laws, the absence whereof would betray her unto the lusts of tyrants; and these I conceive to be the principles upon which Aristotle and Livy (injuriously accused by Leviathan for not writing out of nature) have grounded their assertion that a commonwealth is an empire of laws and not of men. But they must not carry it so. For, saith he, 'the liberty whereof there is so frequent and honourable mention in the histories and philosophy of the ancient Greeks and Romans, and the writings and discourses of those that from them have received all their learning in the politics, is not the liberty of particular men, but the liberty of the commonwealth'. He might as well have said that the estates of particular men in a commonwealth are not the riches of particular men, but the riches of the commonwealth; for equality of estates causeth equality of power, and equality of power is the liberty not only of the commonwealth, but of every man. But sure a man would never be thus irreverent with the great authors, and positive against all antiquity, without some certain demonstration of truth; and what is it? Why, 'there is written

on the turrets of the city of Lucca in great characters at this day the word LIBERTAS, yet no man can thence infer, that a particular man hath more liberty or immunity from the service of the commonwealth there, than in Constantinople. Whether a commonwealth be monarchical or popular, the freedom is the same.' The mountain hath brought forth, and we have a little equivocation! For to say that a Lucchese hath no more liberty or immunity from the laws of Lucca than a Turk hath from those of Constantinople, and to say that a Lucchese hath no more liberty or immunity by the laws of Lucca than a Turk hath by those of Constantinople, are pretty different speeches. The first may be said of all governments alike, the second scarce of any two; much less of these, seeing it is known that whereas the greatest bashaw is a tenant, as well of his head as of his estate, at the will of his lord, the meanest Lucchese that hath land is a freeholder of both, and not to be controlled but by the law; and that framed by every private man unto no other end (or they may thank themselves) than to protect the liberty of every private man, which by that means comes to be the liberty of the commonwealth.

James Harrington, *The Commonwealth of Oceana and A System of Politics*, ed. J. G. A. Pocock (Cambridge: Cambridge University Press, 1992), pp. 19–20.

Chapter 17

John Locke, from *Two Treatises of Government* (1690)

57. The Law that was to govern *Adam*, was the same that was to govern all his Posterity, the *Law of Reason*. But his Off-spring having another way of entrance into the World, different from him, by a natural Birth, that produced them ignorant and without the use of *Reason*, they were not presently *under that Law*: for no Body can be under a Law, which is not promulgated to him; and this Law being promulgated or made known by *Reason* only, he that is not come to the Use of his *Reason*, cannot be said to be *under this Law*; and *Adam*'s Children being not presently as soon as born, *under this Law of Reason* were not presently *free*. For *Law*, in its true Notion, is not so much the Limitation as *the direction of a free and intelligent Agent* to his proper Interest, and prescribes no farther than is for the general Good of those under that Law. Could they be happier without it, the *Law*, as an useless thing would of it self vanish; and that ill deserves the Name of Confinement which hedges us in only from Bogs and Precipices. So that, however it may be mistaken, *the end of Law* is not to abolish or restrain, but *to preserve and enlarge Freedom*: For in all the states of created beings capable of Laws, *where there is no Law, there is no Freedom*. For *Liberty* is to be free from restraint and violence from others which cannot be, where there is no Law: But Freedom is not, as we are told, *A Liberty for every Man to do what he lists*: (For who could be free, when every other Man's Humour might domineer over him?) But a *Liberty* to dispose, and order, as he lists, his Person, Actions, Possessions, and his whole Property, within the Allowance of those Laws under which he is; and therein not to be subject to the arbitrary Will of another, but freely follow his own.

John Locke, *Two Treatises of Government*, ed. P. Laslett (Cambridge: Cambridge University Press, 1960), pp. 305–6.

Chapter 18

Charles de Secondat, Baron de Montesquieu, from *The Spirit of the Laws* (1748)

Book 11
On the Laws that Form Political Liberty in Its Relation with the Constitution

Chapter 3
What Liberty Is

It is true that in democracies the people seem to do what they want, but political liberty in no way consists in doing what one wants. In a state, that is, in a society where there are laws, liberty can consist only in having the power to do what one should want to do and in no way being constrained to do what one should not want to do.

One must put oneself in mind of what independence is and what liberty is. Liberty is the right to do everything the laws permit; and if one citizen could do what they forbid, he would no longer have liberty because the others would likewise have this same power.

Chapter 4
Continuation of the Same Subject

Democracy and aristocracy are not free states by their nature. Political liberty is found only in moderate governments. But it is not always in moderate states. It is present only when power is not abused, but it has eternally been observed that any man who has power is led to abuse it; he continues until he finds limits. Who would think it! Even virtue has need of limits.

So that one cannot abuse power, power must check power by the arrangement of things. A constitution can be such that no one will be constrained to do the things the law does not oblige him to do or be kept from doing the things the law permits him to do.

Book 12
On the Laws that Form Political Liberty in Relation to the Citizen

Chapter 2
On the Liberty of the Citizen

Philosophical liberty consists in the exercise of one's will or, at least (if all systems must be mentioned), in one's opinion that one exerts one's will. Political liberty consists in security or, at least, in the opinion one has of one's security.

This *security* is never more attacked than by public or private accusations. Therefore, the citizen's liberty depends principally on the goodness of the criminal laws.

The knowledge already acquired in some countries and yet to be acquired in others, concerning the surest rules one can observe in criminal judgments, is of more concern to mankind than anything else in the world.

Liberty can be founded only on the practice of this knowledge, and in a state that had the best possible laws in regard to it, a man against whom proceedings had been brought and who was to be hung the next day would be freer than is a pasha in Turkey.

Charles de Secondat, Baron de Montesquieu, Book 11, chs. 3 and 4; Book 12, ch. 2, from Anne Cohler et al. (eds.), *The Spirit of the Laws* (Cambridge: Cambridge University Press, 1989), pp. 155–6, 188.

Chapter 19

Isaiah Berlin, from "Two Concepts of Liberty" (1969)

VI The Search for Status

There is yet another historically important approach to this topic, which, by confounding liberty with her sisters, equality and fraternity, leads to similarly illiberal conclusions. Ever since the issue was raised towards the end of the eighteenth century, the question of what is meant by 'an individual' has been asked persistently, and with increasing effect. In so far as I live in society, everything that I do inevitably affects, and is affected by, what others do. Even Mill's strenuous effort to mark the distinction between the spheres of private and social life breaks down under examination. Virtually all Mill's critics have pointed out that everything that I do may have results which will harm other human beings. Moreover, I am a social being in a deeper sense than that of interaction with others. For am I not what I am, to some degree, in virtue of what others think and feel me to be? When I ask myself what I am, and answer: an Englishman, a Chinese, a merchant, a man of no importance, a millionaire, a convict – I find upon analysis that to possess these attributes entails being recognised as belonging to a particular group or class by other persons in my society, and that this recognition is part of the meaning of most of the terms that denote some of my most personal and permanent characteristics. I am not disembodied reason. Nor am I Robinson Crusoe, along upon his island. It is not only that my material life depends upon interaction with other men, or that I am what I am as a result of social forces, but that some, perhaps all, of my ideas about myself, in particular my sense of my own moral and social identity, are intelligible only in terms of the social network in which I am (the metaphor must not be pressed too far) an element.

The lack of freedom about which men or groups complain amounts, as often as not, to the lack of proper recognition. I may be seeking not for what Mill would wish me to seek, namely, security from coercion, arbitrary arrest, tyranny, deprivation of certain opportunities of action, or for room within which I am legally accountable to no one for my movements. Equally, I may not be seeking for a rational plan of social life, or the self-perfection of a dispassionate sage. What I may seek to avoid is simply being ignored, or patronised, or despised, or being taken too much for granted – in short, not being treated as an individual, having my uniqueness insufficiently recognised, being classed as a member of some featureless amalgam, a statistical unit without identifiable, specifically human features and purposes of my own. This is the degradation that I am fighting against – I am not seeking equality of legal rights, nor liberty to do as I wish (although I may want these too), but a condition in which I can feel that I am, because I am taken to be, a responsible agent, whose will is taken into consideration because I am entitled to it, even if I am attacked and persecuted for being what I am or choosing as I do.

This is a hankering after status and recognition: 'The poorest he that is in England hath a life to live as the greatest he.' I desire to be understood and recognised, even if this means to be unpopular and disliked. And the only persons who can so recognise me, and thereby give me the sense of being someone, are the members of the society to which, historically, morally, economically, and perhaps ethnically, I feel that I belong.[1] My individual self is not something which I can detach from my relationship with others, or from those attributes of myself which consist in their attitude towards me. Consequently, when I demand to be liberated from, let us say, the status of political or social dependence, what I demand is an alteration of the attitude towards me of those whose opinions and behaviour help to determine my own image of myself.

And what is true of the individual is true of groups, social, political, economic, religious, that is, of men conscious of needs and purposes which they have as members of such groups. What oppressed classes or nationalities, as a rule, demand is neither simply unhampered liberty of action for their members, nor, above everything, equality of social or economic opportunity, still less assignment of a place in a frictionless, organic State devised by the rational lawgiver. What they want, as often as not, is simply recognition (of their class or nation, or colour or race) as an independent source of human activity, as an entity with a will of its own, intending to act in accordance with it (whether it is good or legitimate, or not), and not to be ruled, educated, guided, with however light a hand, as being not quite fully human, and therefore not quite fully free.

This gives a far wider than a purely rationalist sense to Kant's remark that paternalism is 'the greatest despotism imaginable'. Paternalism is despotic, not because it is more oppressive than naked, brutal, unenlightened tyranny, nor merely because it ignores the transcendental reason embodied in me, but because it is an insult to my conception of myself as a human being, determined to make my own life in accordance with my own (not necessarily rational or benevolent) purposes, and, above all, entitled to be recognised as such by others. For if I am not so recognised, then I may fail to recognise, I may doubt, my own claim to be a fully independent human being. For what I am is, in large part, determined by what I feel and think; and what I feel and think is determined by the feeling and thought prevailing in the society to which I belong, of which, in Burke's sense, I form not an isolable atom, but an ingredient (to use a perilous but indispensable metaphor) in a social pattern. I may feel unfree in the sense of not being recognised as a self-governing individual human being; but I may feel it also as a member of an unrecognised or insufficiently respected group: then I wish for the emancipation of my entire class, or community, or nation, or race, or profession. So much can I desire this, that I may, in my bitter longing for status, prefer to be bullied and misgoverned by some member of my own race or social class, by whom I am, nevertheless, recognised as a man and a rival – that is, as an equal – to being well and tolerantly treated by someone from some higher and remoter group, someone who does not recognise me for what I wish to feel myself to be.

This is the heart of the great cry for recognition on the part of both individuals and groups, and, in our own day, of professions and classes, nations and races. Although I may not get 'negative' liberty at the hands of the members of my own society, yet they are members of my own group; they understand me, as I understand them; and this understanding creates within me the sense of being somebody in the world. It is this desire for reciprocal recognition that leads the most authoritarian democracies to be, at times, consciously preferred by their members to the most enlightened oligarchies, or sometimes causes a member of some newly liberated Asian or African State to complain less today, when he is rudely treated by members of his own race or nation, than when he was governed by some cautious, just, gentle, well-meaning administrator from outside. Unless this phenomenon is grasped, the ideals and behaviour of entire peoples who, in Mill's sense of the word, suffer deprivation of elementary human rights, and who, with every appearance of sincerity, speak of enjoying more freedom than when they possessed a wider measure of these rights, become an unintelligible paradox.

Yet it is not with individual liberty, in either the 'negative' or the 'positive' sense of the word, that this desire for status and recognition can easily be identified. It is something no less profoundly needed and passionately fought for by human beings – it is something akin to, but not itself, freedom; although it entails negative freedom for the entire group, it is more closely related to solidarity, fraternity, mutual understanding, need for association on equal terms, all of which are sometimes – but misleadingly – called social freedom. Social and political terms are necessarily vague. The attempt to make the vocabulary of politics too precise may render it useless. But it is no service to the truth to loosen usage beyond necessity. The essence of the notion of liberty, in both the 'positive' and the 'negative' senses, is the holding off of something or someone – of others who trespass on my field or assert their authority over me, or of obsessions, fears, neuroses, irrational forces – intruders and despots of one kind or another. The desire for recognition is a desire for something different: for union, closer understanding, integration of interests, a life of common dependence and common sacrifice. It is only the confusion of desire for liberty with this profound and universal craving for status and understanding, further confounded by being identified with the notion of social self-direction, where the self to be liberated is no longer the individual but the 'social whole', that makes it possible for men, while submitting to the authority of oligarchs or dictators, to claim that this in some sense liberates them.

Much has been written on the fallacy of regarding social groups as being literally persons or selves, whose control and discipline of their members is no more than self-discipline, voluntary self-control which leaves the individual agent free. But even on the 'organic' view, would it be natural or desirable to call the demand for recognition and status a demand for liberty in some third sense? It is true that the group from which recognition is sought must itself have a sufficient measure of 'negative' freedom – from control by any outside authority – otherwise recognition by it will not give the claimant the status he seeks. But is the struggle for higher status, the wish to escape from an inferior position, to be called a struggle for liberty? Is it mere pedantry to confine this word to the main senses discussed above, or are we, as I suspect, in danger of calling any improvement of his social situation favoured by a human being an increase of his liberty, and will this not render this term so vague and distended as to make it virtually useless? And yet we cannot simply dismiss this case as a mere confusion of the notion of freedom with that of status, or solidarity, or fraternity, or equality, or some combination of these. For the craving for status is, in certain respects, very close to the desire to be an independent agent.

We may refuse this goal the title of liberty; yet it would be a shallow view that assumed that analogies between individuals and groups, or organic metaphors, or several senses of the word 'liberty', are mere fallacies, due either to assertions of likeness between entities in respects in which they are unlike, or simple semantic confusion. What is wanted by those who are prepared to barter their own and others' liberty of individual action for the status of their group, and their own status within the group, is not simply a surrender of liberty for the sake of security, of some assured place in a harmonious hierarchy in which all men and all classes know their place, and are prepared to exchange the painful privilege of choosing – 'the burden of freedom' – for the peace and comfort and relative mindlessness of an authoritarian or totalitarian structure. No doubt there are such men and such desires, and no doubt such surrenders of individual liberty can occur, and, indeed, have often occurred. But it is a profound misunderstanding of the temper of our times to assume that this is what makes nationalism or Marxism attractive to nations which have been ruled by alien masters, or to classes whose lives were directed by other classes in a semi-feudal, or some other hierarchically organised, regime. What they seek is more akin to what Mill called 'Pagan self-assertion', but in a collective, socialised form. Indeed, much of what he says about his own reasons for desiring liberty – the value that he puts on boldness and non-conformity, on the assertion of the individual's own values in the face of the prevailing opinion, on strong and self-reliant personalities free from the leading-strings of the official lawgivers and instructors of society – has little enough to do with his conception of freedom as non-interference, but a great deal with the desire of men not to have their personalities set at too low a value, assumed to be incapable of autonomous, original, 'authentic' behaviour, even if such behaviour is to be met with opprobrium, or social restrictions, or inhibitive legislation.

This wish to assert the 'personality' of my class, or group or nation, is connected both with the answer to the question 'What is to be the area of authority?' (for the group must not be interfered with by outside masters), and, even more closely, with the answer to the question 'Who is to govern us?' – govern well or badly, liberally or oppressively, but above all 'Who?' And such answers as 'Representatives elected by my own and others' untrammelled choice', or 'All of us gathered together in regular assemblies', or 'The best', or 'The wisest', or 'The nation as embodied in these or those persons or institutions', or 'The divine leader' are answers that are logically, and at times also politically and socially, independent of what extent of 'negative' liberty I demand for my own or my group's activities. Provided the answer to 'Who shall govern me?' is somebody or something which I can represent as 'my own', as something which belongs to me, or to whom I belong, I can, by using words which convey fraternity and

solidarity, as well as some part of the connotation of the 'positive' sense of the word 'freedom' (which it is difficult to specify more precisely), describe it as a hybrid form of freedom; at any rate as an ideal which is perhaps more prominent than any other in the world today, yet one which no existing term seems precisely to fit. Those who purchase it at the price of their 'negative', Millian freedom certainly claim to be 'liberated' by this means, in this confused, but ardently felt, sense. 'Whose service is perfect freedom' can in this way be secularised, and the State, or the nation, or the race, or an assembly, or a dictator, or my family or milieu, or I myself, can be substituted for the Deity, without thereby rendering the word 'freedom' wholly meaningless.[2]

No doubt every interpretation of the word 'liberty', however unusual, must include a minimum of what I have called 'negative' liberty. There must be an area within which I am not frustrated. No society literally suppresses all the liberties of its members; a being who is prevented by others from doing anything at all on his own is not a moral agent at all, and could not either legally or morally be regarded as a human being, even if a physiologist or a biologist, or even a psychologist, felt inclined to classify him as a man. But the fathers of liberalism – Mill and Constant – want more than this minimum: they demand a maximum degree of non-interference compatible with the minimum demands of social life. It seems unlikely that this extreme demand for liberty has ever been made by any but a small minority of highly civilised and self-conscious human beings. The bulk of humanity has certainly at most times been prepared to sacrifice this to other goals: security, status, prosperity, power, virtue, rewards in the next world; or justice, equality, fraternity, and many other values which appear wholly, or in part, incompatible with the attainment of the greatest degree of individual liberty, and certainly do not need it as a precondition for their own realisation. It is not a demand for *Lebensraum* for each individual that has stimulated the rebellions and wars of liberation for which men have been ready to die in the past, or, indeed, in the present. Men who have fought for freedom have commonly fought for the right to be governed by themselves or their representatives – sternly governed, if need be, like the Spartans, with little individual liberty, but in a manner which allowed them to participate, or at any rate to believe that they were participating, in the legislation and administration of their collective lives. And men who have made revolutions have, as often as not, meant by liberty no more than the conquest of power and authority by a given sect of believers in a doctrine, or by a class, or by some other social group, old or new. Their victories certainly frustrated those whom they ousted, and sometimes repressed, enslaved or exterminated vast numbers of human beings. Yet such revolutionaries have usually felt it necessary to argue that, despite this, they represented the party of liberty, or 'true' liberty, by claiming universality for their ideal, which the 'real selves' of even those who resisted them were also alleged to be seeking, although they were held to have lost the way to the goal, or to have mistaken the goal itself owing to some moral or spiritual blindness. All this has little to do with Mill's notion of liberty as limited only by the danger of doing harm to others. It is the non-recognition of this psychological and political fact (which lurks behind the apparent ambiguity of the term 'liberty') that has, perhaps, blinded some contemporary liberals to the world in which they live. Their plea is clear, their cause is just. But they do not allow for the variety of basic human needs. Nor yet for the ingenuity with which men can prove to their own satisfaction that the road to one ideal also leads to its contrary.

VII Liberty and Sovereignty

The French Revolution, like all great revolutions, was, at least in its Jacobin form, just such an eruption of the desire for 'positive' freedom of collective self-direction on the part of a large body of Frenchmen who felt liberated as a nation, even though the result was, for a good many of them, a severe restriction of individual freedoms. Rousseau had spoken exultantly of the fact that the laws of liberty might prove to be more austere than the yoke of tyranny. Tyranny is service to human masters. The law cannot be a tyrant. Rousseau does not mean by liberty the 'negative' freedom of the individual not to be interfered with within a defined area, but the possession by all, and not merely by some, of the fully qualified members of a society of a share in the public power which is entitled to interfere with every aspect of every citizen's life. The liberals of the first half of the nineteenth century correctly foresaw that liberty in this 'positive' sense could easily destroy too many of the 'negative' liberties that they held sacred. They pointed out that the sovereignty of the people could easily destroy that of individuals. Mill explained, patiently and unanswerably, that government by the people was not, in his sense, necessarily freedom at all. For those who govern are not necessarily the same 'people' as those who are governed, and democratic self-government is not the government 'of each by himself', but, at best, 'of each by all the rest'. Mill and his disciples spoke of 'the tyranny of the majority' and of the tyranny of 'the prevailing opinion and feeling', and saw no great difference between that and any other kind of tyranny which encroaches upon men's activities beyond the sacred frontiers of private life.

No one saw the conflict between the two types of liberty better, or expressed it more clearly, than Benjamin Constant. He pointed out that the transference by a successful rising of unlimited authority, commonly called sovereignty, from one set of hands to another does not increase liberty, but merely shifts the burden of slavery. He reasonably asked why a man should deeply care whether he is crushed by a popular government or by a monarch, or even by a set of oppressive laws. He saw that the main problem for those who desire 'negative', individual freedom is not who wields this authority, but how much authority should be placed in any set of hands. For unlimited authority in anybody's grasp was bound, he believed, sooner or later, to destroy somebody. He maintained that usually men protested against this or that set of governors as oppressive, when the real cause of oppression lay in the mere fact of the accumulation of power itself, wherever it might happen to be, since liberty was endangered by the mere existence of absolute authority as such. 'It is not against the arm that one must rail,' he wrote, 'but against the weapon. Some weights are too heavy for the human hand.' **Democracy may disarm a given oligarchy, a given privileged individual or set of individuals, but it can still crush individuals as mercilessly as any previous ruler.** An equal right to oppress – or interfere – is not equivalent to liberty. Nor does universal consent to loss of liberty somehow miraculously preserve it merely by being universal, or by being consent. If I consent to be oppressed, or acquiesce in my condition with detachment or irony, am I the less oppressed? If I sell myself into slavery, am I the less a slave? If I commit suicide, am I the less dead because I have taken my own life freely? 'Popular government is merely a spasmodic tyranny, monarchy a more centralised despotism.' Constant saw in Rousseau the most dangerous enemy of individual liberty, because he had declared that 'In giving myself to all, I give myself to none.' Constant could not see why, even though the sovereign is 'everybody', it should not oppress one of the 'members' of its indivisible self, if it so decided. I may, of course, prefer to be deprived of my liberties by an assembly, or a family, or a class in which I am a minority. It may give me an opportunity one day of persuading the others to do for me that to which I feel I am entitled. But to be deprived of my liberty at the hands of my family or friends or fellow citizens is to be deprived of it just as effectively. Hobbes was at any rate more candid: he did not pretend that a sovereign does not enslave; he justified this slavery, but at least did not have the effrontery to call it freedom.

Throughout the nineteenth century liberal thinkers maintained that if liberty involved a limit upon the powers of any man to force me to do what I did not, or might not, wish to do, then, whatever the ideal in the name of which I was coerced, I was not free; that the doctrine of absolute sovereignty was a tyrannical doctrine in itself. If I wish to preserve my liberty, it is not enough to say that it must not be violated unless someone or other – the absolute ruler, or the popular assembly, or the King in Parliament, or the judges, or some combination of authorities, or the laws themselves (for the laws may be oppressive) – authorises its violation. I must establish a society in which there must be some frontiers of freedom which nobody should be permitted to cross. Different names or natures may be given to the rules that determine these frontiers: they may be called natural rights, or the word of God, or natural law, or the demands of utility or of the 'permanent interests of man', I may believe them to be valid a priori, or assert them to be my own ultimate ends, or the ends of my society or culture. What these rules or commandments will have in common is that they are accepted so widely, and are grounded so deeply in the actual nature of men as they have developed through history, as to be, by now, an essential part of what we mean by being a normal human being. Genuine belief in the inviolability of a minimum extent of individual liberty entails some such absolute stand. For it is clear that it has little to hope for from the rule of majorities; democracy as such is logically uncommitted to it, and historically has at times failed to protect it, while remaining faithful to its own principles. Few governments, it has been observed, have found much difficulty in causing their subjects to generate any will that the government wanted. The triumph of despotism is to force the slaves to declare themselves free. It may need no force; the slaves may proclaim their freedom quite sincerely: but they are none the less slaves. Perhaps the chief value for liberals of political – 'positive' – rights, of participating in the government, is as a means for protecting what they hold to be an ultimate value, namely individual – 'negative' – liberty.

But if democracies can, without ceasing to be democratic, suppress freedom, at least as liberals have used the word, what would make a society truly free? For Constant, Mill, Tocqueville, and the liberal tradition to which they belong, no society is free unless it is governed by at any rate two interrelated principles: first, that no power, but only rights, can be regarded as absolute, so that all men, whatever power governs them, have an absolute right to refuse to behave inhumanly; and, second, that there are frontiers, not artificially drawn, within which men should be inviolable, these frontiers being defined in terms of rules so long and widely accepted that their observance has entered into the very conception of what it is to be a normal human being, and, therefore, also of what it is to act inhumanly or insanely; rules of which it would be absurd to say, for example, that they could be abrogated by some formal procedure on the part of some court or sovereign body. When I speak of a man as being normal, a part of what I mean is that he could not break these rules easily, without a qualm of revulsion. It is such rules as these that are broken when a man is declared guilty without trial, or punished under a retroactive law; when children are ordered to denounce their parents, friends to betray one another, soldiers to use methods of barbarism; when men are tortured or murdered, or minorities are massacred because they irritate a majority or a tyrant. Such acts, even if they are made legal by the sovereign, cause horror even in these days, and this springs from the recognition of the moral validity – irrespective of the laws – of some absolute barriers to the imposition of one man's will on another. The freedom of a society, or a class or a group, in this sense of freedom, is measured by the strength of these barriers, and the number and importance of the paths which they keep open for their members – if not for all, for at any rate a great number of them.

This is almost at the opposite pole from the purposes of those who believe in liberty in the 'positive' – self-directive – sense. The former want to curb authority as such. The latter want it placed in their own hands. That is a cardinal issue. These are not two different interpretations of a single concept, but two profoundly divergent and irreconcilable attitudes to the ends of life. It is as well to recognise this, even if in practice it is often necessary to strike a compromise between them. For each of them makes absolute claims. These claims cannot both be fully satisfied. But it is a profound lack of social and moral understanding not to recognise that the satisfaction that each of them seeks is an ultimate value which, both historically and morally, has an equal right to be classed among the deepest interests of mankind.

Notes

1   This has an obvious affinity with Kant's doctrine of human freedom; but it is a socialised and empirical version of it, and therefore almost its opposite. Kant's free man needs no public recognition for his inner freedom. If he is treated as a means to some external purpose, that is a wrong action on the part of his exploiters, but his own 'noumenal' status is untouched, and he is fully free, and fully a man, however he may be treated. The need spoken of here is bound up wholly with the relation that I have with others; I am nothing if I am unrecognised. I cannot ignore the attitude of others with Byronic disdain, fully conscious of my own intrinsic worth and vocation, or escape into my inner life, for I am in my own eyes as others see me. I identify myself with the point of view of my milieu: I feel myself to be somebody or nobody in terms of my position and function in the social whole; this is the most 'heteronomous' condition imaginable.

2   This argument should be distinguished from the traditional approach of some of the disciples of Burke or Hegel, who say that, since I am made what I am by society or history, to escape from them is impossible and to attempt it irrational. No doubt I cannot leap out of my skin, or breathe outside my proper element; it is a mere tautology to say that I am what I am, and cannot want to be liberated from

my essential characteristics, some of which are social. But it does not follow that all my attributes are intrinsic and inalienable, and that I cannot seek to alter my status within the 'social network', or 'cosmic web', which determines my nature; if this were the case, no meaning could be attached to such words as 'choice' or 'decision' or 'activity'. If they are to mean anything, attempts to protect myself against authority, or even to escape from my 'station and its duties', cannot be excluded as automatically irrational or suicidal.

Isaiah Berlin, "Two Concepts of Liberty," in *Liberty* (Oxford: Oxford University Press, 2002), pp. 200–12.

Chapter 20

F. A. Hayek, from *The Constitution of Liberty* (1960)

Chapter One
Liberty and Liberties

The world has never had a good definition of the word liberty, and the American people just now are much in need of one. We all declare for liberty: but in using the same word, we do not mean the same thing. . . . Here are two, not only different but incompatible things, called by the same name, liberty.

ABRAHAM LINCOLN

1. We are concerned in this book with that condition of men in which coercion of some by others is reduced as much as is possible in society. This state we shall describe throughout as a state of liberty or freedom. These two words have been also used to describe many other good things of life. It would therefore not be very profitable to start by asking what they really mean. It would seem better to state, first, the condition which we shall mean when we use them and then consider the other meanings of the words only in order to define more sharply that which we have adopted.

The state in which a man is not subject to coercion by the arbitrary will of another or others is often also distinguished as "individual" or "personal" freedom, and whenever we want to remind the reader that it is in this sense that we are using the word "freedom," we shall employ that expression. Sometimes the term "civil liberty" is used in the same sense, but we shall avoid it because it is too liable to be confused with what is called "polit-

ical liberty" – an inevitable confusion arising from the fact that "civil" and "political" derive, respectively, from Latin and Greek words with the same meaning.

Even our tentative indication of what we shall mean by "freedom" will have shown that it describes a state which man living among his fellows may hope to approach closely but can hardly expect to realize perfectly. The task of a policy of freedom must therefore be to minimize coercion or its harmful effects, even if it cannot eliminate it completely.

It so happens that the meaning of freedom that we have adopted seems to be the original meaning of the word. Man, or at least European man, enters history divided into free and unfree; and this distinction had a very definite meaning. The freedom of the free may have differed widely, but only in the degree of an independence which the slave did not possess at all. It meant always the possibility of a person's acting according to his own decisions and plans, in contrast to the position of one who was irrevocably subject to the will of another, who by arbitrary decision could coerce him to act or not to act in specific ways. The time-honored phrase by which this freedom has often been described is therefore "independence of the arbitrary will of another."

This oldest meaning of "freedom" has sometimes been described as its vulgar meaning; but when we consider all the confusion that philosophers have caused by their attempts to refine or improve it, we may do well to accept this description. More important, however, than that it is the original meaning is that it is a distinct meaning and that it describes one thing and one thing only, a state which is desirable for reasons different from those which make us desire other things also called "freedom." We shall see that, strictly speaking, these various "freedoms" are not different species of the same genus but entirely different conditions, often in conflict with one another, which therefore should be kept clearly distinct. Though in some of the other senses it may be legitimate to speak of different kinds of freedom, "freedoms from" and "freedoms to," in our sense "freedom" is one, varying in degree but not in kind.

In this sense "freedom" refers solely to a relation of men to other men, and the only infringement on it is coercion by men. This means, in particular, that the range of physical possibilities from which a person can choose at a given moment has no direct relevance to freedom. The rock climber on a difficult pitch who sees only one way out to save his life is unquestionably free, though we would hardly say he has any choice. Also, most people will still have enough feeling for the original meaning of the word "free" to see that if that same climber were to fall into a crevasse and were unable to get out of it, he could only figuratively be called "unfree," and that to speak of him as being "deprived of liberty" or of being "held captive" is to use these terms in a sense different from that in which they apply to social relations.

The question of how many courses of action are open to a person is, of course, very important. But it is a different question from that of how far in acting he can follow his own plans and intentions, to what extent the pattern of his conduct is of his own design, directed toward ends for which he has been persistently striving rather than toward necessities created by others in order to make him do what they want. Whether he is free or not does not depend on the range of choice but on whether he can expect to shape his course of action in accordance with his present inten-

tions, or whether somebody else has power so to manipulate the conditions as to make him act according to that person's will rather than his own. Freedom thus presupposes that the individual has some assured private sphere, that there is some set of circumstances in his environment with which others cannot interfere.

This conception of liberty can be made more precise only after we have examined the related concept of coercion. This we shall do systematically after we have considered why this liberty is so important. But even before we attempt this, we shall endeavor to delineate the character of our concept somewhat more precisely by contrasting it with the other meanings which the word liberty has acquired. They have the one thing in common with the original meaning in that they also describe states which most men regard as desirable; and there are some other connections between the different meanings which account for the same word being used for them. Our immediate task, however, must be to bring out the differences as sharply as possible.

2. The first meaning of "freedom" with which we must contrast our own use of the term is one generally recognized as distinct. It is what is commonly called "political freedom," the participation of men in the choice of their government, in the process of legislation, and in the control of administration. It derives from an application of our concept to groups of men as a whole which gives them a sort of collective liberty. But a free people in this sense is not necessarily a people of free men; nor need one share in this collective freedom to be free as an individual. It can scarcely be contended that the inhabitants of the District of Columbia, or resident aliens in the United States, or persons too young to be entitled to vote do not enjoy full personal liberty because they do not share in political liberty.

It would also be absurd to argue that young people who are just entering into active life are free because they have given their consent to the social order into which they were born: a social order to which they probably know no alternative and which even a whole generation who thought differently from their parents could alter only after they had reached mature age. But this does not, or need not, make them unfree. The connection which is often sought between such consent to the political order and individual liberty is one of the sources of the current confusion about its meaning. Anyone is, of course, entitled to "identify liberty . . . with the process of active participation in public power and public law making." Only it should be made clear that, if he does so, he is talking about a state other than that with which we are here concerned, and that the common use of the same word to describe these different conditions does not mean that the one is in any sense an equivalent or substitute for the other.

The danger of confusion here is that this use tends to obscure the fact that a person may vote or contract himself into slavery and thus consent to give up freedom in the original sense. It would be difficult to maintain that a man who voluntarily but irrevocably had sold his services for a long period of years to a military organization such as the Foreign Legion remained free thereafter in our sense; or that a Jesuit who lives up to the ideals of the founder of his order and regards himself "as a corpse which has neither intelligence nor will" could be so described. Perhaps the fact that we have seen millions voting themselves into complete dependence on a tyrant has made our generation understand that to choose one's government is not necessarily to secure freedom. Moreover, it would seem that discussing the value of freedom would be pointless if any regime of which people approved was, by definition, a regime of freedom.

The application of the concept of freedom to a collective rather than to individuals is clear when we speak of a people's desire to be free from a foreign yoke and to determine its own fate. In this case we use "freedom" in the sense of absence of coercion of a people as a whole. The advocates of individual freedom have generally sympathized with such aspirations for national freedom, and this led to the constant but uneasy alliance between the liberal and the national movements during the nineteenth century. But though the concept of national freedom is analogous to that of individual freedom, it is not the same; and the striving for the first has not always enhanced the second. It has sometimes led people to prefer a despot of their own race to the liberal government of an alien majority; and it has often provided the pretext for ruthless restrictions of the individual liberty of the members of minorities. Even though the desire for liberty as an individual and the desire for liberty of the group to which the individual belongs may often rest on similar feelings and sentiments, it is still necessary to keep the two conceptions clearly apart.

3. Another different meaning of "freedom" is that of "inner" or "metaphysical" (sometimes also "subjective") freedom. It is perhaps more closely related to individual freedom and therefore more easily confounded with it. It refers to the extent to which a person is guided in his actions by his own considered will, by his reason or lasting conviction, rather than by momentary impulse or circumstance. But the opposite of "inner freedom" is not coercion by others but the influence of temporary emotions, or moral or intellectual weakness. If a person does not succeed in doing what, after sober reflection, he decides to do, if his intentions or strength desert him at the decisive moment and he fails to do what he somehow still wishes to do, we may say that he is "unfree," the "slave of his passions." We occasionally also use these terms when we say that ignorance or superstition prevents people from doing what they would do if they were better informed, and we claim that "knowledge makes free."

Whether or not a person is able to choose intelligently between alternatives, or to adhere to a resolution he has made, is a problem distinct from whether or not other people will impose their will upon him. They are clearly not without some connection: the same conditions which to some constitute coercion will be to others merely ordinary difficulties which have to be overcome, depending on the strength of will of the people involved. To that extent, "inner freedom" and "freedom" in the sense of absence of coercion will together determine how much use a person can make of his knowledge of opportunities. The reason why it is still very important to keep the two apart is the relation which the concept of "inner freedom" has to the philosophical confusion about what is called the "freedom of the will." Few beliefs have done more to discredit the ideal of freedom than the erroneous one that scientific determinism has destroyed the basis for individual responsibility. We shall later (in chap. v) consider these issues further. Here we merely want to put the reader on guard against this particular confusion and against the related sophism that we are free only if we do what in some sense we ought to do.

4. Neither of these confusions of individual liberty with different concepts denoted by the same word is as dangerous as its confusion with a third use of the word to which we have already briefly referred: the use of "liberty" to describe the physical "ability to do what I want," the power to satisfy our wishes, or the extent of the choice of alternatives open to us. This kind of "freedom" appears in the dreams of many people in the form of the illusion that they can fly, that they are released from gravity and can move "free like a bird" to wherever they wish, or that they have the power to alter their environment to their liking.

This metaphorical use of the word has long been common, but until comparatively recent times few people seriously confused this "freedom from" obstacles, this freedom that means omnipotence, with the individual freedom that any kind of social order can secure. Only since this confusion was deliberately fostered as part of the socialist argument has it become dangerous. Once this identification of freedom with power is admitted, there is no limit to the sophisms by which the

attractions of the word "liberty" can be used to support measures which destroy individual liberty, no end to the tricks by which people can be exhorted in the name of liberty to give up their liberty. It has been with the help of this equivocation that the notion of collective power over circumstances has been substituted for that of individual liberty and that in totalitarian states liberty has been suppressed in the name of liberty.

[. . .]

6. It is often objected that our concept of liberty is merely negative. This is true in the sense that peace is also a negative concept or that security or quiet or the absence of any particular impediment or evil is negative. It is to this class of concepts that liberty belongs: It describes the absence of a particular obstacle – coercion by other men. It becomes positive only through what we make of it. It does not assure us of any particular opportunities, but leaves it to us to decide what use we shall make of the circumstances in which we find ourselves.

But while the uses of liberty are many, liberty is one. Liberties appear only when liberty is lacking: they are the special privileges and exemptions that groups and individuals may acquire while the rest are more or less unfree. Historically, the path to liberty has led through the achievement of particular liberties. But that one should be allowed to do specific things is not liberty, though it may be called "a liberty"; and while liberty is compatible with not being allowed to do specific things, it does not exist if one needs permission for most of what one can do. The difference between liberty and liberties is that which exists between a condition in which all is permitted that is not prohibited by general rules and one in which all is prohibited that is not explicitly permitted.

If we look once more at the elementary contrast between freedom and slavery, we see clearly that the negative character of freedom in no way diminishes its value. We have already mentioned that the sense in which we use the word is its oldest meaning. It will help to fix this meaning if we glance at the actual difference that distinguished the position of a free man from that of a slave. We know much about this so far as the conditions in the oldest of free communities – the cities of ancient Greece – are concerned. The numerous decrees for the freeing of slaves that have been found give us a clear picture of the essentials. There were four rights which the attainment of freedom regularly conferred. The manumission decrees normally gave the former slave, first, "legal status as a protected member of the community"; second, "immunity from arbitrary arrest"; third, the "right to work at whatever he desires to do"; and, fourth, "the right to movement according to his own choice."

This list contains most of what in the eighteenth and nineteenth centuries were regarded as the essential conditions of freedom. It omits the right to own property only because even the slave could do so. With the addition of this right, it contains all the elements required to protect an individual against coercion. But it says nothing about the other freedoms we have considered, not to speak of all the "new freedoms" that have lately been offered as substitutes for freedom. Clearly, a slave will not become free if he obtains merely the right to vote, nor will any degree of "inner freedom" make him anything but a slave – however much idealist philosophers have tried to convince us to the contrary. Nor will any degree of luxury or comfort or any power that he may wield over other men or the resources of nature alter his dependence upon the arbitrary will of his master. But if he is subject only to the same laws as all his fellow citizens, if he is immune from arbitrary confinement and free to choose his work, and if he is able to own and acquire property, no other men or group of men can coerce him to do their bidding.

7. [. . .] By "coercion" we mean such control of the environment or circumstances of a person by another that, in order to avoid greater evil, he is forced to act not according to a coherent plan of his own but to serve the ends of another. Except in the sense of choosing the lesser evil in a situation forced on him by another, he is unable either to use his own intelligence or knowledge or to follow his own aims and beliefs. Coercion is evil precisely because it thus eliminates an individual as a thinking and valuing person and makes him a bare tool in the achievement of the ends of another. Free action, in which a person pursues his own aims by the means indicated by his own knowledge, must be based on data which cannot be shaped at will by another. It presupposes the existence of a known sphere in which the circumstances cannot be so shaped by another person as to leave one only that choice prescribed by the other.

Coercion, however, cannot be altogether avoided because the only way to prevent it is by the threat of coercion. Free society has met this problem by conferring the monopoly of coercion on the state and by attempting to limit this power of the state to instances where it is required to prevent coercion by private persons. This is possible only by the state's protecting known private spheres of the individuals against interference by others and delimiting these private spheres, not by specific assignation, but by creating conditions under which the individual can determine his own sphere by relying on rules which tell him what the government will do in different types of situations.

The coercion which a government must still use for this end is reduced to a minimum and made as innocuous as possible by restraining it through known general rules, so that in most instances the individual need never be coerced unless he has placed himself in a position where he knows he will be coerced. Even where coercion is not avoidable, it is deprived of its most harmful effects by being confined to limited and foreseeable duties, or at least made independent of the arbitrary will of another person. Being made impersonal and dependent upon general, abstract rules, whose effect on particular individuals cannot be foreseen at the time they are laid down, even the coercive acts of government become data on which the individual can base his own plans. Coercion according to known rules, which is generally the result of circumstances in which the person to be coerced has placed himself, then becomes an instrument assisting the individuals in the pursuit of their own ends and not a means to be used for the ends of others.

F. A. Hayek, *The Constitution of Liberty* (London: Routledge and Kegan Paul, 1960). pp. 11–16, 18–21.

Chapter 21

Philip Pettit, from
Republicanism (1997)

Chapter 2
"Liberty as
Non-domination"

The last chapter gave us a historical introduction to a conception of liberty – a distinctively republican conception, as I believe – that fits on neither side of the now established negative–positive dichotomy. This conception is negative to the extent that it requires the absence of domination by others, not necessarily the presence of self-mastery, whatever that is thought to involve. The conception is positive to the extent that, at least in one respect, it needs something more than the absence of interference; it requires security against interference, in particular against interference on an arbitrary basis.

I believe that this republican conception of freedom, this conception of freedom as non-domination, is of the greatest interest in political theory, and that it is important to put it back on the table in current discussions. My aim in this book is to try to identify the main features of freedom as non-domination, to show what it would mean to take the ideal as a political cause, and to indicate the institutional impact of organizing things so that the ideal is advanced. The book is an exploration of what a neo-republican politics would involve.

[. . .]

I.   Domination
A definition

One agent dominates another if and only if they have a certain power over that other, in particular a power of interference on an arbitrary basis [. . .]. They have sway over the other, in the old phrase, and the sway is arbitrary. It is time now to try to give a more explicit account of what such domination, such arbitrary sway, involves.

In giving this account, I shall often speak as if there are just two individual persons implicated in cases of domination, but that is only for convenience, While a dominating party will always be an agent – it cannot just be a system or network or whatever – it may be a personal or corporate or collective agent: this, as in the tyranny of the majority, where the domination is never the function of a single individual's power. And while a dominated agent, ultimately, will always have to be an individual person or persons, domination may be often be targeted on a group or on a corporate agent: it will constitute domination of individual people but in a collective identity or capacity or aspiration.

There are three aspects to any relationship of domination. Putting the aspects starkly, and without yet adding glosses, someone has dominating power over another, someone dominates or subjugates another, to the extent that

1.   they have the capacity to interfere
2.   on an arbitrary basis

3. in certain choices that the other is in a position to make.

We need to look at this account of domination, clause by clause. What is it to interfere, then, in the manner postulated in the first condition? Interference cannot take the form of a bribe or a reward; when I interfere I make things worse for you, not better. And the worsening that interference involves always has to be more or less intentional in character: it cannot occur by accident, for example, as when I fall in your path or happen to compete with you for scarce goods; it must be at least the sort of action in the doing of which we can sensibly allege negligence [. . .]. Were non-intentional forms of obstruction also to count as interference, that would be to lose the distinction between securing people against the natural effects of chance and incapacity and scarcity and securing them against the things that they may try to do to one another. This distinction is of the first importance in political philosophy, and almost all traditions have marked it by associating a person's freedom with constraints only on more or less intentional interventions by others [. . .].

But interference, as I understand it, still encompasses a wide range of possible behaviours. It includes coercion of the body, as in restraint or obstruction; coercion of the will, as in punishment or the threat of punishment; and, to add a category that was not salient in earlier centuries, manipulation: this is usually covert and may take the form of agenda-fixing, the deceptive or non-rational shaping of people's beliefs or desires, or the rigging of the consequences of people's actions. [. . .]

The variables relevant to an agent's choice are the range of options presented as available, the expected payoffs that the agent assigns to those options, and the actual payoffs – the outcomes – that result from the choice. All interfering behaviours, coercive or manipulative, are intended by the interferer to worsen the agent's choice situation by changing the range of options available, by altering the expected payoffs assigned to those options, or

by assuming control over which outcomes will result from which options and what actual payoffs, therefore, will materialize. Thus physical obstruction and agenda-fixing both reduce the options available; the threat of punishment and the non-rational shaping of desires both affect the payoffs assigned to those options; and punishment for having made a certain choice and disruption of the normal flow of outcomes both affect the actual payoffs. Where the removal of an option from the range of available alternatives is an on-or-off matter, of course, the other modes of interference come in degrees: the expected or actual costs of certain options may be worsened in a greater or a smaller measure.

Context is always relevant to determining whether a given act worsens someone's choice situation, since context fixes the baseline by reference to which we decide if the effect is indeed a worsening. This contextual sensitivity has important implications for the extent to which interference occurs. It means that acts of omission, for example, may count in some circumstances as forms of interference. Consider the pharmacist who without good reason refuses to sell an urgently required medicine, or the judge who spitefully refuses to make available an established sentencing option involving community service instead of prison. Such figures should almost certainly count as interfering with those whom they hurt. The contextual sensitivity will have other effects too. It may mean, for example, that exploiting someone's urgent needs in order to drive a very hard bargain represents a sort of interference. Consider the pharmacist who agrees to sell an urgently required medicine but not for the standard fee – not even for the fee that is standard in the circumstances of an emergency call – only on extortionate terms. Such a person interferes in the patient's choice to the extent of worsening what by the received benchmark are the expected payoffs for the options they face.

But though interference always involves the attempt to worsen an agent's situation, it need not always involve a wrongful act: coercion remains coercion, even if it is morally impeccable. I interfere with you if I obstruct your making a phone call by deliberately occupying the only kiosk available: and this, even though it is perfectly within my rights to occupy that kiosk. I interfere with you if I destroy your custom by deliberately undercutting your prices – assuming I have the required resources – whenever you try to sell your wares: and this, again, even if our market culture tolerates my behaviour. I even interfere with you if I stop you interfering with another, where my act is morally required, not just morally innocent. The notion of interferences, as I employ it here, is entirely unmoralized: whether one person interferes with another is decidable without reference to whether any particular moral offence has occurred; it is decidable just in the light of the facts, albeit the facts as they are seen through the local cultural lens.

So much by way of explicating interference. But what is it to have the capacity to interfere, which the first clause requires? Remember the old joke. 'Can you play the piano?' 'I don't know, I've never tried.' The lesson of that joke is that the capacity to interfere must be an actual capacity, as we might call it – a capacity that is more or less ready to be exercised – not a capacity that is yet to be fully developed: not anything like the virtual capacity of the musically gifted person who has yet to try out the piano. Consider a collection of people who, if they were to constitute themselves as a coherent agent, would have a ready capacity to interfere with someone. Or consider the agent, personal or corporate, who would have such a capacity, did they only recognize the presence of the potential victim, or the availability of causal modes of contact. In such cases there is only a virtual capacity to interfere, not an actual capacity, and I shall not say that there is domination. There is virtual domination, we might say, but not actual domination. Virtual domination may be something. for republicans to guard against, of course, because of the future dangers it represents. But it does not yet constitute the central evil to which they are opposed.

The second clause requires that the person have the capacity to interfere on an arbitrary basis if they are to dominate the other party fully. What makes an act of interference arbitrary, then – arbitrary, in the sense of being perpetrated on an arbitrary basis? An act is perpetrated on an arbitrary basis, we can say, if it is subject just to the *arbitrium*, the decision or judgement, of the agent; the agent was in a position to choose it or not choose it, at their pleasure. When we say that an act of interference is perpetrated on an arbitrary basis, then, we imply that like any arbitrary act it is chosen or not chosen at the agent's pleasure. And in particular, since interference with others is involved, we imply that it is chosen or rejected without reference to the interests, or the opinions, of those affected. The choice is not forced to track what the interests of those others require according to their own judgements.

Notice that an act of interference can be arbitrary in the procedural sense intended here – it may occur on an arbitrary basis – without being arbitrary in the substantive sense of actually going against the interests or judgements of the persons affected. An act is arbitrary, in this usage, by virtue of the controls – specifically, the lack of controls – under which it materializes, not by virtue of the particular consequences to which it gives rise. The usage I follow means that there is no equivocation involved in speaking, as I do speak, either of a power of arbitrary interference or of an arbitrary power of interference. What is in question in each case is a power of interfering on an arbitrary, unchecked basis.

Under this conception of arbitrariness, then, an act of interference will be non-arbitrary to the extent that it is forced to track the interests and ideas of the person suffering the interference. Or, if not forced to track all of the interests and ideas of the person involved – these may make inconsistent demands – at least forced to track the relevant ones. I may have an interest in the state imposing certain taxes or in punishing certain offenders, for example, and the state may pursue these ends according to procedures that conform to my ideas about appropriate means. But I may still not want the state to impose taxes on me – I may want to be an exception – or I may think that I ought not to be punished in the appropriate manner, even though I have been convicted of an offence. In such a case, my relevant interests and ideas will be those that are shared in common with others, not those that treat me as exceptional, since the state is meant to serve others as well as me. And so in these cases the interference of the state in taxing or punishing me will not be conducted on an arbitrary basis and will not represent domination.[1]

The tradition of thinking which we discussed in the last chapter took a distinctive view of what is required for an act of interference – in particular, an act of legal or government interference – to be non-arbitrary, and I follow that tradition in giving this account of non-arbitrariness. Consider Tom Paine's [. . .] complaint against monarchy. 'It means arbitrary power in an individual person; in the exercise of which, *himself*, and not the *respublica*, is the object' [. . .]. What is required for non-arbitrary state power, as this comment makes clear, is that the power be exercised in a way that tracks, not the power-holder's personal welfare or world-view, but rather the welfare and world-view of the public. The acts of interference perpetrated by the state must be triggered by the shared interests of those affected under an interpretation of what those interests require that is shared, at least at the procedural level, by those affected.

When is an interest or idea likely not to be shared with some members of the population and likely to be an inappropriate guide for state action? The operational test suggested by the tradition is: when it is sectional or factional in character. But how to test for what is sectional or factional? The only possible means is by recourse to public discussion in which people may speak for themselves and for the groups to which they belong. Every interest and every idea that guides the action of a state must be open to challenge from every corner of the society; and where there is dissent, then appropriate remedies must be taken. People

must find a higher-level consensus about procedures, or they must make room for secession or conscientious objection or something of that kind.

This is to say that the identification of a certain sort of state action as arbitrary and dominating is an essentially political matter; it is not something on which theorists can decide in the calmness of their studies [. . .]. But though it is political, I should stress that it is not essentially value-laden. There is a fact of the matter as to whether or not the state is effectively forced to track non-sectional interests and ideas when it interferes in people's lives. Politics is the only heuristic available for determining whether the interference of the state is arbitrary or not, but the issue for which it provides a heuristic is still an issue of fact. What has to be established is whether people really are dominated, not whether domination is visible from within some privileged evaluative standpoint. As the facts of the matter, including facts about local culture and context, determine whether a certain act counts as interference, so the facts of the matter determine whether a certain act of interference counts as arbitrary.

Arbitrariness, as we have defined it, may be more or less intense, and this draws attention to the fact that the domination associated with a power of arbitrary interference may be more or less intense too. Suppose that an agent can interfere in the life of another more or less at will: they can act just as their own whim or judgement leads them; they can act at their pleasure. Suppose, moreover, that the agent is subject to no particular difficulty or cost in exercising this capacity to interfere with someone: there is no prospect, for example, of suffering retaliation. And suppose, finally, that the interference in question is the most effective available: it can remove any options that the agent does not like or it can impose unbearable costs on the person's choice of those options. Such an agent will enjoy an absolute power of arbitrary interference over that person. The only brake on the interference that they can inflict is the brake of their own untrammelled choice or their own unchecked judgement, their own *arbitrium*.

Such an absolute power of arbitrary interference may have been available to slave-holders over their slaves in certain dispensations – certainly not in all – and it may have been accessible in some regimes to despotic potentates over their subjects. But it is not likely to be realized in many contexts. Such power is often approximated, however, at lower levels of intensity, even in rule-governed societies. The husband who can beat his wife for disobeying his instructions and be subject, at most, to the mild censure of his neighbours; the employer who can fire his employees as whim inclines him and hardly suffer embarrassment for doing so; the teacher who can chastise her pupils on the slightest excuse or pretence at excuse; the prison warder who can make life hell for inmates, and not worry much about covering her tracks: all such figures enjoy high degrees of arbitrary power over those subject to them. They may not be as common in some societies today as they once were. But they are not as unfamiliar as the slave-holder or potentate, and even where they do not survive, they have often left somewhat less powerful, but still recognizable, progeny in their place.

There are two generic sorts of constraint that we might expect to call on in trying to reduce arbitrariness: that is, in forcing a powerful agent like the state to track relevant interests and ideas. The first sort would put preconditions of action in place which make sectional interference that much more difficult: this, say, in requiring government to follow certain parliamentary procedures or to meet certain legal conditions in the way they act. These constraints are designed to filter or screen out unsuitable acts; they mean, where they are effective, that the agent does not interfere at will. The other sort of constraint would put penalties in place rather than filters: penalties which mean that any agent who perpetrates certain types of interference – violence, fraud, and the like – or who perpetrates otherwise legitimate types of interference under certain conditions – as when a public official has an undeclared interest in the

outcome of their decision – can be called to account and punished. These constraints are designed to expose unsuitable acts of interference to sanction, rather than screening them out; they mean, when they are effective, that the agent cannot interfere with a guarantee of impunity.

And so, finally, to the third clause in our characterization of domination. The main thing to notice about this clause is that it mentions certain choices, not all choices. This highlights the fact that someone may dominate another in a certain domain of choice, in a certain sphere or aspect or period of their life, without doing so in all. The husband may dominate the wife in the home, the employer dominate the employee in the workplace, while that domination does not extend further – not, at least, with the same level of intensity.

We saw in the discussion of the second clause that domination may be more or less intense: a dominating agent may be able to interfere on a more or less arbitrary basis, with greater or lesser ease, and in a more or less severe measure. We see here that domination may also involve a greater or lesser range; it may vary in extent as well as in intensity. This variation in extent will be important insofar as it is better to be dominated in fewer areas rather than in more. But it will also be important insofar as domination in some areas is likely to be considered more damaging than it is in others; better be dominated in less central activities, for example, rather than in more central ones. [. . .]

Common knowledge

The three conditions given are sufficient, as I see things, for domination to occur, though perhaps only in a limited measure, and perhaps only over a restricted domain. But if the conditions obtain to any noticeable degree in a world like ours, for a species like ours, then a further important condition is likely in many cases to be fulfilled too. This is that it will be a matter of common knowledge among the people involved, and among any others who are party to their relationship – any others in the society who are aware of what is going on – that the three base conditions are fulfilled in the relevant degree. The conditions may not be articulated in full conceptual dress, but the possibilities involved will tend to register in some way on the common consciousness. Everyone will believe that they obtain, everyone will believe that everyone believes this, and so on. And so on, at least, in the following pattern: no one will disbelieve that everyone believes this, on one will disbelieve that that is not disbelieved [. . .]

Why is the obtaining of the three conditions likely to mean that it will be a matter of common knowledge that they do in fact obtain? Some plausible empirical assumptions support it. The question as to whether such conditions obtain is going to be salient for nearly everyone involved, since it is of pressing interest for human beings to know how far they fall under the power of others. And the fact that the conditions obtain, if they do obtain, is usually going to be salient for most of the people involved: this, since the kinds of resource in virtue of which one person has power over another tend, with one exception, to be prominent and detectable. There is a salient question, then, and a salient basis for answering the question. And this means, plausibly [. . .], that in cases where the answer is 'Yes' – in cases where the conditions for subjugation are fulfilled – there is a basis for common knowledge, or at least for something approaching common knowledge, that they are indeed fulfilled. Everyone will be in a position, not just to see that the conditions are fulfilled, but to see that everyone else is in a position to see that they are fulfilled, and so on.[2]

The resources in virtue of which one person may have power over another are extraordinarily various: they range over resources of physical strength, technical advantage, financial clout, political authority, social connections, communal standing, informational access, ideological position, cultural legitimation, and the like. They also include the resource of being someone – say, being the only doctor or police officer around – whose help and goodwill the other may need in various possible emergencies. They even include the resource of perceived intractability – at the limit, perceived irrationality – that enables someone to drive a hard bargain.

I said that with one exception such resources tend to be prominent and detectable by those to whose disadvantage they may be deployed, and that this helps ensure that where one person has any dominating power over another, in virtue of an inequality in such resources, it is a matter of common knowledge that that is so. The exception is the case where one person or group is in a position to exercise backroom manipulation, whether manipulation of the options, manipulation of the expected payoffs, or manipulation of the actual payoffs [. . .]. Where domination is achieved by such means, it will not be a matter of common knowledge, unlike most other cases, that in this respect some people fall under the power of others.

When I say that the existence of a certain sort of domination between two parties is going to be a matter of common knowledge amongst them, and amongst their fellows, I should mention that this does not entail that they will evaluate it negatively: it does not entail that they will be aware of the domination as something on a par in any way with slavery. It is possible for those who do the dominating, for example, to take their superiority so far for granted that it does not ever strike them that the parities they dominate may bristle under the yoke. Think of Helmer Thorvald, the husband in Ibsen's play *A Doll's House*. He is clearly aware of dominating Nora, his wife, and indeed clearly believes that this domination is good for her. But he is absolutely blind to the fact that this domination could come to seem irksome and demeaning to Nora herself. No problem there; and no challenge to the claim that such domination is generally a matter of common knowledge. The lesson is that, even where domination exists and is recognized, it may not be seen for what it is when the dominated parties cannot speak for themselves.

Given that the fulfilment of the three original conditions – their fulfilment in any noticeable degree – is generally going to be a matter of something approaching common knowledge, the domination to which the conditions bear testimony will have an important subjective and intersubjective significance. Domination is generally going to involve the awareness of control on the part of the powerful, the awareness of vulnerability on the part of the powerless, and the mutual awareness – indeed, the common awareness among all the parties to the relationship – of this consciousness on each side. The powerless are not going to be able to look the powerful in the eye, conscious as each will be – and conscious as each will be of the other's consciousness – of this asymmetry. Both will share an awareness that the powerless can do nothing except by the leave of the powerful: that the powerless are at the mercy of the powerful and not on equal terms. The master–slave scenario will materialize, and the asymmetry between the two sides will be a communicative as well as an objective reality [. . .].

Conscious of this problem, John Milton deplored 'the perpetual bowings and cringings of an abject people' that he thought were inevitable in monarchies [. . .]. And a little later in the seventeenth century Algernon Sydney [. . .] could observe that 'slavery doth naturally produce meanness of spirit, with its worst effect, flattery'. The theme is given a particularly interesting twist a century later, when Mary Wollstonecraft deplores the 'littlenesses' and 'sly tricks' and 'cunning' [. . .] to which women are driven because of their dependency on their husbands: because of their slavery, as she also calls it. 'It is vain to expect virtue from women till they are, in some degree, independent of man; nay, it is vain to expect that strength of natural affection, which would make them good wives and mothers. Whilst they are absolutely dependent on their husbands they will be cunning, mean, and selfish' [. . .].

What contemporary relationships might illustrate the domination of some by others, with the associated effects on subjectivity and status? We have already got some sense of examples. In the absence of a culture of children's rights and appropriate guards against child abuse, parents individually or jointly will enjoy subjugating power over their children. In the absence of a culture of equal rights that is supportive of battered wives, husbands will enjoy such power over their spouses. In the absence of other employment opportunities and appropriate controls – say, those that a vigilant union might guarantee – employers and managers will enjoy subjugating power over their workers. In the absence of countervailing powers, creditors will often enjoy dominating power over their debtors [. . .]. In the absence of possibilities of appeal or review, bureaucrats and police will certainly enjoy that power over members of the public. And in the absence of some forums and procedures for dealing with minority grievances, a mainstream government may well dominate those in various marginalized groups.

Consent and contestability

It is important to notice that some of the relationships that I mentioned in illustrating domination will have originated historically in consent, while others will not. Whether a relationship sprang originally from a contract or not, whether or not it was consensual in origin, the fact that it gives one party the effective capacity to interfere more or less arbitrarily in some of the other's choices means that the one person dominates or subjugates the other [. . .]. Other considerations apart, this would have given traditional republicans a good reason to be hostile, as they were consistently hostile, towards the slave contract: towards the contract whereby someone, for whatever gain, voluntarily submits to the domination of another [. . .].

The fact that consent to a form of interference is not sufficient as a guard against arbitrariness means that no one who is concerned about domination can be happy about two developments that gathered momentum about the turn of the nineteenth century. One development was the growth of the populist idea, as we described it in the last chapter, that provided the majority rules, all is well. Majority rule may seem to be blessed by its consensual character, but it can clearly involve the domination of minority groups, and no one who resists domination can endorse unconstrained majoritarianism.

The other development that opponents of domination must deplore is the rise of the doctrine of free contract. This is the doctrine that the freedom of contract means the freedom to decide on the terms of a contract, not just the freedom to enter or refuse to enter into a contract, and that the free contract legitimates any treatment of one by another that the parties agree to accept. The law of contract was rapidly evolving and consolidating about the turn of the nineteenth century [. . .]. The development of the doctrine saw freedom of contract invoked in defence of some fairly appalling contractual arrangements, as people ignored the consequences for domination – as they ignored the asymmetries of power established under the contract – and argued that a contract that was not actively coerced was free [. . .]. This development is highly questionable from the point of view of anyone who is worried about domination. It could never have materialized, in all likelihood, had people remained focused on that evil, in particular, had they continued to think that freedom required the absence of domination, not just the absence of interference.

But though consent to interference is not a sufficient check against arbitrariness and domination, is it likely to be a necessary one? Should we hold that any act of interference is arbitrary to the extent that those affected have not consented to the exercise of that sort of power? The belief in the necessity of consent for the legitimacy of government has spawned dubious doctrines of implied or virtual or tacit consent. It would be good if we did not have to think of the consent of those affected by

certain acts of interference – say, by acts of law and government – as necessary for the non-arbitrariness and legitimacy of the interference. For that would mean that we did not have to look to such doctrines in the attempt to legitimate ordinary political realities.

Happily, a little reflection shows that what is required for non-arbitrariness in the exercise of a certain power is not actual consent to that sort of power but the permanent possibility of effectively contesting it. The state will not interfere on an arbitrary basis, by our earlier account, so far as its interference has to be guided by certain relevant interests and ideas and those interests and ideas are shared by those affected. This does not mean that the people must have actively consented to the arrangements under which the state acts. But what it does mean is that it must always be possible for people in the society, no matter what corner they occupy, to contest the assumption that the guiding interests and ideas really are shared and, if the challenge proves sustainable, to alter the pattern of state activity. Unless such contestability is assured, the state may easily represent a dominating presence for those of a certain marginalized ethnicity or culture or gender. The point is familiar from what is now often known as the politics of difference [. . .], and I make much of it in discussing democracy in the second part of the book.

Domination without interference

There are two final points about domination or subjugation that I want to stress, since they connect closely with themes in the last chapter. The first is that the possession by someone of dominating power over another – in whatever degree – does not require that the person who enjoys such power actually interferes, out of good or bad motives, with the individual who is dominated; it does not require even that the person who enjoys that power is inclined in the slightest measure towards such interference. What constitutes domination is the fact that in some respect the power-bearer has the capacity to interfere arbitrarily, even if they are never going to do so. This fact means that the power-victim acts in the relevant area by the leave, explicit or implicit, of the power-bearer; it means that they live at the mercy of that person, that they are in the position of a dependant or debtor or something of the kind. If there is common knowledge of that implication, as there usually will be, it follows that the power-victim cannot enjoy the psychological status of an equal: they are in a position where fear and deference will be the normal order of the day, not the frankness that goes with inter-subjective equality.

Does this point mean that no difference is made by the fact, if it is a fact, that the power-bearer is benign or saintly? That depends. If being benign or saintly means that the person acknowledges that they are subject to challenge and rebuke – if it means that they make themselves answerable in the court of certain considerations – then that entails that they cannot interfere with complete impunity; they can be quoted, as it were, against themselves. Suppose that a power-bearer acknowledges a code of *noblesse oblige*, for example, or just aspires to be a virtuous person. That is going to mean, in itself, that the power they have over someone else is at least less intense that it might have been; there is a certain reduction in the domination they represent, by virtue of their being exposed to the possibility of effective rebuke. This observation is relevant to my argument in the final chapter that the virtue of others represents an indispensable element in the set of safeguards that protects a person from domination.

If, on the other hand, being benign or saintly simply means that the person happens to have inclinations that do no harm to anyone else – in the actual circumstances, they do not lead to interference with anyone – then it will not entail a reduction in the domination of those who are under this person's power. It will remain the case that the person can interfere on an arbitrary basis and that anyone under their power lives, and lives by common

knowledge, at that person's mercy. Even when a dominating agent is benign in this sense, of course, the likelihood of interference will be that much lower. But it is important to see that domination goes with the accessibility of arbitrary interference to another, and that improbability of the kind in question here does not make for inaccessibility. Someone can be in a position to interfere with me at their pleasure, even while it is very improbable that they will actually interfere.

The observation that there can be domination without interference connects with the theme highlighted in the last chapter, that slavery and unfreedom is consistent with non-interference: that is can be realized in the presence of a master or authority who is beneficent, and even benevolent. As Richard Price [. . .] stated the point: 'Individuals in private life, while held under the power of masters, cannot be denominated free, however equitably and kindly they may be treated.'

Interference without domination

The second point I wish to emphasize about domination is that while the enjoyment of dominating power over another is consistent with never actually interfering, it is equally true that one agent may actually interfere with another without dominating that person. The public official or authority who interferes with people in a way that is forced to track their interests and ideas fails to enjoy subjugating power over the person affected. The official is subject to such screening and sanctioning devices, at least in the ideal, that they can be relied upon to act on a non-factional basis: on a basis that is supported by non-sectional interests and ideas. They interfere, since they operate on the basis of coercive law, but their interference is non-arbitrary.

The parliament or the police officer, then, the judge or the prison warden, may practise non-dominating interference, provided – and it is a big proviso – that a suitably constraining, constitutional arrangement works effectively. The agent or agency in question may not have any discretion in the treatment of a person affected, so that they cannot interfere at will, only under constitutionally determined conditions. Or if they have certain areas of discretion – for example, in the way in which the judge may have some discretion in sentencing – then their ability to exercise is to the intentional detriment of the person is severely limited: their actions may be subject to appeal and review, so that they are exposed to sanction in the event of using that discretion in a way that is not properly controlled by non-sectional interest and judgement.

Suppose that a constitutional authority – say, a judge or a police officer – operates under discriminatory laws and suppose that those laws severely constrain such agents in how they act. Do we have a complaint to make in the case of such constitutional discrimination? We certainly have. The fact that the laws are discriminatory means that they do not track the relevant interests or ideas of the group against whom discrimination is practised. Those who implement such laws, therefore, act on an arbitrary basis from the point of view of the group in question. It is true that they may have no option but to act in that way; by hypothesis they operate under severe legal constraint. But the fact that they are forced to interfere on an arbitrary basis with members of the group is consistent with their being able to interfere in that way; the fact that they are under a legal obligation to interfere on an arbitrary basis is consistent with their having the capacity to interfere on that basis.[3]

Like the first point made, this second one connects directly with the discussion in the last chapter. It bears on the question of whether law itself represents an abrogation of liberty: a restriction on people's pre-existing liberty which is justified by the effect it has in realizing a greater liberty and happiness overall. It should be clear that the law need not itself represent a form of domination, under the account of domination advanced here, and that the relation of law to liberty need not be represented in Hobbesian or Benthamite

terms. There will be systems of law available, at least in principle, which are entirely undominating and entirely consistent with freedom: not only will they inhibit potential dominators and reduce unfreedom, they will do so without representing a form of domination in their own right. And equally there will be systems of law that do introduce arbitrary control at some point and that do thereby embody domination and unfreedom: systems that are more or less authoritarian, in the fashion of Hobbes's Leviathan, or America's British legislature. These, in the old republican phrases, will represent the empire of men, not the empire of law [. . .].

Notes

1   Notice that this means, under a conception of freedom as non-domination, that neither a tax levy, nor even a term of imprisonment, need take away someone's freedom. But while such burdens do not compromise someone's freedom, still, as I put it later in this chapter, they do condition it. And so, while they do not compromise someone's freedom as non-domination, they do allow us to say that the person is not free to spend or to travel as they wish.

2   [The] argument, briefly, is this. The fact that the resources in question are available to the powerful person is compelling for everyone; it can be seen by everyone to be compelling for nearly everyone; and it serves for everyone to indicate that the conditions obtain. And so, assuming that people ascribe common information and inductive standards to one another, the fact that the resources are available will be seen by everyone to indicate that the conditions obtain, will be seen by everyone to be seen by everyone to indicate this, and so on.

3   An alternative line would be to say that while the constrained agents do not dominate members of the group, the legislators who make the laws or who are in a position to change the laws certainly do; they are the principal whose wishes are carried out by the constrained agents.

Philip Pettit, "Liberty as Non-domination," from *Republicanism* (Oxford: Oxford University Press, 1997), pp. 51–66.

Chapter 22

Quentin Skinner, from *Liberty before Liberalism* (1998)

II

Hobbes's incapacity (or perhaps refusal) to see any connection between public and private liberty was undoubtedly influential, but most critics of the neo-roman writers acknowledged that the desire to establish such a connection lay at the heart of their argument. Among these critics, however, two further objections were commonly raised against what we can now see to be the most basic contention of the ideology I have been examining, namely that it is only possible to escape from personal servitude if you live as an active citizen under a representative form of government.

A number of critics argued that, even if this contention is not actually incoherent, the suggestion that an equal right to participate in government is indispensable to the maintenance of civil liberty is so utopian as to make it irrelevant to the political world in which we live. This objection was widely canvassed at the time of the American and French revolutions, with William Paley coming forward in his *Principles of Moral and Political Philosophy* in 1785 as perhaps the most influential spokesman for what became the classical liberal case. As Paley urges in minatory tones, 'those definitions of liberty ought to be rejected, which by making that essential to civil freedom which is unattainable in experience, inflame expectations that can never be gratified, and disturb the public content with complaints'. Paley's warning takes on an added significance in the light of the fact that his *Principles* became a leading text-book for the teaching of political theory throughout the nineteenth century.

I shall not attempt to counter Paley's criticism, save by observing that I have never understood why the charge of utopianism is necessarily thought to be an objection to a theory of politics. One legitimate aspiration of moral and political theory is surely to show us what lines of action we are committed to undertaking by the values we profess to accept. It may well be massively inconvenient to suggest that, if we truly value individual freedom, this commits us to establishing political equality as a substantive ideal. If this is true, however, what this insight offers us is not a critique of our principles as unduly demanding in practice; rather it offers us a critique of our practice as insufficiently attentive to our principles.

I want to concentrate, however, on the other and more knock-down objection commonly levelled against the theory I have been laying out. According to a number of eminent critics, the analysis of the concept of liberty underlying the claim that it is only possible to live freely in a free state is itself misleading and confused. Those who have raised this objection commonly mount their attack in two waves. First they reaffirm the Hobbesian principle that the extent of your individual liberty depends on the extent to which the performance of actions within your powers is or is not physically or legally constrained. As Paley, for example, puts it, 'the degree of actual liberty' will always bear 'a reversed proportion to the number and severity of the *restrictions*' placed on your ability to pursue your chosen ends. But the neo-roman theorists, according to Paley, are not talking about this situation. They are talking about the extent to which the performance of such actions may or may not be free from the possible danger of being constrained. But this, Paley goes on, is to confuse the idea of liberty with a wholly different value, that of enjoying security for your liberty and exercise of your rights. So the neo-roman writers 'do not so much describe liberty itself, as the safeguards and preservatives of liberty: for example, a man's being governed by no laws, but those to which he has given his consent, were it practicable, is no otherwise necessary to the enjoyment of civil liberty, than as it affords a probable security against the dictation of laws, imposing arbitrary and superfluous restrictions upon his private will'.

The second wave of the attack then follows at once. As soon as this confusion is uncovered, we can see that the basic claim made by the neo-roman theorists to the effect that you can only be free in a free state is simply a mistake. The extent of your freedom as a citizen depends on the extent to which you are left unconstrained by the coercive apparatus of the law from exercising your powers at will. But this means that what matters for civic liberty is not who makes the laws, but simply how many laws are made, and thus how many of your actions are in fact constrained. This in turn shows that there is no necessary connection between the preservation of individual liberty and maintenance of any particular form of government. As Paley concludes, there is no reason in principle why 'an absolute form of government' might not leave you 'no less free than the purest democracy'.

The objection seems a not unnatural one; even Philip Pettit, the most powerful advocate of the neo-roman theory among contemporary political philosophers, has felt inclined to concede it.[1] It seems to me, however, that Paley's line of criticism fails to come to terms

with the most basic and distinctive claim that the neo-roman theorists are labouring to make about the concept of civil liberty. The claim is implicit in the analysis I have already given, but it is now time to spell it out.

The neo-roman writers fully accept that the extent of your freedom as a citizen should be measured by the extent to which you are or are not constrained from acting at will in pursuit of your chosen ends. They have no quarrel, that is, with the liberal tenet that, as Jeremy Bentham was later to formulate it, the concept of liberty 'is merely a negative one' in the sense that its presence is always marked by the absence of something, and specifically by the absence of some measure of restraint or constraint. Nor have they any wish to deny that the exercise of force or the coercive threat of it must be listed among the forms of constraint that interfere with individual liberty.[2] Despite what a number of recent commentators have implied, they are far from merely wishing to put forward an alternative account of unfreedom according to which it is held to be the product not of coercion but only of dependence.[3]

What, then, divides the neo-roman from the liberal understanding of freedom? What the neo-roman writers repudiate *avant la lettre* is the key assumption of classical liberalism to the effect that force or the coercive threat of it constitute the only forms of constraint that interfere with individual liberty. The neo-roman writers insist, by contrast, that to live in a condition of dependence is in itself a source and a form of constraint. As soon as you recognise that you are living in such a condition, this will serve in itself to constrain you from exercising a number of your civil rights. This is why they insist, *pace* Paley, that to live in such a condition is to suffer a diminution not merely of security for your liberty but of liberty itself.[4]

The issue, in short, is how to interpret the underlying idea of constraint. Among the writers I have been considering, the question surfaces most challengingly in Harrington's response to the satirical comments on the neo-roman theory made by Hobbes in *Leviathan*. Hobbes speaks with scorn of the self-governing republic of Lucca and the illusions fostered by its citizens about their allegedly free way of life. They have written, he tells us, 'on the Turrets of the city of *Lucca* in great characters at this day, the word LIBERTAS'. But they have no reason to believe that, as ordinary citizens, they have any more liberty than they would have had under the sultan in Constantinople. For they fail to realize that what matters for individual liberty is not the source of the law but its extent, and thus that 'whether a Common-wealth be Monarchical, or Popular, the Freedome is still the same'.

Harrington retorts with the lie direct. If you are a subject of the sultan, you *will* be less free than a citizen of Lucca, simply because your freedom in Constantinople, however great in extent, will remain wholly dependent on the sultan's goodwill. But this means that in Constantinople you will suffer from a form of constraint unknown even to the humblest citizen of Lucca. You will find yourself constrained in what you can say and do by the reflection that, as Harrington brutally puts it, even the greatest bashaw in Constantinople is merely a tenant of his head, liable to lose it as soon as he speaks or acts in such a way as to cause the sultan offence. The very fact, in other words, that the law and the will of the sultan are one and the same has the effect of limiting your liberty. Whether the commonwealth be monarchical or popular, the freedom is *not* still the same.

Notes

1   Pettit, for example, appears to concede that, whereas a classical liberal theorist like Paley analyses

unfreedom in terms of interference, the rival tradition analyses it in terms of security from interference [. . .] Pettit accordingly confines himself to objecting that what Paley fails to recognise is that the neo-roman writers seek only a specific kind of security, and seek it only against a specific kind of interference. [. . .] But cf. Pettit, *Republicanism* (1997), p. 5, where he more forthrightly declares that persons 'subject to arbitrary sway' are 'straightforwardly unfree'.

2   Pettit imputes to the defenders of 'republican' freedom the view that, since it is only arbitrary domination that limits individual liberty, the act of obeying a law to which you have given your consent is 'entirely consistent with freedom' (Pettit 1997, p. 66; cf. pp. 55, 56n., 104, 271). The writers I am discussing never deal in such paradoxes. For them the difference between the rule of law and government by personal prerogative is not that the former leaves you in full possession of your liberty while the latter does not; it is rather that the former only coerces you while the latter additionally leaves you in a state of dependence. [. . .]

3   For the idea of an 'alternative ideal', according to which 'freedom is defined as the antonym of domination' rather than interference, see Pettit 1997, pp. 66, 110, 273. But cf. Pettit 1997, pp. 51, 148, where he instead argues that the alternative tradition demands, in the name of freedom, something more than absence of interference. The latter formulation implies that, according to the neo-roman theorists, unfreedom can be produced either by interference or by dependence, which seems to me correct.

4   One might say that the neo-roman and classical liberal accounts of freedom embody rival understandings of autonomy. For the latter, the will is autonomous provided it is not coerced; for the former, the will can only be described as autonomous if it is independent of the danger of being coerced.

Quentin Skinner, *Liberty before Liberalism* (Cambridge: Cambridge University Press, 1998), pp. 77–86.

Part III

Freedom and the Mind

Introduction to Part III

Is a contented slave free? An issue with which the readings in this part are centrally concerned might appropriately be labeled as the "Stoic Problem." Epictetus famously argued that "freedom is secured by the removal of desire." So a slave – someone standardly subject to numerous enforced restrictions on what she may do – could, on this Stoic suggestion, nonetheless considerably liberate herself simply by shedding those of her desires which the restrictions prevent her from fulfilling. Indeed, on this suggestion, she might even be assisted in achieving that liberation by the very persons who restrict her, if they can devise effective methods of inducing the shedding of those desires.

For most writers, however, this conception of freedom is unacceptable. As Isaiah Berlin suggests, by making the absence of any unfulfilled desire a sufficient condition of being free, this conception implies that one's lack of freedom can be self-inflicted, insofar as one fails to rid oneself of that desire: it implies a view of freedom that is intrapersonal and not interpersonal, i.e. not a social or political conception of freedom. Thus, it is often insisted that a person's being free (or unfree) to do an action A is independent of her desiring or not desiring to do A.

Nevertheless, many authors find some grain of truth in Epictetus' otherwise erroneous claim. For it is true that, in considering which actions we are free or unfree to do, we do commonly take explicitly into account only those which we desire to do or, more generally, those which we imagine might be worthwhile doing: we would not, typically, describe ourselves as free to cut off our left ears, even in the absence of enforced restrictions against our doing so.

Can these two thoughts be reconciled? Some writers, including J. P. Day, simply deny that they can. For them, a person's attitude toward an action is utterly irrelevant to the question whether the person is free to perform it: all that matters is whether she is prevented or unprevented from doing so. Others, such as Charles Taylor and John Gray, have constructed arguments that would, if valid, allow the relation between a person's attitudes and an action to play some role in determining whether the person is free to perform it. Thus it has been variously argued that only those actions for which a person's desire can survive her rational and/or informed reflection are ones which the person can be either free or unfree to do. Actions that are desired by her because she has been brainwashed, or because she is driven by phobias or compulsions, or because she is ignorant, are not actions which she can sensibly be described as free to do, despite the fact that she is unprevented from doing them. Nor, on such views, would she be rendered unfree if she were prevented by other people from doing those actions in such circumstances. In all these cases, the relevant state of her desires is presumed to be beyond her power to alter, and this is taken to be a sufficient condition for the avoidance of the Stoic Problem of a self-inflicted lack of freedom. Brainwashing, phobias, and compulsions create or function as "internal constraints" on her acting – constraints which are as real as externally imposed obstacles and which, therefore, are held to deny her the freedom to act in ways contrary to their direction. (The excerpt from Kramer, which also views many psychological constraints as genuine restrictions on freedom, is otherwise quite different in its analysis of their constraining effects. For example, while agreeing with other theorists that people who perform actions under the influence of mind-control or veritable compulsions are not free to perform any contrary actions, Kramer also contends that such people are free to act as they do.)

A notable feature of such arguments, then, is their presupposition that the identification of "not unfree to do A" with "free to do A" is mistaken: there are actions which fall into a third category, as ones which we are "neither free nor unfree" to perform. This assumption stands in marked contrast with a view that freedom is a *bivalent* concept: that for any conceivable action, one is either free to perform it (if unprevented by others) or unfree to perform it (if so prevented).

A difference of views, similar to that concerning the relevance of desires to freedom, also prevails in regard to the relation between *abilities* and freedom. Are we free to perform actions of a *kind* that we are unable to perform? Again, writers who assume bivalence answer in the affirmative. Others trivalently insist that it makes no sense to describe persons as free to do actions which they are generically incapable of performing: even if no one places obstacles in the way of our doing these actions, we are said to be better described as being neither free nor unfree to do them. Few (if any) people, we can safely suppose, are prevented by others from performing extremely complex mathematical calculations in their heads in five seconds. On some bivalent views, they are accordingly free to perform them, whereas the proponents of trivalent conceptions would deny this.

Further Reading

Hirschmann, Nancy J., *The Subject of Liberty: Toward a Feminist Theory of Freedom* (Princeton, NJ: Princeton University Press, 2003) ⟨feminist argument for the relevance of desires and internal constraints⟩.

Kramer, Matthew H., *The Quality of Freedom* (Oxford: Oxford University Press, 2003), pp. 41–60, 360–1 ⟨critique of bivalent conceptions of freedom⟩.

Kristjansson, Kristjan, *Social Freedom: The Responsibility View* (Cambridge: Cambridge University Press, 1996), ch. 5 ⟨discussion of different kinds of internal constraint⟩.

Pettit, Philip, *A Theory of Freedom* (Cambridge: Polity Press, 2001), chs. 2–4 ⟨account of freedom as requiring deliberative control⟩.

Steiner, Hillel, "Freedom and Bivalence", in Ian Carter and Mario Ricciardi (eds.), *Freedom, Power and Political Morality: Essays for Felix Oppenheim* (London and New York: Palgrave, 2001) ⟨defense of bivalent conceptions of freedom⟩.

Chapter 23

Thomas Hobbes, from
Leviathan (1651)

Chapter XXI
"OF THE LIBERTY OF SUBJECTS"

2. And according to this proper, and generally received meaning of the word, a FREEMAN, *is he, that in those things, which by his strength and wit he is able to do, is not hindered to do what he has a will to.* But when the words *free*, and *liberty*, are applied to any thing but *bodies*, they are abused; for that which is not subject to motion, is not subject to impediment: and therefore, when 'tis said (for example) the way is free, no liberty of the way is signified, but of those that walk in it without stop. And when we say a gift is free, there is not meant any liberty of the gift, but of the giver, that was not bound by any law, or covenant to give it. So when we *speak freely*, it is not the liberty of voice, or pronunciation, but of the man, whom no law hath obliged to speak otherwise than he did. Lastly, from the use of the word *free-will*, no liberty can be inferred of the will, desire, or inclination, but the liberty of the man; which consisteth in this, that he finds no stop, in doing what he has the will, desire, or inclination to do.

3. Fear and liberty are consistent; as when a man throweth his goods into the sea for *fear* the ship should sink, he doth it nevertheless very willingly, and may refuse to do it if he will: it is therefore the action, of one that was *free*: so a man sometimes pays his debt, only for *fear* of imprisonment, which because nobody hindered him from detaining, was the action of a man at *liberty*. And generally all actions which men do in commonwealths, for *fear* of the law, are action, which the doers had *liberty* to omit.

4. *Liberty*, and *necessity* are consistent: as in the water, that hath not only *liberty*, but a *necessity* of descending by the channel; so likewise in the actions which men voluntarily do: which, because they proceed from their will, proceed from *liberty*; and yet, because every act of man's will, and every desire, and inclination proceedeth from some cause, and that from another cause, in a continual chain, (whose first link is in the hand of God the first of all causes,) they proceed from *necessity*. So that to him that could see the connexion of those causes, the *necessity* of all men's voluntary actions, would appear manifest. And therefore God, that seeth, and disposeth all things, seeth also that the *liberty* of man in doing what he will, is accompanied with the *necessity* of doing that which God will, and no more, nor less. For though men may do many things, which God does not command, nor is therefore author of them; yet they can have no passion, nor appetite to any thing, of which appetite God's will is not the cause. And did not his will assure the *necessity* of man's will, and consequently of all that on man's will dependeth, the *liberty* of men would be a contradiction, and impediment to the omnipotence and *liberty* of God. And this shall suffice, (as to the matter in hand) of that natural *liberty*, which only is properly called *liberty*.

Thomas Hobbes, ch. xxi, from J. C. A. Gaskin (ed.), *Leviathan* (Oxford: Oxford University Press, 1996).

Chapter 24

J. S. Mill, from
On Liberty (1859)

Again, trade is a social act. Whoever undertakes to sell any description of goods to the public, does what affects the interests of other persons, and of society in general; and thus his conduct, in principle, comes within the jurisdiction of society: accordingly, it was once held to be the duty of governments, in all cases which were considered of importance, to fix prices, and regulate the processes of manufacture. But it is now recognized, though not till after a long struggle, that both the cheapness and the good quality of commodities are most effectually provided for by leaving the producers and sellers perfectly free, under the sole check of equal freedom to the buyers for supplying themselves elsewhere. This is the so-called doctrine of Free Trade, which rests on grounds different from, though equally solid with, the principle of individual liberty asserted in this Essay. Restrictions on trade, or on production for purposes of trade, are indeed restraints; and all restraint, *quâ* restraint, is an evil: but the restraints in question affect only that part of conduct which society is competent to restrain, and are wrong solely because they do not really produce the results which it is desired to produce by them. As the principle of individual liberty is not involved in the doctrine of Free Trade, so neither is it in most of the questions which arise respecting the limits of that doctrine; as for example, what amount of public control is admissible for the prevention of fraud by adulteration; how far sanitary precautions, or arrangements to protect workpeople employed in dangerous occupations, should be enforced on employers. Such questions involve considerations of liberty, only in so far as leaving people to themselves is always better, *caeteris paribus*, than controlling them: but that they may be legitimately controlled for these ends, is in principle undeniable. On the other hand, there are questions relating to interference with trade, which are essentially questions of liberty; such as the Maine Law, already touched upon; the prohibition of the importation of opium into China; the restriction of the sale of poisons; all cases, in short, where the object of the interference is to make it impossible or difficult to obtain a particular commodity. These interferences are objectionable, not as infringements on the liberty of the producer or seller, but on that of the buyer.

One of these examples, that of the sale of poisons, opens a new question; the proper limits of what may be called the functions of police; how far liberty may legitimately be invaded for the prevention of crime, or of accident. It is one of the undisputed functions of government to take precautions against crime before it has been committed, as well as to detect and punish it afterwards. The preventive function of government, however, is far more liable to be abused, to the prejudice of liberty, than the punitory function; for there is hardly any part of the legitimate freedom of action of a human being which would not admit of being represented, and fairly too, as increasing the facilities for some form or other of delinquency. Nevertheless, if a public authority, or even a private person, sees any one evidently preparing to commit a crime, they are not bound to look on inactive until the crime is committed, but may interfere to prevent it. If poisons were never bought or used for any purpose except the commission of murder, it would be right to prohibit their manufacture and sale. They may, however, be wanted not only for innocent but for useful purposes, and restrictions cannot be imposed in the one case without operating in the other. Again, it is a proper office of public authority to guard against accidents. If either a public officer of any one else saw a person attempting to cross a bridge which had been ascertained to be unsafe, and there were no time to warn him of his danger, they might seize him and turn him back, without any real infringement of his liberty; for liberty consists in doing what one desires, and he does not desire to fall into the river. Nevertheless, when there is not a certainty, but only a danger of mischief, no one but the person himself can judge of the sufficiency of the motive which may prompt him to incur the risk: in this case, therefore (unless he is a child, or delirious, or in some state of excitement or absorption incompatible with the full use of the reflecting faculty), he ought, I conceive, to be only warned of the danger; not forcibly prevented from exposing himself to it. Similar considerations, applied to such a question as the sale of poisons, may enable us to decide which among the possible modes of regulation are or are not contrary to principle. Such a precaution, for example, as that of labeling the drug with some word expressive of its dangerous character, may be enforced without violation of liberty: the buyer cannot wish not to know that the thing he possesses has poisonous qualities.

John Stuart Mill, *On Liberty and Other Essays*, ed. J. Gray (Oxford: Oxford University Press, 1991), pp. 105–7.

Chapter 25

Isaiah Berlin, from
Four Essays on Liberty (1969)

Introduction

I wish to correct a genuine error in the original version of *Two Concepts of Liberty*. Although this error does not weaken, or conflict with, the arguments used in the essay (indeed, if anything, it seems to me to strengthen them), it is, nevertheless, a position that I consider to be mistaken. In the original version of *Two Concepts of Liberty* I speak of liberty as the absence of obstacles to the fulfilment of a man's desires. This is a common, perhaps the most common, sense in which the term is used, but it does not represent my position. For if to be free – negatively – is simply not to be prevented by other persons from doing whatever one wishes, then one of the ways of attaining such freedom is by extinguishing one's wishes. I offered criticisms of this definition, and of this entire line of thought in the text, without realizing that is was inconsistent with the formulation with which I began. If degrees of freedom were a function of the satisfaction of desires, I could increase freedom as effectively by eliminating desires as by satisfying them; I could render men (including myself) free by conditioning them into losing the original desires which I have decided not to satisfy. Instead of resisting or removing the pressures that bear down upon me, I can 'internalize' them. This is what Epictetus achieves when he claims that he, a slave, is freer than his master. By ignoring obstacles, forgetting, 'rising above' them, becoming unconscious of them, I

can attain peace and serenity, a noble detachment from the fears and hatreds that beset other men – freedom in one sense indeed, but not in the sense in which I wish to speak of it. When (according to Cicero's account) the Stoic sage Posidonius, who was dying of an agonizing disease, said, 'Do your worst, pain; no matter what you do, you cannot make me hate you', thereby accepting, and attaining unity with, 'Nature', which, being identical with cosmic 'reason', rendered his pain not merely inevitable, but rational, the sense in which he achieved freedom is not that basic meaning of it in which men are said to lose freedom when they are imprisoned or literally enslaved. The Stoic sense of freedom, however sublime, must be distinguished from the freedom or liberty which the oppressor, or the oppressive institutionalized practice, curtails or destroys. For once I am happy to acknowledge the insight of Rousseau: to know one's chains for what they are is better than to deck them with flowers. Spiritual freedom, like moral victory, must be distinguished from a more fundamental sense of freedom, and a more ordinary sense of victory, otherwise there will be a danger of confusion in theory and justification of oppression in practice, in the name of liberty itself. There is a clear sense in which to teach a man that, if he cannot get what he wants, he must learn to want only what he can get may contribute to his happiness or his security; but it will not increase his civil or political freedom. The sense of freedom, in which I use this term, entails not simply the absence of frustration (which may be obtained by killing desires), but the absence of obstacles to possible choices and activities – absence of obstructions on roads along which a man can decide to walk. Such freedom ultimately depends not on whether I wish to walk at all, or how far, but on how many doors are open, how open they are, upon their relative importance in my life, even though it may be impossible literally to measure this in any quantitative fashion. The extent of my social or political freedom consists in the absence of obstacles not merely to my actual, but to my potential choices – to my acting in this or that way if I choose to do so. Similarly absence of such freedom is due to the closing of such doors or failure to open them, as a result, intended or unintended, of alterable human practices, of the operation of human agencies; although only if such acts are deliberately intended (or, perhaps, are accompanied by awareness that they may block paths) will they be liable to be called oppression. Unless this is conceded, the Stoic conception of liberty ('true' freedom – the state of the morally autonomous slave), which is compatible with a very high degree of political despotism, will merely confuse the issue.

Isaiah Berlin, "Introduction," from *Four Essays on Liberty* (Oxford: Oxford University Press, 1969), pp. xxxviii–xl.

Chapter 26

J. P. Day, from "On Liberty and the Real Will" (1987)

Appendix

The preceding essay [see Chapter 11 in this volume] was completed before the publication of Berlin's *Four Essays on Liberty*. But since he raises in the Introduction an interesting point which bears directly on my main thesis, a short Appendix may be excused. Berlin there corrects an error in his 'Two Concepts of Liberty' to which a critic has drawn attention. Namely, that he begins this essay by expounding '*A* is free' as '*A* is not restrained from doing what he wants by *B*', notwithstanding that in the rest of the essay he criticises this notion of liberty. One criticism to which it is exposed is that 'if degrees of freedom were a function of the satisfaction of desires, I could increase freedom as effectively by elimination desires as by satisfying them'.

It is of more than historical interest that one famous theory of liberty, the Stoic, amounts to precisely this. In the words of Epictetus: '. . . freedom is secured not by fulfilling of men's desires, but by the removal of desire'. Apparently Epictetus, like Hobbes, Mill and others, believes mistakenly that Liberty presupposes Desire (See Sec. 2) For it is indeed true that, if '*A* is free to *D*' presupposes '*A* wants to *D*', then *A* cannot be unfree to *D* if he suppresses his desire to *D*; which seems to present the unfree with a solution to their problem.

However, this 'solution' is so unsatisfactory as to constitute no solution at all. For firstly, although it follows from the presupposition thesis that *A* cannot be *unfree* to *D* if he suppresses his desire to *D*, it also follows that, if he does this, he cannot be *free* to *D* either. Sec-ondly, it is absurd to claim that the difficulty of *A*'s unfreedom to *D* can be surmounted by bringing about a state of affairs in which the question of his being free, or unfree, to *D* just does not arise. Common sense recognises that it is not only morally repulsive, but also logically outrageous, to tell the autocrat's subjects that the way out of their difficulty in being politically unfree is to suppress their desire to have the vote. One might as well argue that, since Liberty presupposes Ability, the way to dispose of the problem of a prisoner's unfreedom of movement is to amputate his limbs (See Sec. 2) Thirdly, the Stoic doctrine is in any case simply false, because if the people did suppress their desire to have the vote they would nevertheless still *be* just as politically unfree as they were before they did so, since Desire is irrelevant to Liberty. But they would indisputably no longer *feel* politically unfree if they suppressed this desire; for it is as true that '*A* is free to *D*' presupposes '*A* wants to *D*' as it is false that '*A* is free to *D*' presupposes '*A* wants to *D*'. Presumably Epictetus too was misled into his paradoxical position through confusing being free with feeling free. However, it is also plausible to suppose that what he was really concerned to do was to abolish or mitigate the sense of unfreedom and not unfreedom itself. Indeed, his teaching probably provides the best anodyne available to despairing slaves. But he has nothing to say to those who hope to become, or to remain, freemen.

J. P. Day, "On Liberty and the Real Will" from *Liberty and Justice* (London: Croom Helm, 1987), pp. 16–17.

Chapter 27

John Gray, from "On Negative and Positive Liberty" (1980)

Freedom, Power and the Real Will

It is Berlin's central claim that, whereas there are two distinct and coherent conceptions of liberty, 'negative' and 'positive', positive liberty suffered a transformation as a result of which values other than liberty, such as the values of self-realization and of an integrated community, came to be misrepresented as aspects of liberty itself. While the idea of negative liberty, too, is recognized by Berlin to have been gravely abused as a licence for exploitation, there is a sense in which the perversion of the positive conception is morally and logically more culpable, since it involves the metamorphosis of a doctrine of limitation on political authority into a doctrine of the equivalence of authoritarian determination with individual self-mastery. Berlin distinguishes as 'the essence of liberty, both in the "positive" and "negative" senses' what he calls 'the holding off of something or someone . . . of others who trespass on my field or assert their authority over me, or of obsessions, fears, neuroses, irrational forces . . . intruders and despots of one kind or another'. It is the mutation in the concept of liberty in its positive variants in their legitimate form as conceptions of self-determination in such writers as Spinoza and Kant into the idea of government by objective reason as expressed in the institutions of the State which we find in the later Fichte and in the English Idealists that warrants Berlin's claim that:

It is only the confusion of desire for liberty with this profound and universal craving for status and understanding, further confounded by being identified with the notion of social self-direction, that makes it possible for men, while submitting to the authority of oligarchs and dictators, to claim that this in some sense liberates them.

While what Berlin says here seems to me to be both true and important, I want to draw attention to what I think is an unresolved (and perhaps insuperable) difficulty in one variant of the negative conception of liberty, which he contrasts with the authentic germ of the positive notion of rational self-determination. This is that no viable conception of liberty can altogether dispense with considerations deriving from the difficult idea of the real or rational will. Speaking of the way in which the positive conception of freedom as self-mastery has supported the division of the human personality into two parts, one transcendental and rational and the other empirical and contingent, Berlin comments that this fact illustrates the obvious truth that 'conceptions of freedom directly derive from views of what constitutes a self, a person, a man'. Later, in criticism of Kantian positive libertarianism, Berlin says that 'the authority of reason and the duties it lays upon man is identified with individual freedom, on the assumption that only rational ends can be the "true" objects of a "free" man's "real" nature'. He comments:

I have never . . . understood what reason means in this context: and here wish merely to point out that the *a priori* assumptions of this philosophical psychology are not compatible with empiricism: that is to say, with any doctrine founded on knowledge derived from experience of what men are and seek.

Now it is undoubtedly true that some positive conceptions of liberty depend crucially on a rationalist philosophical psychology in which a noumenal or rational self can be distinguished from a phenomenal empirical personality. This seems to be true of Rawls's theory of justice as fairness, for example, in that there the project of developing a 'moral geometry', in which questions of rightness and distributive justice are definitively answerable, appears to founder unless a conception of the rational self is invoked and given philosophical plausibility. Again, in the case of J. S. Mill, to whom Berlin attributes a mainly negative conception of liberty, it is arguable that the idea of a free man which is at the centre of *On Liberty* requires for its support a philosophical psychology decisively different from, and incompatible with, that empiricist view of the self expounded (with some reservations) in Mill's 'official' philosophical writings (such as that *System of Logic* and *Hamilton*).

Whilst it is importantly true then, that questions about liberty cannot be insulated from controversial metaphysical commitments in the areas of the philosophy of mind and action, it remains the case that there are good reasons to doubt that any coherent conception of liberty can avoid incorporating requirements to do with the conditions of rational choice. One set of reasons why this is so is suggested by Benn and Weinstein, who in a well-known paper reject the conception of freedom as the absence of impediments or restraints and develop the most systematic argument we have so far for an account of freedom as the non-restriction of options. Claiming that it is apposite to discuss whether a man is free to do something only if it is a possible object of reasonable choice, they declare programmatically that: 'Our conception of freedom is bounded by our notions of what might be worthwhile doing . . . Incomprehension, not hostility, is the first obstacle to toleration.' Now it might seem that we are here approaching a conception of freedom as rational self-determination of just the sort Berlin has always resisted. The claim we are advancing is that comparative judgments about freedom always invoke judgments about the preferences of the standard rational chooser, and the suggestion I am noting is that there is something at least problematic about counting as a freedom an opportunity to act which no reasonable man would ever take. Are we not approaching a conflation of acting freely with acting reasonably? In his important paper, 'From hope and fear set free', Berlin has criticized the belief that individual and social freedom are necessarily or always augmented by an increase of knowledge and has attacked the identification of the rational life with the life of a free man. He has emphasized, there and elsewhere, that the freedom of societies, as well as of individuals, must comprehend opportunities for actions which are wilful, perverse, and even consciously irrational. It might seem then that Berlin is at one with those (often moral and practical) sceptics, who sever freedom to act from any requirements of rationality. Such a position, it seems to me, is stronger than any that Berlin explicitly embraces in his writings. In 'From hope and fear set free', the object of his criticism is a thesis of metaphysical rationalism which implies, in the area of practical reasoning, that every dilemma of choice has one right answer. Certainly, Berlin is committed to repudiating any view of freedom as the non-restriction of options which incorporates such a rationalist picture of practical deliberation. This is not the same as denying the relevance to questions of social freedom of any of the requirements of rational choice. Further, I suggest that the conception of rational choice that is appropriate is a minimalist and meagre one, stipulating only that an agent should *have a reason* for what he does. What such a requirement disqualifies as rational conduct is only the behaviour of a delirious agent, where no goal or end may be imputed to him which renders intelligible what he does. True, this minimal requirement of rational choice is liable to be extended so as to disqualify the incorrigibly delusional, the phobia-ridden and the hypnotized agent, and such an extension undoubtedly revives some notion of the rational or real will. My claims are, first, that we need to invoke this difficult notion since no viable conception of social freedom can altogether dispense with it. Second, I suggest that some useful variant of the idea of a real or rational will may survive the demise of the rationalist metaphysics and philosophical psychology in which it has traditionally been embedded. Third, whereas Berlin has nowhere endorsed this line of thought about freedom, I claim there is nothing in his writings which is strictly inconsistent with it.

One way of making these points is to say that, while the distinction between social freedom and power or ability is an important one, it is one which is difficult or impossible to make where the powers and abilities in question have to do with the subjective conditions of choice. Nor is this conclusion surprising when we recall Berlin's observation that conceptions of freedom derive directly from views of the self. Once Berlin has recognized that options are not discrete, countable entities like apples, but are individuated by reference to evaluative judgments endorsing disputable views of the nature of the self, it seems intuitively incongruous that he goes on to deny that whether a man really has an option to do something depends, in part, on whether that action is subjectively available to him. Feinberg has pointed out that much will turn on how we draw the boundaries of the self, and there are obvious difficulties in using a purely spatial criterion to do so. Any view of freedom as the non-restriction of options is bound to remain radically incomplete, however, in the absence of an account of the nature and powers of the self whose options it is that are opened and closed by human action and omission.

These questions arise clearly in the problem – as yet unresolved, in my view – of the avowedly contented slave. As Berlin recognizes in the introduction to the revised version of his lecture, his original definition of negative freedom as the absence of the interferences of others in the area in which an individual wishes to act, though it identifies a paradigm case of freedom, has damagingly paradoxical implications. For it makes the measure of an agent's freedom relative to his desires. Since it can never be assumed in advance of empirical research what are a man's desires, there is an important sense in which negative freedom (as Berlin originally conceives of it) is consistent with the presence and absence of any conditions whatsoever. In other words, expect in so far as they contain references to the state of mind of the agent, or presuppose the truth of some general proposition about human wants, attributions of negative freedom or its absence can (logically) tell us nothing informative about the actual alternatives available to an agent. Since, on Berlin's original account, the degree of a man's freedom is the extent to which his desires are frustrated by the interferences of others, a man may always increase his freedom by trimming his desires. And this has the consequence that we are precluded from describing as unfree the wholly contented slave – or, more generally, from lamenting the lack of liberty in a perfectly engineered *brave new world* in which desires and opportunities always coincide. Nor does Berlin's revised account, in which possible desires are included in the judgement, satisfactorily resolve the question. For, unless we have some principle of counting which is non-neutral, as between the slave and the non-slave, there will be desires which the slave could satisfy, and which in the non-slave will necessarily be frustrated. Only by invoking some norm of human nature which is discriminatory as to the wants which are to be counted, and which includes evaluations of the agent's states of mind, can the intuition that the wholly contented slave remains unfree be supported. This suggests that what we might call the phenomenonological and the sociological aspects of freedom cannot, after all, be hermetically sealed off from one another. It must be pointed out, however, that since invoking a norm of human nature in the way I have suggested is bound to be a highly questionable procedure, Berlin's account of this matter is not without difficulties. They are not difficulties peculiar to his account, however, but rather obstacles in the way of any political theory which recognizes the dependency of views of freedom on conceptions of man.

John Gray, "On Negative and Positive Liberty," from *Liberalisms* (London: Routledge, 1989), pp. 57–60.

Chapter 28

Richard J. Arneson, from "Freedom and Desire" (1985)

Muddles can be instructive. The clarifying confusion to be examined in this paper is Isaiah Berlin's intelligent vacillation on the issue of whether or not the extent of a person's freedom depends on his desires.[1] Is the amount of freedom an agent possesses determined solely by his objective circumstances or is it also partly a function of his subjective tastes and preferences? In clarifying this question I shall suggest that Berlin has trouble answering it because he almost perceives that interpersonal cardinal measurement of freedom, if possible at all, is possible only on a subjective basis. Yet as Berlin eloquently reminds us measuring freedom according to a subjective metric generates paradox. Whether commonsense ideas of freedom are consistent and reasonable is not purely an academic issue, for we do often make political judgments to the effect that one or another policy, or a movement to one or another form of society, can be expected to reduce or enlarge human freedom. If freedom is not measurable these judgments are merely hortatory.

This paper concentrates on one issue, the meshing of freedom and desire, to the exclusion of other significant puzzles regarding the nature of freedom. I do not attempt a full analysis of the concept of freedom. Nor do I have much to say about Berlin's celebrated reasons for championing 'negative' conceptions of liberty against 'positive' rivals. I should also mention that the terms 'liberty' and 'freedom' are interchangeable in this paper.

My starting point is Berlin's preferred negative conception of liberty, according to which the extent of a person's freedom centrally involves the question, 'What is the area within the subject – a person or group of persons – is or should be left to do or be what he is able to do or be, without interference by other persons' (121–2).

In the terms of this spatial metaphor, my question is: how do we measure the 'area' within which the person's opportunities for action are not constrained by the interference of other agents? I here presume that measurement will somehow involve identifying and measuring the opportunities or options for action available to the individual in various settings. To measure freedom one must measure options, but unfortunately options turn out to be elusive entities.

Suppose the police arrest Smith and Jones, and the question arises, whose freedom is more greatly diminished at the hands of the police. Smith is interrogated and quickly released onto the streets, and resumes the normal freedom to live as the chooses, expect that his thumbs have been hurt slightly and require splints. Jones is confined to a cell, and bound tightly from head to foot like a mummy, except that his thumbs protrude from his binding. Jones is then free to do nothing save move his thumbs back and forth. He can, however, move his thumbs in an indefinitely large number of trivially different ways, so it would seem that he is free to choose among an indefinitely large agglomeration of possible actions, each of these actions being a variety of thumb-wiggling. Regarding the extent of their freedom, then, Smith and Jones would appear to be on a par, for each has suffered a loss of countless options of action at the hands of the police, and each has remaining countless options from which to choose. Of course common sense will nonetheless see Smith as suffering far less restriction of freedom than Jones. The basis for so distinguishing Smith and Jones is the reasonable presumption that a great many options that matter to Smith are left open, while the options Jones cares about are foreclosed. (To see that this is the presumption that sways our judgment, imagine it altered: both Smith and Jones are fanatical adherents of an obscure religion which places overwhelming value on the performance each day of a great array of devotional exercises performed with the thumbs.) There may be ways of specifying how to count a person's options for the purpose of measuring his freedom that do not appeal to the desires and interests of the person whose freedom is being measured, yet do not give wildly counter-intuitive results for cases like the one we have been discussing.[2] None, however, has been developed in any detail to date in the literature on freedom. The conclusion to which we seem to be drawn is that variations on an act count as distinct options only to the degree that the differences among the variations are judged significant by the acting person. The individuation of options is relative to what matters to us.

Although Berlin does not explicitly call attention to this line of thought, its pressure on his essay is apparent.

If freedom is to be measured by counting a person's options as weighted by their importance to that person, then quite obviously one possible strategy for enlarging one's freedom is to bring it about that one takes an enlarged view of the significance of one's available options. In Berlin's words, 'If I find that I am able to do little or nothing of what I wish, I need only contract or extinguish my wishes, and I am made free' (139). This stoic strategy

Berlin labels the 'retreat to an inner citadel' (135) and characterizes as a 'sublime' form of the 'doctrine of sour grapes' (139); for him any analysis of the concept of freedom that permits freedom to be increased in this way thereby shows its inadequacy.

What troubles Berlin about the stoic strategy can be brought out by contrasting two slaves, one contented, one discontented, both being subject to exactly the same restrictions. The contented slave succeeds in adjusting his desires to his opportunities so that they mesh perfectly. He attaches no more value whatsoever to the satisfaction of any desire except the desire to do whatever his master commands. In contrast, the discontented slave finds that he is free to do precious little of what matters to him. Surely this example shows that the satisfaction of desire or the fulfillment of one's personal values is one thing and freedom quite another. Berlin proceeds to envisage an even more depressing scenario, in which the source of the slave's contentment is not any self-conditioning process voluntarily undertaken, rather a conditioning process imposed by the master in order to reconcile the slave to his situation (139–40). Surely becoming reconciled to one's situation in this fashion does not render that situation one of freedom. Yet before this conviction attracts our unqualified allegiance, we recall the reasons questioning the possibility of counting a person's options except as weighted by his desires. Clearly we have a problem.

A flickering recognition of this difficulty is registered in a famous footnote in Berlin's essay:

> The extent of my freedom seems to depend on (a) how many possibilities are open to me (although the method of counting these can never be more than impressionistic. Possibilities of action are not discrete entities like apples, which can be exhaustively enumerated); (b) how easy or difficult each of these possibilities is to actualize; (c) how important in my plan of life, given my character and circumstances, these possibilities are when compared with each other; (d) how far they are

open and closed by deliberate human acts; (e) what value not merely the agent, but the general sentiment of the society in which he lives, puts on the various possibilities. (130)

Now (c), as several commentators have noticed, appears to permit precisely what Berlin appears to want to deny in the 'inner citadel' or 'sour grapes' discussion – namely, that the stoic strategy can enlarge one's freedom. Proviso (e) might be calculated to prevent (c) from generating counter-intuitive judgments regarding examples such as that of the contented slave. Even if the slave succeeds in ridding himself of the desires that slavery frustrates, a consensus in the culture to the effect that the options slavery denies are of great value will suffice to show that despite appearances the contented slave has very little freedom. If this is the aim of proviso (e), it fails of its purpose. The dominant sentiment in slave societies tends to be that slaves are inferior creatures who require regimentation for their own good. When the contented slave discounts his desire say to roam about the countryside at will he is following, not opposing, the conventional evaluation of that option by his society. Anyway it is odd to think that how others evaluate a person's options should even partially determine the extent of that very person's freedom. It is peculiar to hold that the amount of freedom a person possesses rises and falls depending on the vicissitudes of cultural fads in which he does not participate.

Note also that in the footnote quoted from a paragraph back, Berlin cannot decide whether freedom is measurable or not. To ask whether a given policy would raise one person's freedom more than it would lower the freedom of three others taken together is, he asserts, 'logically absurd.' Measuring can only be impressionistic. Yet, 'we can given valid reason for saying that the average subject of the King of Sweden is, on the whole, a good deal freer than the average citizen of Spain or Albania' (130). Since both these judgments involve cardinal inter-personal comparisons of freedom, the distinction Berlin draws between

them is obscure to me. How can one measure averages without measuring the instances from which averages are calculated?[3]

Berlin returns to the stoic strategy problem with a sense of chagrin in his 'Introduction' to the 1969 reprint of his essay. He acknowledges that in the original 'Two Concepts' he both denies and permits the stoic strategy, and undertakes to set matters straight. He writes: 'The Stoic sense of freedom, however sublime, must be distinguished from the freedom or liberty which the oppressor, or the oppressive institutionalized practise, curtails or destroys' (xxxix). To characterize the latter idea of freedom he employs a metaphor of doors open and shut:

> The sense of freedom, in which I use this term, entails not simply the absence of frustration (which may be obtained by killing desires), but the absence of obstacles to possible choices and activities – absence of obstructions on roads along which a man can decide to walk. Such freedom ultimately depends not on whether I wish to walk at all, or how far, but on how many doors are open, how open they are, upon their relative importance in my life, even though it may be impossible literally to measure this in any quantitative fashion. The extent of my social or political freedom consists in the absence of obstacles not merely to my actual, but to my potential choices – to my acting in this or that way if I choose to do so. Similarly absence of such freedom is due to the closing of such door or the failure to open them . . . (xxxix–xl)

As John Gray has noticed, Berlin's inclusion of the phrase 'upon their relative importance in my life' readmits the stoic strategy once again. It is as though Berlin has spun all the way round in a revolving door and returned to the starting point he supposedly wished to abandon. Berlin's nervous disclaimer of the possibility of 'quantitative' measurement is also puzzling, for the problem of the contented slave pursuing his stoic strategy only arises on the supposition that freedom does admit of measurement.

My instinct is that there is something worth developing in Berlin's suggestion that the extent of one's freedom is a function of one's potential as well as actual desires. As it stands, however, the main difficulty with Berlin's 'open doors' metaphor is that it tends to beg the crucial question of how to identify and count options available to a person. For we have a reasonably clear idea of what a door is and how to tell whether it is open or shut, whereas the difficulty in measuring freedom is precisely that the notion of an 'option' is not so comfortably determinate. Once it is agreed to identify the problem of measuring freedom with the problem of counting open and closed doors, the idea that the extent of one's freedom varies with one's desires comes to look silly, for surely the question of how many doors I am free to enter is independent of the question whether I want to enter any of them.

In an essay addressed to Berlin's problem Joel Feinberg gives a more elegant version of this metaphor, but even as refined the metaphor remains an unsuitable basis for discussion. Feinberg asks us to 'think of life as a kind of maze of railroad tracks connected and disjoined, here and there, by switches. Where there is an unlocked switch, which can be pulled one way or the other, there is an "open option," wherever the switch is locked in one position the option is closed.' In the terms of this metaphor, I suppose we are to think of the extent of our freedom as given by the length of track we are free to travel upon, or by the number of switches we can reach, or perhaps by a weighted such of these two rankings. The metaphor, which Feinberg cautiously notes is 'inadequate in a number of respects,' admirably helps us to see the relevance to the ¿ measure of our freedom of what Feinberg calls the 'fecundity' of our options: the more an option opens the way to further options, the more fecund it is. Still, the major difficulty is that the railroad maze metaphor like the open doors metaphor is question-begging with respect to the point at issue between those who assert and those who deny that how an option meshes with our desires affects the extent to which having the option enlarges our freedom. *If* options of action are like switches on railroad tracks, then clearly the identification of options is not relative to desire. But are options like that? The metaphor by itself does not give any guidance in resolving this question but only arbitrarily prejudges it.

What are we to make of Berlin's wobbling on the issue which the open doors metaphor only very feebly tries to settle? When a theorist of distinction announces, 'here is a mistake which I have made and which I shall now correct,' and then proceeds to offer a revised position in which the original 'mistake' survives fully intact, this is a clue that the supposed mistake contains a truth which resists easy assimilation into the structure of our thought. In this case, the 'mistake' that haunts Berlin's account of freedom is the *desire thesis: The amount of freedom a person possesses varies directly with the extent to which his desires (or personal values) are satisfiable under the options available to him.* Considering the case of the contented slave, it would seem that we must reject the desire thesis in order to sustain our firm conviction that the contented slave is not more free than the discontented slave similarly situated. Is what seems so really so? Let us explore the possibilities for saving the desire thesis or some portion thereof in the teeth of brave new world examples.

The comparison of the contented and the discontented slave raises several issues at once, some of them in an aggravated form. Before we can reasonably decide whether the example should budge us from the desire thesis, these several issues need separate consideration. In what follows I isolate seven such issues and try to determine to what extent they motivate rejection or revision of the desire thesis.

I Formation-of-desire Worries

Suppose you were the subject of a tyrant or slave master who forcibly attached an electrode to your head, or beamed a special ray at you, the effect of which was to cause you to desire whatever the tyrant or master wishes you to desire. The tyrant can alter your desires at will by means of a mechanical device that he controls. In this extreme case manipulation of your desires can bring it about that your desires are perfectly satisfied no matter what restrictions are imposed on you, but it is counterintuitive to say that this meshing of desire and opportunity for satisfaction increases your freedom. Yet a refusal to judge that here freedom varies directly with the extent to which desires are satisfiable is not tantamount to rejection of the desire thesis. For the desires satisfied are not *your* desires; desires are yours only when they are of 'home growth.' In less extreme cases it will be controversial whether the desires an individual experiences as his own are properly to be counted as his, given that some suspect process has tampered with their formation. I don't believe the literature on freedom has succeeded in articulating any clear criterion for separating the desires of home growth from those of alien growth, but that doesn't matter for present purposes. What does matter is to understand that moral qualms about the processes that form desires, qualms that are certainly present in some versions of the contented slave examples, do not supply any reason to reject or revise the desire thesis. Rather, they simply show that its phrase 'his desires' requires careful glossing.

Moreover, it is important to notice that even if we had a clear criterion for counting desires as one's own for the purposes of measuring one's freedom with the help of the desire thesis, that would not alleviate all the concerns that the contented slave example prompts. To see this, recall that the contented slave may have attained his contentment by means of a voluntarily undertaken desire alteration therapy, rather than through any process of manipulation or deliberate conditioning at the hands of another. Whatever exactly desires of home growth turn out to be, desire that the individual voluntarily strives to attain will uncontroversially qualify as home-grown. Without impugning the process by which the contented slave acquires the desires that

render him contented, we are yet unwilling to allow his contentment to count as freedom.

In an interesting essay Jon Elster has denied this last point. He agrees with Berlin that one should not equate freedom with freedom to do what one wants, regardless of the causal origins of those wants. Instead Elster identifies the extent of a person's freedom with the extent to which the person is free to satisfy home-grown or what Elster call's autonomous' wants: 'Being a free man is to be free to do all the things that one autonomously wants to do.'[4] In section (VI) below I argue against identifying freedom with the satisfiability of any constellation of wants, home-grown or otherwise.

II Conflation of Autonomy and Freedom

Moral autonomy as conceived in the tradition of Kant and Rousseau is an admirable character trait and as such is to be sharply distinguished from freedom as a social benefit, the latter being the concern of political philosophy and of this essay. A person is morally autonomous to the degree that she acts only so as to conform to self-imposed rules; as Rousseau says, 'moral liberty' is 'obedience to a law which we prescribe to ourselves.' Presumably there is a dispositional element to autonomy as well. If life happens to make it very easy for a person to act autonomously, but we have good reason to believe that the person was ready to forfeit her autonomy in the presence of even a modest temptation, to that extent we judge the person less morally autonomous than if she were disposed to stand fast by self-imposed rules come what may. Autonomy so understood is a possession of a certain sort of character. Normally attainment of autonomy is an achievement, perhaps requiring heroic effort of will, though in some cases persons attain autonomy effortlessly. Now obviously moral autonomy construed in this way is not the same as freedom construed as a benefit that can be doled out to a person, consisting in a range of opportunity open to that person. The distinction is slightly trickier, but still manifest, if we understand freedom as a meshing of opportunity and desire, attainable either by altering opportunities to fit antecedent desires or by altering desires to fit antecedent opportunities. In either case possession of freedom might represent an achievement; perhaps one had to fight to gain the opportunities or struggle to change one's desires. But in ascribing autonomy to a person we are saying she behaves or is disposed to behave a certain way, whereas in ascribing freedom to a person we are saying she stands in a relationship to her environment that counts as having a benefit (however she might choose to behave or not behave in response to the benefit). If we failed to mark the distinction between autonomy and freedom, and if we judge the contented slave to be lacking in autonomy, through confusion we might wrongly think that this judgment has some relevance to the question of how much freedom the contented slave possesses. Ordinary usage of the terms 'freedom,' 'autonomy,' and 'liberty' is not regimented at all in terms of the distinction we have been describing, so the distinction is easy to miss.

To say a person is morally autonomous is to say nothing about her situation. A person can be fully morally autonomous while subject to the most extreme deprivation of freedom. Think of an imprisoned person who steadfastly refuses to betray her cause or to reveal secrets under interrogation and torture. But we might have good empirical grounds for suspecting that some situations are more hospitable to the development and maintenance of widespread moral autonomy than others, and these suspicions could provide autonomy-regarding grounds for favoring one or another social situation. Such suspicions might well be part of our grounds for hating slavery. I myself believe these suspicions to be well-founded. My point again is simply to insist that opposition to slave institutions based upon the ten-

dency of slavery to breed heteronomous character has nothing to do with the further question of how to measure how much freedom a contented slave possesses. These matters are quite independent of one another.

Freedom and autonomy can come in conflict. For example, consider Rousseau's choice between residence in Paris in Geneva. Living in Paris offers more freedom but will cause one's disposition to autonomy to be weakened. Freedom and autonomy can be rival values, but it is misleading to think of them as rival specifications of the same concept. One of the reasons that Berlin's celebrated antithesis between negative and positive liberty is confusing is that he bundles under the positive category conceptions of freedom in competition with their negative cousins along with various other values (such as autonomy) that, on his understanding of them, could not be candidate conceptions of freedom at all. The negative and positive contrast as Berlin draws it is not a contrast between two families of ideas about freedom but between one family and a menagerie.

III   Strategic Choice of Desires

Let us say a desire for something is *basic* if that thing is desired for its own sake, not as a means to some further end. Let us also stipulate that what is basically desired is valued – if I experience a craving and consider that satisfying the craving would be worthless, such a craving is not a basic desire. 'Basic desire' is roughly synonymous with 'personal value.' To some extent, such desires are chosen in the light of our circumstances, and in choosing desires we may be making the best if a bad situation. One might hold that sometimes an individual can just adopt a desire more or less at will, or one might hold that one can choose one's desires only indirectly, by choosing to act in ways that one reasonably predicts will give rise to a certain desire. Either way, the point still holds that in order to further our goals we may choose to bring it about that we acquire a new basic desire. If I am choosing basic desires in order to make a prudent adjustment to a terrible situation, a situation let us say of little liberty, there is a natural reluctance to judge that my success in following this rationally prudent strategy increases my freedom. After all my situation does not change, *I* do.

This reluctance to credit the stoic strategy with increasing one's freedom is, so far as I can see, completely independent of our evaluation of the desires chosen for such strategic, prudential reasons. Enslavement by a cultured master might supply motivation to alter one's desires in the direction of the 'higher' pleasures. Still, one might deny that the resultant fit between what the slave comes to want and what the master demands is a good reason to judge the contented slave more free than he would have been had he stayed discontented, unregenerately attached to the 'lower' pleasures. To the extent that unease of this sort underlies our reaction to the contented slave problem, it is doubtful that the appropriate lesson to be learned from this problem is that on the basis of our objective knowledge of the Good Life for Man we should discount the satisfaction of slavish desires because such satisfactions will block the slave's attainment of a Good Life. Hence I disagree with John Gray's proposal for coping with the contented slave problem, if I understand him. He writes: 'Only by invoking some norm of human nature which is discriminatory as to the wants which are to be counted, and which includes evaluations of the agent's states of mind, can the intuition that the wholly contented slave remains unfree be supported.' But I have isolated a reason for discriminating wants and wants, and denying that the satisfiability of the desires of the rationally prudent contented slave contributes to his freedom, and I further claim my reason makes no appeal to a norm of human nature nor to any negative evaluation of the slave's mental states. We may applaud the exemplary prudent adaptive behavior of the slave while denying that the alterations of desire he contrives enlarge his freedom.

However, it will not do to qualify the desire thesis so: strategically chosen basic desires are to be excluded from the calculation of the degree to which a person's desires are satisfiable under given options. This will not do because on this proposal, if my desires change through any process except deliberate choice, the resultant change in the degree of fit between my options and my desires will affect the extent of my freedom – whereas if I deliberately and self-consciously and successfully seek to alter my basic desires to gain some further goal, the resultant changes in the fit between my options and desires will have no impact whatever on my freedom. This does not square with common sense.

IV   Vital and Inert Options

Part of the basis for the judgment that the contented slave possesses very little freedom is assessment along a dimension not yet charted. Suppose a person is considering the impact on his freedom of a new option which he presently lacks and which a proposed policy would grant to him. Let us say an option is *vital* for a person to the extent that its very availability will bring it about that the person acquires an increased basic desire either for having the option or exercising it or both. An option is *inert* to the extent that its very availability will have no effect on the basic desires of the person regarding that option. (In passing we note the possibility of *morbid* options whose very availability lessens people's basic desires for them. In the case of extremely morbid options, you want them only so long as you cannot have them.) The 'very availability' of an option enhances its attraction if the following holds: a person notices or samples the option, or notices other persons noticing or sampling it, or hears persuasive arguments for the desireability of the option (none of which would have happened had the option been unavailable), and in consequence acquires a heightened appreciation of it. Also, the greater the amount of time that elapses before an option, once made available, has an influence on basic desires, the less the vitality of the option.

The suggestion I wish to make is that judgments of the vitality and inertness of options affect our measurements of freedom. The more a proposed change in a person's situation makes vital options available to the person, the more that change increases that person's freedom, other things being equal. Our confidence that making arbitrary finger-wiggling options available to an imprisoned man does not increase his freedom is a function of our confidence that those options are utterly inert for him, and similarly our judgment that emancipation would render the perfectly contented slave more free reflects our judgment that many of the options emancipation makes available are extremely vital for the slave. A sign that this is so is that where our confidence proves misplaced, our judgments of freedom shift. If Dr. Manette is so devastated by Bastille imprisonment that release from prison will neither help him to satisfy his present wants nor have any impact upon his future wants, release does not give an increase of freedom. To decide whether ceding an option to a person enhances his freedom, one must consider not just his present wants but his future wants as well, at least where the availability of the option itself affects his wants.

It may be doubted that considering the vitality of options helps to distinguish the case of a slave about to be free from the case of a free man about to be enslaved. Granting that the options that emancipation opens are vital, we may wonder if the same is not true of the options that enslavement gives. Suppose that slaves are permitted a midafternoon break for a smoke. A rest period for smoking might hold no attraction for a person before enslavement, while under conditions of slavery this option might come to be relished. Does the vitality of this option give reason to think that enslavement increases freedom? Perhaps one could maintain that it is not the very availability of the smoking option that

enhances its attractiveness for the slave, rather the fact that the person has been deprived of other and much more valued options. But there is no need to deny that there could be a case in which the new availability of an option, when other options are restricted, does render that option more attractive than it was previously. This does not undermine the claim that as a matter of fact such cases are rare, so considering vitality does introduce an asymmetry into the situation of the free man and the slave as regards their comparative freedom.

If I am right that the extent to which an option increases a person's freedom depends on its vitality for that person, this fact explains how Berlin could have thought that the extent of an individual's freedom depends on the evaluation that the 'general sentiment of the society' (130) puts on the possibilities of action open to that individual. Prevailing views as to the value of an option are not criteria of his vitality, but they surely are very reliable indicators. Humans are sufficiently similar that if most people find an option grows more attractive once it is made available, that is evidence that any given person will respond similarly. Berlin's point is then not true, but close to true.

It should be evident that the claim that the vitality of an option affects the extent to which it contributes to freedom is compatible with the spirit and letter of the desire thesis. The more vital are a person's newly acquired options, the more the person's desires will change in response to these options so that they come to be highly valued. Other things being equal, the more a shift to a new situation provides vital options, the greater the extent to which the person's desires (weighted by their importance) will be satisfiable in the new situation, compared to the old one. Other things being equal, an option that once made available would enhance your desire for it, adds more to your freedom than an inert option that has negligible impact upon desire. Only your own desires, not anybody else's, determine the extent of your freedom. But the desires that you would come to have in given situations, as well as the desires that you now actually have, play a role in deciding the extent of your freedom.

Any analysis of freedom must allow that freedom is one value among others, that persons sometimes choose lesser freedom. The desire thesis might seem to threaten to collapse freedom into desire satisfaction. If a person finds her desires more easily satisfiable after a change, doesn't this show her freedom is thereby increased? Noticing that the vitality of options affects their contribution to freedom permits us to avert the threatened disappearance of freedom as a distinctive value. Consider two persons who choose to remain in military service rather than enter civilian life. One person places no value on the options that military life lacks and civilian life makes available, and moreover correctly believes that the availability of these civilian options would not enhance their attractiveness. The second person foresees that civilian life would introduce options whose availability would induce undesired changes in her desires. To avoid this result, which she identifies as corruption, the second person remains in the military. On my view the second person is choosing to have less freedom, while from what has been said so far the first person would not gain in freedom by opting for civilian life.

There is another reason why acceptance of the desire thesis need not lead to conflation of freedom and happiness construed as overall high level of satisfaction of desire. Desires can be satisfiable in a situation but not actually satisfied in that situation, if we allow that an agent can fail to satisfy his desires due to various incapacities.[5] It may be prudent for a person to prefer one situation to another, even though more of his desires are satisfiable under the second, if he has good reason to believe that more of his desires will actually be satisfied under the first. Here prudence and the aim of maximizing one's freedom are in conflict.

Notes

1 Isaiah Berlin, 'Introduction' and Two Concepts of Liberty,' in *Four Essays on Liberty* (Oxford: Oxford University Press 1969), ix–lxiii and 118–72. Further references to this book are given in parentheses in the text.

2 A possible alternate basis for distinguishing options is degree of perceptual dissimilarity. For example if we take photographs of Smith's thumb-wiggling options, he and we will have difficulty distinguishing one from another. Whereas if Smith has to choose between walking in the Grand Canyon, trekking over Arctic wastes, and strolling along a Paris boulevard, he and we will readily distinguish these options even if he is as utterly uninterested in their differences as he is in the differences among various thumb gestures. Yet the walking options might seem significantly distinct options that do enlarge Smith's freedom, whatever his desires. But perceptual dissimilarity doesn't begin to be a generalizable criterion. Writing a check for $1 is from many standpoints perceptually indistinguishable from writing a check for $1,000,000. Section (IV) below suggests another way of handing the walking/wiggling examples.

3 That this question is not merely rhetorical is shown by the example of mean kinetic energy. But anyone who thinks freedom is measurable on a macro- but not on a micro-level owes us an account of how this is so.

4 Jon Elster, 'Sour Grapes,' in Amartya Sen and Bernard Williams, eds., *Beyond Utilitarianism* (Cambridge: Cambridge University Press 1982), 277–8. Elster's phrase 'being a free man' leaves it unclear whether he is talking about freedom as a social benefit one might receive or as a desirable character trait one might achieve.

5 I assume here something like the usual contrast between freedom and incapacity or inability. So far as my freedom goes, my desire to swim is satisfiable in a situation if nothing prevents me from satisfying that desire except my own inability to swim. I rely on the freedom/capacity contrast but find it problematic. Compare Smith's freedom and mine in two cases. Smith is very much stronger that I am, and has quicker reflexes. Park rules being liberal, he and I are equally free to climb El Capitan, but I lack the ability to do so. Now suppose the highwayman brandishing a knife says to each of us. 'Your money or your life.' My freedom is restricted; I am forced

to hand over my money. By virtue of his personal endowments, Smith can disarm the highwayman effortlessly, costlessly, at no risk to himself, without suffering moral qualms. His freedom is not restricted by the threat; he is as free to do whatever he wants with his money after the threat as prior to it. Let us suppose the very same differences in our capacities explain why Smith, unlike me, is able to climb and to remain free under the highwayman's threat. In each case the external circumstances we face are identical. In one case incapacity is properly said to affect the amount of freedom an agent has, but not in the other. What explains this asymmetry?

Note also that the desire thesis commences a slide away from the stance of denying that internal constraints affect one's freedom. If my desires affect the extent of my freedom, why not likewise my degree of self-knowledge, the extent to which I am tangled be neurosis, and so on to my other capacities? On this point see Charles Taylor, 'What's Wrong with Negative Liberty?', in Alan Ryan, ed., *The Idea of Freedom: Essays in Honour of Isaiah Berlin* (Oxford: Oxford University Press 1979), 175–93.

Richard J. Arneson, "Freedom and Desire," *Canadian Journal of Philosophy* 15 (1985), pp. 425–40.

Chapter 29

John Christman, from "Liberalism and Individual Positive Freedom" (1991)

The Concept

The idea of positive freedom has been variously rendered. The notion I will be defending represents an attempt to capture the requirement that free agents must be, in a fundamental sense, self-governing. This notion will be equivalent to the concept of individual autonomy as that is sometimes discussed. The distinction between this idea and the concept of *negative* liberty is between seeing freedom as simply the absence of restraints (of any kind) and seeing freedom as (in addition to this) the capacity for self-mastery and self-government.[1] Defenders of positive liberty claim that the concept of a restraint – no matter how embellished an account one gives of it – will not capture the ways that people can be manipulated and conditioned in relation to the very makeup of desires and values.

Imagine, for example, a woman who is raised in a culture which fiercely inculcates in her the idea that women should never aspire to be anything but subservient and humble domestic companions to their husbands, no matter how unhappy this makes them or how abusive their husbands are. Imagine further that this person is suddenly placed in a new culture where opportunities abound for women to pursue independent activities. She nevertheless shuns these opportunities and remains married to an oppressive husband from the old culture. The only "restraint" she faces (to pursuing the opportunities for an independent life-style) are her desires themselves (which remain the sort she was taught to have). She simply does not *wish* to act in any other way, turning a deaf ear to the reasons people give her to consider a less subservient posture. (Imagine that her husband abuses her but tells her she can leave him any time she wants, and she continues to want to stay.) Defenders of positive liberty insist that such a woman is unfree, and precisely because the processes by which her character and values were developed were themselves oppressive. These methods did not allow her to reflect on her emerging values in light of reasonable alternatives. So the presence of opportunities – the absence of restraints – is irrelevant to the true nature of her unfreedom. This shows that negative liberty is simply incomplete as a full accounting of human freedom. The free person must be guided by values that are her own. This is what the idea of positive liberty attempts to express.

Positive freedom, in the sense I want to discuss, will apply principally to *individuals*. I should therefore say a word about the connection which has traditionally been recognized between liberty in the positive sense and political participation – self-government in the collective sense. The relation between positive freedom and political participation is a complex one, but it is a connection which is not, on the view discussed here, *conceptually* necessary. The connection traditionally recognized can be explained this way: self-government means being guided by forces which are self imposed; the institutions of one's government and society to a large extent shape a person's attitudes and values (as well as actions); so unless one participates in the fair democratic institutions of government, it cannot be said that those laws and social forces truly emanate from one's will; and hence, only via participation is one self-governing. This argument depends heavily on the premise concerning the determining force of social and legal institutions. To maintain the conceptual separateness of the notion of positive liberty and democratic participation, one need only point out the contingent nature of the linking premise that our attitudes and values are molded by our society (in some strong sense). In a modern (and large) industrial society, a good many of my concerns are not severely dictated to me by the reigning governmental institutions of the day. So insofar as this is true, I can be to a large extent (individually) self-governing even if the institutions of the state and I keep a respectful distance. But in any case my claim here is only that the notion of *individual* positive liberty is of a piece with the tradition and also does not make participation in democratic institutions a conceptual necessity.

For an individual to be self-governing it at least must be the case that she is not moved by desires and values that have been oppressively imposed upon her, even if she faces no restraints in performing actions such desires motivate. Her character must be formed in a certain manner. What is needed, then, is an account of how desire changes take place, which is an expression of the ideal of the fully free person. Preference changes cannot be the result of oppressive conditions or blind, unreflective conformity to limited choices. Self-mastery means more than having a certain attitude toward one's desires at a time. It means in addition that one's values were formed in a manner or by a process that one

had (or could have had) something to say about. It is in this way that positive freedom will be a property of the "true self," but this self need not be metaphysically set apart (e.g., from the "phenomenal" self) or ontologically mysterious.

There has been much work in recent years on the concept of individual autonomy which is relevant here. Typical of this is the view that "a person is autonomous if he identifies with his desires, goals, and values, and such identification is not influenced in ways which make the process of identification in some way alien to the individual." This approach has faced various objections, most of which focus on the vagueness of the identification requirement and the threat of an infinite regress of the conditions. As my remarks so far have suggested, I would urge that what is needed is an account, at the level of preferences, of what processes of self-change preserve autonomy and which ones do not, an account which does not depend on the condition of identification or on the requirement of an infinite string of self-chosen desires. This can be accomplished, I think, when it is insisted that the conditions of autonomy essentially bear on the *formation* of preferences, not on their structure at any one time. The account would go something like this: whatever forces or factors explain the generation of changes in a person's preference set, these factors must be ones that the agent was in a position to reflect upon and resist for the changes to have manifested the agent's autonomy. In addition, this reflection and possible resistance cannot have been the result of other factors which – as a matter of psychological fact – constrain self-reflection.

This latter condition is needed to prevent an infinite regress of self-chosen desires as being necessary for autonomy. What must be true of the agent's acceptance (or rejection) of the processes of preference change is that at some level this was done in a "clear-headed" manner. That is, such things as drugs or emotional stress – that is, any factors which we know cloud a person's normal ability to reflect at all – were absent in the self-reflective processes that took place (or would have taken place). This is not to say that these factors must be absent at every level, for someone might autonomously choose to expose herself to reflection-inhibiting factors; but then in the case of *that* choice, or one at some more basic level, reflection-inhibiting factors must be absent. This requirement avoids a regress of the conditions for freedom. It also captures the intuition that freedom demands more than the condition that desires must be self-chosen, it must also be the case that these (meta-) choices are made under conditions free of external manipulation and interference.

We can articulate, then, the following conditions for autonomous generation of preferences. A person P is autonomous relative to some desire D if:

1. P was in a position to reflect upon the processes involved in the development of D;
2. P did not resist the development of D when attending to this process of development, or P *would not have* resisted that development had P attended to the process;
3. The lack of resistance to the development of D did not take place (or would not have) under the influence of factors that inhibit self-reflection (unless exposure to such factors was autonomously chosen, in which case that choice had to be made without such factors); and
4. The judgments involved in this self-reflection, plus the desire set that results, are minimally rational for P.

[. . .]

The inner citadel argument

This argument is roughly as follows: if liberty is construed as rational self-mastery, then I am made more free when, instead of removing restraints faced by my real wishes, I am manipulated into giving up those wishes. If freedom means doing what one wants, a person is made more free either by the removal of restraints on her choices or by the dissolution of the restrained choices themselves. This well-known difficulty is underscored this way by Berlin: "It is as if I were to say: 'I have a wounded leg. There are two methods of freeing myself from pain. One is to heal the wound. . . . But . . . [the other is to] get rid of the wound by cutting off my leg.'" I am made more free by retreating into "the inner citadel" of those core desires that form my true – free – self. Berlin labels this implication a "paradox" and suggests that any conception of liberty that entails it is thereby implausible.

Consider, for example, the familiar comparison between two types of slave: one is a person who hates her chains and longs for the things slavery prevents and is consequently miserable; the other is, like Epictetus, properly "adjusted" to her confinement and has expunged any of those desires that her situation has made impossible for her. Now on any conception of freedom which, like positive freedom, insists that an agent is free insofar as she can carry out those desires that are truly her own, then it must be concluded – implausibly – that the second slave is freer than the first.

Now as many have noted (and Berlin admitted), this example is not only a problem for the positive account of freedom. (In fact, I would suggest that the positive account is considerably better equipped than the negative view to capture our intuitions concerning such happy slave examples.) On *any* account of freedom, the very conception of a restraint will need to make reference to actual or possible desires of an agent. If freedom consists in unrestrained *possible* desires, then the concept of liberty becomes vacuous due to the impossibility of enumerating restraints. For example, the books on my shelf apparently are not a restraint. However, if I decide to walk in a line that crosses through where they are (say a fire starts and they block what becomes my only escape route), then they are. This shows how the number of restraints I face at any given time is virtually immeasurable and hence so is freedom.

On the other hand, if objects are counted as restraints only if they frustrate *actual* desires, the status of objects as possible constraints changes according to alterations in desires of the agent. Thus any conception of liberty that counts restraints in accordance with desires faces the possibility that freedom is increased or decreased by changes in desires rather than in external circumstances. This points exactly to the paradox of the happy slave, or so it is claimed.

I think, however, that commentators on this problem have mislocated the locus of the paradox in such "happy slave" cases. What gives the examples the air of paradox is not simply the structural form it takes: "the presence of a desire and a restraint plus the removal of the desire equals an increase in freedom." For certainly if I undergo a self-conscious and (let us say) rational program of character change, and, well after I am successful, some object or force appears that would have prevented me from fulfilling some previously discarded desire, then this object is no barrier to me, and it has no effect on my freedom. It is just like the books on my shelf (without the fire). And this scenario has the same "structure" as the happy slave cases. The paradox, on the other hand, arises when there is a suspicion that the preference change resulted from the very *presence* of the new restraint, bearing down on the agent and (forcefully) causing the change in desire. Calling *these* types of desire changes an increase in freedom is indeed implausible. What this shows is that, while it might be admitted that freedom can be a function of desires (since restraints are defined with reference to them), it cannot be that freedom is increased when desire changes take place directly *because of* the forceful presence of the new barrier.

The application to this problem of the model of positive liberty we have developed is direct: if a person acts upon desires that were not developed in accordance with the conditions set out above, then the person is not acting freely. Restraints can be characterized as those barriers to the carrying out of "autonomously formed" desires. Hence, if the "happy slave" has expunged her desires for freedom only as a result of the oppressive presence of the restraints she faces, then she is not more free after the change. For it is not the case that her desires were formulated in a manner that she could have resisted (and, we imagine, she would have). The chains she feels still constrain those desires for free movement which were (we can suppose) freely formed according to the above formula. So they are still restraints, and she is not more free after the change.

But if desire changes take place, and these changes are autonomous in the above sense, the person will remain free (positively) when forces are introduced that hinder those jettisoned desires. If the desire change in question occurs autonomously then the presence of such a "barrier" does not affect the freedom of the agent. And this is a conclusion free, I think, of paradox and incoherence.

Richard Arneson doesn't agree that this kind of move solves the inner citadel problem. On his view, even if desires are expunged by a process of self-reflective character change, the contented slave is not more free than the miserable one. I think, however that his doubts stem from a failure to take seriously the results of the person's change in character. When the "barriers" in question are things like locks and chains, and the actions being prevented seem so fundamental to normal human flourishing, it is hard to accept that a person could be *truly* indifferent to the presence of those restrictions. And this speculation is quite plausible. But it remains the case that if the Epictetan slave truly *does* extinguish the desires in question, in a way that is admittedly hard to imagine but not impossible, then those "restrictions" can no more be counted as restraints than can my books on a normal day. To make the example more believable, imagine that the desire changes take place well *before* the placing of the "restrictions," so that there is no hint of the possibility that the newly placed objects are the (illicit) cause of the preference change. Imagine that the "happy slave" is a Tibetan monk who has spent the last several years in the same room meditating and sitting quietly (being fed by acolytes) and from which he will never desire to move. If chains are then put on the door to the room, a room he does not want to leave, then his freedom of action is simply unaffected by these chains.

So if a full account of desire formation along the lines described in the first section of this article can be worked out and defended, the idea of positive liberty which contains this as a component will no longer be subject to the inner citadel argument. And I should stress that this was a problem for both positive and negative conceptions of freedom, and it is the positive conception that is most able to accommodate it.

[. . .]

On this view, if the desires and values that a person develops are generated in accordance with the *procedural* conditions of autonomous preference formation that are constitutive of freedom, then no matter what the "content" of those desires, the actions which they stimulate will be (positively) free. There are good theoretical reasons for a content neutral conception. For any desire, no matter how evil, self-sacrificing, or slavish it might be, we can imagine cases where, given the conditions faced, an agent would have *good reason* to have such a desire. That is, there may be many cases where I freely pursue a strategy of action that involves constraining my choices and manipulating my values. But if this is part of an autonomous pursuit of a goal, it is implausible to claim that the resulting actions or values do not reflect my autonomy. So since we can imagine *any* such preference as being autonomously formed, given a fantastic enough situation, then it cannot be the *content* of the preference that determines its autonomy. It is always the *origin* of desires that matters in judgments about autonomy. This of course implies that some extremely

constrained individuals will count as positively free because they (autonomously) choose to be under those constraints. But this is no more counterintuitive than the idea that I act freely when I have to shut off certain options to myself in order to achieve certain goals.

So while I take seriously the liberal objections to the traditional idea of positive liberty – a notion whose roots are in the political theory of the Romantic age – I do not regard this as the only understanding of the ideal of self-government. Rather than throw out the baby of self-government with the Jacobean bathwater, I am insisting on the development of a conception of *individual* positive freedom that avoids these worries of tyranny. What these arguments point to is that theories of justice should include central regard for such self-government in the concept of freedom which they defend. What is left of liberalism after such an inclusion, though, must remain for further discussion.

Note

1   Gerald MacCallum argued, of course, that there is not a true distinction between positive and negative liberty ("Negative and Positive Freedom," *Philosophical Review* 76 [1967]: 312–34). His view is that freedom of any sort is always a triadic relation among a person, an action, and a restraint. But even accepting MacCallum's formal elements, it is nonetheless a crucial aspect of classical liberal doctrine to regard freedom as being increased or decreased *simply* as a function of the presence or absence of restraints. John Rawls, e.g., discusses the MacCallum variables and admits that there are possible variations in what shall be counted to fill in for the 'X' placeholder (the concept of the person). But all he considers for such variants are the "various kinds of agents who may be free – persons, associations, states" (*A Theory of Justice* [Cambridge, Mass.: Harvard University Press, 1971], p. 202). So if one narrows this range to persons, then on the liberal view, the only variable left in the quantification of freedom is the number of restraints.

John Christman, "Liberalism and Individual Positive Freedom," *Ethics* 101 (1991), pp. 344–7, 351–4, 359.

Chapter 30

Charles Taylor, from "What's Wrong with Negative Liberty" (1979)

Isaiah Berlin points out that negative theories are concerned with the area in which the subject should be left without interference, whereas the positive doctrines are concerned with who or what controls. I should like to put the point behind this in a slightly different way. Doctrines of positive freedom are concerned with a view of freedom which involves essentially the exercising of control over one's life. On this view, one is free only to the extent that one has effectively determined oneself and the shape of one's life. The concept of freedom here is an exercise-concept.

By contrast, negative theories can rely simply on an opportunity-concept, where being free is a matter of what we can do, of what it is open to us to do, whether or not we do anything to exercise these options. This certainly is the case of the crude, original Hobbesian concept. Freedom consists just in there being no obstacle. It is a sufficient condition of one's being free that nothing stand in the way.

But we have to say that negative theories *can* rely on an opportunity-concept, rather than that they necessarily do so rely, for we have to allow for that part of the gamut of negative theories mentioned above which incorporates some notion of self-realisation. Plainly this kind of view can't rely simply on an opportunity-concept. We can't say that someone is free, on a self-realisation view, if he

is totally unrealised, if for instance he is totally unaware of his potential, if fulfilling it has never even arisen as a question for him, or if he is paralysed by the fear of breaking with some norm which he has internalised but which does not authentically reflect him. Within this conceptual scheme, some degree of exercise is necessary for a man to be thought free. Or if we want to think of the internal bars to freedom as obstacles on all fours with the external ones, then being in a position to exercise freedom, having the opportunity, involves removing the internal barriers; and this is not possible without having to some extent realised myself. So that with the freedom of self-realisation, having the opportunity to be free requires that I already be exercising freedom. A pure opportunity-concept is impossible here.

But if negative theories can be grounded on either an opportunity-or an exercise-concept, the same is not true of positive theories. The view that freedom involves at least partially collective self-rule is essentially grounded on an exercise-concept. For this view (at least partly) identifies freedom with self-direction, i.e., the actual exercise of directing control over one's life.

But this already gives us a hint towards illuminating the above paradox, that while the extreme variant of positive freedom is usually pinned on its protagonists by their opponents, negative theorists seem prone to embrace the crudest versions of their theory themselves. For if an opportunity-concept is incombinable with a positive theory, but either it or its alternative can suit a negative theory, then one way of ruling out positive theories in principle is by firmly espousing an opportunity-concept. One cuts off the positive theories by the root, as it were, even though one may also pay a price in the atrophy of a wide range of negative theories as well. At least by taking one's stand firmly on the crude side of the negative range, where only opportunity concepts are recognised, one leaves no place for a positive theory to grow.

Taking one's stand here has the advantage that one is holding the line around a very simple and basic issue of principle, and one where the negative view seems to have some backing in common sense. The basic intuition here is that freedom is a matter of being able to do something or other, of not having obstacles in one's way, rather than being a capacity that we have to realise. It naturally seems more prudent to fight the Totalitarian Menace at this last-ditch position, digging in behind the natural frontier of this simple issue, rather than engaging the enemy on the open terrain of exercise-concepts, where one will have to fight to discriminate the good from the bad among such concepts; fight, for instance, for a view of individual self-realisation against various notions of collective self-realisation, of a nation, or a class. It seems easier and safer to cut all the nonsense off at the start by declaring all self-realisation views to be metaphysical hog-wash. Freedom should just be tough-mindedly defined as the absence of external obstacles.

Of course, there are independent reasons for wanting to define freedom tough-mindedly. In particular there is the immense influence of the anti-metaphysical, materialist, natural-science-oriented temper of thought in our civilisation. Something of this spirit at its inception induced Hobbes to take the line that he did, and the same spirit goes marching on today. Indeed, it is because of the prevalence of ths spirit that the line is so easy to defend, forensi-cally speaking, in our society.

Nevertheless, I think that one of the strongest motives for defending the crude Hobbes–Bentham concept, that freedom is the absence of external obstacles, physical or legal, is the strategic one above. For most of those who take this line thereby abandon many of their own intuitions, sharing as they do with the rest of us in a post-Romantic civil-isation which puts great value on self-realisation, and values freedom largely because of this. It is fear of the Totalitarian Menace, I would argue, which has led them to abandon this terrain to the enemy.

I want to argue that this not only robs their eventual forensic victory of much of its value, since they become incapable of defending liberalism in the form we in fact value it, but I want to make the stronger claim that this Maginot Line mentality actually ensures defeat, as is often the case with Maginot Line mentalities. The Hobbes–Bentham view, I want to argue, is indefensible as a view of freedom.

To see this, let's examine the line more closely, and the temptation to stand on it. The advantage of the view that freedom is the absence of external obstacles is its simplicity. It allows us to say that freedom is being able to do what you want, where what you want is unproblematically understood as what the agent can identify as his desires. By contrast an exercise-concept of freedom requires that we discriminate among motivations. If we are free in the exercise of certain capacities, then we are not free, or less free, when these capacities are in some way unfulfilled or blocked. But the obstacles can be internal as well as external. And this must be so, for the capacities relevant to freedom must involve some self-awareness, self-understanding, moral discrimination and self-control, otherwise their exercise couldn't amount to freedom in the sense of self-direction; and this being so, we can fail to be free because these internal conditions are not realised. But where this happens, where, for example, we are quite self-deceived, or utterly fail to discriminate properly the ends we seek, or have lost self-control, we can quite easily be

doing what we want in the sense of what we can identify as our wants, without being free; indeed, we can be further entrenching our unfreedom.

Once one adopts a self-realisation view, or indeed, any exercise-concept of freedom, then being able to do what one wants can no longer be accepted as a sufficient condition of being free. For this view puts certain conditions on one's motivation. You are not free if you are motivated, through fear, inauthentically internalised standards, or false consciousness, to thwart your self-realisation. This is sometimes put by saying that for a self-realisation view, you have to be able to do what you really want, or to follow your real will, or to fulfil the desires of your own true self. But these formulas, particularly the last, may mislead, by making us think that exercise concepts of freedom are tied to some particular metaphysic, in particular that of a higher and lower self. We shall see below that this is far from being the case, and that there is a much wider range of bases for discriminating authentic and inauthentic desires.

[. . .]

There are some considerations one can put forward straight off to show that the pure Hobbesian concept won't work, that there are some discriminations among motivations which are essential to the concept of freedom as we use it. Even where we think of freedom as the absence of external obstacles, it is not the absence of such obstacles *simpliciter*. For we make discriminations between obstacles as representing more or less serious infringements of freedom. And we do this, because we deploy the concept against a background understanding that certain goals and activities are more significant than others.

Thus we could say that my freedom is restricted if the local authority puts up a new traffic light at an intersection close to my home; so that where previously I could cross as I liked, consistently with avoiding collision with other cars, now I have to wait until the light is green. In a philosophical argument, we might call this a restriction of freedom, but

not in a serious political debate. The reason is that it is too trivial, the activity and purposes inhibited here are not really significant. It is not just a matter of our having made a trade-off, and considered that a small loss of liberty was worth fewer traffic accidents, or less danger for the children; we are reluctant to speak here of a loss of liberty at all; what we feel we are trading off is convenience against safety.

By contrast a law which forbids me from worshipping according to the form I believe in is a serious blow to liberty; even a law which tried to restrict this to certain times (as the traffic light restricts my crossing of the intersection to certain times) would be seen as a serious restriction. Why this difference between the two cases? Because we have a background understanding, too obvious to spell out, of some activities and goals as highly significant for human beings and others as less so. One's religious belief is recognised, even by atheists, as supremely important, because it is that by which the believer defines himself as a moral being. By contrast my rhythm of movement through the city traffic is trivial. We don't want to speak of these two in the same breath. We don't even readily admit that liberty is at stake in the traffic light case. For *de minimis non curat libertas*.

But this recourse to significance takes us beyond a Hobbesian scheme. Freedom is no longer just the absence of external obstacle *tout court*, but the absence of external obstacle to significant action, to what is important to man. There are discriminations to be made; some restrictions are more serious than others, some are utterly trivial. About many, there is of course controversy. But what the judgement turns on is some sense of what is significant for human life. Restricting the expression of people's religious and ethical convictions is more significant than restricting their movement around uninhabited parts of the country; and both are more significant than the trivia of traffic control.

But the Hobbesian scheme has no place for the notion of significance. It will allow only for purely quantitative judgements. On the toughest-minded version of his conception, where Hobbes seems to be about to define liberty in terms of the absence of physical obstacles, one is presented with the vertiginous prospect of human freedom being measurable in the same way as the degrees of freedom of some physical object, say a lever. Later we see that this won't do because we have to take account to legal obstacles to my action. But in any case, such a quantitative conception of freedom is a non-starter.

Consider the following diabolical defence of Albania as a free country. We recognise that religion has been abolished in Albania, whereas it hasn't been in Britain. But on the other hand there are probably far fewer traffic lights per head in Tirana than in London. (I haven't checked for myself, but this is a very plausible assumption.) Suppose an apologist for Albanian Socialism were nevertheless to claim that this country was freer than Britain, because the number of acts restricted was far smaller. After all, only a minority of Londoners practise some religion in public places, but all have to negotiate their way through traffic. Those who do practise a religion generally do so on one day of the week, while they are held up at traffic lights every day. In sheer quantitative terms, the number of acts restricted by traffic lights must be greater than that restricted by a ban on public religious practice. So if Britain is considered a free society, why not Albania?

So the application even of our negative notion of freedom requires a background conception of what is significant, according to which some restrictions are seen to be without relevance for freedom altogether, and others are judged as being of greater and lesser importance. So some discrimination among motivations seems essential to our concept of freedom. A minute's reflection shows why this must be so. Freedom is impotant to us because we are purposive beings. But then there must be distinctions in the significance of different kinds of freedom based on the distinction in the significance of different purposes.

[. . .]

This creates some embarrassment for the crude negative theory, but it can cope with it by simply adding a recognition that we make judgements of significance. Its central claim that freedom just is the absence of external obstacles seems untouched, as also its view of freedom as an opportunity-concept. It is just that we now have to admit that not all opportunities are equal.

But there is more trouble in store for the crude view when we examine further what these qualitative discriminations are based on. What lies behind our judging certain purposes/feelings as more significant than others? One might think that there was room here again for another quantitative theory; that the more significant purposes are those we want more. But this account is either vacuous or false.

It is true but vacuous if we take wanting more just to mean being more significant. It is false as soon as we try to give wanting more an independent criterion, such as, for instance, the urgency or force of a desire, or the prevalence of one desire over another, because it is a matter of the most banal experience that the purposes we know to be more significant are not always those which we desire with the greatest urgency to encompass, nor the ones that actually always win out in cases of conflict of desires.

When we reflect on this kind of significance, we come up against what I have called elsewhere the fact of strong evaluation, the fact that we human subjects are not only subjects of first-order desires, but of second-order desires, desires about desires. We experience our desires and purposes as qualitatively discriminated, as higher or lower, noble or base, integrated or fragmented, significant or trivial, good and bad. This means that we experience some of our desires and goals as intrinsically more significant than others: some passing comfort is less important than the fulfilment of our lifetime vocation, our *amour propre* less important than a love relationship; while we experience some others as bad, not just comparatively, but absolutely: we desire not to be moved by spite, or some childish desire to impress at all costs. And these judgements of significance are quite independent of the strength of the respective desires: the craving for comfort may be overwhelming at this moment, we may be obsessed with our *amour propre*, but the judgement of significance stands.

But then the question arises whether this fact of strong evaluation doesn't have other consequences for our notion of freedom, than just that it permits us to rank freedoms in importance. Is freedom not at stake when we find ourselves carried away by a less significant goal to override a highly significant one? Or when we are led to act out of a motive we consider bad or despicable?

The answer is that we sometimes do speak in this way. Suppose I have some irrational fear, which is preventing me from doing something I very much want to do. Say the fear of public speaking is preventing me from taking up a career that I should find very fulfilling, and that I should be quite good at, if I could just get over this 'hang-up'. It is clear that we experience this fear as an obstacle, and that we feel we are less than we would be if we could overcome it.

Or again, consider the case where I am very attached to comfort. To go on short rations, and to miss my creature comforts for a time, makes me very depressed. I find myself making a big thing of this. Because of this reaction I can't do certain things that I should like very much to do, such as going on an expedition over the Andes, or a canoe trip in the Yukon. Once again, it is quite understandable if I experience this attachment as an obstacle, and feel that I should be freer without it.

Or I could find that my spiteful feelings and reactions which I almost can't inhibit are undermining a relationship which is terribly important to me. At times, I feel as though I am almost assisting as a helpless witness at my own destructive behaviour, as I lash out again with my unbridled tongue at her. I long to be able not to feel this spite. As long as I feel it,

even control is not an option, because it just builds up inside until it either bursts out, or else the feeling somehow communicates itself, and queers things between us. I long to be free of this feeling.

These are quite understandable cases, where we can speak of freedom or its absence without strain. What I have called strong evaluation is essentially involved here. For these are not just cases of conflict, even cases of painful conflict. If the conflict is between two desires with which I have no trouble identifying, there can be no talk of lesser freedom, no matter how painful of fateful. Thus if what is breaking up my relationship is my finding fulfilment in a job which, say, takes me away from home a lot, I have indeed a terrible conflict, but I would have no temptation to speak of myself as less free.

Even seeing a great difference in the significance of the two terms doesn't seem to be a sufficient condition of my wanting to speak of freedom and its absence. Thus my marriage may be breaking up because I like going to the pub and playing cards on Saturday nights with the boys. I may feel quite unequivocally that my marriage is much more important than the release and comradeship of the Saturday night bash. But nevertheless I wouldn't want to talk of my being freer if I could slough off this desire.

The difference seems to be that in this case, unlike the ones above, I still identify with the less important desire, I still see it as expressive of myself, so that I couldn't lose it without altering who I am, losing something of my personality. Whereas my irrational fear, my being quite distressed by discomfort, my spite – these are all things which I can easily see myself losing without any loss whatsoever to what I am. This is why I can see them as obstacles to my purposes, and hence to my freedom, even though they are in a sense unquestionably desires and feelings of mine.

Before exploring further what's involved in this, let's go back and keep score. It would seem that these cases make a bigger breach in the crude negative theory. For they seem to be cases in which the obstacles to freedom are internal; and if this is so, then freedom can't simply be interpreted as the absence of *external* obstacles; and the fact that I'm doing what I want, in the sense of following my strongest desire, isn't sufficient to establish that I'm free. On the contrary, we have to make discriminations among motivations, and accept that acting out of some motivations, for example irrational fear or spite, or this too great need for comfort, is not freedom, is even a negation of freedom.

But although the crude negative theory can't be sustained in the face of these examples, perhaps something which springs from the same concerns can be reconstructed. For although we have to admit that there are internal, motivational, necessary conditions for freedom, we can perhaps still avoid any legitimation of what I called above the second-guessing of the subject. If our negative theory allows for strong evaluation, allows that some goals are really important to us, and that other desires are seen as not fully ours, then can it not retain the thesis that freedom is being able to do what I want, that is, what I can identify myself as wanting, where this means not just what I identify as my strongest desire, but what I identify as my true, authentic desire or purpose? The subject would still be the final arbiter of his being free/unfree, as indeed he is clearly capable of discerning this in the examples above, where I relied precisely on the subject's own experience of constraint, of motives with which he can't identify. We should have sloughed off the untenable Hobbesian reductive-materialist metaphysics, according to which only external obstacles count, as though action were just movement, and there could be no internal, motivational obstacles to our deeper purposes. But we would be retaining the basic concern of the negative theory, that the subject is still the final authority as to what his freedom consists in, and cannot be second-guessed by external authority. Freedom would be modified to read: the absence of internal or external obstacle to what I truly or authentically want. But

we would still be holding the Maginot Line. Or would we?

I think not, in fact. I think that this hybrid or middle position is untenable, where we are willing to admit that we can speak of what we truly want, as against what we most strongly desire, and of some desires as obstacles to our freedom, while we still will not allow for second-guessing. For to rule this out in principle is to rule out in principle that the subject can ever be wrong about what he truly wants. And how can he never, in principle, be wrong, unless there is nothing to be right or wrong about in this matter?

That in fact is the thesis our negative theorist will have to defend. And it is a plausible one for the same intellectual (reductive-empiricist) tradition from which the crude negative theory springs. On this view, our feelings are brute facts about us; that is, it is a fact about us that we are affected in such and such a way, but our feelings can't themselves be understood as involving some perception or sense of what they relate to, and hence as potentially veridical or illusory, authentic or inauthentic. On this scheme, the fact that a certain desire represented one of our fundamental purposes, and another a mere force with which we cannot identify, would concern merely the brute quality of the affect in both cases. It would be a matter of the raw feel of these two desires that this was their respective status.

In such circumstances, the subject's own classification would be incorrigible. There is no such thing as an imperceptible raw feel. If the subject failed to experience a certain desire as fundamental, and if what we meant by 'fundamental' applied to desire was that the felt experience of it has a certain quality, then the desire couldn't be fundamental. We can see this if we look at those feelings which we can agree are brute in this sense: for instance, the stab of pain I feel when the dentist jabs into my tooth, or the crawling unease when someone runs his fingernail along the blackboard. There can be no question of misperception here. If I fail to 'perceive' the pain, I am not in pain. Might it not be so with our fundamental desires, and those which we repudiate?

The answer is clearly no. For first of all, many of our feelings and desires, including the relevant ones for these kinds of conflicts, are not brute. By contrast with pain and the fingernail-on-blackboard sensation, shame and fear, for instance, are emotions which involve our experiencing the situation as bearing a certain import for us, as being dangerous or shameful. This is why shame and fear can be inappropriate, or even irrational, where pain and a frisson cannot. Thus we can be in error in feeling shame or fear. We can even be consciously aware of the unfounded nature of our feelings, and this is when we castigate them as irrational.

Thus the notion that we can understand all our feelings and desires as brute, in the above sense, is not on. But more, the idea that we could discriminate our fundamental desires, or those which we want to repudiate, by the quality of brute affect is grotesque. When I am convinced that some career, or an expedition in the Andes, or a love relationship, is of fundamental importance to me (to recur to the above examples), it cannot be just because of the throbs, *élans* or tremors I feel; I must also have some sense that these are of great significance for me, meet important, long-lasting needs, represent a fulfilment of something central to me, will bring me closer to what I really am, or something of the sort. The whole notion of our identity, whereby we recognize that some goals, desires, allegiances are central to what we are, while others are not or are less so, can make sense only against a background of desires and feelings which are not brute, but what I shall call import-attributing, to invent a term of art for the occasion.

Thus we have to see our emotional life as made up largely of import-attributing desires and feelings, that is, desires and feelings which we can experience mistakenly. And not only can we be mistaken in this, we clearly must accept, in cases like the above where we want

to repudiate certain desires, that we are mistaken.

For let us consider the distinction mentioned above between conflicts where we feel fettered by one desire, and those where we do not, where, for instance, in the example mentioned above, a man is torn between his career and his marriage. What made the difference was that in the case of genuine conflict both desires are the agent's, whereas in the cases where he feels fettered by one, this desire is one he wants to repudiate.

But what is it to feel that a desire is not truly mine? Presumably, I feel that I should be better off without it, that I don't lose anything in getting rid of it, I remain quite complete without it. What could lie behind this sense?

Well, one could imagine feeling this about a brute desire. I may feel this about my addiction to smoking, for instance – wish I could get rid of it, experience it as a fetter, and believe that I should be well rid of it. But addictions are a special case; we understand them to be unnatural, externally-induced desires. We couldn't say in general that we are ready to envisage losing our brute desires without a sense of diminution. On the contrary, to lose my desire for, and hence delectation in, oysters, mushroom pizza, or Peking duck would be a terrible deprivation. I should fight against such a change with all the strength at my disposal.

So being brute is not what makes desires repudiable. And besides, in the above examples the repudiated desires aren't brute. In the first case, I am chained by unreasoning fear, an import-attributing emotion, in which the fact of being mistaken is already recognised when I identify the fear as irrational or unreasoning. Spite, too, which moves me in the third case, is an import-attributing emotion. To feel spite is to see oneself and the target of one's resentment in a certain light; it is to feel in some way wounded, or damaged, by his success or good fortune, and the more hurt the more he is fortunate. To overcome feelings of spite, as against just holding them in, is to come to see self and other in a different light, in particular, to set aside self-pity, and the sense of being personally wounded by what the other does and is.

(I should also like to claim that the obstacle in the third example, the too great attachment to comfort, while not itself import-attributing, is also bound up with the way we see things. The problem is here not just that we dislike discomfort, but that we are too easily depressed by it; and this is something which we overcome only by sensing a different order of priorities, whereby small discomforts matter less. But if this is thought too dubious, we can concentrate on the other two examples.)

Now how can we feel that an import-attributing desire is not truly ours? We can do this only if we see it as mistaken, that is, the import or the good it supposedly gives us a sense of is not a genuine import or good. The irrational fear is a fetter, because it is irrational; spite is a fetter because it is rooted in a self-absorption which distorts our perspective on everything, and the pleasures of venting it preclude any genuine satisfaction. Losing these desires we lose nothing, because their loss deprives us of no genuine good or pleasure or satisfaction. In this they are quite different from my love of oysters, mushroom pizza and Peking duck.

It would appear from this that to see our desires as brute gives us no clue as to why some of them are repudiable. On the contrary it is precisely their not being brute which can explain this. It is because they are import-attributing desires which are mistaken that we can feel that we would lose nothing in sloughing them off. Everything which is truly important to us would be safeguarded. If they were just brute desires, we couldn't feel this unequivocally, as we certainly do not when it comes to the pleasures of the palate. True, we also feel that our desire to smoke is repudiable, but there is a special explanation here, which is not available in the case of spite.

Thus we can experience some desires as fetters, because we can experience them as not ours. And we can experience them as not ours because we see them as incorporating a quite erroneous appreciation of our situation and of what matters to us. We can see this again if we contrast the case of spite with that of another emotion which partly overlaps, and which is highly considered in some societies, the desire for revenge. In certain traditional societies this is far from being considered a despicable emotion. On the contrary, it is a duty of honour on a male relative to avenge a man's death. We might imagine that this too might give rise to conflict. It might conflict with the attempts of a new regime to bring some order to the land. The government would have to stop people taking vengeance, in the name of peace.

But short of a conversion to a new ethical outlook, this would be seen as a trade-off, the sacrifice of one legitimate goal for the sake of another. And it would seem monstrous were one to propose reconditioning people so that they no longer felt the desire to avenge their kin. This would be to unman them.[1]

Why do we feel so different about spite (and for that matter also revenge)? Because the desire for revenge for an ancient Icelander was his sense of a real obligation incumbent on him, something it would be dishonourable to repudiate; while for us, spite is the child of a distorted perspective on things.

We cannot therefore understand our desires and emotions as all brute, and in particular we cannot make sense of our discrimination of some desires as more important and fundamental, or of our repudiation of others, unless we understand our feelings to be impot-attributing. This is essential to there being what we have called strong evaluation. Consequently the half-way position which admits strong evaluation, admits that our desires may frustrate our deeper purposes, admits therefore that there may be inner obstacles to freedom, and yet will not admit that the subject may be wrong or mistaken about these purposes – this position doesn't seem tenable. For the only way to make the subject's assessment incorrigible in principle would be to claim that there was nothing to be right or wrong about here; and that could only be so if experiencing a given feeling were a matter of the qualities of brute feeling. But this it cannot be if we are to make sense of the whole background of strong evaluation, more significant goals, and aims that we repudiate. This whole scheme requires that we understand the emotions concerned as import-attributing, as, indeed, it is clear that we must do on other grounds as well.

But once we admit that our feelings are import-attributing, then we admit the possibility of error, or false appreciation. And indeed, we have to admit a kind of false appreciation which the agent himself detects in order to make sense of the cases where we experience our own desires as fetters. How can we exclude in principle that there may be other false appreciations which the agent does not detect? That he may be profoundly in error, that is, have a very distorted sense of his fundamental purposes? Who can say that such people can't exist? All cases are, of course, controversial; but I should nominate Charles Manson and Andreas Baader for this category, among others. I pick them out as people with a strong sense of some purposes and goals as incomparably more fundamental than others, or at least with a propensity to act the having such a sense so as to take in even themselves a good part of the time, but whose sense of fundamental purpose was shot through with confusion and error. And once we recognise such extreme cases, how avoid admitting that many of the rest of mankind can suffer to a lesser degree from the same disabilities?

What has this got to do with freedom? Well, to resume what we have seen: our attributions of freedom make sense against a background sense of more and less significant purposes, for the question of freedom/unfreedom is bound up with the frustration/fulfilment of our purposes. Further, our significant purposes can be frustrated by our own desires, and where these are sufficiently based on misappreciation, we consider them as not really ours, and experience them as fetters. A man's freedom can therefore be hemmed in by internal, motivational obstacles, as well as external ones. A man who is driven by spite to jeopardise his most important relationships, in spite of himself, as it were, or who is prevented by unreasoning fear from taking up the career he truly wants, is not really made more free if one lifts the external obstacles to his venting his spite or acting on his fear. Or at best he is liberated into a very impoverished freedom.

If through linguistic/ideological purism one wants to stick to the crude definition, and insist that men are equally freed from whom the same external obstacles are lifted, regardless of their motivational state, then one will just have to introduce some other term to mark the distinction, and say that one man is capable of taking proper advantage of his freedom, and the other (the one in the grip of spite, or fear) is not. This is because in the meaningful sense of 'free', that for which we value it, in the sense of being able to act on one's important purposes, the internally fettered man is not free. If we choose to give 'free' a special (Hobbesian) sense which avoids this issue, we'll just have to introduce another term to deal with it.

Moreover since we have already seen that we are always making judgements of degrees of freedom, based on the significance of the activities or purposes which are left unfettered, how can we deny that the man, externally free but still stymied by his repudiated desires, is less free than one who has no such inner obstacles?

But if this is so, then can we not say of the man with a highly distorted view of his fundamental purpose, the Manson or Baader of my discussion above, that he may not be significantly freer when we lift even the internal barriers to his doing what is in line with this purpose, or at best may be liberated into a very impoverished freedom? Should a Manson overcome his last remaining compunction against sending his minions to kill on caprice, so that he could act unchecked, would we consider him freer, as we should undoubtedly consider the man who had done away with spite or unreasoning fear? Hardly, and certainly not to the same degree. For what he sees as his purpose here partakes so much of the nature of spite and unreasoning fear in the other cases, that is, it is an aspiration largely shaped by confusion, illusion and distorted perspective.

Once we see that we make distinctions of degree and significance in freedoms depending on the significance of the purpose fettered/enabled, how can we deny that it makes a difference to the degree of freedom not only whether one of my basic purposes is frustrated by my own desires but also whether I have grievously misidentified this purpose? The only way to avoid this would be to hold that there is no such thing as getting it wrong, that your basic purpose is just what you feel it to be. But there is such a thing as getting it wrong, as we have seen, and the very distinctions of significance depend on this fact.

But if this is so, then the crude negative view of freedom, the Hobbesian definition, is untenable. Freedom can't just be the absence of external obstacles, for there may also be internal ones. And nor may the internal obstacles be just confined to those that the subject identifies as such, so that he is the final arbiter; for he may be profoundly mistaken about his purposes and about what he wants to repudiate. And if so, he is less capable of freedom in the meaningful sense of the word. Hence we cannot maintain the incorrigibility of the subject's judgements about his freedom, or rule out second-guessing, as we put it above. And at the same time, we are forced to abandon the pure opportunity-concept of freedom.

For freedom now involves my being able to recognise adequately my more important purposes, and my being able to overcome or at least neutralise my motivational fetters, as well as my way being free of external obstacles. But clearly the first condition (and, I would argue, also the second) require me to have become something, to have achieved a certain condition of self-clairvoyance and self-understanding. I must be actually exercising self-understanding in order to be truly or fully free. I can no longer understand freedom just as an opportunity-concept.

In all these three formulations of the issue – opportunity-versus exercise-concept; whether freedom requires that we discriminate among motivations; whether it allows of second-guessing the subject – the extreme negative view shows up as wrong. The idea of holding the Maginot Line before this Hobbesian concept is misguided not only because it involves abandoning some of the most inspiring terrain of liberalism, which is concerned with individual self-realisation, but also because the line turns out to be untenable. The first step from the Hobbesian definition to a positive notion, to a view of freedom as the ability to fulfil my purposes, and as being greater the more significant the purposes, is one we cannot help taking. Whether we must also take the second step, to a view of freedom which sees it as realisable or fully realisable only within a certain form of society; and whether in taking a step of this kind one is necessarily committed to justifying the excesses of totalitarian oppression in the name of liberty; these are questions which must now be addressed. What is certain is that they cannot simply be evaded by a philistine definition of freedom which relegates them by fiat to the limbo of metaphysical pseudo-questions. This is altogether too quick a way with them.

Note

1   Compare the unease we feel at the reconditioning of the hero of Anthony Burgess's *A Clockwork Orange*.

Charles Taylor, "What's Wrong with Negative Liberty," from A. Ryan (ed.), *The Idea of Freedom* (London: Oxford University Press, 1979), pp. 177–193.

Chapter 31

Christopher Megone, from "One Concept of Liberty" (1987)

Having established that we have a notion of strongly evaluated desires, Taylor's goal is to tie this to freedom. He asks 'is freedom not at stake when we find ourselves carried away by a less significant goal to override a highly significant one? Or when we are led to act out of a motive we consider bad or despicable?'

[. . .]

His reply is that 'we do sometimes speak in this way'. My short answer is 'no'. What conception of freedom does his answer give? It claims that I am free to the extent that I act in line with my 'real' desires; that is, my strongly evaluated desires, and that there can be aspects of my personality which count as internal obstacles and thus are constraints on my freedom. It is important to be clear on what aspects count as internal obstacles. They are not desires I merely evaluate less highly. To be an internal obstacle, a desire which fetters, the desire must be something that I do not strongly evaluate at all (that is, strongly evaluate as of zero worth) – a desire that is not truly mine. Such desires I can lose without losing any of my personality, 'even though they are unquestionably desires and feelings of mine'.

This means that in a case where I have a conflict of desires, even where I value one of the desires much less than the other, I am not in any sense unfree. But the valueless desires constitute internal obstacles. And thus,

according to Taylor, 'in the meaningful sense of free, that for which we value it, in the sense of being able to act on one's important purposes, the internally fettered man is not free'.

I have some doubt about the existence of desires not strongly evaluated at all, on which this argument depends. There are three further preliminary points. First, this view has the odd consequence that some weak-willed or acratic acts turn out to be politically unfree. For if one characterizes weakness of will, very roughly, as acting on a first-order desire against a second-order desire, such an action will, apparently, be politically unfree. This view shares this peculiarity with certain accounts of what it is to act of one's own free will. But acratic action is supposed to be free intentional irrational action. On this account, secondly, it seems that political liberty at least in this respect has nothing to do with the arrangements and institutions of society, except, perhaps, contingently – in so far as they affect the ability of each to act on his strongly evaluated desires, to rid himself of internal obstacles.

Thirdly, it seems to change what is at stake in living in a society where one is at liberty to pursue one's own course. For whereas the negative conception of liberty rests on the idea that external obstacles restrict the *opportunity* of the agent for action, here, despite the term 'obstacle' being applied to the internal case, it is no longer a restriction on opportunity, but on the agent's ability. Perhaps this reveals the fact that although Taylor is able to appeal to the use of the same term 'obstacle', a subtle change has occurred in the move from inner to outer.

But why not accept this as part of an account of political freedom? Two main reasons seem to arise. First of all it presupposes an odd conception of the self. For as Taylor admits, these bad desires are certainly mine, so that in so far as I am unfree it is because one part of me is an obstacle to *me*. It seems possible to accept Taylor's careful account of strongly evaluative, import-attributing desires without being required to think that the lesser part of me can be viewed as a chain on the real entity. This idea implicitly relies on identifying the agent with his real desires, since it is that real-desire agent who is obstructed by the lesser motives. But it is hard to see why I should now be identified with my 'real' desires rather than the bundle of desires and emotions I actually possess. This is perhaps made clear by an argument which is the corollary of one put forward by Hillel Steiner. As he points out, both positive and negative conceptions share the view that *Red* is unfree if his acting is restrained, but not by *Red*. (This seems to be central to the positive view that *Red* is free in so far as *he* controls his actions.)

Taylor's claim is that *Red* is here being restrained, but the source of restraint is not *Red*. But since the desires are my desires, it must be not *Red*, the agent acting, but a different referent – *Red*, the autonomous self – which is constricted. Not I, but my autonomous self is unfree. At the very least more argument is needed for the claim that I am this autonomous self, comprising my 'real' desires, rather than the self I am ordinarily taken to be – comprising all the desires I actually have.

The second reason for rejecting this account will emerge if we consider again the sense in which my desires, even those I strongly evaluate at zero, are obstacles to my purposes. They are desires which, if I had full self-knowledge, I would not value; or perhaps which, if I could, I would be rid of. But on each occasion of action I make a choice, and I may choose to act either in line with my real desires or in accord with these bad desires. In what sense are these desires obstacles? In no way do they *rule out* any action. But it may be said that external obstacles do not rule out actions. External obstacles may, though, make certain actions very difficult. Destruction of church buildings may prevent public worship; destruction of independent presses may help to prevent free expression of opinion. But perhaps external obstacles cannot rule out actions. Certainly traffic lights do not rule out crossing the junction. Yet their effect seems different from an inner 'obstacle'. External obstacles do, at the minimum, prevent one acting without (potential) punishment (for example, one cannot drive through a red traffic light without potential punishment). But inner obstacles do not do that; they do not rule out doing what one really wants unpunished. For if the choice is to act on the real desire rather than one characterized as not being part of the real you, then no punishment follows. You simply do what you really want. And acting thus, rather than on a desire you desire to be without, cannot involve punishment.

These zero-rated desires do not constrain choice. Their only effect is to make it seem there is a choice, where really there is no choice. In this way they are quite unlike external obstacles. The only case which gives any plausibility to the notion of their being an obstacle is the case of a kleptomaniac. Here the agent chooses in line with his 'real' desires, but on every occasion is prevented from acting on that choice. Because the choice is obstructed every time, we have an obstacle (of a metaphorical sort) of exactly the same nature as the external obstacles. Thus the plausibility of saying the kleptomaniac is unfree comes from the fact that his internal obstacle *does* parallel external obstacles.

To go further, why not say that the man who acts on his real desire, rather than one he wishes he were rid of, is a better man rather than more free? Taylor comes close to this when saying that in failing to overcome an irrational fear, 'we feel that we are *less* than we would be if we could overcome it'. In ridding myself of a desire I do not identify with, do I not improve, rather than free myself? It is possible that goodness and the good life are here confused with freedom. If I act on my real purposes I do indeed fulfil or realize myself, but that seems constitutive of a good life, not freedom. In making this point I have presumed that a man's real desire, rather than one he wishes he were rid of, will have a morally better goal. On a certain interpretation of 'real' desire this might be so. But one might also allow that if the man misconceives the good, his real desire will be evil, so that in acting on it he will be a worse man. In this case what seems at issue is the man's being true to himself (whether as good or evil): a form of integrity. So again it is integrity, not freedom, or lack of it, which is at stake. Perhaps the point may be generalized through the suggestion that these cases can be charac-terized in moral terms, rather than in terms of freedom (above all *political* freedom) or its lack. Cooper gives a description of someone who has achieved 'Promethean' freedom. (Such an account incorporates Taylor's, but goes beyond it.) 'A man who, in control of his material desires, resistant to whim and fashion, regulates his life through rationally adopted principles and plans.' This seems to be an account of the practically wise man, not of the free man. Of course we value such a condition, but is it valuable as freedom? Intuitively it seems that a man can be completely free and yet use that freedom to do a bad act. The fact that he uses opportunities badly does not make a man unfree. If we value freedom because it is a necessary condition for doing what one wants because one wants it, it does not follow that when one fails to do what one wants, one is unfree.

Christopher Megone. "One Concept of Liberty," *Political Studies* 35 (1987), pp. 611, 620–2.

Chapter 32

Richard E. Flathman, from *The Philosophy and Politics of Freedom* (1987)

Freedom$_1$ and Unfreedom$_1$ or Freedom and Unfreedom of Movement

Self-activated movement plus the possibility of impediments to the movement in question.

Freedom$_2$ and Unfreedom$_2$ or Freedom and Unfreedom of Action

Action attempted by an agent plus the possibility of impediments to that action placed or left by another agent or other agents acting with the intention of placing or leaving those impediments.

Freedom$_3$ and Unfreedom$_3$ or Autonomy and Heteronomy

Action attempted by an agent in the pursuit of a self-critically chosen plan or project that the agent has reason to believe is consonant with defensible norms or principles, plus the possibility of impediments to that action placed or left by another agent or other agents acting with the intention of placing or leaving those impediments.

Freedom$_4$ and Unfreedom$_4$ or Communal Freedom and Unfreedom

Action attempted by an agent in pursuit of a plan or project chosen to satisfy, and in fact satisfying, norms or principles that are authoritative in the agent's community, plus the possibility of impediments to that action placed or left by another agent or other agents acting with the intention of placing or leaving those impediments.

Freedom$_5$ and Unfreedom$_5$ or Fully Virtuous Freedom and Unfreedom

Action attempted by an agent in the pursuit of a plan or project self-critically chosen to satisfy, and in fact satisfying, certifiably worthy norms or principles, plus the possibility of impediments to that action placed or left by another agent or other agents acting with the intention of placing or leaving those impediments.

[. . .] If widely received opinion about psychosis is correct, and if positive theorists are also correct to extend the same or a strongly analogous analysis to a further range of cases, the appropriate inference would not be that those for whom the opinion or the analysis holds are unfree; it would rather be that questions about freedom and unfreedom arise about them only if we are thinking of freedom$_1$ and unfreedom$_1$. Such persons do not satisfy conditions requisite to predication of freedoms$_{2-5}$ and unfreedoms$_{2-5}$. Putting the matter this way, it seems to me, sharpens the edge of the following question: Is this the appropriate way to think about those who would like to be cooperative, and forgiving but are persistently selfish, obstinate, and vindictive? Is it the way to regard those who agonize about their overeating, their smoking, their poor work habits, but who, perhaps despite every assistance and encouragement from family, friends, and fellow-workers, do not succeed in breaking these habits or reversing these tendencies?

In the hope of addressing those questions in an orderly manner, I posit a continuum moving from individuals entirely lacking in control over forces internal to them to those with control so complete as to be able to eliminate such forces. Anchoring one end of this continuum are the psychotics I have been discussing. Setting aside views such as Foucault's and Laing's, it is part of a widely influential understanding of such persons that they are so incapable of "responsibility for self" that they can be said to be unfree only in the sense of unfreedom$_1$. There is *energeia* or self-activation and of course there can be impediments and obstacles to the movements produced. But questions about freedoms$_{2-5}$ and unfreedoms$_{2-5}$ arise about such persons only in the sense that others might attempt to cure their illnesses and thereby render them capable of moral and political freedom and unfreedom.

The other end of the continuum I am positing is occupied by creatures familiar enough in imagination and even belief but hard to come by empirically. Some conceptions of gods and goddesses, perhaps of angels, saints, and holy persons in certain religious traditions, are expressions of this ideal. In the more worldly (but far from mundane) realm of secular (or apparently secular) thought, this notion has been expressed in the ideal of a human life of fully self-critical, entirely presuppositionless, judgments and actions, an ideal that has been the aspiration of hubristic philosophers from Plato to Jürgen Habermas.

This continuum might be thought of as moving from entire unfreedom to perfect freedom. But this would be a mistake on several counts. In respect to the psychotic it would confuse unfreedom$_1$ – and hence a lack of capacity for freedoms$_{2-5}$ and unfreedoms$_{2-5}$

– with unfreedoms$_{2-5}$. In respect to gods and god-like philosophers it would either confuse omniscience with omnipotence or make the Stoic's mistake encountered earlier, namely, *equating* freedom and control of self. Most generally, and most importantly for the theory of human freedom and unfreedom, it would be to ignore such facts as that freedom in one respect often conflicts with freedom in another and that the value we place on freedom varies depending on the importance we assign to the actions we are free to take and the objectives we are free to pursue. Someone not far removed from the psychotic on the continuum might be free in ways very important to her or might have relatively few goals and objectives and hence might rarely experience the necessity of choosing among actions all of which she is free to do. On the other hand, because not even the most god-like of philosophers can be in two places at one time, entire control over their internal forces would not make their freedom "perfect" or "full." It makes good sense to talk of more and less freedom, but the notion of complete, or full, or perfect freedom is a misunderstanding.

A person's location on the continuum, then, may be relevant to assessing her freedom but it cannot itself settle that assessment. With this proviso in mind, let us consider a few of the large number of "stages" that might be singled out between the psychotic – call this position (a) – and the god-like philosopher. Leaving aside undoubted cases of organic disorders (such as epilepsy) and addictions that are agreed to be at least in part neurophysiological or biochemical, a next stage (b) might be occupied by persons suffering obsessions, phobias, and compulsions. Here again the ordinary uses of these terms attribute to the compulsive such characteristics as being "in the grip of" or "overcome by" some inner force. The kleptomaniac "cannot help herself"; when surrounded by the cornucopia of goods displayed in a supermarket or a department store her best efforts are not enough to prevent her from slipping items into her purse or under her coat. The

acrophobic simply cannot maintain compo-
sure at the top of the Eiffel Tower. If she is so
foolish as to ascend, she will all but certainly
panic and do harm to herself unless restrained.

In certain respects, then, notions like
"phobia" and "obsession" overlap with "psychosis" and "insane." The reflection, deliberation, intention formation and revision, the
choosing, deciding, explaining and justifying,
the adapting to changed circumstances and
accommodation to other persons, the following of rules, routines, and recipes, the making
and correcting of mistakes – none of these
components of "ordinary" or "standard"
action and acting are present in those aspects
of the phobic's or the compulsive's life in
which the phobia or the compulsion holds
sway. (Of course the compulsive or phobic,
just as with the psychotic, may be the very paradigm of the ordinary or standard agent or
actor in some or much of her conduct.) For
these reasons, the responsibility of compulsives and phobics, and the appropriateness of
blaming and praising, punishing and rewarding them for the specifically compulsive and
phobic behaviors, is minimal if not nonexist-
ent. Because these abnormalities are often
quite specific and coexist with ordinary capacity for action in other respects, we expect those
who suffer them to take such precautions as
they can against their occurrence and their
effects. But when they do occur our role is to
help and to sympathize, not to blame or
punish.

Here again, then, we can make good sense
of the notion of inner forces taking control of,
even (if we remember that it is metaphorical)
enslaving, human beings. Nor is there reason
to doubt that persons who suffer compulsions
and obsessions would like to be freed of or
from them. But this too is unfreedom$_1$, at
most the aspiration to freedoms$_{2-5}$. In respect
to her obsessions and phobias, the genuine
compulsive or phobic is incapable of action
and hence of freedoms$_{2-5}$ and unfreedoms$_{2-5}$.
To relate to her on any other assumption, for
example to accuse her of inadequate responsibility for self or to read her lectures about her

failings of character, would be either stupid
or cruel.

The movement of my continuum toward its
appointed termination with the god-like
philosopher could proceed in a wide variety of
ways or through a considerable diversity
of "stages." One perhaps not implausible
sequence would be the following: (c) habits in
the at least mildly perjorative sense in which
we say that smoking and pot-taking are habits;
(d) a wide variety of so-called akratic behaviors, cases in which a person fails to act in the
manner or in pursuit of the end or goal that
she herself identifies as right or best by criteria that she herself endorses; (e) habits in the
benign or even favorable usage of theorists
such as Edmund Burke and Michael
Oakeshott; (f) the purely preferential and
instrumental but perhaps exquisitely calculated choices of some utilitarianisms and of
classical and neoclassical economic theories;
(g) character traits or settled but principled
dispositions à la Aristotle and such contemporary writers as Bernard Williams and Charles
Taylor; (h) the casuistries, firmly practical,
elegant in formulation, and deeply grounded
in an elaborate system of reflections, of
the scholastic moralist; (i) the thoughts and
actions of the philosopher who would be
divine if only she hadn't suffered the indignity
of being created mortal.

I comment briefly on some of these (most
particularly habits and the moderately technical notion of *akrasia*) just below. But I will
assume that the idea informing the progres-
sion from stage to stage is at least as available
and as intuitively clear to readers of this book
as are the notions of psychosis and obsessions,
compulsions and phobias. For present purposes what is needed is not a detailed explication of these familiar notions but rather
consideration of the bearing, if any, of the
similarities and differences among them on
theories of freedom and unfreedom.

It appears to me to be the Hegelian and the
neo-Hegelian view that unfreedom, or no
better than a thin, insignificant freedom, prevails until we reach (e) or even (f) on this con-

tinuum and that rich, fully significant freedom is a possibility only for those who have arrived at least at stage (g), perhaps at (h) in this sequence. (Note that in principle a person could be at various stages in respect to the several dimensions or aspects of life. At least this could be true up to [h] or [i].) If I am correct about this, two now familiar ways of interpreting this view emerge from my previous discussions. One of these is that the view equates freedom with various other values or ideals such as virtue, good character, authenticity, and the like. Those at states (c) through (e) or (f) fall short of their own or their community's ideals in various ways and to various degrees. As we move from (f) or (g) toward (i), the degree and quality of freedom increase along with the extent to which the individual achieves (so far as she is not prevented from doing so by others) whatever ideals are in question. The second interpretation is the one I have been considering and that led me to posit the continuum. Movement along the continuum is not calibrated in terms of more or less virtue, higher or lower levels of achievement of valued objectives or states. Rather, it is from little or seriously inadequate control over inner forces to entire control over them. On this second interpretation, persons at stages (c) through (f) are treated as remarkably similar to psychotics in respect to their psychoses and obsessives in respect to their obsessions. Those who eat too much, work inefficiently, live fragmented, disorganized lives, have poor relationships with others, above all persons who are cowardly, selfish, unjust, illiberal, and the like are said to be in the grip of or overcome by some sort of internal but alien force. It is in this sense, it is for this reason, that they are unfree or enjoy no more than an impoverished freedom.

At least in respect to Charles Taylor, both of these interpretations are partly correct. Freedom is a kind of virtue and virtue is knowledge of self-in-community that makes possible rational control of action. Unfreedom is a kind of vice or evil when vice is an absence or failure of knowledge of self-in-community and of self-command which leaves the individual at the mercy of the irrational and nonrational forces that lurk in the subhuman recesses of the self. In a manner at least reminiscent of earlier versions of the theory of positive freedom, neo-Hegelian arguments combine these two doctrines.

If we exclude ordinary desires and compositional evaluations on the grounds presented in Chapter 2 [of *The Philosophy and Politics of Freedom*], and if we set aside psychosis and compulsions for the reasons discussed in this chapter, the plausibility of the second doctrine is left to depend on those occurrences in human affairs that we would place at stages (c), (d), and possibly (e) on my continuum. In both (c) and (d) and perhaps in (e), certain of the elements that are prominent in our ordinary notion of action are thought to be very little in evidence or perhaps missing altogether. In the case of habits in the at least mildly pejorative sense expressed by talk of having the habit of smoking, the elements alleged to be missing are critical self-consciousness, deliberation, rationality, and even decision and choice. There are those who invariably reach for a cigarette as they swing their legs out of bed in the morning, on the appearance of a cup of coffee, in the course of starting their cars, answering their telephones, beginning lectures to their classes, and so forth. Their smoking in these and other circumstances is as if by rote or by the numbers. They pause for not so much as an instant. There seems to be no evidence of their asking themselves whether they want to smoke, should smoke, have already smoked enough that day, would do better to save their remaining cigarettes for later, or anything of the sort. In the more inclusive case of (d), which on some interpretations would in fact encompass (c), there may be reflection, an abundance of self-examination and criticism, ambivalence, dissonance, hesitation, vacillation, agonizing, and so forth. The akratic, in short, may give an appearance very different from the person "locked into" a habitual mode of behavior. Here the missing or inadequately represented element is more like Harry Frankfurt's "will" to act on the conclusions of one's deliberations, to implement one's "choices" in the sense of the results of one's deliberations. For all of her agonizing and self-castigation about past failures, despite her elaborate preparations, strategies, and scheming, the akratic cannot resist the cigarette, the rich dessert, the nasty comment about a colleague, the putting herself first. If the habitual smoker is "in a rut," of which she may no longer be aware and from which she does not try to escape, the akratic is aware of her deficiencies and failings but fails to correct or overcome them. In both cases, perhaps for different reasons or by different psychological mechanisms, it appears that the persons are controlled by some force or forces that are alien or at least inauthentic. Hence they are unfree. It also appears that they could be made free, or that their freedom could be enhanced, if other agents or agencies would remove them, even if forcibly, from their rut or would prevent them from acting in ways that they themselves may regret and even despise.

We do frequently talk in ways that seem to warrant such conclusions about habitual and akratic conduct. I will comment on these forms of speech in a moment. But we should first note some additional characteristics of each of these modes, characteristics that support quite different conclusions about them. Habitual conduct is properly contrasted with decisions reached and choices made as the more or less direct or immediate conclusion of reflection and deliberation. It is "matter of course" in the sense that the conduct occurs without critical reflection about its propriety or desirability when the agent finds herself (or thinks she finds herself) in the kind of circumstance or situation in which it has previously served. The person does not, in Hannah Arendt's phrase, "stop to think" [. . .]. There is no turning inward, no consideration of alternatives, no seeking of further information or advice. Nevertheless, even the most settled, the least reflective of habitual behaviors are only "robot-like," not the movements of robots. Even the monotonous, the dreary regularity with which Able, a member of my car pool, lights up as she settles into the back seat each morning is broken if she hasn't seen to having cigarettes and matches in her purse. Nor is Able literally a "smoking machine"; her deadly instrument moves irregularly from hand-to-hand and hand-to-mouth, she puffs rapidly and then slowly, exhales first in my direction and then in that of another sufferer, she flicks her ashes sometimes on the floor, sometimes out the window, occasionally in the ashtray. These depressing sequences, moreover, are learned and practiced. Able knows how and how not to smoke. She conceives of herself as smoking in a sophisticated manner. There are many ways in which she would "not be caught dead" smoking. The angle at which she hold her head and her arm, the manner in which she holds the cigarette in her yellowing fingers, the ways in which she uses her inhaling and exhaling to punctuate her speech and to express her mood, all of this is ritual. If it is a ritual by now performed largely or even entirely without deliberation, if it is thoughtless in numerous senses of that word, it is nevertheless replete with intentionality and with purposiveness and it manifests choice and decision throughout. Although repeated many times each day by Able, and many times each day by millions of other human beings, each of these repetitions is a chosen, an enacted, performance, one that differs from every other.

Owing to these characteristics, each of these habitual performances is subject to evaluation. Each of them can be carried out elegantly or inelegantly, smoothly or awkwardly, efficiently or wastefully. More important for present purposes, as with any and all habits, the habit itself (taken to be the ensemble of actions that constitutes having the habit of smoking) is subject to evaluation as a good or a bad habit. Perhaps my morning companion no longer asks herself this question. Perhaps she hasn't asked herself this question for years. But at some point in her life history, at some level of self-consciousness, Able asked and answered it. Her habit developed because she repeatedly answered some formulation of the question in the affirmative. Having become satisfied with her answer, she has since had no more occasion to continue to ask it than a dispositionally courageous person has to ask herself whether she should be a coward. But any one of a wide array of events or occurrences might prompt her to ask it again. And if Able doesn't ask it, or asks it but comes to what others think is the wrong conclusion concerning it, she is subject to criticism. If those who know her are convinced that the habit has become to "deeply ingrained" that it is genuinely difficult for her to reconsider it or to consider it in an open-minded, balanced, manner, they may be sympathetic, patient, and gentle with her. They may decide that the habit has come to occupy so central a place in her life that it is better not to bring the matter up at all. But the same assessment, if combined with the view that smoking is a very bad habit indeed, that it is deeply harmful to herself or to others, may convince others that they are justified in employing measures so severe that they deprive Able of freedoms she had previously been enjoying (the same freedoms that will continue to be enjoyed by persons whose habits are judged to be good).

According to Amelie Rorty and other recent students of akrasia, akratic behavior is itself habitual [. . .]. It differs from habits such as I have just discussed in that it typically occurs when there is a conflict among two or more of a person's habits. On this account of the phenomenon, the Able of my car pool is a likely candidate for akrasia. Her habit of smoking coexists with a variety of others such as attending to her health and her good physical appearance, seeking the approval of others and avoiding actions distressing or annoying to them, being frugal about her money, and so forth. She took up smoking before it came to be thought harmful to health, when it was considered fashionable by all but the unfashionably ascetical or puritanical and even a mark of liberation on the part of a woman, and

before her government had come to appreciate its potential as a source of revenue. As changes occur in these regards, Able's habit of smoking will increasingly conflict with other of her dispositions and inclinations and she may decide that it would be better if she "kicked" it. Not smoking may become what Rorty calls her "preferred judgment," continued smoking an "*akratic* alternative" to that preferred judgment. If she nevertheless continues to smoke she will in that respect become an *akrates*. Despite her sincere belief that she should not smoke, her concerted efforts to act on that belief, and her regret and perhaps even self-disgust at her failure to do so, her smoking continues unabated.

Traditional analyses of akrasia support the view that the akrates is unfree. For Socrates, a person who takes an action or follows a course of action that is wrong or less attractive than available alternatives is either ignorant of what she is doing (doesn't realize the consequences of her action or doesn't appreciate that it falls under a principle she rejects) or under some kind of compulsion. Plato simplified this view by treating all wrongdoing as a result of ignorance of the good. As Rorty points out, however, these analyses, and even Aristotle's more plausible view that akrasia is explained by mistakes of fact or of practical reasoning, "explain" the phenomenon by denying its existence. Their explanations do not explain akrasia, they explain it away. My smoker Able is by now well-informed about smoking. She knows the grim statistics about lung cancer, heart disease, and emphysema; she is intensely aware of the disapproval of other; she keeps accurate account of the money she spends on cigarettes and adverts frequently to the other pleasures she must therefore forego. In other regards, morever, she maintains a close and effective discipline over her conduct. Although fond of rich desserts, she ends her meals with black coffee in order to remain trim and to save money; although intensely disliking her boss, she never permits herself so much as the mildest criticism of her. In most respects she is a paradigm of the "responsible self."

Of course there is weakness here, weakness that may deserve understanding and sympathy on the part of friends and acquaintances that would never occur to them in respect to other aspects of Able's conduct. Moreover, Able may talk about her smoking in ways which, if taken literally, suggest more than mere weakness. For example, she may say that she "can't help" smoking, or that it is "impossible" for her to stop doing so. These and many related locutions, which are characteristic of persons experiencing akrasia, might seem to support the view that the akrates is unfree.

The most serious difficulty with this analysis can be seen by noting that the akrates herself, despite using language that suggests unfreedom, continues to describe her smoking as mistaken or regrettable at least in the sense of not being the most desirable or best or right thing for her to do. Rorty argues that this does not mean that akrasia always involves conduct of a deeply or seriously mistaken kind; conduct that is immoral or seriously harmful to the agent or to others. On her analysis, the concept applies even if the akrates has no more a mild preference for some alternative pattern of conduct. But as the traditional term "weakness of will" suggests, akrasia involves some sense of shortcoming or deficiency, some at least mildly negative or critical self-assessment. Weakness and shortcoming, however, are not unfreedom. If the akrates were unfree, such self-criticism would be out of place. I cannot at once be unfree and *make* a mistake. If I am unfree in a particular respect I cannot *act* in that respect and hence I am not subject to criticism, by myself or by others, in that respect. (Of course I might be subject to criticism for past actions that led to my present unfree condition.) It is a condition of the applicability of "mistake," "criticism," and a whole host of evaluational concepts that I am an agent engaged in action.

Statements that appear to claim unfreedom should be understood, rather, as expressions of a two- or perhaps a three-fold regret, but a regret that is at least partially qualified. (i) Able regrets her continued smoking; there is an obvious alternative, one that she genuinely and sincerely prefers. (ii) She regrets the fact that she allows herself to be influenced by considerations – the anticipated pleasure of the cigarettes, the comradely support of other smokers – over which she could exercise control if she made a sufficient effort. (iii) She regrets earlier decisions and actions that established her habit of smoking and that make her susceptible to the continuing influence of considerations such as in (ii). But the regret is qualified or partial, not entire. From early in the history of her habit Able genuinely enjoyed smoking and she continues to do so. The cigarettes do taste good to her, do give her other pleasurable sensations; she enjoys the ritual, likes to discuss the differences among brands with other smokers, finds satisfaction in the thought that, unlike earlier generations of women, members of her generation are at liberty to smoke if they see fit. If she gave up smoking her sense of achievement would be qualified by regret over the loss of these pleasures. The considerations that influence the partially regretted action are not alien or external or inauthentic to her. They influence her, they have weight with or for her, because of beliefs, inclinations, and preferences that are among her characteristics as a person. She may succeed in changing herself in these respects, but until she does so her smoking remains an action that she takes.

I suggested that positive theorists exaggerate the significance, for the moral and political theory of freedom, of the idea that desires, interests, inclinations, and so forth "enslave" the agent. There is no denying that something like this notion is frequently encountered outside of the pages of philosophical works. My argument that positive theorists exaggerate the significance of the notion is in two stages. I concede, *arguendo*, that "enslavement" occurs in cases of psychoses and obsessions and compulsions. But I contend that these are cases of freedom₁, and hence are relevant to moral and political theory only insofar as it is possible to cure psychosis and addiction and hence make those who have suffered them eligible for predication of freedoms$_{2-5}$ and unfreedoms$_{2-5}$. To put this thesis somewhat differently, in the cases in which the language of brute and alien forces, and hence absence of agency, is appropriate, talk of "enslavement" is metaphorical and the "enslaving" forces should not be assimilated to the desires and interests that operate at stages (c) through (e) or (f) on the continuum I have posited. Secondly, I contend that talk of "enslavement" in respect to stages (c), and (d) is inappropriate; these stages – and more obviously (e) and (f) – should be understood in ways that leave agency largely if not entirely intact. Taylor is correct in his sometimes implicit thesis that notions such as making a mistake remain available in the cases that concern him, and hence he is also correct that freedoms$_{2-5}$ and unfreedoms$_{2-5}$ can be predicated of the actors in such cases. But he is mistaken in his view that evidence of the kinds he considers is sufficient to justify saying that those agents are unfree if we are thinking of unfreedoms$_{2-5}$.

In the light of these reflections, it appears that the versions of the positive theory of freedom I have examined combine, in an inappropriate manner, the two views that I suggested as ways of interpreting it. These theorists *are* working with an ideal of virtue or authenticity or integrity or good personal adjustment. They value and hope for persons whose actions are deliberately chosen to satisfy norms and principles that those persons correctly believe to be morally and otherwise worthy. And they are disposed to say that actions which do not meet these criteria are unfree. But they are unwilling to adopt in an unvarnished form the position that equates freedom and virtue or freedom and authenticity, unfreedom and vice or unfreedom and inauthenticity. Hence they seek plausibility for their use of "freedom" and (especially) "unfreedom" by treating actions that are not morally or otherwise worthy as compelled by inner forces. I suggest that this move, although seeming to find support from certain ordinary modes of speech, misinterprets the

locutions that appear to support it and leads to incoherence in the theory of freedom.

If we recur now to Feinberg's schema, it is evident that the foregoing remarks are primarily concerned with constraints of the internal, positive variety. Not only obsessions and compulsions but unevaluated desires, passions, habits, and so forth are treated by positive theorists as forces preventing the agent from acting as she should and as compelling untoward or inadmissible "actions." So understood, their discussions give an apparent plausibility to the argument that such persons are unfree.

The same passages to which I have been responding support the interpretation that the positive theory equates freedom with ideals of virtue and character. To see this, we need do no more than shift our focus to Feinberg's category of constraints that are internal but negative. In this perspective, those persons whom positive theorists regard as unfree (in ways that negative theories of freedom cannot accommodate) lack the qualities of character that are necessary conditions of proper action. Just as a person who is suffering from the negative external constraint of lack of money cannot buy a new car, so persons who lack the qualities that positive theorists celebrate cannot act in a proper manner. By implicitly adopting Feinberg's notion of negative, internal constraints, they connect freedom with virtue without explicitly using an unvarnished version of the position that assimilates freedom and virtue.

My objection to the positive theory, then, is at three levels. In respect to psychotics, genuine compulsives, and the like, I allow that there is no action or agency and hence a kind of unfreedom. But this is unfreedom only if we are thinking of unfreedom$_1$. Questions about freedoms$_{2-5}$ do not arise about psychotics and compulsives. The second and third levels of my objection concern habitual actions and actions taken to satisfy evaluated passions, desires, and interests, objectives and purposes, evaluations that positive theorists disapprove and that the agent herself may regret in the qualified senses discussed above. I contend that such actions are the agent's own. The evaluations and choices that prompt them are authentic to the actor as she is and as she understands herself and should not be regarded, in Feinberg's language, as positive, internal constraints that compel movements or behaviors on the agent's "part." In the absence of external, positive impediments or constraints, these actions, however objectionable, are feely done, are done in freedom.

The third level of my objection can be put by stressing the respect in which the second objection is in effect conceded by positive theorists. When actions are called base as opposed to noble, cowardly as opposed to courageous, mean as opposed to generous, spiteful or vindictive as opposed to understanding, forgiving, or magnanimous, the actor is *criticized* and *blamed*. Such criticism abandons the view that the person in question was compelled by internal or any other forces. To save the notion that the actor is nevertheless unfree, a conceptual move is made that can be described in any one of three interrelated ways: in a vocabulary that equates freedom and virtue; by using "freedom" to refer to my kinds of freedom$_{4-5}$; as a readiness to treat the absence of virtue or good character as a negative, internal constraint that allows the agent to act but prevents her from acting in a noble, courageous, generous, understanding, forgiving, or magnanimous fashion.

Having separated this move from the positions criticized at my first two levels, how should we assess it? It will help to note again the difference between freedom$_4$ and freedom$_5$. As introduced in Chapter 1 [of *The Philosophy and Politics of Freedom*], freedom$_4$ requires that the plan of action followed by the actor satisfy the criteria that purportedly inform the actions in question. This formulation does not specify *who* is to make the judgment whether the actions taken in fact satisfy those criteria. Most important, it does not specify whether (for purposes of assessing the freedom or unfreedom of the act and the actor) that judgment is to be made by the

actor herself or by other parties. By contrast, freedom$_5$ clearly posits some species of interpersonally defensible judgment concerning the worthiness of the agent's objectives and hence excludes the possibility that the agent's own judgment, as such, could be conclusive.

In respect to freedom$_4$, the move that I am discussing takes plausibility from the fact that the agent who acts habitually says or shows that she partially regrets her action because it does not fully satisfy the criteria that she accepts and aims to satisfy. Able aims to have cordial, harmonious relations with Baker and she partially regrets it when her actions produce tension and ill-feeling. Thus she criticizes herself for not having fully satisfied her own objectives. The language of freedom and unfreedom appears to obtain a foothold in this setting. Able does not want to disavow responsibility for the outcome, does not want to "cop out" or "pass the buck" to someone else. Yet something stands between her and her objectives. Because of this feature, it is not inconceivable that she would say or herself that she would be more free if that something were removed or brought under control.

I have argued, however, that if such talk is taken literally – whether by the agent herself or by other parties – it is incoherent. A person cannot at once, that is in respect to one and the same act or failure to act, claim that she was unfree and that she has *made* a mistake. Persons who talk themselves into such an incoherence in respect to their own conduct are either confused or, more likely, suffering from a more or less serious case of that mode of self-deception that existentialists call *mauvaise foi* (or perhaps it is deception of others and should be called, less esoterically, bad faith). Persons who interpret such talk on the part of others in this literal-minded way either misunderstand it (perhaps because they accept a certain theory of freedom) or are taken in by it.

The position of positive theorists is yet less plausible if we assign to other parties the judgment whether Able's actions serve Able's own objectives or meet her own criteria. Let us focus on cases in which Able is, on balance, satisfied with her actions but Charlotte and Dorothy, although raising no questions about Able's objectives, conclude that her actions in fact disserve those objectives and betray inadequate responsibility for self. For example, Able aspires to good relationships with her academic colleagues but frequently publishes sharply critical analyses of their scholarly work. Some at least of Able's colleagues resent this practice and are cool to her because of it. Charlotte and Dorothy attribute Able's conduct to jealousy and personal insecurity and urge Able to seek counseling so as to better understand and control her inclinations. They argue that following this course would enhance Able's freedom.

Able admits to a degree of jealousy of some of her colleagues and to insecurity about her own professional standing and achievements. She even allows that she would be happier if she were rid of these feelings. But she contends that the actions in question conform to the norms of academic life as she understands and accepts them and that she takes the actions for this reason. The resentment and cool relationships are the fault of her colleagues' failure to understand collegiality at its best.

Pressed by Charlotte and Dorothy, Able may be induced to claim that she is "free" to alter her practice out of deference to the feelings of colleagues. She may also contend that her colleagues are equally "free" to adopt her understanding of collegiality and thus to appreciate rather than to resent her practice. I suggest, however, that even such talk on Able's part would be an inappropriate concession to an unfortunate misconception held by Charlotte and Dorothy. The issue is not whether Able or her friends are free; that issue is already settled, indeed tacitly acknowledged to have been settled. Rather, the issue is whether she or they are justified in their respective views concerning the norms that do and/or that should inform and govern academic life. The freedom of Able and her friends is a supposition of the disagreement between them concerning this normative issue. In attempting to transform the normative issue into a question about Able's freedom, Charlotte and Dorothy patronize – that is, insult – Able. If Able is a patient (or perhaps a charitable) as well as a clear-headed sort, she will explain this distinction to Charlotte and Dorothy. If they persist in their views despite her explanation, she will be presented with a choice between sympathizing with their incapacity and resenting their obnoxious conduct.

We can now set aside as irrelevant the differences between freedom$_4$ and freedom$_5$. Questions about the worthiness of Able's projects and objectives presuppose Able's freedom to choose and to pursue them. If she were unfree in these respects, the projects and objectives would not be *hers* and criticism of her would be misdirected. Given that she has chosen and pursued her projects and objectives, any number of issues can be raised about the merits of her choices and actions. To treat these as issues about freedom is to confuse the question whether Able is free with the quite different matter of the merits of Able's use of whatever freedom she has.

In sum, the concepts of freedom and unfreedom encompass my kinds of freedom$_{1-3}$. Persons or other creatures characterized by no more than freedom$_1$ are as yet neither free nor unfree by the criteria of freedoms$_{2-3}$, that is, by the criteria of the only kinds of freedom that can be thought of as moral and political in character. My supposed freedoms$_{4-5}$ and unfreedoms$_{4-5}$ are not kinds of freedom and unfreedom at all. They are made to appear as such (and positive theories are made to appear to be theories of freedom) by equating (confusing) freedom with abilities and virtues or unfreedom with the absence thereof (that is, with internal, negative constraints). All instances of freedoms$_{2-3}$ and unfreedoms$_{2-3}$ are situated as opposed to "brute," and most if not all such instances are situated in further respects that remain to be explored.

Richard Flathman, *The Philosophy and Politics of Freedom* (Chicago: Chicago University Press, 1987), pp. 91–107, 322.

Chapter 33

Matthew H. Kramer, from *The Quality of Freedom* (2003)

6. Freedom and Psychological Incapacities

In this final main section of the present chapter, we shall investigate an array of problems relating to the psychological capacities of various individuals. We need to inquire whether psychological incapacities ever in themselves deprive individuals of liberty; and, if they do, we need to ascertain the conditions under which the freedom-reducing effects occur. A number of difficulties must be skirted or defused if an exposition of negative liberty is to be adequately protected against collapsing into a theory of determinism-versus-free-will or into a positive-liberty doctrine. On the one hand, that is, we have to guard against transforming all questions of social and political freedom into questions of natural or metaphysical freedom. Were we to go down that route, we would very likely arrive at the outlandish conclusion that the only sociopolitical freedoms in any community are those presupposed by the actions and states and processes which people in the community actually undertake and undergo. At the same time, while seeking not to become embroiled in debates over natural or metaphysical determinism, we must recognize the incapacitating effects of some mental deficiencies – without embracing the sweeping verdict that each person is never free to engage in any of the courses of action which he is not in a position to consider or envisage. That sweeping verdict, though not as far-reaching as the transformation of all questions of social and political liberty into questions of metaphysical liberty, would unduly narrow the range of circumstances in which we can appositely ascribe freedoms to each person. In short, while resolutely acknowledging that some psychological incapacities do destroy freedoms, this final section of Chapter 3 will also aim to cabin that acknowledgement properly.

6.1 Every thought taken captive

Among the conditions that will be pondered in our exploration of psychological incapacities, the extreme variety is that of outright mind-control. If somebody's brain has fallen completely under the sway of someone else through surgical or chemical or electronic means, then the victim has become the living marionette of the controlling person. Every intention harboured by the former is determined fully by the manipulations and designs of the latter. As has been remarked in Chapter 2 [of *The Quality of Freedom*], there are two principal ways in which such a situation can be analysed. First is an approach not favoured here. Under that approach, a person whose mind has been completely taken over by somebody else is deemed no longer to be anyone to whom freedom or unfreedom can pertinently be ascribed. In other words, the lot of such a victim is assimilated to that of a dead person. In each case, somebody once endowed with sundry freedoms and unfreedoms has ceased to exist in a state that warrants our attributing any freedoms and unfreedoms to her. She has become a mere extension and device of the people who have seized control over her mind. We should not attribute social and political liberty to an ostensible person in that condition, any more than to a mechanical robot that is steered by electrical signals from its owner. That ostensible person is not an agent endowed with freedoms and unfreedoms any more than is a corpse. Like the body of the elderly patriarch Abraham as described by St Paul, she is as good as dead. Such, at any rate, is the conclusion generated by one line of analysis that might be adopted in our efforts to come to grips with the vexed issues surrounding the take-over of anybody's mind.

As has been indicated in Chapter 2 [of *The Quality of Freedom*], a preferable treatment of this matter proceeds quite differently. Although the person whose mind has been thoroughly taken over is no longer an autonomous agent by any reckoning, such a person is still an agent inasmuch as her dealings with the world are carried on through beliefs and attitudes and intentions. To be sure, in a crucial sense, those beliefs and attitudes and intentions are not her own; they are directly implanted into her by the nefarious manoeuvres of the people who control every aspect of her psyche. Still, while wholly devoid of autonomy, she differs from a robot or any other machine in harbouring beliefs and attitudes and intentions. She interacts with her environment consciously and rationally, even though her consciousness and rationality are piloted by others who shape and channel her thoughts. Because she differs in this fundamental respect form machines and corpses, she is someone to whom freedom and unfreedom can appositely be attributed.

At the same time, of course, we must take account of the freedom-curtailing character of her condition. Indeed, one of the principal reasons for designating her as someone to whom freedom and unfreedom can be ascribed is that we thus enable ourselves to affirm that she has been made unfree in countless respects by the people who exert dominion over her mind. Were we to rule out attributions of freedom and unfreedom to her, we could not say that her mind's captors are rendering her unfree in any way as they firmly direct her attitudes and beliefs and inclinations. If we instead allow that she is somebody who can be free or unfree in any number of respects, we can chart how the conquest of her mind has affected her freedom and unfreedom – along the lines suggested tersely in my second chapter. On the one hand, that is, we should recognize that she is free to behave in all the ways in which she does behave. Given that everything actual is possible, the modes of conduct in which she actually engages are perforce modes of conduct that are possible for her. She is consequently free to undertake those very modes of conduct. Her freedom to undertake them consists, after all, in nothing more and nothing less than her being unprevented from undertaking them. She obviously *is* unprevented from adopting those modes of behaviour, for she does in fact adopt them. Indeed, even under an unduly narrow conception of liberty as freedom of choice, we would have to conclude that she is free to engage in those modes of conduct. Although her choices to engage in them have been pre-ordained by the people with dominion over her mind, they are nonetheless choices. She is unprevented from choosing what she in fact chooses. Of course, if the control of the brainwashers over their victim's mind is minutely exhaustive, the unpreventedness of her performing the actions which she chooses is accompanied by the preventedness of her performing any other actions. When the masters of her mind pre-decide her in favour of certain paths of conduct, they preclude her from opting for other such paths. Nevertheless, the availability of the chosen paths is evident from the fact that they are indeed pursued.

A victim of mind-control, then, is free to carry out any actions which she in fact carries out. Does she enjoy any other particular freedoms? Two main points are relevant here. First, irrespective of how minutely the brainwashers regulate her thoughts and attitudes, she will be subject to mischances and the vicissitudes of her circumstances. For example, if the brainwashers have prompted her to walk along a certain road, she may stumble and thus depart from the straightforward ambulation which they had envisioned. Such non-volitional movements of her body are events which she is free to undergo, in so far as they happen to her. When she stumbles, her body is unprevented from falling or lurching. No amount of fine-grained control by her mind's captors will be guaranteed to avert such occurrences, and therefore she will be free to undergo any non-volitional bodily movements that are not so averted. Such bodily movements might arise from the complete overpowering of her by some other human being(s) or by a natural force such as a whirlwind. If Dorothy is a victim of thorough mind-control, she will nonetheless be free to soar through the air as she is driven by a whirlwind along a trajectory which the masters of her mind have not anticipated or ordained. She is unprevented from being heaved along that trajectory by the impetus of the wind, notwithstanding that her flight is at odds with the designs of the people who manipulate all her thoughts and intentions.

A second set of particular freedoms that might be enjoyed by a victim of mind-control – apart from her freedoms to perform the actions which she actually performs – will depend on the looseness of that control. On the one hand, the captors of her mind might direct every attitude and belief and intention of hers in the minutest detail. If so, then the only actions which she is free to perform are the actions which she actually performs. (As my last paragraph has indicated, she is also free to undergo any non-volitional processes or states that force themselves upon her.) On the other hand, the brainwashers might exert a more relaxed grip over her mental faculties. They might prevent her from harbouring certain thoughts and forming certain intentions, but they might leave her with some latitude in regard to thoughts and intentions which they have not excluded. In other words, instead of closely regulating every element and impulse of the operations of her mind, they might simply set constraints within which those operations can unfold. Within those constraints, nothing is either preordained or debarred. If the regimen of brainwashing is indeed along these more relaxed lines, then the victim will not only be free to perform whatever actions she in fact does perform; she will in addition be free to perform any of the actions (within her capabilities) that are not excluded by the masters of her mind. In essentially the same way in which a normal person is free to carry out myriad actions which she does not actually carry out, the victim of a relatively lenient system of mind-control will be free to engage in quite a number of actions which she does not actually choose. Furthermore, of course, she will be free to undergo non-volitional processes and states that take hold of her.

More important than the freedom of the victim is her unfreedom. To the extent that the mind-control renders her unfree, it does so only in regard to actions which are not beyond her own capacities and which are not precluded by external impediments or restraints other than the mind-control itself. Many such actions, of course, are not prevented by the mind-control any more than by other potential curbs on her freedom. Hence, the precise set of actions in respect of which the victim has been rendered unfree by the mind-control is the set comprising every action that partakes of the following three characteristics: (1) the action is within the capacities of the victim; (2) it is unprevented by any factors other than the mind-control itself; and (3) it is prevented by the mind-control. That set of actions is what Ian Carter has in mind when he writes that 'if I force you to think certain thoughts, then there are also likely to be many actions that I am preventing you from performing, so that it can at least be said that forcible hypnosis and brainwashing can entail great reductions in freedom'.[1] Plainly, the greater or lesser thoroughness of the mind-control will affect the expansiveness of the set of actions which the victim has been made unfree-to-perform as a result of that control. If the direction of her mind is minutely exhaustive, then the aforementioned set will comprise every action which she does not actually perform and which has not been ruled out by internal or external preventative factors other than the mind-control itself. By contrast, if the regimen of brainwashing is more relaxed, the relevant set will fall short of comprising every not-otherwise-prevented action which the victim does not actually perform. Instead, it comprises only the not-otherwise-prevented actions which the brainwashing has excluded. *Ex hypothesi*, given that the regulation of the mind of the victim is relatively light-handed, that latter set of actions is smaller than the set of not-otherwise-prevented actions which she does not actually perform. As we naturally would expect, a system of mind-control that leaves the victim more latitude in arriving at her intentions and beliefs and attitudes is a system that creates less unfreedom for her.

In short, the taking over of a person's mind by others does not remove her status as someone to whom freedoms and unfreedoms can be imputed. Nor does it deprive the person altogether of her freedom, by any means. She is still unprevented from performing all the actions which she does perform; and, if the regimen of brainwashing is relatively unintrusive, she will likewise be unprevented from performing quite a few other actions. Nevertheless, even a fairly light-handed programme of mind-control imposes constraints on the objectives and intentions that she can form. It therefore imposes limits on the actions which she can carry out. She is unfree to carry out the excluded actions. To be sure, the mind-control does not impose limits on non-volitional movements of her body, in the presence of factors that occasion

such movements. However, because such factors will often be absent and because when present they will sometimes be evaded by the people who direct her consciousness, the mind-control often renders her unfree to move her body in any ways which those people rule out. By clamping curbs on her thoughts and dispositions, the captors of her mind clamp curbs on her actions and effectively on her bodily movements. They thereby create unfreedom for her.

6.2   Determinism defused

Mind-control qualifies as a source of unfreedom because it operates as a preventive factor whose effects as such are not dependent on the truth of any doctrine of natural or metaphysical determinism. Such a doctrine adverts to the inexorable succession of events in causal chains that are strictly and comprehensively preordained by all the preceding events in the chains and by the applicable laws of nature. A full-blown principle of determinism maintains that the process of inexorable succession just mentioned is characteristic of the unfolding of every event. As Carl Ginet remarks, a theory of 'determinism says that, given the state of the world at any particular time, the laws of nature determine all future developments in the world, down to the last detail'.[2] Let us suppose that some version of such a doctrine is correct. If so, then the character of every occurrence follows perforce from the total array of antecedent occurrences and the applicable laws of nature – which means that the total array of antecedent occurrences and the applicable laws of nature preclude the character of every occurrence from being other than what it is. Within the ineluctable flow of happenings, each thing must emerge with the form and substance that have been predetermined for it by all previous things. Nothing can ever emerge with any form or substance different from that with which it is actually endowed. No event can take any path other than that which it actually takes. Now, if a doctrine of predestination along these lines is correct, there would seem to be no place left for social and political liberty beyond the liberty of each person to behave in exactly the manner in which he or she does behave. After all, *ex hypothesi*, each person could not have behaved in any other manner. To presume that he or she could have behaved in other ways is to presume that the events constituting his or her behaviour have not been fully determined by earlier events – which is to depart from the assumption that has been adopted by us *arguendo*, to the effect that determinism prevails. If we cleave to that assumption instead of abandoning it, we shall have to conclude that nobody has ever been able to do anything other than what he or she actually does. Nor has anybody ever been able to undergo any non-volitional bodily movements other than those which he or she actually undergoes. Thus, if socio-political freedoms are understood as abilities – as they clearly are understood within my theory – we apparently have to conclude that people never enjoy socio-political freedoms to perform any acts which they do not perform. Despite appearances to the contrary, no one is ever free to do anything unless he or she actually does it. Must we accept such an unpalatable verdict?

One way of resisting that verdict, of course, is to impugn the doctrine of causal determinism. Somebody can point, for example, to the areas of quantum physics that tend to belie such a doctrine. However, even if we grant that the universe is not thoroughly deterministic, we cannot infer therefrom that the exceptions to strict determinism are of the right sort to enable the occurrence of volitions and actions other than those which actually materialize. As Ginet observes:

[I]f determinism is incompatible with free will . . . then we have the freedom of will we like to think we have only if determinism is false in certain specific ways, only if the laws of nature and the antecedent states of the world leave open all or most of the alternative actions we like to think are open to us. But that determinism is false in all those specific ways does not follow from indeter-

ministic quantum theory. So even if we know that indeterministic quantum theory is true, we cannot know by deduction therefrom that determinism has all the right exceptions. And it is clear that we do not know this in any other way either.[3]

At present, then, the truth-status of deterministic claims about human behaviour remains far from clear. In application to such behaviour, a doctrine of determinism may well be true notwithstanding its apparent falsity in application to the subatomic events studied by quantum physicists. In any case, given that the truth or falsity of that doctrine in application to human actions is currently unresolved and irresolvable, one should not logically commit oneself to an outright rejection of determinist theses. If we are to eschew the unpalatable verdict broached in my last paragraph, we should do so on the assumption that determinist claims about human behaviour might be true. Should that assumption ultimately prove to be unfounded, the problem addressed in this subsection will no longer have to be addressed. We cannot at present enjoy the luxury of ignoring that problem, however, and the ultimate resolution of the debates about the truth of determinist doctrines may reveal that we shall never enjoy such a luxury.

How, then, can we avoid the unpalatable verdict delineated two paragraphs ago? A circumvention of that verdict is indeed essential, for otherwise we shall have to accept that all questions of social and political liberty collapse into questions concerning what has happened and what will happen. Political philosophy's treatment of freedom will have been completely displaced by the natural sciences or by predestinarian religion. An exit from this unhappy predicament has been signalled at the outset of this subsection. If mind-control is a source of socio-political unfreedom partly because its status as such does not depend on the truth of determinist doctrines, then a comparable test or criterion should be applied to other preventive factors. Even though we may assume herein that some determinist doctrine is true, we should never rely on the truth of such a doctrine as a reason for classifying anything as a source or manifestation of the impairedness of somebody's socio-political freedom. Thus, for example, if Herbert has just scratched his own nose at some time t, that act will not have betokened a lack of socio-political freedom on his part to abstain from scratching his nose at t. Until the moment for this abstention from scratching at t has passed, Herbert enjoys the socio-political liberty to abstain therefrom at that time. We can know that his scratching of his nose at t does not warrant our inferring that he has theretofore lacked the socio-political freedom to abstain from scratching at that time, since – except in the presence of special circumstances such as thoroughgoing mind-control, which we may assume to be absent – any such inference would have to rely on the truth of a determinist theory. Because we are not allowed to invoke the actuality of determinism as a premise from which to draw conclusions about social and political liberty, we are not allowed to infer that Herbert's scratching of his nose at t is indicative of his having thitherto lacked the social and political liberty to abstain from scratching at t. Instead, we have to infer that Herbert has enjoyed the liberty-to-abstain-from-scratching, and that he has declined to exercise it.

These remarks on Herbert's act of scratching his nose can and should be generalized to other instances of conduct. No such instance should count as a source or manifestation of any limits on someone's socio-political freedom, unless its status as such is independent of the truth of determinist credos. If that status would obtain notwithstanding that all such credos might prove to be false, then the specified instance of conduct can rightly be regarded as promotive or indicative of restrictions on social and political liberty. By contrast, if that status depends on the truth of determinist doctrines, then the specified instance of conduct is not in itself promotive or indicative of any such restrictions.

This test aptly ensures that inquiries about social and political freedom/unfreedom are not collapsed into inquiries about natural or metaphysical determinism. The test does so, moreover, without presuming that any determinist theories are false. It prescinds from the truth-values of the claims of such theories, instead of denying those claims. Nevertheless, the test may strike some readers as question-begging or as suspiciously pat. Does not it presuppose the very distinctness of the two sets of inquiries just mentioned? The answer to this question, of course, is 'yes'. So what? My discussion in this subsection takes as given that an effacement of the distinction between those two sets of inquiries is unacceptable. A thesis about the unacceptability of any such effacement is not a conclusion for which I have sought to argue or for which I should be seeking to argue; rather, it is the central starting point that underlies the devising of this subsection's test. Taking that thesis as given is not an instance of begging the question but is instead a matter of pursuing the question. What is at issue in this subsection is not whether metaphysical and scientific enquiries into the existence of freedom-of-the-will should be separated from political-philosophical enquiries into the existence of anybody's socio-political freedoms or the extent of anybody's socio-political freedom. The need for such a separation is here treated as axiomatic. What is at issue, rather, is whether a suitable test can be devised for effecting that separation. Such a test must satisfy two main requirements. On the one hand, it cannot assume the falsity of determinist theses. As has been noted, a presupposition of the falsity of those theses would not currently be justifiable and might never be justifiable. At the same time, an appropriate test must distinguish between problems of freedom-of-the-will and problems of socio-political freedom in a manner that forestalls any thoroughgoing subsumption of the latter by the former. It must carve out a place for the latter set of problems that will accommodate the array of issues normally addressed by a conception of negative liberty within the domain of political philosophy (by my own conception, for example, as encapsulated in my F Postulate and U Postulate). Both of these requirements for a pertinent test can best be fulfilled by our abstracting from the truth-values of determinist doctrines. While not at all presuming that those doctrines are false, we should not accept any claim about restriction-on-freedom that indispensably presupposes the truth of those doctrines. By filtering out every such claim, we shall end up with an account of negative liberty that can stand firmly as a theory in political philosophy.

6.3 Psychological constraints

When we defuse determinist doctrines by not allowing them to serve as bases for claims about limits on socio-political liberty, we gain ample leeway to affirm that people are free to do things other than the things which they actually do. We gain such leeway because we prescind from the possibility that people are unable to form intentions and beliefs and attitudes other than those which they actually harbour. Having done as much, we should not hastily conclude that we must forbear from taking any notice of constraints on the formation of intentions and beliefs and attitudes. In my discussion of mind-control, of course, we have already taken notice of one source of such constraints. In this subsection we shall briefly look at some other conditions and afflictions that might qualify as further sources.

Among the conditions and maladies that might seem to curtail the liberty of anybody who suffers therefrom are cowardice, ignorance, phobias, compulsive habits, unintelligence, psychoses, severe depression, schizophrenia, mental retardation, diffidence, shyness, strong enticements, and infatuations. Clearly, a negative-liberty theory as opposed to a positive-liberty theory will decline to classify many of these factors as abridgements of freedom. For example, if cowardice disposes someone to avoid most dangers and ostensible dangers, the person's pusillanimous disposition falls short of an outright inability and thus falls short of an absence of any particular freedoms. Instead of maintaining that a cowardly person lacks the freedom to face certain hazards, we should maintain that he is strongly inclined not to exercise the freedom which he enjoys. Given that we are not allowing determinist theses to serve as bases for claims about curtailments of freedom, we should not accept that a coward is strictly unable and thus unfree to confront various dangers and scary situations which he sedulously avoids. He is free to watch a frightening film, for example, even if he is determinedly disinclined to exercise that freedom. Of course, there are undoubtedly some dangers which he is genuinely unable to handle. For instance, he may be unable to walk on a tightrope suspended between two high points, because he lacks the physical dexterity to do so. In general, however, actions that are physically possible for him are not strictly precluded by his being timorously undisposed to perform them. His cowardice is an aversion to perceived dangers; like other aversions, it should not be taken into account when we ascertain his particular liberties and his overall liberty. A young boy is free to eat broccoli even if he is fiercely uninclined to do so. Similarly, a coward is free to undertake a number of actions from which he shudderingly shrinks. For the purposes of a negative-liberty theory that insists on the desire- independence of the existence of freedoms and unfreedoms, his faint-heartedness is not a factor that should be registered in our enquiries and calculations. Much the same can be said in connection with diffidence and shyness and infatuations and strong enticements, which do not amount to veritable mind-control. Each of those conditions will doubtless make certain modes of conduct (self-assertive conduct or self-restrained conduct) extremely unpleasant, but none of them is a genuinely preventive factor.

Ignorance is a more complicated condition, in the present context. It will often be a straightforwardly disabling factor and will thus impair a person's overall liberty. For instance, if a man has never learned the Italian language, and if he is capable of learning that language through instruction that would have been available to him if he had sought it, his ignorance is what prevents him from reading an Italian newspaper and from understanding an Italian conversation. Were it not for his ignorance, he would enjoy a set of freedoms with which he is not currently endowed. In very different settings as well, ignorance produces freedom-diminishing effects. Let us recall Chapter 2's depiction of Dave who is interned in a cell with only one door, which is sealed with a computerized lock that is formidably unyielding unless Dave manages to type in a 200-digit number correctly. His ignorance of the correct sequence of digits radically lowers the probability of his being able to emerge from the cell, in comparison with a situation in which he has been informed of the exact array of digits that will enable him to escape. Indeed, gauged from any realistic perspective, his chances of typing the correct number and thus of emerging from the cell are effectively nil. With the knowledge of the relevant sequence of digits, Dave would be free to disengage the lock quite soon and would then be free to leave the cell. In the absence of such knowledge, he is almost certainly unfree to disengage the lock and is therefore almost certainly unfree to depart from the dungeon. In this setting, then, ignorance is a severely freedom-constricting and unfreedom-promoting condition.

In other settings, however, ignorance does not affect a person's liberty. Suppose that Bob has abducted Kathy and has placed her in a shed. Inadvertently, he leaves the door to the shed unlocked. A simple turn of the knob by Kathy would open the door and would thus enable her to escape altogether with very little effort. Nonetheless, because Kathy wrongly believes that the door is firmly locked – either because Bob has told her as much, or else because she simply assumes that no kidnapper would be so stupidly remiss as to leave his victim in a wholly unsecured shed – she does not even attempt to open the door, and consequently she does not discover that she can readily escape. Her ignorance in this case does not deprive her of her freedom-to-leave-the-shed; instead, it simply leads her to fail to exercise that freedom. She could very easily have learned of her possession of that freedom and could therefore have easily exercised it. She has neglected to take advantage of an opportunity that has been present all the same. Her situation is markedly different from that of Dave, whose chances of discovering the proper sequence of digits for the computerized lock are practically zero. Unlike Kathy, Dave has not been presented with a significant opportunity which he has neglected to exploit in spite of having been able to exploit it easily. Rather, he has not been presented with any significant opportunity whatsoever.

Ignorance, then, amounts to a freedom-curtailing condition in proportion to the difficulty of its being overcome. When it can be dispelled with hardly any effort, it has no effect or virtually no effect on one's overall freedom. By contrast, when the difficulty of overcoming it is staggeringly formidable – as is true in the situation of Dave in the dungeon – ignorance severely reduces one's overall freedom. These divergences between the effects of ignorance in different situations are, plainly, matters of probability. When one's ignorance can be rectified very easily, there is nearly a 100 per cent probability that one will be able to take advantage of opportunities that would remain unavailable if and only if the ignorance could not be rectified. Whether or not one does take advantage of them, one will almost certainly be *able* to take advantage of them. When one's ignorance is virtually insurmountable, by contrast, there is approximately a 0 per cent probability that one will be able to take advantage of opportunities that would become genuinely available if and only if the ignorance were to be rectified. Countless other settings will involve intermediate levels of difficulty in the overcoming of ignorance. In each case, the probabilistic qualification attached to any ascription of freedom will reflect the likelihood of the dissolution of a person's ignorance if the person were indeed to endeavour (without any blunders) to achieve such a dissolution. When the probabilities are extremely high, we can safely say that a person is free to do whatever his ignorance would prevent him from doing if the ignorance were not susceptible to being dissipated. When the probabilities are almost unimaginably low, we can safely say that for all practical purposes a person is not free to do anything that his undissipated ignorance disenables him from doing – for example, Dave's typing in of the correct sequence of 200 digits. When the probabilities are at intermediate levels, we are best advised to frame our ascriptions of freedom or unfreedom in an overtly probabilistic manner. Hence, whenever the probabilities fall short of being extremely high, ignorance will perceptibly diminish a person's overall liberty. After all, as has been suggested already in this book and as will be explained more lengthily in Chapter 5, the probabilistic qualifications attached to our ascriptions of freedom and unfreedom are entered directly into our measurements of overall liberty. By significantly affecting the probability that a person will be able to perform this or that action, ignorance significantly affects the property which we measure as the person's overall freedom.

Note, incidentally, that the foregoing remarks on ignorance do not imply a relationship of entailment between the following two propositions: (1) 'Subject to some probability p, Charles is free to perform some action A', and (2) 'Subject to some probability p, Charles will perform some action A if he endeavours to do so'. We can fully recognize the disabling effects of ignorance and the empowering effects of knowledge while also recognizing that people sometimes make mistakes which they know how to avoid or which they could very easily have learned how to avoid. Precisely such mistakes have been designated as 'blunders' at the several junctures in this chapter where the parenthetical phrase 'without any blunders' has been included. Because of the abiding possibility of blunders by any human being, the first of the propositions above does not entail the second. By

contrast, if the phrase 'do one's best' is stipulatively defined to mean 'endeavour without any blunders', a relationship of entailment does obtain between the following two propositions: (3) 'Subject to some probability p, Charles is free to perform A', and (4) 'Subject to some probability p, Charles will perform A if he does his best to perform it'. In short, because my conception of liberty is focused strictly on abilities rather than on the care or patience with which those abilities are used, it leaves room for a situation in which someone is able and thus free to do something which he tries and fails to do.

Let us move on. Phobias are further potential constraints on any person's liberty. On the one hand, if a phobia amounts simply to a strong fear or dread or revulsion, we should regard it – within our calculations of a person's overall freedom – in much the same way that we regard cowardice and shyness. That is, we should view such a phobia as an aversion that bears on the *palatableness* of options (for the person with the phobia) rather than on the *existence* of those options as such. In other cases, however, phobias can physically restrict people from engaging in various actions. In any such case, a phobia removes some of a person's particular freedoms and thereby reduces his or her overall freedom. Consider, for example, a phobia concerning blood and needles. Such a phobia may go well beyond a strong sense of squeamishness or revulsion, and may lead a person to lose consciousness or to become debilitatingly nauseated in circumstances that activate the phobia. In so far as a phobia does tend to inflict physical incapacitation of this sort on the phobia-sufferer in the aforementioned circumstances, it eliminates some of her particular freedoms and some of her combinations of conjunctively exercisable freedoms. And such affliction, which effectively immobilizes its victim under certain conditions, will clearly have impaired the victim's overall liberty.

Compulsive habits are likewise potential curbs on freedom. On the one hand, compulsive habits are sometimes merely strong urges that can be treated here as the inverse counterparts of strong aversions. In such forms, compulsive habits do not amount to veritable constraints on what people can do or abstain from doing. Refraining from indulging a strong and inveterate urge may be a highly disagreeable option, but it is indeed an option. On the other hand, compulsive habits sometimes involve considerably more than strong urges. In some cases, compulsively habitual movements of the body are carried out non-volitionally. In any such case, the movement is performed not just inadvertently or unreflectively but without any volition at all. If so, and if the movement cannot always be stifled through conscious effects to suppress it, then the person plagued by it is not free to keep his body from twitching or contorting (or moving in other ways) quite frequently. In such a situation, of course, the irresistible movement is not an action at all – any more than is a muscular reflex or the trembling of the hands of someone who suffers from Parkinson's disease.

In other contexts as well, compulsive habits are full-fledged limits on people's freedom. Perhaps the most striking cases of freedom-curtailing habits are instances of outright addiction to drugs such as heroin or alcohol. People who have become abjectly dependent on such drugs are not free to desist from them without undergoing a number of physically debilitating effects. Throughout the duration of those effects, a person's ability to undertake many activities will be substantially impaired. Consequently, even if we submit that addicts are typically free to extricate themselves from their state of dependence, we should recognize that the process of extrication will physically incapacitate them (to a greater or a lesser degree) for quite a while. At the very least, in other words, an addict's sorry state removes many of his combinations of conjunctively exercisable freedoms. It thereby reduces his overall liberty quite sharply.

Even when addictive drugs are not involved, a compulsive habit can amount to an encroachment on the overall liberty of a person. When such a habit is a product of a neurosis or some other mental disorder, the eschewal of it can involve debilitation comparable to that undergone by an addicted person who seeks to shake off his dependence on drugs. That is, even when a person's neurotic habit is not strictly non-volitional – in that it can be controlled through conscious efforts to keep it in check – it can eliminate many of the person's combinations of conjunctively exercisable freedoms. The person may be free to restrain his body from moving in its habitual pattern, but the debilitation attendant on that self-restraint will scotch many of his other freedoms for quite some time. In such circumstances, then, his neurotic habit significantly limits his overall liberty.

Most of the remaining conditions and maladies listed near the outset of this subsection can be discussed here very briefly, since they clearly lie outside the control of anybody who is affected by them. An unintelligent person, for example, is different from a merely ignorant person in that the former cannot overcome his condition by applying himself earnestly. He can undoubtedly improve his mind in some respects through painstaking endeavours, but, if he is genuinely unintelligent, he will never be capable of performing the intellectual feats that can be accomplished by someone with a much sharper mind. He is not free to perform such feats. We should note, moreover, that a generally smart person can be afflicted by a paucity of intelligence in some specific area(s). Some people are incapable of learning foreign languages proficiently, for example, regardless of how diligently they try. Other generally intelligent people are incapable of understanding mathematics beyond a fairly elementary level. No matter how carefully they might strive to follow the reasoning and concepts in more advanced mathematics, they remain uncomprehending. They are not free to engage in sophisticated mathematical reasoning, just as the irredeemably monolingual people are not free to speak and write proficiently in foreign languages.

Even more clearly insusceptible to being transcended trough persistent efforts is mental retardation or insanity. Although such afflictions can be alleviated in certain respects, and although some types of insanity can be largely or wholly cured over time, no such condition is remediable through sheer exertions of will on the part of the person who suffers from it. Indeed, no such condition is remediable at all in the short term. Throughout the duration of a state of insanity, then, any actions rendered impossible for the insane person by that state will be actions which he is not free to perform. Similarly, throughout the life of a mentally retarded person, any actions or achievements ruled out by his unfortunate condition are things which he is not free to do. Broadly the same can be said about serious mental illnesses such as schizophrenia and severe depression. Notwithstanding that severe depression is typically much more ephemeral than mental retardation or insanity, it incapacitates a person in many respects while it lasts. Likewise, although schizophrenia is often intermittent (with sustained periods of remission) and is sometimes curable, it produces a number of freedom-curtailing effects when it is present. A person afflicted by some strain of the disease cannot keep himself from behaving in ways that are impelled by the disorder of his mind. Whether the schizophrenia is of a kind that induces lethargy or is instead of a kind that inspires strange bursts of energy, it seizes at least partial control of somebody's mind. In that respect – though not necessarily in other respects – it resembles many different psychological incapacities. Like those other incapacities, it diminishes the freedom of anyone who remains within its grip. When psychological afflictions are genuine constraints on freedom, they can be powerful constraints indeed.

In sum, even though full-blown determinist theses cannot serve as bases for claims about restrictions on socio-political liberty, the volition-channelling effects of various psychological maladies are unquestionably to be taken into account when we seek to measure such liberty. We can and should recognize that those maladies circumscribe the range of people's options (often acutely), since our acknowledgement of that point does *not* commit us to an unacceptable reliance on determinist theses. When we submit that certain well-defined mental conditions and afflictions constrict people's socio-political freedom, we are hardly thereby accepting that every formation of a preference is a limit on such freedom. My observations in this subsection do not go any way toward collapsing all questions about socio-political liberty into metaphysical or scientific questions about the existence of freedom-of-the-will.

Notes

1 Ian Carter, *A Measure of Freedom* (Oxford: Oxford University Press, 1999).
2 Carl Ginet, *On Action* (Cambridge: Cambridge University Press, 1990) [Ginet, *Action*], p. 92. I do not here need to take any position in debates concerning whether determinism and freedom-of-the-will are compatible or incompatible. Even if compatibilism is correct, it cannot be so in any way that would eliminate the problem which I am addressing in this subsection.
3 Ginet, *Action*, p. 94.

Matthew H. Kramer, *The Quality of Freedom* (Oxford: Oxford University Press, 2003), pp. 255–71.

Part IV
Freedom and Morality

Introduction to Part IV

Can we be free to perform morally impermissible actions? On the face of it, most people would unhesitatingly answer this question affirmatively. After all, morally impermissible actions do, regrettably, occur. And there seems to be something outlandish about denying that their perpetrators were thus free to perform them. Many writers, such as Felix Oppenheim, accepting the force of this argument, accordingly suggest that there is simply no conceptual connection to be found between the moral permissibility or impermissibility of an act and a person's freedom or lack of freedom to perform it.

Others disagree, offering a variety of accounts of how freedom and morality are indeed related. William Connolly challenges the very idea that freedom can be defined non-evaluatively. Since its meaning is so politically contested, he says, any analysis of it must be understood as an exercise in "persuasive definition" – an attempt to capture freedom's undoubtedly positive connotations on behalf of some particular ideological position. Some writers, such as S. I. Benn and W. L. Weinstein, advance the less bold view that the class of actions to which freedom judgments apply consists of only those which most persons would standardly consider worth doing. On each of these views, an action's actually being performed would not in itself imply that its doer is free to do it, if that action is one lacking the requisite permissibility or worth. Closely related to such views is a frequently drawn distinction between *liberty* and *license*, whereby only the former is identified with freedom, and licentious acts are thus consigned to the category of actions which persons are neither free nor unfree to perform (i.e. regardless of whether others would prevent their occurrence or not).

A more complex view of the relation between freedom and morality directs our attention not to the evaluation of the action that a person may be prevented or unprevented from performing, but instead to the moral quality of the constraint that other persons might employ to prevent that performance. One such argument, advanced by Robert Nozick and criticized by G. A. Cohen, holds that, if the person imposing a preventive constraint on another's action is acting within his moral rights, then the former is not making the latter unfree to perform that action. Thus, if we forcibly prevent you from entering a house or factory, and if we are the morally rightful owners of those premises (or persons acting on their behalf), then you are not rendered unfree to enter them but instead are neither free nor unfree to do so. Similarly, an egalitarian might argue that if the government forcibly taxes away part of your income in order to fund some morally desirable program, it does not thereby make you unfree to spend that money. In both cases, the question of your freedom to do those prevented actions is said not to arise. It is evidently this form of argument that is often at work in political arguments over whether it is capitalism or socialism that provides the basis of a free society.

Another constraint-focused account of how freedom is connected to morality revolves around the notion of *moral responsibility*. On some views of freedom, like that of Oppenheim, one person's being *causally* responsible for the prevention of another's action is a sufficient ground for regarding the latter as unfree to perform that action. Thus, if I lock a closet and, unbeknown to me, you are inside it, I would be making you unfree to exit the closet and also unfree to do various other actions that could only occur outside that closet. However, on the moral responsibility view of the matter, David Miller suggests that my locking that closet with you inside it would render you unfree only if I was morally responsible for your consequent confinement in the closet. Among the possible grounds for my *not* being morally responsible for your confinement might be that I had a moral obligation to lock the closet that I performed non-negligently, e.g. by first checking to see if someone was inside, but not seeing you because you had deliberately hidden from view.

Further Reading

Carter, Ian, *A Measure of Freedom* (Oxford: Oxford University Press, 1999), pp. 69–74 〈critique of justice-based definitions of freedom〉.

Dworkin, Ronald, "Do Liberty and Equality Conflict?" in P. Barker (ed.), *Living as Equals* (Oxford: Oxford University Press, 1996) 〈defense of an equality-based conception of freedom〉.

Olsaretti, Serena, *Liberty, Desert and the Market. A Philosophical Study* (Cambridge: Cambridge University Press, 2004), ch. 5 〈critique of the moralized freedom-based defense of the free market〉.

Pettit, Philip, *Republicanism: A Theory of Freedom and Government* (Oxford: Oxford University Press, 1997), ch. 2 〈moralized definition of freedom in terms of common interests〉.

Swanton, Christine, *Freedom: A Coherence Theory* (Indianapolis, IN: Hackett, 1992), pp. 1–10 〈appraisal of the view that freedom is an essentially contested concept〉.

Chapter 34

John Locke, from *Two Treatises of Government* (1690)

Chapter II
Of the State of Nature

4. To understand Political Power right, and derive it from its Original, we must consider what State all Men are naturally in, and that is, a *State of perfect Freedom* to order their Actions, and dispose of their Possessions, and Persons as they think fit, within the bounds of the Law of Nature, without asking leave, or depending upon the Will of any other Man.

A *State* also *of Equality*, wherein all the Power and Jurisdiction is reciprocal, no one having more than another: there being nothing more evident, than that Creatures of the same species and rank promiscuously born to all the same advantages of Nature, and the use of the same faculties, should also be equal one amongst another without Subordination or Subjection, unless the Lord and Master of them all, should by any manifest Declaration of his Will set one above another, and confer on him by an evident and clear appointment an undoubted Right to Dominion and Sovereignty.

[. . .]

6. But though this be a *State of Liberty*, yet it is *not a State of Licence*, though Man in that State have an uncontroleable Liberty, to dispose of his Person or Possessions, yet he has not Liberty to destroy himself, or so much as any Creature in his Possession, but where some

nobler use, than its bare Preservation calls for it. The *State of Nature* has a Law of Nature to govern it, which obliges every one: And Reason, which is that Law, teaches all Mankind, who will but consult it, that being all equal and independent, no one ought to harm another in his Life, Health, Liberty, or Possessions. For Men being all the Workmanship of one Omnipotent, and infinitely wise Maker; All the Servants of one Sovereign Master, sent into the World by his order and about his business, they are his Property, whose Workmanship they are, made to last during his, not one anothers Pleasure. And being furnished with like Faculties, sharing all in one Community of Nature, there cannot be supposed any such *Subordination* among us, that may Authorize us to destroy one another, as if we were made for one anothers uses, as the inferior ranks of Creatures are for ours. Every one as he is *bound to preserve himself*, and not to quit his Station willfully; so by the like reason when his own Preservation comes not in competition, ought he, as much as he can, *to preserve the rest of Mankind*, and may not unless it be to do Justice on an Offender, take away, or impair the life, or what tends to the Preservation of the Life, the Liberty, Health, Limb or Goods of another.

John Locke, *Two Treatises of Government*, ed. P. Laslett (Cambridge: Cambridge University Press, 1960), pp. 269–71.

Chapter 35

Felix E. Oppenheim, from *Political Concepts* (1981)

4.1 Social Unfreedom

I shall first examine the concept of social unfreedom because it is the simpler one, because it is connected with the concepts of social power we have analyzed, and because it will in turn help to define the concept of social freedom. I shall spell out what it means to say that one person or group is, wrt [with respect to] another, unfree to act in a certain way. There are two ways in which an actor can make another unfree to do something: he may make it either impossible or punishable for him to do so. The defining expression will indicate these two methods.

Definition: Wrt P, R is unfree to do x iff P prevents R from doing x or would punish him if he did x.

Analogously, we might say that, wrt P, R is unfree not to do x (or that it is mandatory for R to do x) iff P makes it either necessary for R to do x or punishable for R to abstain from doing x. However, I shall deal explicitly only with the former expression, as 'wrt P, R is unfree to do x' dovetails with 'P has power over R's not doing x' – the expression on which we focused in chapter 2.

4.1.1 Preventing

Clearly, someone who either restrains or prevents me from acting in a certain way (or coerces me to do something or makes it necessary for me to do so) does limit my freedom in that respect. By making R unable to do x, P not only has control over R's not doing x, but also makes him unfree to do x. If the guard either restrains or prevents a prisoner from breaking out, the latter is, wrt the former, unfree to leave. Similarly, the owner who encloses his property by a high wall makes everybody unable, and unfree as well, to trespass. The same relationship of unfreedom holds between the gunman who uses coercive threats and his victim. Offers "one cannot refuse" also render the person to whom they are made unfree to disobey. The same is true of legal impediments. If divorce is not legalized in a given country, its citizens are, wrt their government, unfree to divorce, including those citizens who do not contemplate such a step.

Unfreedom is not synonymous with inability. A person is not unfree to do what he cannot do unless his inability is caused, at least in part, by another person or jointly by several individuals or a group, intentionally or not (as I shall point out later). A kleptomaniac may be psychologically unable to refrain from stealing, but he is not unfree to refrain – wrt any other actor. As J. P. Day points out, his behavior is compulsive, but not compelled (by anyone else) [...]. Someone who lacks the skill to wiggle his ears or to play the violin is not interpersonally unfree to do so. On the other hand, a prisoner, unable to leave his cell, is under the power of the guards who would push him back if he tried to break out *and* unfree to do so wrt the guards. What if P has made it difficult rather than impossible for R to do x? Has he made him unfree to do so? Here we must remember what we said about impossibility in connection with control. Strict impossibility shades over into difficulty, unpleasantness, and risk; hence, unfreedom is, like control, a matter of degree. (This aspect will be examined in 4.3.)

Whether an actor's incapacity to act in a certain way is the result of the intervention of some other person or group or is due to other factors is often a matter of controversy. That the high cost of television time renders this medium inaccessible to most does not appear to constitute a limitation of freedom of speech. Or could it be considered an instance of social unfreedom after all? If the rate has been set by a few monopolistic networks, is it then not true that those who cannot afford the media are unfree to use them – unfree wrt the broadcasting companies whose rates have made them unable to take advantage of their facilities? (I am assuming that monopolistic prices are set by specifiable actors, but non-monopolistic prices by "the market.") Were workers in the mid-nineteenth century just unable to earn a living wage because of the generally prevailing economic, social, and political conditions? Or were they also unfree to earn more, and if so, wrt whom? Wrt the employers who did not offer higher wages? Wrt the government because it failed to enact minimum wage laws? Was the inability of many to find employment in 1929 merely the result of the Depression, or was the Depression in turn a consequence of Herbert Hoover's policies? If so, the unemployed did not merely lack the possibility of finding work; they were also unfree to secure employment – wrt Herbert Hoover and whoever else caused the Depression.

It might be argued that governments, by not introducing social legislation, failed to enable workers to earn higher wages and on this account made them unfree to do so. However, we have seen that, by not enabling R to do x, P does not necessarily make R unable to do so. Only when P makes it impos-

sible for R to do x is there power and – we may now add – unfreedom. So the question is: did the legislators, by not enacting minimum wage laws, merely fail to enable workers to secure an adequate living standard, or did the course taken by the former prevent the latter from earning more and make them unfree to do so? Similarly, did the American government in 1929 merely abstain from adopting measures of full employment, or did its policy make it impossible for many to find jobs?

Professor Macpherson considers "an important source of unfreedom the capitalist property institutions whose necessary . . . result was the coercion of the non-owning class".[1] Given the proposed definitions, coercion by *institutions* is not an instance of social unfreedom, unless their existence is in turn "the result of arrangements made by other human beings," as the author claims in another passage.[2] To deny this, he holds, is to "suggest or imply that the poverty of the poor is entirely their own fault".[3] But this is not implied. Poverty can be viewed as the "fault" not of either the poor or the wealthy, but of economic and political institutions not shaped by the actions of any particular group or class. (Even Marx explained low wages in contemporary industrial society as the necessary consequence of an economic system in which capitalists were enmeshed no less than wage earners.) Whether poverty under capitalism constitutes unfreedom depends, then, on the general theory of the causes of poverty one adopts. Some tend to explain poverty and unemployment in terms of anonymous causal factors inherent in that, or perhaps any, economic system; others are inclined to lengthen the causal chain to arrive at specific persons or groups whom they *accuse* of being the cause of what they consider to be instances of unfreedom. Thus Macpherson "counts as deprivations of an individual's liberty the indirect interference imposed by withholding from him the means of life or means of labor".[4] The words 'interference' and 'imposed' point toward specifiable actors who, moreover, not merely failed to enable the individual to secure the means of life and labor, but 'withheld' them from him, i.e., made it impossible for him to secure them. The choice between such rival explanatory theories is then likely to be affected by ideological and normative considerations. Conceptual analysis cannot provide general objective criteria to distinguish between agents and other causes of inability, and to decide when the causal chain becomes too long to be subsumed under the concept of unfreedom. Since 'unfreedom' has a negative valuational connotation in ordinary language, there is a tendency to apply the term to any situation of which one disapproves. On the basis of the proposed "value-free" language, to deny that poverty or unemployment under capitalism is an instance of social unfreedom is not to justify capitalism, and to hold that it is implies no condemnation of that economic system.

4.1.2   Punishability

Unfreedom is often taken as applying only to prevention. E.g., "An individual is unfree is, *and only if*, his doing of any action is rendered impossible by the action of another individual".[5] It seems to me that, if another individual (or group) makes it punishable for the former to perform a certain action, he must also be considered unfree to do so. Wrt P, R is unfree to do x not only to the extent that P makes it impossible for R to do x, but also to the extent that P would carry out an explicit or implied threat of punishment if he found R guilty of having done x. One might object that I myself previously considered punishability a form of prevention and that 'prevention' can therefore be taken as a synonym of 'unfreedom'. The reply is that P, by making it punishable for R to do x, makes it impossible for R to do x *without being punished*, but does not prevent him from doing x.

It has, in fact, been objected that "[t]he existence of a threatened punishment does not in itself create unfreedom. To say that a man is unfree to perform an activity he in fact performs is logically most cumbersome".[6] It seems to me that this interpretation of social unfreedom does not even deviate from common usage. We do say currently that a speeder does something he is officially unfree to do. Nor does this common use of language seem cumbersome to me. (Incidentally, a conclusion cannot be "logically cumbersome," but only logically false – or true, as this statement is, given the proposed definition.)

This interpretation of unfreedom has also been criticized for implying "that a man can be socially unfree to do something he has already done".[7] I do not claim that P, by punishing R at time t2 for having done x at time t1, makes R *retroactively* unfree to do what he did. From the fact that R is being punished for speeding at t2, I infer that R *was* unfree to speed when he did (at t1), not that he is *now*, at t2, unfree "to do something he has already done." If R was not caught speeding at t1, it follows by definition that R was not unfree to speed *on that occasion* (but free to speed or not to speed, as we shall see). At t1, we can only say that R is unfree to speed with a certain degree of probability, depending on the likelihood that he will be fined. And so is everyone else. Another driver who stays within the speed limit at t1 is just as unfree to speed as R who speeds, unfree to the extent of the probability of the counterfactual statement: were he to speed, he would be fined. If punishment is certain, his unfreedom is maximal; but if the law is not being enforced at all, he is not unfree to speed (but free to do so), no more so than if there were no legal speed limit. If the Highway Department applies speeding laws to 40 percent of all speeders, it follows that *everyone* is to a degree of 40 percent unfree to speed – speeders (any speeder has a 40 percent chance of being fined), would-be speeders, and those who do not consider speeding, including nondrivers (there is a 40 percent probability that any of them would be fined if he speeded). Everyone is also under a legal obligation to keep within the speed limits – to 100 percent. The higher the degree of law enforcement, the closer the correspondence between the range of behavioral unfreedom and of illegal behavior.

Does it sound odd to say that someone did something that, we found out later, he was unfree to do (more precisely, unfree to have done), or that he is doing something now that, it will turn out later, he is unfree (more precisely, he will have been unfree) to do? We do not hesitate to affirm that one actor was punished by another for an action he performed previously, or to predict that the latter will punish the former for what he is doing now. In our ordinary language, there is unfortunately no transitive verb referring to unfreedom analogous to 'punishing' (or 'influencing', 'deterring', 'coercing'); one does not say, 'P unfrees R'. We can say that P makes R unfree to do x by preventing R from doing x or by making it punishable for R to do x. Here P's action y is temporally prior to R's potential action x. But it would indeed be odd to say that P, by punishing R now for having done x, makes R now unfree to do x or to have done x. Ordinary language leaves us no choice but to put ourselves in the shoes of R, rather than of P, as it were, when referring to actual punishment as an instance of unfreedom, and to say, if P punished R for having done x, then R was, wrt P, unfree to do x. It becomes then more practical to use, as the defining expression in our restructured language, 'wrt P, R is unfree to do x' to cover prevention and punishability, including actual punishment.

The application of legal sanctions by government to citizens who act illegally is only one kind of social unfreedom through punishability. Such relationships hold among all kinds of persons or groups. Wrt a union, a company is unfree to withhold certain benefits from union members if otherwise the union would picket the company. Members of an organization who would be expelled if they did not conform to certain, perhaps unwritten, norms are unfree to deviate from such rules wrt the organization or its leadership. Wrt Saudi Arabia, the United States is unfree to increase its military aid to Israel if Saudi Arabia would in that case further increase its oil price, and the more unfree, the higher the price. On the other hand, the United States is not unfree to acquire oil from Saudi Arabia if that country would in that case ask for a higher price, because that would not constitute a punishment of the United States for wanting to acquire the oil. Rather, this is a bargaining situation. On the other hand, if I tell B that I am "not free for dinner" because I have accepted A's dinner invitation, this is not to be taken literally. Wrt A, I am not unfree to dine with B, since presumably A would not hinder me from going with B or punish me if I did. 'I am not free for dinner' does not refer to interpersonal unfreedom at all (nor to unfreedom in any other sense). It means that I have a prior engagement and subscribe to the principle that promises should be kept. Perhaps "my conscience" would "punish me with guilt" if I broke my engagement with A; but my superego is not *another actor*.

[. . .]

8
Normative Interpretations

In the preceding chapters, I have been criticizing other definitions of some basic political concepts, thereby indirectly justifying my own analysis. In this chapter I shall have to adopt a more defensive strategy. I must defend my approach against the view that political concepts like those I have been analyzing are not purely descriptive, but have a normative component; that these are two sides of the same coin; and that statements using these concepts are therefore bound to function simultaneously as factual assertions and moral judgments.

[. . .]

While power and unfreedom are held to involve blame, "freedom is a benefit"[8] and the concept of social freedom has "positive normative import"[9] and should therefore not be taken as a purely descriptive concept.

> In the ordinary language of political life and in more formal systems of political inquiry the normative dimensions in the idea of freedom are not attached to it as "connotations" that can be eliminated; without the normative point of view from which the concept is formed we would have no basis for deciding what "descriptive terms" to include or exclude in the definition.[10]

First of all, what is *the* normative point of view allegedly involved in the idea of freedom? Here the variety of moral outlooks is perhaps even greater than in connection with power. Plato thought that government should *not* give its citizens much freedom (which he defined, quite descriptively, as being allowed to do what one likes [*Republic*, VIII, 557]). Furthermore, as mentioned earlier, it is empirically impossible to favor "a freedom" such as freedom of speech without also approving of the necessary limitations of freedom. Also, one kind of freedom deemed desirable must be weighed against other freedoms incompatible with the former, as well as against other goals such as welfare or equality.

For rhetorical purposes, it may be good strategy to use the *word* 'freedom' only in a laudatory way, and to call a freedom one opposes 'license': "If unbridled license of speech and of writing be granted to all, nothing will remain sacred and inviolate. . . . Thus, truth gradually being obscured by darkness, promiscuous and manifold error, as too often happens will easily prevail. Thus, too, license will gain what liberty loses" (Encyclical *Libertas*, 1888). Here, unfreedom to propagate "error" becomes freedom – to affirm "truth" – and freedom of opinion becomes "license."

My point is this. If 'freedom' is taken by everyone as a moral notion to refer to all, and only to, relationships of *both* freedom and unfreedom of which he approves, everyone will agree on one point only: that "freedom" is something good. But there will be dis-

agreement on what states of affairs are the desirable ones. Meaningful disagreement about the desirable extent and limit of some specific kind of social freedom presupposes agreement about the meaning of 'freedom'. I believe that such agreement is possible on the basis of the analysis of the concept of social freedom I have provided. The proposed interpretation does not even deviate from "the ordinary language of political life," except that it detaches the concept from what I consider to be its moral *connotation*. Since it incorporates no "normative point of view," it can be applied by anyone to determinate states of affairs, regardless of his moral, political, or ideological convictions.

[. . .]

[. . .], the concept of social freedom is often restricted to being able to do what others *should* make it possible to accomplish. To give just one example of this familiar conception, "Personal freedom means the power of the individual to buy sufficient food, shelter and clothing to keep his body in good health and to gain access to sufficient teaching and books to develop his mind".[11] Such definitions confuse social freedom with freedom of action. Furthermore, they restrict the meaning of the latter to an actor's capacity to bring about something *specific* such as a certain level of well-being.

Denying, as I do, that inabilities resulting from impersonal factors are instances of social unfreedom has been interpreted as a defense of laissez-faire capitalism (see e.g., Macpherson 1973, p. 91). More generally, defining social freedom the way I have done has been tied to viewing society – and approvingly so – as consisting of Hobbesian, isolated, self-interested, utility-maximizing individuals. I do not believe that my interpretation of social freedom and unfreedom has any normative implications, no more so than my attempt to construct a valuationally neutral concept of power. Proponents of this *definition* of negative liberty need not be "[p]roponents of negative liberty".[12] To deny that inabilities caused by capitalism (rather than by capitalists) are limitations of freedom is not to approve of these inabilities or to defend capitalism, and to deny that providing full employment and social benefits are matters of freedom is not to oppose such measures.

Defining "freedom in general" as being able or being permitted to do what one wants – thus confusing social freedom with the feeling of freedom – is also linked to normative considerations, in this case the conviction that people should normally be enabled and permitted to fulfill their desires. The same normative standpoint accounts for the related view that an individual has *more* freedom if the range within which he is free to act includes the alternative he wants to pursue most than if it does not. "Clearly, there can be no simple or direct relationship between the range of available alternatives and the extent of freedom. However numerous the alternatives between which a man may choose, he will not admit himself to be free if the one alternative that he would most prefer is the one which is excluded".[13] He may not *admit* or even realize that he remains free to perform any of the actions he wants to perform less or not at all. He may not *feel* free if it is his favored course of action he is being made unfree to pursue. However, we have seen that my not wanting to do something does not count against my being free to do so, that the range of my freedom depends exclusively on the number of alternatives I am free to pursue, and that this range is indeed *one* of the dimensions of the extent of my freedom. Given the proposed definition of social freedom and the ordinary usage of the term as well, it just is not true that "a person who is prevented from doing something which is of some importance to him is suffering a greater curtailment of liberty than [if it is not]" and that "the degree to which his liberty is thereby curtailed depends (other things being equal) on how important the course of action in question is to him".[14] Conversely, it is not the case that a person's freedom is greater if what he is free to do happens to include what is important to him and that the degree of his freedom is the

greater, the stronger his desire to perform that particular action. As pointed out in chapter 4, we should not confuse the *extent* of my freedom, how much (or how little) I *value* being free in that respect, and how valuable it is to me to be able (as well as free) to pursue *some particular* course of action.

Indeed, even if what I want to do most is included in the range of my freedom, in most cases the opportunity to do what I desire is what I value, rather than my freedom to do so *or to do something else*, just as, when I am unable but free to realize my desire, I value being given the opportunity I lack, not the freedom I already have. After the revocation of the Edict of Nantes, Frenchmen became free to be Protestants or Catholics. Protestants cared mainly about being no longer unfree to practice their faith, and some would not have minded if Protestantism became the mandatory state religion. Catholics did not value their *freedom* of religion either. The principle of freedom of religion for all was advocated by some philosophers. I mentioned, too, that there are many circumstances in which most prefer being compelled to do certain things, i.e., being made unfree to act otherwise. I deny therefore that "[n]o matter what values men hold, the freedom to pursue these values is important for them".[15] Being free to do one thing or another becomes important only if one values the possibility of deciding for oneself whether to do this or that. This is the meaning of valuing freedom – or better: valuing some specific social freedom like freedom of opinion – either for oneself or for others or for all. But restricting 'freedom' by definition to doing, or being permitted to do, what one desires is usually a disguise for *advocating* that people *should* be left free to make their own decisions *in some specific area*.

Notes

1 C. B. Macpherson, *Democratic Theory* (Oxford: Oxford University Press, 1973), p. 99.

2 Ibid., p. 98.

3   Ibid., p. 100.

4   Ibid., p. 118.

5   Hillel Steiner, "Individual Liberty," *Proceedings of the Aristotelian Society* 75 (1975): 33; italics added.

6   C. W. Cassinelli, *Free Activities and Interpersonal Relations* (The Hague: Nijhoff, 1966), p. 34.

7   William Parent, "Some Recent Work on the Concept of Liberty," *American Philosophical Quarterly* II (1974), p. 157.

8   Gerald C. MacCallum, Jr., "Negative and Positive Freedom," *Philosophical Review* 76 (1967), p. 312.

9   William Connolly, *The Terms of Political Discourse* (Lexington, MA: Heath, 1974), p. 143

10   Ibid., p. 141.

11   Sidney Webb and Beatrice Webb, *The Decay of Capitalist Civilization*, 3rd ed. (Westminster: Fabian Society, 1923), p. 45.

12   Macpherson, *Democratic Theory*, p. 98.

13   P. H. Partridge, "Freedom," in Paul Edwards (ed.), *Encyclopedia of Philosophy* (New York: Macmillan, 1967), p. 223.

14   Ernest Loevinsohn, "Liberty and the Redistribution of Property," *Philosophy and Public Affairs* 6 (226) (1976), p. 232.

15   Christian Bay, *The Structure of Freedom* (Stanford, CA: Stanford University Press, 1958), p. 15.

Felix E. Oppenheim, *Political Concepts* (Oxford: Basil Blackwell, 1981), pp. 53–9, 150, 153–4, 158–60.

Go to page
299

Chapter 36

William E. Connolly, from *The Terms of Political Discourse* (1983)

Freedom as a Contested Concept

Freedom is perhaps the most slippery and controversial of the concepts we shall discuss. We can best hope to cope with the notion if we come to terms with just why it is the subject of such intense and continuing controversy. One tradition of conceptual analysis approaches the problem in the following way: The idea of freedom, fairly clear in itself, is today surrounded by positive normative "connotations." These positive connotations encourage advocates of different ideologies to define it persuasively, to advance definitions, that is, that bring the values and goals they favor within the rubric of freedom. As a result, the concept becomes increasingly vague and unclear; misused by competing ideologists, the concept itself threatens to lose its utility in neutral empirical inquiry.

The task of conceptual analysis, according to this view, is first to purge the concept of all normative or value connotations and then to explicate it in ways that enable all investigators, regardless of the ideological orientation they "happen" to adopt, to use it in description and explanation of social and political life. Such an approach will allow us to transcend the current confusions permeating studies in which the concept figures and will in fact make it possible to pinpoint our normative differences. For now all investigators will have access to the same conceptual system, neutral

with respect to opposing ideologies, in which they can discuss their differences about the extent to which freedom is properly prized as an ideal of political life. Perhaps the ideological differences will not be fully resolved, it is argued, but at least the factual issues that can be brought to bear on these questions will be stated with clarity in a neutral language. In a book that has contributed valuable insights into the concept of freedom, Felix Oppenheim states this view. "Meaningful disagreement about the value of freedom depends," he contends, "on agreement on that about which one disagrees." To achieve this goal we must "arrive at a system of definitions acceptable to everybody because they do not conflict with anybody's political ideology." Reviewing in a recent article his own efforts to fulfill this objective, he asserts:

> Thus, in the case of the concept of social, political, or interpersonal freedom, the expression we must explicate is, "With respect to B, A is free to do x." This expression can be defined by: "B makes it neither impossible nor punishable for A to do x." Not only does this definition remain close to ordinary usage, it is also descriptive, and in two ways: the defining expression consists exclusively of descriptive terms, and it is "value-free" in the sense that it can be applied to determinate states of affairs by anyone independently of his political convictions.

The concern here expressed for clarity is laudable, but I shall argue, the approach adopted and the presuppositions it embodies are inappropriate to the objective stated. In the ordinary language of political life and in more formal systems of political inquiry the normative dimensions in the idea of freedom are not attached to it as "connotations" that can be eliminated; without the normative point of view from which the concept is formed we would have no basis for deciding what "descriptive terms" to include or exclude in the definition. Debates about the criteria properly governing the concept of freedom are in part debates about the extent to which the proposed criteria fulfill the normative point of the concept and in part about exactly what that point is. To refuse to bring these considerations into one's deliberations about 'freedom' is either to deny oneself access to the very considerations that can inform judgment about the concept or to delude oneself by tacitly invoking the very considerations formally eschewed. That is the charge I shall defend.

The alternative approach pursued here does not promise to issue in a neutral definition couched in criteria acceptable to all regardless of normative commitments; it does promise, though, to clarify the issues underlying conceptual disputes about freedom; and it does purport to help the investigator clarify explicitly the considerations that move him to adopt one formulation over others.

The thesis to be advanced is that 'freedom' is contested partly because of the way it bridges a positivist dichotomy between "descriptive" and "normative" concepts. Though considerations in support of this thesis will be offered throughout this essay, we will devote the rest of this section to linguistic evidence from ordinary discourse, which provides it with preliminary support.

To capture the grammar of 'free' tacitly accepted in ordinary discourse, Alan Ryan has compared words with the suffix 'free' to others that have the suffix 'less'. We draw subtle distinctions between these ideas, he concludes, that determine which suffix properly applies in particular contexts. Thus a driver might be carefree as he drives down an empty highway just after his car has passed a safety check, but he is careless if he adopts a similar attitude on a crowded thoroughfare with an old car on the way to a safety check. Care*free* motoring and care*less* motoring each call our attention to different aspects of the driver and his situation. We speak of a dust-free room because of our belief that a room without dust is more pleasant and healthy than one with great quantities of dust, but we call a painting worthless (rather than worth*free*) when we conclude that it lacks artistic value. Similarly we speak of being penniless, but not pennyfree when we are out of money. And it would be odd indeed to say that a person without means of defense in the face of a massive attack is defensefree; surely we would describe him as defenseless in that situation. Note that it is proper to say that we would *describe* him as defenseless.

In comparing the circumstances in which these suffixes apply it is clear that in general 'free' applies to situations or outcomes that are advantageous or helpful to the agent involved, while 'less' applies to situations that are deleterious to, involve some deprivation, or relate to the lack of needed or useful resources to, the agent. The difference between these suffixes, *both* of which typically apply to situations in which something is missing, is not adequately captured by saying they describe the same things, but attach different normative appraisals to those things. A dustfree room, for instance, describes a fairly complex phenomenon: a room without dust, which is, *for that reason*, more comfortable to the inhabitants. As Ryan himself concludes, "Clearly the use of 'free' rather than 'less' implies a good deal about people's wants and purposes, about people's duties, about the uses of objects, and so on. Talking of the so-called fact-value dichotomy here is of little relevance, because there is more to be said."

These two suffixes pick out different elements in situations that refer in the broadest sense to the absence of something; and they pick out different elements *because* each notion bears a different relationship to the wants, interests, and purposes of the agents implicated in those situations. The one suffix, then, does not simply have "value connotations" different from the other; for that choice of words suggests that the use of one suffix rather than the other is determined by the different *feelings* people project onto situations that are *descriptively identical*. But in fact the suffixes pick out different aspects of situations that are only similar in some respects. The choice of "connotation" to capture the difference between 'free' and 'less' is deficient in another respect: Connotations are emotive attitudes that happen to cluster around a word; they can be stripped from the idea itself without altering or emasculating it. The positive normative import of 'free', though, is not attached to it accidentally but flows from its identification of factors pertinent to human well-being in situations where something is absent. And that normative import in turn sets general limits to the sort of situations to which the idea of freedom can be applied. Instead of seeking to strip the idea of its positive "associations," we must ask, Why does 'freedom' carry positive normative significance and what import might the answer have for our shared understanding of, and disputes about, the idea itself?

William E. Connolly, *The Terms of Political Discourse*, 3rd edn. (Oxford: Blackwell, 1993), pp. 139–43.

Chapter 37

Robert Nozick, from *Anarchy, State and Utopia* (1974)

How Liberty Upsets Patterns

It is not clear how those holding alternative conceptions of distributive justice can reject the entitlement conception of justice in holdings. For suppose a distribution favored by one of these non-entitlement conceptions is realized. Let us suppose it is your favorite one and let us call this distribution D_1; perhaps everyone has an equal share, perhaps shares vary in accordance with some dimension you treasure. Now suppose that Wilt Chamberlain is greatly in demand by basketball teams, being a great gate attraction. (Also suppose contracts run only for a year, with players being free agents.) He signs the following sort of contract with a term: In each home game, twenty-five cents from the price of each ticket of admission goes to him. (We ignore the question of whether he is "gouging" the owners, letting them look out for themselves.) The season starts, and people cheerfully attend his team's games; they buy their tickets, each time dropping a separate twenty-five cents of their admission price into a special box with Chamberlain's name on it. They are excited about seeing him play; it is worth the total admission price to them. Let us suppose that in one season one million persons attend his home games, and Wilt Chamberlain winds up with $250,000, a much larger sum than the average income and larger even than anyone else has. Is he entitled to this income? Is this new distribution D_2, unjust? If so, why? There is *no* question about whether each of the people was entitled to the control over the resources they held in D_1; because that was the distribution (your favorite) that (for the purposes of argument) we assumed was acceptable. Each of these persons *chose* to give twenty-five cents of their money to Chamberlain. They could have spent it on going to the movies, or on candy bars, or on copies of *Dissent* magazine, or of *Monthly Review*. But they all, at least one million of them, converged on giving it to Wilt Chamberlain in exchange for watching him play basketball. If D_1 was a just distribution, and people voluntarily moved from it to D_2, transferring parts of their shares they were given under D_1 (what was it for if not to do something with?), isn't D_2 also just? If the people were entitled to dispose of the resources to which they were entitled (under D_1), didn't this include their being entitled to give it to, or exchange it with, Wilt Chamberlain? Can anyone else complain on grounds of justice? Each other person already has his legitimate share under D_1. Under D_1, there is nothing that anyone has that anyone else has a claim of justice against. After someone transfers something to Wilt Chamberlain, third parties *still* have their legitimate shares; *their* shares are not changed. By what process could such a transfer among two persons give rise to a legitimate claim of distributive justice on a portion of what was transferred, by a third party who had no claim of justice on any holding of the others *before* the transfer?[1] To cut off objections irrelevant here, we might imagine the exchanges occurring in a socialist society, after hours. After playing whatever basketball he does in his daily work, or doing whatever other daily work he does, Wilt Chamberlain decides to put in *overtime* to earn additional money. (First his work quota is set; he works time over that.) Or imagine it is a skilled juggler people like to see, who puts on shows after hours.

Why might someone work overtime in a society in which it is assumed their needs are satisfied? Perhaps because they care about things other than needs. I like to write in books that I read, and to have easy access to books for browsing at odd hours. It would be very pleasant and convenient to have the resources of Widener Library in my back yard. No society, I assume, will provide such resources close to each person who would like them as part of his regular allotment (under D_1). Thus, persons either must do without some extra things that they want, or be allowed to do something extra to get some of these things. On what basis could the inequalities that would eventuate be forbidden? Notice also that small factories would spring up in a socialist society, unless forbidden. I melt down some of my personal possessions (under D_1) and build a machine out of the material. I offer you, and others, a philosophy lecture once a week in exchange for your cranking the handle on my machine, whose products I exchange for yet other things, and so on. (The raw materials used by the machine are given to me by others who possess them under D_1, in exchange for hearing lectures.) Each person might participate to gain things over and above their allotment under D_1. Some persons even might want to leave their job in socialist industry and work full time in this private sector. I shall say something more about these issues in the next chapter. Here I wish merely to note how private property even in means of production would occur in a socialist society that did not forbid people to use as they wished some of the resources they are given under the socialist distribution D_1.

The socialist society would have to forbid capitalist acts between consenting adults.

The general point illustrated by the Wilt Chamberlain example and the example of the entrepreneur in a socialist society is that no end-state principle or distributional patterned principle of justice can be continuously realized without continuous interference with people's lives. Any favored pattern would be transformed into one unfavored by the principle, by people choosing to act in various ways; for example, by people exchanging goods and services with other people, or giving things to other people, things the transferrers are entitled to under the favored distributional pattern. To maintain a pattern one must either continually interfere to stop people from transferring resources as they wish to, or continually (or periodically) interfere to take from some persons resources that others for some reason chose to transfer to them. (But if some time limit is to be set on how long people may keep resources others voluntarily transfer to them, why let them keep these resources for *any* period of time? Why not have immediate confiscation?) It might be objected that all persons voluntarily will choose to refrain from actions which would upset the pattern. This presupposes unrealistically (1) that all will most want to maintain the pattern (are those who don't, to be "reeducated" or forced to undergo "self-criticism"?), (2) that each can gather enough information about his own actions and the ongoing activities of others to discover which of his actions will upset the pattern, and (3) that diverse and far-flung persons can coordinate their actions to dovetail into the pattern. Compare the manner in which the market is neutral among persons' desires, as it reflects and transmits widely scattered information via prices, and coordinates persons' activities.

It puts things perhaps a bit too strongly to say that every patterned (or end-state) principle is liable to be thwarted by the voluntary actions of the individual parties transferring some of their shares they receive under the principle. For perhaps some *very* weak patterns are not so thwarted. Any distributional pattern with any egalitarian component is overturnable by the voluntary actions of individual persons over time; as is every patterned condition with sufficient content so as actually to have been proposed as presenting the central core of distributive justice. Still, given the possibility that some weak conditions or patterns may not be unstable in this way, it would be better to formulate an explicit description of the kind of interesting and contentful patterns under discussion, and to prove a theorem about their instability. Since the weaker the patterning, the more likely it is that the entitlement system itself satisfies it, a plausible conjecture is that any patterning either is unstable or is satisfied by the entitlement system.

Note

1. Might not a transfer have instrumental effects on a third party, changing his feasible options? (But what if the two parties to the transfer independently had used their holdings in this fashion?) I discuss this question below, but note here that this question concedes the point for distributions of ultimate intrinsic noninstrumental goods (pure utility experiences, so to speak) that are transferrable. It also might be objected that the transfer might make a third party more envious because it worsens his position relative to someone else. I find it incomprehensible how this can be thought to involve a claim of justice. On envy, see Chapter 8 [of *Anarchy, State, and Utopia*].

Here and elsewhere in this chapter, a theory which incorporates elements of pure procedural justice might find what I say acceptable, *if* kept in its proper place; that is, if background institutions exist to ensure the satisfaction of certain conditions on distributive shares. But if these institutions are not themselves the sum or invisible-hand result of people's voluntary (nonaggressive) actions, the constraints they impose require justification. At no point does *our* argument assume any background institutions more extensive than those of the minimal night-watchman state, a state limited to protecting persons against murder, assault, theft, fraud, and so forth.

Robert Nozick, *Anarchy, State and Utopia* (New York: Basic Books/Oxford: Blackwell, 1974), pp. 160–4, 262–5.

Chapter 38

G. A. Cohen, from "Illusions about Private Property and Freedom" (1981)

Freedom to buy and sell is one freedom, of which in capitalism there is a great deal. It belongs to capitalism's essential nature. But many think that capitalism is, quite as essentially, a more comprehensively free society. Very many people, including philosophers, who try to speak carefully, use the phrase 'free society' as an alternative name for societies which are capitalist. And many contemporary English-speaking philosophers and economists call the doctrine which recommends a purely capitalist society 'libertarianism', not, as might be thought more apt, 'libertarianism with respect to buying and selling'.

It is not only the libertarians themselves who think that is the right name for their party. Many who reject their aims concede the name to them: they agree that unmodified capitalism is comprehensively a realm of freedom. This applies to *some* of those who call themselves 'liberals'.

These liberals assert, plausibly, that liberty is a good thing, but they say that it is not the only good thing. So far, libertarians will agree. But liberals also believe that libertarians wrongly sacrifice other good things in too total defence of the one good of liberty. They agree with libertarians that pure capitalism is liberty pure and simple, or anyway *economic* liberty pure and simple, but they think the various good things lost when liberty pure and simple is the rule justify restraints on liberty.

They want a capitalism modified by welfare legislation and state intervention in the market. They advocate, they say, not unrestrained liberty, but liberty restrained by the demands of social and economic security. They think that what they call a free economy is too damaging to those, who, by nature or circumstance, are ill placed to achieve a minimally proper standard of life within it, so they favour, within limits, taxing the better off for the sake of the worse off, although they believe that such taxation reduces liberty. They also think that what they call a free economy is subject to fluctuations in productive activity and misallocations of resources which are potentially damaging to everyone, so they favour measures of interference in the market, although, again, they believe that such interventions diminish liberty. They do not question the libertarian's description of capitalism as the (economically) free society. But they believe that economic freedom may rightly and reasonably be abridged. They believe in a compromise between liberty and other values, and that what is known as the welfare state mixed economy achieves the right compromise.

I shall argue that libertarians, and liberals of the kind described, misuse the concept of freedom. This is not a comment on the attractiveness of the institutions they severally favour, but on the rhetoric they use to describe them. If, however, as I contend, they misdescribe those institutions, then that is surely because the correct description of them would make them less attractive, so my critique of the defensive rhetoric is indirectly a critique of the institutions the rhetoric defends.

My central contention is that liberals and libertarians see the freedom which is intrinsic to capitalism, but do not give proper notice to the unfreedom which necessarily accompanies it.

To expose this failure of perception, I shall criticise a description of the libertarian position provided by Antony Flew in his *Dictionary of Philosophy*. It is there said to be 'wholehearted political and economic liberalism, opposed to any social or legal constraints on individual freedom'. Liberals of the kind I described above would avow themselves unwholehearted in the terms of this definition. For they would say that they support certain (at any rate) legal constraints on individual freedom.

Now a society in which there are *no* 'social and legal constraints on individual freedom' is perhaps imaginable, at any rate by people who have highly anarchic imaginations. But, be that as it may, the Flew definition misdescribes libertarians, since it does not apply to defenders of capitalism, which is what libertarians profess to be, and are.

For consider. If the state prevents me from doing something I want to do, it evidently places a constraint on my freedom. Suppose, then, that I want to perform an action which involves a legally prohibited use of your property. I want, let us say, to pitch a tent in your large back garden, because I have no home or land of my own, but I have got hold of a tent, legitimately or otherwise. If I now try to do what I want to do, the chances are that the state will intervene on your behalf. If it does, I shall suffer a constraint on my freedom. The same goes for all unpermitted uses of a piece of private property by those who do not own it, and there are always those who do not own it, since 'private ownership by one person . . . presupposes non-ownership on the part

of other persons'. But the free enterprise economy advocated by libertarians rests upon private property: you can sell and buy only what you respectively own and come to own. It follows that the Flew definition is untrue to its *definiendum*, and that 'libertarianism' is a questionable name for the position it now standardly denotes.

How could Flew publish the definition I have criticised? I do not think he was being dishonest. I would not accuse him of appreciating the truth of this particular matter and deliberately falsifying it. Why then is it that Flew, and libertarians like him, see the unfreedom in prospective state interference with your use of your property, but do not see the unfreedom in the standing intervention against my use of it entailed by the fact that it *is* your private property? What explains their monocular vision?

One explanation is a tendency to take as part of the structure of human existence in general, and therefore as no 'social or legal constraint' on freedom, any structure around which, *merely as things are*, much of our activity is organised. In capitalist society the institution of private property is such a structure. It is treated as so *given* that the obstacles it puts on freedom are not perceived, while any impingement on private property itself is immediately noticed. Yet private property pretty well *is* a distribution of freedom *and* unfreedom. It is necessarily associated with the liberty of private owners to do as they wish with what they own, but it no less necessarily withdraws liberty from those who do not own it. To think of capitalism as a realm of freedom is to overlook half of its nature. (I am aware that the tendency to this failure of perception is stronger, other things being equal, the more private property a person has. I do not think really poor people need to have their eyes opened to the simple conceptual truth I emphasise. I also do not claim that anyone of sound mind will for long deny that private property places restrictions on freedom, once the point has been made. What is striking is that the point so often needs to be made, against what should be *obvious* absurdities, such as Flew's definition of 'libertarianism').

I have supposed that to prevent someone from doing something he wants to do is to make him, in that respect, unfree: I am unfree whenever someone interferes, *justifiably or otherwise*, with my actions. But there is a definition of freedom which is implicit in much libertarian writing, and which entails that interference is *not* a sufficient condition of unfreedom. On that definition, which I shall call the *moralised* definition, I am unfree only when someone does or would *unjustifiably* interfere with me. If one now combines this moralised definition of freedom with a moral endorsement of private property, one reaches the result that the protection of legitimate private property cannot restrict anyone's freedom. It will follow from the moral endorsement of private property that you and the police are justified in preventing me from pitching my tent on your land, and, because of the moralised definition of freedom, it will then further follow that you and the police do not thereby restrict my freedom. So here we have another explanation of how intelligent philosophers are able to say what they do about capitalism, private property and freedom. But the characterisation of freedom which figures in the explanation is unacceptable. For it entails that a properly convicted murderer is not rendered unfree when he is justifiably imprisoned.

G. A. Cohen, "Illusions about Private Property and Freedom," from J. Mepham and D. H. Ruben (eds.), *Issues in Marxist Philosophy*, vol. 4 (Brighton: Harvester, 1981), pp. 225–8.

Chapter 39

S. I. Benn and W. L. Weinstein, from "Being Free to Act, and Being a Free Man" (1971)

It is now something of a commonplace that to know whether a man is free we must know what he is supposed to be free from, and what free to do. The concept "freedom" includes, as it were, two variables, which must be supplied either explicitly or contextually. However, we cannot assign just *any* value to these variables, for there are certain characteristics of the concept that limit what in general one can appropriately say one is free from, and free to do. One object of this paper is to identify these restrictive conditions; another, to show that they arise in moral and political discourse, in part at least from the normative functions of "freedom". From the analysis of certain paradoxical situations, as where one wants to say that a man was not free to do something that he nevertheless did freely, we shall argue that underlying and presupposed by the concept of freedom of action there is another but related concept, that of autonomy – of the free man as chooser.

I

In a recent article, Gerald C. MacCallum questioned whether one could properly distinguish between "freedom from . . ." and "freedom to . . ." in relation to actions and agents, as though there were here two distinct concepts of "freedom". Whenever the freedom of agents is in question, he says, it always refers (explicitly or by contextual implication) to a triadic relation, between an agent, some preventing conditions said to be absent, and "actions, or conditions of character of circumstance" (that the agent is free to do, become, or attain). MacCallum's claim is restricted to freedom of agents; there are other, dyadic uses of "free of" and "free from", as in "the sky is now free from clouds", "his record is free of blemish", but in such cases "free of/from" means simply "rid of" or "without".

Now although our present discussion will be mainly about "freedom" in political discourse, these more primitive dyadic uses suggest certain pointers. It is appropriate to say that a man is free from sin, fault, or awkwardness, but not from merit, virtue, or skill. We congratulate ourselves on being free from care, poverty, and fatigue; but cannot correspondingly complain that we are free from nourishment, riches, or rest. It seems that whenever we say of a person that he is free from X, or free of X, X is either a flaw, or it is some condition contrary to that person's supposed interest. To say that he was now free of his wealth would be to say, in a deliberately paradoxical way, that he was better off without it; indeed, it would be a way of revising accepted standards of what is in man's interest.

What sort of things is it appropriate to say we are free to *do*? To run, to invest one's money, or to steal are all things that anyone might without eccentricity want to do, either for the satisfaction of just doing them, or because they promised some advantage. And there is nothing odd in rejoicing that one is free to do them, or in complaining that one is not. But there is something paradoxical about saying that a person is either free or not free to starve, cut off his ears, or to die; one would commonly add the ironic qualification: "if he wants to", precisely on account of the standard association between "being free" and experiences or activities normally regarded as worthwhile, either intrinsically or instrumentally. Of course, one can appropriately say that Jones is or is not free to do something, like bird-watching in the gardens of Buckingham Palace, without *his* having an actual interest in doing it. Nevertheless it is apposite to discuss whether he is free to do it only if it is a possible object of reasonable choice; cutting off one's ears is not the sort of thing anyone, in a standard range of conditions, would reasonably do, *i.e.* "no one in his senses would think of doing such a thing" (even though some people have, in fact, done it). It is not a question of logical absurdity; rather, to see the point of saying that one is (or is not) free to do X, we must be able to see that there might be some point in doing it. Our conception of freedom is bounded by our notions of what might be worthwhile doing; it is out of its element when we find its objects bizarre. Incomprehension, not hostility, is the first obstacle to toleration.

II

Since only acts that have some point are appropriate complements for "freedom to . . .", the scope of the concept is governed by whatever criteria determine what such actions are. Similarly, there are criteria governing what one can appropriately complain of not being free from, i.e. what counts as an interference or as restricting choice. These criteria, we shall argue, also depend on standards of reasonable conduct and expectation.

Liberty (according to Hobbes) is the absence of all the impediments to action that are not contained in the nature and intrinsical quality of the agent. As for example, the water is said to descend freely, or to have liberty to descend by the channel of the river, because there is no impediment that way, but not across, because the banks are impediments. And though the water cannot ascend, yet men never say it wants the *liberty* to ascend, but the *faculty* or *power*, because the impediment is in the nature of the water, and intrinsical.

The point of Hobbes's definition was to give a meaning to "liberty" consistent with a determinist theory of human action; if the motions of material objects could be free while causally determined, so could the actions of human beings. Yet the cause of the water's natural motion is not, after all, contained in the nature of the water – "intrinsical", but in its gravitational relation with the earth; and if we continue to talk about free flow and free fall, it is because we are presupposing a system of normal or standard conditions, with correspondingly normal or natural motions, which may, however, be deflected or inhibited by forces external to the system (like dams or parachutes). It turns out, then, that the distinction between intrinsic and extrinsic causes makes between sense in respect of agents of whom we can say that they try and decide, than it does for the motion of water or falling bodies. For whatever causal account, if any, that one may wish to give of trying and deciding, when one says "he did not go to the opera because he wanted to go to bed early instead", one implies that he could have gone had he wanted, *i.e.* he was free to go – it was his own decision, not something external to him like a car breakdown, nor something physical that just happened to him like a stroke, that made it impossible for him to go.

Now this distinction between internal and external determination takes us only a little way. For if I decide against a course of action to avoid threatened penalties am I free or unfree, determined by intrinsic or extrinsic factors? And if unfree, is the man who decides *for* that course, in spite of the penalty, freer on that account? And is the man who does the only thing the law permits him to do, but who would have done it anyway, freer than either, though one can quite properly say of him "he really had to choice"? The conception of freedom as the absence of impediments or constraints in unsatisfactory precisely because neither the man who would have acted in the same way in any event, nor the one who goes ahead despite the penalty, seems to be impeded, but only the one actually deterred; but it is odd to say that he alone is therefore unfree.

The phrase "he really had no choice" suggests that a better way of characterizing conditions of unfreedom is that they restrict choice by making alternatives unavailable or ineligible. So *all* the following cases would now qualify as instances of unfreedom:

(1)   where the act done would *not* have been done had the alternative been available;

(2)   where another act *would* have been done, had it not been made unavailable (the obverse of (1));

(3)   where the act enjoined and performed would still have been chosen had alternatives been available (here, however, one might say that "compliance is given freely");

(4)   where the alternative is unavailable, but the agent decides to take it all the same. This is the case where the agent freely does what he is unfree to do.

(3) and (4) clearly raise new problems, which we shall explore more fully later. Before doing so, however, we have to consider what constitutes a restriction on choice. This comes close to the heart of the question "What are the criteria for freedom of action?"

[. . .]

IV

Since freedom is a principle, whatever interferes with it demands to be justified; conse-

quently, only those determining conditions for which rational agents (God or man) can be held responsible can qualify as interfering with it. But it does not follow that whenever one man's act influences or even frustrates another's, the characteristic demand for justification can appropriately be made. There are influences that do not restrict their subject's range of choice, and therefore do not need to be justified as interferences with freedom. There are others, like offering bribes or invasions of privacy, that do need justification, but on the grounds that they interfere with interests other than freedom.

The least problematic influence is a simple request. Suppose John asked George to lend him £50; George may have inquired why he wanted it, but it would have been out of place to ask John what *right* he had to make the request; for John did not have to have a right – everyone is at liberty to ask, just as everyone is at liberty to refuse. John's asking impaired no interest of George's (though if he agreed to it George may have impaired his own). It did not even interfere with George's most primitive freedom, to be allowed to go his own way. Nevertheless, John's request may have influenced George – George would not have given him £50 had he not asked. But that is not enough to constitute it an interference with George's range of choices; for that, it would have had to be not merely a necessary but a sufficient condition for George's decision – and we have no reason for saying it was. A request may confront one with a new alternative; but one decides oneself whether to adopt it. Suppose, however, that John manipulates George's feelings, *e.g.* of guilt about his wealth; this pressure may be a sufficient condition for George's compliance, and therefore an interference with his freedom. Of course, in some circumstances such an interference may be perfectly justified; but justified or not, it *needs* justifying, as the simple request does not.

John's influence over George's conduct may be decisive in other ways; for instance he may point out facts that he has overlooked, make clear what alternatives *are* open to him, or offer him disinterested advice. In none of these cases would John normally be called on to justify his action, though he may, of course, be required to give grounds for his opinion. Offering advice as such – even bad advice – calls for no justification; for George may disregard it if he likes; the mere offering of it puts no pressure on him. Moreover, though it may seem to George that courses that he formerly contemplated as possible alternatives have now been closed to him, those he now sees as impossible always were; and those he now sees only as undesirable are still open – his rejecting them makes them no less available to be chosen. So John has done nothing to restrict George's options and nothing, therefore, that needs justification as affecting George's freedom. However, tendering uncalled-for advice or asking for a loan may require justification because they invade not his freedom but his privacy. The liberty to act in these ways is restricted, in some cultures at least, to people standing in a particular social relation; the intruder causes embarrassment, and is thus, if in only a minor way, attacking a legitimate interest. But such an interference does not make George unfree; no option is closed that would otherwise be open. The offence, such as it is, touches him in quite a different way.

Making an offer, of trade or employment, is another way of influencing a person's action which calls for no justification since it limits no otherwise available alternatives. On the contrary, it enlarges them; one may either accept an offer or do precisely what one would have done had it not been made; one cannot be less free than before. So far, at least, there is nothing to justify.

Considering freedom as the non-restriction of options, rather than as the absence of impediments, we can readily distinguish straightforward business offers from extortion. The shopkeeper who offers eggs at 62 cents a dozen rather than giving them away might be said to impede my obtaining eggs if I have no money. But it would be odd to say

that he interferes with my freedom, like the highwayman who takes my purse as the price of my passing. This is because the general framework of property relations is taken to define the normal conditions of action, and therefore the initial opportunities or alternatives available, just as the laws of mechanics determine the conditions under which we can fly. The earth's gravitation could be said to impede my flying – but it could as well be said to define the opportunities for flying available to me – *e.g.* if I have an aeroplane or a balloon, but not otherwise. Given the laws of property, I cannot complain that I am being deprived of free eggs as I can of the highwayman's denying me free passage. Having free eggs was never open to me anyway. Of course, it is a well-established move in radical argument to call in question the hitherto given initial conditions, like property institutions, by arguing that they *do* close alternatives otherwise available, because there is nothing illegitimate nor logically nor practically absurd, in envisaging a social order in which they would be absent, or at least different. Short of a revision of this kind, however, trading or market offers do not narrow options – on the contrary, they enlarge them, to the advantage of the respondent, and, *prima facie*, injuring no one else. But does not a bribe also enlarge the respondent's opportunities? Indeed, it does; but then, from the point of view of the respondent's freedom it is unobjectionable. Offering a bribe is properly an offence not because it makes anyone unfree but because it attacks the public interest, giving someone a motive for betraying a trust or neglecting a duty.

But this is clearly not the full story. For a man really desperate for money the offer of a bribe may be quite irresistible. Indeed, his defence might be that in accepting it he was not responsible for what he was doing – he was not a free agent.

Or consider the case of exploitation: Esau, faint unto death, was in no position to haggle with Jacob over the price of a bowl of soup. Though the form of an offer may suggest that the respondent can decide for himself whether to take it or leave it, it may still put pressure on him to accept it as effective as any threat. Exploitation – using some special bargaining power to demand more than a commodity would cost in some normal circumstances, or offering less for a service (*e.g.* in wages) than it is worth (by some similar standard) – is always *unfair*; but it is only when to turn the offer down would be to suffer real deprivation, so that one could say "I have no alternative but to accept" (*e.g.* Esau's situation, or that of an unemployed worker offered a poorly-paid job in a depression) that we are inclined to talk not only of injustice but also of unfreedom. Even so, it might still be objected that though Esau was not free to refuse Jacob's offer, this was because there happened to be no other alternative course that a reasonable, prudent man would consider eligible – not that Jacob had *deprived* him of alternatives to accepting. For he had not. All the same, we should certainly regard Esau as having contracted under duress, a condition sufficient to void the contract. But it is because the price is unreasonably high that one calls it duress; desperate need alone would not be sufficient if the price were reasonable. Jacob used the power fortuitously given him by Esau's abnormal situation to induce him to agree to a bargain that, by *normal standards and in normal circumstances* would be contrary to his interests, and therefore unreasonable. The concept of duress thus involves two standards, first, a standard price that it is reasonable to pay for a type of good or service; and second, a standard of what would be a reasonable alternative, in the absence of which one is vulnerable to pressure. Thus one may plead unfreedom in order to rebut contractual claims if one can argue both that the consideration one derives from the agreement is incommensurate with the sacrifice incurred, and that one would not have made such an agreement but for one's being in an abnormally weak bargaining position, that is to say, not having the kind of reasonable alternative normally available. In practice, the Courts may interpret these standards very strictly; they may be very reluctant to deter-

mine whether the consideration derived from a contract is incommensurate with the cost incurred. Our object here, however, is to point out the standards implied by a plea of duress, whether or not it is acceptable.

This analysis of duress suggests that the source of unfreedom is not merely the exploiter's price, but also the circumstances that give him his bargaining power. And this helps to explain a difference between the classical economic liberal and the socialist radical. An unemployed worker may be unable to refuse a poorly-paid job when no more favourable opportunities are open to him. But for the liberal, unless the employer has arranged things this way himself (*e.g.* by a blacklist or by monopoly), he is merely acting appropriately in economic conditions that are not of his making – he is not responsible for the other party's desperate need; neither is he committing an injustice in offering the wage he does. For the only available standard by which to judge the reasonableness of the wage is the competitive market rate. So the worker cannot complain of duress, but only of misfortune. No one makes him unfree. The radical socialist, however, claims that the worker's wage can be judged against a standard of need, or of what it might be in a different economic order. By such a standard, it is unreasonable. Moreover, he believes the system could be changed; society alone, or its ruling minority, is responsible for there being no reasonable alternative to the job offered. In the absence of such an alternative, the worker is vulnerable to pressure, and therefore under duress.

V

We are now in a position to return to two problems referred to earlier, (1) whether the man is free who would do anyway, of his own free will, what the law requires him by threats to do, *e.g.* the situation of the conscientious Church member when tithing is compulsory; and (2) whether Francis who is unfree by law to murder Gerald but does so all the same, must on that account be said to have been free to do so.[1]

The tithing case calls for a distinction between the conditions under which one can say that a man in doing something does it freely, and the conditions in which one can speak of his having freedom in that respect. If tithing is compulsory, I have no choice but to pay even though if I had such a choice, I should still pay. The range of alternatives open to me does not depend on my preference for one rather than another; consequently, to eliminate an otherwise available alternative, *i.e.* non-tithing with impunity, is just as much an interference with freedom, whether or not I should have chosen it had it been available. To abridge the possibility of choice is to abridge freedom. Nevertheless, we obviously want to be able to distinguish the man who acts as he does only *because* this is the only possibility left open, from the man who would act in the same way whatever the possibilities, to whose *action* the absence of other possibilities is irrelevant. Yet even for him, the possibility of reviewing his action, of deciding whether to go on acting in this way, or indeed of regretting having done so up till now, is closed – for it is pointless to regret the unavoidable.

We have been arguing so far as though any legal prescription to which a sanction is attached automatically puts all alternative courses out of reach. But this, of course, cannot be true, since people wittingly break the law. Nevertheless, it remains important to retain a way of distinguishing the unfreedom of the man who will be punished if (and because) he does what he wants, from the freedom of the man who will not. To have to say (as some recent behavioural political scientists have said) that "the greater an actor's desire to perform a punishable action, the penalty remaining constant, the greater his freedom to do so",[2] is to pay too high a price for a solution to the paradox that criminals freely commit crimes they are not free to commit. Consider Hobbes's way of dealing with the problem: "All actions", wrote Hobbes, "that men do in commonwealths for

fear of the law are actions which the doers had liberty to omit." For to give a man an additional motive for action (*i.e.* fear of punishment) to set against whatever motives he may have, makes him no less free. He may choose to disobey if he will and take the consequences:

> as when a man throweth his goods into the sea for fear the ship should sink, he doth it nevertheless very willingly, and may refuse to do it if he will . . . So a man sometimes pays his debt only for fear of imprisonment, which because nobody hindered him from detaining, was the action of a man at liberty. (*Leviathan*, chapter XXI).

This looks, to a liberal, wilfully perverse. Action under coercion or threat is, for the liberal, the very paradigm of unfreedom; the incompatibility of freedom and coercion is, after all, what classical Liberalism is all about. For all that, Hobbes's paradox can help to distinguish the kind of unfreedom we have been mainly concerned with so far, from that which arises from manipulation by certain techniques of persuasion and conditioning. It also illuminates the sort of action model that Hobbes, like many other liberal social philosophers, regarded as standard.

The model is that of a man wanting to do something, threatened with legal penalties if he does it, and freely deciding it would not be worth it. Still, when Hobbes remarks "that in all kinds of actions by the laws praetermitted, men have the liberty, of doing what their own reasons shall suggest, for the most profitable to themselves" (*Leviathan*, chapter XXI), he implies that in those things forbidden by the law, men are not free, at least in the same sense. It is, of course, true that there is a rule-derived sense in which a person is unfree to do anything forbidden by a rule (*i.e.* not "praetermitted"), irrespective of any sanction, as one is unfree to move a pawn backwards in chess. If A has undertaken to have dinner with B this evening, A is not free to accept another invitation. He has already limited the alternatives he is *entitled* to choose among. But he *could* break his promise, all the same – there is nothing to stop him. So he is free to decide whether to honour his obligation or not. But suppose a penalty is attached to his breaking faith; now, quite apart from wholly rule-derived unfreedom, he is not free to do what he would otherwise like to do (to do X) because he cannot now do X without also attracting the penalty (P), and X is not worth doing on those terms. Hobbes would maintain that this is consistent with freedom – A would have chosen X had it been open to him, but in fact it is not – it is X + P rather than X that is the available alternative to not-X. A sensibly prefers not-X. There *are* people who might prefer X + P and, as Cassinelli remarks,[3] it is "logically most cumbersome to say that a man is unfree to perform an activity he in fact performs." Can a conscientious objector in prison for refusing to obey orders claim that he was unfree to refuse? Yet another, less steadfast, might very well explain that, his appeal having been rejected, he was no longer free to refuse – it was quite unreasonable to expect anyone to do X if he also had to suffer P; only someone with a disordered scale of values, or one of quite superhuman steadfastness, a fanatic or a saint, would make such a choice. The unfreedom now in question is more substantial than pure rule-derived unfreedom: it is not merely that one is not *entitled* to consider X among the available alternatives; it is that X simpliciter no longer *is* available – but only X + P. The claim now is that by attaching penal sanctions to a course of action, the law has made it unavailable to any reasonably prudent man.

Still, even someone arguing in this way presupposes a kind of freedom – the freedom of a rational being, an economic man, making the most prudent choice he can among alternatives with different (if all rather unsatisfactory) utilities. The choice, it is true, may be rigged against him by someone with power to allot rewards or penalties (analogous to a monopolistic price-fixer), but given the conditions, he makes his own choice – he is still his own master. But if we accept this model, the man who submits to the law does so as freely, no more, no less, than the man who deliberately defies it.

How adequate a model is it?

There is a range of politically important forms of utterance in which "freedom" and "unfreedom" occur, each making its own characteristic kind of point. How far, then, do these forms all presuppose a model of rational choice? One such form has already emerged: we have shown that the man whose freedom is restricted by a law backed by a sanction may also be seen as choosing between obedience and disobedience. If he obeys or intends to obey, his account of his position as being unfree contains *an evaluation*, namely that it would be unreasonable to expect anyone in such circumstances to break the law, though admittedly some rash or unusually determined individuals might be able to break it in spite of the consequences.

This evaluation might be challenged by insisting that the law does not sufficiently foreclose other alternatives: "But you *could* still break the law." If to obey is to abandon some vital principle or some paramount interest or objective, the point of claiming "You still have a choice", in spite of the fact that choosing X incurs P, is to insist on the agent's responsibility for what he does in obeying, and perhaps to charge him with lack of will or faith. And this one does only if there is some good reason, overriding his prudential calculations, why he should disobey. So to insist that he was free to act is to alter his moral position; for example, it would expose to blame a soldier who complied with an order to torture prisoners. The point of denying that a threatened penalty is sufficient to determine the agent's action is to challenge the usual prudential defence. The agent's counter-plea that in his circumstances only a saint or a fanatic would have disobeyed, is a claim that the wrong standards are being applied to him, *i.e. he* could not be expected to disregard normal prudence.

Notes

1 Cf. C. W. Cassinelli, *Free Activities and Inter-personal Relations* (The Hague, 1966): "the frequency of premeditated murder . . . raises doubts whether the law ever makes men who contemplate murder unfree to commit it" (p. 33). ". . . if Francis made an attempt on Gerald's life, the law against murder obviously had not made him unfree to do so" (p. 34).

2 F. E. Oppenheim, *Dimensions of Freedom* (New York, 1961), p. 189. Cf. also C. W. Cassinelli, op. cit.

3 Op. cit., p. 34.

S. I. Benn and W. L. Weinstein, "Being Free to Act, and Being a Free Man," *Mind* 80 (1971), pp. 194–7, 200–8.

Chapter 40

David Miller, from "Constraints on Freedom" (1983)

Among the most intractable questions that political theorists are asked to consider are those concerning the overall amounts of freedom provided by particular social systems. Given that one such system offers to its members a specified set of opportunities and restrictions, promised rewards and threatened punishments, and so forth, how are we to judge the quantity of freedom enjoyed by a representative member? To make this more specific, consider two conflicting accounts of the freedom enjoyed by the majority of men under capitalism. On the first account, which I shall dub "libertarian," freedom under capitalism is restricted only by rules of law backed by sanctions and by such occurrences of force and fraud as the law fails to prevent.[1] Thus whatever the extent of inequality generated by the workings of the economy, the representative man enjoys a very great deal of freedom indeed, even if he lacks the ability or opportunity to perform a number of the actions that he is free to perform, such as becoming an employer of labor or dining at the Ritz. Capitalism, in this view, deserves its self-applied title "the free society," since it imposes only such restrictions on freedom as are necessary to secure an equal amount of freedom for all. On the second view, which I shall dub "socialist," this is very far from the case. Freedom under capitalism is unequally distributed, since freedom depends not only on the absence of legal restrictions, force, and fraud, but on having the effective opportunity to pursue courses of action. Moreover, since the major-

ity of men under capitalism are hired workers and since they lack the effective opportunity to perform many actions important to them, the average degree of freedom is small – indeed possibly smaller than under systems which impose many more legal restrictions on human action.

[...] The dispute is about narrower and broader conceptions of "constraint." I shall argue that this dispute cannot be definitively resolved because it depends upon ascriptions of moral responsibility for barriers to action, which depend in turn on the view taken of the obligations owed by one man to another. Libertarians and socialists may disagree ultimately because they hold conflicting theories of interpersonal moral obligation; by the same token, judgments about freedom cannot be wholly value-neutral, even leaving aside the aggregation problem. These conclusions will be reached through a close examination of the notion of a constraint. Finally I shall offer a persuasive defense of the socialist view, making it clear at what points the defense rests on assumptions about moral obligation.

I

Discussions of freedom and constraint usually and properly start from the distinction between being free to do something, being able to do it, and desiring to do it. A commonplace example illustrates the distinction in question. Suppose that I enjoy taking walks along the bank of a certain river, and consider the following three possibilities:

1. The local authority which administers the river bank erects fences around it and employs a warden to keep people off. When this happens I shall say that I am no longer free to take my walk.
2. Brambles grow and block the path so that I can't walk on the bank without tearing my clothes. In this event I shall say that although I am still free to walk there, I am no longer able to do so.
3. The river becomes littered with offensive debris. Under these circumstances I shall say that, although I am both free and able to walk, I no longer wish to do so.

We have here three changes in my environment, each of which has the same behavioral consequence (namely, that I cease walking on the river bank) but which we describe in different terms. In order to clarify the distinction we need to understand the point of making it. If we were only interested in behavior and its explanation, it might seem prodigal to have three alternative descriptions for the same behavioral change. But in fact we are equally interested in questions of justification. From that point of view, the source of an obstacle to potential action may be as important as its very existence. The concepts of ability and desirability make no reference to the genesis of the set of possible actions open to an agent, and the distinction between them is merely one of degree; that is, we say that an agent is unable to perform an action when it is literally impossible for him to perform it, or the performance would be so costly that it is effectively excluded from the scope of his consideration, while we say that an action is simply undesirable when the costs outweigh the benefits but not so overwhelmingly.[2] We use the notion of freedom, however, in the subclass of cases where the presence of an obstacle can be attributed to the action of another human being or beings, and we do so in order to draw attention to that fact. There are, in other words,

numerous instances which can equally properly be described as cases of unfreedom or of inability, and our choice of terms will depend on whether we want to emphasize the human source of the obstacle. If, in example 1 above, I wish merely to lament the fact that a pleasurable activity is no longer open to me, I may well say that I am unable to walk on the river bank; but if, in addition, I want to draw attention to the human agency responsible for the deprivation, I shall use the language of freedom.

This question about the origins of an obstacle is closely linked to a question about justification. Our language embodies a presumption that humans should not obstruct one another's activity. When we say of an obstacle that it renders a person unfree to act, we make a charge that stands in need of rebuttal. Reasons have to be given for the continued presence of the obstacle. Of course such reasons may not be far to seek. Many restrictions of freedom are justified, whether to protect the freedom of other agents, to promote competing values such as welfare and equality, or to protect the agent himself. It is a mistake to think that to describe a state of affairs as involving unfreedom is to settle a political argument; it is, however, to make a *move* in a political argument.[3] There is no such presumption in cases of inability which are not also describable as cases of unfreedom. Someone's inability to act in a certain way is morally or politically relevant only where the inability serves to bring other values into play. The fact that a speleologist is unable to escape from a cave moves us to act because we are independently concerned for his welfare; but the fact that millions of men are unable to fly to the moon moves us not at all.

In embodying this presumption our language of freedom reflects the view that "the nature of things does not madden us, only ill will does." From certain perspectives this view may appear irrational. A full-blooded determinist will see no relevant difference between obstacles brought about by human agency and obstacles arising from natural causes. If we were examining a society of robots and wanted to describe the options open to one particular robot, there would be no point in distinguishing actions that he was unfree to perform from actions that he was free but unable to perform. The behavior of the other robots would not appear to be a circumstance that was relevantly different from the rest of the environment. The language of social freedom presupposes a view of human agents as (in another sense) free and responsible for their actions.[4] We are thereby licensed to complain about restrictions of freedom in a way that would be inappropriate in the case of natural obstacles. This view of the human agent need not be a matter of controversy between libertarians and socialists. It is true that some socialists have wanted to define freedom as, for instance, the opportunity to satisfy all of one's needs, a definition which appears to obliterate the distinction between humanly caused and naturally occurring obstacles. But this might arise from the belief that all obstacles to the satisfaction of needs are as a matter of fact humanly caused, together with the belief that ordinary definitions of freedom invite too narrow an interpretation of the notion of constraint. (I hope that by the end of this essay the latter fear will be allayed.) It is hard to believe that anyone would, on political grounds alone, wish to obliterate the distinction between unfreedom and inability altogether. In any social system we can presently imagine, there will be some people with physical handicaps who are (as we should say) unable, though free, to act in various ways. Is it proposed that their disabilities should be treated as on a par with humanly imposed obstructions? What distortions in the allocation of resources might not arise if this equation were to be made? If the point is granted, the question becomes one of drawing the line between (mere) disability and unfreedom or, in other words, of determining when an obstacle should be considered a constraint on freedom. This, it seems to me, is the proper site for the contest between libertarians and socialists. The metaphysical challenge posed by a strong version of determinism can be kept to one side.

II

Having examined the context in which the problem about constraints arises we can now begin to investigate the problem itself. It has two main dimensions. First, what causal history must an obstacle to action have in order for it to count as a constraint on freedom? Up to now I have loosely contrasted "natural" obstacles with obstacles "attributable to human agency." How is this contrast to be made more precise? Second, how large must the obstacle itself be for it to count as a constraint? Must it, at one extreme, be an obstruction which renders the proposed action impossible? Or, at the other extreme, should any unwelcome feature that has been attached to an action count as a reduction in one's freedom to perform it? These two dimensions are obviously separate, but it will turn out that resolving the first issue helps to resolve the second. For the sake of clarity, I shall begin by considering cases where an action has been rendered impossible in order to tackle the causal history problem and then go on to look at various ways in which the hurdle might be lowered.

Take a simple, if mildly improbable, example. Suppose that I am the unfortunate possessor of a room whose door can only be opened from the outside, and consider the following ways in which I might become trapped in the room.

1. I am working in my room. Y, knowing that I am inside and wishing to confine me, pushes the door shut.
2. Y walks along the corridor and, without checking to see whether anybody is inside, closes my door.
3. The wind blows the door shut. It is Y's job to check rooms at 7 P.M. each evening, but he is engaged on a private errand, and this evening he fails to do so.
4. The wind blows the door shut. At 6.30 P.M. I call to a passerby to unlock the

door, but the passerby, who knows about Y's duties, is busy and pays no attention.

5. Y, whose job it is to check rooms, comes to my room and looks round it. I have concealed myself in a cupboard and he closes the door without having seen me.

6. The wind blows the door shut. There is no one assigned to check rooms, and no passerby within earshot.

We are likely to be most confident in our judgments about cases 1 and 6. In case 1 I am rendered unable to leave my room by the deliberate action of another human being, and this is clearly a case where I have been made unfree to leave by Y. On the other hand, in case 6 the cause of my imprisonment is entirely natural and we should say that I am free but unable to leave.[5] The intermediate cases are more complex. In cases 2 and 5 Y's action is the main cause of my confinement, but in another respect the cases are significantly different. In case 2 Y, although not intending to imprison me, behaves in a negligent fashion. Shutting doors without checking to see whether anyone is behind them is, in the circumstances, likely to lead to people being trapped. Y ought to know this. In case 5, by contrast, Y does everything that could reasonably be expected of someone whose job it is to check rooms. My imprisonment results from a quite unforeseeable combination of circumstances, notwithstanding the fact that Y's action is its direct cause. We should normally mark this difference by saying that Y was responsible for my imprisonment in case 2 but not in case 5. "Responsible" here must plainly mean "morally responsible" rather than "causally responsible," since Y's causal role is approximately the same in both cases. I suggest that this gives us grounds for saying that Y has rendered me unfree to leave in case 2 but not in case 5.

Before considering more fully why this should be so, let me deal with cases 3 and 4. In case 3 the main cause of my imprisonment is a natural event, but a contributory cause is

Y's omission, his failure to check the room at the appropriate time. Y has an obligation to check rooms and so is morally responsible for my subsequent confinement. In case 4, on the other hand, the passerby is so placed that he could if he wished release me, but in the circumstances he has no obligation to do so.[6] From a causal point of view his omission is partly responsible for my confinement, but from a moral point of view he is not responsible at all. This difference permits us to say that in case 3 I am unfree to leave my room from 7 P.M. on (when Y is supposed to check), whereas in case 4 I am merely unable to leave from 6.30 P.M. and 7 P.M. (between the passerby's passing and Y's arriving).

I have identified three cases in which some Y may be held morally responsible for the existence of an obstacle to some X's action: Y may have imposed the obstacle intentionally, he may have imposed it negligently, or he may have failed to remove it despite having an obligation to do so. Why should moral responsibility so understood be the appropriate criterion for distinguishing between constraints on freedom and other hindrances to action? Notice that to say someone is morally responsible for a state of affairs is *not* to say that he is blameable for it, though it is to say that he is liable to blame if he fails to provide a justification for his conduct. Thus in case 3 Y might admit that he was responsible for my imprisonment but defend himself by stressing the importance of his private mission. This feature of the concept of moral responsibility precisely mirrors a feature of the concept of freedom which has already been noted. When we describe a person as unfree to do something we imply that an obstacle exists which stands in need of justification, and we are in effect calling upon the human race collectively to vindicate its behavior in permitting the obstacle to exist. At the same time we allow that such justification may be forthcoming: we distinguish unfreedom from unjustified unfreedom.[7] This suggests very strongly that the appropriate condition for regarding an obstacle as a constraint on freedom is that some other person or persons can be held morally responsible for its existence. When that condition obtains, we have achieved our two desiderata, namely, that the obstacle stands in need of justification and that justification may nonetheless be possible.

If this criterion were to be rejected, what other possibilities might be open to us? First we might say that obstacles were constraints on freedom only when they were deliberately imposed by other human agents. Second, we might argue that the relevant dividing line lay between obstacles that human beings had imposed (deliberately or not) and those they had merely failed to remove. Third, we might propose that a constraint on freedom was any obstacle for whose existence other humans were causally responsible, in whole or in part. Each of these proposals is unsatisfactory, as I shall try to show.

The first suggestion has some defenders – for instance it serves as the starting point for Berlin's classic account of negative liberty, though Berlin does not hold the position consistently – and it seems to capture the idea that "ill will" is what maddens us. But reflecting a little further along these lines, it is difficult to see why we should always resent deliberate obstruction more than, say, obstruction which is a by-product of action in pursuit of other ends. If a law is passed which is aimed at preventing me from leaving the country, I should regard it as an infringement of my freedom. But equally if a law is passed which requires me to repay the costs of my professional training (which I cannot as it happens do without remaining in the country), I shall to the same degree regard myself as unfree to leave. Indeed I may rail more strongly against incompetent legislators who fail to foresee the consequences of their actions than against misguided legislators who act in the light of sincere (though in my view mistaken) convictions.

The second proposal relies on a distinction between acts and omissions, between what people do and what they fail to do. It therefore faces two critical difficulties connected with that distinction. The first is simply one of drawing the dividing line in a clear way. If I allow trees to grow on my land which prevent you from driving your car into your garage, have I blocked your drive or merely failed to keep it clear? Either description of my behavior – as an act or as an omission – seems about as plausible as the other. The distinction might perhaps be firmed up in some ingenious way. But then the second problem is that by itself it seems to have no moral significance. For although the distinction might be *correlated* to some extent with features of behavior that are morally significant, the bare contrast between an act and an omission is not. It may, for instance, turn out that agents are morally responsible for the results of a larger proportion of those pieces of behavior we should call acts than of those pieces of behavior we should call omissions; but it does not of course follow from this that to describe a piece of behavior as an act (or an omission) is to say anything morally relevant about it. Now since I have assumed that the distinction between unfreedom and mere inability is morally loaded, it seems unlikely that it should rest on a distinction that is not.

What the supporter of the second proposal has to show is that there are no cases in which agents are rendered unfree by others' omissions. But consider the case in which I am caving with a companion who is trapped by a fall of rock. If I fail to make reasonable attempts to extricate him, how can I avoid conceding that he is now unfree to escape? To load the moral dice still further, suppose that I deliberately leave him trapped because I have designs upon his wife. My omission is then intentional but it is still on any reasonable account an omission. Why should this state of affairs be described differently in terms of freedom from one in which I precipitate the rock fall myself?

The final suggestion is that any obstacle for which human agents are in some way or other causally responsible should be regarded as a constraint on freedom. This might on the face of it seem a reasonable way of explaining the distinction between naturally occurring and humanly caused obstacles. But if the proposal is not to collapse into some version of the acts-and-omissions doctrine, the notion of causal responsibility must be interpreted very broadly indeed. A constraint will have to be defined as any obstacle which it is possible for human beings to remove or fail to impose. This means in effect that the scope of mere inability will shrink almost to vanishing point; for who can say what impediments to individual action might not be removed by the concerted efforts of men? For instance, all those who wished to fly to the moon might be able to do so, if human resources were devoted entirely to this end, at the expense of all the other projects on which we are now engaged. In that case we should have to say that men are now unfree to fly to the moon; among the causal conditions of their inability is the fact that the rest of the human race has not devoted itself single-mindedly to that aim.[8] It seems clear to me that this is not a helpful extension of the concept of freedom; it fails entirely to capture the intentions of those who want to retain a distinction between inability and unfreedom. One should, in other words, either abandon the distinction altogether or reject the third proposal as extending the limits of unfreedom absurdly far.

Having eliminated several alternatives, we may return to my original proposal that constraints should be identified as those obstacles for whose existence other men are morally responsible. The practical implications of this proposal will depend on the account we give of moral responsibility: for how much of our conduct can we be made to answer morally? Here our view of moral obligation is crucial. In the series of examples involving the self-locking door, I tacitly invoked an everyday understanding of obligations, for instance those of janitors and casual passerby. A utilitarian view of obligation would on the other hand produce what has been called the "strong doctrine of responsibility," namely, that we are morally responsible for outcomes to the extent to which we are causally respon-

sible for them. Acceptance of this view would bring us by a different route to the unacceptable conclusions of the third proposal outlined above. I assume, therefore, that our theory of freedom will rest on a view of obligation that does not entail our being obliged to do everything in our power to promote human welfare; in other words, on a view of limited obligation and therefore of limited responsibility. This still leaves open, as we shall see later, a wide field for controversy.

[…]

V

We may now begin to apply our analysis of freedom to the debate between libertarians and socialists outlined at the beginning of the paper. The key question is whether the distribution of wealth and the structure of opportunities facing the members of a capitalist society is relevant to an assessment of the degree of freedom each enjoys. One conclusion that follows directly from our analysis is that nothing in the nature of a wealth-and-opportunity distribution disqualifies it from featuring in a discussion of freedom. If it is impossible for me to obtain education of a certain kind because none is available, or if large price tags are attached to goods that I desire, these obstacles potentially constrain my freedom as much as legal prohibitions. From the point of view of social freedom, legal obstacles have no special status. Equally, it is not a decisive argument against regarding a wealth-and-opportunity distribution as constraining that no one has intended the distribution to take the form that it has. Intention is not a necessary condition of moral responsibility.

Interestingly enough, even such committed libertarians as Hayek and Nozick concede that the price attached to a good may infringe the freedom of potential consumers in the special case of a monopoly. Both discuss the example of a person who owns the only water hole in the desert and charges extravagantly for water. Both regard this as an exception to the normal rule that refusing to supply others with things except at your price does not reduce their freedom. But in attempting to distinguish such a monopolistic exchange from other market transactions they set out along different paths. Hayek concentrates on the position of the person who needs the water and argues that the exchange is potentially coercive only because one party faces severe deprivation if the exchange fails to occur. "So long as the services of a particular person are not crucial to my existence or the preservation of what I most value, the conditions he exacts for rendering these services cannot properly be called 'coercion.'" Nozick, on the other hand, focuses on the well owner, arguing that he has violated the "Lockean proviso" – that one may acquire property only when there is "enough and as good left in common for others" – unless he can show that the well's continuing to flow is attributable to his efforts. The difficulty with Hayek's view is that it introduces an unwanted subjective element into judgments about freedom: whether someone's refusal to supply me with a good except on his own terms constitutes a constraint will depend on whether the good is "crucial to my existence or the preservation of what I most value," so the scope of freedom will change as my values change. The difficulty with Nozick's argument is that it applies equally to the fair-minded well owner who charges only a moderate price for his water, say a price that covers his costs and gives him an average return for his labor in the prevailing economic conditions. Such a person cannot plausibly be seen as constraining his customers.

Neither argument is satisfactory because each tries to handle the problem of monopoly without introducing positive interpersonal moral obligations. The libertarian position rests on the premise that all one man owes another is noninterference with his actions. I may not kill or imprison you, but I have no obligation to keep you alive or release you from natural entombment (these things may be morally desirable, but are not obligatory). Charging a price for some good cannot be

seen as interference, and so it can only be brought within the scope of unfreedom by an ad hoc maneuver in the case of monopoly. But we cannot properly understand what is objectionable about the practice of the monopolist without bringing in positive obligations. In the earlier discussion of the circumstances under which a shopkeeper might be judged to interfere with the freedom of his customers through the prices he attached to his goods, I invoked two such obligations: the obligation to ensure that the needs of others are met, and the obligation to deal fairly with people placed in a dependent position. Together, these imply, first, that a water-hole monopolist is obliged to supply water to those in need, so withholding water can properly be regarded as an infringement of freedom. But this by itself dose not settle the terms on which the water is to be offered. The second condition requires that the price be fair – that is, not what the consumer might be prepared to pay given his needy condition and his dependence on one supplier, but the price that could be charged under "normal" circumstances. The relevant benchmark here may be either what the customer would pay if he were not in need or what the supplier could charge if forced to compete with other suppliers.[9] The price that is actually charged will be a constraint to the extent that it rises above the fair price.

But having invoked these obligations in order to give a satisfactory explanation of our intuitive view (shared by Hayek and Nozick) that the monopolist might constrain his customers, we must next ask whether a capitalist economy in general may be viewed in the same light. Let us consider first the obligation to satisfy needs and its corollary that a failure to meet needs infringes the freedom of the needy. Clearly the practical implications of this principle will depend on the view one takes of "needs." Given a suitably expanded definition, any society that does not distribute goods entirely according to need (and indeed does not ensure that enough is produced in the first place) will be an unfree society. But this may be too high a price to pay for a condemnation of capitalism, since as the scope of "needs" expands, we are likely to become less sure that satisfying needs is obligatory. A more moderate view would confine "needs" to "basic needs" and conclude that whereas laissez-faire capitalism did infringe the freedom of large sections of the working class, welfare-state capitalism does not, on that score at least.[10]

Attention then switches to the second obligation, the obligation not to exploit those placed in a dependent position. A great deal now depends on how we conceive the relationship between a worker and the capitalist who employs him. Socialists often advance the oversimple argument that workers are unfree just because they are forced to work for capitalists. This is open to the fair riposte that they are in any case obliged to work to stay alive. The relevant question is whether the terms offered by the capitalist – the package of hours, conditions, and pay – are exploitative, which depends in turn upon taking a view about the relative bargaining strengths of the two parties. It is interesting that Nozick chooses to handle this question by analogy with a marriage market in which liaisons between the more attractive members of either sex progressively reduce the options open to the less attractive. These reduced options do not amount to limitations of freedom, Nozick claims, because each person had a right to marry whom he chose – in our terms, none had an obligation to leave wider marriage options open to the others. The analogy softens us nicely for the blow that follows ("Similar considerations apply to market exchanges between workers and owners of capital"), but it does so partly because we assume that individuals compete in the marriage market on roughly equal terms. Suppose that this were not so – suppose for instance that great inequalities of wealth allowed some men to bribe a number of women to remain available as mistresses – then we should begin to think that the freedom of badly-off participants had been infringed. Power to control other's fates activates obligations of fairness,

and failure to meet these obligations infringes freedom.

The socialist view of capitalism makes the revised analogy more appropriate than the original. The bargain struck between worker and capitalist is not like a contract between buyer and seller in a fully competitive market, but an unequal deal between two parties of very uneven strength. The reason, to put the matter simply, is that any particular worker needs the capitalist more than the capitalist needs him. This depends, first, on the fact that a failure to contract leaves the worker considerably worse off than the capitalist, and, second, on the fact that the capitalist has more alternative contractual partners than the worker, capital being scarce relative to labor.[11] Rather than seeing the capital–labor relationship as fully competitive, therefore, we should regard the capitalist class as standing collectively in a position of monopoly vis-à-vis the working class. The analogy here would be with a state of affair in which, although there were several water holes to choose from in the desert, the supply of water was always scarce in relation to the demand, so that each owner could charge a price containing a monopoly element on top of the cost-covering and labor-rewarding components.

When dealing with the water-hole case, it was useful to compare the amount that a monopolist might extract from a desperate customer with the amount he could charge in a competitive market. What might serve as an analogous point of comparison in the present instance? I suggest that the relevant benchmark would be a state of affairs in which each person had equal access to capital. That is, anyone wishing to do so could obtain capital to use by himself or in cooperation with others. If, under these circumstances, anyone chose to contract to work for a capitalist, the terms would have to be such that his freedom was not restricted. Under the existing capitalist regime, however, workers are constrained to the extent of the difference between those terms and the terms they now obtain. They are constrained because the capitalist class collectively attaches conditions to their making a living that can only be attached because of the dependent condition of the working class, and which therefore violate the obligation not to exploit.

Notes

1 A more extreme view still, attributable to Hayek, is that rules do not restrict freedom, since freedom consists in the absence of *arbitrary* coercion. This is gilding the capitalist lily. As John Gray has pointed out, Hayek's venture along this path leads him directly to a positive conception of liberty. See J. Gray, "Hayek on Liberty, Rights, and Justice," *Ethics* 92 (1981): 73–84.

2 We make a distinction here between "being able to" do something and "having the ability to" do it. The latter notion is narrower and refers to the agent's physical or psychological capacity. The former also covers cases where an agent has the capacity to act but is deterred by the costliness of an option. We should say of a badly paid worker, e.g., that he is unable to take a holiday abroad, but not that he hasn't the ability to do so.

3 This error may underlie Hayek's attempt to show that rules of law do not diminish freedom – so that freedom under capitalism is almost complete. See n. 1 above.

4 The freedom at issue here is freedom of the will. I have not wanted to be drawn into the debate about the compatibility of determinism and free will. The relevant line of division for our purposes lies not between determinists and indeterminists, but between strong, or "incompatibilist," determinists, who maintain that the truth of determinism makes ordinary notions of human choice and responsibility redundant, and the rest.

5 An alternative view here is that when I am unable to do A, the question of my freedom to do A does not arise; I can properly be described neither as free nor as unfree to do A. This view gains its strength from the observation that it is often pointless and sometimes cynical to say that men are free to do things which they are clearly unable to do. It may nonetheless be conceptually proper to say such a thing. In defense of the view taken in the paper, consider the case where the government decides to fence off Scafell Pike. We may well want to say that this action makes everyone unfree to climb Scafell

Pike, without waiting to make an elaborate calculation of the number of people able to climb it in the first place.

6 I assume as part of the story that when I call to the passerby I manifest no signs of distress. If I were to, then, with a few other conditions added, the passerby would have an obligation to come to my aid.

7 This should make it clear that the definition of freedom I am offering is not a moralized definition of the sort that G. A. Cohen has found objectionable ("Capitalism, Freedom and the Proletariat," in *The Idea of Freedom*, ed. A. Ryan [Oxford: Oxford University Press, 1979], pp. 12–13), though it is not a morally neutral definition either.

8 William Connolly has argued that an obstacle to action should count as a constraint when its removal is feasible and when such removal is regarded as sufficiently important by the person obstructed. This sounds much like view I am attacking here. But Connolly also implies that judgments of feasibility must take into account the costs of removing the obstacle. "The notion of a constraint, then, involves the idea of a normal range of conduct people can be expected to undertake or forgo when doing so restricts the options of others." See W. E. Connolly, *The Terms of Political Discourse* (Lexington, Mass.: D. C. Heath & Co., 1974), pp. 160–70.

9 A similar thought may lie behind Hayek's proposal that the remedy for monopolistic coercion is to require the monopolist to charge every customer the same price.

10 Small sections of the population may be left below the "need" line; but these are not likely to be employed workers.

11 Marxists may object to an analysis of exploitation that focuses on the relative market advantage of capital over labor, arguing that the source of exploitation lies in production – the performance of surplus labor – rather than exchange. But the market advantage analysis is necessary to show why the capitalist can extract surplus labor in the first place: how can he impose terms that require the worker to labor for so many hours a day? Hence Marxist references to "the reserve army of the unemployed" are very much to the point, as indicating one source of the capitalist's advantage. For discussion of alternative theories of exploitation, see J. Elster, "Exploring Exploitation," *Journal of Peace Research* 15 (1978): 3–17.

David Miller, "Constraints on Freedom," *Ethics* 94 (1983), pp. 66–75, 81–5.

Chapter 41

Felix E. Oppenheim, from "'Constraints on Freedom' as a Descriptive Concept" (1985)

Are freedom and unfreedom essentially contestable moral notions, or can they be explicated descriptively? David Miller maintains that "judgments about freedom cannot be wholly value neutral" because the defining expression unavoidably refers to moral responsibility. Consequently, libertarians and socialists who "hold conflicting theories of interpersonal moral obligation" are bound to disagree as to whether, for example, the poor are unfree, or merely unable, to fulfill their basic needs.

I believe that the concept of constraints on freedom can be defined without reference to moral obligation, using only descriptive terms. This definition captures the core meaning of 'unfreedom' in ordinary language, abstracting only from negative valuational overtones. This way, moral philosophers and political scientists (if not political orators and politicians) with different moral convictions can nevertheless agree as to whether a given situation is to be characterized as one of unfreedom. A critical comparison between Miller's moral notion and the proposed descriptive explication will clarity this issue.

I. I agree with Miller that 'unfreedom' should be taken as a subcategory of 'inability'. Only obstacles 'attributable to human agency' constitute limitations of freedom, whereas "'natural' obstacles" render X unable, but not unfree, to do x. However, Miller narrows the category of unfreedom further by considering

X, whom Y prevents from doing x, unfree to do x only if Y is morally responsible for the obstacle. This criterion does indeed involve moral evaluations and possible moral disagreement. Are those at present unable to find work in the United States unfree to work? Yes, if the Reagan administration is to be blamed for producing unemployment; not so, according to proponents of "Reaganomics." Furthermore, applying this standard has implications at variance with common usage. It would follow that a prisoner unable to leave his cell because the guard locked it is, at least with respect to the guard, not unfree to leave (but free?) if the guard is not morally responsible for his confinement; and if he is jailed by virtue of a just conviction, there is nobody who restricted his freedom.

I accept a proposal Miller rejects, "that any obstacle for which human agents are in some way or other causally responsible should be regarded as a constraint on freedom" – causally, not morally, responsible. Whether the unemployed are unfree to work depends on whether and to what extent their plight is due to governmental policies, regardless of whether we approve of them. The guard who caused the prisoner's inability to leave did make him unfree to escape. I don't agree with Miller's criticism of this interpretation "as extending the limits of unfreedom absurdly far". It leaves outside the range of constraints on freedom not only physical or psychological inabilities and natural obstacles but also incapacities caused by anonymous demographic or economic or institutional conditions. Some consider unemployment as due not to specific governmental policies but to impersonal economic circumstances (or "capitalism").

Let us apply Miller's criteria and mine to his six cases. Y locks M (Miller) up in his room, in case 1 deliberately, in case 2 negligently, and in case 5 accidentally. I consider M's freedom to have been restricted in all three cases since Y's locking the door is a direct cause of M's confinement. Miller, too, interprets 1 and 2 as instances of unfreedom, but 2 for the different reason that M acted negligently. I would regard M no less unfree to leave if it were not Y's job to check the room. To Miller, 5 does not involve unfreedom because Y is not morally responsible for M's inability to leave. To me, this is a relationship of unfreedom like that between the guard and the prisoner. In cases 3, 4, and 6, M's confinement is due to the wind's blowing the door shut. I conclude that M is unable but free to leave not only when nobody is around (6 – here Miller agrees) but also in 3, where Y fails to do his job of checking the room, and in 4, where M calls in vain to a passerby to unlock the door. Miller subsumes 3 under unfreedom because Y is morally responsible for M's confinement. We both agree that 4 does not involve unfreedom, but Miller's reason is that the passerby had no moral duty to answer M's call. My own analysis does not involve any moral considerations.

II.   Miller interprets cases 3 and 4 as restraints on freedom for the further reason that Y and the passerby fail to unlock M's door. According to Miller, Y makes X unfree to do *x* if Y (irresponsibly) either makes X unable to do *x* or does not enable him to do so. Here my objection is that whoever is unable to do something would be unfree to do it with respect to anyone who happens not to make it possible for him to do so. In cases 3 and 4, M would be unfree to leave with respect to everyone who does not unlock his

door, including those unaware of his predicament. It is quite true that "this means in effect that the scope of mere inability will shrink almost to the vanishing point". This difficulty can be avoided by subsuming under constraints on freedom only cases of preventing, not those of failure to enable.[1] No doubt it is sometimes difficult to distinguish between these two categories, as Miller's caving example well illustrates. At least, they, too, do not involve valuational considerations.

III.   I agree that the concept of unfreedom must cover more than situations of Y making it literally impossible for X to do *x* but that it should not extend to cases in which Y makes it only slightly less attractive for X to do *x* than it would be without Y's intervention. "How large must the [man-made] obstacle itself be for it to count as a constraint" of freedom? Here Miller uses again an ethical standard. Only if Y is "morally responsible for an obstacle to X's action" does Y limit X's freedom. It follows that the local monopolist in Miller's example who raises the price "in violation of an obligation of fairness," however slightly, renders customers unfree to buy the product but that a justifiable, even prohibitive increase does not limit their freedom. Indeed, "the sheer size of the obstacle [has] no intrinsic importance". I would instead take Miller's expanded criterion of impossibility as a criterion for unfreedom: with respect to Y, X is also unfree to do *x* if Y makes doing *x* "so costly that it is effectively excluded from the scope of his consideration". A clear example would be: "Your money or your life!" It might be objected that a poor taxi driver considers a small parking fine prohibitive but that a millionaire considers it insignificant. I would therefore say that Y makes X unfree to do *x* if he makes it either strictly or practically impossible to do *x*, and by 'practical impossibility' I mean making it so difficult or unpleasant or costly or risky for any actor in normal circumstances (thus not for a specific person) to do *x* that he has practically no choice but to abstain. Again, this criterion is not of a moral kind.

IV. I agree that punishability should be taken as an "additional condition" of unfreedom. Accordingly, with respect to Y, X is unfree to do *x* if Y makes it either impossible (strictly or practically) for X to do *x* or punishable for him to do so. There are several reasons for subsuming both prevention and punishability under unfreedom but also for distinguishing between them. (1) As Miller points out, punishment is by definition intentional, while placing an obstacle need not be.[2] (2) Y's punitive action is based on his belief (true or false) that X committed an offense *x* (as defined by some rule, which need not be legal), and this enables us to distinguish between imposing a penalty (e.g., a parking fine) and a cost (e.g., a parking fee). (3) 'Punishability' implies that Y would actually mete out the punishment if he believed that X did *x*. A mere "threat of punishment may deter someone from acting in a certain way, but does not make him unfree to disregard the threat."[3] (4) Imposing even a small penalty restricts freedom, but only an obstacle amounting to practical impossibility does so. Accordingly, a highly credible threat of a very severe sanction is an instance of both punishability and prevention.[4]

V. Miller does not distinguish between the degree of a person's freedom and the value to him of having a freedom. These are independent variable. Those who like to travel and those who prefer to stay home are equally free to go, but this freedom is valuable only to the former. The same parking fine makes every driver equally unfree to park, but the fine is more burdensome to a taxi driver than to a millionaire. The degree of one's unfreedom depends on such factors as the severity of the sanction, the probability of its application, the difficulty of surmounting the obstacle, and the number of alternatives closed.

VI. Miller might object that a purely descriptive analysis of 'unfreedom' disregards the negative valuational aspect of this concept in ordinary language and the corresponding laudatory connotation of 'freedom.' To claim that "our language embodies a presumption that humans should not obstruct one another's activity" seems to me too broad a generalization. We approve of laws against speeding, polluting, and committing statutory crimes, and we want to be constrained to contribute to the production of public goods, provided others are not left free to withhold their share. Miller himself asserts that "many restrictions of freedom are justified". I don't think we say so merely in rebuttal against a presumption to the contrary.

VII. Let us return to the debate between libertarians and socialists. According to the former, those lacking basic necessities are unable but free to acquire them. The latter hold that the needy are unfree in that respect because government erects obstacles in disregard of its moral obligation to secure everyone's basic needs. This is the socialist's view expressed in Miller's language. Were they instead to use the conceptual scheme proposed here, they could well agree with the libertarians that, under a laissez-faire system, even the destitute have freedoms which they lack in a welfare state. Indeed, the impossibility to secure basic necessities may well be due to the economic, social, and political system. Contrariwise, for example, minimum wage laws do restrict the freedom of employees as well as of employers. This purely descriptive characterization is perfectly compatible with the normative view that freedom ought to be restricted as far as necessary "to promote competing values such as welfare and equality". An agreed descriptive language is a prerequisite for a fruitful discussion of normative issues.

Notes

1 It is therefore not true that "a constraint *will have to be* defined as any obstacle which it is possible for human beings to remove or fail to impose" (italics added). Such a definition would indeed be too broad, just as the one discussed under I seems to me too narrow.

2 I agree that Y may punish X "*either* as retribution for X's having done *A or* to discourage X from

doing *A* again *or* to deter others from doing actions like *A*". However, I do not think that such a clause needs to be included in the definition of punishability.

3 Felix E. Oppenheim, *Political Concepts: A Reconstruction* (Chicago: University of Chicago Press, 1981), p. 60. I do not "say that all threats of punishment infringe on the addressee's freedom" (p. 78). They do not. Other arguments in the text are also based on this work, chaps. 2, 4.

4 It is therefore not true "that Oppenheim's definition would exclude all cases where cost-imposing action is intentional but nonpunitive" or that "he neglects the important class of situations where there is no intention to penalize and yet freedom is infringed". Unfreedom includes prevention as well as punishability, and prevention includes imposing costs (even unintentionally) high enough to amount to practical impossibility. On the other hand, nonpunitive and nonprohibitive cost-imposing actions (like normal parking fees) do not restrict freedom.

Felix E. Oppenheim, "'Constraints on Freedom' as a Descriptive Concept," from *Ethics* 95 (1985), pp. 305–9.

Chapter 42

David Miller, from "Reply to Oppenheim" (1985)

Felix Oppenheim has raised a number of questions in his reply to my "Constraints on Freedom." I propose to look closely at what I take to be the central point at issue between us – the proper criterion for describing something as a constrain on freedom – and to add a few remarks about whether it makes sense to try to analyze the idea of freedom in a descriptive, value-neutral manner.

Oppenheim and I both share the primary intuition that obstacles standing in a person's path which are attributable to human agency constrain that person's freedom, whereas obstacles that arise "naturally" merely make him less able to act in certain ways. We disagree, however, about how the expression "attributable to human agency" should be interpreted. My proposal was that an impediment to action should be counted as a constraint when some person (or persons) could be held morally responsible for its existence, either because he (they) had imposed it, deliberately or negligently, or because he (they) had failed to remove it, despite having an obligation to do so. Oppenheim finds this unsatisfactory and suggests instead that any obstacle for which human agents are causally responsible should be counted as a constraint. As his argument unfolds, however, it becomes clear that he is interpreting "causally responsible" in a fairly narrow sense. He makes a distinction between preventing someone from acting in a certain way and failing to enable that person to act in that way. This distinction is not explored, but the only way I can make sense

of it is to suppose that it is equivalent to the distinction between acts and omissions, a view I discussed [in 'Constraints']. On this view, an obstacle will count as a constraint if human beings have done something to bring it into existence but not if its existence merely reflects a failure to act of some kind.

Comparing our two criteria extensionally, Oppenheim would count as constraints (but I would not) obstacles brought about by human action where the agent is not morally responsible for the outcome – for instance, obstacles that arise from my action in some unforeseeable way. On the other hand, I would count as constraints (but Oppenheim would not) obstacles arising from omissions, for which the agent is responsible because he has a moral obligation to remove them. In many other cases, our respective criteria will deliver the same verdict.

If Oppenheim's criterion is to be of any use, it must (*a*) be capable of reasonably clear explication and (*b*) fit our considered judgments about freedom and constraint. I will try to show that the only plausible explication fails to meet the second condition.

It may at first sight seem relatively simple to distinguish between acting failing to act; our language is replete which idioms that embody such a distinction (killing and letting die; hindering and failing to help; preventing and failing to enable; etc.). But this apparent simplicity vanishes as soon as we begin to lengthen and complicate the causal chain between agent and outcome. Consider a rudimentary case. Jones owns a piece of land on which stands a large tree overhanging a neighboring highway. If Jones saws the tree down, it seems uncontroversial to say that he has blocked the highway and (using Oppenheim's criterion) constrained potential travelers. If, on the other hand, the tree blows down (but would not have done so if Jones had erected props to hold it up), we should say that Jones has merely failed to stop the tree falling and (by extension) failed to enable the travelers to travel. But now consider two more difficult cases. In the first, the tree will blow down if (and only if) Jones tills the soil around it, weakening the roots. In the second, the tree will blow down if (and only if) Jones does not till the soil (doing which would allow moisture to penetrate). In each of these cases, would the tree's falling and the blocking of the highway result from an act or an omission? Would the first result from an act and second from an omission because we would naturally describe the human cause in the active voice in the first case ("tilling the soil") but in the passive voice in the second ("leaving the soil untilled")? But we could easily describe the relevant acts in such a way that the voices were reversed – "failing to keep the ground firm" in the first case and "keeping the ground firm" in the second. If we describe the cases in this way, there will be constraint in the second case if the tree falls but not in the first.

If the acts/omissions distinction is not to fall prey to linguistic arbitrariness, we must supply it with an objective basis. The only explication known to me that meets this condition is Jonathan Bennett's distinction between positive and negative instrumentality.[1] Bennett's idea is that an agent A is positively instrumental at T in bringing about a result R if, of all the things he might have done at T, only a small proportion lead to R, whereas a large proportion lead to – R.[2] Thus if Jones saws the tree down, he is positively instrumental in bringing it about that the tree blocks the road because, of all the actions he might have performed at that time, only a tiny percentage would have the result that the tree

lies across the road. Negative instrumentality is the converse of this. If the tree falls because Jones fails to prop it up, he is negatively instrumental in bringing about this outcome because nearly all of the actions that he might have performed at the relevant time would have the result that the tree would fall. In theory we should be able to apply this criterion to our two more difficult cases and so decide whether to count Jones's behavior as an act or an omission in each instance.

As Bennett observes, the resulting distinction between acts and omissions is morally neutral. It neither rests on moral considerations nor, by itself, has any moral implications (that is, if two pieces of behavior are relevantly similar in every respect except that one is an act and the other an omission, they are morally equivalent). In my article, I took this as a reason against resting the distinction between unfreedom and inability on that between acts and omissions, believing that the former distinction was morally loaded. Oppenheim, however, does not share this belief. He holds that freedom and constraint are value-neutral terms, capable of being explicated descriptively. This is why Bennett's distinction between positive and negative instrumentality is particularly suitable for his purposes.

To see what is wrong with analyzing freedom and constraint in this way, we need to look at cases of accidental acts and at cases of deliberate omissions. These can be made as fantastic as one pleases. Suppose I am picnicking on a cliff top and casually toss aside an apple. A pip takes root, grows into a small tree, and at some later time precipitates a cliff fall that traps Smith in a recess below. Assuming that I am positively instrumental in bringing about this result (which means, roughly, that the fall wouldn't have occurred unless the apple had landed more or less where it did, etc.), Smith has been constrained and his freedom impaired (on Oppenheim's criterion). Suppose, on the other hand, that a cliff fall will trap Smith (and I know this) unless I pick up and set aside a small stone on the top. Disliking Smith intensely, I hold back and allow the fall to occur. Since (on reasonable assumptions) I am negatively instrumental in bringing about this result, Smith's freedom remains untouched, and I have merely not enabled him to leave the cliff face.

These two judgments seem paradoxical because they clash with our primary intuition that constraints are obstacles attributable to human agency. In both cases the result depends on a combination of natural factors and human behavior. But "human agency" means both more and less than positive instrumentality in the technical sense analyzed above. It means that the humans in question knew what they were doing or, if not, that they should have done. In the first case there is positive instrumentality, but the result is neither willed nor intended nor foreseen (nor even perhaps capable of being foreseen). In the second case there is both foresight and intention even though the instrumentality is negative. It seems to me that Smith's confinement can properly be attributed to human agency in the second case but not in the first and that our judgments about his freedom should follow suit.

The criterion I proposed to capture such a view was that constraints were obstacles for which some person or persons could be held morally responsible. This criterion clearly fits the two cases above (I am not responsible for Smith's later confinement when I throw the apple aside, but I am responsible when I deliberately fail to remove the crucial stone).[3] Oppenheim takes this to imply that all restrictions of freedom are unjustified. No such implication can be drawn, as I tried to make clear in my article. To be responsible for something is to be answerable for it; it is not necessarily to be blamable. The judge who sends a felon to jail is responsible for that person's confinement and has restricted his freedom, but if he has acted according to the provisions of a justified law, he is in no way blamable. Responsibility, one might say, opens the door to questions of praise and blame without deciding them. In the same way, showing that an obstacle is a constraint on someone's

freedom raises the question of its justifiability but does not resolve it.

The view that the idea of freedom has no built-in evaluative force seems to me incredible. If showing that the enactment of a certain law increases or decreases freedom or that people in society A generally enjoy more freedom than people in society B were merely an exercise in technical classification, what purpose would it have? We are interested in deciding when obstacles are properly seen as constraints because, other things being equal, we wish not to be constrained. Of course other things are never equal, and there are large and important arguments about how freedom should be balanced against other political goods. But these arguments themselves would make no sense unless freedom were seen as a good whose loss could only be offset by gains of other kinds.

Oppenheim sees that presently there is disagreement about the proper application of the concept of freedom. But he believes it should be possible to reach agreement, presumably through a convergence in our judgments about social causation (i.e., about which outcomes can be attributed to human acts rather than omissions in the sense outlined above). The argument advanced in my article, and reiterated here, is that causal inquiry, although important, may not settle the issue because attributing responsibility also raises questions about moral obligation. Suppose the government cuts unemployment benefits, and as a result some people are reduced to poverty. There may be no dispute that human agents (in this case government ministers) were positively instrumental in bringing about the outcome. There may, however, still be dispute about whether the people in question were responsible for the results of their actions because it may not be agreed that there is a general obligation on the part of governments to relieve poverty. Since disagreements of the latter kind seem to be endemic, I conclude that concepts affected by them, such as the concept of freedom, are usefully described as essentially contestable.

Notes

1   Jonathan Bennett, "Morality and Consequences" in *The Tanner Lectures on Human Values*,
vol. 2, ed. Sterling M. McMurrin (Salt Lake City:
University of Utah Press, 1981).

2   Because of worries about the idea of negative
actions, Bennett expresses the criterion in terms of
propositions referring to A at T; for simplicity of
exposition, I have put it back into the material mode.

3   This second judgment rests on the belief that
where at little or no cost to oneself one could avert
some serious harm to another, one has an obligation to do so. This view is not universally accepted,
so the assertion that I am responsible for Smith's
confinement when I leave the stone in place is
potentially challengeable.

David Miller, "Reply to Oppenheim," *Ethics* 95 (1985),
pp. 310–14.

Chapter 43

Kristján Kristjánsson, from
Social Freedom (1996)

It is vital at this juncture to be quite clear on the difference (*a*) between a *moral* and a *moralised* account of freedom, and (*b*) between *moral* and *causal responsibility*. A moralised account (such as Nozick's) links constraints on freedom with moral wrongness or culpability; a moral account (such as Miller's) links them with moral responsibility. It must be re-emphasised that holding *A* mor-ally responsible for a state of affairs is not saying that he is blameworthy: 'Responsi-bility . . . opens the door to questions of praise and blame without deciding them'. Perhaps the janitor's errand in case 3 was of such vital significance that he cannot by any means be blamed for failing to do his profes-sional duty; he could, for example, have been taking his critically ill wife to hospital. But that does not change the original conclusion about his being morally responsible for *B*'s unfree-dom. A failure to grasp this difference leads Oppenheim badly astray in his reply. He adduces as critical ammunition against Miller the story I used earlier: of the prison guard who locks up a justly convicted criminal in his cell. Oppenheim claims that in Miller's account the prisoner is free to leave in such a case since the guard is not morally responsible for his confinement. This is, of course, misconstruing the very point of Miller's definition. The guard may well be morally responsible for the imprisonment, by locking the door of the cell, but this does not mean that he is blameworthy for it, that he is doing the *wrong* thing. Responsibil-ity is not the same as culpability. Oppenheim's example, as we saw, is telling against a *moralised* definition, but not against a *moral* definition.

[. . .]

In the final part of 'Constraints on Freedom', where Miller argues for his respon-sibility view (sec. 2.3), he aims to apply his account to the ongoing debate between liber-tarians and socialists.[1] That debate tends to focus on the distribution of wealth in the world, and a question which often crops up is whether such distribution is relevant to an assessment of people's freedom. Miller's basic observation is that nothing in the nature of *financial* obstacles disqualifies them from fea-turing in a discussion of freedom. Like any other obstacles, they count as constraints if there are agents who can be held morally responsible for not suppressing them. So, to decide whether a certain distribution of wealth is freedom-restricting, more than a conceptual analysis is needed; the moral responsibility in question must be established. According to Miller's analysis, this 'requires in turn a theory of moral obligation'.[2] Thus, in order to clarify the socialist point of view, Miller finds it nec-essary to invoke two general obligations: that of ensuring that the needs of others are met, and that of dealing fairly with people placed in dependent positions. However, for Miller the existence of these obligations is irreducibly controversial. Generally, his claim is that because libertarians and socialists hold conflicting theories of interpersonal moral obligations, *ultimate disagreements* between them are inevitable. Often what the former call freedom, the latter would call unfreedom – and there is no rational way to decide who is right.[3]

I am not the only reader of Miller's paper to wonder if, in making these apparent concessions, he is not cutting off the branch from which his own theory hangs. Any attentive reader will be somewhat taken aback by the sudden change of tone toward the end of his piece. Up to that point, the whole exposition has a very optimistic air. What Miller seemed to be showing by his 'office-stories' was this: once we realise how the notion of a constraint on freedom is tied up with that of responsibility, we can decide when an obstacle is freedom-restricting. Thus, Miller's aim appeared to be that of providing us with a decision procedure for locating and defining constraints on freedom; a procedure that somehow claimed the acceptance of every perspicuous thinker. The reader may be excused for believing that here we had finally reached the conceptual common ground on which meaningful, substantive controversies about the value of particular freedoms could be staged.

Maybe this was never Miller's point; at least he ultimately backs away from this conclusion. But, once the assumption of a firm common ground has been abandoned or relaxed, the whole edifice of his theory begins to crumble. Obviously, we cannot understand Miller to be claiming, on the one hand, that there is a consensus on responsibility and, on the other hand, that moral obligations are a matter of irresolvable dispute, without imputing to him a glaring inconsistency. It is therefore of vital importance to find out where exactly Miller goes wrong in his analysis.

The cause of Miller's apparent about-face must lie somewhere in the links he supposes to obtain between responsibility, justification, and the (prima facie) obligation to suppress a given obstacle. Since the last of these three is, for Miller, prior in the order of explanation, it is the concept of obligation, or more precisely

of prima facie obligation, that turns out to be the logical foundation of his analysis. His eventual claim is that having a prima facie obligation to suppress an obstacle is a necessary and a sufficient condition of an agent's moral responsibility for that obstacle and, hence, for its counting as a constraint on freedom.

It is reasonable to suppose that Miller understands 'prima facie obligation' in a deontological or a quasi-deontological sense. Typically for the deontologist, prima facie obligations are obligations which are *real* but not *absolute*. That is, they exist unless overridden – usually by other obligations but perhaps sometimes by other things: I have an obligation to meet you for dinner tomorrow if I have promised to do so, but if I should have to save someone's life tomorrow, my obligation to dine with you is overridden. Hence, it is not an absolute but a prima facie obligation. Consequentialists may well use the notion of 'prima facie obligation' to serve some purpose in their theories, but the notion is not as naturally at home there as in the deontological ones since consequentialists consider one and only one obligation as overriding: that of promoting the best state of affairs. Anyway, we shall see in the sequel that Miller's interest is in deontological prima facie obligations.

There, however, a fundamental problem confronts us. It is well known that deontologists disagree on what obligations we have and, also, which of those obligations (if any) are absolute. However, most of them define 'obligation' rather tightly; it would be difficult to imagine the usefulness of invoking the term if we had, for instance, an obligation (even prima facie) to promote whatever another person happens to want. In the context of a responsibility view of freedom, it seems implausible to hold that the only time we are morally responsible for the non-suppression of an obstacle is when we have a prima facie obligation to suppress it. Would it not be stretching the concept of obligation beyond the breaking point to claim that the reason why a jailer, who locks up a justly convicted criminal in his cell, thereby constrains the prisoner's freedom, is that the jailer has a prima facie obligation not to lock him up? Or, to take another example, would we want to say that a fireman rescuing a semi-conscious person from a burning house has, *qua* fireman, a prima facie obligation to leave him in there, if he knows that the person lit the fire himself in order to commit suicide? I take it that we would probably not want to say that, although we would grant that the fireman is restricting the person's freedom to commit suicide.

These cases seem to indicate that there is an extensional difference between being morally responsible for not suppressing an obstacle, on the one hand, and violating a prima facie obligation to suppress it, on the other. The jailer and the fireman would easily fall under the former description, but scarcely under the latter. If Miller insists that they do fall under the latter also, he is using the term 'prima facie obligation' in a more permissive way than most deontologists would allow. Not that I have anything against such deviant usage; deontological theories contain in general much baggage that I do not want to carry. But this creates problems for Miller's own view. *First*, it means that he can no longer use prima facie obligations to *explain* the onus of justification and thus moral responsibility; the former are no longer prior in the order of explanation. For on this permissive reading, 'having a prima facie obligation to suppress an obstacle' simply turns out to mean the same as 'being obliged to justify the non-suppression of the obstacle', that is, 'having the onus of justification for its non-suppression placed on you'. Now, it is clear what would be meant by saying that the jailer and the fireman are morally responsible for the non-suppression of the relevant obstacles because they are obliged to justify their action/inaction (in the above sense of having the onus of justification placed on them), although we could still ask *why* they are obliged to do so. But it would not add anything to say that they are so obliged *because* they have a prima facie obligation to suppress the obstacles, if they are *ex hypothesi*

deemed to have such a prima facie obligation whenever they are obliged to justify their non-suppression.

So, to explain the two apparently clear-cut cases of unfreedom above, Miller would have to adopt a very permissive definition of 'prima facie obligation' that is at best synonymous with, and at worst less clear than, the notion it was supposed to explain. I am not denying that we would understand what Miller was saying if he claimed that the jailer had *qua* human being a general prima facie obligation not to lock anyone up. There is even a sense in which it is true to say that my account of constraints of freedom presupposes a theory of moral obligation. However – and here we come to the *second* problem – when Miller starts to discuss different moral claims of 'socialism' and 'libertarianism', it is not this permissive sense that he has in mind at all, but the more traditional and narrow one; he imagines different deontological systems with conflicting views of prima facie obligations. In the light of that, he considers it a matter of controversy whether we have even a prima facie obligation to help people in need; such an obligation must, he thinks, be 'invoked' by the socialist in a way that the libertarian is not forced to accept. In other words, Miller would need the permissive definition to account for many common cases of unfreedom, but he uses the narrow definition to show that judgements about freedom are bound to be the object of an irresolvable disagreement. However, he has not produced any convincing arguments for the claim that there is a link between moral responsibility and prima facie obligations on the narrow reading. In fact, the cases above indicate that there is no such link. Whether one is a socialist or a libertarian, a deontologist or a non-deontologist, the jailer is restricting the prisoner's freedom to leave his cell.

Perhaps obstructing a person by violating such prima facie obligations toward him as are recognised within a certain deontological system – say, a libertarian system – is a *sufficient* condition of a constraint on freedom;

but there is no reason to believe that it is a *necessary* one. So, there could well be an uncontroversial sense in which we are morally responsible for the non-suppression of obstacles despite its being controversial when we are morally obliged to suppress them; it is not true that because deontological views of prima facie obligations differ, judgements about freedom will necessarily differ, too.

In sum, Miller's claims about the link between moral responsibility and the onus of justification, on the one hand, and prima facie obligations, on the other, are either *trivial* or *wrong*. They are trivial on the permissive definition of 'prima facie obligation' and wrong on the narrow one.

4.3   Responsibility and Reasons

Instead of criticising further attempts to define the moral responsibility in question, I shall now suggest and argue for the following view: An agent *A* is morally responsible for the non-suppression of an obstacle *O* to *B*'s choices/action when it is appropriate to request from *A* a justification of his non-suppression of *O*, and that in turn is when there is an objective *reason*, satisfying a minimal criterion of plausibility, why *A*, given that he is a normal, reasonable person, could have been expected (morally or factually) to suppress *O* – however easily overridable this reason is.

When I talk about there being an objective reason for the suppression of *O*, I am emphasising that *objective*, not *subjective*, standards of appropriate requests are being referred to. In general, if we ask whether *C* has a good reason to request a justification from *A* of his actions, the answer will depend on many factors having to do with *C*'s position. For example, if *C* sees a child, *B*, being forced to opt out of a ball-game because its shoelaces have become untied while *A*, whom *C* takes to be *B*'s father, sits immobile on a bench nearby, it seems appropriate for *C* to ask *A* for a justification of his inaction. Meanwhile, another observer

(*D*) knows that *A* is totally paralysed and/or that *A* is in fact not *B*'s father; hence, it does not seem appropriate for *D* to make the same request. But surely, *A*'s responsibility cannot depend on what *C* and *D* happen to know about him. To overcome this problem, my definition implies that a rational agent, *C*, can be mistaken about *A*'s responsibility, because of his lack of knowledge, and that he may have to admit after becoming aware of the facts: 'I thought there was a reason to ask for a justification, but now I know there wasn't; that's why I mistakenly believed *A* was constraining *B*'s freedom.' Note that this 'adequate knowledge condition' does not mean that *C* must be omniscient or able to read *A*'s mind; it is only meant to rule out the possibility that the reason for *C*'s requesting a justification from *A* merely lies in his ignorance of the basic details of the situation, such as who *A* is, whether *A* would be able to do something about the relevant obstacle, etc.

One advantage of the proposed definition is that it honours the subtle distinction between *imperfect* responsibility and *no* responsibility, mentioned earlier. It is incumbent on the Icelandic government to justify why it does not help the starving Ethiopians, because there must always be at least a minimally good reason why people in a life-threatening situation should be helped, if possible. However, the justification for not doing so may be easy to find since the responsibility in this case is imperfect. On the other hand, there is no reason why the father could be expected to tie the loose laces of all the children in the city (barring the unlikely possibility that he has been employed especially to perform that function). The responsibility here is not imperfect; it is non-existent. For if we held that, even in this case, there was a reason of the above kind, we would have robbed that notion of any significance in our language. There would no longer be any difference between a reason for doing *x* and the possibility of doing *x*.

The case of the jailer and the prisoner may be a little thornier. However, I think it is fair to say there that we have a grip on a reason, satisfying a minimal criterion of plausibility, why the jailer should not lock up the prisoner. He is preventing another person from doing something that happens to be of paramount importance to people in general. We would understand the point of the claim that there was a reason for not locking up people at all, although we might find this reason outweighed by other considerations – or at least put no blame on the jailer for doing his job.[4] On the other hand, we would not understand the point of the claim that we have a reason for walking around the city all day, looking for any loose shoelaces we could possibly tie. That claim may be *intelligible* but it is *unreasonable* or foolish. As these examples show, we must look at each case on its own merits and check whether an appropriate reason presents itself there.

My proposed account of *A*'s responsibility for the non-suppression of *O* also supplies us, I believe, with the correct moral test for which we were looking at the end of chapter 3, a test which can determine when threats do constitute constraints on freedom. For instance, in the *Drug Case I*, it is surely appropriate to ask *B*'s normal supplier for a justification of his threat not to sell *B* more dope unless *B* kills a certain person. However, in the *Drug Case II*, the question is inappropriate, for there is no sense (moral, factual or otherwise) in which *B* could reasonably expect the stranger to offer him dope anyway. Furthermore, in the *Slave Case*, the slaveholder's threat 'Unless you do *x*, I'll continue to beat you up tomorrow', does constitute a constraint on *B*'s freedom (*contra* Feinberg), for, although the slaveholder could be *statistically* expected to continue the beating, it is surely possible to give a good reason of another kind (here a moral one) why he should be expected to stop the beating and, hence, it is not inappropriate to ask him for a justification.

It is now time to consider charges of *relativity* that could be brought against my test of moral responsibility. An objector may complain that I have eliminated various *material* ways of specifying what a person's moral responsibilities are and replaced them with a merely *formal* criterion that leaves it all up to intuitions. To be sure, he might say, there must be a reason why *A* could have been expected to suppress *O*, but the point of substance at issue between the rejected accounts above is exactly this: *when* is there such a reason? In reply, there is no denying the fact that all conceptual studies are partly dependent on our intuitions [. . .]. However, the main line of argument I have tried to indicate is this: the rejected accounts suggest various tests of responsibility which fail to account for paradigmatic cases of freedom or constraints on freedom. These shortcomings can be ameliorated if we introduce the notion of a minimally plausible reason for suppressing an obstacle, a notion I have tried to explicate by means of examples. It is not true that this notion merely supplies us with a formal test of responsibility, for anyone who understands what constitutes such a reason will readily accept that:

1. There may be a minimally plausible reason why *A* can be expected to suppress *O* oven though such a suppression is not the standard convention – which leads to the refection of Benn and Weinstein's 'standard choice-situation model'.
2. There is not a minimally plausible reason for expecting *A* to suppress all possibly- or feasibly-suppressible obstacles – which leads to a rejection of the 'strong doctrine' of responsibility and Connolly's 'feasibility view'.
3. There may be a minimally plausible reason why *A* can be expected to suppress *O* although he has no prima facie obligation to do so within a given deontological system – which leads to the rejection of Miller in his restrictive mood.

However, there may be little to choose between my analysis and that of Miller in the first part of his paper, where he tacitly invokes a more permissive notion of 'prima facie obligation'. So, why not simply tighten up the account of such obligations rather than jettisoning it in favour of a talk of minimally plausible reasons, which in the end may come down to more or less the same thing? My answer here is much the same as my earlier response to Miller. I think it is desirable in a moral inquiry to retain Miller's narrow definition of 'prima facie obligation', which allows for disagreement among different moral systems over the prima facie obligations we have. Recall that on Miller's view, an agent is responsible for the non-suppression of an obstacle when he is obliged to justify its non-suppression, and that in turn is when he has a prima facie obligation to suppress it. Note that my account explains what the onus of justification (being obliged to justify the non-suppression) really amounts to, without recourse to a prima facie obligation to suppress, a recourse which proved either to be wrong (on the narrow definition) or trivial (on the permissive one). In other words, my account allows for there being a good reason to expect *A* to suppress *O* without *A*'s necessarily having a prima facie obligation to suppress it. A libertarian could, for example, justify his non-suppression of obstacles in certain cases by pointing out that he had no obligation, not even a prima facie one, to suppress them: 'To be sure, I constrained this person's freedom but I had no obligation not to do so.' This seems much more plausible than insisting that since he had no prima facie obligation to suppress the obstacle to *B*'s choices, he could not have constrained his freedom. Thus, although there is a sense in which my account, like Miller's, presupposes a theory of moral obligation, namely, the obligation to *justify* a given non-suppression, this sense is quite distinct from that of Miller's.

To clarify further the point about justification, we can ask what exactly is true in the claim, commonly made by proponents of the responsibility view, that there is a 'principle of freedom' embodied in our language. It cannot be right that this principle amounts to a general presumption against restricting the choices of others or obstructing their activity, for we are doing so all the time without there being any reason for us not to; the father is, for instance, restricting the possible choices of those children whose loose laces he does not tie. What is true, on the other hand, is that there is a presumption against constraining other people's freedom. When there is some minimally plausible reason why *A* could have been expected to suppress *O*, we expect him to come up with a justification for his non-suppression. Thus, freedom is a 'principle' in the sense that when the onus of justification can be placed on us for the non-suppression of an obstacle, to avoid blame we must be able to explain satisfactorily our non-suppression. This means that the connection between the principle of freedom and the onus of justification is more intimate than previous writers may have realised. It is not, as Connolly suggests, that once we have decided that a description of unfreedom correctly applies, there is a presumption against that relationship. We do not *first* locate instances of unfreedom and *then* place the onus of justification on the constraining agents; this onus is a defining characteristic of what constitutes unfreedom in the first place. When it can be placed on a specific person, *A*, that person is responsible for the given obstacle to *B*'s choice and, hence, *A* has constrained *B*'s freedom.

Notes

1   Miller, 'Constraints on Freedom'.
2   Ibid.
3   At the very end of Miller's paper, however, he claims a kind of a victory on points for the socialists. For though their case rests 'on a view of obligation that is in principle contestable', it 'derives persuasive force from the fact that the obligations it invokes must be invoked even by the

libertarian to handle cases of monopoly satisfactorily' (ibid.).

4 This also solves the problem, which at first might seem a daunting one for the responsibility theorist, how a law against, say, child-abuse curbs the freedom of the potential malefactors. For what objective reason (factual or moral) could there be for expecting the law-giver to permit such atrocities? The answer would be that the sanctions imposed by the law (extended imprisonment, etc.) are such that we could reasonably question their moral legitimacy.

Krystján Krystjánsson, *Social Freedom* (Cambridge: Cambridge University Press, 1996), pp. 32–3, 70–9.

Chapter 44

Richard E. Flathman, from
The Philosophy and Politics of Freedom (1987)

Questions about virtue and vice, good and evil, right and wrong, are of course importantly related to freedom and unfreedom. To begin with, in our culture freedom is itself widely regarded as a good and various particular freedoms are regarded as especially valuable and important. Whether and why this should be the case will be our concern in later chapters. If we simply accept the fact for now, for this reason the question whether an action is right or wrong, good or evil, virtuous or unvirtuous, often cannot be decided apart from, independently of, whether it is or will be done in freedom or in the exercise of a particular freedom. If Mr. Harding in Trollope's *Barchester Towers* had thought Eleanor's (supposed) willingness to marry Mr. Slope had been coerced or even manipulated, his readiness to accommodate himself to that arrangement would have diminished or disappeared. Although he despised the match itself, his belief that his daughter was acting in freedom was important in convincing him that he ought to accept it. If a despicable racist harangue is regarded as an exercise of freedom of speech, our estimate of the importance of that freedom convinces many that the act should not only be allowed but protected. In short, the freedom or unfreedom of actions is itself sometimes a consideration in our moral and other evaluations of those actions. In addition, actions and proposed or attempted actions typically raise further moral or normative questions, questions about which our thinking may be influenced but is seldom settled by the fact that they are or would be done in freedom. Let us assume that Mr. Harding was right to respect his daughter's freedom and that we are right to protect the racist's speech. Let us further assume that Eleanor and the racist have a right to act as they see fit in these regards. It may nevertheless be that Eleanor would have been wrong to marry Slope and that the racist would be wrong to give her speech. The moral good that is freedom, even the good that is a freedom protected by an established right, coexists and often conflicts with other moral goods. If we tried to assess these actions without attending to the fact that freedom is involved (as Dr. Grantly was disposed to do and as opponents of racism sometimes do) our identification of the issues before us would be incomplete and prejudicial. But we might recognize and attach great significance to these features of the actions and yet conclude that other considerations, other values in question in the circumstances, should properly take precedence. For example, we might desist from any active attempt to prevent the actions and yet think less well of the agents for persisting in them.

As against theorists of Pure Negative Freedom, theorists of positive freedom are therefore correct in thinking that the theory of freedom is an integral part of the more general theory of morality. Questions about freedom are typically moral questions. But these theorists make the wrong kind of connection between freedom and other moral concepts. By making the question whether an action is done in freedom equivalent to the question whether it is virtuous, by equating freedom and virtue, they lose the independence of the concept and the value of freedom and they distort and simplify moral issues. On their construction, the moral good of freedom and of particular freedoms cannot conflict with the moral goods with which freedom is equated. If the racist is morally wrong to hold and to express her views, she is *therefore* unfree in doing so. As we have seen, on the "enslaved by desires" dimension of the positive theory, it follows that the racist cannot be criticized or blamed for the particulars of (what appears to be her thought and action but in reality is) her behaviors. At most we can criticize her for the train of failures of responsibility for self that have left her in the grip of such vile impulses. Setting this consequence aside, we now see that it is impossible for us to conceptualize the issue posed by her proposed speech as involving a conflict between (genuine) freedom and other moral values. Quite apart from anything we may or may not do, the racist is already

unfree (or enjoying no better than an impoverished freedom); hence there can be no such conflict (or the conflict will be easily resolved against the impoverished freedom). Difficult and vitally important moral and political questions disappear.

Of course this or that theorist of positive freedom might well reach correct substantive conclusions about any number of moral issues. The theory of positive freedom might be regarded as a theory of freedom in the powerfully moralized sense of a theory that tells us who *ought to be* free to do what. But equating "freedom" with "morally virtuous (or otherwise right or proper) action" conceals an important part of what is at issue in the judgments that the theory urges on us. We are conceptually blinded to the fact that the judgments propose limitations on freedom itself. Not knowing what is at issue, we are in no position to assess the merits of proposed resolutions of it. In the name of wedding freedom to reason and morality, the positive theory diminishes our ability to deal intelligently with moral issues involving freedom.

Richard E. Flathman, *The Philosophy and Politics of Freedom* (Chicago: Chicago University Press, 1987), pp. 105–7.

Chapter 45

Hillel Steiner, from *An Essay on Rights* (1994)

Thomas Scanlon and G. A. Cohen correctly detect a "moralised definition" of freedom at work in part of Robert Nozick's account of distributive justice. This account famously asserts that "taxation of earnings from labour is on a par with forced labour." But what makes the paying of such taxes "forced," according to Nozick, is *not* the fact that the tax authorities would employ force to prevent the labourer's withholding funds. Contrary to what one might infer from the interdefinability of forcing and preventing, it's not that the former prevent the latter from forbearing to pay the tax. It is, rather, that such a forcibly imposed tax violates what Nozick sees as the moral rights of the labourer. Hence this kind of prevention of some of his action-possibilities is to be distinguished from preventions in "other cases of limited choices which are not forcings." "Other people's actions place limits on one's available opportunities. Whether this makes one's resulting action non-voluntary depends upon whether these others had the right to act as they did." On this view not all preventions, not all actions placing limits on one's opportunities, count as forcings. My action is non-voluntary – I am describably unfree to forbear it – only if others' actions which prevent me from forbearing it are ones which are impermissible for them to do. In Nozick's account, only such ineligible preventions are instances of unfreedom.

Another way in which freedom judgements are thought to be predicated on the eligibility of preventions is illustrated in the following set of examples adapted from an argument offered by David Miller. Suppose that I'm the unfortunate occupant of a room whose door can be opened only from the outside, and consider the following ways in which I might become trapped in the room.

1. I'm working in my room. Knowing that I'm inside and wishing to confine me, you shut the door.
2. You walk along the corridor and, without checking to see whether anybody is inside, shut my door.
3. You shut my door because there's a pack of wild animals roaming the corridors and posing a considerable danger to the building's occupants.
4. You, whose job it is to check rooms, come to my room and look round it. I've concealed myself in a cupboard and you shut the door without having seen me.

Miller's claim is that, although your causal role in preventing me from leaving my room is exactly similar in all four cases, you can be said to have made me unfree to do so in only the first three. The first three are respectively characterized as instances of deliberate, negligent and justified prevention. More precisely, and following Miller's contention that "when we describe a person as unfree to do something we imply that an obstacle exists which stands in need of justification," we can array these instances as follows: (i) deliberate and unjustified, (ii) non-deliberate and unjustified, and (iii) deliberate and justified. What's said to unite all these instances and qualify them as constraints on freedom is that you are "morally responsible" for the preventions they involve.

However, according to Miller, you are *not* morally responsible for the prevention in the fourth case. This prevention can be characterized as (iv) non-deliberate and justified. Just why this conjunction of characteristics, which are each disjunctively possessed by the second and third preventions for which you *are* morally responsible, negates your moral responsibility for the fourth prevention is unclear. At any rate, Miller's view too is that only ineligible preventions – here, ones which lack the joint quality of being both non-deliberate and justified – count as instances of unfreedom.

Yet another attempt to distinguish eligible from ineligible preventions, and to deem only the latter as restrictive of liberty, is to be found in [an] argument of Jan Narveson:

> A might be drunk, for instance, or acting thoughtlessly, or contrary to what A has previously represented to be A's own best interests. Does the right to liberty . . . permit or forbid interference in such cases? . . . If I try to prevent A from doing x, where x is what A currently seems to want to do but is contrary to what A has clearly insisted are A's own deeper desires or best interests, I am still respecting A's liberty . . .

Here the eligibility of the prevention, implying that it's not an instance of unfreedom, is due to the ineligibility of the action it prevents. On this understanding of what it is to be free or unfree, John Stuart Mill's famous proscription – of paternalistic curtailments of the liberty to do self-harming acts – would not be mistaken: it would be simply unintelligible.

What we've been looking at, then, is a collection of proposals that emanate from various avowedly negative accounts of liberty and that impose far greater restrictions, than does the pure negative conception, on the sorts of preventing occasion that warrant describing someone as "unfree." For these "impure negative" conceptions, the preventing of an action is not an instance of unfreedom if either the prevented act lacks eligibility or the preventing act doesn't or both. In this regard, it's worth noting Charles Taylor's cogent arguments for the untenability of such "hybrid or middle positions": that is, ones lying between pure negative liberty and characteristic formulations of positive liberty. Be this as it may, what possible motivations might lie behind these proposed restrictions?

Well one, of course, is the ever equivocal guidance of our ordinary usage of freedom. We just don't feel comfortable saying, as in the familiar caricature of the negative conception, that "Rich and poor alike are free to sleep under the bridges of London" (assuming that no one prevents them from doing so). Affirming the intelligibility and possible truth of this claim is part of the price which Blue has to pay for her intuitions. Is it too high a price?

Acknowledging the undesirability of sleeping under the bridges of London and deploring the sort of society in which the poor have no better place to sleep, don't we still want to be able to distinguish between that situation and one in which the police actually do prevent people from sleeping under the bridges? And doesn't part of that distinction consist in saying that people are unfree in the latter situation, but not in the former, to sleep under the bridges of London? Conversely and responding to Nozick's argument, do we really think that the fact that the police would be acting permissibly and exercising the public's right to have its property thus cleared of vagrants is a reason for denying that they thereby make them unfree?

If discomfort in uttering things like the previous irony is one motivation of those wishing to modify the pure negative conception, it's closely related to another more general motivation recorded by Miller: namely "a presumption that humans should not obstruct one another's activity." No doubt we do entertain such a presumption – allowing it to be overridden, as Miller suggests, only when we don't hold the obstructer morally responsible for his obstruction. But it's one thing to entertain this moral presumption, along with that caveat, and quite another to insist that suitably qualified obstructions are not restrictions of freedom at all.

Trivially, ascriptions of moral responsibility, being predicated on judgements about justifiability, presuppose particular moral values. Persons and cultures often entertain different sets of moral values and, hence, differ over what obstructions people may be held morally responsible for. For example, from some moral standpoints you, as Miller's case (4) roomchecker, might be held not to have fulfilled your duty in merely glancing round my room before shutting the door. In which event, you *would* be morally responsible for locking me in, as in case (2), and you *would* be deemed to have made me unfree.

The cost of letting Miller's moral presumption inform our judgements of *whether* persons are free or unfree is that we would be linguistically disabled from urging our moral opponents to allow people to have certain freedoms. This disability would not be due, as one might normally suppose, to our opponents' obduracy in clinging to their moral values. Rather, it would be due precisely to their acceptance of Miller's proposed modification and their consequent sheer incomprehension of our belief that their obstructive practices actually are sources of unfreedom, much less ones which they should discontinue. Such disablement does seem a high price to pay for modifying the pure negative conception of liberty. And it's evidently a purchase which many ordinary language users are as yet unwilling to make.

Hillel Steiner, *An Essay on Rights* (Oxford: Blackwell, 1994), pp. 12–15.

Chapter 46

Matthew H. Kramer, from *The Quality of Freedom* (2003)

Let us consider first the F Postulate, which declares what is necessary and sufficient for the existence of any particular freedom:

F Postulate: A person is free to φ if and only if he is able to φ.

In this formulation, the Greek letter 'φ' (which stands for any germane verb or set of verbs plus any accompanying words) can denote one's performance of some action or one's existence in some condition or one's undergoing of some process. Any ability of a person, to which the F Postulate refers, will consist not only in his power to φ – that is, his power to φ if left unimpeded – but also in the very condition of unforeclosedness that leaves open at least one opportunity for the exercise of his power to φ. To be free to φ is both to be capable of φ-ing and to be unprecluded from exerting that capability, whether one actually exerts it or not. Alternative formulations of the F Postulate are 'A person is free to φ if and only if it is possible for him to φ' and 'A person is free to φ if and only if he is unprevented from φ-ing'.

Just as important as the necessary and sufficient conditions for the existence of particular freedoms are the necessary and sufficient conditions for the existence of particular unfreedoms. Let us consequently ponder an additional postulate:

U Postulate: A person is unfree to φ if and only if both of the following conditions obtain: (1) he would be able to φ in the absence of the second of these conditions; and (2) irrespective of whether he actually endeavours to φ, he is directly or indirectly prevented from φ-ing by some action(s) or some disposition(s)-to-perform-some-action(s) on the part of some other person(s).

A person *P* who is unfree to φ would be able to φ if left unconstrained by everyone else, but is prevented from φ-ing by some action(s) which at least one other person performs or which at least one other person is disposed to perform in the event of *P*'s attempting to φ. [...]

1.4 Freedom as Normative Condition and Freedom as Physical Fact

1.4.1 Some general philosophical observations

In the F Postulate and the U Postulate with which this book has sought to encapsulate the conditions for the existence of particular freedoms and unfreedoms, the central points of reference are the modal categories of possibility and impossibility. By contrast, the deontic categories of permissibility and impermissibility do not figure at all. As should be quite plain, then, the states of freedom and unfreedom on which this book principally concentrates are non-normative. A person *P* is non-normatively free-to-φ if and only if he is physically unprevented from φ-ing. *P* is non-normatively unfree-to-φ if and only if he is physically unable-to-φ as a result of some action(s) by some other person(s). (In these statements, the word 'physically' is not to be construed in contrast with 'mentally' or 'psychologically'. We do not have to delve very deeply into the mind–body relationship to realize that somebody mentally or psychologically precluded from φ-ing is likewise physically precluded from φ-ing. If the physical preclusion did not obtain, then the psychological preclusion would not genuinely consist in preventedness. A person is mentally incapacitated from learning how to read, for example, only if it is not possible for him to undertake and undergo the full set of physical processes – chiefly cerebral processes – that would constitute his learning how to read. In sum, regardless of how one perceives the mind–body relationship, one should recognize that psychological impossibility and physical impossibility are both indeed conditions of sheer preventedness. Precisely that common characteristic is what separates them from normative impermissibility, which consists in forbiddenness rather than in precludedness. Instead of being implicitly contrasted with 'mentally,' then, the word 'physically' throughout this subsection is to be construed in opposition to 'normatively'.)

Normative liberty consists not in the physical fact of unpreventedness, but in a state of permittedness that is implicitly or explicitly established by authoritative norms such as laws or moral precepts or institutional rules. Any action which those norms allow is something which a person is normatively free to do. Contrariwise, any action which those norms forbid is something which a person is normatively unfree to do. When we are enquiring into someone's normative freedom or unfreedom, the categories that inform our investigation are deontic rather than modal. That is, we are asking whether particular modes of conduct are unprohibited or prohibited, rather than whether they are possible or infeasible. We are

seeking to discover not whether a person is *capable* of doing certain things, but whether he is *entitled* to do them.

Normative freedom as a state of permittedness and normative unfreedom as a state of forbiddenness are different in crucial respects from non-normative freedom and unfreedom. For one thing, 'free' and 'unfree' in their normative senses are bivalent; 'normatively not free' is equivalent to 'normatively unfree', and 'normatively not unfree' is equivalent to 'normatively free'. A person *P* is normatively at liberty to φ – for instance, morally or legally at liberty to φ – if and only if he is not prohibited from φ-ing by any authoritative norms such as moral precepts or laws. *P* is normatively unfree-to-φ if and only if he is prohibited from φ-ing by some authoritative norm(s). When our focus is on normative states of affairs, no gap obtains between 'unfree' and 'not free'. Of course, there are different varieties of authoritative normativity. *P* can be morally free-to-φ while being legally unfree-to-φ, and vice versa. Nevertheless, so long as we are talking about authoritative normativity generally or about a single variety of such normativity, any application of the predicate 'not free' is equivalent to an application of the predicate 'unfree'. Likewise, any application of the predicate 'not unfree' is equivalent to an application of the predicate 'free'.

Perhaps even more important than the foregoing difference between non-normative liberty and normative liberty is the difference between them as a state of unpreventedness and a state of unforbiddenness respectively. Equally significant, of course, is the difference between non-normative unfreedom as a state of preventedness and normative unfreedom as a state of forbiddenness. Whenever someone is non-normatively free to do *A*, she is able to do it – irrespective of whether she is permitted to do it. She *can* do it, whether or not she *may* do it (that is, whether or not she can do it legitimately). She might be transgressing moral or legal norms in the process, but she is non-normatively at-liberty-to-do-*A* inasmuch as she is unprecluded from doing it. Ability, not permissibility, is the key category for non-normative freedom. Quite the reverse is true for normative freedom. Whenever somebody is normatively free to do A, she is allowed to do it by any authoritative norms that might be applicable. If none of those norms imposes on her a duty to abstain from doing A or to abstain from doing something that would be indispensable for the doing of A, then the performance of A is something which she is normatively free to undertake. She enjoys normative freedom in respect of A inasmuch as she is not required by any authoritative norms to forgo A. However, her normative latitude to carry out A will not necessarily be accompanied by any non-normative freedom to do it. She might be wholly unable to perform A, either because of her own incapacities or because of some external preventive factor. For example, while not being under any legal or moral duty to refrain from running a mile in less than four minutes, and while likewise not being under any duty to refrain from engaging in some activity (such as regular practice) that would be indispensable for the performance of such a feat, Mary is utterly unable to run a mile so swiftly. Though she is normatively at liberty to run a mile in less than four minutes, she lacks the capacity to do so, and therefore she does not enjoy any non-normative liberty to run with such celerity.

Whenever someone is non-normatively unfree to do A, he is unable to do it, and his inability has been caused by some action(s) of some other person(s). He might be perfectly entitled to do A – that is, he might be normatively at liberty to do it – but at least one action by some other person(s) has physically prevented him from doing it. In other words, even if he enjoys the normative freedom to do A, the actions or dispositions of some other person(s) have made him unable to exercise that freedom (whether or not he endeavours to exercise it). Permissibility and impossibility can coincide. Much the same can be said, conversely, about the potential coincidence of possibility and impermissibility. Whenever somebody is normatively unfree to do A, he is

prohibited from doing it by some authoritative norm that imposes a duty on him to eschew A or to eschew some action(s) that would be indispensable for his performance of A. Because of the forbiddenness of A or the forbiddenness of an essential prerequisite thereof, he cannot perform A without disobeying the requirements of some moral or legal or other authoritative norms. Nonetheless, although he cannot perform A without disobeying those requirements, he might be able to perform it with ease. These need not be and frequently will not be a convergence between what is barred by legal or moral mandates and what is rendered impossible by the physical facts of a situation. Those facts frequently enable occurrences which the prevailing legal or moral norms prohibit. As was noted earlier, even the regular enforcement of legal mandates will seldom preclude violations of their requirements. That enforcement is usually *post hoc* rather than anticipatory. In short, impermissibility and possibility very frequently coincide – which means, of course, that the normative unfreedom-to-φ and the non-normative freedom-to-φ very frequently coincide. We have seen above that there is no necessary correlation between instances of normative freedom and instances of non-normative freedom, and we have seen here that a similar point obtains in regard to normative and non-normative *un*freedom.

Another dissimilarity between normative freedom or unfreedom and non-normative freedom or unfreedom pertains to the isolability of actions that are proscribed or precluded. The removal of someone's non-normative freedom-to-do-X will sometimes require the removal of his non-normative freedom-to-do-things-that-are-crucially-prerequisite-to-his-performance-of-X, whereas a prohibition on his doing X (that is, the removal of his normative liberty-to-do-X) will never require the prohibition of any prerequisite actions that are logically distinct from his doing X. If somebody retains the non-normative freedom to take steps that are immediately antecedent to his performance of X, then the prevention of his doing X – that is, the removal of his non-normative liberty-to-do-X – will typically depend on monitoring and rapid interventions by other people to an extent that will sometimes not be feasible. To be sure, such monitoring and interventions will often be feasible, in connection with many activities. For example, just as King Uzziah was about to offer incense on the altar of the ancient temple of Judah, dozens of priests interposed themselves between him and the altar, and they thrust him away. In some circumstances, however, last-minute preventive intrusions of this sort are not realistically possible. An intervention at an earlier stage will sometimes be essential if a person's non-normative liberty-to-do-X is genuinely to be eliminated. Nothing similar is ever essential for the removal of someone's normative liberty-to-do-X. Suppose, for illustration, that somebody in a queue for a bus has assaulted somebody else in the queue. The assault was legally and morally forbidden, even though the close physical proximity of the two people in the queue – essential for the perpetration of the assault – was not itself illegal or immoral. That is, the assailant had no normative liberty to commit the assault, even though he did enjoy normative liberty (as well as non-normative liberty) to do virtually everything prerequisite to his commission of the assault. Precisely because the elimination of any person's normative liberty-to-do-X concerns what is impermissible rather than what is impossible, that elimination is always perfectly consistent with the fact that the person retains the normative liberty to do just about everything that is physically indispensable for his undertaking of X. (Of course, sometimes a person will not enjoy the normative liberty to take steps that immediately lead up to his proscribed performance of X. What I have argued

here is simply that the absence of his normative liberty to take those steps is never necessary for the absence of his normative liberty to perform X itself.)

Still another divergence between normative unfreedom and non-normative unfreedom is evident from the first chief subsection of this chapter. As was argued there, a person whose mind has not been completely taken over by someone else or by a severe mental illness will retain the non-normative freedom to eschew any particular action. At the very least, such a person will always have the option of surrendering in a wholly passive manner to the operations of external forces. In other words, there is no such thing as a physically unavoidable action. When we cross from the realm of the non-normative to the realm of the normative, we encounter a very different situation. Any person P can be normatively unfree to forgo certain instances of conduct. For example, every person whose income is subject to taxation will be legally unfree – and perhaps morally unfree – to abstain from doing what is necessary in order to pay any taxes that are owed. Though P is always physically free (albeit perhaps at great cost) to refrain from signing the requisite forms and cheques for the payment of his taxes in a timely fashion, he is normatively unfree to hold back in that manner. He is legally obligated and perhaps morally obligated to sign the relevant documents. A moral or legal obligation can render the doing of A normatively mandatory, by rendering impermissible a failure to do A. In that respect, as well as in other respects, the mandatoriness created by legal or moral requirements is distinguishable from the necessity created by physical constraints.

Matthew H. Kramer, *The Quality of Freedom* (Oxford: Oxford University Press, 2003), pp. 59–65.

Part V
Coercion

Introduction to Part V

Like the concept of freedom, the concept of coercion is employed on both sides of the political spectrum. Coercion is a form of power – forcing others to act in accordance with one's will – and many political thinkers of both the right and the left regard such power as prima facie unjust. Friedrich von Hayek defined freedom as the absence of coercion, and held that the minimization of coercion requires the enforcement of the rules of private property and voluntary contract. Socialist thinkers, on the other hand, have traditionally claimed that workers in a capitalist economy lack freedom because they are forced to sell their labor power at exploitatively low prices. Philosophers have tried to shed light on these and similar disagreements by analyzing the meaning of coercion and clarifying its relation to freedom.

Some philosophers have suggested that, pace Hayek, being negatively unfree is not essentially a matter of being coerced. There is a difference, they point out, between being free to perform an action and performing that action freely. The former involves having an opportunity (and is what negative freedom consists in), while the latter involves exercising an opportunity in a certain way (specifically, in a non-coerced way). Coercion is a limiting of the freedom *with which* a person does something.

Distinguishing in this way between "the freedom to act" and "acting freely" tends to lead in the direction of the "pure negative" conception of freedom, which is defended in this section by Hillel Steiner. According to this conception, the freedom to do something is removed only by the physical impossibility of doing that thing. Since coercion operates by means of its effect on the *will* of the coerced, it does not amount to the physical prevention of options. For Steiner, coercing someone into doing x – for example, by threatening to kill them should they fail to do x – removes neither their freedom to do x nor their freedom not to do x. Some theorists, like Serena Olsaretti, sympathize with this view but are nevertheless interested in examining the concept of coercion in its own right. Olsaretti suggests that coercion limits another important attribute, the "voluntariness" of actions, so that if I am forced to do something under threat of death, while I remain free to do or not to do that thing, I nevertheless do it involuntarily. Others see the pure negative conception as stretching common usage too far, and prefer to say that if a person may only do *x* on pain of death, then that person is unfree to do *x*. In either case, we are still left with the problem of defining coercion, either as a possible source of unfreedom or as an independent phenomenon.

One of the tasks that have most puzzled philosophers in attempting to characterize coercion is that of sorting out the roles played by threats and offers. It is generally agreed that threats are coercive, but there is less certainty over whether offers can be coercive. Some, like David Zimmerman, argue that an employer who offers an unemployed person a badly paid job can be seen as making a "coercive offer." Others, like Michael Gorr, deny that offers can ever be coercive in themselves.

One of the reasons for this disagreement lies in the difficulty of distinguishing threats from offers in the first place. We tend to think that not giving in to a threat makes one worse off than one would otherwise have been, whereas declining an offer does not. This thought helps to explain the intuition that offers do not coerce. But what is meant by, "how well off one would otherwise have been"? This would seem to depend on what the normal and expected course of events would have been in the absence of the intervention (the offer/threat). But how are we to characterize this normal and expected course of events? If Mary stumbles across a badly injured man lying alone in the street, and agrees to take him to hospital only if he pays her $5,000, is she making an offer (to take him to hospital) or issuing a threat (to leave him lying in the street)? Robert Nozick suggests that, despite initial appearances, we tend on reflection to see this as a threat, the reason being that the normal and expected course of events involves the taking of the injured man to hospital (once Mary has stumbled across him) either free of charge or for a fee well below $5,000. For Nozick, this implies that what counts as a threat depends on moral norms, because the concept of the "normal and expected course of events" depends on what is *morally* normal and expected.

A similar line of reasoning might be employed by the socialist in order to claim that capitalist "wage offers" are really threats in disguise. However, there is also a rival understanding of coercion, according to which the relevant "normal and expected course of events" can and should be characterized without reference to moral norms. Zimmerman's account of coercive wage offers, for example, is based on a non-moral account of coercion, and refers instead to the preferences of the recipients of the offers.

As will be seen from the writings in this part, an adequate characterization of coercion requires some fairly complex work specifying the necessary and sufficient conditions for coercion's existence. This is partly due to the number of factors involved, which may include the intentions of the coercer, the preferences or well-being of the coerced, and the beliefs of both the coercer and the coerced.

Further Reading

Cohen, G. A., *History, Labour and Freedom. Themes from Marx* (Oxford: Clarendon Press, 1988), Part III ⟨analysis of the Marxist claim that workers are forced to sell their labor power⟩.

Day, J. P., "Threats, Offers, Law, Opinion and Liberty," in J. P. Day, *Liberty and Justice* (London: Croom Helm, 1987) ⟨defense of the view that threats restrict negative liberty⟩.

Lamond, Grant, "The Coerciveness of Law," *Oxford Journal of Legal Studies* 20 (2000), pp. 39–62 ⟨analysis of the different ways in which law is coercive⟩.

Lyons, Daniel, "Welcome Threats and Coercive Offers," *Philosophy* 50 (1975), pp. 425–36 ⟨analysis and defense of the notion of coercive offers⟩.

Ryan, Cheyney C., "The Normative Concept of Coercion," *Mind* 89 (1980), pp. 481–98 ⟨defense of a normative conception of coercion⟩.

Chapter 47

F. A. Hayek, from *The Constitution of Liberty* (1960)

Chapter Nine
Coercion and the State

For that is an absolute villeinage from which an uncertain and indeterminate service is rendered, where it cannot be known in the evening what service is to be rendered in the morning, that is where a person is bound to whatever is enjoined to him.

HENRY BRACTON

1.   Earlier in our discussion we provisionally defined freedom as the absence of coercion. But coercion is nearly as troublesome a concept as liberty itself, and for much the same reason: we do not clearly distinguish between what other men do to us and the effects on us of physical circumstances. As a matter of fact, English provides us with two different words to make the necessary distinction: while we can legitimately say that we have been compelled by circumstances to do this or that, we presuppose a human agent if we say that we have been coerced.

Coercion occurs when one man's actions are made to serve another man's will, not for his own but for the other's purpose. It is not that the coerced does not choose at all; if that were the case, we should not speak of his "acting." If my hand is guided by physical force to trace my signature or my finger pressed against the trigger of a gun, I have not acted. Such violence, which makes my body someone else's physical tool, is, of course, as bad as coercion proper and must be prevented for the same

reason. Coercion implies, however, that I still choose but that my mind is made someone else's tool, because the alternatives before me have been so manipulated that the conduct that the coercer wants me to choose becomes for me the least painful one. Although coerced, it is still I who decide which is the least evil under the circumstances.

Coercion clearly does not include all influences that men can exercise on the action of others. It does not even include all instances in which a person acts or threatens to act in a manner he knows will harm another person and will lead him to change his intentions. A person who blocks my path in the street and causes me to step aside, a person who has borrowed from the library the book I want, or even a person who drives me away by the unpleasant noises he produces cannot properly be said to coerce me. Coercion implies both the threat of inflicting harm and the intention thereby to bring about certain conduct.

Though the coerced still chooses, the alternatives are determined for him by the coercer so that he will choose what the coercer wants. He is not altogether deprived of the use of his capacities; but he is deprived of the possibility of using his knowledge for his own aims. The effective use of a person's intelligence and knowledge in the pursuit of his aims requires that he be able to foresee some of the conditions of his environment and adhere to a plan of action. Most human aims can be achieved only by a chain of connected actions, decided upon as a coherent whole and based on the assumption that the facts will be what they are expected to be. It is because, and insofar as, we can predict events, or at least know probabilities, that we can achieve anything. And though physical circumstances will often be unpredictable, they will not maliciously frustrate our aims. But if the facts which determine our plans are under the sole control of another, our actions will be similarly controlled.

Coercion thus is bad because it prevents a person from using his mental powers to the full and consequently from making the greatest contribution that he is capable of to the community. Though the coerced will still do the best he can do for himself at any given moment, the only comprehensive design that his actions fit into is that of another mind.

2 Political philosophers have discussed power more often than they have coercion because political power usually means power to coerce. But though the great men, from John Milton and Edmund Burke to Lord Acton and Jacob Burckharkt, who have represented power as the archevil, were right in what they meant, it is misleading to speak simply of power in this connection. It is not power as such – the capacity to achieve what one wants – that is bad, but only the power to coerce, to force other men to serve one's will by the threat of inflicting harm. There is no evil in the power wielded by the director of some great enterprise in which men have willingly united of their own will and for their own purposes. It is part of the strength of civilized society that, by such voluntary combination of effort under a unified direction, men can enormously increase their collective power.

It is not power in the sense of an extension of our capacities which corrupts, but the subjection of other human wills to ours, the use of other men against their will for our purposes. It is true that in human relations power and coercion dwell closely together, that great powers possessed by a few may enable them to coerce other, unless those powers are contained by a still greater power; but coercion is

neither so necessary nor so common a consequence of power as is generally assumed. Neither the powers of a Henry Ford nor those of the Atomic Energy Commission, neither those of the General of the Salvation Army nor (at least until recently) those of the President of the United State, are powers to coerce particular people for the purposes they choose.

It would be less misleading if occasionally the terms "force" and "violence" were used instead of coercion, since the threat of force or violence is the most important form of coercion. But they are not synonymous with coercion, for the threat of physical force is not the only way in which coercion can be exercised. Similarly, "oppression," which is perhaps as much a true opposite of liberty as coercion, should refer only to a state of continuous acts of coercion.

3 Coercion should be carefully distinguished from the conditions or terms on which our fellow men are willing to render us specific services or benefits. It is only in very exceptional circumstances that the sole control of a service or resource which is essential to us would confer upon another the power of true coercion. Life in society necessarily means that we are dependent for the satisfaction of most of our needs on the services of some of our fellows; in a free society these mutual services are voluntary, and each can determine to whom he wants to render services and on what terms. The benefits and opportunities which our fellows offer to us will be available only if we satisfy their conditions.

This is as true of social as of economic relations. If a hostess will invite me to her parties only if I conform to certain standards of conduct and dress, or my neighbor converse with me only if I observe conventional manners, this is certainly not coercion. Nor can it be legitimately called "coercion" if a producer or dealer refuses to supply me with what I want except at his price. This is certainly true in a competitive market, where I can turn to somebody else if the terms of the first offer do not suit me; and it is normally no less true when I face a monopolist. If, for instance, I would very much like to be painted by a famous artist and if he refuses to paint me for less than a very high fee, it would clearly be absurd to say that I am coerced. The same it true of any other commodity or service that I can do without. So long as the services of a particular person are not crucial to my existence or the preservation of what I most value, the conditions he exacts for rendering these services cannot properly be called "coercion."

A monopolist could exercise true coercion, however, if he were, say, the owner of a spring in an oasis. Let us say that other persons settled there on the assumption that water would always be available at a reasonable price and then found, perhaps because a second spring dried up, that they had no choice but to do whatever the owner of the spring demanded of them if they were to survive: here would be a clear case of coercion. One could conceive of a few other instances where a monopolist might control an essential commodity on which people were completely dependent. But unless a monopolist is in a position to withhold an indispensable supply, he cannot exercise coercion, however unpleasant his demands may be for those who rely on his services.

It is worth pointing out, in view of what we shall later have to say about the appropriate methods of curbing the coercive power of the state, that whenever there is a danger of a monopolist's acquiring coercive power, the most expedient and effective method of preventing this is probably to require him to treat all customers alike, i.e., to insist that his prices be the same for all and to prohibit all discrimination on his part. This is the same principle by which we have learned to curb the coercive power of the state.

The individual provider of employment cannot normally exercise coercion, any more than can the supplier of a particular commodity or service. So long as he can remove only one opportunity among many to earn a living, so long as he can do no more than cease to pay certain people who cannot hope to earn

as much elsewhere as they had done under him, he cannot coerce, though he may cause pain. There are, undeniably, occasions when the condition of employment creates opportunity for true coercion. In periods of acute unemployment the threat of dismissal may be used to enforce actions other than those originally contracted for. And in conditions such as those in a mining town the manager may well exercise an entirely arbitrary and capricious tyranny over a man to whom he has taken a dislike. But such conditions, though not impossible, would, at the worst, be rare exceptions in a prosperous competitive society.

A complete monopoly of employment, such as would exist in a fully socialist state in which the government was the only employer and the owner of all the instruments of production, would possess unlimited powers of coercion. As Leon Trotsky discovered: "In a country where the sole employer is the State, opposition means death by slow starvation. The old principle, who does not work shall not eat, has been replaced by a new one: who does not obey shall not eat."

Except in such instances of monopoly of an essential service, the mere power of withholding a benefit will not produce coercion. The use of such power by another may indeed alter the social landscape to which I have adapted my plans and make it necessary for me to reconsider all my decisions, perhaps to change my whole scheme of life and to worry about many things I had taken for granted. But, though the alternatives before me may be distressingly few and uncertain, and my new plans of a makeshift character, yet it is not some other will that guides my action. I may have to act under great pressure, but I cannot be said to act under coercion. Even if the threat of starvation to me and perhaps to my family impels me to accept a distasteful job at a very low wage, even if I am "at the mercy" of the only man willing to employ me, I am not coerced by him or anybody else. So long as the act that has placed me in my predicament is not aimed at making me do or not do specific things, so long as the intent of the act that harms me is not to make serve another person's ends, its effect on my freedom is not different from that of any natural calamity – a fire or a flood that destroys my house or an accident that harms my health.

4 True coercion occurs when armed bands of conquerors make the subject people toil for them, when organized gangsters extort a levy for "protection," when the knower of an evil secret blackmails his victim, and, of course, when the state threatens to inflict punishment and to employ physical force to make us obey its commands. There are many degrees of coercion, form the extreme case of the dominance of the master over the slave or the tyrant over the subject, where the unlimited power of punishment exacts complete submission to the will of the master, to the instance of the single threat of inflicting an evil to which the threatened would prefer almost anything else.

Whether or not attempts to coerce a particular person will be successful depends in a large measure on that person's inner strength: the threat of assassination may have less power to turn one man from his aim than the threat of some minor inconvenience in the case of another. But while we may pity the weak or the very sensitive person whom a mere frown may "compel" to do what he would not do otherwise, we are concerned with coercion that is likely to affect the normal, average person. Though this will usually be some threat of bodily harm to his person or his dear ones, or of damage to a valuable or cherished possession, it need not consist of any use of force or violence. One may frustrate another's every attempt at spontaneous action by placing in his path an infinite variety of minor obstacles: guile and malice may well find the means of coercing the physically stronger. It is not impossible for a horde of cunning boys to drive an unpopular person out of town.

In some degree all close relationships between men, whether they are tied to one another by affection, economic necessity, or physical circumstances (such as on a ship or an expedition), provide opportunities for coercion. The conditions of personal domestic service, like all more intimate relations, undoubtedly offer opportunities for coercion of a peculiarly oppressive kind and are, in consequence, felt as restrictions on personal liberty. And a morose husband, a nagging wife, or a hysterical mother may make life intolerable unless their every mood is obeyed. But here society can do little to protect the individual beyond making such associations with others truly voluntary. Any attempt to regulate these intimate associations further would clearly involve such far-reaching restrictions on choice and conduct as to produce even greater coercion: if people are to be free to choose their associates and intimates, the coercion that arises form voluntary association cannot be the concern of government.

The reader may feel that we have devoted more space than is necessary to the distinction between what can be legitimately called "coercion" and what cannot and between the more severe forms of coercion, which we should prevent, and the lesser forms, which ought not to be the concern of authority. But, as in the case of liberty, a gradual extension of the concept has almost deprived it of value. Liberty can be so defined as to make it impossible of attainment. Similarly, coercion can be so defined as to make it an all-pervasive and unavoidable phenomenon. We cannot prevent all harm that a person may inflict upon another, or even all the milder forms of coercion to which life in close contact with other men exposes us; but this does not mean that we ought not to try to prevent all the more severe forms of coercion, or that we ought not to define liberty as the absence of such coercion.

5. Since coercion is the control of the essential data of an individual's action by another, it can be prevented only by enabling the individual to secure for himself some private sphere where he is protected against such interference. The assurance that he can

count on certain facts not being deliberately shaped by another can be given to him only by some authority that has the necessary power. It is here that coercion of one individual by another can be prevented only by the threat of coercion.

The existence of such an assured free sphere seems to us so much a normal condition of life that we are tempted to define "coercion" by the use of such terms as "the interference with legitimate expectations," or "infringement of rights," or "arbitrary interference." But in defining coercion we cannot take for granted the arrangements intended to prevent it. The "legitimacy" of one's expectations or the "rights" of the individual are the result of the recognition of such a private sphere. Coercion not only would exist but would be much more common if no such protected sphere existed. Only in a society that has already attempted to prevent coercion by some demarcation of a protected sphere can a concept like "arbitrary interference" have a definite meaning.

If the recognition of such individual spheres, however, is not itself to become an instrument of coercion, their range and content must not be determined by the deliberate assignment of particular things to particular men. If what was to be included in a man's private sphere were to be determined by the will of any man or group of men, this would simply transfer the power of coercion to that will. Nor would it be desirable to have the particular contents of a man's private sphere fixed once and for all. If people are to make the best use of their knowledge and capacities and foresight, it is desirable that they themselves have some voice in the determination of what will be included in their personal protected sphere.

The solution that men have found this problem rests on the recognition of general rules governing the conditions under which objects or circumstances become part of the protected sphere of a person or persons. The acceptance of such rules enables each member of a society to shape the content of his protected sphere and all members to recognize what belongs to their sphere and what does not.

We must not think of this sphere as consisting exclusively, or even chiefly, of material things. Although to divide the material objects of our environment into what is mine and what is another's is the principal aim of the rules which delimit the spheres, they also secure for us many other "rights," such as security in certain uses of things or merely protection against interference with our actions.

6 The recognition of private or several property is thus an essential condition for the prevention of coercion, though by no means the only one. We are rarely in a position to carry out a coherent plan of action unless we are certain of our exclusive control of some material objects; and where we do not control them, it is necessary that we know who does if we are to collaborate with others. The recognition of property is clearly the first step in the delimitation of the private sphere which protects us against coercion; and it has long been recognized that "a people averse to the institution of private property is without the first element of freedom" and that "nobody is at liberty to attack several property and to say at the same time that he values civilization. The history of the two cannot be disentangled." Modern anthropology confirms the fact that "private property appears very definitely on primitive levels" and "the roots of property as a legal principle which determines the physical relationships between man and his environmental setting, natural and artificial, are the very prerequisite of any ordered action in the cultural sense."

In modern society, however, the essential requisite for the protection of the individual against coercion is not that he possess property but that the material means which enable him to pursue any plan of action should not be all in the exclusive control of one other agent. It is one of the accomplishments of modern society that freedom may be enjoyed by a person with practically no property of his own (beyond personal belongings like clothing – and even these can be rented) and that we can leave the care of the property that serves our needs largely to others. The important point is that the property should be sufficiently dispersed so that the individual is not dependent on particular persons who alone can provide him with what he needs or who alone can employ him.

That other people's property can be serviceable in the achievement of our aims is due mainly to the enforcibility of contracts. The whole network of rights created by contracts is as important a part of our own protected sphere, as much the basis of our plans, as any property of our own. The decisive condition for mutually advantageous collaboration between people, based on voluntary consent rather than coercion, is that there be many people who can serve one's needs, so that nobody has to be dependent on specific persons for the essential conditions of life or the possibility of development in some direction. It is competition made possible by the dispersion of property that deprives the individual owners of particular things of all coercive powers.

In view of a common misunderstanding of a famous maxim, it should be mentioned that we are independent of the will of those whose services we need because they serve us for their own purpose and are normally little interested in the uses we make of their services. We should be very dependent on the beliefs of our fellows if they were prepared to sell their products to us only when they approved of our ends and not for their own advantage. It is largely because in the economic transactions of everyday life we are only impersonal means to our fellows, who help us for their own purposes, that we can count on such help from complete strangers and use it for whatever end we wish.

The rules of property and contract are required to delimit the individual's private sphere wherever the resources or services needed for the pursuit of his aims are scarce and must, in consequence, be under the control of some man or another. But if this is true of most of the benefits we derive from men's efforts, it is not true of all. There are some kinds of services, such as sanitation or roads, which, once they are provided, are normally sufficient for all who want to use them. The provision of such services has long been a recognized field of public effort, and the right to share in them is an important part of the protected sphere of the individual. We need only remember the role that the assured "access to the King's highway" has played in history to see how important such rights may be individual liberty.

We cannot enumerate here all the rights to protected interests which serve to secure to the legal person a known sphere of unimpeded action. But, since modern man has become a little insensitive on this point, it ought perhaps to be mentioned that the recognition of a protected individual sphere has in times of freedom normally included a right to privacy and secrecy, the conception that a man's house is his castle and that nobody has a right even to take cognizance of his activities within it.

7.   The character of those abstract and general rules that have been evolved to limit coercion both by other individuals and by the state will be the subject of the next chapter. Here we shall consider in a general way how that threat of coercion which is the only means whereby the state can prevent the coercion of one individual by another can be deprived of most if its harmful and objectionable character.

This threat of coercion has a very different effect from that of actual and unavoidable coercion, if it refers only to known circumstances which can be avoided by the potential object of coercion. The great majority of the threats of coercion that a free society must employ are of this avoidable kind. Most of the rules that it enforces, particularly its private law, do not constrain private persons (as distinguished from the servants of the state) to perform specific actions. The sanctions of the law are designed only to prevent a person from doing certain things or to make him perform obligations that he has voluntarily incurred.

Provided that I know beforehand that if I place myself in a particular position, I shall be coerced and provided that I can avoid putting myself in such a position, I need never be coerced. At least insofar as the rules providing for coercion are not aimed at me personally but are so framed as to apply equally to all people in similar circumstances, they are no different from any of the natural obstacles that affect my plans. In that they tell me what will happen *if* I do this or that, the laws of the state have the same significance for me as the laws of nature; and I can use my knowledge of the laws of the state to achieve my own aims as I use my knowledge of the laws of nature.

8.   Of course, in some respects the state uses coercion to make us perform particular actions. The most important of these are taxation and the various compulsory services, especially in the armed forces. Though these are not supposed to be avoidable, they are at least predictable and are enforced irrespective of how the individual would otherwise employ his energies; this deprives them largely of the evil nature of coercion. If the known necessity of paying a certain amount in taxes becomes the basis of all my plans, if a period of military service is a foreseeable part of my career, then I can follow a general plan of life of my own making and am as independent of the will of another person as men have learned to be in society. Though compulsory military service, while it lasts, undoubtedly involves severe coercion, and though a lifelong conscript could not be said ever to be free, a predictable limited period of military service certainly restricts the possibility of shaping one's own life less than would, for instance, a constant threat of arrest resorted to by an arbitrary power to ensure what it regards as good behavior.

The interference of the coercive power of government with our lives is most disturbing when it is neither avoidable nor predictable. Where such coercion is necessary even in a free society, as when we are called to serve on a jury or to act as special constables, we mitigate the effects by not allowing any person to possess arbitrary power of coercion. Instead, the decision as to who must serve is make to rest on fortuitous processes, such as the drawing of lots. These unpredictable acts of coercion, which follow from unpredictable events but conform to known rules, affect our lives as do other "acts of God," but do not subject us to the arbitrary will of another person.

[. . .]

F. A. Hayek, *The Constitution of Liberty* (London: Routledge and Kegan Paul, 1960), pp. 133–43.

Chapter 48

Robert Nozick, from "Coercion" (1969)

Conditions for Coercion

I shall begin by considering an account of coercion obtained from combining some things said on this subject in Hart and Honoré's *Causation in the Law* (Oxford, 1961) with some remarks of Hart in his *The Concept of Law* (Oxford, 1959). According to this account, person P coerces person Q into not doing act A if and only if

(1) P threatens to do something if Q does A (and P knows he's making this threat).

(2) This threat renders Q's doing A substantially less eligible as a course of conduct than not doing A.

(3) P makes this threat in order to get Q not to do A, intending that Q realize he's been threatened by P.

(4) Q does not do A.

(5) P's words or deeds are part of Q's reason for not doing A.[1]

Conditions 1–5 do not appear to be sufficient for coercion. For example, P threatens Q, saying that if Q performs a particular action, a rock will fall and kill him. P thinks Q knows of his (P's) infamous procedure of murdering people, but Q thinks that P is telling him about some strange natural law that holds independently of human action, namely whenever someone performs this action, he gets killed by a falling rock. That is, Q understands what P says, not as a *threat* but as a *warning*. If Q refrains from performing the action, P has not coerced him into not doing it, even though the five conditions are satisfied. This suggests that we add as a further condition:

(6) Q knows that P has threatened to do the something mentioned in 1, if he, Q, does A (or, to handle cases of anonymous threats, Q knows that someone has threatened to do something mentioned in (1) if he, Q, does A).

It is not clear that the conditions thus far listed are sufficient. You threaten to do something if I do A, thinking that I don't want this something done. But in fact, I don't mind it or even slightly want it. However I realize that you must feel very strongly about my doing A, since you've threatened me, and that you will be very upset if I do A (*not* that you will *choose* to be upset to punish me for doing A). Since I don't want you to be upset, I refrain from doing A. You did not coerce me into not doing A, though it seems that the conditions listed are satisfied; in particular it seems that the relevant conditions 5 and 2 are satisfied. Or, if they can be so interpreted so that they're not satisfied, it would be well to make this interpretation explicit, replacing 5, 1 and 2 by:

(5') Part of Q's reason for not doing A is to avoid (or lessen the likelihood of) the thing which P has threatened to bring about or have brought about.[2]

(1′) P threatens to bring about or have brought about some consequence if Q does A (and knows he's threatening to do this).

(2′) A with this threatened consequence is rendered substantially less eligible as a course of conduct for Q than A was without the threatened consequence.

Must P make the threat *in order* to get Q not to do A? Must condition 3 be satisfied? In normal situations it will be satisfied; e.g., a highwayman says 'If you don't give me your money, I'll kill you,' making this threat in order to get me to give him my money. But suppose that we are conducting an experiment for the Social Science Research Council, to study people's reactions in the highwayman situation. We don't care how he reacts to our threat (if he gives over the money we must turn it over to the SSRC; if he resists we are empowered to kill him and, let us suppose, have no moral scruples about doing so). We do not say 'your money or your life' in order to get him to give us his money, but in order to gather data. We might even suppose that I think him very brave and have bet with you that he'll resist and be killed. After making the bet, I want him *not* to hand over the money, and I don't make the threat in order to get him to hand it over. In the grip of fear and trembling, he hands over the money. Surely we coerced him into doing so. This suggests replacing 3 by a more complicated condition:

(Part of) P's reason for deciding to bring about the consequence or have it brought about, if Q does A, is that P believes this consequence worsens Q's alternative of doing A (i.e. that P believes that this consequence worsens Q's alternative of doing A, or that Q would believe it does[3]).

The SSRC example satisfies this condition, since (part of) the researchers' reason for deciding to kill Q if he doesn't turn over the money is that they believe this consequence worsens Q's alternative of not giving them the money.

But the condition formulated is not broad enough, for we want to cover cases where P has not decided to bring about the consequence if Q does A, but is bluffing instead, or neither intends nor intends not to bring it about if Q does A. This suggests disjoining another condition with the one above:

If P has not decided to bring about the consequence, or have it brought about, if Q does A, then (part of) P's reason for saying he will bring about the consequence, or have it brought about, if Q does A is that (P believes) Q will believe this consequence worsens Q's alternative of doing A.[4]

One is tempted to say that this disjunctive condition is superfluous, because it is built into the notion of threatening, and hence follows from condition 1′. That is, one is tempted to say that if this condition is not satisfied, if P's reasons or motives are not as described, then P has not *threatened* Q. I shall have more to say about this later.

The conditions listed still do not appear to be sufficient. Consider cases where Q wants to do A in order to bring about x, and P says that if Q does A, he (P) will do something which just prevents A from bringing about x. This makes A substantially less eligible as an alternative for Q (Q now, we may suppose, has no reason to do A), and the other conditions may well be satisfied. Yet, at least some cases of this sort ('If you say another word, I shall turn off my hearing aid') are not cases of coercion.[5]

Cases of this sort suggest the following condition:

(7) Q believes that, and P believes that Q believes that, P's threatened consequence would leave Q worse off, having done A, than if Q didn't do A and P didn't bring about the consequence.

In the application of this condition, in deciding how well or poorly off Q is having done A and having had his purpose x thwarted, one must ignore Q's wasted effort, humiliation at having failed to bring about x, and (in some cases) Q's foregoing opportunities. Similarly in deciding how well or poorly off Q would be not doing A and not having P bring about the consequence, one must ignore any regret Q might feel at not doing A.[6]

According to our account of 'P coerces Q into doing A,' the following cases are *not* cases in which P coerces Q into doing A.

(1) Q mishears P as having said 'Your money or your life' and hands over his money, but P said something else, or said this as a questions about something he thought Q said, etc.

(2) P doesn't speak English, but has picked up the sentence 'Your money or your life' from a movie, though he does not know what it means. To be friendly, P utters this one sentence to Q who is sitting next to him in a bar (perhaps while showing Q his unusual knife for Q to admire). Q hands over his money.

(3) Q walks into a room, and unbeknownst to him there is a tape recorder in the next room playing part of the soundtrack of a movie. Q hears 'Put all of your money on the table and then leave, or I'll kill you.' Q puts his money on the table, and leaves.

I suggest that in these cases, though Q feels coerced and thinks he is coerced, P does not coerce Q into giving over the money. (In the third case there is no plausible person P to consider.) Those who refuse to accept this might hold the view that though P does not coerce Q into giving over the money, nonetheless Q is coerced into giving over the money. Such a person would reject the view that 'Q is coerced into doing A' is equivalent to 'there is a P who coerces Q into doing A,' and perhaps suggest that Q is coerced into doing A if and only if

(1) There is a P who coerces Q into doing A.

or (2) Q is justified in believing that there is a P who has threatened to bring about a consequence which significantly worsens his alternative of not doing A (and that P has the appropriate reasons and intentions), and (past of) Q's reason for doing A is to avoid or lessen the likelihood of this consequence he believes was threatened.

I should mention that a threat need not be verbally expressed; it may be perfectly clear from actions performed what the threat is, or at least that something undesirable will occur if one doesn't perform some appropriate action. For example, members of a street gang capture a member of a rival gang and ask him where that gang's weapons are hidden. He refuses to tell, and they beat him up. They ask again, he refuses again, they beat him again. And so on until he tells. He was coerced into telling. His captors didn't have to *say*, 'if you don't tell us we will continue to beat you up or perhaps eventually do something worse.' This is perfectly clear to all involved in the situation. In many situations the inflication of violence is well understood by all parties to be a threat of further infliction of violence if there is noncompliance. Nothing need be *said*. It may be for reasons such as this that some writers (e.g. Bay) say that all infliction of violence constitutes coercion. But this is, I think, a mistake. If a drunken group comes upon a stranger and beats him up or even kills him, this need not be coercion. For there need have been no implicit threat of further violence if the person didn't comply with their wishes, and it would indeed be difficult for this to be the case if they just come upon him and kill him.[7]

There is another type of situation very similar to the one we have thus far been concerned with, for which similar conditions can be offered. I have in mind cases where no one threatens to inflict some damage on Q if he does A, but someone sets things up so that damage is automatically inflicted if Q does A. It's not that if you do A, I will bring about a consequence which you consider to be bad, but rather that I now do something (the doing of which is not conditional upon your doing A) which is such that if you do A after I have done this thing, there will be a consequence which you consider to be bad. Though in such situations a person is deterred from doing something, it is not obvious to me that he is coerced into not doing it. If it is coercion then the account of coercion would say that P coerces Q into not doing A if and only if either of the two sets of conditions is satisfied.

I suggest that it is as a case of this sort of situation, rather than the one discussed earlier, that we are to understand the following: some adult's mother says to him, 'If you do A I'll have a heart attack, or the probability = p that I'll have a heart attack.' I have in mind a case where the mother does not *choose* to have a heart attack if her son does A or to do something which will bring on or raise the probability of a heart attack. She just knows she will (or that the probability = p). It seems to me that the mother's statement is not plausibly construed as a threat to (choose to) do something or bring about a consequence if her son does A. To use a distinction which will be discussed later, what the mother issues is not a threat but rather a nonthreatening warning. If we look just at the first sort of situation, we will conclude that the mother did not coerce the son into not doing A. But this example can plausibly be viewed as a case of the second sort of situation, in which before Q does A, P does something, making this known to Q, which worsens Q's alternative of doing A. And if this counts as coercion, then the mother may coerce the son. We should look, in this case, at the mother's act, prior to her son's doing A, of telling him that she will or probably will have a heart attack if he does A. We may suppose that without her announcement the consequence of her son's doing A is some probability of her having a heart attack and some probability of his feeling guilty (a function of the probability of his realizing why she

died and the probability that he will feel guilty anyway because he did something she didn't like and then she died) and some probability of A's having quite nice consequences. And we may suppose that after the mother's announcement the consequences of his doing A are changed significantly. For now there is some probability of her dying and his feeling *enormously* guilty (because he ignored her warning), and even if she won't die because of his doing A, if he does A he will worry over this possibility, feel guilty about doing something he knows upsets her, etc. Her act of making her announcement before he did A worsened the consequence of his doing A. If we suppose, furthermore, that one of her reasons for making the announcement was to worsen the consequences, and that one of his reasons for not doing A was *this* worsening of consequences, then we have a situation of the second sort. And if this sort of situation counts as coercion, the son was coerced into not doing A.

[. . .]

Threats and Offers

The notion of a threat has played a central role in what has been said thus far. In this section we shall consider the differences between threats and offers, and in the next section we shall consider the differences between threats and warnings.

If P offers Q substantially more money than Q is earning at his current job to come to work for P, and Q accepts because he wants to increase his income, has P coerced Q into working for him? Some writers (Hale, Bay) would say that P has; the threat being 'come to work for me or I won't give you the money.' On this view, every employer coerces his employees, every employee his employer ('give me the money or I won't work for you'), every seller of an object coerces his customers ('give me the money or I won't give you the object'), and every customer the person from whom he buys. It seems clear that normally these aren't cases of coercion. Offers of inducements, incentives, rewards, bribes, consideration, remuneration, recompense, payment do not normally constitute threats, and the person who accepts them is not normally coerced.

As a first formulation, let us say that whether someone makes a threat against Q's doing an action or an offer to Q to do the action depends upon how the consequence he says he will bring about changes the consequences of Q's action from what they would have been in the normal or natural or expected course of events. If it makes the consequences of Q's action worse than they would have been in the normal and expected course of events, it is a threat; if it makes the consequences better, it is an offer.[8] The term 'expected' is meant to shift between or straddle *predicted* and *morally required*. This handles pretty well the clear cases of threats and offers. Let us see how it fares with more difficult examples.

(a) P is Q's usual supplier of drugs, and today when he comes to Q he says that he will not sell them to Q, as he normally does, for $20, but rather will give them to Q if and only if Q beats up a certain person.

(b) P is a stranger who has been observing Q, and knows that Q is a drug addict. Both know that Q's usual supplier of drugs was arrested this morning and that P had nothing to do with his arrest. P approaches Q and says that he will give Q drugs if and only if Q beats up a certain person.

In the first case, where P is Q's usual supplier of drugs, P is *threatening* not to give Q the drugs. The normal course of events is one in which P supplies Q with drugs for money. P is threatening to *withhold* the supply, to *deprive* Q of his drugs, if Q does not beat up the person. In the second case, where P is a stranger to Q, P is not *threatening* not to supply Q with drugs; in the normal course of events P does not do so, nor is P expected to do so. If P does not give Q the drugs he is not

withholding drugs from Q nor is he *depriving* Q of drugs. P is *offering* Q drugs as an inducement to beat up the person. Thus in the second case, P does not *coerce* Q into beating up the person, since P does not threaten Q. (But the fact that P did not coerce Q into beating up the person does not mean that it would not be true for Q to say, in some legitimate sense of the phrase: 'I had no choice.')

There is a further point to be considered about the first case in which P is Q's usual supplier of drugs. In addition to threatening to withhold the drugs if Q doesn't beat up a certain person, hasn't P made Q an offer? Since in the normal and expected course of events Q does not get drugs for beating up the person, isn't this a case in which P then offers Q drugs as an incentive to beat up the person? And if P *has* made this offer, why do we view the overall situation as one in which P threatens Q, rather than as one in which P makes Q an offer? We have here a situation in which P takes a consequence viewed as desirable by Q (receiving drugs) off one action (paying $20) and puts it onto another action (beating up the person). Since Q prefers and P believes that Q prefers paying the money and receiving the drugs to beating up the person and receiving the drugs, and since Q would rather not beat up the person, P's statement is a threat to withhold the drugs if Q doesn't beat up the person, and this threat predominates over any subsidiary offer P makes for Q to beat up the person, making the whole situation a threat situation.

But instead of subtracting a desirable consequence from one of Q's actions and tagging the *same* consequence onto another of Q's actions, P may subtract a desirable consequence C from one of Q's actions A_1 and add a *more* desirasble consequence C' onto another action A_2 available to Q. for example, the dope peddler might say to Q, 'I will not give you drugs if you just pay me money, but I will give you a better grade of drugs, without monetary payment, if you beat up this person.' It seems plausible to think that as one increases the desirability of C' to Q, at some point the situation changes form one predominantly involving a threat to deprive Q of C if he does A_1 (doesn't to A_2) to one which predominantly involves an offer to Q of C′ if he does A_2. And it seems plausible to claim that this turning point from threat to offer, as one increases the value of C′ for Q, comes at the point where Q begins preferring A_2 and C′ to A_1 and C (stops preferring the latter to the former?).

The following principle embodies this claim, and also covers the case where it is the same consequence which is switched from one action to another as in the earlier example. It also is meant to apply to obvious mixtures of threats and offers, e.g., 'If you go to the movies I'll give you $10,000. If you don't go, I'll kill you.'

> If P intentionally changes the consequences of two actions A_1 and A_2 available to Q so as to lessen the desirability of the consequences of A_1, and so as to increase the desirability of the consequences of A_2, and part of P's reason for acting as he does is to so lessen and increase the desirabilities of the respective consequences then
> (a) This resultant change predominantly involves a threat to Q if he does A_1 if Q prefers doing the old A_1 (without the worsened consequences) to doing the new A_2 (with the improved consequences).
> (b) This resultant change predominantly involves an offer to Q to do A_2 if Q prefers doing the new A_2 (with the improved consequences) to the old A_1 (without the worsened consequences).

This principle ties in nicely with something we shall say later. For when the change predominantly involves a threat, Q would normally not be willing to have this change made (since he'd rather do the old A_1 than either of the two alternatives after the change), whereas when the change predominantly involves an offer, Q would normally be willing to have the

change made (since he'd rather do the new A_2 than the old A_1, and if he prefers doing one of the old alternatives (A_1) to doing the new A_2, he can still do it.) I shall claim later that this willingness or unwillingness to make the change marks an important difference between offers and threats.[9]

If a statement's being a threat or an offer depends upon how the carrying out of the statement affects the normal or expected course of events, one would expect that there will be situations where it is unclear whether a person is making a threat or an offer because it is unclear what the normal and expected course of events is. And one would expect that people will disagree about whether something is a threat or an offer because they disagree about what the normal and expected course of events is, which is to be used as a baseline in assessing whether something is a threat or an offer. This is indeed the case.

Consider the following example. Q is in the water far from shore, nearing the end of his energy, and P comes close by in his boat. Both know there is no other hope of Q's rescue around, and P knows that Q is the soul of honesty and that if Q makes a promise he will keep it. P says to Q 'I will take you in my boat and bring you to shore if and only if you first promise to pay me $10,000 within three days of reaching shore with my aid.' Is P offering to take Q to shore if he makes the promise, or is he threatening to let Q drown if Q doesn't make the promise? If one views the normal or expected course of events as one in which Q drowns without P's intervention, then in saying that he will save Q if and only if Q makes the promise, P is *offering* to save Q. If one views the normal or expected course of events as one in which a person in a boat who comes by a drowning person, in a situation such as this, saves him, then in saying that he will save Q if and only if Q makes the promise, P is *threatening* not to save Q. Whether P's saying that he will save Q if and only if Q makes the promise is an *offer* to save Q or a *threat* not to save Q depends upon what the normal or expected course of events is.

Since it is likely to be clear to the reader which course of events he wants to pick out as normal and expected as the background against which to assess whether P's statement is an offer or a threat (namely, the one that makes it a threat) we should sharpen the example. Suppose in addition to the foregoing that P knows that Q has greatly wronged P (or others), but that Q cannot be legally punished for this (no law covered the wrong, a legal technicality, the statute of limitations has run out, or some such thing). Or P knows that Q will go on to do monstrous deeds if rescued. In some such situations it will be unclear what P is morally expected to do, and hence unclear whether his statement is a threat or an offer. For other such situations it will be clear that P is morally expected to let Q drown, and hence his statement will be an offer.[10]

Thus far we have considered threats as introducing certain deviations from the normal and expected course of events. The question arises as to whether the normal or expected course of events itself can be coercive. Suppose that usually a slave owner beats his slave each morning, for no reason connected with the slave's behaviour. Today he says to his slave, 'Tomorrow I will not beat you if and only if you now do A.' One is tempted to view this as a threat, and one is also tempted to view this as an offer. I attribute these conflicting temptations to the divergence between the normal course of events, in which the slave is beaten each morning, and the (morally) expected course of events, in which he is not. And I suggest that we have here a situation of a threat, and that here the morally expected course of events takes precedence over the normal course of events in assessing whether we have a threat or an offer.

One might think that in deciding whether something is a threat or an offer, the (morally) expected course of events always takes precedence over the normal or usual course of events, where these diverge. It is not obvious that this is so. I have in mind particularly the example mentioned earlier, where your normal supplier of dope says that he will continue to supply you if and only if you beat up a certain person. Here, let us suppose, the morally expected course of events is that he doesn't supply you with drugs, but the course of events which forms the background for deciding whether he has threatened you or made you an offer is the normal though not morally expected course of events (in which he supplies you with drugs for money); it is against this background that we can obtain the consequence that he's threatened you.

Thus, in both the slave and addict examples the normal and morally expected courses of events diverge. Why do we pick one of these in one case, and the other in the other as the background against which to assess whether we have a threat or an offer? The relevant difference between these cases seems to be that the slave himself would prefer the morally expected to the normal course of events whereas the addict prefers the normal to the morally expected course of events. It may be that when the normal and morally expected courses of events diverge, the one of these which is to be used in deciding whether a conditional announcement of an action constitutes a threat or an offer is the course of events that the recipient of the action prefers.[11]

I have raised the question of whether the normal and expected course of events itself can be coercive, and was led to consider cases where the normal and (morally) expected courses of events diverged. I now would like to consider this question again, for cases where they do not diverge. Can P, by saying that he will bring about a consequence if Q does A (where this consequence is such that if Q does A, P would bring it about in the normal *and* (morally) expected course of events), coerce Q into not doing A? Suppose that in the normal *and* morally expected course of events, people get punished for theft. Aren't some people coerced into not stealing by the legal apparatus?

One might say that if a *type* of action or consequence is itself part of the normal and expected course of events if Q does A, one should use the normal and expected course of events minus this type of action or consequence as a background against which to assess whether a statement is a threat. If the consequences of an action would be worse, if the statement is carried out, than they would be in this *new* course of events (i.e. the normal and expected course of events without the type of action or consequence) then the statement is a threat. But who knows what the world would be like if there was no punishment for crimes? It might well be that things would be so bad that the institution of punishing crimes would improve the consequences of almost all actions, and hence count, according to this suggestion, as making offers to people.

An alternative procedure seems more reasonable; namely, to consider the normal and expected course of events, if Q does A, without P's particular act or without the particular consequence P will bring about, and against this background assess whether P's statement that if Q does A he will do a particular act or bring about a particular consequence constitutes a threat (i.e. whether P's statement, if carried out, makes Q's A worse than it would be in *this* new course of events).

There remain some problems about knowing what the course of events would be without this act, but these seem manageable. On this view, even though in the normal and expected course of events Q gets punished for theft, the statement that he will be punished for theft counts as a threat since the act of punishment, if Q steals, unfavourably affects the consequences of one act of Q's (stealing) against the background of the normal and expected course of events minus *this* act of punishment.[12]

According to the account offered earlier of (the first sort of) coercion, threats are necessary for coercion. One might extend the account to include some offers, if there were clear situations in which Q is coerced into doing A even though Q does A because P offered to do B if Q did A. Despite my inclination to say that one is never coerced when one does something because of an offer, there

is one sort of case, where the offer is closely tied to coercion or attempted coercion, which I find it difficult to decide about. Suppose that P knows that Q has committed a murder which the police are investigating, and knows of evidence sufficient to convict Q of this murder. P says to Q, 'If you give me $10,000 I will not turn over the information I have to the police.' Let us assume that were P unable to contact Q and present his proposal he would turn the information over to the police. Furthermore, in this situation P is (morally) expected to turn the information over to the police. So in the normal and expected course of events, P turns the information over to the police (whether or not Q gives him $10,000). It would seem, therefore, that P is *offering* not to turn the information over to the police, rather than *threatening* to turn it over. Yet one is strongly tempted to say, when Q pays P $10,000 because he accepts the offer, that Q was coerced by P into paying the $10,000.[13]

If the following principle were correct, then this would be a case of coercion:

> If P offers to refrain from aiding the threatener of a coercive consequence for Q's A from bringing about this consequence, in exchange for Q's doing B, and if the credible threat of this consequence[14] if Q didn't perform B would coerce Q into doing B, then when Q does B because of the offer, Q was coerced into doing B.

A case similar to the previous one, is one in which the police arrest Q for a crime, believing that he has committed it and having sufficient evidence to convict him of it. In the course of questioning Q, they come to believe that Q knows who has committed some other crime, and they say that Q will not be prosecuted if and only if he tells them who has committed this other crime. Since if the police did not think Q knew who committed the other crime they would have prosecuted, and since they are morally expected to have him prosecuted, the police have *offered* not to have Q prosecuted rather than *threatened* to have him prosecuted. If Q names the person who committed the other crime, in order to escape being prosecuted, some are strongly tempted to say that he was coerced into giving the information. The above principle would yield this consequence. Though I do not deny that one may say, in some legitimate sense of these expressions, 'Q was forced to do what he did,' 'Q had no choice,' I am unable to decide whether, in the above cases, Q was coerced into doing so, and I leave this an open question.

The two previous cases are cases where P is morally expected or required to do the act, and would normally do so (turn the murderer over to the police, have Q prosecuted). It is worth mentioning cases where P has a legal and moral right to do the act, but would not decide to do so (even if Q didn't do A) were he not trying to get Q to do A. For example, P has a right to build on his land blocking Q's view, or foreclose Q's mortgage, or bring legal action against Q (on a valid and enforcible claim) but would not decide to do so (it's not worth the trouble, P has no pressing need for funds, etc.) were it not for his wanting Q to do A. P tells Q that unless he does A, he (P) will build on his land, foreclose Q's mortgage, bring legal action against Q, etc. Since P's action is not part of the morally expected course of events (not that P is morally expected *not* to do it) and since in the normal course of events P wouldn't do it, the account yields the result that one would wish: In these cases P is threatening to perform his actions rather than offering not to do so.

[...]

Threats, Offers, and Choices

I have claimed that normally a person is not coerced into performing an action if he performs it because someone has offered him something to do it, though normally he is coerced into performing an action if he does so because of a threat that has been made against his not doing so. Writers who count offers as coercive do so, I suspect, because they accept something roughly like the following statement:

If Q has available to him the actions in a set A, and as a result of what P has done or will do
(a) act A_1 is significantly higher in utility to Q than the other actions in A
(b) act A_2 is significantly lower in utility to Q than the other actions in A

whereas it wasn't before, and Q
(a) does A_1 because of this
(b) refrains from A_2 because of this

then Q was coerced into
(a) doing A_1
(b) not doing A_2

According to this view, any action of P's which results in A_1's being significantly greater or A_2's being significantly less in utility than the other actions in A may coerce Q. It makes no difference, according to this view, how the difference in utility is brought about; whether in (a) A_1 is absolutely raised in utility or all the other members of A are absolutely lowered in utility, or whether in (b) A_2 is absolutely lowered in utility, or all the other members of A are absolutely raised in utility. It is only the resulting *relative* positions, however arrived at, which count. This view is mistaken, and I shall assume that we can all think of examples that show to our satisfaction that this is so. I now want to consider whether anything illuminating can be said about *why* the notion of coercion isn't so wide as to encompass all bringing about of actions by the bringing about of difference in relative position. The question I'm asking may seem bogus. After all, there will be some terms which apply both to getting someone to do something via threats, and to getting someone to do something via offers, e.g., 'getting someone to do something.' And there will be some terms which apply to one and not the other. Am I just asking why the word 'coercion' is among those that apply to only one of these and not to both? And why expect the answer, presumably going back to the word's Latin roots, to be philosophically interesting? So let me state my task differently.

I would like to make sense of the following claims: when a person does something because of threats, the will of another is operating or predominant, whereas when he does something because of offers this is not so; a person who does something because of threats is subject to the will of another, whereas a person who acts because of an offer is not; a person who does something because of threats does not perform a fully voluntary action, whereas this is normally not the case with someone who does something because of offers; when someone does something because of threats it is not his own choice but someone else's, or not fully his own choice, or someone else has made his choice for him; when a person does something because of threats he does it unwillingly, whereas this is normally not the case when someone does something because of offers. (There are other ways to approach this area. One might ask why we say that we *accept* offers, but we go along with threats rather than accept them.)

I would like to make sense of these claims in the face of the following three roughly true statements, which seem to indicate that threat and offer situations are on a par so far as whose will operates, whether the act is fully voluntary, whose choice it is, and so forth.

(1)   A person can be gotten to do something which someone else wants him to do, which he otherwise wouldn't do, by offers as well as by threats.

(2)   A person can choose to do what there is a threat against his doing, just as a person can choose to do what there is an offer for him not to do. ('just as'?)

(3)   Sometimes a threat is so great that a person cannot reasonably be expected not to go along with it, but also sometimes an offer is so great that a person cannot reasonably be expected not to go along with it (that is, not to accept it).

I shall consider only a partially described person, whom I shall call the Rational Man, and unfortunately shall not get to us. The Rational Man, being able to resist those temptations which he thinks he should resist, will normally welcome credible offers,[15] or at any rate not be unwilling to have them be made. For he can always decline to accept the offer, and in this case he is no worse off than he would have been had the offer not been made. (Here I ignore the 'costs' of making decisions, e.g. time spent in considering an offer.) Why *should* he be unwilling to be the recipient of an offer? On the other hand, the Rational Man will normally not welcome credible threats, will normally be unwilling to be threatened even if he is able to resist going along with them. It is worth mentioning some cases which are or seem to be exceptions to this. A person might not mind threats if he was going to do the act anyway. But, since in this case he (probably) wasn't coerced, he needn't concern us here. A person might welcome threats which restrict the acts he can reasonably be expected to perform, and therefore improve his bargaining position with a third party, e.g. an employer negotiating with a labour union might welcome publicly known threats against raising wages by more than n per cent. But what he welcomes is not his being coerced into not raising wages by more than n per cent (he is not coerced), but its looking to others as though he is coerced. This needn't concern us here.

But there are other cases which are somewhat more difficult. For example, P tells Q that he'll give Q $10,000 if in the next week someone, without prompting, threatens Q. Someone does and Q welcomes the threat. Or, P is jealous of Q's receiving certain sorts of offers and tells Q that if he (Q) receives another offer before P does, then P will kill Q. Q cringes when the next offer comes. Or Q believes that having at least five threats (offers) made to one in one week brings good (bad) luck, and so is happy (unhappy) at the coming of the fifth threat (offer) in a week. Or for tax purposes Q welcomes a threat to illegally take some of his money. And so forth. I want to say that in such cases when threats are welcomed and offers shunned, they are done so for extraneous reasons, because of the special context. (One is tempted to say that in these contexts what would normally be a threat (offer) isn't really one.) I find it difficult to distinguish these special contexts from the others, but the claim that threats are normally unwelcome whereas offers are not, is not meant to apply to contexts where some special 'if-then' is believed to obtain, where it is believed to be the case that if a threat (offer) is made, resisted (accepted), or carried out then something good (bad) will happen to the recipient of the threat (offer) (where this good (bad) consequence is not 'internal' to the threat (offer)), and this belief on the part of the recipient of the threat (offer) overrides other considerations. It is along such lines that I suggest viewing the person who welcomes a threat because it affords him the opportunity to prove to others or test for himself his courage. Finally, let me mention the case where a person is in an n-person prisoners' dilemma situation. In this case, he may most prefer everyone *else's* being coerced into performing a dominated action while he is left free to perform the dominant action. He may also prefer everyone's being coerced into performing a specific dominated action (e.g. paying taxes) to no one's being so coerced. And since he realizes that the policy he most prefers, which treats him specially, isn't a feasible alternative, he may welcome the threat to everyone including himself.[16] But though he welcomes the system which threatens everyone, he might still be coerced into performing his particular action (e.g. paying his taxes). This too seems to me not to be a counter-example to the claim that threats are unwelcome, but one of the special contexts, with special if-thens tagged onto the making of the threat, to which the claim is not meant to apply.

I have said that the Rational Man would normally be willing to have credible offers made to him, whereas he would not normally be willing to be the recipient of credible threats. Imagine that the Rational Man is given a choice about whether someone else makes him an offer (threatens him). For example, the Rational Man is asked, 'Shall I threaten you (make you an offer)?' If he answers 'yes', it is done. I am supposing that no offer is made to the Rational Man to say 'yes' to this question, and no threat is made against his not saying 'yes'; i.e. that no threats of offers are involved in *this* choice about whether a threat (offer) is to be made. Let us call the situations before a threat or offer is made, the presituation. (I shall speak of the prethreat and preoffer situations, in anticipation of what is to come.) And let us call the situations after a threat or offer is made the threat and the offer situations respectively.

Looking first at offers:

(a) The Rational Man is normally willing to go and would be willing to choose to go from the preoffer to the offer situation.

(b) In the preoffer situation, the Rational Man is normally willing to do A if placed in the offer situation.

(c) The Rational Man, in the preoffer situation, is unwilling to do A. (We're concerned with the case where he does A [partly] because of the offer.)

(d) The Rational Man, when placed in the offer situation, does not normally prefer being back in the preoffer situation.

Turning to threats:

(a) The Rational Man is normally unwilling to go and unwilling to choose to go from the prethreat situation to the threat situation.

(b) In the prethreat situation, the Rational Man is normally willing to do A if placed in the threat situation.

(c) The Rational Man, in the prethreat situation, is unwilling to do A, and would not choose to do it. (We're concerned with the case where he does the act [partly] because of the threat.)

(d) The Rational Man, when placed in the threat situation, would normally prefer being back in the prethreat situation, and would choose to move back.

The two significant differences between these two lists are:

(1) The Rational Man would be willing to move and to choose to move from the preoffer to the offer situation, whereas he would normally not be willing to move or to choose to move from the prethreat situation to the threat situation.

(2) The Rational Man, once in the offer situation, would not prefer being back in the preoffer situation, whereas the Rational Man in the threat situation would normally prefer being back in the prethreat situation.

If we concentrate solely on the choices made in the threat and offer situations, we shall be hard put to find a difference between these situations which seems to make a difference as to whose will is operating, whose choice it is, whether the act is fully voluntary, done willingly or unwillingly, and so forth. If, however, we widen our focus and look not only at the choices made in the postsituations, but look *also* at the choice that would be made about moving from the presituation to the postsituation, then things look more promising. For now we face not just two choices but two pairs of choices:

(1) To move from the preoffer to the offer situation, and to do A in the offer situation.

(2) To move from the prethreat to the threat situation, and to do A in the threat situation.

And the Rational Man would (be willing to) make both choices in (1), whereas he would

not make both choices in (2). This difference in what choices are or would be made (when other factors are appropriately the same) seems to me to make the difference, when someone else intentionally moves you from the presituation to the postsituation, to whose choice it is, whose will operates, whether the act is willingly or unwillingly done, and to whether or not the act is fully voluntary.

One would like to formulate a principle that is built upon the preceding considerations, but I find it difficult to formulate one that I am confident is not open to very simple counterexamples. Very hesitantly and tentatively, I suggest the following plausible-looking principle:

> If the alternatives among which Q must choose are intentionally changed by P, and P made this change in order to get Q to do A, and before the change Q would not have chosen (and would have been unwilling to choose) to have the change made (and after it's made, Q would prefer that it hadn't been made), and before the change was made Q wouldn't have chosen to do A, and after the change is made Q does A, then Q's choice to do A is not fully his own.

Notice that I have *not* said that the feature I am emphasizing which is mentioned in the principle, namely, being willing to choose to move from one situation to another, is by itself sufficient for a choice in the latter situation to be not fully one's own, but instead I have said that this feature, *in conjunction* with the other features listed in the antecedent of the principle, is sufficient.

Since this principle presents a sufficient condition for Q's choice not being fully his own, it does not yield the consequence that in the offer situation, normally Q's choice is fully his own. A detailed discussion of when choices *are* fully one's own, or fully voluntary, yielding this consequence, would take us far afield. Here I just wish to suggest that the crucial difference between acting because of an offer and acting because of a threat *vis-à-vis* whose choice it is, etc., is that in one case (the offer case) the Rational Man is normally willing to move or be moved from the presituation to the situation itself, whereas in the other case (the threat case) he is not. Put baldly and too simply, the Rational Man would normally (be willing to) choose to make the choice among the alternatives facing him in the offer situation, whereas normally he would not (be willing to) choose to make the choice among the alternatives facing him in the threat situation.

The principle seems to me to be on the right track in concentrating not *just* on the choice of whether or not to do A, but also on the choice to move into the threat or offer situation. But it is difficult to state a principle, which gets all the details right, and which is not trivial and unilluminating (as one would be which said: if P moves Q from S_1 to S_2 via threats then . . .). It seems that rather than speaking (just) of act A being fully one's own choice, one should speak of its being fully one's own choice to do A rather than B. I have in mind the following sort of case. P intentionally breaks Q's leg (intentionally moving him from S_1 [no broken leg] to S_2 [broken leg]). Q would prefer not making this move, and afterwards would prefer not having made it. But once Q has a broken leg, he chooses to have a decorated cast put on it, rather than a plain white one. If we just look at the act of wearing a decorated cast, we will have difficulties, for surely it is not Q's own choice (he was forced into a position where he had to wear a cast, etc.), yet in some sense it is. It seems to me more illuminating to say that wearing a cast rather than none was not fully Q's own choice, wearing a decorated cast rather than a plain one *was* fully Q's own choice, and wearing a decorated cast rather than none was not fully Q's own choice. It is not clear how to state a principle which takes this and similar complications into account, and is not open to obvious difficulties. I do, however, want to suggest that we shall not be able to understand why acts done because of threats are not normally fully voluntary, fully

one's own choice, etc. where as this is not normally the case with acts done in response to offers, if we attend only to the choice confronting the person in the threat and offer situations. We must look also at the (hypothetical) choice of getting (and willingness to get) into the threat and offer situations themselves.

We have said that if P coerces Q into not doing A then (part of) Q's reason for not doing A is to avoid or lessen the likelihood of P's threatened consequence. Assuming that all of the conditions in the first section of this paper are satisfied, then

(a) In the case where Q's whole reason for not doing A is to avoid or lessen the likelihood of P's threatened consequence (ignoring his reasons for wanting to avoid this consequence), P coerces Q into not doing A.[17]

(b) In the case where P's threatened consequence is not part of Q's reason for not doing A (even if it is a reason Q has for not doing A) then P does not coerce Q into not doing A.

But the case is more difficult when P's threatened consequence is part of Q's reason for not doing A, and other reasons which Q has for not doing A (which do not involve threats) are also part of his reason for not doing A. For in this case, Q contributes reasons of his own; it is not solely because of the threat that he refrains from doing A. If we had to say either that this situation was one of coercion, or was not one of coercion we would, I think, term it coercion.[18] But, I think, for such cases one is inclined to want to switch from a classificatory notion of coercion to a quantitative one.

Let me indulge in a bit of science fiction. Suppose that one were able to assign weights to the parts of Q's reasons for not doing A, which indicated what fraction of Q's total reason for not doing A any given part was. One might then say, if P's threat was n/mth of Q's total reason for not doing A, that Q was n/m-coerced into not doing A. If P's threat is Q's whole reason for not doing A (no part of Q's reason for not doing A) then Q is 1-coerced (o-coerced) or, for short, coerced (not coerced). And, in the absence of precise weights, one might begin to speak of someone's being partially coerced, slightly coerced, almost fully coerced into doing something, and so forth. Furthermore, without claiming that a person is *never* to be held responsible for an act he was coerced into doing, we might, for some cases in which his reasons (other than the threat) for doing an act aren't sufficient to get him to decide to do the act, be led to speak of a person's being (held) partially responsible for his act; not completely responsible because he did it partly because of the threat, and not complete absence of responsibility because he didn't do it solely because of the threat, but contributed some reasons of his own. I would end by saying that the consideration of such a view of responsibility, and the tracing of the modifications in what has been said thus far introduced by a thorough-going use of the notion of n/m-coerced, would require another paper – were it not for the thought that some readers might take this as a threat.

Notes

1   Hart and Honoré list one further condition: Q forms the intention of not doing A only after learning of P's threat. That Q formed the intention of not doing A after learning of P's threat may be reason for thinking that he did A because of the threat. But Q may have refrained from doing A because of the threat even though he formed the intention of not doing it before learning of the threat. For example, Q intends to visit a friend tomorrow. P threatens him with death if he doesn't go. Q then learns that this friend has a communicable disease such that were it not for the threat, Q wouldn't visit him. But Q goes because of P's threat, though he'd formed the intention of going before learning of the threat, and never lost this intention. Though Hart and Honoré's further condition is not satisfied, P coerced Q into going.

2   This condition requires further refinements to handle cases in which unbeknownst to P, Q wants to avoid P's inflicting the threatened consequence only because this will lead to some further consequence detrimental to P, which Q (only out of concern for P's interest) wants to avoid. For example, Q refrains from A because he knows that P will feel enormously guilty after he's inflicted the consequence, and Q doesn't want this to happen. Or, Q refrains from A in the face of P's threat to fire him only because without Q working for him, P will go bankrupt, and Q doesn't want this to happen. I shall not pursue here the details of a principle which would exclude these as cases of coercion.

3   I included the latter disjunct since I can threaten you with a consequence which I don't believe would actually worsen your alternative of doing A, but which I know that you believe would do so. Subtle questions arise about cases where it is the making of the threat itself that causes the person to believe that one consequence is worse than another. For example, a Gestapo agent questioning a prisoner believes that two concentration camps are equally bad, and the prisoner too initially believes this. The Gestapo agent tells the prisoner, in a threatening voice, that he will be sent to a concentration camp in any case, but if he cooperates during the questioning he will be sent to the first camp, whereas if he does not, he will be sent to the second camp. Here it is the very making of the threat which causes the prisoner to think that the second camp is worse than the first.

I might note one refinement of this condition, to handle cases where (part of) P's reason for so deciding is as described in the condition, but this part drops away and P sticks with his decision for another reason entirely and thereafter announces the decision. It might be more appropriate to say something like: (Part of) P's reason, at the time he informs Q he will bring about the consequence or have it brought about if Q does A, for planning to bring about the consequence or have it brought about if Q does A, is that P believes. . . .

The condition in the text should also be interpreted or extended so as to cover cases in which the worsening of Q's alternative of doing A is not part of P's reason for deciding to bring about the consequences if Q does A, but rather

(a)   P decides to bring about the consequences if Q does A because he believes he has a duty or obligation to do so.

(b) P knows this consequence would worsen Q's alternative of doing A.

(c) Part of the reason for P's bringing about of such a consequence if Q does A originally being thought to be his duty or obligation, or being continued to be so thought, is that such a consequence worsens Q's alternative of doing A.

4   This disjunction is condition 3′. Thus the full condition 3′ is: (Part of) P's reason for deciding is . . ., *or*, if P hasn't decided, (part of) P's reason for saying is. . . . An alternative condition would be just: (Part of) P's reason for saying is to get Q not to do A, or to worsen. . . . This alternative condition differs from the one under consideration for cases where P has decided to bring about the consequence if Q does A, and no part of his reason or motive is as described, but part of his reason for *telling* Q that he will bring about the consequence if Q does A, *is* to get Q not to do A. I find it difficult to decide between these conditions, though I lean towards the one presented in the text. A specific example for which the condition in the text and the alternative condition diverge is discussed (as case 3) in the section on Threats and Warnings.

5   Note the difference, with respect to coercion, between saying to a man who intends to do A in order to bring about x:

(1) If you do A, I'll do something which (just) prevents your A from bringing about x.

(2) If you do B, I'll do something which would, were you to do A, (just) prevent your A from bringing about x.

6   I should note that I do not discuss in this paper, and wish here to leave open, two further conditions. (Hart mentions something in the area of the first.)

(1) The consequence which P has threatened *is* so weighted by Q as to override the weight which Q (morally) *ought* to give to not doing A.

For example, Q who is not in dire financial condition, and would just slightly rather not kill people (he feels about killing people as most people do about killing flies), kills R because P has threatened not to return the $100 he's borrowed from Q unless Q kills R. Did P coerce Q into killing R?

(2) The weight which Q *does* give to not doing A does not fall far short of the weight he (morally) *ought* to give to not doing A.

For example, Q destroys R's home because P has threatened a consequence, if Q does not destroy the home which R has laboriously built, which Q weights *and* anyone (morally) ought to weight as worse than destroying R's home. However, Q just *slightly* would rather not destroy R's home. Did P coerce Q into destroying R's home?

7   Complication: Suppose that as the stranger is being beaten, he says that if they stop and promise to release him, he'll sign over a traveller's cheque to them for $1,000. They stop, he signs it over, they release him. Was he coerced into signing it over?

8   A more complicated statement would be required to take into account condition 7 in the section on Conditions for Coercion.

9   The notion discussed here should be distinguished from another in which both threatening Q with x if he does A and offering him y if he doesn't do A are said to predominantly involve an offer (threat) if for almost any action B, if Q is both threatened with x if he does B and offered y if he does B, Q will prefer to do B (not do B).

10   I ignore problems arising from a divergence between what P believes to be the morally expected course of events and what is the morally expected course of events, e.g., where P believes he's morally required to let Q drown, although he's morally required to save Q.

11   Let me suggest as a fertile area for testing intuitions and theories, the following, where the normal and morally expected courses of events may diverge, and where it may not be clear what the morally expected course of events is. Suppose some nation N were to announce that it will in the future give economic aid to some other countries provided that these other countries satisfy certain conditions (e.g., do not vote contrary to N on important issues before the United Nations, do not trade with specific nations, do not have diplomatic relations with specific nations). Would this announcement constitute an offer to give these nations aid, or a threat not do so? Relevant factors (to list just two of many) are whether or not N has an obligation or is morally required to give these nations economic aid (independently of whether they satisfy the conditions), and whether or not N has previously given these nations economic aid independently of whether they satisfy the conditions.

12 Though this seems to me to be the correct thing to say, there is a problem, which I have not yet been able to solve, which I should briefly mention.

Letting P = you are punished
    C = you commit a crime

the officials in the society might say
    P if and only if C

or equivalently
    not-P if and only if not-C.

Interpreted truth-functionally, each of these is equivalent to either (P and C) or (not-P and not-C). The two remaining possibilities are (P and not-C), and (C and not-P). The back-ground we want to use in deciding whether a threat is involved is C and not-P. If we were to use the remaining possibility, P and not-C, as the background, then it would turn out that an offer is involved here. The problem is to formulate criteria, in cases where the biconditional is itself part of the normal and expected course of events, which pick out C and not-P rather than P and not-C in this and other threat cases, and which would pick out the appropriate background for offer cases as well.

13 This is a case of blackmail which presumably should be legally forbidden because allowing it increases the probability that crimes will go undetected. Other reasons apply to other cases, but note that it is not obvious that one wants to legally forbid all cases which fit the description: saying that one will make public some information about Q unless Q pays money. For example.

(a) P's saying that he will make public the information that Q has not paid P the money Q owes him, unless Q pays the money.

(b) P is writing a book, and in the course of his research comes across information about Q which will help sell many copies of the book. P tells Q he will refrain from including this information in the book if and only if Q pays him an amount of money equal to the expected difference in his royalties between the book containing this information and the book without the information.

14 More precisely, the credible threat of raising the probability of this consequence from what it is without P's aiding in bringing it about, to what it would be with P's aid.

15 I omit consideration of offers to do acts such that, if the offer is made, the act cannot be done without accepting the offer, e.g. one cannot work at certain government jobs without receiving a salary of at least one dollar per year. The Rational Man may sometimes prefer doing the act without the offer's having been made, so that it will be clear to others, and perhaps himself, *why* he does the act (e.g. not for the money). I also shall not consider the case of a person's not welcoming an offer for him to perform a malicious act because of what it shows about the person making the offer. Note the importance of our restricting our attention here to the Rational Man. Another person might not, for example, welcome an offer of $50,000 for him to kill Jones, because he's afraid he may be tempted to (and unable to resist the temptation to) accept the offer. In considering only the Rational Man, I am leaving part of my task undone. For I do not argue, as I would wish to, that even for someone who sometimes succumbs to temptations which he believes he ought to resist, there is a significant difference between offers and threats.

16 For a discussion of the prisoners dilemma, cf. R. D. Luce and Howard Raiffa, *Games and Decisions* (New York, 1957), pp. 94–102. On dominance principles, see my 'Newcomb's Problem and Two Principles of Choice' in N. Rescher *et. al.*, eds., *Essays in Honor of Carl G. Hempel* (Reidel, 1969). One often finds this argument applied to questions about the provision of a public good for a group. For example, each inhabitant of an island might prefer that others contribute to the construction of barriers against the sea while he does not, yet prefer everyone's being forced to contribute to contributions being left purely voluntary in which case, let us suppose, the barriers won't get constructed. (For a discussion of the conditions under which a public good for a group will be provided, cf. Mancur Olson, *The Logic of Collective Action* (Harvard, 1965). James M. Buchanan and Gordon Tullock, in *The Calculus of Consent* (Michigan, 1962), argue that public goods for a group will be provided more often than one might think.)

One must be wary of concluding too quickly from this line of argument that there will be unanimous consent to the provision of the public good by forcing everyone to contribute. For there will generally be alternative ways in which the public good can be provided, and individuals even if they all agree that each of these ways is preferable to the purely voluntary situation, may differ about which of the ways should be used. Should the good be paid for from funds gathered via a system of proportional taxation, or one of progressive taxation? And so forth. It is not obvious how unanimous consent to one *particular* way of providing the good is supposed to arise.

17　Even if Q has other reasons for not doing A. We distinguish between 'Q has a reason *r* for not doing A,' and '*r* is (part of) Q's reason for not doing A.'

18　This indicates an asymmetry between doing something (partly) because of a threat, and doing something partly because of an offer. For suppose that the other reasons Q has for not doing A which are part of his reasons for not doing A, include an offer by R for Q not to do A. Using a classificatory notion of coercion, doing A partly because of a threat shows the person was coerced, whereas doing something partly because of an offer does not show that he was not coerced.

Robert Nozick, "Coercion" from P. Laslett et al. (eds.), *Philosophy, Politics, and Society*, 4th series (Oxford: Blackwell, 1994), pp. 102–9, 112–20, 127–35.

Chapter 49

Robert Nozick, from *Anarchy, State, and Utopia* (1974)

Voluntary Exchange

Some readers will object to my speaking frequently of voluntary exchanges on the grounds that some actions (for example, workers accepting a wage position) are not really voluntary because one party faces severely limited options, with all the others being much worse than the one he chooses. Whether a person's actions are voluntary depends on what it is that limits his alternatives. If facts of nature do so, the actions are voluntary. (I may voluntarily walk to someplace I would prefer to fly to unaided.) Other people's actions place limits on one's available opportunities. Whether this makes one's resulting action non-voluntary depends upon whether these others had the right to act as they did.

Consider the following example. Suppose there are twenty-six women and twenty-six men each wanting to be married. For each sex, all of that sex agree on the same ranking of the twenty-six members of the opposite sex in terms of desirability as marriage partners: call them A to Z and A' to Z' respectively in decreasing preferential order. A and A' voluntarily choose to get married, each preferring the other to any other partner. B would most prefer to marry A', and B' would most prefer to marry A, but by their choices A and A' have removed these options. When B and B' marry, their choices are not made non-voluntary merely by the fact that there is something else they each would rather do. This other most preferred option requires the cooperation of others who have chosen, as is their right, not to cooperate. B and B' chose among fewer options than did A and A'. This contraction of the range of options continues down the line until we come to Z and Z', who each face a choice between marrying the other or remaining unmarried. Each prefers any one of the twenty-five other partners who by their choices have removed themselves from consideration by Z and Z'. Z and Z' voluntarily choose to marry each other. The fact that their only other alternative is (in their view) much worse, and the fact that others chose to exercise their rights in certain ways, thereby shaping the external environment of options in which Z and Z' choose, does not mean they did not marry voluntarily.

Similar considerations apply to market exchanges between workers and owners of capital. Z is faced with working or starving; the choices and actions of all other persons do not add up to providing Z with some other option. (He may have various options about what job to take.) Does Z choose to work voluntarily? (Does someone on a desert island who must work to survive?) Z does choose voluntarily if the other individuals A through Y each acted voluntarily and within their rights. We then have to ask the question about the others. We ask it up the line until we reach A, or A and B, who chose to act in certain ways thereby shaping the external choice environment in which C chooses. We move back down the line with A through C's voluntary choice affecting *D*'s choice environment, and *A* through *D*'s choices affecting *E*'s choice environment, and so on back down to *Z*. A person's choice among differing degrees of unpalatable alternatives is not rendered non-voluntary by the fact that others voluntarily chose and acted within their rights in a way that did not provide him with a more palatable alternative.

We should note an interesting feature of the structure of rights to engage in relationships with others, including voluntary exchanges.[1] The right to engage in a certain relationship is not a right to engage in it with anyone, or even with anyone who wants to or would choose to, but rather it is a right to do it with anyone who has the right to engage in it (with someone who has the right to engage in it . . .). Rights to engage in relationships or transactions have hooks on them, which must attach to the corresponding hook of another's right that comes out to meet theirs. My right of free speech is not violated by a prisoner's being kept in solitary confinement so that he cannot hear me, and my right to hear information is not violated if this prisoner is prevented from communicating with me. The rights of members of the press are not violated if Edward Everett Hale's "man without a country" is not permitted to read some of their writings, nor are the rights of readers violated if Josef Goebbels is executed and thereby prevented from providing them with additional reading material. In each case, the right is a right to a relationship with someone else who *also* has the right to be the other party in such a relationship. Adults normally will have the right to such a relationship with any other consenting adult who has this right, but the right *may* be forfeited in punishment for wrongful acts. This complication of hooks on rights will *not* be relevant to any cases we discuss. But it does have implications; for example it complicates an immediate condemnation of the disruption of speakers in a *public* place, solely on the grounds that this disruption violates the rights of other people to *hear* whatever opinions they choose to listen to. If rights to engage in relationships go out only half-way, these others do have a right to hear whatever opinions they please, but only from persons who have a right to communicate them. Hearers' rights are not violated *if* the speaker has no hook to reach out to join up with theirs. (The speaker can lack a hooked right only because of something he has done, not because of the *content* of what he is about to say.) My reflections here are not intended to justify disruption, merely to warn against the too simple grounds for condemnation which I myself have been prone to use.

Note

1   Since I am unsure of this point, I put this paragraph forward very tentatively, as an interesting conjecture.

Robert Nozick, *Anarchy, State, and Utopia* (New York: Basic Books/Oxford: Blackwell, 1974), pp. 262–5.

Chapter 50

G. A. Cohen, from *Self-ownership, Freedom, and Equality* (1995)

[. . .]

7. I now examine Nozick's section on 'Voluntary Exchange', which I presumed [. . .] to be his more extended treatment of the problem of the effect of market transactions on persons not party to them, including the as yet unborn. Nozick allows that agreed exchanges between *A* and *B* may reduce *C*'s *options*, but he implies that they do not thereby reduce *C*'s *freedom*. He explicitly says that they do not render involuntary anything that *C* does. And since what *C* is forced to do he does involuntarily, it follows that, for Nozick, the actions of *A* and *B*, though reducing *C*'s options, cannot have the result that *C* is *forced* to do something that he might not otherwise have done.

The last claim entails a denial of a thesis central to the socialist critique of capitalism, which may usefully be expressed in the terms of Nozick's doctrine of natural rights, without commitment to the truth of the latter.

For Nozick, every person has a natural right not to work for any other. If one is a slave, then, unless one contracted freely into slavery [. . .], one's rights were violated, as they are in slave states, which do not confer on everyone as a matter of civil right the rights that he enjoys naturally. And natural rights would remain violated if the law permitted slaves to choose for which master they should labour, as long as it forbade them to withhold their services from all masters whatsoever.

One difference between a modern capitalist state and a slave state is that the natural right not to be subordinate in the manner of a slave is a civil right in modern capitalism. The law excludes formation of a set of persons who are legally obliged to work for other persons. That status being forbidden, everyone is entitled to work for no one. But the power matching this right[1] is differentially enjoyed. Some *can* live without subordinating themselves, but most cannot. The latter face a structure generated by a history of market transactions in which, it is reasonable to say, they are *forced* to work for some or other person or group. Their natural rights are not matched by corresponding effective powers.

This division between the powerful and the powerless with respect to the alienation of labour power is the heart of the socialist objection to claims on behalf of the justice and freedom of capitalist arrangements. The rights Nozick says we have by nature we also have civilly under capitalism, but the matching powers are widely lacking. That lack is softened in contemporary rich capitalist countries, because of a hard-won institutionalization of a measure of protection for working-class people. In Nozick's capitalism such institutionalization would be forbidden on the ground that it was coercive, and the lack would be greater.

But Nozick, in the course of his full reply to the problem of 'third parties', denies that even the most abject proletarian is *forced* to work for some capitalist or other. Addressing himself to 'market exchanges between workers and owners of capital', he invites us to reflect on the situation of a certain *Z* (so-called because he is at the bottom of the heap in a twenty-six-person economy) who is 'faced with working [for a capitalist] or starving':

> the choices and actions of all other persons do not add up to providing *Z* with some other option. (He may have various options about what job to take.) Does *Z* choose to work voluntarily? . . . *Z* does choose voluntarily if the other individuals *A* through *Y* each acted voluntarily and within their rights . . . A person's choice among differing degrees of unpalatable alternatives is not rendered nonvoluntary by the fact that others voluntarily chose and acted within their rights in a way that did not provide him with a more palatable alternative . . . [Whether other people's option-closing actions] makes one's resulting action non-voluntary depends on whether these others had the right to act as they did.[2]

One might think that people of necessity lack the right so to act that someone ends up in *Z*'s position, a view that I put forward later [. . .]. But here we suppose, with Nozick, that all of *A* through *Y* acted as impeccably upright marketeers and therefore did nothing wrong. If so, says Nozick, *Z* is not *forced* to work for a capitalist. If he chooses to, the choice is voluntary.

Notice that Nozick is not saying that *Z*, although forced to work *or* starve, is not forced to *work*, since he may choose to starve. Rather, he would deny that *Z* is forced to work-or-starve, even though *Z* has no other alternative, and would accept that *Z* is indeed forced to work, if, contrary to what Nozick holds, he is forced to work or starve. For Nozick believes that

(8) if *Z* is forced to do *A* or *B*, and *A* is the only thing it would be reasonable for him to do, and *Z* does *A* for this reason, then *Z* is forced to do *A*.[3]

Nozick holds that

(9) *Z* is forced to choose between working and starving only if human actions caused his alternatives to be restricted in that way,

and that

(10) *Z* is forced so to choose only if the actions bringing about the restriction on his alternatives were illegitimate.

Both claims are false, but we need not discuss (9) here. For we are concerned with choice restriction which Nozick himself attributes to the actions of persons, *viz.*, some or all of *A* through *Y*. We need therefore only reject his claim that if someone is forced to do something, then someone acted *illegitimately*: we need to refute (10) only.

Let me once again display the text in which (10) is affirmed:

> Other people's actions may place limits on one's available opportunities. Whether this makes one's resulting action non-voluntary depends upon whether these others had the right to act as they did.[4]

But there is no such dependence, as the following pair of examples shows.

Suppose farmer Fred owns a tract of land across which villager Victor has a right of way. Then, if Fred erects an insurmountable fence around the land, Victor is forced to use another route, as Nozick will agree, since Fred, in erecting the fence, acted illegitimately. Now consider farmer Giles, whose similar tract is regularly traversed by villager William, not as of right, but because Giles is a tolerant soul. But then Giles erects an insurmountable fence around his land for reasons which justify him in doing so. According to Nozick, William may not truly say that, like Victor, he is now forced to use another route. But the examples, though different, do not so contrast as to make such a statement false. William is no less forced to change his route than Victor is. (10) is false even if – what I also deny – (9) is true, and the thesis that Z is forced to place his labour power at the disposal of some or other member of the capitalist class is sustained.

8. Nozick's claim about Z is so implausible that it may seem puzzling, coming as it does from an extremely acute thinker. Can it be that he is driven to it because it occupies a strategic place in his defence of libertarian capitalism? How is libertarian capitalism *libertarian* if it erodes the liberty of a large class of people?

Still, we can imagine Nozick granting that Z is forced to work for a capitalist, and attempting to recoup his position by saying this: Z is indeed so forced, but, since what brings it about that he is forced is a sequence of legitimate transactions, there is no moral case against his being so forced, no injustice in it. [. . .]

That would be less impressive than the original claim. Nozick is in a stronger position – could he but defend it – when he holds that capitalism does not deprive workers of freedom than if he grants that the worker is forced to subordinate himself yet insists that, even so, his situation, being justly generated, is, however otherwise regrettable, unexceptionable from the standpoint of justice. For the original claim, if true, entitles Nozick to say, given his other theses, that capitalism is not only a just but also a free society; while the revised claim makes him say that capitalism is just, but not entirely free. When Z is accurately described capitalism is less attractive, whatever we may say about it from the standpoint of justice.

Turning to that standpoint, and bearing Z in mind, it seems reasonable to add to the constraints on just acquisition a provision that no one may so acquire goods that others suffer severe loss of liberty as a result.

Notes

1 The concept of a *power which matches a right* is explicated in section (2) of Chapter VIII of my *Karl Marx's Theory of History*. The basic idea: power *p* matches right *r* if and only if what X is *de jure* able to do when X has *r* is what X is *de facto* able to do when X has *p*.
2 Robert Nozick, *Anarchy, State and Utopia* (New York: Basic Books, 1974), pp. 262, 263–4.
3 Robert Nozick, 'Coercion', in *Philosophy, Politics and Society*, ed. P. Laslett et al. (Oxford: Blackwell, 1994), p. 446. I derive (8) above from principle (7) of the 'Coercion' essay on the basis of Nozick's commitment to: Z is forced to do A if and only if there is a person P who forces Z to do A. See (9) in the next sentence of the text above.)
4 *Anarchy*, p. 262.

G. A. Cohen, *Self-ownership, Freedom, and Equality* (Cambridge: Cambridge University Press, 1995), pp. 34–7.

Chapter 51

Hillel Steiner, from *An Essay on Rights* (1994)

Liberty

BLUE: But surely you aren't denying that he was free to do it.

RED: I most certainly am.

BLUE: But . . . but . . . we both know that he actually did it!

RED: What's that got to do with it?

That's one conversation. Here's another:

BLUE: Look, it says here in the newspaper that they're going to stop us doing that from now on. We're going to be less free than before.

RED: I don't see why we are. No rational, prudent or decent person would ever do that anyway.

BLUE: What's that got to do with it?

And yet another:

BLUE: Look, it says here in the newspaper that they're going to stop us doing that from now on. We're going to be less free than before.

RED: I don't see why we are. They're perfectly entitled to stop us from doing that.

BLUE: What's that got to do with it?

Not everyone, it must be admitted, shares Blue's linguistic intuitions here. For that is what they are: linguistic intuitions. A good deal of philosophical debate consists, among other things, in duelling with linguistic intuitions. And you don't need to have spent long years toiling in the fields of political philosophy – nor even, indeed, in the cosier confines of common parlance – to know that our uses of the word "free" and other cognate terms rest upon diverse and often opposed intuitions.

Blue's intuition is that there is something more than a little odd about conceptions of liberty that logically commit us heroically to denying that you were free to do what you, in fact, did. And she is similarly troubled by the idea that someone's stopping you from doing things doesn't curtail your freedom. Put this way, perhaps Blue's intuitions are shared by all of us.[1] Unfortunately, not all of us are entitled to share them.

A point of order is called for. It's assuredly not the job of philosophers to legislate on which linguistic (much less, moral) intuitions we may hold nor, therefore, on what conception of liberty we may employ. They utterly lack the authority to do so. Rather, their brief is the more modest one of indicating which set of intuitions can be held *consistently*. Intuitions have implications. Conceptions carry logical commitments. And the job of philosophers is to tell us when our several uses of a word like "free" are inconsistent – inconsistent inasmuch as the conceptions respectively underpinning them deliver mutually contradictory judgements in particular cases.

When such inconsistencies occur, the court of first appeal must unquestionably be ordinary language. We need to ask ourselves which of the opposed judgements more closely reflects the way in which normal speakers of that language employ that word. The trouble is that, in the case of "free" and its cognates, this court frequently refuses to pronounce on such appeals. Ordinary usage's treatment of freedom is not univocal and it stubbornly persists in licensing such inconsistencies. In effect, it leaves the litigants to settle their differences in the time-honoured fashion of duelling with their intuitions.

How do we duel with these intuitions? The non-univocality of ordinary usage suggests that, very often, it's *we* who are amongst our most determined opponents. That is, we each use the word "free" inconsistently ourselves, as well as in ways that are inconsistent with other persons' uses. What's worrying is that these several uses, however mutually inconsistent, probably each reflect some entrenched intuition we have about a kind of circumstance in which a person is describable as free.

To achieve consistency, we have to expel some of these reflections from our usage, to silence the intuitions they express. This is never an easy thing to do. It means having to face an uncomfortable linguistic future in which we're bound to find some of our own uses of "free," as well as our appraisals of others' uses, distinctly counter-intuitive. Accordingly, in picking and choosing among our intuitions, we should take some care to silence only those whose absence from our usage promises to cause us less discomfort than would the absence of those it continues to reflect. And, of course, that usage can continue to reflect any set whose absence is not a requirement of consistency. For although consistency is surely worth its price in counter-intuitiveness, we don't want to pay over the odds for it.

What, then, is the price of Blue's intuitions? What conception of freedom is she invoking in the previous conversations? What are its more salient attributes and implications? And which uses, ordinary or otherwise, of the words "free" and "unfree" does it deny us? Like Blue, I find it especially difficult to let go of the idea that persons are free to do what they actually do. They're also free to do many of the things they don't do and would never consider doing. Simply stated, the rest of this chapter is devoted to looking at some implications of an unswerving commitment to those ideas.

Broadly speaking, it suggests that a person is unfree to do an action if, and only if, his doing that action is rendered impossible by the action of another person. We ordinarily regard an action as rendered impossible by another action if the latter either (i) does occur, or (ii) would occur if the former were attempted, and the latter's occurrence implies the impossibility of the former's occurrence. When these two actions are the respective actions of two different persons, one of them makes the other unfree inasmuch as one prevents the other from acting.[2] Thus I'm ordinarily unfree to leave my prison cell if the guard has locked my door, or even if he hasn't done so but would do so were I to attempt to leave.

Traditionally, arguments about the nature of liberty have taken the form of disputes over the relative merits of various positive and negative conceptions of liberty. Salient aspects of these disputes are best understood as rival attempts to address two questions. The first asks whether one person's rendering another's action *ineligible* – as distinct from impossible – makes the latter unfree to do it. And the second asks whether one person's prevention of another's action implies the latter's unfreedom to do it, only if that prevented action possesses eligibility or the preventing action lacks it. In both questions "eligibility" is meant to cover diverse moral or motivational conditions which proponents of rival conceptions variously impose on ascriptions of freedom and unfreedom. Somewhat surprisingly, in my view, the affirmative replies standardly offered by positive libertarians to these two questions have been repeated rather than rejected by many negative libertarian accounts.

In exploring the implications of Blue's intuition, the present account firmly rejects these affirmative replies. Blue's conception of liberty is thus a particular type of negative conception – one famously associated with Hobbes but probably more consistently employed by Bentham. In recent years it has been carefully distinguished and appropriately labelled by Michael Taylor as "pure negative liberty" and, less approvingly, by Charles Taylor as "crude negative liberty."

This pure negative conception is uncontroversially an empirical or descriptive one. That is, statements using it to describe a person as free or unfree to do a particular action presuppose nothing about the significance or permissibility either of that action or of any action preventing it. Nor, for that matter, do they presuppose anything about whether someone believes either of those actions to be significant or permissible. However disparagingly, Charles Taylor is not mistaken in identifying this conception as the one which is also at work when scientists and engineers refer to the "freedom of some physical object, say a lever."

There can be little doubt that our ordinary language does contain such a purely descriptive conception. And even if it cannot claim a monopoly on the use of the words "liberty," "freedom" and their cognates, we should be loath simply to abandon it – not least, because we typically want to retain the linguistic capacity to express intelligible and non-redundant judgements about the freedoms which people do and do not want or should and should not have. As we'll presently see, other conceptions of liberty rather oppressively consign such judgements to either redundancy or nonsense.

Actions and Eligibility

Current philosophical discussion of the concept of liberty often takes, as its starting point, Sir Isaiah Berlin's inaugural lecture "Two Concepts of Liberty." In his introduc-tion to the revised version of that seminal work, Berlin undertakes to correct what he considers to be a serious error in the negative libertarian argument of the original version. That earlier version had claimed that liberty, properly understood, consists in not being prevented by other persons from doing whatever one *desires* to do and, thus, that one is free to the extent that one is not prevented by another from doing what one desires to do. "If I am prevented by others from doing what I want I am to that degree unfree." Berlin now acknowledges that this formulation of the negative conception paradoxically licenses the positive libertarian inference that my unfreedom can be reduced by the suppression of my desires, i.e. those which others prevent me from satisfying. And conversely, it implies that my unfreedom can increase merely by virtue of an increase in my desires and without any increase in the restrictive treatment meted out to me by those others. In short, this formulation suggests that ultimately one's oppressor is oneself.

In a similar vein, J. P. Day has pointedly remarked that ridding oneself of the desire to do an action which is prevented by another does not make one free to do that action. He suggests that to treat an action's being desired as a necessary condition of the actor's being free or unfree to do it is to confuse the condition of *being free* with that of *feeling free*. Thus Blue, Day and the later Berlin concur that, if there are persons who would make it impossible for me to import heroin into this country, then I'm unfree to do so. And I'm unfree to do so irrespective of whether I want to do so, am indifferent to doing so or want not to do so. Being imprisoned makes me unfree to go to the theatre regardless of whether I want to go to the theatre or not.

Obviously, the extent to which such prevention engenders a feeling of frustration in me, the extent to which I experience it as an obstacle to my satisfaction or contrary to my interests, *does* depend on what I actually desire to do. Perhaps the only freedom that really matters to me is the freedom to do what I desire to do. But it doesn't follow from this that I can be free or unfree to do only those actions which I want to do. We have no problem understanding the statement "I am free to go to the theatre, i.e. am not prevented from doing so, though I have no desire to do so." And it's equally intelligible to say, "I am unfree to go to the theatre and don't want to do so." Since ordinary usage evidently embraces such claims without strain, it really is incumbent on those who suggest that desires cannot be excluded from any analysis of the meaning of liberty to account for these perfectly common pieces of counter-evidence.

Much the same would seem to be true of actions whose relation to their agents is specified in various evaluative terms. When we ask whether a person is free to do a particular action, we typically don't imagine ourselves to be asking an evaluative question. Rather we're asking a factual question, the (affirmative) answer to which is presupposed by any evaluative question about his doing that action, since "is prevented" implies "cannot" whereas "ought" implies "can." How, after all, could persons ever do actions which they ought not to do unless they're unprevented from doing them?

Banal as it is, one cannot point out too often that *such actions do happen.* And Blue's intuition is that their doers must *ipso facto* have been free to do them. She thus emphatically rejects the claim that "our conception of freedom is bounded by our notions of what might be worthwhile doing."[3] Such claims embrace the evaluative counterpart of the failure to distinguish "being free" from "feeling free." They neglect the difference, noted by John Rawls, between liberty and the worth of liberty.

These considerations suggest that statements to the effect that "Blue is free to do B" do not imply or presuppose statements to the effect either that "Blue wants to do B" or that "It is contrary to Blue's interests or duties to refrain from doing B." Nor therefore do they imply or presuppose statements about what Blue really wants or what it is in her real interests to do. Judgements about whether an agent is free to do an action are logically independent of any judgement concerning the eligibility of that action.

[. . .]

Deeply embedded in our thinking about liberty is the idea that we are unfree to do an action when we are threatened by others with a penalty – or at least a serious penalty – for doing it. While preventing (making impossible) a person's action is commonly acknowledged to be the paradigm form of unfreedom, most accounts have no hesitation in speaking of prevention *and* penalizability in the same breath as if there were no relevant distinction between them so far as unfreedom is concerned.

The object of this section is to show that for Blue's pure negative conception of liberty, and perhaps for others too, there is indeed such a distinction. And inattention or indifference to it generates a good deal of descriptive imprecision in our thinking about freedom. Specifically, I shall argue that although penalization does indeed curtail our freedom, the penalizability of an action does not make us unfree to do it.

Suppose that I'm offered a teaching post at a university other than the one that currently employs me. Suppose, further, that the duties and privileges attached to the offered post are quite similar to those of my present post except that the offered salary is considerably greater than my present one. And suppose, finally, that I'm not averse to receiving a higher salary and would positively welcome it. Is there some significant sense in which this offer makes it *impossible* for me to remain in my present post?

Alternatively, suppose that I have no offer of a teaching post other than the one I currently occupy. Suppose, further, that the university authorities have informed me that unless I substantially increase the amount of teaching I am to do in the next academic session, my contract of employment will be terminated. And suppose, finally, that I'm utterly loath to surrender still more of my time to teaching as I much prefer to spend it reading and writing. Is there some significant sense in which this threat makes it *impossible* for me to reject the extra teaching?

Offers and threats are interventions by others in persons' practical deliberations. They are intended by their authors to influence how their recipients act, by altering the extent to which they actually desire to do a particular action: that is, by altering that action's eligibility. If the interveners are correct in their assessment of the recipients' desires and if they have designed their interventions accordingly, they necessarily succeed in bringing about the intended alteration in those desires.[4] However, despite this shared characteristic of interventions which are offers and interventions which are threats, few negative libertarians regard the making of an offer as curtailing the liberty of its recipient, whereas many of them do so regard threats. (Positive libertarians allow that both offers and threats, as heteronomous influences, may curtail personal liberty.) Four questions thereby suggest themselves:

1. What, if any, are the grounds for distinguishing offers from threats?
2. If such a distinction can be established, does it imply a difference between the ways in which offers and threats affect the practical deliberations of their recipients?
3. If such a difference exists, does it supply a reason for claiming that threats, but not offers, reduce personal liberty?
4. And if no such difference exists, can we nevertheless claim (as positive libertarians do) that both threats and offers may reduce personal liberty?

Cinema-goers will recall that in the popular Hollywood film *The Godfather* the *padrone*, when periodically confronted with an uncooperative business associate, orders his subordinates to make the recalcitrant "an offer he can't refuse." That the wonderful irony of this phrase has been so widely appreciated might readily be taken as evidence that we are all perfectly able to distinguish an offer from a threat, because we can distinguish a gain from a loss. But if a distinction of this kind can be drawn, it cannot be done simply upon such grounds as these. For what's true of both offers and threats is that acceding to them promises to make their recipients better off than not doing so. So the differences that must exist if a distinction is to be drawn between offers and threats are those (i) between the gains of acceding to an offer and a threat respectively and, correspondingly, (ii) between the losses of not acceding to an offer and a threat respectively.

It's unnecessary to rehearse the accounts supplied by the literature on this subject to appreciate that the existence of such differences presupposes a conception of *normalcy* into which the threatening or offering action is taken to be an extraneous intrusion. The need for such a presupposition is evident from the casual distinction commonly drawn between offering and threatening interventions: that acceding to the former promises to increase wellbeing whereas not acceding to the latter promises to decrease it. This distinction tends to obscure the fact that not acceding to offers promises a relative decrease in wellbeing, while acceding to threats promises a relative increase in wellbeing.

To establish the distinction between offers and threats it's therefore necessary to suppose that the accession-consequences of the former, and the non-accession-consequences of the latter, respectively promise not merely relative increments and decrements of wellbeing but absolute ones. And this entails a baseline or norm from which such consequences are deemed to be departures. In the literature, the conception of this norm is the description of the normal and predictable course of events: that is, the course of events (and associated level of wellbeing) that would confront the recipient of the intervention were that intervention not to occur.

Given this conception of the norm, we can derive a simple configuration of the alternative consequences posed by various types of intervention. For an offer – "You may use my car whenever you wish" – the accession-consequence promises a situation which is more desired than the norm, while the non-accession-consequence is on the norm, no more or less desired than it because identical to it. For a threat – "Your money or your life" – the accession-consequence (no money) is less desired than the norm, but the non-accession-consequence (no life) is still less desired. We can additionally identify a third kind of intervention which I'll call a *throffer*: "Kill this man and you'll receive £1000; fail to kill him and I'll kill you." Here the accession-consequence may be more desired than the norm, while the non-accession-consequence is definitely less desired than the norm.

This configuration can be displayed diagrammatically (Figure 51.1). The vertically aligned pairs of points represent the alternative consequences promised by offers (1, 2), threats (3, 4) and throffers (5, 6); and the odd-numbered points represent accession-consequences, with the even-numbered points representing non-accession-consequences. (It need not be assumed that levels of wellbeing are cardinally measurable.) Hence it appears that the answer to the first of our four questions is an affirmation that we *can* distinguish offers from threats and that the grounds for doing so consist in the fact that the alternative consequences posed by the former occupy different positions relative to the norm than do those posed by the latter.

Let's consider our answer to the second question in the light of this distinction. Does this difference between offers and threats imply any difference between the ways in which each respectively affects the practical deliberations of their recipients? The short answer is "no." For the way in which both offers and threats affect their recipients consists in the *reversal* of the relative preferability of doing an action with that of not doing it. Whereas in the normal and predictable course of events – in the absence of an intervention – Blue's desire to do B (use my car, surrender her money, kill this man) is less than her desire not to do it, in the presence of an intervention her desire to do B is greater than her desire not to do it.

What is salient for Blue's deliberations is not whether the alternatives confronting her are above, on, or below the norm. Rather, it is the fact, true of both offers and threats, that acceding promises to leave her in a more desired position than does not acceding. The *modus operandi* of an intervention – its method of promoting an acceding response – consists in promising a non-zero difference when the wellbeing associated with not acceding is deducted from that associated with acceding. This is true irrespective of where the

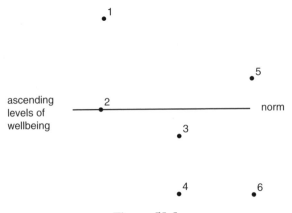

Figure 51.1

two alternative consequences lie in relation to the norm: that is, irrespective of whether the intervention is an offer or a threat.

And while it's certainly true that acceding to an offer is more desired than acceding to a threat, it's very far from being true that the promised non-zero difference in wellbeing is always greater in the case of offers than in the case of threats. This simply means, as we already know from common experience, that offers are not invariably more resistible or less impelling than threats. With respect to any intervention, it's the existence of this difference that affects the practical deliberations of the recipient.[5]

If (and only if) this argument is correct, it should be true that the factor determining the relative strength of a recipient's desire to accede to an intervention is the size of this difference and not the distance of either of its consequences from the norm. That this is indeed the case can be seen by comparing the following threats:

1. Give me £100 or I'll kill you.
2. Give me £1000 or I'll kill you.
3. Give me £1000 or I'll kill you and your brother.
4. Give me £100 or I'll kill you and your brother.

Making the usual assumptions about persons' relative preferences concerning money, personal survival and fraternal welfare (i.e. that the latter two are preferred to the former), we can readily see that Blue's desire to accede would be greatest in the case of (4) and least in the case of (2). What this indicates is that the strength of a threat is not a function of how much less its accession-consequence is desired than the norm: (2) is weaker than both (1) and (4). Nor is its strength a function of how much less its non-accession-consequence is desired than the norm: (3) is weaker than (4), and (2) is weaker than (1). Differences in wellbeing between consequences and the norm are utterly irrelevant in assessing the strength of a threat. All that's relevant is the extent of the difference between acceding and not acceding.

In that respect, it's not strictly mistaken (as it is in the case of threats) to regard the strength of an offer as a function of the promised difference between its accession-consequence and the norm. But this provides no reason to suppose that the strength of offers is determined by considerations different from those pertaining to threats. For it's simply an analytic fact, true by definition, that the non-accession-consequence of an offer lies on the norm. The strength of an offer, like that of any sort of intervention, is purely a function of the promised difference between its alternative consequences. That this is true of all interventions is further borne out by a comparison of the following throffers:

1. Do B and I'll give you £100; fail and I'll kill you.
2. Do B and I'll give you £1000; fail and I'll kill you.
3. Do B and I'll give you £100; fail and I'll kill you and your brother.
4. Do B and I'll give you £1000; fail and I'll kill you and your brother.

Again, on the same relative preference assumptions, it's clear that the greatest desire to accede arises in (4) and the least in (1). This ordering, in terms of capacity to affect the desire to accede, exactly corresponds to the ordering of these throffers in terms of the promised difference between their alternative consequences. It doesn't correspond to their ordering in terms of the difference between acceding and the norm, nor of the difference between not acceding and the norm.

A further point should be made in this connection. Thus far I've been talking about how offers and threats affect their recipients' *desires*, that is, about the relative *preferability* of acceding and not acceding. But it's equally possible to formulate a parallel discussion in terms of how such interventions affect their recipients' *duties*, that is, in terms of the *morality* of acceding and not acceding. So whereas in the normal course of events Blue may have no duty to refrain from doing B, in the presence of an offer or a threat she may have this duty. The only difference between the descriptive account and the prescriptive one is that, in the latter case, the relative positioning of the two alternatives is not necessarily a matter of the difference between them being a positive quasi-numerical one. Interventions, in the prescriptive account, do not make the recipient better off by acceding than by not acceding. Rather, acceding becomes obligatory and not acceding becomes prohibited. The difference in the prescriptive account is, so to speak, one of quality rather than quantity. This, however, doesn't alter the point that whether interventions affect desires or duties, the ways in which these are affected are of the same form: namely, the creation of a difference between the value of acceding and that of not acceding.

Briefly then, both the *modus operandi* of an intervention and its strength are determined without reference to the norm. What the normal course of events would have been simply has no bearing on the impact an intervention has on its recipient. Since it's with reference to the norm that we define offers and threats and distinguish between them, we may conclude – in answer to our second question – that there is no difference between the ways in which offers and threats respectively affect their recipients' practical deliberations.

And this provides us with the answer to the third question as well. Since no such difference exists, it cannot constitute a reason for claiming that threats, but not offers, reduce personal liberty. Which brings us to the fourth question. This asks whether, in the absence of such a difference, it is nevertheless possible to claim – as do positive libertarians – that both threats and offers may reduce liberty.

We've already seen, in the previous section, that "Blue is free to do B" implies or presupposes neither that "Blue wants to do B" nor that "Blue has no duty to refrain from doing B." Whereas in the normal course of events it might be the case that "Blue wants to do B" or that "Blue has no duty to refrain from doing B," the occurrence of Red's threat or offer to Blue may cause it to be the case that "Blue wants to refrain from doing B" or that "Blue has a duty to refrain from doing B." But neither of these latter two statements, nor the fact that they are true because of another's action, implies that "Blue is unfree to do B." They do not imply that the event "Blue doing B" is impossible. Of course, the truth of the first of these statements rules out the possibility of "Blue doing B eagerly" and the truth of the second rules out "Blue doing B justifiably." But that is another matter.

Hence neither the making of threats nor the making of offers reduces liberty. When an aspiring Casanova reports that "The look she gave me *stopped* me in my tracks," we know that he's speaking metaphorically regardless of whether the look was an offer or a threat. Interventions don't count as preventions.

The claim to the contrary would be that Red's intervening action A, in behalf of "Blue refraining from doing B," *does* render "Blue doing B" impossible. For this claim to be true it must be the case that making accession (not doing B) preferable or morally superior to non-accession (doing B), implies rendering the latter impossible and the former therefore necessary. And this in turn implies that only that one, which is the preferred or morally superior of the two alternative courses of action, can be done. Clearly however, this is just false with respect to any *morally superior* alternative since its being a moral alternative implies that it's possible not to do it.

Is it nonetheless true of *preferred* alternatives? If it were, then we should have to say that Red's intervening action A must be preferred by him to not doing A. And this would imply, on this account, that "Red not doing A" is impossible and thus that "Red doing A" is necessary. But observe that if this were so, then "Red doing A" – as a necessary event –

must itself be a constituent part of the normal and predictable course of event, since it's analytically true that all necessary events are predictable events. In which case, however, "Red doing A" cannot be construed as an intervention, that is, as an extraneous intrusion into the normal and predictable course of events.

So the view that intervention is prevention is self-contradictory because anyone entertaining it is committed both to affirming and denying that an intervening action is part of the normal and predictable course of events. This contradiction seems to me to be implicit in the writings of many of those who embrace positive conceptions of liberty. And it's therefore all the more surprising to discover it in the opposing arguments of some negative libertarians.

Taking exception to the general argument just advanced, J. P. Day has proposed a different account of why threats do, but offers don't, reduce negative liberty. Day agrees that one is to be described as unfree to do an action only if others render one's doing of that action impossible. But he contends that threats, unlike offers, make their recipients unfree because they render impossible their doing a *complex* (conjunctive) action. The highwayman's threat to the traveller – "Your money or your life" – is said to render impossible the traveller's doing the complex action of keeping his money *and* keeping his life.

I suggest, however, that we need to consider carefully whether this alleged impossibility can be the effect of the highwayman's threat. If Red's threat against "Blue keeping money" renders impossible the complex action of "Blue keeping money and keeping life," what can be the effect of Red's *execution* of his threat? On Day's argument, it's hard to see how Red's act of executing the threat can add anything further to Blue's unfreedom than has already been achieved by Red's act of issuing the threat. If Blue withholds her money and Red executes his threat, is Blue thereby released from her unfreedom to do that complex action?

Suppose that Blue does withhold her money and the execution is nonetheless not forthcoming. This entails that Blue keeps her money and her life. Day concedes that it is "illogical" to describe a person as unfree to do an action (simple or complex) which she in fact does. Hence, anticipating this rejoinder, he suggests that threats are generally executed. But this empirical generalization, even if true, is insufficient to imply what is in any case patently false: namely, that it is the threat and not its execution that is doing whatever prevention occurs in such circumstances. Neither threats nor warnings nor, for that matter, friendly advice about the malign intentions of third parties serve to render impossible any action (simple or complex) of their recipients. Intervention, we must conclude, is simply not the same as prevention.

Notes

1 Assuming, as she is, that the liberty under consideration here is not liberty in the normative sense of that word (signifying the absence of a duty to refrain from, and the consequent permissibility of, doing something).

2 This also covers "compelling." See G.H. von Wright, *Norm and Action* (London: Routledge & Kegan Paul, 1963), pp. 54–5: "There are two types of act which . . . relate to one agent's ability to interfere with the ability of another to perform a certain act. These are the types of act which we call *hindering* or *preventing* and *compelling* or *forcing*. These two types of act are obviously interdefinable. Therefore we can here limit discussion to one of them. To compel an agent to do something is the same as to prevent him from forbearing this thing. And to hinder an agent from doing something is the same as to force him to forbear it."

3 S. I. Benn and W. L. Weinstein, "Being Free to Act and Being a Free Man," *Mind* 80 (1971), p. 195.

4 If they are *not* correct in their assessments of those desires – if they underestimate their recipients' attachment to the non-compliant alternative – and/or fail to design their interventions

appropriately, they *a fortiori* cannot succeed in altering the action's eligibility. [. . .]

5   A plausible suggestion is that persons *resent* receiving threats whereas this is not the case with offers. But, though true, this does not imply a recipient's greater willingness to accede to offers than to threats since the (thereby augmented) undesirability of acceding to the latter simply reduces the wellbeing differential between doing and not doing so. It can't be presumed to make it less than the corresponding differential for any offer, much less, to eliminate it.

Hillel Steiner, *An Essay on Rights* (Oxford: Blackwell, 1994), pp. 6–11, 22–30.

Chapter 52

David Zimmerman, from "Coercive Wage Offers" (1981)

Is the wage bargain in a capitalist labor market coercive if the worker is limited to a choice between unpalatable alternatives, for example, working at a low-paying job and starving? This is an old controversy which endures even in contemporary western economies where much of the work force is unionized and wage levels are more frequently set by bargaining than by markets. These workers have a choice between taking a well-paid (but still relatively unsatisfying) job and going on welfare (which is usually somewhat worse). In a recent polemic, C. B. Macpherson insists:

> What distinguishes the capitalist economy from the simple exchange economy is the separation of capital and labour, that is, the existence of a labour force without its own sufficient capital and therefore without a choice as to whether to put its labour into the market or not. Professor Friedman would agree that where there is no choice there is coercion.[1]

Robert Nozick disagrees:

> Z [a worker] is faced with working or starving; the choices and actions of all other persons do not add up to providing Z with some other option. . . . Does Z choose to work voluntarily? . . . Z does choose to work voluntarily if the other individuals A through Y [capitalists and those workers who got the better jobs] each acted voluntarily *and within their rights.*[2]

Macpherson and Nozick disagree on at least two distinct points: whether workers in a capitalist economy actually do have sufficient access to capital and to jobs outside of the private sector so that their own wage bargain is uncoerced, and whether this wage bargain would be uncoerced even if workers had *no* such access. The first question is factual, the second more-or-less conceptual. In this paper I am mainly concerned with the second: I want to examine the nature of coercive relationships in order to determine what conditions would have to be satisfied for acceptance of a wage bargain to count as coerced.

Nozick's claim that A through Y coerce Z only if *they do not act within their rights* is striking in that it makes "coercion" out to be an essentially moral concept, in the sense that its conditions of application contain an ineliminable reference to moral rightness or wrongness. Note that if "coercion" did prove to be an essentially moral concept, then the enduring dispute over the coerciveness of capitalist wage proposals would be wholly parasitic on the prior moral question of those rights and wrongs, in particular, on the question of whether capitalist relations or production are morally acceptable on grounds of justice or utility.[3] But this flies in the face of appearances. The dispute has endured so long and has generated so much heat because all the parties to it, socialists and laissez-faire liberals alike, have embraced the conviction that coercion is prima facie morally wrong, so that if capitalist wage bargains did involve coercion, that would be one moral strike against them. And the intuitive idea underlying this moral conviction is that coercion *undermines freedom* – this is what is ultimately prima facie morally wrong. To be sure, defenders of capitalism are perfectly prepared to argue that this economic system is morally acceptable and apologists to argue that it is not, but they have generally been under the impression that the dispute over the *coerciveness* of capitalist relations of production is a dispute about freedom, not justice or utility.

[. . .]

Nozick advances an essentially moral condition for coercion with the best of theoretical motives: he wants to account for the special quality of certain proposals which are welcomed by their recipients and which thus satisfy a plausible set of conditions for being counted as genuine offers, but which nonetheless seem coercive. I argue, however, that with some elaboration of the non-moral framework for distinguishing threats from offers the phenomenon of "coercive offers" can be accommodated without any assumptions about prior rights and wrongs.

[. . .]

In developing a completely non-moral account of coercion, the main task is to accommodate intuitions about the coerciveness of proposals like the slave-owner's, which count as offers when reckoned in terms of the normally expected course of events, but to do this in a way which has no recourse to a moral baseline set by prior rights and wrongs. My suggestion is that we retain the normally expected course of events as the relevant pre-proposal situation in *all* cases, and then broaden the framework as follows to account for the coerciveness of certain offers. The slave does in fact prefer to move from the pre-proposal situation in which he is beaten every day to the proposal situation in which he is spared the customary beating for performing the disagreeable task, so let us concede, for the sake of theoretical uniformity, that the slave-owner is making a genuine offer. We can

account for its being a coercive offer by bringing into the picture an *alternative pre-proposal situation* which the slave strongly prefers to the actual one. This suggests a hypothesis: an offer is coercive only if Q would prefer to move from the normally expected pre-proposal situation to the proposal situation, *but he would strongly prefer even more to move from the actual pre-proposal situation to some alternative pre-proposal situation*. The slave, for example, would strongly prefer not being a slave to having a choice between being beaten and being spared a beating for performing a disagreeable task.

Now this hypothesis obviously will not do as it stands, for there are no doubt many alternative pre-proposal situations Q would strongly prefer to the actual one, but not all of them can be relevant in establishing the coerciveness of P's proposal. The theoretical task, then, is to come up with some way of limiting this range to take the place of Nozick's reliance on the morally required course of events.

First, there has to be some kind of *feasibility* condition: in assessing the coerciveness of offers, we do not need to take into account alternative pre-proposal situations which are *not possible*, historically, economically, technologically, or the like, however much Q prefers them to the actual pre-proposal situation. When set in terms of what is *historically* or *technologically* possible, this condition is intuitively obvious, it looks trivial in fact, but it does have genuinely interesting implications when applied to various capitalist wage proposals [. . .].

When set in terms of *economic* possibilities, however, the feasibility condition raises questions. For example, if P can improve the terms of his proposal only at great cost to himself, should this be taken into account in estimating the feasibility of the alternative pre-proposal situation Q highly prefers? Cost to P clearly does not always affect feasibility. The slave-owner, for example, would suffer a great loss if he were to free the slave, but even though emancipation would take him far below his "minimum transfer price," it is feasible nonetheless. Since I am trying to work out a *non*-moral account of the structure of coercion, it will not do to explain this situation in terms of the slave-owner's moral obligation to free the slave. My problem is to determine when *P*'s costs render an alternative pre-proposal situation unfeasible *without* making any appeal to what it would be obligatory or supererogatory for him to do.

I suggest that *P*'s costs do count against feasibility when his role in the unavailability of the pre-proposal situation *Q* highly prefers is merely one of *not giving Q* what he needs to gain it, and that *P*'s costs do not count against feasibility when he plays an active role in *preventing Q* from gaining it. There is an independent rationale for insisting on this distinction, in any event, for a coercive offer is not merely an extremely unattractive offer which *Q* cannot afford to refuse: it is all-important *how Q* came to be in such a vulnerable position. I would claim that for *P*'s offer to be genuinely coercive it must be the case that *he actively prevents Q from being in the alternative pre-proposal situation Q strongly prefers.*

Consider the difference between these two cases. *A* kidnaps *Q*, brings him to the island where *A*'s factory is located and abandons him on the beach. All the jobs in *A*'s factory are considerably worse than those available to *Q* on the mainland. The next day *A* approaches *Q* with the proposal "Take one of the jobs in my factory and I won't let you starve." Coercive or uncoercive? *B* also owns a factory (the only other one) on the island, in which the jobs are just as bad. Seeing *Q*'s plight, he beats *A* to the scene and makes the same kind of proposal. Coercive or uncoercive? Let us concede that both *A* and *B* make genuine offers, for in each case *Q* would presumably prefer to go from the actual pre-proposal situation in which he starves on the beach to the proposal situation in which he has a choice between working at a terrible job or starving.

Let us also concede that both *A* and *B exploit Q*'s misfortune by offering such bad terms. (Whether their terms are unfair we can leave to the theory of justice.) The question is whether they both coerce *Q*.

Some philosophers are inclined to think that exploiting another's misfortune by extracting a commitment from him on grossly unfavorable terms is a form of coercion. Frankfurt, for example, claims that *P* coerces *Q* if he "exploits his dependency and need." And Lyons claims that "*P* used his superior bargaining power to force *Q* into a hard bargain whenever the *y* which *P* got from *Q* is worth far more than the minimum transfer price required to persuade *P* to give up *x*, while *Q* got hardly more than his minimum transfer price." I would claim, on the other hand, that only *A* makes a coercive offer. The intuitive idea underlying coercion is that *the person who does the coercing undermines, or limits the freedom* of the person who is coerced, so coercing goes beyond exploiting, however morally objectionable the latter may be. If the island wage-level is unfairly low, then *B* wrongs the dependent *Q* in only one way: he offers him an exploitive wage. But *A* wrongs him in two ways: first, he places *Q* in a dependent position where he is vulnerable to exploitation, and then he offers him an exploitive wage.

[. . .]

Questions can he raised, however, about just what counts as preventing *Q* from having the pre-proposal situation he prefers. Suppose *P* quietly corners the market in penicillin and then offers to sell some to the infected *Q* at an outrageously high price. Is this just a case of monopolistic exploitation, or is *P* to be counted as preventing *Q* from having any of the commodity on better terms, and therefore as coercing him? I am inclined to say that this monopolist does coerce his customer. Contrast this with a case of "natural monopoly" in which all the pencillin in the world, except for *P*'s, is simultaneously destroyed through no action of *P*, and he then charges the same outrageously high price. Here I am inclined to say that *P* exploits but does not coerce his customer.

Does the coerciveness of an offer depend at all on the *intention* with which P prevents Q from having the alternative pre-proposal situation he strongly prefers? Consider a pair of non-economic cases. Prosecutor A believes he has a very strong case so he brings a charge of trafficking in heroin against Q. It then occurs to him that he would be able to get valuable information from Q if he offered to let him plead guilty to the lesser charge of possession in return for his giving evidence against his accomplices. So A offers the plea-bargain. Prosecutor B, on the other hand, believes he has a weak case on both the stronger and lesser charges. But he knows that Q does not know just how weak, so he also brings the stronger charge initially, with the intention of using it to scare Q into accepting his offer to let Q plead guilty to a lesser charge. Both prosecutors make an offer, since Q would undoubtedly prefer to face the lesser charge of possession, but my intuitions are that only B's offer is coercive. Both prosecutors initially bring the stronger charge and thereby prevent Q from being in the pre-proposal situation he strongly prefers, namely not being up against a charge at all, but only B does this with the intention of rendering Q vulnerable to the eventual plea-bargain; A does it because he knows he can sustain the stronger charge. If my intuition about the coerciveness of B's offer is correct, then an independent intention condition is required in some (all?) cases, since this seems to be the only salient difference between the two cases. To be sure, there is also a difference in what the prosecutors would have done in some base-line situation: A would have brought the stronger charge anyway and B would not. But these counterfactual states of affairs cannot be identified without reference to A's and B's intentions: A would have brought the stronger charge *even if* he had not intended to make Q vulnerable to his offer, whereas B would have brought it *only if* he had so intended.

[. . .]

Macpherson is right to insist that non-access to better terms is part of what makes a wage bargain coercive, but he is wrong to suggest that it is sufficient. And though Nozick has made a significant contribution to our understanding of the structure of coercive relationships, he is wrong to suppose that the coerciveness of capitalist wage proposals turns on the question of prior rights and wrongs. What I have tried to do here is work out a non-moral account of coercion which can be used to settle at least the conceptual side of the enduring dispute. Capitalist wage proposals generally do count as genuine offers, because workers generally do want to make the move from actual pre-proposal situations, even the relatively prosperous ones available in a welfare state, to the proposal situations capitalists make available. And a wage offer counts as coercive if and only if (1) an alternative pre-proposal situation workers would strongly prefer to the actual one is technologically and economically feasible when the offer is made, and (2) capitalists prevent workers from having at least one of these feasible alternative pre-proposal situations.[4]

This account leaves many empirical and moral issues open. [. . .] I make no real attempt to determine whether or not these conditions are actually satisfied in the real world of capitalist relations of production. If they are satisfied, and if the common conviction that coercion is prima facie wrong is sound, then the most that follows from my account is that capitalist wage offers are *prima facie wrong*. It would take a lot more discussion to determine whether they are wrong *all things considered*.

Notes

1 C. B. Macpherson, "Elegant Tombstones: A Note on Friedman's Freedom," in *Democratic Theory* (Oxford: Oxford University, 1973), p. 146.
2 Robert Nozick, *Anarchy, State and Utopia* (New York: Basic Books, 1974), p. 263.
3 Some defenders of a moral account of coercion will object to setting the baseline, as Nozick does, exclusively in terms of prior rights, and will wish to

include considerations of utility-maximization. I owe this observation to Daniel Lyons.

4 When I speak of jointly sufficient conditions here, the reader should keep in mind that I am assuming the satisfaction of whatever rationality and credibility conditions might also be needed. [. . .] [Earlier] I confessed that I am unclear about whether *P's intention* to render *Q* vulnerable is generally necessary for the coerciveness of a proposal. I am also unclear about the necessity of this condition for the coerciveness of capitalist wage proposals in particular, though if it were necessary, there would in most cases be little difficulty, I think, in showing that it was satisfied.

David Zimmerman, "Coercive Wage Offers," *Philosophy and Public Affairs* 10 (1981), pp. 121–4, 131–4, 137–8, 144–5.

Chapter 53

Christine Swanton, from *Freedom: A Coherence Theory* (1992)

The Nature of Threats and Offers

The ultimate purpose of the next two sections is to examine the question of the effect on freedom of threats and offers. I shall suggest that the current thinking on this issue is radically misguided. To show this, I first need to discuss the distinction between threats and offers, and my opposition to current analyses.

In his article "Coercive Offers," Robert Stevens[1] argues against the account of threats and offers proposed by Steiner,[2] claiming that it is vulnerable to counterexample. I shall suggest that Stevens's own account is also susceptible to counterexample. More importantly, I shall claim, this susceptibility, shared by both Steiner and Stevens, is symptomatic of a radical mistake made by both Stevens and those whom he criticizes. The current thinking on the nature of threats and offers shares a common presupposition which I shall question.

Threats and offers are currently distinguished by focusing on the proposee's preference schedule, relative to a baseline of what Steiner calls a concept of "normalcy" – a baseline from which threats and offers are deemed to be specific kinds of departure. Authors differ on the details of this basic idea, however. For Steiner, the standard of normalcy is "the course of events which would confront the recipient of the intervention were the intervention not to occur" (op. cit., p. 39). An intervention is an *offer* relative to this norm, if and only if "the compliance-consequence represents a situation which is preferred [by the recipient] to the norm while the noncompliance-consequence represents a situation on the norm, no more or less preferred than it because identical to it" (op. cit., p. 39). An intervention is a *threat* relative to this norm, if and only if "the compliance-consequence represents a situation which is less preferred than the norm . . . but the noncompliance-consequence represents a situation which is still less preferred . . ." (op. cit., p. 39).

In disagreeing with Steiner's account, Stevens offers the following counterexample:

> Suppose *P* offers *Q* a handful of beans for her cow. It is likely that *P* prefers her cow to a handful of beans (unless they are magic beans). If so, the desirability to *Q* of noncompliance with *P*'s offer . . . is greater than the desirability to *Q* of compliance with *P*'s offer (op. cit., p. 84).

Stevens's account of offers is as follows. *P*'s proposal to *Q* that *Q* do *A* is an offer if and only if the desirability to *Q* of *Q*'s doing *A* relative to what it would have been if *P* made no proposal is increased, and the desirability to Q of Q's doing not A relative to what it would have been if P made no proposal is unchanged; or the desirability to Q of Q's not doing A relative to what it would have been if P made no proposal is increased, and the desirability to Q of Q's doing A relative to what it would have been been if P made no proposal is unchanged (op. cit., p. 85).

This account accommodates the cow for beans case, in that Q presumably prefers giving away her cow in exchange for beans to giving away her cow simpliciter. Stevens's account, too, is vulnerable to counterexample. Assume that I have a number of garden gnomes in my garage which I cannot sell. I offer Q a dozen of my choicest gnomes for her cow. Q, though, hates garden gnomes and does not want the bother of getting rid of them. Q prefers giving away her cow simpliciter to giving away her cow in exchange for gnomes. The desirability to Q of giving away her cow relative to what it would have been had there been no proposal is decreased, and the desirability to Q of not giving away her cow relative to what it would have been had there been no proposal is unchanged. So, on Stevens's account, the proposal of gnomes for cow is not an offer. Yet surely my proposal, though unfortunate and perhaps even misguided, is still an offer?

I shall claim that both Steiner and Stevens make the same radical mistake. Stevens follows a long line of accounts that distinguish threats and offers by focusing on their effect on the preferences of the proposee. In short, they treat threats and offers as perlocutionary acts. A treatment of threats and offers as illocutionary acts would lead to quite different results. The reason the gnome lover's proposal is an offer despite the preferences of the gnome hater has to do with the conventions surrounding the making of offers and the context surrounding the proposal.

More specifically, the fact that the proposal is an offer has nothing to do with the preferences of the person to whom the offer is directed: preferences that determine the perlocutionary effect of the offer but not the nature of the proposal as an offer. The proposal to exchange gnomes for the cow is an offer, given the following:

(i) The proposal falls within the accepted range of locutions conventionally assigned to the making of offers: paradigmatically the uttering of the words: "Would you care for my gnomes in exchange for your cow?" rather than, e.g., a locution designed for insulting: "If you don't prefer my gnomes to your miserable beast, you're even more of an idiot than I thought."

These conventions are designed for:

(a) Securing a certain uptake (viz., ". . . bringing about the understanding of the meaning and of the force of the locution,"[3] even though that uptake may not be secured on a given occasion (the offeree did not hear, for example).

(b) Taking effect in a certain way (whereby ". . . in consequence of the performance of this [illocutionary] act, such and such a future event, *if* it happens, will be *in order*, and such-and-such other events, *if* they happen, will not be in order").[4] For example, rolling up one's sleeves may be in order as a consequence of the slight to one's animal and one's intelligence, but definitely not in order as a consequence of the offer of exchange.

(c) Inviting further acts that are responses or sequels (in the case of offers, acceptance or rejection by the offeree, and if there is acceptance, the offerer's honoring his offer).

(ii) The procedure for making an offer is invoked in appropriate circumstances: in a context where an exchange of cows for gnomes can be made. If there are no gnomes to exchange, if the context is a play, or a joke on a desert island, there is no genuine offer.

(iii)   The proposal is designed for use by persons having certain intentions, expectations, and hopes: e.g., the hope or expectation that the offeree will perceive the offer as a benefit, and the intention not to harm the offeree by the offer. Consequently, if the proposer believes the gnomes are filled with explosives and hopes to maim the proposee, the offer will be, to use Austin's words, "unhappy" (though Austin did not believe the performance to be "void" in these circumstances).

I have denied that Stevens's account provides a necessary condition of offers. The root problem is his failure to appreciate the conventional aspects – illocutionary force – of offers. The same problem underlies the failure of his account to provide a sufficient condition of offers. Consider his following example:

> Highwayman *P* wants money. So *P* points a gun at traveller *Q*'s head and says to *Q* 'I am going to kill you.' Some time later *P* still holding the gun at *Q*'s head says to *Q* 'Your money or your life.' Preferring to keep her life to keeping her money *Q* gives *P* her money (op. cit., p. 93).

It is a consequence of Stevens's view that this is an offer, and he accepts this consequence. Yet, surely, it has all the conventional force of a threat.

It may be argued that the problem lies in the standard of normalcy that Stevens has proposed. Perhaps the pre-offer situation that is the baseline for comparison should be prior to the context of the coercive setup within which the so-called offer is made. This suggestion does not help in the case of other counterexamples, however, which reinforce my claim that the real problem lies in the failure to appreciate that offers and threats should be understood as illocutionary acts. Consider again the standard highway robber's proposal: "Your money or your life!" Imaging that I, the proposee, am suicidal. Being of a cowardly disposition, I have failed to take my own life by

the traditional methods. The highway robber provides me with just the situation I crave. By refusing to yield, I am able to end my miserable existence, and on a high note: my fantasies of dying while resisting the forces of evil are splendidly realized. Yet, surely, despite my bizarre preferences, the proposal is a threat.[5] The problem with Stevens's account is not that he fixes on the wrong baseline for comparison of preferences, but that he focuses on the preferences of the proposee at all. The reason the highway robber makes a threat is that the proposal has the illocutionary force of a threat. "Your money or your life" is text-book threatening language designed to invite the responses and sequels appropriate to threats; the context is appropriate to the issuing of genuine threats – one of attempted armed robbery; the robber has the appropriate expectations and intentions: his aims are not ones of the benevolent mercy killer, but are those of the traditional highway robber. In no way does the proposal have the illocutionary force of an offer. Yet on Stevens's account, the highwayman's proposal to me that I hand over my money is an offer. It is an offer, since one of the sufficient conditions for offers is satisfied: the desirability to me of my not handing over the money relative to what it would have been if the highwayman had made no proposal is increased, and the desirability to me of handing over my money relative to what it would have been if the highwayman had made no proposal is unchanged.

Although Stevens's account provides neither necessary nor sufficient conditions for proposals being offers, accounts such as his (and those he criticizes) are right to focus on the important distinction between the point of threats and offers: the point that distinguishes their illocutionary force. Threats are designed to limit options, whereas offers are designed to expand them. But Stevens's account, like those he criticizes, interprets this idea in terms of perlocutionary effect on the individual proposee, instead of the illocutionary force of the proposal. Whether or not a proposal is an offer does not depend on whether or not *in fact* the proposal expands options. It depends on whether the context is one in which it has the illocutionary force of an offer – on whether or not it is a conventionally recognized, context-sensitive, signal for option-expansion.

Do Threats and Offers Limit Freedom?

Whether or not threats and offers limit freedom depends on their perlocutionary effects. Because threats and offers have been standardly analyzed in terms of their perlocutionary effects, there has been a tendency to believe that getting straight on the distinction between threats and offers will answer the question about their relationship to freedom. Since the nature of threats and offers depends on their illocutionary force, however, and not on their perlocutionary effects, this belief is mistaken.

Threats and offers have many perlocutionary effects, not all of which determine their effect on freedom. As the background theory suggests, the relevant perlocutionary effects are whether or not the threat or offer limits the individual's potential in agency. There are two areas that are relevant: limitation of *autonomy*, and limitation of *options*. Both threats and offers may limit autonomy by subverting the deliberative process through debilitating fear or irresistible temptation. Since this chapter is concerned with eligibility of options, the autonomy factor will be deferred until chapter 9.

Consider first, threats. I shall argue that though threats paradigmatically limit options and therefore freedom, not all threats do, since threats are not defined in terms of their perlocutionary effects. First, however, we must consider an argument of Steiner's suggesting that *no* threats limit freedom. His argument is based on a similarity between threats and offers. People can be brought to do things that they otherwise would not do by both threats and offers, since both operate by manipulating the relative desirability of compliance and noncompliance. It is not nec-

essarily the case that the difference in desirability between compliance and noncompliance is greater where the intervention is a threat as opposed to an offer: furthermore, both threats and offers can be so irresistible that reasonable people cannot be expected not to comply. Steiner concludes that "it is not necessarily true that offers are more resistible or exert less influence than threats" (op. cit., p. 40). From this conclusion, he draws the inference that, since there is no difference between the way in which threats and offers affect the practical deliberations of their recipients, no such difference can "constitute a reason for asserting that threats, but not offers, diminish personal liberty" (op. cit., p. 43). He concludes that neither threats nor offers limit freedom.

This conclusion is at odds with the endoxa, e.g.,

E4: The man who hands over his money, having yielded to credible threat at gun point, does not perform a free act.

E16: The professional tennis player who accepts the promoter's offer of $50,000 merely to appear in a tournament in which he otherwise would not have appeared performs a free act, even though he could not be reasonably expected to turn down the offer.

The background theory not only demonstrates that the endoxa can be saved, and their worthiness of preservation, but also what is wrong with Steiner's argument. The question the argument raises is: Why should the perlocutionary effect of relative degree of influence of a proposal determine a proposee's freedom? Surely a piece of advice may be so timely and apt that any reasonable person would be expected to go along with it. Admittedly, a threat may similarly powerfully influence a reasonable person, but surely the advice and the threat are not in the same boat as far as freedom is concerned. Why is this? According to the background theory, freedom is affected only where influence is seen as a *limitation* on the practical process.

A typical mistake (to be discussed more fully in the next chapter) has manifested itself in Steiner's argument. The mistake is a confusion between the material and the formal properties of freedom. Certainly, a frequent concomitant of freedom-limiting factors is relative irresistibility of influence on an agent's practical deliberations. This material property does not constitute a freedom-limiting factor, however, unless it is also true that it constitutes some kind of infelicity or untoward factor, viz., a flaw, limitation, or breakdown in the practical process. The advice does not limit agency: it enhances it.

The reason proposals manipulating costs and benefits restrict freedom as far as eligibility is concerned is that some *limit* options, whereas others expand them. According to Benn and Weinstein, for example, threats standardly constitute limitations on options, whereas offers do not. This is the reason that threats, but not offers, standardly limit freedom. Although threats paradigmatically limit freedom by limiting options, not all proposals having the illocutionary force of threats do so. An example is the threat to the suicidal person discussed in the previous section.

Let us now turn our attention to the even more controversial area of offers. It may be thought that some offers limit freedom since they actually limit options. The problem is that whether or not an offer is regarded as a *limitation* depends on what counts as the "choice situation." An offer to beat a slave less if he works harder constitutes an expansion of options relative to the current level of beating but does not constitute an expansion of options relative to the "norm," viz., a state of nonbeating. Hence, it may be asked: Should not the offer be seen as a "limitation" because it is a limitation relative to the relevant norm? More specifically, David Zimmerman holds the view that the "offer" is coercive – being a limitation of freedom – because it is a limitation on options in the following sense. The slave owner prevents the slave from acting on

his own or with the help of others to procure an *alternative* proposal situation that is strongly preferred to the actual one [. . .].

In order to answer this challenge, we must be clearer about the notion of a limitation of options. On our view, a restraint R that renders an action A_i ineligible is held to *limit* P's options with respect to A_i, if and only if for some pair of alternatives $(A_i \ldots A_j)$, where P must choose either A_i or A_j, R produces more restraint attached to P's performance of A_i and A_j taken together than that which prevailed before R came into being. This view is distinct from the view that R limits options, if and only if for some large set of actions $A_i \ldots A_m$, R produces more restraint attached to P's performance of those actions taken together than would have been the case without R. The much criticized view [of Locke] that "that ill deserves the name of confinement which hedges us in only from bogs and precipices" looks quite reasonable on the latter account of what counts as a limitation of options, provided it is assumed that the absence of the putative confinement would sufficiently increase the probability of falling into bogs and over the precipices. On my view, then, to claim that R limits freedom *with respect to the eligibility of P's performance of A_i* does presuppose comparison with other actions, but the relevant comparison class is that action that P must perform if she does not perform A_i: it is not some larger set of actions. The larger set is relevant only *a propos P's overall* freedom with respect to eligibility. An important caveat must be made. Whether or not a cost/benefit manipulation limits options *from the standpoint of ineligibility* does not depend on the preferences of the proposee, even though there is, as we have already noted, a richer sense of limiting options where the degree of limitation is a function of both degree of restraint and degree of significance of alternatives.

We can now reply to the views of Zimmerman, Virginia Held, and others. In assessing whether or not an agent is unfree in a certain respect, it is essential to specify the action with respect to which he is unfree, and the partic-ular restraint that renders the agent unfree in that respect. My point is that, although Zimmerman correctly focuses on an area of unfreedom, viz., the action of attaining the strongly preferred proposal situation, the restraint that prevents or hinders the slave from attaining that goal is *not* the making of the offer to beat the slave less if he works harder. It is a quite different restraint or set of restraints: it is the restraints that prevent or hinder the slave from leading a life free of beatings. The offer itself is not a limitation with respect to the slave's options of not working harder or working harder. Similarly, the issuing of a threat, such as "Your money or your life," may enhance your options, where it involves the cancellation of a previ-ous credible threat, "Your money, or the lives (after protracted torture) of all your children." But, of course, this does not alter the fact that the issuing of either threat involves a reduc-tion of overall freedom relative to the tranquil situation that obtained before the robber impinged on your life.

Notes

1 Robert Stevens, "Coercive Offers," *Aus-tralasian Journal of Philosophy* 66 (1988), pp. 83–95.
2 Hiller Steiner, "Individual Liberty," *Proceedings of the Aristotelian Society* 75 (1975), pp. 33–50.
3 J. L. Austin, *How To Do Things with Words* (New York: Oxford University Press, 1962), p. 166.
4 J. L. Austin, "Performative-Constative," in J. Searle (ed.), *The Philosophy of Language* (New York: Oxford University Press, 1971), p. 14.
5 It should be acknowledged that there is a sense of 'making a threat' where this is a perlocutionary act: X threatens Y only if Y is actually threatened by the threat. In this respect 'threaten' shares the ambiguity of 'warn'.

Christine Swanton, *Freedom: A Coherence Theory* (Indianapolis: Hackett, 1992), pp. 104–13.

Chapter 54

Michael J. Gorr, from *Coercion, Freedom, and Exploitation* (1989)

[...]

[...] what exactly *is* an act of coercion? The following analysis seems to be both intuitively attractive and yet sufficiently precise to be of value for moral theorizing:

D1   By doing A P directly coerces Q into doing (not doing) B = ₍def₎

(1)   A is an act (or combination of acts) on P's part by which P intentionally communicates to Q the proposition that P will intentionally bring about (or attempt to bring about) some consequence R if and only if Q does not do (does) B.

(2)   Q does (does not do) B intentionally.

(3)   Q prefers (and P believes that Q prefers) that, all else equal, it not be the case that P bring about R.

(4)   In doing (not doing) B, Q is motivated by his desire that it not be the case that P bring about R and his belief that doing (not doing) B will prevent P from bringing about R.

(5)   P's bringing about R would not consist in P's simply omitting to perform some action but in P's actively bringing about some state of affairs.

(6)   It is not the case that Q prefers that P not bring about R solely because P's bringing about R would be incompatible with P's bringing about some other states of affairs the obtaining of which Q desires.

[...]

Perhaps the central source of controversy in the literature on coercion has been the nature of the coercive act. Must it always be a threat or can it sometimes be an offer? Disagreement has persisted, I believe, largely because of a failure to systematically sort out the issues involved in a clear and careful manner. What follows is intended to help remedy this deficiency.

As Frankfurt has observed, coercive proposals are almost always (at least implicitly) biconditional in nature. Thus, when the highwayman says, "Your money or your life!" this is usually shorthand for the biconditional assertion "You may have your life if and only if you give me your money." Usually, that is, a coercive proposal A issued by P to Q will consist in the communication to Q of a proposition of the following form:

"I will bring about consequence R if and only if you do not do (do) B." Given that p iff q is logically equivalent to the conjunction of the two conditionals, if q then p and if not-q then not-p, we may reformulate the content of the proposal as the conjunction of the following:

If you do not do (do) B, then I will bring about R.

and

> If you do (do not do) B, then I will not bring about R.

It is my view that a biconditional proposal of this sort is coercive only if at least one of its constituent proposals is a *threat*. Furthermore, I do not believe that, strictly speaking, an *offer* can ever be coercive in and of itself. My argument for these assertions is implicit in the following analysis of the difference between a threat and an offer:

D2 By doing A P conditionally threatens Q = def

(1) A is an act (or combination of acts) on P's part by which P intentionally communicates to Q the proposition that P will intentionally bring about (or attempt to bring about) some consequence R if Q does not do (does) B.

(2) Q prefers (and P believes that Q prefers) that, all else equal, it not be the case that P bring about R.

(3) P's bringing about R would not consist in P's simply omitting to perform some action but in P's actively bringing about some state of affairs.

(4) It is not the case that Q prefers that P not bring about R solely because P's bringing about R would be incompatible with P's bringing about some other state of affairs the obtaining of which Q desires.

D3 By doing A P makes Q a conditional offer = def

(1) Same as (1) above.

(2) Q prefers (and P believes that Q prefers) that, all else equal, P bring about R.

(3) Same as (3) above.

(4) It is not the case that Q prefers that P bring about R solely because P's bringing about R would be incompatible with P's bringing about some other state of affairs the non-obtaining of which Q desires.

This account of what a conditional offer is

makes clear why they are characteristically welcomed by their recipients. For, decision-making costs aside, all rational persons prefer increased opportunities to bring about states of affairs they find desirable. (It should be noted that condition (3) is required because my proposing, in return for some action or omission on your part, not to inflict upon you an unwanted consequence that would not otherwise threaten surely does not constitute an offer. Condition (4) is required because we would not want to count as an offer my proposing, in return for some action or omission on your part, to walk away if the *only* reason you desire me to walk away is that doing so would be incompatible with my beating you up, the action you believe I would otherwise perform). Similarly the account of what a threat is makes it clear why they are generally unwelcome: a rational person will not normally look with favor upon a proposal to attach an undesirable consequence to the performance of an action that he is now able to perform without fear of such a consequence. Finally this account makes clear the primary relationship between threats and coercion: (direct) coercion is what occurs when and only when a conditional threat is successful in inducing compliance with its terms. Hence the conditions that must be satisfied for the occurrence of a conditional threat are a proper subset of the conditions that must be satisfied for the occurrence of coercion.

It might be thought that there are counterexamples to the thesis that rational persons always find threats unwelcome. Nozick suggests the following:

> . . . P tells Q he'll give Q $10,000 if in the next week someone, without prompting, threatens Q. Someone does and Q welcomes the threat.

Nozick argues that proposals of this sort are not really exceptions to his thesis since they are welcomed "for extraneous reasons, because of the special context." Unfortunately he goes on to admit that he finds it difficult to distinguish such contexts from those which are not so special.

What examples of this sort show, I think, is that the original thesis needs to be restated more carefully. For a proposal to count as a threat it is not necessary (through it will characteristically be the case) that a rational person will not welcome the *making* of the proposal; rather, what he must be averse to is the proposed *consequence* of his failure to accede to the terms of the proposal. In Nozick's example Q may welcome the making of the threat but, if it is to count as a genuine threat, he must not desire that what is threatened actually be done. In cases where a person does welcome the proposed consequence (even if only because of some desirable further consequence that it is expected to lead to), then I think the proposal ought not to be counted as a threat. This, of course, is compatible with holding that the person who made the proposal may well have been *trying* to make a threat.

[. . .]

Of course not every proposal to bring about (or not bring about) a change in the world is either a threat or an offer. Consider again the paradigm coercive proposal, "Your money or your life!" As I indicated earlier, this is equivalent to the conjunction of the following two conditional assertions:

(1.1)   If you don't give me your money, I will kill you.

(1.2)   If you do give me your money, I will not kill you.

(1.1) is clearly a threat (thus insuring the coerciveness of the proposal as a whole). (1.2), however, seems to be neither a threat nor an offer since the speaker is not proposing to *bring about* any consequence whatever, desired or undesired. He is, in effect, simply indicating his willingness to take the money without any further ado if the victim chooses to surrender it. Let us therefore term propos-

als such as (1.2) "neutral" conditional proposals and define them as follows:

D4   By doing A P makes a neutral conditional proposal to Q = $_{def}$

A is an action (or combination of actions) on P's part by which P intentionally communicates to Q either

(i)   the proposition that P will intentionally bring about some consequence R if Q does (does not do) some action B, where R is a consequence to which Q is indifferent,

or

(ii)   the proposition that P will intentionally bring about some consequence R if Q does (does not do) some action B, where P's bringing about R would be either

(a)   not preferred by Q solely because P's bringing about R would be incompatible with P's bringing about some other state of affairs the obtaining of which Q desires,

or

(b)   preferred by Q solely because P's bringing about R would be incompatible with P's bringing about some other state of affairs the non-obtaining of which Q desires,

or

(iii)   the proposition that P will intentionally omit to bring about some consequence R if Q does (does not do) some action B.

The reason for clause (i) should be evident; if I indicate that I intend (say) to burn my copy of *Silas Marner* unless you perform a specified task, it would be very counterintuitive to regard my proposal as constituting either a threat or an offer since what I am proposing to do will (ordinarily) make you neither better nor worse off. The function of clause (ii) is to deal with some cases excluded (for the reasons already indicated) by the analyses of what constitutes a conditional offer and of what constitutes a conditional threat. Clause (iii) is needed because it does not seem plausible to regard as either an offer or a threat a proposal *not* to interfere with what we might term the "natural" course of events, i.e., with what would happen in the absence of any interference on one's part. Of course clause (iii) would also serve to exclude cases in which we might be inclined to regard the proposal as a threat precisely because the proposer has, by his own previous actions, so arranged things that his victim has *become* vulnerable to his proposal. Suppose, for example, that P secretly adds poison to Q's wine and then, after Q has emptied his glass, insists that Q give him his money if he desires P to provide him with the antidote. I concede that it does not seem wholly implausible to claim that, should Q comply, he will have been coerced into doing so. Although my reasons for resisting the temptation to so characterize P's proposal will not become fully clear until [. . .] [later in this work] three points may be noted here: (1) What, in my view, is most characteristic of coercion is the manipulation of behavior via the *making* of a threat, yet the case in question is one in which the "threat," so to speak, has *already* been made; (2) We can explain why P has acted wrongly without accusing him of coercing Q – all we need point out is that P has acted so as to increase unjustifiably the risk of serious harm to Q and then followed this with a proposal which takes unfair advantage of Q's newly-acquired vulnerability; and (3) Denying that Q has been coerced does not rule out the possibility of arguing that Q has nevertheless been *compelled* to comply with P's proposal. (The general analysis of compulsion needed to support such an argument will not, however, be attempted here.)

A paradigmatic non-coercive proposal would be the following: "I'll sell you my car for $1500." This is most plausibly interpreted as equivalent to the following pair of conditionals:

(2.1) If you give me $1500, I will give you my car.

(2.2) If you don't give me $1500, I will not give you my car.

Here (2.1) clearly counts as an offer (at least under ordinary circumstances) while (2.2) is entirely neutral. What I shall term "standard" non-coercive proposals are those which are analyzable as combinations of appropriately related conditional offers and neutral conditional proposals; similarly what I shall term "standard" coercive proposals (where by a "coercive" proposal I mean one which would constitute coercion if complied with) are those which are reducible to combinations of appropriately related conditional threats and neutral conditional proposals. (In accordance with the usual practice, however, I shall generally refer to any non-coercive biconditional proposal as an "offer" and any coercive biconditional proposal as a "threat".) [. . .]

Some Illustrations

To test the adequacy of my account, I shall briefly consider its application to a few of the more problematic cases that have been suggested in the literature.

C1 (Nozick)

> Suppose that P knows that Q has committed a murder which the police are investigating, and knows of evidence sufficient to convict Q of the murder. P says to Q, "If you give me $10,000 I will not turn over the information I have to the police."

Here the relevant conditionals are:

(C1.1) If you give me $10,000 I will not turn over the information I have to the police.

(C1.2) If you do not give me $10,000 I will turn over the information I have to the police.

Nozick states that he is unsure how to deal with this case. He admits that it appears to involve coercion but maintains that, if this is so, it must be because the proposal encompasses a coercive *offer*, not a threat. Yet he also confesses to an "inclination to say that one is never coerced when one does something because of an offer . . ."

On my analysis the proper classification of the proposal is simple and straightforward: (C1.1) is a neutral proposal while (C1.2) is clearly a threat; hence should Q acquiesce and pay P, it would be proper to say that P coerced Q into doing so. Nozick's reason for not accepting a solution like the one I have proposed is the fact that he accepts the following criterion for distinguishing threats from offers: a proposal by P to bring about R unless Q does (does not do) B is a threat only if R makes the consequences of Q's not doing (doing) B worse for Q then they would have been in "in the normal and expected course of events." He adds, by way of explanation, that "the term 'expected' is meant to shift or straddle *predicted* and *morally required*." But since, in the above example, P's turning over his information to the police is both predictable *and* required, Nozick concludes that "P is *offering* not to turn the information over to the police, rather than *threatening* to turn it over."

It is by now pretty well agreed that Nozick's criterion is an unsatisfactory way of determin-ing whether a proposal to intervene in a certain way is a threat or an offer. Its principal deficiencies seem to be these: (1) it wrongly recommends that we compare what people propose to do with what they have customarily done in the past rather than, as Frankfurt suggests, "with what would *now* happen but for their proposed intervention;" (2) by allow-ing "expected" to serve as a surrogate for either "predicted" *or* "morally required," it makes coercion an essentially normative concept; and (3) since the theory is a two baseline account it is objectionable on grounds of explanatory simplicity since, as Zimmerman observes, it "forces the theorist to produce two distinct explanations for [the] prima facie wrongness [of coercion]."

It is also worth noting, I think, that in cases where the baseline established by what is morally required diverges from the baseline set by what is normally expected, Nozick maintains that the coerciveness of a proposal is to be deter-mined by using whichever baseline is *preferred* by the recipient of the proposal. If preferences are so important here, however, it is unclear why they should be less so in cases where the two baselines coincide. A virtue of my account, I think, is that it makes the subject's preferences a controlling factor in *all* cases.

[. . .]

Michael J. Gorr, *Coercion, Freedom and Exploitation* (New York: Peter Lang, 1989), pp. 20–1, 24–7, 29–34.

Chapter 55

Alan Wertheimer, from
Coercion (1987)

Coercion as Contextual

Normative Force and Truth Conditions. I now want to argue, in some detail, that coercion claims are emphatically and technically contextual. To deepen and broaden our understanding of this point, I shall describe several contexts in which we use the family of coercion terms, although the categories are neither exhaustive nor mutually exclusive. The list is designed to show two things. First, in each context, the coercion claim has a certain point. In some, the point is mainly *descriptive.* In others, the point is primarily *normative* – that A is acting wrongly, that B is not responsible for his action, and so forth. Call this the *normative* or *moral force* of a coercion claim. To illustrate: the normative (legal) force of a coercion claim in a contract case is that the contract is voidable; the normative force of a coercion claim in a criminal trial is that the defendant is not guilty.

Second, a coercion claim with a given descriptive or normative force will have certain correlative *truth conditions.* Roughly speaking, the truth conditions of a coercion claim are what must be the case for the coercion claim to be valid or acceptable. (I do not want to put much weight on the term "truth.") In some cases, the truth conditions will be (more or less) factual. In other cases, the truth conditions will include normative judgments.

Coercion Contexts. In assembling the following list of coercion contexts, I deliberately include situations in which we would not normally use the *word* "coercion," but would,

instead, prefer a related expression, for example, "B was forced to do X," "B had no choice but to do X," or "B did X involuntarily." Once again, I do not deny that the linguistic differences may reflect distinctions of moral importance. Nonetheless, if we were to attend only to contexts in which "coercion" is at home, there is a substantial risk that we would beg important philosophical questions. For that reason, I continue to cast my net widely. We may still make such linguistic distinctions later, should it prove desirable to do so (although I shall argue that it is not desirable to do so).

1. As I noted in Part One [of *Coercion*], we sometimes use coercion claims to describe cases in which the agent's actions or movements are nonvolitional. The typical normative force of such coercion claims is that the agent is not legally or morally responsible for his action.

2. We sometimes use coercion claims in legal and moral contexts to describe cases of constrained volition. Such claims are meant to cancel the normal legal and moral effects of one's act – to deny one's obligation to keep a promise, to cancel the effects of the waiver of a right, or to absolve one of moral or legal responsibility for one's immoral act. There is, however, at least one important difference between the way coercion claims work in legal contexts and the way they work in moral contexts. The law generally makes *binary*

judgments: a court will hold that B was (or was not) coerced and therefore is not (or is) responsible. Moral discourse allows for finer-grained distinctions. If A applies coercive pressure to B, a judge cannot say, "B has some but not much legal obligation to perform on his contract," but *we* can say that B has a weaker moral obligation that he otherwise would.

3.   A coercion claim can *explain* or *justify* to others (or to ourselves) what might otherwise be a puzzling or criticizable action. The normative force of such claims is that certain background conditions have created a situation in which B has only one *prudent* or *reasonable* choice. B may want others to understand that this is so, that he is not stupid, irrational, or cowardly. A football coach may defend his decision not to punt on fourth down by saying, "We were behind, it was late in the game, and we had to go for it." The seller of a house might say, "We were moving in a few weeks, so I was forced to lower the price." A mugger's victim might say, "He had a knife, so I had no choice but to give him my wallet." Here, as in many contexts, one can make a perfectly plausible coercion claim without any expectation that it will nullify one's responsibility for one's actions.[1]

4.   A coercion claim may convey the *spirit* in which one acts – in particular, that one is not *happy* about one's action, that one acts reluctantly. A college professor might say "I was forced into signing the loyalty oath" to indicate that he would have preferred not to do so, but that it was a condition of employment. Voters frequently make such claims about their choice of candidates.

5.   We can use coercion claims to draw attention to a person's very limited options, or to express the view that more options should be made available. We may say that "she was forced to become a prostitute" to stress the absence of welfare support or other, decent job opportunities, or that the poor are

"forced" to join the military because they have few civilian career opportunities. We may also use coercion claims to describe cases in which a previously available option is no longer available: "I used to be able to cut through the yard, but now I'm forced to go around."

6.   A frequently invoked and important type of coercion claim captures the fact that the state has required some behavior as a matter of *law*. Whereas coercion claims often indicate moral disapproval, this is not so here, where we may want only to distinguish between actions undertaken in response to legal prohibitions and those that are not or to distinguish between legal processes which involve punishment and those that do not (as in the distinction between coercion, regulation, and taxation).[2] We may say, "Wearing a seat belt is compulsory in New York" and "Australia has compulsory voting," while approving of the former and disapproving of the latter. Although the truth conditions of coercion claims are often quite problematic, here they are quite straightforward. A statute or court order will generally do.[3]

7.   Analogously, a coercion claim may signify the use of nonlegal penalties or requirements. We may say "This university compels its students to take a foreign language" to point out that completion of foreign language courses is a degree requirement. Similarly, we might say "That child was forced into playing the violin" to note that he did so in response to parental pressure rather than because he wanted to.

8.   We sometimes use coercion claims to emphasize the efficacy or unfairness of informal pressures that do not involve specific penalties. We may say, for example, "Students at that university are virtually compelled to join a fraternity," or "Socialization forces women into adopting traditional life styles." It has, in this vein, been argued that athletes who use steroids to improve their strength are, in

effect, coercing other athletes into doing so as well. These sorts of coercion claims have moral force: they are often intended to signify that there are good moral reasons for changing the relevant background situation. But even when that is so, they do not necessarily serve to bar or mitigate individual responsibility.

9. Analogously, inducements are sometimes described as coercive, particularly when they are thought to be inappropriate or so great as to make refusal completely irrational. When the federal government threatens to withhold state highway funds if a state does not raise its drinking age to twenty-one, it may be said that it is "forcing" (or "blackmailing") the states into compliance. Or suppose, for example, that a mandatory national health insurance plan had premiums for nonsmokers which were 50 percent lower than the premiums for smokers. One might say that the government was coercing citizens into not smoking. Indeed, even small incentives may be described as coercive if we want to contrast actions undertaken in response to incentives with those undertaken in the absence of incentives. Richard Titmuss, for example, argues that to pay people for giving blood makes such donations less than fully voluntary.

10. We sometimes use a noncoercion claim to note that a certain *form* of pressure was *absent*, even though we know that the action was performed under (sometimes very great) pressure. Thus we may say that a suspect turns himself in "voluntarily," although he may do so only because he fears being brought in involuntarily, or that the Japanese imposed "voluntary import quotas," although, had they not done so, Congress would have imposed quotas for them.

11. Although coercion claims frequently serve to negate moral *blame*, they can also nullify the ascription of moral (or legal) *credit*. Of the philistine who is attending an opera, we may say, "Don't be misled, his wife forced him to go." Credit-denying coercion claims perplex some philosophers. Because it is generally wrong to make coercive threats (and we sometimes call them coercive only if they are wrong), some conclude that legitimate threats cannot be coercive. Suppose, for example, that A finds B assaulting his wife and threatens to shoot B if he does not stop. Cheyney Ryan claims that because A is not acting wrongly, it is "absurd" to say that A has coerced B into not raping his wife. But it is *not* absurd. In cases where B ceases a wrong act, it is often important to know whether or not B acts in response to a proposal to harm him if he does not.

Conclusion

What does all this show? It does *not* show that coercion claims are meaningless or that we can make them in any way we want. It does show, first, that there is no reason to think that coercion claims have only one sort of moral force. We might, of course, *stipulate* that "coercion" refers only to those claims which serve to bar the ascription of responsibility, but we would then need other expressions to make coercion claims (broadly speaking) with different moral force. Unlike the family of "homicide expressions," which in our language contains the distinction between "murder" and "killing," each of which has different moral force, the family of coercion words contains no comparable linguistic placemarks. I suppose that we could try to introduce such distinctions. But rather than create an artificial linguistic precision, it seems best simply to remain sensitive to the contextual character of coercion claims.

Second, I hope to have shown that coercion claims do not have one set of *truth conditions*. In some cases, informal pressures are sufficient to coerce; in other cases, only those pressures sufficient to negate responsibility are coercive. Once again, we could *stipulate* that "coercion" always involves specific and serious threats, but then we would need to know whether other pressures could have comparable moral force – whether, for example, such pressures could invalidate an agreement. Whatever their advantages for analytic purposes (and I think these are negligible), such linguistic stipulations would settle nothing of substantive moral importance.

Third, and joining the two previous points, a coercion claim with a specific moral force may have specific correlative truth conditions. Just as "X is a murder" has different moral force than "X is a killing," it also has different truth conditions. "X is a murder" must be supported by more and different sorts of facts – for example, that the killing is not in self-defense. As with "killing," so, too, with coercion. A claim that A coerces B in a way that nullifies B's responsibility must be supported by different underlying facts than a claim which signifies only that B's background conditions should be changed.

Consider Frankfurt's example once again, this time in syllogistic form.

(4)   4a.   Coerced confessions are not valid.
      4b.   A coerced B into confessing.
      4c.   B's confession is not valid.

(5)   5a.   Agents are not responsible for acts they are coerced into performing.
      5b.   A coerced B into confessing.
      5c.   B is not responsible for confessing.

What can we say about these arguments? First, we can say that (4) and (5) have different normative force. Second, we can say that (4) and (5) may have different truth conditions. The facts sufficient to support (4b) may *not* establish the truth of (5b).

The point might be put this way. It may be claimed that coercion claims have identical truth conditions. Call this the *equivalence thesis*. With respect to any two coercion claims, the equivalence thesis may or may not be true. With respect to (4) and (5), I believe that the equivalence thesis is false.

Is the equivalence thesis a problem? Consider this analogy. Derek Parfit has noted that,

in one sense, all of a person's relatives are equally his relatives. On this use of "relative," a person's cousins are as much his relatives as his children are. Although there is a point to this claim, it is not, as Parfit points out, a "deep truth." And although it is technically misleading, it rarely, in fact, misleads.

It may also be true that all forms of coercion are equally forms of coercion. Nonetheless, with respect to coercion, this claim does not represent a deep truth. Does it *mislead*? Here I believe that it does. The problem, I think, is that philosophers have typically developed their analyses of coercion claims because of an interest in specific substantive moral and political questions. At the same time, the conceptual or linguistic analyses are often based on contexts in which coercion claims have a normative force and, therefore, truth conditions that are distinct from those of coercion claims in the contexts that motivated the analysis in the first place. Many philosophical analyses proceed as if the equivalence thesis were true generally, as if it were possible and desirable to identify a single set of necessary and sufficient truth conditions for all coercion claims.

[. . .]

Objections to a Moralized Theory Reconsidered

I have argued that politically inspired critiques of a moralized theory of coercion lose much of their (philosophical) power if we understand that coercion claims can have different moral force. This also explains how justified coercion is possible. As I argued in Chapter 10 [of *Coercion*], there is a standard sort of coercion claim which allows us to say that A coerces B into doing X just in case A proposes to punish B if B does not do X. Justified coercion is possible because the truth conditions of the coercion claim embedded in "The state is justified in coercing citizens to pay taxes" are not identical with the truth conditions of the coercion claim embedded in "B's agreement is not binding because A coerced B."

Why is this so? One reason is this. In most coercion contexts, B's action would change his moral or legal status – were it not for the coercion. He would, for example, be obligated to do something he was otherwise not obligated to do. By contrast, the state's coercive threats typically give B prudential reasons to do what he is morally obligated to do in any case (not kill, not steal, pay his taxes, and so forth). Because the coercion does not change B's moral status, whether the state is exercising coercion is not problematic. Put slightly differently, the moral considerations that (help) determine whether someone is coerced (in the sorts of responsibility-affecting contexts on which I have focused) are importantly distinct from the sorts of moral considerations that figure in the justification of state coercion. In any case, the claim that some (state) coercion is justified does no damage to the moralized theory of coercion that I advance.

There is another objection to a moralized theory which I shall briefly consider. What might be called a "dialectical" objection to a moralized account of coercion stems from a broader critique of the use of moralized concepts. It is claimed that we can intelligently disagree about the morality of the use of coercion only if we start from a morally neutral account of coercion itself. This argument does not assert that moralized concepts are "false" or that nonmoral concepts are "true". For concepts are neither true nor false. Rather, the argument asserts that coercion (or freedom) *can* be defined in nonmoral terms, and that there are analytical and argumentative advantages in doing so.

While I am generally quite skeptical of stipulative or "constructive" definitions of crucial concepts, I am not concerned to defend ordinary language. My principal response to the objection is this. First, there is no a priori reason to believe that fruitful moral discourse requires that we begin with nonmoral concepts. Second, there is no evidence (broadly construed) that moral discourse which rests on nonmoral accounts of crucial concepts is, in fact, more fruitful than moral discourse which rests on moralized accounts of those concepts (establishing this would, of course, require a controversial metric of moral fruitfulness).

Still, I have not answered all the objections to a moralized theory [. . .] Recall the *circularity* objection. If A's proposal is coercive only *if* it is wrong, can we also say, without circularity, that A acts wrongly *because* he makes a coercive proposal to B? Perhaps not. But even if this special sort of coercion argument is circular (and that is not clear), the coercion arguments in which I have been interested do not have this particular form. Consider the following sort of argument.

(1) Coerced agreements are not binding.
(2) A makes a coercive proposal only if A acts wrongly (in the requisite way).
(3) Because A acts wrongly (in the requisite way), A makes a coercive proposal.
(4) A coerces B (by whatever further conditions are necessary if A's coercive proposal is to coerce B).
(5) B is not bound by his agreement.

There is no circularity in this argument if the moral judgment expressed in (5) is not *identical* to that identified in (2) and presupposed in (3) and (4). And they are not identical. For (5) expresses a judgment about what we should do in the *light* of B's moral baseline as determined by (2) *and* further facts contained in (3) and (4).

If the circularity objection can be defused, is there not still something to the *triviality* objection? Even if the moral judgment identified in (2) and presupposed in (3) is not *identical* to the moral judgment made in (5), is it not also true that once the criteria for (2) have been settled and applied in (3), (5) adds little of moral interest? Not entirely. For [. . .] the move from (3) to (5) is by no means automatic. (5) also presupposes (4), which rests on different moral criteria than those applied in (3).

All the same, there is, I think, a sense in which the triviality objection is essentially *right*. For by the time we have settled (3), we are at least well down the road to our argument for (5). Is this a cause for concern? I do not think so. The reason is this. Lurking beneath most conceptual analyses of coercion is, I think, the hope that by getting clear about the *concept* of coercion, we shall be in a position to resolve *substantive* moral, legal, and political problems. And if the conceptual analysis were to yield a nonmoral account of coercion, we would be able to go from non-moral premises to (important) moral conclusions. It would, of course, be nice to make progress on substantive moral problems in ways that do not, themselves, require substantive moral arguments. Yet to set up the motivation for the analysis of coercion in this way is to make this hope seem implausible from the outset. There is simply no reason to think that we can generate interesting moral conclusions from some combination of careful conceptual analysis and rigorous empirical investigation.

Now it may be objected that I have overstated the case. Assuming that we accept a basic moral principle, we can sometimes go fairly directly from an empirical claim to a moral conclusion. Consider:

(1)   X is killing.
(2)   Therefore, it is wrong to X.

It is generally noncontroversial whether X is killing, so identifying X as killing is often sufficient to establish that X is wrong. The attentive reader will, of course, quickly object that it is not always uncontroversial whether X is the *sort* of killing that it is *wrong* to commit.

Is killing in self-defense included? Is killing in a (just) war? Is capital punishment? No analysis of the concept of killing along with even a complete account of the relevant facts will establish whether a nonstandard killing is the sort of act it is wrong to commit. That is a job – it *has* to be a job – for moral analysis.

So, too, for coercion. Perhaps there *can* be a nonmoral account of coercion. It might be possible to define coercion so that all proposals of a readily identifiable type would be classified as coercive. But it is a bit far-fetched to think that such a definition could tell us much about plea bargaining, contracts, experimentation with prisoners, capitalism, and the like. Interesting and difficult moral questions will always be answered by moral argument.

Notes

1   Indeed, one may take *pride* in seeing that there is only one prudent decision, particularly when others are not similarly astute.
2   One might say that characterizing the law as coercive is not completely neutral, for we would not identify the use of legal prohibitions in this way unless we thought there was some moral significance in doing so. I think that is true. But this does not entail that we make moral judgments of approval and disapproval in characterizing the use of the law as coercive.
3   Interestingly, it does *not* follow just because the state coerces its citizens (in this sense) that citizens have "no choice" (in the prudential sense) but to comply with the law, if, for example, the legal penalties are slight or rarely applied.

Alan Wertheimer, *Coercion* (Princeton, NJ: Princeton University Press, 1987), pp. 184–91, 255–8.

Chapter 56

Serena Olsaretti, from *Liberty, Desert, and the Market* (2004)

That a satisfactory account of choice needs to make a sharp distinction between freedom and voluntariness is shown by the following two examples, which depict situations where judgements of freedom and voluntariness pull in different directions.

> *The Desert City.* Daisy is the inhabitant of a city, located in the middle of a desert, which she is free to leave. However Daisy, who would wish to leave, knows with absolute certainty that if she leaves the city, she will not be able to survive the hardship of the desert and she will die. Her choice to remain in the city is not a voluntary one.

> *The Wired City.* Wendy is the inhabitant of a city fenced with electrifying wire, which she is unfree to leave. However, her city has all that anyone could ever ask for, and Wendy, who is perfectly happy with her life there, has no wish of leaving it. She voluntarily remains in her city.

In the first example, freedom does not suffice for voluntariness; in the second, unfreedom (that is, lack of the freedom to not perform the action one does perform) does not undermine voluntariness.

A satisfactory account of voluntary choice, I suggest, has to steer away from two opposed but similarly misguided tendencies. The first is to conflate questions of voluntariness with questions of freedom, to suppose that, *given* that the agent whose voluntary choice is under discussion is free to act as he does, and does what he does, it follows that he acts voluntar-ily. The second mistake that is sometimes made consists in (rightly) separating questions of freedom and questions of voluntariness, and in then (wrongly) suggesting that there are no structural features of an individual's 'choice conditions' which are of moral interest. I suggest, by contrast, that considerations about the choice conditions an individual faces are germane to the voluntariness of her choice, and, for that reason, do have moral signifi-cance. An account of voluntariness that can deal with cases of limited choice needs to specify precisely under what conditions an individual's choice counts as voluntary: given that the individual has made a choice or given his consent, there is a genuine issue as to whether the conditions under which this choice was carried out vitiate its voluntariness.

When, then, is a choice voluntary? [. . .] I suggest that a choice is voluntary if and only if it is not made *because* there is no acceptable alternative to it. Conversely, a claim that a person was forced to do *x* (she did *x* non-voluntarily) means that she did *x* because she had no acceptable alternative to it.[1] Claims of force, in my view, are claims of vitiated voluntariness, not of curtailed freedom. Notice that when we refer to someone acting voluntarily (or freely), we refer both to vol-untary *choice* and to voluntary *doings*. Both the case in which an individual voluntarily chooses the option he chooses among a pool of them, and the case in which, al-though no choice among several options is involved, an individual nonetheless does the thing he does voluntarily, are cases in which the individual acts voluntarily, that is, he does not act as he does because no acceptable alternative is available. As I suggested before, the standard of acceptability by which options are assessed is an objective one that views basic needs satisfactions as central, so that choices made so as to avoid having one's basic needs go unmet are non-voluntary ones.[2]

This definition of voluntariness needs further specification, and I will develop it somewhat more fully [later in *Liberty, Desert, and the Market*]. What I want to emphasise here is the distinction between claims of freedom, which are claims about the options an individual faces, and claims of voluntariness, which are claims about how the nature of those options affect an individual's will. In other words, freedom is about the options we face, whereas voluntariness is about the choices we make.[3] Judgements of freedom identify the circumstances in which an individual is situated; judgements of voluntariness and of force, by contrast, are primarily claims about why an agent acts as she does.

Freedom and voluntariness, then, are distinct. Freedom does not guarantee voluntariness; and unfreedom does not undermine it. *Some* freedom, however, is necessary for *some* voluntariness. In order for P to do *x* voluntarily, it must be the case that P is free to do *x*. This, it must be noted, is not a claim about the relationship between freedom and voluntariness, but about freedom and action. For P to do *x* at all, whether voluntarily or non-voluntarily, it must be the case that P is free to do *x*. Once we recognise this, we are able to make sense of G. A. Cohen's claim that when someone is forced to do something, she is free to do it. The truth of that claim hinges, quite simply, on this: if someone is forced to do something, then she does that thing. And if she does that thing, she was free to do that thing. We cannot do what we are not free to do. Insofar as voluntariness is a quality of our *actions*, and insofar as, in order to act, we must be free to act, then the freedom to do *x* is required for someone to do *x* voluntarily. But,

as I suggested above, it is not always necessary that someone be free to do anything else, including not-*x*, in order to choose to do *x* voluntarily. Hence my emphasis on the fact that *some* freedom is necessary for some voluntariness.

Further, it is the case that even this limited freedom is not always necessary for voluntariness. Since voluntariness can be a quality of our choices as well as our actions, and since choices do not necessarily result in action, it is possible for someone to *choose to do* something voluntarily, even if she does not, after all, do that thing, and she is not free to do it. Hence my emphasis on the fact that some freedom is necessary for *some* voluntariness. Since in what follows I am going to be concerned with the voluntariness of actions that people in fact do perform, the freedom to perform those actions is a necessary condition for those actions to have been carried out voluntarily.

But the distinction between freedom and voluntariness remains crucial. First, 'being free to do *x*' is a necessary condition for 'doing *x* voluntarily, or freely' only because 'being free to do *x*' is a necessary condition for 'doing *x*' at all. The required freedom is not required for voluntariness as such, but for action generally. Second, no other freedom than the freedom to do *x* is necessary.[4] And finally and most interestingly, even if the freedom to do *x* is a necessary condition for someone to do *x* voluntarily, it is not a sufficient one. Freedom does not guarantee voluntariness.

[. . .] The distinction between freedom and voluntariness, so I believe, helps us to better understand the concept of coercion, by which I refer to the deliberate interference of one person with another, typically through the use of threat of force.[5] Coercion, as I have mentioned, is often taken by libertarians to be the paradigmatic form of illegitimate, justice-disrupting interference. As one libertarian states, 'the essential ingredient in all this [in the libertarian idea] is freedom from coercion by others. This is one's basic and inalienable right'.[6] Libertarians also claim that coercion involves a loss of negative freedom, and imply that, in the absence of coercion, all transactions are voluntary. They then conclude that, since the free market hosts only mutually advantageous and therefore non-coercive transactions, it is a realm in which freedom and voluntariness alike are respected.

However, just how coercion affects freedom, voluntariness or both are questions that merit more careful examination than libertarians have given them. To see this, consider the following example. Burt's coercive threat to Audrey to do *y* if Audrey does *x* leads Audrey to abstain from doing *x*, since she wants to avoid *y*. However, unbeknown to Audrey, Burt is bluffing and would be unable to carry through his threat. In this case, Audrey has been coerced not to do *x*, although it is also true that she was not rendered unfree by Burt. Unlike freedom, voluntariness is always undermined by coercion, *independently* of whether the agent who is coerced not to do *x* has been rendered unfree to do anything. In the example above, Audrey has acted non-voluntarily. Does it mean, then, that coercion is characterised by undermined voluntariness rather than unfreedom? Does a commitment to protecting people against coercion therefore require something altogether different from giving them freedom? And if coercion does undermine voluntariness and the latter is what makes coercion illegitimate, should we not also ask whether it is sufficient, to ensure that people make voluntary choices, that they not be coerced?

[. . .] I suggest that when we talk about an individual being coerced, we are primarily making claims of vitiated voluntariness, so that coercion is really a type of forcing. This has the following implications for the libertarian defence of the free market: since coercion is primarily a type of forcing, and since the concern behind condemning coercion lies (at least in part) in the fact that the coerced agent has not chosen voluntarily, then that concern also seems to justify taking seriously cases of vitiated voluntariness where coercion is not present. Libertarians overlook this important

fact and wrongly conclude, from the fact that coercion is not present on the free market, that all free market transactions are voluntary and justice-preserving. In fact, libertarians' own anti-coercion stance justifies a concern with reducing the forced transactions individuals enter in a free market society as much as it minimises the coercive interference by the more-than-minimal state.

[. . .]

Freedom, Coercion, and Voluntariness in Two Critiques of Libertarianism

So far I have claimed that a satisfactory account of voluntariness must reflect the fact that claims of voluntariness and of force on the one hand, and claims of freedom and unfreedom on the other, are distinct. But, as I have said, this distinction has been overlooked by critics of libertarianism as much as by libertarians themselves. Critics of Nozick's moralised definition of freedom have failed to identify the moralised definition of voluntariness, and, in fact, have referred to the passage in which Nozick appeals most clearly to rights-defined voluntariness as an illustration of his use of rights-defined freedom.[7] This is because, like Nozick, they have failed to distinguish between freedom and voluntariness. Further, they have contributed to clouding the distinction between freedom and voluntariness by presenting their discussion of Nozick's account as one of 'the moralised theory of coercion'. Since coercion is thought to undermine both freedom and voluntariness, the issue of the conditions for voluntary choice has been presented as being primarily an issue about coercion, thus resulting in – or at least reinforcing – the contention that coercion exhausts non-voluntariness. The debate is further muddled due to the ambiguous use of the idea of 'being forced', which is sometimes equated with that of 'being coerced', sometimes broadly opposed to the idea of 'being free' and yet at other times opposed to the idea of 'acting voluntarily'. In this section I would like to bring what I have said about freedom, voluntariness and coercion to bear on the assessment of some existing critiques of libertarianism.

Consider, first, G. A. Cohen's discussion of libertarianism. It is indicative of the confusion between freedom and voluntariness that Cohen, who has been a main critic of the libertarian use of the moralised definition of freedom, has failed to notice the extent to which his critique of Nozick, and his own thesis about freedom, actually rests on notions of voluntariness rather than freedom. This is very apparent in one of Cohen's central claims, namely, his interpretation of what 'being forced' means, and in his claim, which I have already mentioned, that when one is forced to do something, one is free to do that thing. According to Cohen, someone is forced to do something if she has no reasonable or acceptable alternative to doing something, which is compatible with saying that she is free to do that thing. As Cohen points out, the dispute between the Left and Right about whether workers are forced to take hazardous jobs is the result of a failure to see that *both* Left and Right are right, insofar as workers are free, as well as forced, to take hazardous jobs.[8]

I too would endorse that claim. Unlike Cohen, however, I believe that its truth is nothing but an illustration of the distinction between being free to do something and doing something voluntarily. Workers are free to take hazardous jobs – they are not prevented from taking those jobs – and yet, because, *ex hypothesi*, they take them *because* they have no acceptable alternative, they are also forced to take them, that is, their choice to take those jobs is not a voluntary one. Cohen identifies an important point, but the way he makes sense of it is misguided. He implies that 'being forced to do something' makes one unfree on the first sense of freedom, rather than it being an explanatory

claim, one about the vitiated voluntariness of people's choices.

The claim that workers are both free and forced to sell their labour may well show, as Cohen says, that both the Left and the Right are right, insofar as each can uphold the claim that is dear to them. But the reason why they can each uphold their favoured claim lies in nothing other than the distinction between freedom and voluntariness, so the fact that workers are free to sell their labour does not imply that, when they sell their labour, they sell it voluntarily. When the Right and the Left each insist on claiming that establishing that workers are free to sell their labour could either support or refute the claim that workers are forced to sell their labour, they are both mistaken, insofar as they both imply that judgements of freedom suffice to settle judgements about voluntariness and force.[9]

The attempt to criticise the libertarian thesis by arguing that capitalist wage offers are coercive is also problematic in a similar way, that is, insofar as it carries forward, rather than overcomes, some of the problems with the libertarian thesis. Reconsider the first of the two examples I mentioned at the beginning of this chapter, in which Daisy is the inhabitant of a city, located in middle of a desert, which she is free to leave. Daisy, who would wish to leave, knows with absolute certainty that, if she leaves the city, she will not be able to survive the hardship of the desert and she will die. Her choice to remain in the city is not a voluntary one. No coercion is involved, that is, no forcing by means of threats is at stake. Daisy is not coerced, but she is nonetheless forced to remain in her city.

The point I would like to emphasise here is a point I made in the previous section, namely, that we can flesh out the conditions for voluntary choice along exactly the same lines as the conditions for non-coerced, voluntary choice are usually understood. What makes choices carried out under coercion non-voluntary is exactly what also makes other types of limited choices non-voluntary. The alternative faced by the man who hands over the money when threatened with a gun is to be killed; the alternative of a worker who sells his labour power for whatever price is to remain unemployed and suffer severe hardship. The relevant condition which undermines voluntariness in the first case is also present in the second, namely, the absence of an acceptable alternative. The options of handing over the money or of accepting a hazardous job are chosen because the alternatives – to risk being shot or to suffer severe hardship – are unacceptable. This consideration, and *not* the consideration of whether the gunman and the employer act within their rights (unlike what Robert Nozick suggests), or of how and by whom the alternative option was brought about, is what is relevant for assessing the voluntariness of the choice at issue.

If what I have said so far is true, then it becomes clear why the attempt to show that capitalist wage offers are coercive is unsatisfactory. In particular, it encounters two main problems. Firstly, it stretches needlessly the notion of coercion, it contributes to obscuring the distinction between coercion and other types of forcings, while at the same time it lends credibility to the (mistaken) libertarian thesis that only coercion undermines voluntariness. Secondly, this type of claim focuses on the wrong side of the coin, so to speak. Since the underlying concern is with the cogency of the libertarian thesis about the justice of capitalist wage offers, and since that thesis hinges on the claim that no one's freedom of choice, not even the worker's, is reduced, insofar as each voluntarily chooses to sell his or her labour, then it is on the voluntariness of the worker's choice that we should focus. When we ask whether capitalist wage offers can be coercive, the concern is with whether the person who is thus constrained acts voluntarily or, by contrast, is forced to act as she does. But if this is what the question asks, then it is more appropriate to pose the question in just this way, rather than to talk about coercive offers. Once again: since coercion is only one type of forcing – one which

utilises threats – it is misleading to treat it as the only type of forcing.

Notes

1 My definitions could be restated as follows. A person is forced to do *x* if and only if (i) there is no acceptable alternative to doing *x*, *and* (ii) the fact that there is no acceptable alternative to doing *x* motivates that person. A person chooses to do *x* voluntarily if and only if (i) there is an acceptable alternative to doing *x*, and she knows this when she does *x*; *or* (ii) *x* is an option which she finds very attractive or choiceworthy, and which she is motivated to choose by the fact that she finds it very attractive or choiceworthy. Note that if a person chooses a course of action out of mixed motives when faced with one or more unacceptable options, then, in order to ascertain whether she has chosen voluntarily, we would ask whether she would have made that choice even if she had had an acceptable alternative. So, for example, suppose that Burt faces the choice of whether to become a teacher on the one hand and suffer hardship on the other, and chooses the former both because he likes the prospect of being a teacher and because the alternative is unacceptable. Is Burt's choice forced? The answer is affirmative only if, had Burt an acceptable alternative to becoming a teacher, he would choose that over becoming a teacher.

2 When talking about actions, choices or consent, I use 'non-voluntary' and 'forced' interchangeably.

3 The term 'choice' is ambiguously used to refer both to an option and to the choosing of an option. In order to avoid this ambiguity, throughout I use 'choice' to refer to 'the choosing of an option'.

4 This, of course, will depend on the individual's preferences.

5 'Coercion' is sometimes used more loosely, so as to refer to the deliberate interference of one person with another, without necessarily involving the use of threat. Even when they use the notion of coercion so defined, libertarians subscribe to the view that choices made in response to offers and choices made in limited choice circumstances not deliberately created by other agents do not count as coercive. These two claims are the ones I focus on in what follows, when contesting libertarians' emphasis on coercion as the only type of forcing. The fact that I take 'coercion' to refer to

interference that typically involves the use of threat, therefore, does not matter for my argument below.

6   J. Hospers, 'What Libertarianism Is', in T. R. Machan and D. B. Rasmussen (eds.), *Liberty for the 21st Century. Contemporary Libertarian Thought* (Maryland: Rowman & Littlefield, 1995), pp. 5–17, at p. 8.

7   Hence, [...] when arguing that Nozick adopts the rights-definition of freedom in the previous chapter, Cohen quotes as evidence the passage from Nozick (*Anarchy, State, and Utopia* (Oxford: Blackwell, 1974), p. 262) where the latter offers a rights-definition of voluntariness. Steiner makes the same mistake. See Steiner, *Essay on Rights*, p. 12. Notice that, in an earlier piece, Steiner does object to Nozick's moralised definition of voluntariness (Cf. H. Steiner, 'Capitalism, Justice and Equal Starts', *Social Philosophy and Policy* 5 (1987), pp. 49–71, at p. 55, note 8), but there he does not address the question of the relationship between freedom and voluntariness. Although I have not defended here the adoption of a negative conception of freedom, I believe that one reason for adopting such a conception lies in the fact that, by so doing, we can draw a clear distinction between freedom and voluntariness and thereby achieve greater clarity about many otherwise ambiguous claims about freedom.

8   Some contributions in labour history commit a mistake along these lines, by focusing on labour as 'free' as opposed to 'coerced'. Further, since what they actually focus on are issues of *legal* freedoms, they overlook how labour that is free in this sense may nonetheless be forced labour. And, by opposing free labour with coerced labour, they also suggest that coercion is the only form of unfreedom and the only type of forcing. See: R. J. Steinfield and S. L. Engerman, 'Labor – Free or Coerced? A Historical Reassessment of Differences and Similarities', in T. Brass and M. van der Linden (eds.), *Free and Unfree Labour. The Debate Continues* (Bern: Peter Lang, 1997), pp. 11–42; R. J. Steinfield, *The*

Invention of Free Labor (Chapel Hill: University of North Carolina Press, 1991).

9   Cohen has come to embrace the explanatory account of forcings I defend. See G. A. Cohen, 'Once More into the Breach of Self-Ownership: Reply to Narveson and Brenkert', *Journal of Ethics* 2 (1998), pp. 57–96. In this article Cohen says that he has come to endorse the explanatory account of what 'being forced' means: 'one is forced to do something if and only if one does it *because* one is forced to do it' (p. 82). I think that Cohen's definition of force remains problematic. Let us refer to this claim as (EF), for 'the explanatory account of forcings'. Cohen here formulates the explanatory account by retaining his original use of 'forced', according to which to say that someone is forced to do A means 'doing A *when* one has no acceptable alternative to A' (p. 82, emphasis mine). Let us refer to this claim as (DF), for 'the descriptive account of forcings'. Strictly speaking, this formulation of the explanatory account is misleading, since, by unfolding DF as part of EF, we get the contention that 'one is forced to do something only if one does it *because* one does it when one has no acceptable alternative to it'. But this cannot be right. So, the correct version of EF is that 'one is forced to do something only if one does it *because* one has no acceptable alternative to it', where the original, non-explanatory sense of 'being forced' would then only indicate that 'one has no acceptable alternative to what one chooses'. This, however, is implausible, since claims about an agent being forced, whether of the non-explanatory or of the explanatory sort, must make reference to the agent's *acting*. The preferable formulation of the explanatory account, then, is the one that does without the descriptive notion of 'force' altogether, simply stating that a person is forced to do A if and only if she does A because she has no acceptable alternative to it.

Serena Olsaretti, *Liberty, Desert, and the Market* (Cambridge: Cambridge University Press, 2004), pp. 138–43, 148–50.

Part VI

Autonomy

Introduction to Part VI

Autonomy is intimately related to a number of other concepts discussed in this anthology: many positive theories of freedom could equally well be classed as theories of autonomy, but for the fact that they are formulated in opposition to an exclusive emphasis on negative freedom (see "Negative and Positive Freedom"); the presence of "internal constraints" on an agent's freedom can often and equally be characterized as a diminution of his or her autonomy (see "Freedom and the Mind"); theorists of coercion clearly make use of the concept of autonomy when they claim that coerced people act "involuntarily" (see "Coercion"). The present part of the anthology contains a few representative writings that focus on the concept of autonomy in its own right.

Taken literally, autonomy means self-legislation, or obeying only one's own rules (its opposite, heteronomy, means obedience to the rules of others). But what, exactly, does self-legislation mean? Can *any* rules count as the rules autonomous persons set for themselves? What is it to set oneself a rule? How is the relevant self to be conceived?

One common way of conceiving of the self is as a bundle of beliefs and desires. This, however, immediately raises the following problem: if one's actions are caused by one's beliefs and desires, and one's beliefs and desires are themselves all caused in one way or another, then none of one's reasons for acting as one does would seem to be of one's own making. A much-canvassed solution to this problem consists in thinking of autonomous behavior as behavior caused by beliefs and desires *of a certain sort*. For example, it seems plausible to say that one is autonomous to the extent that one's beliefs and desires have been *formed* in certain ways – as a result of rational and informed reflection, without coercion, deception or manipulation, and so on. An argument along these lines by John Christman can be found in Part III ("Freedom and the Mind") and similar positions are taken in the present section by Stanley Benn and Gerald Dworkin.

Another, related way of singling out autonomous behavior, defended by Gerald Dworkin among others, involves distinguishing between first-order desires and second-order desires. Second-order desires are desires about desires

– for example, the desire not to have the desire to smoke or, more generally, the desire to have a certain set of aesthetic tastes or moral values. One's second-order desires are about the kind of person one would like to be; when one's behavior conforms to those desires, one is conforming to one's own ideals and is therefore autonomous.

Kantian philosophers reject the above accounts of autonomy on the grounds that they still fail to overcome the problem of causal determination. Regardless of whether desires are called "second-order" or "first-order," and regardless of whether their occurrence is mediated by reflection or by coercion, if one continues to explain actions within an empiricist, causal framework, then all actions will continue to be dependent and therefore heteronomous. Onora O'Neill argues that, in order to account for our view of autonomous action as independent action, we need to offer an explanatory account of actions that provides an alternative to the causal model – one that refers not to causes but to maxims. O'Neill's own account of autonomy is based on a Kantian theory of action according to which human actions are caused empirically but nevertheless are guided by human agents in accordance with maxims that are rational.

But the Kantian conception of autonomy has difficulties of its own. Many contemporary philosophers prefer to steer clear of the metaphysically controversial notion of a self capable of guiding its actions independently of the causal world. The Kantian interpretation of autonomy as rationality is also seen by some as an overdemanding ideal.

Notions of autonomy have played an important role in radical social and political theories. Marxism and feminism identify the heteronomy of workers or women in the present world and propose political and social changes aimed at rendering them autonomous. Marx famously claimed that the capitalist division of labor subjected human beings to an "alien power" of their own making, and he contended that communist society would allow them to realize their diverse creative capacities. Feminists often claim that women's roles in society involve heteronomy, both because they are chosen involuntarily and because the roles themselves involve subjection. Such claims are controversial, however, even among radical philosophers. While defending a feminist stance on sex roles, Janice Moulton and Francine Rainone deny that female roles are any less freely chosen than many unobjectionable social roles, and they suggest that social roles are themselves essential for rational deliberation and choice.

Like its close cousin positive freedom, the ideal of autonomy bears a complex relation to that of negative freedom, as several of the authors in this section point out. Restricting the negative freedom of people may affect their deliberations and ultimately their fundamental desires, leading to reductions in their levels of autonomy. On the other hand, a weak-willed person is not necessarily rendered less autonomous by external constraints if, by preventing weak-willed actions, such constraints help her in the long term to act more rationally of her own accord. Nor are people necessarily heteronomous simply because they opt to have their own negative freedom curtailed.

Further Reading

Christman, John (ed.), *The Inner Citadel: Essays on Individual Autonomy* (Oxford: Oxford University Press, 1989) ⟨representative collection of essays by various authors⟩.

Frankfurt, Harry, "Freedom of the Will and the Concept of the Person," *Journal of Philosophy* 68 (1971), pp. 829–39 ⟨influential account of autonomy in terms of first- and second-order desires⟩.

Hill, Thomas E., Jr., *Autonomy and Self-respect* (Cambridge: Cambridge University Press, 1991) ⟨examination of the Kantian notion of autonomy⟩.

O'Neill, Onora, *Constructions of Reason: Explorations of Kant's Practical Philosophy* (Cambridge: Cambridge University Press, 1989) ⟨more detailed critique of the empiricist account of action⟩.

Young, Robert, *Personal Autonomy: Beyond Negative and Positive Liberty* (New York: St. Martin's Press, 1986) ⟨refinements of the Dworkin–Frankfurt model⟩.

Chapter 57

Stanley I. Benn, from *A Theory of Freedom* (1988)

8   Freedom as autarchy

The free-choice Situation

Chapters 5 and 6 [of *A Theory of Freedom*] dealt with the principle of noninterference, which, it was claimed, was grounded in our conception of a natural person, and in the conceptual linking of natural and moral personality. From the principle of respect for persons which follows from this linking derives not only the principle of noninterference but also the principle of equal consideration of interests. In Chapter 7 coercion, duress, and extortion were distinguished from other influences on actions, such as counseling, providing an agent with fresh information, or making him offers, which, in standard cases, would not count as the kind of interferences for which justification need be provided, because they do not restrict the options available to a decision maker or a chooser.

Handcuffing Alan, clearing all the pebbles in his vicinity to prevent his engaging in his favorite pastime of splitting pebbles on the beach, imposing penalties on anyone caught splitting pebbles, charging $1,000 for a pebble-splitter's license, or under some conditions demanding exorbitant rates for the right to split pebbles on the only pebbly bit of the beach would be paradigmatic ways of interfering with Alan's freedom to split pebbles. Taken together, these presuppose an agent in a standard choice situation with four components:

(1)   The agent has a range of powers and capacities, a determinate set of resources at his disposal, such as pebbles and money, which are the conditions enabling him to act, and a range of possible impediments, such as handcuffs, which are standardly absent.

(2)   He is confronted by a set of opportunity costs: If he goes for x he must forgo y.

(3)   He has a set of beliefs about (1) and (2), for example, about the extent of his resources, their substitutability, their usefulness as means to his ends, and so forth.

(4)   There are certain activities which he believes are worth engaging in and certain states of affairs to be approved and admired or disapproved and deplored; these form an ordered set of ends and principles, a set of preferences which, in combination with (3), generate his intentions and practical decisions.

I shall refer to (1) and (2), which are states of the world independent of the agent's beliefs, as the *objective choice conditions*. Conditions (3) and (4) I call *subjective choice conditions* because they are states of the agent's beliefs about both himself and the world at large. Whether or not they correspond to the objective conditions, to the extent that the agent is practically rational they will shape his intentions, and someone capable of manipulating them will be interfering with his freedom of action. The physical conditions affecting the agent's mobility, the size of his muscles as well as the shackles on his wrists, count as objective conditions just because his physical capacities and the various restraints which can deprive him of them exist independently of his beliefs about them. Hamlet "bounded in a nut-shell" would have only a very little room in which to move, objectively speaking, however he might count himself "king of infinite space."

Standard cases of one person's making another unfree to act involve actual or possible interferences affecting one or more of these conditions. This may be done by an interference that changes the conditions (e.g., by threatening penalties) or by a failure to alter them on the part of an agent, such as a jailer, who is both able to alter them and, in the absence of overriding reasons justifying constraint, could reasonably be expected or required to alter them to remove the impediment to action. A jailer who was liable to be punished for letting his prisoner go free would himself be unfree to release the prisoner even if he wanted to. The responsibility for the prisoner's unfreedom would then lie with the authorities who have restricted the options of both; for, given the threatened punishment, the jailer cannot do otherwise. That, at least, would be one way of excusing himself when the prisoner begs him to let him go. "It's more than my job – or my life – is worth," he might say.

A coercive or deterrent threat makes a course of action, otherwise attractive to the agent, relatively unattractive to the point of ineligibility, by attaching to it costly consequences that it would not have but for the intention of the threatener. This amounts to an interference that rigs the opportunity costs, as in (2). Or someone can be rendered unfree to leave an island by depriving him of his boat, a case of altering the resources at his disposal, as in (1).

Freedom of action can be interfered with, however, by altering the subjective choice conditions as well as by altering the objective ones. Because a person's practical decisions depend on his beliefs, his actions can be determined by someone else if the latter can shape those beliefs. A person can be misled by false information about the resources at his disposal into believing that he is unable to do what he can in fact do; or he may be wrongly informed about the environment which provides and constrains his opportunities. Censorship may deny him access to information that would otherwise correct his false beliefs and make him aware of options and opportunities which already exist. Or his preferences may be manipulated, for example by media exploitation, advertising techniques, or religious and political ritual practices, such as mass rallies and revivalist meetings, which make him vulnerable to nonrational suggestion. With his beliefs and preferences so managed, his actions can be controlled with no alteration to his objective choice conditions, effectively depriving him of the freedom to do what he nevertheless has the power or capacity to do.

In treating such management as interference with freedom of action, we accept as the model of a free decision-making agent, one who possesses at least a certain minimal kind of rationality. A person is acting under duress if and only if (1) he believes that some of the costs of adopting a certain option he would otherwise favor would be so heavy as to make that course ineligible and (2) those costs would not have had to be borne but for someone's making it ineligible or for someone's not acting in some expected way to remove the conditions that make it ineligible, precisely for the purpose of influencing the subject to decide against his otherwise preferred option. To threaten him with those costs would be pointless if he were incapable of assessing possible courses of action in terms of their outcomes, weighing costs against benefits, and of arriving at a decision on the basis of an ordered set of preferences. Similarly, deception and censorship would be pointless if the subjects were not expected to form their beliefs on evidence and to suit their actions to their beliefs. A necessary constituent of the model decision situation is, accordingly, a decision-making subject satisfying certain minimal conditions of both cognitive and practical rationality.

Autarchy and Autonomy

The condition of a decision maker who satisfies these minimum rationality conditions I call *autarchic* – self-directing. I distinguish it both from conditions which fall short of it, which I shall call *impulsions*, and from an ideal that transcends it, which I shall call *autonomy*. Most writers make no distinction between autarchy and autonomy, using "autonomy" to cover both concepts. I have coined the term "autarchy" (which, though to be found in the *Oxford English Dictionary*, is not generally used in quite my way) because, without a way of distinguishing autarchy from autonomy, one cannot make clear that the two states generate reasons for action of quite distinct kinds. Furthermore, despite the need for the neologistic usage, the concept is not itself an innovation, but is deeply embedded in our moral thinking; its isolation is a necessary step in understanding our beliefs about persons and what they commit a person to in his dealings with others.

Autarchy is a condition of human normality, both in the statistical sense, that the overwhelming majority of human beings satisfy it, and in the further sense that anyone who does not satisfy it falls short in some degree as a human being. This is because the standard instance of an autarchic agent is a human person. We need the notion primarily for thinking about entities who are also human, and the conception of autarchy has been formed, along with the concept of rationality, in the experience that human beings have had in dealing with one another, rather than from their dealings with cows and sheep. But it does not follow that autarchy is an exclusively human property; it is at least logically possible that some nonhuman beings might be autarchic – angels, perhaps, or appropriately equipped aliens from outer space or dolphins.

Neither does it follow from the closeness of the tie between rationality and humanity that every human being is autarchic. Some with defects of rationality fall short of it.

Autonomy goes beyond autarchy. It is an excellence of character for which an autarchic person may strive, but which persons achieve in varying degrees, some hardly at all. It is an ideal, not a normal condition. A human being is not defective either as human or as a person because he falls short of it, any more than he would be defective as a human person for the lack of the wisdom of a sage or the creativity of Mozart. To be autonomous is to live (in Rousseau's phrase) "according to a law that one prescribes to oneself." But to understand what that might mean and why it should be seen as an ideal must be left until we have a better grasp of autarchy. If, however, we do have reason to value autonomy, and to admire people who possess it, it can, as an ideal, generate reasons for action – to foster it, for instance, by educational practices which encourage independence of mind rather than an unquestioning acceptance of authority or to combat attitudes and institutions, such as race or sex discriminations, which discourage autonomy by fostering self-depreciation and deference.

But because a person may fall very short of autonomy and yet qualify as autarchic, and someone defective in autarchy may nevertheless qualify as a person, neither autonomy nor autarchy is a necessary condition for the application of the principle of noninterference. That principle, however, does not proscribe interference; it only places a burden of justification on the interferer and puts certain constraints on what can serve as a justification. So defective autarchy may justify interferences that would not otherwise be acceptable, interferences in particular that override the agent's own judgment of his own interests. Correspondingly, it may be held to diminish an agent's responsibility for his actions. The respect that is owed to a person may generate different rights and immunities where the person is nonautarchic. What remains unchanged, however, is the condition that the person shall not be used merely as the means to another person's ends. Where paternalist interference is justifiable on grounds of defective autarchy, it must be exercised as a trust in the interest of the beneficial subject, not of the trustee, or for the sake of whatever projects the latter might deem valuable. Defective autarchy is not a justification, for instance, for treating a person as an available experimental object, as one might a fruit-fly.

Nonautarchic Persons: Impulsion

No term in common use corresponds precisely to the concept of autarchy, perhaps because we rarely need it. For ordinary practical purposes we know well enough what a normal person is like and an unqualified reference to someone as a person licenses the assumption that that person is autarchic. Lord Bowen's celebrated reference to "the man on the Clapham omnibus" was a way of glossing "the reasonable man," the autarchic person's counterpart in the law of negligence. And just as the man on the Clapham omnibus "has not the courage of Achilles, the wisdom of Ulysses, or the strength of Hercules," so autarchy may fall short of the ideal autonomy. For practical, nontechnical purposes, we are more likely to be in need of precise ways of identifying and differentiating deviations from the norm rather than of an accurate formulation of its criteria. Nevertheless, such a formulation was sought in 1843, when the English judges, being called upon to state the conditions under which an accused person might plead insanity as a defense in criminal law, committed themselves in the M'Naghten Rules to minimal criteria for criminal responsibility, which attempted to codify conditions of normality, and therefore for punishability. They relied, however, as much on a specification of the defects that would rebut the presumption of sanity as on a precise characterization of the conditions sufficient for it.

Correspondingly, if autarchy is the norm for human beings, one way to grasp its requirements is to consider what neurotic and psy-

chotic states are deemed to qualify, in whole or in part, someone's responsibility and his entitlement, under the principle of respect for persons, to exercise independent judgment. These states, if severe, might be grounds, for instance, not only for deeming him not liable to blame or punishment for his actions, but for declaring someone incompetent to manage his own affairs, or for putting him under preventive constraint to protect either himself or others from the harm he might inflict on them. They are defects broadly of three kinds: of epistemic rationality, practical rationality, and psychic continuity.

[. . .]

9 Autonomy and Positive Freedom

The Characterization of Autonomy as an Ideal

[. . .]

The difference between autonomy and autarchy lies first in the addition of the idea of *nomos* to the characterization of the decision maker. The *nomos* corresponds to the positive freedom theorist's notion of law, which confers on the life of the autonomous person a consistency and a coherence deriving from the consistency and coherence that he can achieve in the network of beliefs by which his actions are governed. To the extent that a person lacks that coherence, he is *anomic*, acting on impulse or on whim, not because he is impelled or compulsive, but because he acknowledges nothing as a reason for doing otherwise. Caring for nothing, the inclination of the moment is his only source of action commitments. He is autarchic in that he does not lack the capacity to order his preferences according to a coherent set of beliefs and to act on them; it is only that he possesses no principles that could structure such an ordering. In an extreme case it would be hard to tell someone who was autarchic but anomic from a psychopath. But whereas psychopaths are thought to be defective in the capacity to order their lives differently, so that they could not be taught to live by principles or ordered values instead of by responding to the immediacy of an expected gratification, anomic persons are thought to have a capacity to grasp a more considered way of living but have simply never learned how to do it or to value anything which living by a *nomos* could offer in return for the postponement of gratification.

A heteronomous person also possesses the capacity to order his life according to a *nomos*, and, unlike the anomic one, he really does so; his life may be as coherent, indeed, as that of the autonomous person. The heteronomous person, however, receives his *nomos* ready-made, as a well-trained, well-drilled soldier may live punctiliously according to the *Manual of Military Law* and battalion orders. His actions can be quite properly seen as appropriate responses to the world as he apprehends it, but that apprehension is structured by beliefs he has simply introjected uncritically and unexamined from his social milieu, from parents, teachers, workmates, bosses, his priest, or the sergeant-major. It is not that he is incapacitated from independent judgment; he is not like the heterarchic person, whose attempt at critical appraisal of key beliefs would be blocked by acute anxiety. This one governs himself, but by a *nomos* simply borrowed from others, which he has done nothing to make his own. Of course, there are soldiers whose training has been so thorough as to deprive them of autarchy, but these belong to the pathologies of military discipline; heterarchic soldiers are not good at responding flexibly and with initiative to emergency situation in battle, however well they may perform on the barrack square. Good soldiers are heteronomous rather than heterarchic. Autonomy is not a disqualification, but it may not be good for discipline.

Fundamental to a person's autarchy is his consciousness of himself as the author of intentional changes in the world. Admittedly, the person who has a place on an assembly line, so far as concerns that role alone, is not likely to see himself as an originator. The total product is remote from his performance, and his sense of personal responsibility for its creation is likely to be weak. But of course his whole life need not be like that; if he fries an egg for his breakfast, he can recognize this at least as his own work and can judge whether he has done it well or ill. Admittedly, if the greater part of his waking hours is spent in mindless repetitive routines he perceives rather as molding him than as ways in which he molds the world, the remaining activities in which he perceives himself as able to make a difference to how they are done may be so insignificant that he loses his grip on autarchy in a kind of schizoid consciousness. But though radical critics have pointed to this as an aspect of that pathology of industrialism they call "alienation", it is obviously an exaggeration to treat this as the standard mode of self-perception, even among the people whose work comes closest to this paradigm.

[. . .]

One might say that to be autonomous a person's *nomos* must be his own, not merely picked up from *heterotes*, from others about him. But how can anyone be the author of his own *nomos*? Surely everyone is governed by the basic presuppositions of the culture which has furnished the very conceptual structure of his world, the traditions into which he has been inducted, the demands of roles he has internalized? The very canons of rationality that he employs when he thinks himself most independent in his judgment have been learned as part of his cultural heritage. One's range of options, both in belief and action, is as much circumscribed by such mental furniture as the highest speed at which one can travel is governed by the prevailing technology.

The distinction between autonomy and heteronomy, however, is not affected by this truism; it is a distinction between character types, all of which are subject to these conditions. It is certainly necessary to a person's autonomy that he be capable of rational choice, and for that he needs criteria, rules of inference, and a conceptual scheme for grasping the options from which the choice is to be made. To be autonomous one must have reasons for conjuring action commitments out of nowhere. And for reasons one must have a system of beliefs from which action commitments derive and into which new evidence can be assimilated, yielding new commitments. How could anyone come by these bits of basic equipment except by learning them in the first instance from parents, teachers, friends, and colleagues? Someone who had escaped such a socialization process would not be free, unconstrained, able to make *anything* of himself that he chose; he would be able to make nothing of himself, being hardly a person at all.

Within this conception of a socialized individual, however, there is still room to distinguish as autonomous a person who is committed to a critical, creative, and conscious search for coherence within his system of beliefs. He rests neither on the unexamined shibboleths and conventions of a traditional culture nor on the fashionably outrageous heresies of a radical one when they lead him into palpable inconsistencies. The resources on which he will rely for this critical exploration must lie, necessarily, within the culture itself, supplemented, perhaps, by those elements of alien cultures with which he has become acquainted. But such elements, too, have to be assimilated into the network of his own cultural beliefs, to be located in and related to the overall framework of his intelligible world, before they can be accessible to him. Within this complex web – perhaps "tangle" would be more appropriate – he will try to create his own consistent pattern, appraising one aspect of it by critical canons derived from another. As an artist or a scientist must draw on the resources of an existing tradition to contribute creatively to its development, so an autarchical man must construe it for himself to become autonomous.

[. . .]

Because the concept of autonomy has been formulated in terms of criticism *within* a culture or a tradition, it does not presuppose that there be ultimate and objectively valid principles or evaluative truths in terms of which received beliefs are to be assessed. Suppose it were a logical truth that someone reared in a tradition that took little account of some very general principle, such as respect for persons, or some value, such as the value of human life, could not be persuaded by reasoned argument into adopting it as a practical belief, because his culture (or language) lacked essential concepts for the formulation of such principles. He might have no way of questioning, for instance, his own indifference to the claims of other persons to be told the truth or not to be treated as means to his own ends, even though he understood that other people held such beliefs which he, however, could see no point in. His inability to question his belief that lying was unobjectionable would not then be inconsistent with his being autonomous, but only because *ex hypothesi* to question it would be logically impossible. This is quite different from being incapacitated from questioning beliefs by a socialization process which, by instilling guilty feelings, has inhibited questioning he might otherwise have freely undertaken. If he held beliefs that were logically impregnable, which differed from corresponding beliefs held by others, they would have to be regarded as defining elements of his character – he would be a species of person who held such beliefs, and there would be other species which held different ones. There could be sociological explanations of these differences, but they would not entail that all these people were necessarily heteronomous. For the autonomous person is not necessarily one who can give reasons for *all* his beliefs; it is required only that he be alive to, and disposed to resolve by rational reflection and decision, incoherences in the complex tradition that he has internalized. Such criticism would always be internal; the reasons on which he could draw would always be, in that sense, within himself. Though he is open to persuasion, it can succeed only by invoking principles as beliefs to which he is already committed at least as firmly as to the ones under attack. For rationally persuading someone to abandon a belief requires that he be shown that to continue to hold the belief would be inconsistent with believing something else it would be still more difficult for him not to believe.

It appears, then, that autonomy is an ideal available only within a plural tradition, for it requires that two conditions be satisfied. In the first place, it requires that the subject's beliefs be coherent and consistent; secondly, their coherence must be the outcome of a continuing process of critical adjustment within a system of beliefs in which it is possible to appraise one sector by canons drawn from another. A monolithic system, in which, for instance, social and environmental conditions had remained virtually unchanging for centuries, and in which ways of acting had been routinized by a kind of natural selection process for all the major eventualities, and which encountered no alien cultures, would simply lack the incoherences which leave space for autonomous development. Where there is no work to be done, none can claim credit for doing it. Autonomy has become a conscious ideal in modern Europe since the Renaissance and the Reformation displayed great rifts in its culture, demanding that men and women define what they believed, without being able to rely upon unshaken and unshakeable authority. [. . .]

Stanley I. Benn, *A Theory of Freedom* (Cambridge: Cambridge University Press, 1988), pp. 152–7, 176–7, 179–80, 181–2.

Chapter 58

Gerald Dworkin, from *The Theory and Practice of Autonomy* (1988)

[. . .]

III

The central idea that underlies the concept of autonomy is indicated by the etymology of the term: *autos* (self) and *nomos* (rule or law). The term was first applied to the Greek city state. A city had *autonomia* when its citizens made their own laws, as opposed to being under the control of some conquering power.

There is then a natural extension to persons as being autonomous when their decisions and actions are their own; when they are self-determining. The impetus for this extension occurs first when questions of following one's conscience are raised by religious thinkers. Aquinas, Luther, and Calvin placed great stress on the individual acting in accordance with reason as shaped and perceived by the person. This idea is then taken up by the Renaissance humanists. Pico della Mirandola expresses the idea clearly in his "Oration on the Dignity of Man." God says to Adam:

> We have given thee, Adam, no fixed seat, no form of thy very own, no gift peculiarly thine, that . . . thou mayest . . . possess as thine own the seat, the form, the gift which thou thyself shalt desire . . . thou wilt fix the limits of thy nature for thyself . . . thou . . . art the molder and the maker of thyself.

The same concept is presented by Berlin under the heading of "positive liberty":

> I wish to be an instrument of my own, not other men's acts of will. I wish to be a subject, not an object . . . deciding, not being decided for, self-directed and not acted upon by external nature or by other men as if I were a thing, or an animal, or a slave incapable of playing a human role, that is, of conceiving goals and policies of my own and realizing them.

But this abstract concept only can be understood as particular specifications are made of the notions of "self," "my own," "internal," and so forth. Is it the noumenal self of Kant, or the historical self of Marx? Which mode of determination (choice, decision, invention, consent) is singled out? At what level is autonomy centered – individual decision, rule, values, motivation? Is autonomy a global or a local concept? Is it predicated of relatively long stretches of an individual's life or relatively brief ones?

Let me begin by considering the relationship between the liberty or freedom of an individual and his autonomy. Are these two distinct notions? Are they linked, perhaps, in hierarchical fashion so that, say, interference with liberty is always interference with autonomy, but not vice-versa? Are they, perhaps, merely synonymous?

Suppose we think of liberty as being, roughly, the ability of a person to do what she wants, to have (significant) options that are not closed or made less eligible by the actions of other agents. Then the typical ways of interfering with the liberty of an agent (coercion and force) seem to also interfere with her autonomy (thought of, for the moment, as a power of self-determination). If we force a Jehovah's Witness to have a blood transfusion, this not only is a direct interference with his liberty, but also a violation of his ability to determine for himself what kinds of medical treatment are acceptable to him. Patient autonomy *is* the ability of patients to decide on courses of treatment, to choose particular physicians, and so forth.

But autonomy cannot be identical to liberty for, when we deceive a patient, we are also interfering with her autonomy. Deception is not a way of restricting liberty. The person who, to use Locke's example, is put into a cell and convinced that all the doors are locked (when, in fact, one is left unlocked) is free to leave the cell. But because he cannot – given his information – avail himself of this opportunity, his ability to do what he wishes is limited. Self-determination can be limited in other ways than by interferences with liberty.

Both coercion and deception infringe upon the voluntary character of the agent's actions. In both cases a person will feel used, will see herself as an instrument of another's will. Her actions, although in one sense hers because she did them, are in another sense attributable to another. It is because of this that such infringements may excuse or (partially) relieve a person of responsibility for what she has done. The normal links between action and character are broken when action is involuntary.

Why, then, should we not restrict our categories to those of freedom, ignorance, and voluntariness? Why do we need a separate notion of autonomy? One reason is because not every interference with the voluntary character of one's action interferes with a person's ability to choose his mode of life. If, as is

natural, we focus only on cases where the person wishes to be free from interference, resents having his liberty interfered with, we miss an important dimension of a person's actions.

Consider the classic case of Odysseus. Not wanting to be lured onto the rocks by the sirens, he commands his men to tie him to the mast and refuse all later orders he will give to be set free. He wants to have his freedom limited so that he can survive. Although his behavior at the time he hears the sirens may not be voluntary – he struggles against his bonds and orders his men to free him – there is another dimension of his conduct that must be understood. He has a preference about his preferences, a desire not to have or to act upon various desires. He views the desire to move his ship closer to the sirens as something that is no part of him, but alien to him. In limiting his liberty, in accordance with his wishes, we promote, not hinder, his efforts to define the contours of his life.

To consider only the promotion or hindrance of first-order desires – which is what we focus upon in considering the voluntariness of action – is to ignore a crucial feature of persons, their ability to reflect upon and adopt attitudes toward their first-order desires, wishes, intentions.

It is characteristic of persons, and seems to be a distinctively human ability, that they are able to engage in this kind of activity. One may not just desire to smoke, but also desire that one not have that desire. I may not just be motivated by jealousy or anger, but may also desire that my motivations be different (or the same).

A person may identify with the influences that motivate him, assimilate them to himself, view himself as the kind of person who wishes to be moved in particular ways. Or, he may resent being motivated in certain ways, be alienated from those influences, prefer to be the kind of person who is motivated in different ways. In an earlier essay I suggested that it was a necessary condition for being autonomous that a person's second-order identifications be congruent with his first-order motivations. This condition, which I called "authenticity," was to be necessary but not sufficient for being autonomous.

I now believe that this is mistaken. It is not the identification or lack of identification that is crucial to being autonomous, but the capacity to raise the question of whether I will identify with or reject the reasons for which I now act. There are a number of considerations that tell against my earlier view.

First, autonomy seems intuitively to be a global rather than local concept. It is a feature that evaluates a whole way of living one's life and can only be assessed over extended portions of a person's life, whereas identification is something that may be pinpointed over short periods of time. We can think of a person who today identifies with, say, his addiction, but tomorrow feels it as alien and who continues to shift back and forth at frequent intervals. Does he shift back and forth from autonomy to nonautonomy?

Second, identification does not seem to be what is put in question by obvious interferences with autonomy. The person who is kept ignorant or who is lobotomized or who is manipulated in various ways (all obvious interferences with autonomy) is not having his identifications interfered with, but rather his capacity or ability either to make or reject such identifications.

Third, there seems to be an implication of the position that is counterintuitive. Suppose that there is a conflict between one's second-order desires and one's first-order desires. Say one is envious but does not want to be an envious person. One way of becoming autonomous is by ceasing to be motivated by envy. But another way, on the view being considered here, is to change one's objections to envy, to change one's second-order preferences.

Now there may be certain limits on the ways this can be done that are spelled out in the other necessary condition which I elaborated: that of procedural independence. So, for example, it wouldn't do to have oneself hypnotized into identifying with one's envious motivations. But even if the procedures used were "legitimate," there seems to be something wrong with the idea that one becomes more autonomous by changing one's higher-order preferences.

Fourth, this view breaks the link between the idea of autonomy and the ability to make certain desires effective in our actions. On this view, the drug addict who desires to be motivated by his addiction, and yet who cannot change his behavior, is autonomous because his actions express his view of what influences he wants to be motivating him. This seems too passive a view. Autonomy should have some relationship to the ability of individuals, not only to scrutinize critically their first-order motivations but also to change them if they so desire. Obviously the requirement cannot be as strong as the notion that "at will" a person can change his first-order preferences. Indeed, there are certain sorts of inabilities of this nature that are perfectly compatible with autonomy. A person who cannot affect his desires to act justly or compassionately is not thought by that fact alone to be nonautonomous. Perhaps there is still the idea that if justice were not a virtue or that if, in a given case, hardness and not compassion were required, the agent could adjust his desires. Susan Wolf has suggested the requirement that a person "could have done otherwise if there had been good and sufficient reason."

The idea of autonomy is not merely an evaluative or reflective notion, but includes as well some ability both to alter one's preferences and to make them effective in one's actions and, indeed, to make them effective because one has reflected upon them and adopted them as one's own.

It is important both to guard against certain intellectualist conceptions of autonomy as well as to be candid about the ways in which people may differ in their actual exercise of autonomy. The first error would be to suppose that my views imply that only certain types or classes of people can be autonomous. If we think of the process of reflection and identification as being a conscious, fully articulated, and explicit process, then it will appear that it is mainly professors of philosophy who exercise autonomy and that those who are less educated, or who are by nature or upbringing less reflective, are not, or not as fully, autonomous individuals. But a farmer living in an isolated rural community, with a minimal education, may without being aware of it be conducting his life in ways which indicate that he has shaped and molded his life according to reflective procedures. This will be shown not by what he says about his thoughts, but in what he tries to change in his life, what he criticizes about others, the satisfaction he manifests (or fails to) in his work, family, and community.

It may be true, however, that there is empirical and theoretical evidence that certain personality types, or certain social classes, or certain cultures are more (or less) likely to exercise their capacity to be autonomous. I do not suppose that the actual exercise of this capacity is less subject to empirical determination than, say, the virtue of courage. To the extent that this is borne out by the evidence, we must be on guard against the tendency to attribute greater value to characteristics which are more likely to be found in twentieth-century intellectuals than in other groups or cultures.

To return to our original question of the relation between autonomy and liberty, I would claim that the two are distinct notions, but related in both contingent and noncontingent ways. Normally persons wish to act freely. So, interfering with a person's liberty also interferes with the ways in which he wants to be motivated, the kind of person he wants to be, and hence with his autonomy. But a person who wishes to be restricted in various ways, whether by the discipline of the monastery, regimentation of the army, or even by coercion, is not, on that account alone, less autonomous. Further, I would argue that the condition of being a chooser (where one's choices are not defined by the threats of another) is not just contingently linked to being an autonomous person, but must be the standard case from which exceptions are seen

as precisely that – exceptions. Liberty, power, control over important aspects of one's life are not the same as autonomy, but are necessary conditions for individuals to develop their own aims and interests and to make their values effective in the living of their lives.

Second-order reflection cannot be the whole story of autonomy. For those reflections, the choice of the kind of person one wants to become, may be influenced by other persons or circumstances in such a fashion that we do not view those evaluations as being the person's own. In "Autonomy and Behavior Control" I called this a failure of procedural independence.

Spelling out the conditions of procedural independence involves distinguishing those ways of influencing people's reflective and critical faculties which subvert them from those which promote and improve them. It involves distinguishing those influences such as hypnotic suggestion, manipulation, coercive persuasion, subliminal influence, and so forth, and doing so in a non ad hoc fashion. Philosophers interested in the relationships between education and indoctrination, advertising and consumer behavior, and behavior control have explored these matters in some detail, but with no finality.

Finally, I wish to consider two objections that can (and have) been raised to my views. The first is an objection to introducing the level of second-order reflection at all. The second is why should we stop at the second level and is an infinite regress not threatened.

The first objection says that we can accomplish all we need to by confining our attention to people's first-order motivation. After all, on my own view of the significance of procedural independence, we have to find a way to make principled distinctions among different ways of influencing our critical reflections, so why not do this directly at the first level. We can distinguish coerced from free acts, manipulated from authentic desires, and so forth. My reply is that I think we fail to capture something important about human agents if we make our distinctions solely at the first level.

We need to distinguish not only between the person who is coerced and the person who acts, say, to obtain pleasure, but also between two agents who are coerced. One resents being motivated in this fashion, would not choose to enter situations in which threats are present. The other welcomes being motivated in this fashion, chooses (even pays) to be threatened. A similar contrast holds between two patients, one of whom is deceived by his doctor against his will and the other who has requested that his doctor lie to him if cancer is ever diagnosed. Our normative and conceptual theories would be deficient if the distinction between levels were not drawn.

The second objection is twofold. First, what is particularly significant about the second level? Might we not have preferences about our second-order preferences? Could I not regret the fact that I welcome the fact that I am not sufficiently generous in my actions? I accept this claim, at least in principle. As a theory about the presence or absence of certain psychological states empirical evidence is relevant. It appears that for some agents, and some motivations, there is higher-order reflection. If so, then autonomy will be thought of as the highest-order approval and integration. As a matter of contingent fact human beings either do not, or perhaps cannot, carry on such iteration at great length.

The second part of this objection concerns the acts of critical reflection themselves. Either these acts are themselves autonomous (in which case we have to go to a higher-order reflection to determine this, and since this process can be repeated an infinite regress threatens) or they are not autonomous, in which case why is a first-order motivation evaluated by a nonautonomous process *itself* autonomous. My response to this objection is that I am not trying to analyze the notion of autonomous *acts*, but of what it means to be an autonomous person, to have a certain capacity and exercise it. I do claim that the process of reflection ought to be subject to the requirements of procedural independence, but if a person's reflections have not been manipulated, coerced, and so forth and if the person does have the requisite identification then they are, on my view, autonomous. There is no conceptual necessity for raising the question of whether the values, preferences at the second order would themselves be valued or preferred at a higher level, although in particular cases the agent might engage in such higher-order reflection.

Putting the various pieces together, autonomy is conceived of as a second-order capacity of persons to reflect critically upon their first-order preferences, desires, wishes, and so forth and the capacity to accept or attempt to change these in light of higher-order preferences and values. By exercising such a capacity, persons define their nature, give meaning and coherence to their lives, and take responsibility for the kind of person they are.

Gerald Dworkin, *The Theory and Practice of Autonomy* (Cambridge: Cambridge University Press, 1988), pp. 12–20.

Chapter 59

Onora O'Neill, from "Autonomy, Coherence, and Independence" (1992)

Many of the political philosophers who now lay most store by autonomy speak of themselves as Kantians. By this they often mean only that they are not Utilitarians: they do not judge actions right because they maximize the good, or specifically because they maximize happiness. Their fundamental ethical category is that of the right, and often specifically that of rights. Typically they vindicate the primacy of right(s) by stressing the importance of human autonomy and then pointing out the vital role of rights both in fostering autonomy of character and in allowing for its expression in autonomous acts. Rights are to be shown crucial for securing both dispositional and occurrent autonomy.

However, the conception of action that most contemporary proponents of 'Kantian' ethics rely on, like that favoured by the Utilitarians whom they oppose, construes action in broadly empiricist terms as a matter of choosing instrumentally rational ways of pursuing an agent's preferences. Even Rawls' supposedly Kantian account of justice takes an empiricist view of action, choice and rationality. So do Nozick, Ronald Dworkin and Feinberg. So do many who write specifically on autonomy. Hence there is little need for present purposes to make much of the fashionable distinction between 'Kantians' and Utilitarians.

[. . .]

The problem for an account of autonomy that starts with any empiricist account of action is to show why some but not all instrumentally rational ways of pursuing given preferences in the light of given beliefs should count as autonomous. This is often done at a surface level by suggesting that certain acts are independent and coherent in the relevant, 'autonomous' way simply because they reflect the self or agency or freedom of the agent in peculiar measure. Yet a deeper account along these lines proves elusive once the empiricist starting point is accepted. If we view the self as nothing but a set of mental states, agency as nothing but the pursuit of preference, or freedom as nothing but the absence of constraint, how are we to explain how some acts can be more central than others to the self, agency, freedom, identity or integrity of an agent? There have been various proposals for an account of autonomy that fits within an empiricist framework; I have not yet met a convincing one. Some examples will indicate the sorts of difficulties that arise.

Some of these proposals suggest that preferences with a specific sort of *content* bear the hallmarks of autonomy. For example, Mill insists that there are certain 'higher pleasures', whose pursuit more truly reflects the self or person. He takes as the hallmark of a pleasure being 'higher' that the experts (those who know both sorts of pleasure) prefer it. This demarcation was meant to serve as a moral criterion, and has often been criticized as such and also for dispersing the evident conceptual rigour and economy of a bolder utilitarianism.

However, from the point of view of an account of autonomy, the deficiencies are more basic. Put simply, it is unclear why the pursuit of any category of pleasures should be thought of as escaping from the fundamental picture of pleasures or preferences as states of affairs which befall some but not other choosers. The criticism is, so to speak, not that we have not been shown that poetry is better than pushpin, but that we have not been shown whether or why a preference for poetry is other than one more of life's accidents, susceptible of causal explanation, but not in itself evidence of liberty, self-rule, sovereignty, freedom of the will, dignity, integrity, individuality, independence, responsibility, self-knowledge, self-assertion, critical reflection, freedom from obligation let alone of absence of external causation. Mere preference for poetry (or other 'higher' affairs) does not guarantee any notable forms of independence or of coherence.

Others contend that it is not the content but the *structure* of effective preferences that distinguishes autonomous from non-autonomous action. Autonomous action is still pursuit of preference but is guided, for example, by second-order preferences. On such views, common-or-garden eating, that only aims at enjoyment and satisfaction of hunger or conformity to daily routine, is not autonomous, but witting eating, that not merely satisfies hunger and taste, but also fulfils a preference for having, or 'being a person who has', these or those attitudes to food – e.g. a gourmet, an ascetic, a vegetarian – is autonomous action.

However, such attempts to pick out what makes actions autonomous by reference to the structure of preferences do not on reflection seem convincing either. How, for example, are we to construe the idea of a preferred or 'reflectively endorsed' preference? If we are not covertly to introduce a notion of self or free will that is suspect for empiricists, it seems that we will need to interpret the notion entirely formally, so that any preference that refers to and endorses other preferences (of the same individual) thereby counts as a second-order preference. In that case the interlocking structure of human preferences – the very ground of the coherence constraints which empiricist explanations of action invoke and models of rational choice demand – will guarantee that an enormous amount of human action including most trivial acts, count as autonomous. Most trivial preferences are not merely congruent with, but guided by or components of larger preferences, hence automatically receive second-order endorsement: any preference will be reflectively endorsed in so far as it is seen as an element or instance of a wider preference. Examples spring to mind: a teenager who rejects childish dependence may dress to defy parental demands. The preference for clothes the parents dislike but which conform to youth fashion, receives second-order endorsement, since the teenager wants to be a person who rejects parental demands. A patient who develops a dependent relationship with a doctor may have a preference for health that endorses all preferences for doing what the doctor orders. Yet there is no reason to think that teenagers who follow fashion or dependent patients manifest the sorts of independence or coherence that constitute autonomy. Second-orderedness is just too commonplace to guarantee significant coherence or any independence.

[. . .]

The history of the notion of autonomy until its contemporary proliferation of interpretations is remarkably specific. The term was used in Greek political writings to characterize independence from tyranny or foreign rule: autonomous polities are those that make their own laws. Autonomy is not discussed in Mediaeval political theory, but the term enters political discussion via early modern jurisprudence, and retains a significant use in international relations and political theory. Its extended use to describe a property of agents is entirely attributable to Kant. His choice of this term can be connected historically with traditions of political theory, in that he uses the term to characterize an extended conception of what Rousseau called '*liberté morale*'.

However, it is in Kant's writing that we first meet the idea that human agents, rather than polities, are the primary locus of autonomy. In Kant's work autonomy is for the first time treated as pivotal for human freedom and for morality. It is also from his writings that we inherit the modern conception of human autonomy as combining independence and coherence. However, in Kant's work these two ideas are understood in ways that fit together. Incoherence threatens only when we seek to transfer the Kantian connection between independence and coherence into other, especially into empiricist, accounts of action.

[...]

Kant's best known discussion of autonomy is in the third chapter of his *Groundwork*. In broad terms this chapter analyses the connections between freedom and morality, and argues that we can provide no proof but only a 'deduction' (i.e. vindication) [...] or 'defence' [...] of human freedom. The conception to be vindicated is a strong conception of 'positive' freedom, or autonomy. Kant argues that if we are to understand the idea of freedom at all, we must understand it as belonging to a will which is 'able to work independently of *determination* by alien causes'. [...] Such 'negative' freedom by itself would not, however, suffice for human action or for morality. For absence of 'alien causation' could be simply the absence of all causation, that is of all law-likeness. Random action (if it exists) would be free from determination by alien causes, so negatively free, because it is free from *all* modes of determination. Kant characterizes such action as 'lawless' (literally: not lawlike; [...]), and regards it as antithetical to morality.

The central claim of *Groundwork*, ch. III is that agents who are capable of negative freedom must also be capable of positive freedom. Action manifests positive freedom only if law-like. However, lawlikeness in the action of a negatively free being cannot be a matter of subjection to 'alien' causes, but must reflect determination by 'self-imposed law'.

The term 'autonomy', which originally characterized cities that made their own laws, is evidently an appropriate label for such 'positive freedom'. 'What else', Kant asks, 'can freedom of the will be but autonomy – that is, the property which will has of being a law to itself?' [...]. Even more starkly he asserts: '. . . on the presupposition that the will of an intelligence is free there follows necessarily its *autonomy* as the formal condition under which alone it can be determined' [...].

It is immediately clear that this account of autonomy introduces a robust, positive conception of independence 'from alien causes', that goes beyond morally indeterminate independence from particular events or powers. It is less clear whether Kantian autonomy invokes any strong idea of coherence. However, a little thought shows that the notion of 'lawfulness' itself demands coherence of a certain sort. To put the point – the point that Murdoch misses in her assimilation of Kant to existentialism – in terms of the political origins of the notion of autonomy, Kant holds that autonomy is a matter not merely of *self-imposed* law, but specifically of self-imposed *law*.

One common objection to this conception of autonomy is that the demand for 'independence from alien cause' introduces some metaphysically extravagant conception of self, which is to be thought of as 'universal legislator' as independent of all social bonds, and as a sort of monster of wilfulness. This suspicion lies behind Murdoch's identification of Kantian man with Lucifer, behind Rawls' reluctance to go the whole way with Kant, and behind Sandel's polemic against something that he calls the 'deontological self' and attributes to Kant and to contemporary 'Kantians'. Many commentators think that Kant's account of freedom and autonomy is not only intrinsically implausible, but that it flies in the face of his own critique of transcendent metaphysics, by introducing the notions of a 'noumenal' or 'intelligible' self and world, and treating these as the grounds of freedom and autonomy. In short, Kant's analysis of the way in which autonomous action is independent of 'alien causes' is subject to perennial suspicions. These are serious issues, for freedom 'from alien causes' cannot be merely a matter of independence from 'external' events and states; Kant is quite clear that events and states which we think of as 'internal' to agents also count as 'alien' if they are the naturally caused effects of other 'alien' causes. In particular, preferences, desires, inclinations might all be 'alien' causes.

[...]

The basis of Kant's conception of autonomy as combining lawlikeness with (negative) freedom from 'alien' causes is a non-empiricist account of action. Although Kant holds that an empiricist framework is needed to explain the origins and causal connections between events, including acts, he insists that the account of action that we need for practical purposes – for acting – is quite different. He rejects the empiricist view that normative and theoretical approaches to action differ only in the uses to which they put a single, encompassing theoretical model of action.

Kant takes it that human actions are individuated by the various descriptions under which they fall, rather than by their supposed position in a causal net. Acts have propositional content: they are intelligible. Any act satisfies a variety of descriptions, one of which may be said to be its *maxim*. The maxim of an act may not be the agent's conscious intention; rather it is to be seen as the fundamental principle that can be used to explain the various descriptions which the act satisfies. The maxim of an act is the principle that would require *this* specific enactment in *this* situation, as understood by the agent. Since agents are opaque to themselves – and to others – it may often be uncertain what the maxim of a given agent in a certain situation is. The hermeneutics of daily life, of history and of social understanding, may not be enough to resolve all ambiguities. However, even if judgement of cases is uncertain, we can still distinguish between maxims that can and others that cannot be universally adopted.

Only the former can be self-imposed laws: non-universalizable maxims are simply incompetent for this role.

The role of preferences in this account of action is quite different from their role in empiricist theories of action. Kant is well aware that maxims often refer to agents' preferences. He speaks of lives which systematically give maxims of satisfying preferences priority as based on a fundamental maxim of self-love [...]. However, he denies that maxims have to be subordinated to a principle of self-love. Negative freedom is the ability to adopt maxims that are not modes of self-love, that are independent of contingent ('alien') preferences as well as of other more clearly 'external' features.

This conception of freedom from alien causes should not be read as mere puritanism. Although there are much-quoted passages where Kant depicts preferences and inclinations as in themselves morally suspect [...] there are also passages where he insists that they are good. He writes, for example, 'Natural inclinations, *considered in themselves*, are *good*, that is, not a matter of reproach, and it is not only futile to want to extirpate them but to do so would also be harmful and blameworthy' [...]. The most plausible reading of Kant's position is not (as often alleged) that preferences and inclinations are bad, hence to be opposed by reason and morality, but that their relation to action may not be that of empirical cause to effect. Although actions have natural causes, we cannot take for granted that these are preferences and inclinations. The sense in which preferences *can* determine action is that agents who choose to act on maxims that refer to their preferences thereby adopt maxims of a determinate form. Preferences may determine action in the sense that when referred to in maxims they become part of the formal, intelligible rather than of the efficient, natural causes of action.

By distinguishing between the intelligible and the natural 'causes' of action, and their respective practical and theoretical tasks, Kant allows for action that, without being merely random, is neither causally nor conceptually bound to agents' preferences. However, he needs also to show that preference-following is in fact avoidable. If he cannot, his account of autonomy fails, for although it is open to him to insist that autonomous action *if possible* would have to be law-like, hence coherent, he would have failed to show that it is possible. He would have formulated an account of coherent, but none of independent, action. His account of positive freedom would fail because his account of the negative freedom that it presupposes would fail. Kant himself concedes that proof of freedom is impossible and that 'analysis of freedom' leads us only into a circle [. . .]. The only exit from this circle that he detects is via a critique of reason, which is said to offer reasons why freedom is not to be denied.

The strategy of argument that Kant uses to argue for freedom in the critical sections of *Groundwork*, ch. III [. . .] can be understood as a way of throwing doubt not on the *merits* but on the *scope and sufficiency* of the empiricist framework, within which the conception of acts as naturally caused by states of agents (that are ultimately the product of 'alien' causes) is confined. That conception of human action places it squarely within a natural order whose causal structure Kant regards as exceptionless. The 'empirical character' of human action is entirely within the scope of causal explanation: there is incontrovertible textual evidence that Kant's conception of noumenal freedom is not a conception that depends on claiming that there are gaps or discontinuities in the natural order [. . .]. What Kant disputes is the thought that empiricism can provide a *sufficient* account of action. On his view, causal judgement itself presupposes a capacity to distinguish within the flux of experience between those sequences that are objective (the agent could not have varied them) and those which are in part subjective (the agent could have varied them in some respect). Two fundamental features of the Kantian vindication of causal explanation are that it is a restricted,

conditional vindication – it provides a basis only for conditional, incomplete explanations – and that it presupposes a capacity to distinguish action from passivity. Knowledge of causes, including those that constitute the 'empirical character' of human beings, is attainable only by free agents.

[. . .]

This rapid and far from complete survey of Kant's account of autonomy provides a vantage point for some reflections on current discussions of autonomy. It may seem that in arguing from within an empiricist framework that no robust conception of autonomy is available there, I was merely trying to pull the rug out from under current debates. This was not my aim, since many of those debates have serious concerns. However, if we think that an adequate conception of autonomy must bring together robust notions of coherence and of independence, yet that empiricism undermines the latter by construing preferences and beliefs themselves as dependent, then (it seems to me) we have no choice but to step outside an empiricist framework. One way in which we could move – a plausible one given that this is the origin of many of our intimations about autonomy as linking coherence and independence in morally significant ways – would be in Kant's direction.

Yet it is easy to find strong reasons for resisting the pull back to Kant, which will weigh even with those who judge empiricist accounts of autonomy incoherent and Kant's account of what it takes to link independence and coherence impressive. A common objection is that Kant makes autonomy *too* central, that he does not give due recognition to human frailty, vulnerability and dependence, but that such difficulties are central to our concerns in daily and professional discussions of autonomy.

[. . .]

[. . .] Kant simply says too little about the institutional and social settings which constrain and form our capacities to act, including our capacities to enact what autonomy requires. He does not explore the ways in which the formation and structure of these capacities may require certain sorts of dependence as well as certain sorts of independence from others. Recent empiricist attempts to characterize autonomy often suggest that capacities for choice and morality are formed in part by restraint, or more specifically that negative liberty cannot flourish without a particular formation of positive liberty. These points may not in the end be coherently formulable within an empiricist account of action, because no conception of positive liberty can fit there. Yet their analogues outside that framework may be of great importance. Respect for autonomy demands sensitivity to ways in which ordinary, relational sorts of independence sometimes foster and at other times damage agents' fundamental capacities for action.

Although Kant does not say enough about social and institutional means of supporting capacities for autonomy, his approach leaves room to develop a critical account of these conditions. Since he does not identify autonomy with specific (relational, graduated) forms of independence, his conception of autonomy provides a standard for judging the moral importance and acceptability of those sorts of independence – and dependence. Kant offers no reasons for admiring either mere, sheer choice, or choices which simply mirror preferences agents happen to have. In a Kantian approach, social relations of independence – or of dependence – can, however, be judged derivatively by their tendency to sustain or secure abilities to act on principles that a plurality of free agents can share.

A systematic attempt to use a Kantian account of autonomy to think about issues of dependence and independence would have at least four corollaries. First, the value of autonomy would be established not by trying to identify it with whichever of the items Gerald Dworkin lists are judged most 'attractive' or 'optimal', but by testing central arguments that link morality, freedom and rationality. Second, various types of social and personal independence would not automatically be judged morally desirable, but would be evaluated for their contribution to lives of autonomy and to other goods. Third, the various types of social and personal dependence would not automatically be condemned, but would be evaluated for their contribution to lives of autonomy and other goods. Fourth, other characteristics which have at times been conflated with autonomy – e.g. self-sufficiency, individuality and authenticity – could each be taken seriously and their moral and other importance assessed by the same standards.

The last three of these points return us to the context of many worries expressed by communitarians, by feminists and by writers on virtue ethics, about the dangers of excessive admiration of independence, self-sufficiency, self-assertion and the like. Within a Kantian approach, it is not axiomatic that lives of evident external dependence are morally inferior to those of greater external independence. Total external independence is in any case mythical, and the best that can be achieved may be to avoid modes of external *dependence or independence* that damage opportunities or capacities for acting autonomously and to secure institutions and relations that foster these opportunities and capacities. In particular, a Kantian account of autonomy provides a framework for reconsidering popular images of moral achievement, success and 'autonomy' that locate them in certain forms of personal distancing from relations of closeness and dependence. It is in no way obvious that those whose lives eschew closeness with others, or whose 'life-plans' mesh best with 'public' institutions, or who dominate others' lives, have enacted maxims of autonomy or lead better lives than those who live 'private' lives on the margins or in the meshes of 'non-public' institutions. The successful may even be *less* good at living by maxims that could be self-imposed laws for all than are others. Finally, a Kantian understanding of autonomy undercuts all reasons to think that those whose lives are in special ways dependent on others – for example, those who need wheelchairs, or subsidies or special emotional support – must be less autonomous than others in any morally significant way: they are merely more dependent in specific ways that may have no general moral significance. There is no doubt a level of total external dependence (e.g. extreme senility or retardation) which signals a complete loss of capacities for action and so for autonomy. But where there are capacities to act, there are also capacities for Kantianly autonomous action, however awkwardly or tragically the contingencies of life constrain their realization.

Onora O'Neill, "Autonomy, Coherence, and Independence," from D. Milligan et al. (eds.), *Liberalism, Citizenship, and Autonomy* (Aldershot: Avebury, 1992), pp. 205–8, 212–21.

Chapter 60

Janice Moulton and Francine Rainone, from "Women's Work and Sex Roles" (1984)

Most contemporary feminist critics maintain that sex roles ought to be abolished. Their argument is that sex roles restrict freedom and opportunity, and if they were abolished individual freedom would be enhanced and opportunities made more equal. On this view the interests of males as well as females would be served by such a change. We agree that much of what are called sex roles should be changed. But we consider this argument for their abolition to be inadequate because it neither tells us why women in particular are disadvantaged by sex roles, nor does it give a correct account of what is wrong with sex roles. In this essay we will argue that the problem is not that sex roles restrict freedom; rather the problem is that sex roles reinforce the sexual division of labor (SDL) that functions in most existing societies to subordinate women.

The concept of "role" is used quite widely – and very loosely – in contemporary social science. The more specific concept of a "sex role" is equally widespread: every college student who has taken an introductory sociology or psychology class can discuss roles and sex roles. Some have argued that these concepts are hopelessly inexact and foster confused thinking about the way society actually functions. We do not wish to enter into that debate here. Instead, we hope to show that theorists who criticize current sex roles base their criticisms on the wrong grounds. They do not understand what is really wrong with sex roles.

By focusing on sex roles one can easily lose sight of the main problem: subordination. Even if women freely choose their sex roles, these roles are still wrong whenever they subordinate women to men. We believe that sex roles and subordination are in principle independent; only under certain social conditions are sex roles pernicious. Whether or not sex roles are pernicious depends on how they affect the total structure of society. When sex roles are used to effect the subordination of women, to prevent women from having an equal share in the distribution of social resources, they should be changed. On the restricts-freedom view of sex roles, sex roles are intrinsically wrong: because sex roles restrict the freedom of individuals to do certain things they are wrong. In the next section we challenge this claim, arguing that many roles that do restrict freedom are not wrong.

All Roles Restrict Freedom

Dictionaries define a role as a part, an office, a duty, or a function. In addition to roles that people assume are roles that people just have, sometimes by choice and sometimes not. There are actors' roles and advisory roles, personal and professional roles, child, parent, and adult roles. The term "role" is used so broadly that nearly any pattern of behavior or function in a group or system can be called a role.

It is not sufficient for a behavior pattern or function to exist in a society for it to be a role; there must be expectations or standards about the behavior for it to be a role. It might even be said that social roles are characterized more by expectations and standards than by what people actually do. The expectations might be so unrealistic or impossible that no one, or hardly anyone, could ever meet them, but the role would still be characterized by the expectations and not by its fulfillment. For example, very few ballerinas in the world achieve the perfection of Makarova, yet her flawless performances help set the standards for that role. To give a different kind of example, it is almost impossible to be an ideal father, as that role is currently defined. Ideal fathers work long hours to provide the maximum in material benefits for their children, yet they are also supposed to spend long hours playing with and caring for their children. These two demands are incompatible, but they may still form the basis of our expectation of fathers.

On the other hand, people might follow a pattern of behavior or perform a function with no concomitant expectations or standards, which consequently would not be a role. For example, we all, in exhaling carbon dioxide, perform a function, but there are no expectations or standards about such behavior. We are not enjoined to exhale deeply near plants nor expected to produce certain amounts of carbon dioxide. Exhaling carbon dioxide is a pattern of behavior and a function, but it is not a social role.

Where there are expectations and standards in a society, rewards and penalties will be given according to how well people conform to the behavior patterns set by those expectations and standards. Some penalties may be merely the withholding of desired rewards, while in other cases social and legal sanctions may exist

for ensuring conformity. The restrictions on freedom and opportunity that these penalties produce have been the subject of debate in previous discussions of sex roles.

It is certainly true that sex roles limit individual freedom and opportunity, but so do roles other than sex roles. One must be qualified to fill certain roles. The law restricts who may fill some roles and determines penalties for playing disallowed roles. Immigrants cannot be President; convicted felons cannot legally be gun owners. Freedom and opportunity are restricted because having one role can prevent a person from having another. Just as society tells us that men are not supposed to act like women, it also tells us that adults are not supposed to act like children and that lawyers are not supposed to dress like rock stars. One cannot simultaneously take a vow of silence and be on a debating team, have two nine-to-five jobs, be a boxer and a concert pianist, nor be a member of a city council and live in another city.

So sex roles are not alone in imposing limitations. The arguments used against sex roles will apply to any roles whatever: roles in general impose limitations on the people in them, and roles come with expectations about conduct, style, behavior, and so on, incurring sanctions when the expectations are not met.

Yet someone might argue that the sanctions imposed on sex role violators are particularly unfair; that while the severe sanctions imposed on felons and other disrupters of the social order are appropriate, those imposed on people who do not or cannot live up to sex role expectations are unjust. The argument might be that sanctions and restrictions arising from roles freely chosen are justified, but since sex roles are certainly not freely chosen, sex role restrictions are not fair.

This argument does not recognize that a great many occupations and social roles are not freely chosen, but rather are determined by economic necessity, social pressures, or ignorance about alternatives. And many of the roles that are chosen are done so with little information about the actual requirements of the roles. For example, all the roles involved in public entertainment attract many people, but most aspiring performers usually overlook the actual working conditions – low pay, job insecurity, long periods on the road. Influences such as early childhood experience (e.g., exposure, or lack of exposure, to team sports, musical training, or role models) often determine one's roles in later life. It is not clear, for example, that Wanda Landowska's being a harpsichordist was any more freely chosen than was her being a woman. Distinguishing acceptable roles from sex roles cannot be done on the assumption that the first are all freely chosen.

Let us emphasize this conclusion. The claim is that sex roles are unjust because they are not freely chosen. Nevertheless, many roles that most of us would allow to be unobjectionable, fair, and perhaps even beneficial to their holders are not freely chosen. Many factors interfere with free choice: ignorance, economic and social pressures, lack of ability. Yet the roles themselves might be rewarding, enriching, even desirable, and not at all unjust. Therefore it cannot be lack of free choice that makes sex roles unjust. It must be something else.

Many feminist critics argue that sex roles are wrong because they are assigned from birth rather than chosen. But we also do not choose whether we will be tall or short, attractive or ugly; and many roles depend on such attributes. Some might object that this analogy is faulty. It is true that one's height cannot be chosen any more than one's sex. But height materially disqualifies a person from fulfilling certain social roles, while sex does not, because it is not a relevant characteristic for fulfilling any social role. The answer to this objection is that *no* characteristic is relevant to the performance of a role if one is willing to change society and/or develop new technology. Short people could be basketball players with other short basketball players, or if gym shoes were designed to propel their wearers several feet into the air. Wealth would not be a relevant characteristic of potential political

officeholders if campaigns were funded solely by public money. So the question is not what *is* relevant, but what *ought* to count as relevant. We do not believe that sex ought to be a relevant characteristic for the performance of social roles. But we are arguing against the claim that it ought not to be relevant *because* making it relevant limits women's freedom of choice. Let us examine the concept of freedom of choice and how it applies to this issue.

In the ordinary sense of free choice, someone chooses freely if s/he has alternatives, knows what the alternatives are, and chooses among them on the basis of preference rather than as a result of coercion. Unfortunately, it is very difficult to know what counts as coercion. Moreover, after enough coercion, people tend to have certain preferences. The feminist concern about sex role stereotyping in early education stems from this realization. But is it sensible to say, for example, that a 35-year-old woman is coerced into wearing make-up because of influences on her during her childhood and adolescence? And if not, can we say she freely chooses to wear make-up? Even if we could resolve these issues, the argument would still be unconvincing, for two reasons.

First, not all coercion is bad. In fact, education could hardly proceed without it. Children are coerced into learning many rules and types of behavior that curtail their freedom of choice about what sort of adults they become, in ways that we approve of. So proponents of this argument need to distinguish between acceptable and unacceptable coercion. Second, this argument cannot tell us why women are more severely disadvantaged by sex roles, because it ignores the issue of power and domination.

Boys are as coerced as girls to learn their socially determined role. A strong case can be made that men have *less* freedom to choose their sex roles and less latitude of behavior within them. Yet the sex roles of women attract more concern about injustice. This indicates that the real issue about sex roles is not freedom of choice, but the other effects of sex roles on their bearers. The real issue concerns the respective positions of women and men in the distribution of social resources, which result from sex roles. The central effect of sex roles is the perpetuation of a worldwide SDL in which:

> women are one-third of the world's formal labor force, and do four-fifths of all "informal" work, but receive only 10 percent of the world's income and own less than 1 percent of the world's property. [L. Leghorn and K. Parker, *Woman's Worth*]

The fact that sex roles reinforce the SDL, and thereby perpetuate the subordination of women to men, is what makes sex roles wrong. Even if it were true that many housewives had more freedom of choice in their daily lives than their husbands, this would not change the feminist problems with the position of housewives. The issue of whether men or women have more freedom to choose their social roles, or even whether they have any freedom at all, does not address the problem with sex roles. In sum, the free-choice argument is inadequate because it is based on a vague concept of free choice, and because it fails to confront the issues of power and domination.

One could try to distinguish sex roles from acceptable roles by claiming that the acceptable roles are restrictions on occupational roles, while sex roles are restrictions on persons. Restrictions on occupational roles include training and licensing requirements and rules in games and sports, and they are justified by the purpose they serve. But restrictions on persons as persons are not justified. This argument ignores the extent to which sex roles *are* job roles and how important that is for this issue. Let us consider it nonetheless. It claims that sex roles serve no purpose. But don't they? One can claim they tell people how to "play the game," if nothing else, and serve at least as much purpose as any other game. Or one can argue that they tell people what to expect of others. Perhaps they add stability to a culture. In a world where economic

and political roles may fluctuate greatly, sex roles can provide a focus for one's self-identity because they are stable. So sex roles may serve a purpose just as some other roles do. This does not mean that their purpose cannot be served some other way, just as the purposes served by many other roles can be served in other ways. But it does mean that lack of purpose is not a reason for eliminating sex roles.

In addition, restrictions on occupations are, like sex-role restrictions, also restrictions on persons, namely the persons who have those jobs and who must do certain things, and the persons who do not have those jobs and therefore are not allowed to do certain things. A person not accepted to medical or dental school can never legally prescribe certain drugs; that is a restriction on that person whether or not she or he wanted to prescribe drugs. So sex roles do not appear to be significantly different from occupational roles after all.

Suppose one argues that the degree of severity of the sanctions and restrictions makes sex roles wrong. The trouble with sex roles, one might say, is that there are only two, and the social cost of nonconformity is very great. To show that this is true, one would have to show that the social cost of disobeying sex role expectations was greater than that of not living up to other standards and stereotypes. And it is not clear that this is true. It would seem, for example, that the social cost of breaking the law, of being poor or illiterate in an industrialized society, of being handicapped, old, or naive is greater than the social cost of being unmasculine or unfeminine (however they are characterized). One might contradict this by pointing out the threats of violence, the ostracism, or the fear of being locked up or left unprotected that come with sex role nonconformity. Yet felons, the mentally handicapped, and others have the same problems. The sanctions for sex role violations are not essentially different from the sanctions for other role violations. We may think sex role sanctions are worse than other sanctions because we think that they are wrong *and* can be corrected.

Roles Aren't Wrong

Freedom cannot be used to distinguish sex roles from other, acceptable roles. But instead of looking elsewhere to find out what is wrong with sex roles, we might conclude that all roles are wrong – that to guarantee individual freedom there should be no roles at all. We are going to argue that this second alternative is mistaken as well. We shall claim that roles are essential to our freedom because they provide information about what to expect when we make decisions, and that only with roles are informed choices possible. On our view, a society without roles would be impossible; roles could neither be abolished nor ignored when we act.

Suppose there were no roles. How then could we decide what specific activities to undertake, what is worth training for, or whether some activities will be rewarded well in the future? If there were no roles, there would be no expectations about patterns of behavior and functions and therefore no reason to believe that a person's current actions or situation are part of, or prerequisites for, particular future actions or situations. We could not require an education, apprenticeship, or practice to prepare an individual to become an X (driver, teacher, scuba diver) because that would amount to a role restriction. And if we went to school, served an apprenticeship, or practiced with the aim of becoming an X in this society-without-roles, we would be deluded. If there were no roles, no one would be able to gain an advantage by special training to fulfill some X, for that would restrict the people who had not trained to be Xs. We could not say that something was done well or ill because that would impose sanctions, restrictions on the way something was done; it would show that we had standards and expectations about doing X well. Work done toward a goal produces expectations that can, and very often will, be exhibited by rewards for some and punishments for others. If there were no roles, we

could never decide between occupations or hobbies on the grounds that one appeared to involve more interesting activities, or more material rewards, or attracted more praise or respect than another, for all these attributes are part of the rewards and punishments that are supposed to be eliminated. If we chose occupations based on knowledge or beliefs of what we would do in those jobs, we would be using role expectations to make our decisions. Surely such a society without roles is both undesirable and impossible. Different sorts of things to do will always require training for some and produce expectations about performance, with praise for success and penalties for failure.

Consider the following analogy. Our theories and beliefs about the world affect our perceptions by restricting what we perceive, so that we see things one way and not another. But this restriction is what allows us to understand and make sense of the world, by organizing our experience and relating it to other knowledge. Similarly, roles constitute restrictions. They limit our freedom so that some choices are possible and others are not. But in so doing, roles provide information about the future – what behavior is possible, how behaviors are related, what treatment to expect from others. And this information is essential for making choices. If we had no theories and beliefs we would have no coherent perceptions at all, and if we had no roles in our society we would have no reason for making choices. The limitations that roles produce do restrict freedom, but without roles there would be no reason for freedom.

If our arguments so far are correct, we have established that all roles limit freedom and opportunity, but that this does not prove them unjustified. In fact, a world without roles would be impossible. This does not mean that every particular role is justified; far from it. But it does mean that to show what is wrong with sex roles we must show something other than that they limit freedom.

Janice Moulton and Francine Rainone, "Women's Work and Sex Roles," from Carol Gould (ed.), *Beyond Domination: New Perspectives on Women and Philosophy* (Totowa: Rowman and Allanheld, 1984), pp. 189–96.

Chapter 61

Karl Marx and Friedrich Engels, from *The German Ideology* (1846)

[. . .]

Futher, the division of labour implies the contradiction between the interest of the separate individual or the individual family and the communal interest of all individuals who have intercourse with one another. And indeed, this communal interest does not exist merely in the imagination, as the 'general interest', but first of all in reality, as the mutual interdependence of the individuals among whom the labour is divided. And finally, the division of labour offers us the first example of how, as long as man remains in natural society, that is, as long as a cleavage exists between the particular and the common interest, as long, therefore, as activity is not voluntarily, but naturally, divided, man's own deed becomes an alien power opposed to him, which enslaves him instead of being controlled by him. For as soon as the distribution of labour comes into being, each man has a particular, exclusive sphere of activity, which is forced upon him and from which he cannot escape. He is a hunter, a fisherman, a shepherd, or a critical critic, and must remain so if he does not want to lose his means of livelihood; while in communist society, where nobody has one exclusive sphere of activity but each can become accomplished in any branch he wishes, society regulates the general production and thus makes it possible for me to do one thing today and another tomorrow, to hunt in the morning, fish in the afternoon, rear cattle in the evening, criticize after dinner, just as I have a mind, without ever becoming hunter, fisherman, cowherd, or critic. This fixation of social activity, this consolidation of what we ourselves produce into an objective power above us, growing out of our control, thwarting our expectations, bringing to naught our calculations, is one of the chief factors in historical development up till now.

Karl Marx and Friedrich Engels, *The German Ideology*, from D. McLellan (ed.), *Karl Marx: Selected Writings* (Oxford: Oxford University Press, 1977), p. 169.

Part VII

Freedom, Ability, and Economic Inequality

Introduction to Part VII

How, if at all, is freedom affected by the distribution of resources? Libertarians like Robert Nozick (in Part IV on "Freedom and Morality"), Friedrich von Hayek, Murray Rothbard, and Bruno Leoni all deny that the degree to which one is free is affected by how well-off one is in economic terms. Freedom, for these authors, consists in the absence of active interference by others, not in one's power or ability to achieve one's goals. From this they conclude that the freest kind of society will be one in which the state interferes as little as possible with citizens' free exercise of their proprietary prerogatives. In that society, in their view, the state would constrain individuals' actions only as a means of preventing or punishing encroachments upon the rights of others. Rich and poor will enjoy the freedom of such a society to the same degree, for while the poor may be less able to do certain things, they will be no less *free* than the rich to do them. Equal freedom is guaranteed not by equal purchasing power but by the rule of law – that is, by the effective enforcement of wholly general laws applying equally to all.

Egalitarian thinkers like Philippe Van Parijs, G. A. Cohen, and Amartya Sen, on the other hand, favor the identification of freedom with ability and of inability with unfreedom (although Sen speaks of "capability" rather than "ability" – see chapter 76 in Part VIII). For such authors, any form of obstacle to the performance of an action constitutes a constraint on the freedom to perform that action – not only interference by others, but also a lack of means, such as knowledge, personal abilities, and economic and social resources. Whoever lacks the economic means to dine at the Ritz is unfree to dine at the Ritz, and to claim with the libertarians that such a person is "free but unable" to do so is to abandon ordinary language for no good reason. Egalitarians often claim that while the poor are free to dine at the Ritz in a "formal" sense – because no law forbids it – they are nevertheless "materially" or "substantively" or (rather more polemically) "really" unfree to do so.

It is sometimes suggested that the difference between these two outlooks can be characterized as one between negative and positive freedom (see "Negative and Positive Freedom"). However, this suggestion can be misleading. There has indeed been a tendency among proponents of the positive doctrine of liberty, from T. H. Green onward, to see in that doctrine an active role for the state in promoting the personal abilities and economic means of the least advantaged members of society. However, there is no need to appeal to the notion of a "real self" or to refer to "internal constraints" in order to claim that one is rendered less free by a lack of external means. Partly for this reason, both Van Parijs and Cohen avoid the label "positive freedom."

Similarly, it is not always clear that libertarians appeal to a purely negative conception of freedom. One reason for this is that they sometimes base their anti-egalitarian claims on a "moralized" or "rights-based" notion of freedom (see "Freedom and Morality"). Another is that libertarians sometimes suggest or imply that the legal limits imposed by the rule of law, being wholly general and non-discriminatory, do not themselves restrict anyone's freedom. On this view, the rule of law is akin to the law of gravity, which only makes us unable to do certain things, not unfree to do them (see the final part of Hayek's piece in Part V, on "Coercion"). Thus, a society characterized by the rule of law, in which property rights are wholly respected and impartially enforced, does not contain any unfreedom at all. The standard "negative" view, on the other hand, would be that the rule of law creates some unfreedoms in order to promote other (greater, more important, or more fairly distributed) freedoms.

Furthermore, not all egalitarians think that one needs to identify freedom and ability in order to show that economic constraints reduce freedom. Indeed, while Cohen favors such an identification, his central argument depends only on the more modest premise that one is unfree if others prevent one from acting in certain ways. It is wrong, Cohen says, to see a lack of money as on a par with physical disabilities, ignorance, and suchlike personal incapacities. Money is a social relation, and its possession implies the non-prevention of actions: if one hands it over, others abstain from preventing one from doing certain things (like taking home and wearing a sweater that is currently lying on a shelf in a clothes store); if one does not hand the money over, one continues to be subject to the relevant preventions (imposed by the store owner, the police, and the other agents of the state). On Cohen's argument, then, there is a strong empirical correlation between the possession of money and the enjoyment of negative freedom as standardly conceived.

Finally, one should note that not all egalitarians hold the poor to be less free than the rich. Some prefer to acknowledge that freedom and wealth are independent variables – perhaps because they share the libertarians' intuition that the freedom of a society is not something that fluctuates in the same way as the amount and distribution of material resources it contains. At the same time, however, they call for the state to strike a compromise between freedom and economic equality by restricting certain market freedoms (in the name of redistribution) while nevertheless protecting certain fundamental rights. This view forms the basis of John Rawls's famous distinction between liberty (i.e. the enjoyment of certain fundamental rights), which is distributed equally in a just liberal society, and "the worth of liberty," which is enjoyed unequally as a result of social and economic disparities.

Further Reading

Jones, Peter, "Freedom and the Redistribution of Resources," *Journal of Social Policy* 11 (1982), pp. 217–38 ⟨critique of the Hayekian freedom-based argument against redistribution⟩.

Kelley, David, *A Life of One's Own* (Washington D.C.: Cato Institute, 1998), ch. 4 ⟨libertarian critique of positive freedom and welfare rights⟩.

Narveson, Jan, "Equality vs. Liberty: Advantage, Liberty," in E. Frankel Paul, F. D. Miller, Jr., and J. Paul (eds.), *Liberty and Equality* (Oxford: Blackwell, 1985) ⟨critique of redistribution and defense of rights-based libertarianism⟩.

Steiner, Hillel, "Capitalism, Justice and Equal Starts," in E. Frankel Paul, F. D. Miller, Jr., J. Paul, and J. Ahrens (eds.), *Equal Opportunity* (Oxford: Blackwell, 1988) ⟨left-libertarian defense of redistribution on the basis of a right to equal negative freedom⟩.

Waldron, Jeremy, "Homelessness and the Issue of Freedom," in J. Waldron, *Liberal Rights. Collected Papers 1981–1991* (Cambridge: Cambridge University Press 1993) ⟨negative-liberty-based argument to the effect that destitution is a form of unfreedom⟩.

Chapter 62

F. A. Hayek, from *The Constitution of Liberty* (1960)

The transition from the concept of individual liberty to that of liberty as power has been facilitated by the philosophical tradition that uses the word "restraint" where we have used "coercion" in defining liberty. Perhaps "restraint" would in some respects be a more suitable word if it was always remembered that in its strict sense it presupposes the action of a restraining human agent. In this sense, it usefully reminds us that the infringements on liberty consist largely in people's being prevented from doing things, while "coercion" emphasizes their being made to do particular things. Both aspects are equally important: to be precise, we should probably define liberty as the absence of restraint and constraint. Unfortunately, both these words have come also to be used for influences on human action that do not come from other men; and it is only too easy to pass from defining liberty as the absence of restraint to defining it as the "absence of obstacles to the realization of our desires" or even more generally as "the absence of external impediment." This is equivalent to interpreting it as effective power to do whatever we want.

This reinterpretation of liberty is particularly ominous because it has penetrated deeply into the usage of some of the countries where, in fact, individual freedom is still largely preserved. In the United States it has come to be widely accepted as the foundation for the political philosophy dominant in "liberal" circles. Such recognized intellectual leaders of the "progressives" as J. R. Commons and John Dewey have spread an ideology in which "liberty is power, effective power to do specific things" and the "demand of liberty is the demand for power," while the absence of coercion is merely "the negative side of freedom" and "is to be prized only as a means to Freedom which is power."

[. . .] This confusion of liberty as power with liberty in its original meaning inevitably leads to the identification of liberty with wealth; and this makes it possible to exploit all the appeal which the word "liberty" carries in the support for a demand for the redistribution of wealth. Yet, though freedom and wealth are both good things which most of us desire and though we often need both to obtain what we wish, they still remain different. Whether or not I am my own master and can follow my own choice and whether the possibilities from which I must choose are many or few are two entirely different questions. The courtier living in the lap of luxury but at the beck and call of his prince may be much less free than a poor peasant or artisan, less able to live his own life and to choose his own opportunities for usefulness. Similarly, the general in charge of an army or the director of a large construction project may wield enormous powers which in some respects may be quite uncontrollable, and yet may well be less free, more liable to have to change all his intentions and plans at a word from a superior, less able to change his own life or to decide what to him is most important, than the poorest farmer or shepherd.

If there is to be any clarity in the discussion of liberty, its definition must not depend upon whether or not everybody regards this kind of liberty as a good thing. It is very probable that there are people who do not value the liberty with which we are concerned, who cannot see that they derive great benefits from it, and who will be ready to give it up to gain other advantages; it may even be true that the necessity to act according to one's own plans and decisions may be felt by them to be more of a burden than an advantage. But liberty may be desirable, even though not all persons may take advantage of it. We shall have to consider whether the benefit derived from liberty by the majority is dependent upon their using the opportunities it offers them and whether the case for liberty really rests on most people wanting it for themselves. It may well be that the benefits we receive from the liberty of all do not derive from what most people recognize as its effects; it may even be that liberty exercises its beneficial effects as much through the discipline it imposes on us as through the more visible opportunities it offers.

Above all, however, we must recognize that we may be free and yet miserable. Liberty does not mean all good things or the absence of all evils. It is true that to be free may mean freedom to starve, to make costly mistakes, or to run mortal risks. In the sense in which we use the term, the penniless vagabond who lives precariously by constant improvisation is indeed freer than the conscripted soldier with all his security and relative comfort. But if liberty may therefore not always seem preferable to other goods, it is a distinctive good that needs a distinctive name. And though "political liberty" and "inner liberty" are long-established alternative uses of the term which, with a little care, may be employed without causing confusion, it is questionable whether the use of the word "liberty" in the sense of "power" should be tolerated.

In any case, however, the suggestion must be avoided that, because we employ the same word, these "liberties" are different species of the same genus. This is the source of dangerous nonsense, a verbal trap that leads to the most absurd conclusions. Liberty in the sense of power, political liberty, and inner liberty are not states of the same kind as individual liberty: we cannot, by sacrificing a little of the one in order to get more of the other, on balance gain some common element of freedom. We may well get one good thing in the place of another by such an exchange. But to suggest that there is a common element in them which allows us to speak of the effect that such an exchange has on liberty is sheer obscurantism, the crudest kind of philosophical realism, which assumes that, because we describe these conditions with the same word, there must also be a common element in them. But we want them largely for different reasons, and their presence or absence has different effects. If we have to choose between them, we cannot do so by asking whether liberty will be increased as a whole, but only by deciding which of these different states we value more highly.

F. A. Hayek, *The Constitution of Liberty* (London: Routledge and Kegan Paul, 1960), pp. 16–19.

Chapter 63

Bruno Leoni, from *Freedom and the Law* (1961)

[. . .]

Several thinkers, ancient as well as modern, have tried to connect the fact that some people are not free from hunger or from disease with the fact that other people in the same society are not free from the constraint of their fellow men. Of course, the connection is obvious when someone is in bondage to other people who treat him badly and let him die, for instance, through starvation. But the connection is not at all obvious when people are not in bondage to others. However, some thinkers have erroneously believed that whenever someone lacks something he needs or simply desires, he has been unjustly "deprived" of that very thing by the people who do have it.

History is so full of examples of violence, robbery, invasions of land, and so on, that many thinkers have felt justified in saying that the origin of private property is simply violence and that it is therefore to be regarded as irremediably illicit at present as well as in primitive times. The Stoics, for example, imagined that all the land on earth was originally common to all men. They called this legendary condition *communis possessio originaria*. Certain Fathers of the Christian Church, particularly in the Latin countries, echoed this assumption. Thus, Saint Ambrose, the famous archbishop of Milan, could write in the fifth century CE that while Nature had provided for things to be common to all, private property rights were due to usurpation. He quotes the Stoics, who maintained, as he says, that everything in the earth and in the seas was created for the common use of all human beings. A disciple of Saint Ambrose, called the Ambrosiaster, says that God gave everything to men in common and that this applies to the sun and to the rain as well as to the land. The same thing is said by Saint Zeno of Verona (for whom one of the most magnificent churches in the world is named) in reference to the men of very ancient time: "They had no private property, but they had everything in common, like sun, days, nights, rain, life, and death, as all those things had been given to them in equal degree, without any exception, by the divine providence." And the same saint adds, obviously accepting the idea that private property is the result of constraint and of tyranny: "The private owner is without doubt similar to a tyrant, having himself alone the total control of things that would be useful to several other people." Almost the same idea can be found some centuries later in the works of certain canonists. For instance, the author of the first systemization of the rules of the Church, the so-called *decretum Gratiani*, says: "Whoever is determined to keep more things than he needs is a robber."

Modern socialists, including Marx, have simply produced a revised version of this same idea. For instance, Marx distinguishes various stages in the history of mankind: a first stage, in which the production relations had been those of cooperation, and a second stage, in which some people acquired for the first time control of the factors of production, thereby placing a minority in the position of being fed by the majority. The old Archbishop of Milan would say in less complicated and more effective language: "Nature is responsible for a law of things in common; usurpation is responsible for private law."

Of course, we can ask how it is possible to speak of "things common to all." Who decreed that all things are "common" to all men, and why? The usual reply given by the Stoics and their disciples, the Christian Fathers in the first centuries after Christ, was that, just as the moon and the sun and the rain are common to all men, so there is no reason to maintain that other things, such as land, are not also common. These advocates of communism did not bother to make a semantic analysis of the word "common." Otherwise they would have discovered that land cannot be "common" to all men in the same sense in which the sun and the moon are and that it is therefore not altogether the same thing to let people cultivate land in common as it is to let them use moonlight or sunlight or fresh air when they go out for a walk. Modern economists explain the difference by pointing out that there is no scarcity of moonlight, while there is a scarcity of land. Notwithstanding the truistic nature of this statement, a purported analogy between scare things like arable land and abundant things like moonlight has always been a good reason in the eyes of many people for maintaining that the "have-nots" have been "constrained" by the "haves," that the latter have illicitly deprived the former of certain things originally "common" to all men. The semantic confusion in the use of the word "common" introduced by the Stoics and the early Christian Fathers in this connection has been retained by modern socialists of all kinds and lies, I believe, at the origin of the tendency, manifested particularly in recent times, to use the word "freedom" in an equivocal sense that relates "freedom from want" with "freedom from other people's constraint."

This confusion is connected, in its turn, with another. When a grocer or a doctor or a lawyer waits for customers or clients, each of them may feel dependent on the latter for his living. This is quite true. But if no customer or client makes his appearance, it would be an abuse of language to assert that the customers or clients who do not appear constrain the grocer or the doctor or the lawyer to die by starvation. In fact, no one committed any constraint against him for the simple reason that no one put in an appearance. To put the matter in the simplest possible terms, the customers or clients did not exist at all. If we now suppose that a client puts in an appearance and offers a very small fee to the doctor or the lawyer, it is not possible to say that this particular client is "constraining" the doctor or the lawyer to accept his fee. We may despise a man who can swim and does not save a fellow man whom he sees drowning in a river, but it would be an abuse of language to assert that in failing to save the drowning man he was "constraining" the latter to drown. In this connection I must agree with a famous German jurist of the nineteenth century, Rudolph Jhering, who was indignant at the unfairness of the argument advanced by Portia against Shylock and on behalf of Antonio in Shakespeare's *Merchant of Venice*. We may despise Shylock, but we cannot say that he "constrained" Antonio or anybody else to make an agreement with him – an agreement that implied, under the circumstances, the death of the latter. What Shylock wanted was only to constrain Antonio to respect his agreement after he had signed it. Notwithstanding these obvious considerations, people are often inclined to judge Shylock in the same way as they would judge a murderer and to condemn usurers as if they were robbers or pirates, although neither Shylock nor any ordinary usurer can properly be accused of constraining anyone to go to him to ask for money at a usurious rate.

In spite of this difference between "constraint," in the sense of something actually done to cause harm to somebody against his will, and behavior like that of Shylock, many people, especially in the last hundred years in

Europe, have tried to inject into ordinary language a semantic confusion the result of which is that a man who has never committed himself to perform a definite act in favor of other people and who therefore does nothing on their behalf is censured because of his purported "omission" and is blamed as if he had "constrained" others to do something against their will. This is not, in my opinion, in accordance with the proper usage of ordinary language in all the countries with which I am familiar. You do not "constrain" someone if you merely refrain from doing on his behalf something you have not agreed to do.

All socialist theories of the so-called "exploitation" of workers by employers – and, in general, of the "have-nots" by the "haves" – are, in the last analysis, based on this semantic confusion. Whenever self-styled historians of the Industrial Revolution in England in the nineteenth century talk about the "exploitation" of workers by employers, they imply precisely this idea that the employers were exercising "constraint" against workers to make them accept poor wages for hard jobs. When statutes such as the Trade Disputes Act of 1906 in England granted to the trade unions a privilege to constrain employers to accept their demands by unlawful acts, the idea was that the employees were the weaker party and that they could therefore be "constrained" by employers to accept poor wages instead of high wages. The privilege granted by the Trade Disputes Act was based on the principle familiar to the European liberals of that time, and corresponding also to the meaning of "freedom" as accepted in ordinary language, that you are "free" when you can constrain other people to refrain from constraining you. The trouble was that, while the constraint granted to the unions as a privilege by the Act had the usual meaning of this word in ordinary language, the "constraint" that the privilege was designed to prevent on the part of the employers was not understood in the sense that this word had and still has in ordinary language. If we consider things from this point of view, we must agree with Sir

Frederick Pollock, who wrote in his *Law of Torts* that "legal science has evidently nothing to do with the violent empirical operation on the body politic" that the British legislature had thought fit to perform by the Trade Disputes Act of 1906. We have to say also that the ordinary use of language has nothing to do with the meaning of "constraint" that rendered it suitable, in the eyes of the British legislators, to inflict upon the body politic a violent operation of his kind.

Unprejudiced historians, such as Professor T. S. Ashton, have demonstrated that the general situation of the poor classes of the English population after the Napoleonic wars was due to causes that had nothing to do with the behavior of the entrepreneurs of the new industrial era in that country and that its origin is traceable far back into the ancient history of England. What is more, economists have often demonstrated, both by adducing cogent arguments of a theoretical nature and by examining statistical data, that good wages depend on the ratio between the amount of capital invested and the number of workers.

But this is not the main point of our argument. If one gives to "constraint" such different meanings as those we have just seen, one can easily conclude that the entrepreneurs at the time of the Industrial Revolution in England were "constraining" people to inhabit, for example, old and unhealthful houses only because they did not build for their workers a sufficient number of new and good houses. In the same way, one could say that the industrialists who do not make huge investments in machinery, regardless of the returns they can get, are "constraining" their workers to content themselves with low wages. In fact, this semantic confusion is fostered by several propaganda and pressure groups interested in making persuasive definitions both of "freedom" and of "constraint." As a result, people can be censured for the "constraint" they allegedly exercise over other people with whom they have never had anything to do. Thus, the propaganda of Mussolini and Hitler before and during the Second

World War included the assertion that the people of other countries located as far from Italy or Germany as, say, Canada or the United States were "constraining" the Italians and the Germans to be content with their poor material resources and their comparatively narrow territories, although not even one single square mile of German or Italian territory had been taken by Canada or by the United States. In the same way, after the last World War we were told by many people – especially by those belonging to the Italian "intelligentsia" – that the rich landowners of Southern Italy were directly responsible for the misery of the poor workers there or that the inhabitants of Northern Italy were responsible for the depression of the deep South, although no demonstration could be seriously supplied to prove that the wealth of certain landowners in Southern Italy was the cause of the workers' poverty or that the reasonable standard of living enjoyed by the people of Northern Italy was the cause of the absence of such a standard in the South. The assumption underlying all these ideas was that the "haves" of Southern Italy were "constraining" the "have-nots" to make a poor living, in the same way as the inhabitants of Northern Italy were "constraining" those living in the South to be content with agricultural incomes instead of building industries. I must point out too that

a similar semantic confusion underlies many of the demands made upon the peoples of the West (including the United States) and the attitudes adopted toward them by the ruling groups in certain former colonies like India or Egypt.

This results in occasional mutinies, riots, and all kinds of hostile actions on the part of the people who feel "constrained." Another no less important result is the series of acts, statutes, and provisions, at national as well as international levels, designed to help people allegedly "constrained" to counteract this "constraint" by legally enforced devices, privileges, grants, immunities, etc.

Thus, a confusion of words causes a confusion of feelings, and both react reciprocally on each other to confound matters even more.

I am not so naive as Leibniz, who supposed that many political or economic questions could be settled, not by disputes (*clamoribus*), but by a sort of reckoning (*calculemus*) through which it would be possible for all people concerned to agree at least in principle about the issues at stake. But I do maintain that semantic clarification is likely to be more useful than is commonly believed, if only people were put in a condition to benefit from it.

Bruno Leoni, *Freedom and the Law* (Los Angeles: Nash, 1961), pp. 52–8.

Chapter 64

Murray N. Rothbard, from
The Ethics of Liberty (1982)

Isaiah Berlin on Negative Freedom

One of the best-known and most influential present-day treatments of liberty is that of Sir Isaiah Berlin. In his *Two Concepts of Liberty*, Berlin upheld the concept of "negative liberty" – absence of interference with a person's sphere of action – as against "positive liberty," which refers not to liberty at all but to an individual's effective power or mastery over himself or his environment. Superficially, Berlin's concept of negative liberty seems similar to the thesis of the present volume: that liberty is the absence of physically coercive interference or invasion of an individual's person and property. Unfortunately, however, the vagueness of Berlin's concepts led to confusion and to the absence of a systematic and valid libertarian creed.

One of Berlin's fallacies and confusions he himself recognized in a later essay and edition of his original volume. In his *Two Concepts of Liberty*, he had written that "I am normally said to be free to the degree to which no human being interferes with my activity. Political liberty in this sense is simply the area within which a man can do what he wants."[1] Or, as Berlin later phrased it, "In the original version of *Two Concepts of Liberty* I speak of liberty as the absence of obstacles to the fulfillment of a man's desires."[2] But, as he later realized, one grave problem with this formulation is that a man can be held to be "free" in proportion as his wants and desires are extinguished, for example by external conditioning. As Berlin states in his corrective essay,

> If degrees of freedom were a function of the satisfaction of desires, I could increase freedom as effectively by eliminating desires as by satisfying them; I could render men (including myself) free by conditioning them into losing the original desires which I have decided not to satisfy.[3]

In his later (1969) version, Berlin has expunged the offending passage, altering the first statement above to read: "Political liberty in this sense is simply the area within which a man can act unobstructed by others."[4] But grave problems still remain with Berlin's later approach. For Berlin now explains that what he means by freedom is "the absence of obstacles to possible choices and activities," obstacles, that is, put there by "alterable human practices."[5] But this comes close, as Professor Parent observes, to confusing "freedom" with "opportunity," in short to scuttling Berlin's own concept of negative freedom and replacing it with the illegitimate concept of "positive freedom." Thus, as Parent indicates, suppose that X refuses to hire Y because Y is a redhead and X dislikes redheads; X is surely reducing Y's range of opportunity, but he can scarcely be said to be invading Y's "freedom."[6] Indeed, Parent goes on to point out a repeated confusion in the later Berlin of freedom with opportunity; thus Berlin writes that "the freedom of which I speak is opportunity for action" (xlii), and identifies increases in liberty with the "maximization of opportunities" (xlviii). As Parent points out, "The terms 'liberty' and 'opportunity' have distinct meanings"; someone, for example, may lack the *opportunity* to buy a ticket to a concert for numerous reasons (e.g., he is too busy) and yet he was still in any meaningful sense "free" to buy such a ticket.[7]

Thus, Berlin's fundamental flaw was his failure to define negative liberty as the absence of physical interference with an individual's person and property, with his *just property rights* broadly defined. Failing to hit on this definition, Berlin fell into confusion, and ended by virtually abandoning the very negative liberty he had tried to establish and to fall, willy-nilly, into the "positive liberty" camp. More than that, Berlin, stung by his critics with the charge of upholding laissez-faire, was moved into frenetic and self-contradictory assaults on laissez-faire as somehow injurious to negative liberty. For example, Berlin writes that the "evils of unrestricted laissez faire . . . led to brutal violations of 'negative' liberty . . . including that of free expression or association." Since laissez faire precisely means full freedom of person and property, including of course free expression and association as a subset of private property rights, Berlin has here fallen into absurdity. And in a similar canard, Berlin writes of

> the fate of personal liberty during the reign of unfettered economic individualism – about the condition of the injured majority, principally in the towns, whose children were destroyed in mines or mills, while their parents lived in poverty, disease, and ignorance, a situation in which the enjoyment by the poor and the weak of legal rights . . . became an odious mockery.[8]

Unsurprisingly, Berlin goes on to attack such pure and consistent laissez-faire libertarians as Cobden and Spencer on behalf of such confused and inconsistent classical liberals as Mill and de Tocqueville.

There are several grave and basic problems with Berlin's fulminations. One is a complete ignorance of the modern historians of the Industrial Revolution, such as Ashton, Hayek, Hutt, and Hartwell, who have demonstrated that the new industry alleviated the previous poverty and starvation of the workers, including the child laborers, rather than the contrary. But on a conceptual level, there are grave problems as well. First, that it is absurd and self-contradictory to assert that laissez-faire or economic individualism could have injured person *liberty*; and, second, that Berlin is really explicitly scuttling the very concept of "negative" liberty on behalf of concepts of positive power or wealth.

Berlin reaches the height (or depth) of this approach when he attacks negative liberty directly for having been

> used to . . . arm the strong, the brutal, and the unscrupulous against the humane and the weak. . . . Freedom for the wolves has often meant death to the sheep. The bloodstained story of economic individualism and unrestrained capitalist competition does not . . . today need stressing.[9]

The crucial fallacy of Berlin here is insistently to identify freedom and the free market economy with its opposite – with coercive aggression. Note his repeated use of such terms as "arm," "brutal," "wolves and sheep," and "bloodstained," all of which are applicable *only* to coercive aggression such as has been universally employed by the *State*. Also, he then identifies such aggression with its opposite – the peaceful and voluntary processes of free exchange in the market economy. Unrestrained economic individualism led, on the contrary, to peaceful and harmonious exchange, which benefitted most precisely the "weak" and the "sheep"; it is the latter who could *not* survive in the statist rule of the jungle, who reap the largest share of the benefits from the freely competitive economy. Even a slight acquaintance with economic science, and particularly with the Ricardian Law of Comparative

Advantage, would have set Sir Isaiah straight on this vital point.

Notes

1 Isaiah Berlin, *Two Concepts of Liberty* (Oxford: Oxford University Press, 1958), p. 7.
2 Isaiah Berlin, "Introduction," *Four Essays on Liberty* (Oxford: Oxford University Press, 1969), p. xxxviii.
3 Ibid., p. xxxviii. Also see William A. Parent, "Some Recent Work on the Concept of Liberty," *American Philosophical Quarterly* 11(1974), pp. 149–53. Professor Parent adds the criticism that Berlin neglects the cases in which men act in ways which they do not "truly" want or desire, so that Berlin would have to concede that a man's freedom is not abridged if he is forcibly prevented from doing something he "dislikes." Berlin may be sal-

vaged on this point however, if we interpret "want" or "desire" in the formal sense of a person's freely chosen goal, rather than in the sense of something he emotionally or hedonistically "likes" or enjoys doing or achieving. Ibid., pp. 150–2.
4 Berlin, *Four Essays on Liberty*, p. 122.
5 Ibid., pp. xxxix–xl.
6 Furthermore, if one were to prohibit X from refusing to hire Y because the latter is a redhead, then X has had an obstacle imposed upon his action by an alterable human practice. On Berlin's revised definition of liberty, therefore, the *removing of* obstacles cannot increase liberty, for it can only benefit some people's liberty at the expense of others. [. . .]
7 Parent, "Some Recent Work," pp. 152–3.
8 Berlin, *Four Essays on Liberty*, pp. xlv–xlvi.
9 Ibid., p. xlv.

Murray N. Rothbard, *The Ethics of Liberty* (Atlantic Highlands, NJ: Humanities Press, 1982), pp. 215–18.

Chapter 65

John Rawls, from *A Theory of Justice* (1971)

[...] The inability to take advantage of one's rights and opportunities as a result of poverty and ignorance, and a lack of means generally, is sometimes counted among the constraints definitive of liberty. I shall not, however, say this, but rather I shall think of these things as affecting the worth of liberty, the value to individuals of the rights that the first principle [i.e. equal liberty] defines [see chapter 74, pp. 408–9]. With this understanding, and assuming that the total system of basic liberty is drawn up in the manner just explained, we may note that the two-part basic structure allows a reconciliation of liberty and equality. Thus liberty and the worth of liberty are distinguished as follows: liberty is represented by the complete system of the liberties of equal citizenship, while the worth of liberty to persons and groups depends upon their capacity to advance their ends within the framework the system defines. Freedom as equal liberty is the same for all; the question of compensating for a lesser than equal liberty does not arise. But the worth of liberty is not the same for everyone. Some have greater authority and wealth, and therefore greater means to achieve their aims. The lesser worth of liberty is, however, compensated for, since the capacity of the less fortunate members of society to achieve their aims would be even less were they not to accept the existing inequalities whenever the difference principle [giving priority to the economically and socially disadvantaged] is satisfied. But compensating for the lesser worth of freedom is not to be confused with making good an unequal liberty. Taking the two principles together, the basic structure is to be arranged to maximize the worth to the least advantaged of the complete scheme of equal liberty shared by all. This defines the end of social justice.

John Rawls, *A Theory of Justice* (Cambridge, MA: Harvard University Press, 1971), p. 178.

Chapter 66

Philippe Van Parijs, from *Real Freedom for All* (1995)

[...] [A] minimal and pretty uncontroversial feature of anything that can be called a free society is a system of well-defined and effectively enforced property rights or entitlements (in the weaker sense of the term). No society can be free if its members can constantly be prevented from doing what they might want to do by the arbitrary use of force or threats. If this were the case, the freedom of its weaker members would unavoidably be small indeed. And a free society has been understood throughout as a society whose members are *all* free, or as free as possible. I shall in the sequel assume that whatever institutional set-up is being discussed satisfies this condition of rights security, and ask what set-up of this sort has the strongest claim to embodying the ideal of a society of free people. Though in one way very strong – never a thug in your street, never a thief in your bag – this condition is also very weak. It can in principle be satisfied, for example, by both slavery and collectivism, as these regimes have been defined.

So, the next question is: what are the obstacles which the institutional framework of a free society should abolish, or at least minimize. One prominent issue – the key issue according to such authors as Hayek or Buchanan – is whether or not only *coercion* can count as a freedom-restricting obstacle. What is coercion? According to one prima-facie plausible account, coercion is the restriction of a person's opportunity set, relative to what she is legitimately entitled to. Coercing someone into doing (or not doing) something then

consists in making her do (or not do) it by the use of force or threats, that is, by (credibly) suppressing from the range of options open to her some options she has a right to choose. Bullying someone in the street, threatening to take someone's life, to burn down her house, to tarnish her reputation by slander, or to jeopardize the promotion she is entitled to: these are all cases of coercion. By defining coercion in this way, however, one fails to discriminate among different institutional set-ups that satisfy the security condition stated above. A non-coercive society in this sense is nothing but a society with a perfectly enforced system of rights. But it would – unacceptably – be consistent with a very repressive but law-abiding system of slavery.

Could then coercion not be interpreted, secondly, not as a constraint on people's actions stemming from the (threat of a) violation of whatever rights happen to prevail under a given institutional set-up, but rather, more broadly, as the (threat of a) transgression of a framework of rights which comprises the right of self-ownership? And this is indeed a second element which the above discussion [...] has explicitly recognized as an essential ingredient in the ideal of a free society. Note that self-ownership is here to be understood in a sense that is weak enough to be consistent with the impossibility of actually doing anything with oneself, owing, for example, to not being entitled to stand anywhere; but at the same time in a sense that is strong enough to exclude not just slavery or feudal bondages, but also compulsory schooling or military service and the imposition of lump-sum taxes on people's talents. I shall later take up the question of whether some restrictions of self-ownership may be justified for the sake of strengthening the other features of a free society, and there will be room for significant disagreements on this score. But that institutional restrictions of self-ownership are freedom-restricting is hard to dispute. The genuinely controversial issue is whether there is anything else, apart from coercion in the second and broader of the two senses just mentioned, that can be said to restrict freedom.

Formal Freedom versus Real Freedom

Two positive answers to this question have featured in our earlier discussion [. . .]. The standard libertarian answer can be construed as further extending the concept of coercion (or of aggression) to cover institutional violations of pre-existing rights in external objects: 'The libertarian creed rests upon one central axiom: that no man or group of men may aggress against the person or property of anyone else'.[1] But this position, it was argued above, degrades a genuine concern with people's freedom into an obsession with alleged natural rights, and only owes whatever prima-facie plausibility it may have to a confusion between the weak and the strong notion of entitlement. Another answer was suggested as an alternative to the libertarian view. It asserts that security and self-ownership, though necessary to freedom, are not sufficient for it, because doing anything requires the use of external objects which security and self-ownership alone cannot guarantee.

The move proposed in this second answer has been fiercely resisted by those among the advocates of pure capitalism who claim to give freedom a prominent place, whether or not they share the standard libertarian stance just recalled. Thus, Friedrich Hayek complains about the 'confusion of liberty as power with liberty in its original meaning', which 'inevitably leads to the identification of liberty with wealth': 'whether or not I am my own master and can follow my own choice and whether the possibilities from which I must choose are many or few are two entirely different questions.'[2] 'Even if the threat of starvation to me and perhaps to my family impels me to accept a distasteful job at a very low wage, even if I am "at the mercy" of the only man willing to employ me, I am not coerced by him or anybody else',[3] nor therefore unfree, since freedom is nothing but freedom from coercion. James Buchanan's formulation hardly differs: 'Whether or not an individual has the ability or power to undertake the activity that he is at liberty to undertake is a separate matter, and it can only confuse discussion to equate liberty with ability or power or to extend its meaning to include these qualities.' Freedom, he insists, is 'negative liberty': 'an individual is at liberty or free to carry on an activity if he or she is not coerced from so doing by someone else, be this an individual or a group.' According to proponents of a conception of what he calls 'positive liberty', on the other hand, 'if someone lacks the means to take a round-the-world cruise, then that person is not at liberty to take the cruise, even though no individual or institution is constraining such travel. We believe this to represent a serious conceptual confusion.'

Thus, in the language of Hayek and Buchanan, (appropriately labelled) 'negative liberty' consists in the 'absence of constraint by individuals or institutions', whereas (misleadingly labelled) 'positive liberty' is a matter of power, ability, means, wealth, or size of the opportunity-set. As it stands, however, this distinction does not stick. It is, surely, the social institution of private property (or, as the case may be, of public property) that prevents those who 'lack the means' of taking a round-the-world cruise from getting on to the boat. Moreover, no refining of the definition could make nonsense of the following intuitions: if I am penniless, I am not really free to join the cruise; if I have no option but to starve or to accept a lousy job, I am not really free to turn the latter down. I shall call *opportunity* the third component of freedom which these examples point to. The exact nature of this component clearly requires further clarification, but no semantic trick, *à la* Hayek or Buchanan, should blind us to its existence. I shall use the term *real freedom* to refer to a notion of freedom that incorporates all three components – security, self-ownership, and opportunity – in contrast to *formal freedom*, which only incorporates the first two. Unlike the formal freedom, the opportunity, and hence the real freedom, to do whatever one might want to do can only be a matter of degree. The ideal of a free society must therefore be expressed as a society whose members are maximally free – in a sense to be specified shortly – rather than simply free.

It is worth emphasizing that the choice that has just been made amounts to selecting the broadest possible characterization of freedom-restricting obstacles consistent with the view that lacking freedom is being prevented from doing some of the things one might want to do [. . .]. Abstracting for the time being from the time dimension, any restriction of the opportunity-set is relevant to the assessment of freedom. For example, I can lack the real freedom to swim across a lake despite my being the full owner of myself, not just because I would not be granted permission by the private owner of the lake, but also because my lungs or my limbs would give in before reaching the other side. And this would be the case whether or not this physical inadequacy resulted from deliberate action by other human beings, whether or not other human beings played any role in bringing it about, and also whether or not they could do anything to remove it now. Thus, the conception of real freedom presented above does not merely refuse to confine freedom-restricting obstacles to coercion – whether defined as self-ownership-violation or as right-violation. It also refuses to confine them to obstacles external to the person concerned, or to obstacles

that are produced deliberately, indeed produced at all and/or removable by other human beings.

The strongest objection against this broad definition of real freedom is that it fails to capture the important distinction between what I may and what I can, between prohibitions and incapacities. The objection is not only that the language of freedom has more intuitive appeal in the former context than in the latter. While some stretching undoubtedly needs doing, it does not need to reach beyond a recognizably grey area, in which using the word 'free' is still fully intelligible. Even stating that I am not free to travel faster than light is only slightly odd, if at all. More fundamentally, the objection appeals to the observation that what we are concerned with here is the institutional characterization of a free society, and that an institutional set-up is just a way of distributing 'mays', not 'cans'. Hence, stretching the concept of freedom to encompass both the permission dimension and the capacity dimension of the opportunity-set is pointless anyway, since it is only the former that is relevant to our enterprise. Thus formulated, the objection is useful but misguided. It is plainly wrong to assert that because an institutional set-up is a system of permissions, abilities are irrelevant to the task of determining which set-up has the most favourable impact on opportunity-sets. This is so, in part, because what I may is systematically affected by what I can. To illustrate, just think of the warning that appears on a board off Oxford's Magdalen Bridge in the early spring: 'Experienced punters only'. Less trivially, via our earning power, our personal abilities massively affect what we shall be permitted to acquire. Conversely, what I can – over more than the very short term – is systematically affected by what I may. Whether or not I shall stop limping depends on whether or not my wallet or the waiting list will allow me to have the operation I require. Indeed, whether I shall survive at all depends on my entitlements to shelter, food, and drink. Thus, even though only the permission dimension of the opportunity-set is directly affected by the selection of an institutional set-up, the strong two-way causal relation between permissions and abilities makes it altogether impossible to dismiss the ability dimension as irrelevant to the freedom-based choice of such a set-up.

Note, finally, that, though very broad, the characterization of freedom-restricting obstacles that is being proposed is still narrower than some would like it to be. Personal abilities or talents are internal to the person, and it is therefore correct to say that it is possible for freedom, on this conception, to be restricted by internal as well as external obstacles. Moreover, the internal obstacles can take the form of preferences or desires. Addictions or tendencies to burst into fits of anger or to indulge in spiteful behaviour may genuinely reduce a person's ability to do whatever she might want to do, and the inability to resist such tendencies can therefore count as a freedom-restricting obstacle. However, the class of desires that could therefore count as freedom-restricting according to the view of real freedom that is here being proposed does not include all desires that would be regarded as freedom-restricting if one of the 'positive'

conceptions of freedom had been adopted [. . .]. For a desire to restrict a person's real freedom, it is not sufficient that it should not have been chosen by her. It must also be such that the person could not (sufficiently easily) get rid of it, if only she wanted to. Furthermore, for a desire to be real-freedom-restricting, it is of course not sufficient either (nor indeed necessary) that it should diverge from some normative view about what the person ought to desire. Thus, admitting that there can be internal, and even volitional, obstacles to real freedom as defined does not turn the latter into 'positive freedom' in either of the versions rejected above.

Notes

1 Murray Rothbard, *For a New Liberty* (New York: Macmillan, 1973), p. 23.
2 F. A. Hayek, *The Constitution of Liberty* (London: Routledge & Kegan Paul, 1960), p. 17.
3 Ibid., p. 137.

Philippe Van Parijs, *Real Freedom for All* (Oxford: Oxford University Press, 1995), pp. 20–4.

Chapter 67

G. A. Cohen, from *Self-ownership, Freedom, and Equality* (1995)

2a.   In section 8 of Chapter 1 [of *Self-ownership, Freedom and Equality*] I dealt briefly and bluntly with the relationship between freedom and justice in Nozick. I said that he could not claim that a society in which some are forced to sell their labour power on pain of starvation upheld the value of freedom, but I allowed that he might nevertheless claim that such a society is consistent with the idea of justice. There was a certain lack of nuance in that summation of the position. For, in Nozick's conception, freedom and justice are closely related matters. It was, therefore, a little swift to allow that Nozick might rest his case on justice despite its unsustainability on grounds of freedom. In this section further investigation of the relationship between the two concepts will occur.

2b.   A proponent of D1 [see chapter 37 of this anthology] might respond to the Chamberlain argument by proposing a tax on his earnings. The rate of tax, and the destiny of its proceeds, would be decided by the principles underlying D1. Now, taxation for the sake of equality (or whatever D1 is) will often dampen productivity in a capitalist economy. But let us suppose, as might well be true in the Chamberlain case [. . .], that such a tax would not act as a disincentive, so that we can focus on this distinct question: would the contemplated tax policy be unacceptable because it unjustifiably restricts freedom?

2c.   Well, such a policy undoubtedly removes *certain* freedoms. With the taxing policy, Chamberlain loses the freedom to enter a contract under which he plays basketball and earns a cool quarter of a million, and the fans lose the freedom to enter a contract under which they each pay twenty-five cents and he gains the aforementioned sum. But the removal of *certain* freedoms can be in the interest of freedom itself, and before we conclude that a policy of taxing people like Chamberlain restricts freedom *tout court*, or restricts it unjustifiably, we must check to see whether its removal of *certain* freedoms might not promote other ones that also matter.

How much freedom I have depends on the number and nature of my options. And that in turn depends *both* on the rules of the game *and* on the assets of the players: it is a very important and widely neglected truth that it does not depend on the rules of the game alone.

Suppose that I am the sovereign of an island up on which, from time to time, marooned sailors are washed. At the moment, there is only one washed up sailor, sailor One, in residence. He has built himself a shelter, and, by the rules I, the sovereign, have made, he is the owner of that shelter: he need not part with it, or let anyone else use it. Others will be entitled to use it only if he agrees to let them do so, perhaps for a consideration. And now a storm washes up a second sailor, sailor Two, who, battered by the storm, will probably die unless sailor One lets him shelter, temporarily, in his hut. Under the existing rules, sailor One can legitimately demand the life-long slavery of sailor Two in exchange for letting him shelter. The existing rules permit any kind of contract, including that extreme one, and the sailors' assets and motivations might ensure that that would be the contract that occurs. But, because I am a freedom-loving sovereign, I change the rules so that they forbid slave contracts. Now, we can suppose, sailor Two will get a better deal, under which he will enjoy more freedom. Precisely as a result of the prohibition that I laid down, he now has an option superior to slavery which was unavailable when the rules of contract were more permissive.[1] More permissive rules look unambiguously freedom-promoting only when all we look at is the rules and we ignore, unjustifiably, the asset distribution in which they operate. When a socialist society forbids capitalist acts between consenting adults, some of them will be freer than they otherwise would have been just because of that restriction on everyone's, and, therefore, on their own, freedom.

2d. Let me now relate the foregoing reflections to the less drastic case of Chamberlain and his fans. Taxing him pretty unequivocally reduces Chamberlain's freedom: to think otherwise, you have to believe an implausible story about knock-on effects, or fancy Marxist stuff about how deeply free we all really are when we are all equal together. But it is not at all obvious that preventing the fans from entering a contract whose proceeds will be free of tax reduces *their* freedom. For the prohibition creates an option which is otherwise unavailable to them, to wit, the option of paying twenty-five cents to see Wilt play *without* endowing a member of their society with enormous wealth, and at the same time regaining much of what they pay in benefits financed by a suitably constructed tax policy.

That casts doubt on whether the taxing policy, which removes certain freedoms, is, for all that, to be eschewed out of a respect for freedom. But there is another, and partly distinct, point, to be made, which is that although D1's tax rules restrict freedom, they do so because all rules do, and so, therefore, in particular do the rules which would prevail in the private property free market economy favoured by libertarians. It follows that no one can claim that D1's rules restrict freedom, *by contrast* with the rules that libertarians favour.

Nozick presents himself as a defender of unqualified private property *and* as an unswerving opponent of all restrictions on individual freedom. I claim that he cannot coherently be both, if only because no one who is not an anarchist can be the second, and I now want to drive that point home. With a view to doing so, I shall begin by exploiting a banal truth, so banal, indeed, that, as we shall see, my use of it excited a (wholly misplaced) protest from the pen of John Gray: he was unable to believe that something so banal could be polemically consequential. Having laid out the case to which Gray objected, I shall respond to his complaints.

The banal truth is that, if the state prevents me from doing something that I want to do, then it places a restriction on my freedom. Suppose, then, that I want to perform an action which involves a legally prohibited use of your property. I want, let us say, to pitch a tent in your large back garden, perhaps just in order to annoy you, or perhaps for the more substantial reason that I have nowhere to live and no land of my own, but I have got hold of a tent, legitimately or otherwise. If I now try to do this thing that I want to do, the chances are that the state will intervene on your behalf. If it does, I shall suffer a constraint on my freedom. The same goes, of course, for all unpermitted uses of a piece of private property by those who do not own it, and there are always those who do not own it, since 'private ownership by one person presupposes non-ownership on the part of other persons'.[2] But the free enterprise economy rests upon private property: in that economy you sell and buy what you respectively own and come to own. It follows that libertarians cannot complain that a socialist dispensation restricts freedom, *by contrast* with the dispensation that they themselves favour.

2e. Before proceeding further with the present critique of libertarians, I pause to point out that the banal truth pressed against them here also constitutes an objection to the way that anti-libertarian liberals of the American type often describe the modified capitalism that they favour.

According to Thomas Nagel, who is an anti-libertarian liberal of an especially perspicacious kind, 'progressive taxation' entails 'interference' with individual freedom.[3] He regards the absence of such interference as a value, but one which needs to be compromised for the sake of greater economic and social equality, as what he calls the 'formidable challenge to liberalism . . . from the left' maintains.[4] Yet it is quite unclear that social democratic checks on the sway of private property, through devices like progressive taxation and the welfare minimum, represent *any* enhancement of governmental interference with freedom. The government certainly interferes with a landowner's freedom if it establishes public rights of way and a right for others to pitch tents on his land. But it also interferes with the freedom of would-be walkers or tentpitchers when it prevents them from indulging *their* 'individual inclinations'.[5] The general point is that incursions against private property which *reduce* owners' freedom by transferring rights over resources to non-owners thereby *increase* the latter's freedom. In advance of further argument, the net effect on freedom of the resource transfer is indeterminate.

Libertarians are against what they describe as an 'interventionist' policy in which the state engages in 'interference'. Nagel is not, but he agrees that such a policy 'intervenes' and 'interferes'. In my view, the use of words like 'interventionist' to designate the stated policy is an ideological distortion detrimental to clear thinking and friendly to the libertarian point of view. It is, though friendly to that point of view, consistent with rejecting it, and Nagel does reject it, vigorously. But, by acquiescing

in the libertarian use of 'intervention', he casts libertarianism in a better light than it deserves. The standard use of 'intervention' esteems the private property component in the liberal or social democratic settlement too highly, by associating that component too closely with freedom.

2f. My zeal on behalf of anti-ideological clear-mindedness about 'intervention' and 'interference' prompts me to comment on a well-known sequence of political debate, which runs as follows. The Right extols the freedom enjoyed by all in a liberal capitalist society. The Left complains that the freedom in question is meagre for poor people. The Right rejoins that the Left confuses freedom with resources. 'You are free to do what no one will interfere with your doing', says the Right. 'If you cannot afford to do it, that does not mean that someone will interfere with your doing it, but just that you lack the means or ability to do it. The problem the poor face is lack of ability, not lack of freedom'. The Left may then say that ability should count for as much as freedom does. The Right can then reply, to significant political effect: so *you* may think, but our priority is freedom.

In my view, the depicted right-wing stance depends upon a reified view of money. Money is unlike intelligence or physical strength, poor endowments of which do not, indeed, prejudice freedom, where freedom is understood as absence of interference. The difference between money and those endowments implies, I shall argue, that lack of money *is* (a form of) lack of freedom, in the favoured sense of freedom, where it is taken to be absence of interference.[6]

To see this, begin by imagining a society without money, in which courses of action available to people, courses they are free to follow without interference, are laid down by the law. The law says what each sort of person, or even each particular person, may and may not do without interference, and each person is issued with a set of tickets detailing what she is allowed to do. So I may have a ticket saying that I am free to plough this piece of land, another one saying that I am free to go to that opera, or to walk across that field, while you have different tickets, with different freedoms inscribed on them.

Imagine, now, that the structure of the options written on the tickets is more complex. Each ticket lays out a disjunction of conjunctions of courses of action that I may perform. I may do A and B and C and D OR B and C and D and E OR E and F and G and A, and so on. If I try to do something not licensed by my tickets or ticket, armed force intervenes.

By hypothesis, these tickets say what my freedoms (and, consequently, my unfreedoms) are. But a sum of money is nothing but a highly generalized form of such a ticket. A sum of money is a licence to perform a disjunction of conjunctions of actions – actions, like, for example, visiting one's sister in Bristol, or taking home, and wearing, the sweater on the counter at Selfridge's.

Suppose that someone is too poor to visit her sister in Bristol. She cannot save, from week to week, enough to buy her way there. Then, as far as her freedom is concerned, this is equivalent to 'trip to Bristol' not being written on someone's ticket in the imagined non-monetary economy. The woman I have described has the capacity to go to Bristol. She can board the underground and approach the barrier which she must cross to reach the train. But she will be physically prevented from passing through it, or physically ejected from the train, or, in the other example, she will be physically stopped outside Selfridge's and the sweater will be removed. The only way that she will not be prevented from getting and using such things is by offering money for them.

To have money *is* to have freedom, and the assimilation of money to mental and bodily resources is a piece of unthinking fetishism, in the good old Marxist sense that it misrepresents *social relations of constraint as things* that people lack. In a word: money is no object.

2g.   Here is an objection to the banal argument presented in 2d above. In the course of that argument, I supposed that to prevent someone from doing something that he wants to do is to make him, in that respect, unfree: I am *pro tanto* unfree *whenever* someone interferes with my actions, *whether or not I have a right to perform them, and whether or not my obstructor has a right to interfere with me.* But there is a definition of freedom which informs much libertarian writing and which entails that interference is not a sufficient condition of unfreedom. On that definition, which may be called the *rights definition of freedom*, I am unfree only when someone prevents me from doing what I have a right to do, so that he, consequently, has no right to prevent me from doing it. Nozick was using the rights definition of freedom when he wrote the passage from which I had occasion to quote [. . .] [in chapter 50 of this anthology].

> Other people's actions place limits on one's available opportunities. Whether this makes one's resulting action non-voluntary depends upon whether these others had the right to act as they did.[7]

Now, if one combines this rights definition of freedom with a moral endorsement of private property, with a claim that, in standard cases, people have a moral right to the property that they legally own, then one reaches the result that the protection of (legitimate) private property cannot restrict anyone's freedom. It will follow from the moral endorsement of private property that you and the police are justified in preventing me from pitching my tent on your land, and, because of the rights definition of freedom, it will then further follow that you and the police do not thereby restrict my freedom. So, on the rights definition of freedom, which is, after all, the one that Nozick uses, private property need not, as I contend it must, restrict freedom. It does not restrict freedom if and when the formation and protection of private property proceeds congruently with people's legitimate rights.

2h. I have two replies to this manœuvre against my banal argument. The first reply is that the characterization of freedom exercised in the objection is unacceptable. It is false that, in order to determine whether actions which 'place limits on one's available opportunities' make one (*pro tanto*) unfree, it is necessary to investigate whether the resulting limits on opportunities are wrongfully produced. A properly convicted murderer is rendered unfree when he is justly imprisoned.

That first reply to the objection in 2 g invokes the ordinary use of such terms as 'free' and 'freedom'. My second reply to the objection does not rely on how language is ordinarily used.

Suppose that we overrule ordinary usage and we say, with Nozick, that *rightful* interference with someone's action does not restrict his freedom. It cannot then be argued, without further ado, that interference with private property is wrong *because* it restricts freedom. For one can no longer take for granted, what is evident on a rights-neutral ordinary language conception of freedom, that interference with private property *does* reduce freedom. On a rights account of what freedom is one must abstain from that assertion until one has shown that people have moral rights to their private property. Yet libertarians tend *both* to use a rights definition of freedom *and* to take it for granted that interference with his private property diminishes its owner's freedom. But they can take the latter for granted only on the rights *neutral* account of freedom, on which, however, it is equally obvious that the protection of private property diminishes the freedom of *non*-owners, to avoid which consequence they adopt a rights definition of the concept. And so they go, back and forth, between inconsistent definitions of freedom, not because they cannot make up their minds which one they like better, but under the propulsion of their desire to occupy what is in fact an untenable position. Libertarians want to say that interferences with people's use of their private property are unacceptable because they are,

quite obviously, abridgements of freedom, *and* that the reason why protection of private property does not similarly abridge the freedom on non-owners is that owners have a right to exclude others from their property and non-owners consequently have no right to use it. But they can say both things only if they define freedom in two incompatible ways.

2i. The retreat to the rights definition lands Nozick inside a circle. On the rights definition of freedom, a person is entirely free when he is not prevented from performing any action that he has a right to perform: on the rights definition, interfering with a person interferes with his freedom only if the interfering person lacks the right to commit the given interference. Accordingly, to know whether a person is free, in the rights-laden sense of the term, we have to know what his (and others') rights are. But what characterization of people's rights does Nozick provide? Either no characterization at all, or a characterization in terms of freedom, something like: people have those rights the possession of which secures their freedom.

Thereby Nozick locks himself inside a circle. For Nozick, there is justice, which is to say no violation of anyone's rights, when there is lack of coercion, which means that there is justice when there is no restriction on freedom. But freedom is then itself defined in terms of non-violation of rights, and the result is a tight definitional circle and no purchase either on the concept of freedom or on the concept of justice.

2j. Let me show how the circularity in Nozick's conceptions of freedom and justice affects principle (1):

(1) Whatever arises from a just situation by just steps is itself just.

To apply (1), we have to know that makes steps just. Nozick's answer is that they are just when voluntarily performed, or coercion-free. But, when we now ask what voluntary performance is, we are told that someone's action is voluntary, no matter how limited his opportunities were, if and only if there was no injustice in the production of the limitation on his opportunities. And that creates a circle: justice in transfer is defined in terms of voluntariness and voluntariness is defined in terms of justice. I think that the first definition is mistaken and that the second is a ridiculous deviation from ordinary language, but the present different point is that, under such ways with words, we cannot use either freedom or justice as a criterion of evaluation.

Notes

1   To be sure, sailor One loses an option which contributed to his freedom, and, *ceteris paribus*, gains no freedom by way of compensation. Suppose, then, that the (good) sense in which I am a freedom-loving sovereign is that I want the person who is least free to be as free as possible.

2   Karl Marx, *Capital*, Vol. III, p. 812.

3   Nagel believes that libertarians go too far towards the liberty end of a spectrum on which leftists go too far towards the equality end: 'Libertari-

anism . . . fastens on one of the two elements [that is, freedom and equality – GAC] of the liberal ideal and asks why its realization should be inhibited by the demands of the other. Instead of embracing the ideal of equality and the general welfare, libertarianism exalts the claim of individual freedom of action and asks why state power should be permitted even the interference represented by progressive taxation and public provision of health care, education and a minimum standard of living' (Thomas Nagel, 'Libertarianism Without Foundation', *Yale Law Journal* 85 (1975), p. 192).

4   Ibid., p. 191.

5   Ibid., p. 191.

6   Accordingly, poverty should not be bracketed with illness and lack of education and thereby treated in the manner of the Commission on Social Justice, as a restriction on 'what [people] can do with their freedom' [. . .]. Poverty restricts freedom itself, and social democrats needlessly accede to the Right's misrepresentation of the relationship between poverty and freedom when they make statements like the just quoted.

7   Robert Nozick, *Anarchy, State and Utopia* (New York: Basic Books, 1974), p. 262.

G. A. Cohen, *Self-ownership, Freedom, and Equality* (Cambridge: Cambridge University Press 1995), pp. 53–61.

Chapter 68

Amartya Sen, from *Inequality Reexamined* (1992)

Equality of What?

Why Equality? What Equality?

Two central issues for ethical analysis of equality are: (1) Why equality? (2) Equality of what? The two questions are distinct but thoroughly interdependent. We cannot begin to defend or criticize equality without knowing what on earth we are talking about, i.e. equality of what features (e.g. incomes, wealths, opportunities, achievements, freedoms, rights)? We cannot possibly answer the first question without addressing the second. That seems obvious enough.

But if we *do* answer question (2), do we still *need* to address question (1)? If we have successfully argued in favour of equality of x (whatever that x is – some outcome, some right, some freedom, some respect, or some something else), then we have already argued for equality in *that* form, with x as the standard of comparison. Similarly, if we have rebutted the claim to equality of x, then we have already argued against equality in that form, with x as the standard of comparison. There is, in this view, no 'further', no 'deeper', question to be answered about why – or why not – 'equality'. Question (1), in this analysis, looks very much like the poor man's question (2).

There is some sense in seeing the matter in this way, but there is also a more interesting substantive issue here. It relates to the fact that every normative theory of social arrangement that has at all stood the test of time seems to demand equality of *something* – something that is regarded as particularly important in that theory. The theories involved are diverse and frequently at war with each other, but they still seem to have that common feature. In the contemporary disputes in political philosophy, equality does, of course, figure prominently in the contributions of John Rawls (equal liberty and equality in the distribution of 'primary goods'), Ronald Dworkin ('treatment as equals', 'equality of resources'), Thomas Nagel ('economic equality'), Thomas Scanlon ('equality'), and others generally associated with a 'pro equality' view. But equality in some space seems to be demanded even by those who are typically seen as having disputed the 'case for equality' or for 'distributive justice'. For example, Robert Nozick may not demand equality of utility or equality of holdings of primary goods, but he does demand equality of libertarian rights – no one has any more right to liberty than anyone else. James Buchanan builds equal legal and political treatment – indeed a great deal more – into his view of a good society. In each theory, equality *is* sought in some space – a space that is seen as having a central role in that theory.

But what about utilitarianism? Surely, utilitarians do not, in general, want the equality of the total utilities enjoyed by different people. The utilitarian formula requires the maximization of the sum-total of the utilities of all people *taken together*, and that is, in an obvious sense, not particularly egalitarian. In fact, the equality that utilitarianism seeks takes the form of equal treatment of human beings in the space of *gains and losses of utilities*. There is an insistence on equal weights on everyone's utility gains in the utilitarian objective function.

This diagnosis of 'hidden' egalitarianism in utilitarian philosophy might well be resisted on the ground that utilitarianism really involves a sum-total maximizing approach, and it might be thought that, as a result, any egalitarian feature of utilitarianism cannot be more than accidental. But this reasoning is deceptive. The utilitarian approach is undoubtedly a *maximizing* one, but the real question is what is the nature of the objective function it maximizes. That objective function could have been quite inegalitarian, e.g. giving much more weight to the utilities of some than to those of others. Instead, utilitarianism attaches exactly the same importance to the utilities of all people in the objective function, and that feature – coupled with the maximizing format – guarantees that everyone's utility gains get the same weight in the maximizing exercise. The egalitarian foundation is, thus, quite central to the entire utilitarian exercise. Indeed, it is precisely this egalitarian feature that relates to the foundational principle of utilitarianism of 'giving equal weight to the equal interests of all the parties' (Hare), or to 'always assign the same weight to all individuals' interests' (Harsanyi).

What do we conclude from this fact? One obvious conclusion is that being egalitarian (i.e. egalitarian in *some space or other* to which great importance is attached) is not really a 'uniting' feature. Indeed, it is precisely because there are such substantive differences between the endorsement of different spaces in which equality is recommended by different authors that the basic similarity between them (in the form of wanting equality in *some* space that is seen as important) can be far from transparent. This is especially so when the term 'equality' is defined – typically implicitly – as equality in a *particular* space.

For example, in his interesting essay, 'The Case against Equality', with which William Letwin introduces an important collection of papers by different authors on that theme (the volume is called *Against Equality*), he argues against equal distribution of incomes (or commodities) thus: 'Inasmuch as people are unequal, it is rational to presume that they ought to be treated unequally – which might mean larger shares for the needy or larger shares for the worthy' ('A Theoretical Weakness of Egalitarianism', p. 8). But even the demand for equal satisfaction of 'needs' is a requirement of equality (in a particular space), and it has indeed been championed as such for a long time. Even though the idea of individual 'worth' is harder to characterize, the usual formulations of the demand for 'larger shares for the worthy' tend to include equal treatment for equal worth, giving to each the same reward for worth as is given to another. Thus, these critiques of egalitarianism tend to take the form of being – instead – egalitarian in some *other* space. The problem again reduces to arguing, implicitly, for a different answer to the question 'equality of what?'.

Sometimes the question 'equality of what?' gets *indirectly* addressed in apparently discussing 'why equality?', with equality defined in a *specific* space. For example, Harry Frankfurt's well-reasoned paper attacking 'equality as a moral ideal' is concerned mainly with disputing the claims of *economic* egalitarianism in the form of 'the doctrine that it is desirable for everyone to have the same amounts of income and wealth (for short, "money")'.[1] Though the language of the presentation puts 'egalitarianism' as such in the dock, this is primarily because Frankfurt uses that general term to refer specifically to a particular version of 'economic egalitarianism': 'This version of economic egalitarianism (for short, simply "egalitarianism") might also be formulated as the doctrine that there should be no inequalities in the *distribution* of money.'[2]

The choice of space for equality is, thus, central to Frankfurt's main thesis. His arguments can be seen as disputing the specific demand for a common interpretation of economic egalitarianism by arguing (1) that such an equality is of no great intrinsic interest, *and* (2) that it leads to the violation of intrinsically important values – values that link closely to the need for paying equal attention to all in some other – more relevant – way.

Wanting equality of *something* – something seen as *important* – is undoubtedly a similarity of some kind, but that similarity does not put the warring camps on the same side. It only shows that the battle is not, in an important sense, about 'why equality?', but about 'equality of what?'.

Since some spaces are traditionally associated with claims of 'equality' in political or social or economic philosophy, it is equality in one of those spaces (e.g. incomes, wealths, utilities) that tend to go under the heading 'egalitarianism'. I am *not* arguing against the continued use of the term 'egalitarianism' in one of those senses; there is no harm in that practice if it is understood to be a claim about equality in a specific space (and by implication, *against* equality in other spaces). But it is important to recognize the limited reach of that usage, and also the fact that demanding equality in one space – no matter how hallowed by tradition – can lead one to be anti-egalitarian in some other space, the comparative importance of which in the overall assessment has to be critically assessed.

[. . .]

Equality versus Liberty?

The importance of equality is often constrasted with that of liberty. Indeed, someone's position in the alleged conflict between equality and liberty has often been seen as a good indicator of his or her general outlook on political philosophy and political economy. For example, not only are libertarian thinkers (such as Nozick) seen as anti-

egalitarian, but they are diagnosed as anti-egalitarian *precisely because* of their overriding concern with liberty. Similarly, those diagnosed as egalitarian thinkers [. . .] may appear to be less concerned with liberty precisely because they are seen as being wedded to the demands of equality.

In the light of the discussion in the previous sections, we must argue that this way of seeing the relationship between equality and liberty is altogether faulty. Libertarians must think it important that people should have liberty. Given this, questions would immediately arise regarding: *who, how much, how distributed, how equal?* Thus the issue of equality immediately arises as a *supplement* to the assertion of the importance of liberty.[3] The libertarian proposal has to be completed by going on to characterize the distribution of rights among the people involved. In fact, the libertarian demands for liberty typically include important features of 'equal liberty', e.g. the insistence on equal immunity from interference by others. The belief that liberty is important cannot, thus, be in conflict with the view that it is important that the social arrangements be devised to promote equality of liberties that people have.

There can, of course, be a conflict between a person who argues for the equality of some variable *other than* liberty (such as income or wealth or well-being) and someone who wants only equal liberty. But that is a dispute over the question 'equality of *what*?' Similarly, a distribution-independent general promotion of liberty (i.e. promoting it wherever possible without paying attention to the distributive pattern) could, of course, conflict with equality of some other variable, say, income, but that would be (1) partly a conflict between concentrating respectively on liberty and on incomes, and (2) partly one between a concern for distributive patterns (of incomes in this case) and non-distributive aggregative considerations (applied to liberty). It is neither accurate nor helpful to think of the difference in either case in terms of 'liberty *versus* equality'.

Indeed, strictly speaking, posing the problem in terms of this latter contrast reflects a 'category mistake'. They are not alternatives. Liberty is among the possible *fields of application* of equality, and equality is among the possible *patterns* of distribution of liberty.[4]

As was discussed earlier, the need to face explicitly the choice of space is an inescapable part of the specification and reasoned evaluation of the demands of equality. There are, at one end, demands of equal libertarian rights only, and at the other end, various exacting demands of equality regarding an extensive list of *achievements* and also a corresponding list of *freedoms* to achieve. [. . .]

Notes

1 Harry Frankfurt, "Equality as a Moral Ideal," *Ethics* 98 (1987), p. 21.
2 Ibid.

3 There can be quite different ways of defending the importance of liberty. One distinction relates to the different concepts of goodness and rightness. First, liberty can be seen as a *good* thing that people should have, and the violation of liberty may be seen as making the state of affairs less good. Second, liberty may be taken to be not a part of the idea of goodness, but a feature of *right* social arrangements. There are distinctions – not unrelated to the above contrast – also between what duties *others* have if someone's liberties are violated.

4 There can, of course, be some ambiguity regarding what is called a 'pattern'. Sometimes the term 'pattern' may be used to impose particular specifications of constituent characteristics, e.g. the Union Jack demands some blue and some red. The appropriate analogy for equality and liberty is with the distinction between, say, the pattern of intensities of colours (e.g. the same intensity for each unit, or maximal intensity altogether), and the use of particular colours (e.g. blue) the intensities of which are examined.

Amartya Sen, *Inequality Reexamined* (Oxford: Oxford University Press, 1992), pp. 12–16, 21–3.

Part VIII

Liberalism and the Value of Freedom

Introduction to Part VIII

The primary concern of this part of the anthology is not the nature of freedom, but its value. While philosophers disagree over whether the nature of freedom can be discussed independently of ideas about its value, the main concern of the authors of this section is to examine the reasons we have for saying that the state should promote or respect freedom, assuming a prior understanding of what freedom *is*. The positions advocated here can all be called liberal in a broad sense, where "liberalism" is taken to include both the libertarian and the liberal egalitarian positions defended in Part VII. The various authors disagree over what exactly a constraint on freedom amounts to, but they share an interest in investigating why – and in what ways – we value being in a position to make choices among an array of options.

One important question addressed here is whether freedom of choice has intrinsic value, or is only a means to other goods, either for the individual or for society as a whole. This issue has been discussed by Amartya Sen, Thomas Hurka, Joel Feinberg, and Ian Carter among others. If freedom is intrinsically valuable, then it is apparently a good thing in itself for a person to have more options rather than less. Some have objected to this view that it would seem to imply the rationality of an insatiable desire for options. Is it better to have a choice among 50 different brands of soap powder than a choice among 40? Others worry that assigning only instrumental value to freedom will prove incompatible with the liberal belief in freedom as a fundamental value. Still others bite the bullet and deny that liberals prize freedom "as such," claiming instead that only certain specific freedoms have value, and that the value of specific freedoms derives from their contribution to those ideals that *are* fundamental for liberals. This last view is defended by Ronald Dworkin, for whom the fundamental liberal value is that of equal concern and respect.

If freedom has merely instrumental value, what is the good that it brings about? On one influential view dating back at least to the Enlightenment, the relevant good is human progress, which in turn is seen either as an end in itself or as a means to increased human happiness. Such is the view of J. S. Mill, of

Friedrich von Hayek, and of Karl Popper. Because progress involves the discovery of that which is not yet known, we are unable to say in which direction it will take us, and the state is incapable of directing our behavior in such a way as to produce it. Only individual experimentation will show us the way, and people therefore need to be given as much freedom as possible to make mistakes and to learn from them. This argument has been applied to various kinds of progress: not only to economic progress, but also to social and scientific and even moral progress.

The argument from progress posits a large-scale empirical correlation (between freedom and progress), and such correlations are, of course, open to contestation by social scientists. The argument might also be contested at a conceptual level, by those who would deny that we have a clear idea of what progress is or why it is valuable.

Other liberal philosophers, including John Rawls and Joseph Raz, have defended freedom as a means to, or as a constitutive element of, individual well-being, rather than as something that brings about a more distant and collective good, like progress. For them, individual freedom is good because it is good for the individual who possesses it. Many liberals argue that the availability of a range of choice is beneficial because it induces each of us to reflect on our own values and so to behave more autonomously. Rawls avoids assuming that an autonomous life is the best form of life, but nevertheless sees freedom as one of the "primary goods" – or all-purpose means – required for the individual's development of two basic moral powers: the capacity for a conception of the good and the capacity for a sense of justice.

One of the background assumptions in liberal defenses of the value of freedom, especially evident in the work of Rawls, Raz, and Isaiah Berlin, is the presence in society of a plurality of conflicting ideas about what it is to lead a good life. There are at least two ways of taking account of this plurality of conceptions of the good. First, one may simply view it as a fact of life in contemporary societies that people disagree about the nature of the good life – regardless of where one stands oneself on such issues – and one may contend that the only way to respect such conflicting conceptions of the good is by granting the freedom to pursue them within the constraints imposed by a respect for other conceptions of the good. Secondly, and more radically, one may assume value pluralism as a substantive ethical position and claim that the ends of life are themselves many and varied, and indeed incompatible and incommensurable. The value of individual freedom is taken to follow from such a value-pluralist stance on the ground that value pluralism itself renders individual choice among values a basic human need.

It should be emphasized that not all liberals believe in value pluralism as a substantive ethical position. Utilitarians, who often view liberty as a component of individual well-being as well as a means to social progress, see all values – including liberty itself – as ultimately reducible to utility. Historically, the utilitarian tradition has played an important part in the development of liberalism and the promotion of individual freedom and diversity.

Further Reading

Berlin, Isaiah, "John Stuart Mill and the Ends of Life," in I. Berlin, *Liberty* (Oxford: Oxford University Press, 2002) ⟨interpretation of Mill's thought assigning a central role to his views on the value of liberty⟩.

Dworkin, Gerald, *The Theory and Practice of Autonomy* (Cambridge: Cambridge University Press, 1988), ch. 5 ⟨critique of the assumption that more choice is always better than less⟩.

Dworkin, Ronald, *Sovereign Virtue: The Theory and Practice of Equality* (Cambridge, MA: Harvard University Press, 2000), ch. 3 ⟨theory assigning market freedoms an instrumental role in establishing equality of resources⟩.

Hees, Martin van, *Legal Reductionism and Freedom* (Dordrecht: Kluwer, 2000), ch. 8 ⟨analysis of specific versus non-specific value of freedom⟩.

Pettit, Philip, *Republicanism: A Theory of Freedom and Government* (Oxford: Oxford University Press, 1997), chs. 3 and 4 ⟨comparison of the values of negative freedom and freedom as non-domination⟩.

Chapter 69

J. S. Mill, from
On Liberty (1859)

[. . .]

Like other tyrannies, the tyranny of the majority was at first, and is still vulgarly, held in dread, chiefly as operating through the acts of the public authorities. But reflecting persons perceived that when society is itself the tyrant – society collectively, over the separate individuals who compose it – its means of tyrannizing are not restricted to the acts which it may do by the hands of its political functionaries. Society can and does execute its own mandates: and if it issues wrong mandates instead of right, or any mandates at all in things with which it ought not to meddle, it practices a social tyranny more formidable than many kinds of political oppression, since, though not usually upheld by such extreme penalties, it leaves fewer means of escape, penetrating much more deeply into the details of life, and enslaving the soul itself. Protection, therefore, against the tyranny of the magistrate is not enough: there needs protection also against the tyranny of the prevailing opinion and feeling; against the tendency of society to impose, by other means than civil penalties, its own ideas and practices as rules of conduct on those who dissent from them; to fetter the development, and, if possible, prevent the formation, of any individuality not in harmony with its ways, and compel all characters to fashion themselves upon the model of its own. There is a limit to the legitimate interference of collective opinion with individual independence: and to find that limit, and maintain it against encroachment, is as indispensable to

a good condition of human affairs, as protection against political despotism.

[. . .]

The object of this Essay is to assert one very simple principle, as entitled to govern absolutely the dealings of society with the individual in the way of compulsion and control, whether the means used be physical force in the form of legal penalties, or the moral coercion of public opinion. That principle is, that the sole end for which mankind are warranted, individually or collectively, in interfering with the liberty of action of any of their number, is self-protection. That the only purpose for which power can be rightfully exercised over any member of a civilized community, against his will, is to prevent harm to others. His own good, either physical or moral, is not a sufficient warrant. He cannot rightfully be compelled to do or forbear because it will be better for him to do so, because it will make him happier, because, in the opinions of others, to do so would be wise, or even right. These are good reasons for remonstrating with him, or reasoning with him, or persuading him, or entreating him, but not for compelling him, or visiting him with any evil in case he do otherwise. To justify that, the conduct from which it is desired to deter him, must be calculated to produce evil to some one else. The only part of the conduct of any one, for which he is amenable to society, is that which concerns others. In the part which merely concerns himself, his independence is, of right, absolute. Over himself, over his own body and mind, the individual is sovereign.

[. . .]

It is proper to state that I forgo any advantage which could be derived to my argument from the idea of abstract right, as a thing independent of utility. I regard utility as the ultimate appeal on all ethical questions; but it must be utility in the largest sense, grounded on the permanent interests of man as a progressive being. Those interests, I contend, authorize the subjection of individual spontaneity to external control, only in respect to those actions of each, which concern the interest of other people. If any one does an act hurtful to others, there is a prima facie case for punishing him, by law, or, where legal penalties are not safely applicable, by general disapprobation. There are also many positive acts for the benefit of others, which he may rightfully be compelled to perform; such as, to give evidence in a court of justice; to bear his fair share in the common defence, or in any other joint work necessary to the interest of the society of which he enjoys the protection; and to perform certain acts of individual beneficence, such as saving a fellow creature's life, or interposing to protect the defenceless against ill-usage, things which whenever it is obviously a man's duty to do, he may rightfully be made responsible to society for not doing. A person may cause evil to others not only by his actions but by his inaction, and in either case he is justly accountable to them for the injury. The latter case, it is true, requires a much more cautious exercise of compulsion than the former.

To make any one answerable for doing evil to others, is the rule; to make him answerable for not preventing evil, is, comparatively speaking, the exception. Yet there are many cases clear enough and grave enough to justify that exception. In all things which regard the external relations of the individual, he is *de jure* amenable to those whose interests are concerned, and if need be, to society as their protector. There are often good reasons for not holding him to the responsibility; but

these reasons must arise from the special expediencies of the case: either because it is a kind of case in which he is on the whole likely to act better, when left to his own discretion, than when controlled in any way in which society have it in their power to control him; or because the attempt to exercise control would produce other evils, greater than those which it would prevent. When such reasons as these preclude the enforcement of responsibility, the conscience of the agent himself should step into the vacant judgement-seat, and protect those interests of others which have no external protection; judging himself all the more rigidly, because the case does not admit of his being made accountable to the judgement of his fellow creatures.

But there is a sphere of action in which society, as distinguished from the individual, has, if any, only an indirect interest; comprehending all that portion of a person's life and conduct which affects only himself, or if it also affects others, only with their free, voluntary, and undeceived consent and participation. When I say only himself, I mean directly, and in the first instance: for whatever affects himself, may affect others through himself; and the objection which may be grounded on this contingency will receive consideration in the sequel. This, then, is the appropriate region of human liberty. It comprises, first, the inward domain of consciousness; demanding liberty of conscience, in the most comprehensive sense; liberty of thought and feeling; absolute freedom of opinion and sentiment on all subjects, practical or speculative, scientific, moral, or theological. The liberty of expressing and publishing opinions may seem to fall under a different principle, since it belongs to that part of the conduct of an individual which concerns other people; but, being almost of as much importance as the liberty of thought itself, and resting in great part on the same reasons, is practically inseparable from it. Secondly, the principle requires liberty of tastes and pursuits; of framing the plan of our life to suit our own character; of doing as we like, subject to such consequences as may follow:

without impediment from our fellow creatures, so long as what we do does not harm them, even though they should think our conduct foolish, perverse, or wrong. Thirdly, from this liberty of each individual, follows the liberty, within the same limits, of combination among individuals; freedom to unite, for any purpose not involving harm to others: the persons combining being supposed to be of full age, and not forced or deceived.

No society in which these liberties are not, on the whole, respected, is free, whatever may be its form of government; and none is completely free in which they do not exist absolute and unqualified. The only freedom which deserves the name, is that of pursuing our own good in our own way, so long as we do not attempt to deprive others of theirs, or impede their efforts to obtain it. Each is the proper guardian of his own health, whether bodily, or mental and spiritual. Mankind are greater gainers by suffering each other to live as seems good to themselves, than by compelling each to live as seems good to the rest.

John Stuart Mill, *On Liberty and Other Essays*, ed. John Gray (Oxford: Oxford University Press, 1991), pp. 8–9, 13–19.

Chapter 70

J. S. Mill, from
On Liberty (1859)

Of Individuality, as One of the Elements of Well-being

Such being the reasons which make it imperative that human beings should be free to form opinions, and to express their opinions without reserve; and such the baneful consequences to the intellectual, and through that to the moral nature of man, unless this liberty is either conceded, or asserted in spite of prohibition; let us next examine whether the same reasons do not require that men should be free to act upon their opinions – to carry these out in their lives, without hindrance, either physical or moral, from their fellow men, so long as it is at their own risk and peril. This last proviso is of course indispensable. No one pretends that actions should be as free as opinions. On the contrary, even opinions lose their immunity, when the circumstances in which they are expressed are such as to constitute their expression a positive instigation to some mischievous act. An opinion that corn-dealers are starvers of the poor, or that private property is robbery, ought to be unmolested when simply circulated through the press, but may justly incur punishment when delivered orally to an excited mob assembled before the house of a corn-dealer, or when handed about among the same mob in the form of a placard. Acts, of whatever kind, which, without justifiable cause, do harm to others, may be, and in the more important cases absolutely require to be, controlled by the unfavourable sentiments, and, when needful, by the active interference of mankind. The liberty of the individual must be thus far limited; he must not make himself a nuisance to other people. But if he refrains from molesting others in what concerns them, and merely acts according to his own inclination and judgement in things which concern himself, the same reasons which show that opinion should be free, prove also that he should be allowed, without molestation, to carry his opinions into practice at his own cost. That mankind are not infallible; that their truths, for the most part, are only half-truths; that unity of opinion, unless resulting from the fullest and freest comparison of opposite opinions, is not desirable, and diversity not an evil, but a good, until mankind are much more capable than at present of recognizing all sides of the truth, are principles applicable to men's modes of action, not less than to their opinions. As it is useful that while mankind are imperfect there should be different opinions, so is it that there should be different experiments of living; that free scope should be given to varieties of character, short of injury to others; and that the worth of different modes of life should be proved practically, when any one thinks fit to try them. It is desirable, in short, that in things which do not primarily concern others, individuality should assert itself. Where, not the person's own character, but the traditions or customs of other people are the rule of conduct, there is wanting one of the principal ingredients of human happiness, and quite the chief ingredient of individual and social progress.

In maintaining this principle, the greatest difficulty to be encountered does not lie in the appreciation of means towards an acknowledged end, but in the indifference of persons in general to the end itself. If it were felt that the free development of individuality is one of the leading essentials of well-being; that it is not only a co-ordinate element with all that is designated by the terms civilization, instruction, education, culture, but is itself a necessary part and condition of all those things; there would be no danger that liberty should be undervalued, and the adjustment of the boundaries between it and social control would present no extraordinary difficulty. But the evil is, that individual spontaneity is hardly recognized by the common modes of thinking, as having any intrinsic worth, or deserving any regard on its own account. The majority, being satisfied with the ways of mankind as they now are (for it is they who make them what they are), cannot comprehend why those ways should not be good enough for everybody; and what is more, spontaneity forms no part of the ideal of the majority of moral and social reformers, but is rather looked on with jealousy, as a troublesome and perhaps rebellious obstruction to the general acceptance of what these reformers, in their own judgement, think would be best for mankind. Few persons, out of Germany, even comprehend the meaning of the doctrine which Wilhelm von Humboldt, so eminent both as a savant and as a politician, made the text of a treatise – that 'the end of man, or that which is prescribed by the eternal or immutable dictates of reason, and not suggested by vague and transient desires, is the highest and most harmonious development of his powers to a complete and consistent whole'; that, therefore, the object 'towards which every human being must ceaselessly direct his efforts, and on which especially those who design to influence their fellow men must ever keep their eyes, is the individuality of power and development'; that

for this there are two requisites, 'freedom, and variety of situations'; and that from the union of these arise 'individual vigour and manifold diversity', which combine themselves in 'originality'.

Little, however, as people are accustomed to a doctrine like that of von Humboldt, and surprising as it may be to them to find so high a value attached to individuality, the question, one must nevertheless think, can only be one of degree. No one's idea of excellence in conduct is that people should do absolutely nothing but copy one another. No one would assert that people ought not to put into their mode of life, and into the conduct of their concerns, any impress whatever of their own judgement, or of their own individual character. On the other hand, it would be absurd to pretend that people ought to live as if nothing whatever had been known in the world before they came into it; as if experience had as yet done nothing towards showing that one mode of existence, or of conduct, is preferable to another. Nobody denies that people should be so taught and trained in youth, as to know and benefit by the ascertained results of human experience. But it is the privilege and proper condition of a human being, arrived at the maturity of his faculties, to use and interpret experience in his own way. It is for him to find out what part of recorded experience is properly applicable to his own circumstances and character. The traditions and customs of other people are, to a certain extent, evidence of what their experience has taught *them*; presumptive evidence, and as such, have a claim to his deference: but, in the first place, their experience may be too narrow; or they may not have interpreted it rightly. Secondly, their interpretation of experience may be correct, but unsuitable to him. Customs are made for customary circumstances, and customary characters; and his circumstances or his character may be uncustomary. Thirdly, though the customs be both good as customs, and suitable to him, yet to conform to custom, merely *as* custom, does not educate or develop in him any of the qualities which are the distinctive endowment of a human being. The human faculties of perception, judgement, discriminative feeling, mental activity, and even moral preference, are exercised only in making a choice. He who does anything because it is the custom, makes no choice. He gains no practice either in discerning or in desiring what is best. The mental and moral, like the muscular powers, are improved only by being used. The faculties are called into no exercise by doing a thing merely because others do it, no more than by believing a thing only because others believe it. If the grounds of an opinion are not conclusive to the person's own reason, his reason cannot be strengthened, but is likely to be weakened, by his adopting it: and if the inducements to an act are not such as are consentaneous to his own feelings and character (where affection, or the rights of others, are not concerned) it is so much done towards rendering his feelings and character inert and torpid, instead of active and energetic.

He who lets the world, or his own portion of it, choose his plan of life for him, has no need of any other faculty than the ape-like one of imitation. He who chooses his plan for himself, employs all his faculties. He must use observation to see, reasoning and judgement to foresee, activity to gather materials for decision, discrimination to decide, and when he has decided, firmness and self-control to hold to his deliberate decision. And these qualities he requires and exercises exactly in proportion as the part of his conduct which he determines according to his own judgement and feelings is a large one. It is possible that he might be guided in some good path, and kept out of harm's way, without any of these things. But what will be his comparative worth as a human being? It really is of importance, not only what men do, but also what manner of men they are that do it. Among the works of man, which human life is rightly employed in perfecting and beautifying, the first in importance surely is man himself. Supposing it were possible to get houses built, corn grown, battles fought, causes tried, and even churches erected and prayers said, by machinery – by automatons in human form – it would be a considerable loss to exchange for these automatons even the men and women who at present inhabit the more civilized parts of the world, and who assuredly are but starved specimens of what nature can and will produce. Human nature is not a machine to be built after a model, and set to do exactly the work prescribed for it, but a tree, which requires to grow and develop itself on all sides, according to the tendency of the inward forces which make it a living thing.

John Stuart Mill, *On Liberty and Other Essays*, ed. John Gray (Oxford: Oxford University Press, 1991), pp. 62–6.

Chapter 71

Karl R. Popper, from *The Poverty of Historicism* (1957)

[...]

Comte and Mill, it will be remembered, held that progress was an unconditional or absolute trend, which is *reducible to the laws of human nature*. 'A law of succession,' writes Comte, 'even when indicated with all possible authority by the method of historical observation, ought not to be finally admitted before it has been rationally reduced to the positive theory of human nature . . .' He believes that the law of progress is deducible from a tendency in human individuals which impels them to perfect their nature more and more. In all this, Mill follows him completely, trying to reduce his law of progress to what he calls the 'progressiveness of the human mind' whose first 'impelling force . . . is the desire of increased material comforts'. According to both Comte and Mill the unconditional or absolute character of this trend or quasi-law enables us to deduce from it the first steps or phases of history, without requiring any initial historical conditions or observations or data. In principle, the whole course of history should be thus deducible; the only difficulty being, as Mill puts it, that 'so long a series . . . , each successive term being composed of an even greater number and variety of parts, could not possibly be computed by human faculties.'

The weakness of this 'reduction' of Mill's seems obvious. Even if we should grant Mill's premises and deductions, it still would not follow that the social or historical effect will be significant. Progress might be rendered negligible, say, by losses due to an unmanageable natural environment. Besides, the premises are based on only one side of 'human nature' without considering other sides such as forgetfulness or indolence. Thus where we observe the precise opposite of the progress described by Mill, there we can equally well 'reduce' these observations to 'human nature' (Is it not, indeed, one of the most popular devices of so-called historical theories to explain the decline and fall of empires by such traits as idleness and a propensity to over-eat?) In fact we can conceive of very few events which could not be plausibly explained by an appeal to certain propensities of 'human nature'. But a method that can explain everything that might happen explains nothing.

If we wish to replace this surprisingly naïve theory by a more tenable one, we have to take two steps. First, we have to attempt to find *conditions* of progress, and to this end we must apply the principle set out [earlier]: we must try to imagine *conditions under which progress would be arrested*. This immediately leads to the realization that a *psychological propensity alone* cannot be sufficient to explain progress, since conditions may be found on which it may depend. Thus we must, next, replace the theory of psychological propensities by something better; I suggest, by an *institutional* (and technological) analysis of the conditions of progress.

How could we arrest scientific and industrial progress? By closing down, or by controlling, laboratories for research, by suppressing or controlling scientific periodicals and other means of discussion, by suppressing scientific congresses and conferences, by suppressing Universities and other schools, by suppressing books, the printing press, writing, and, in the end, speaking. All these things which indeed might be suppressed (or controlled) are social institutions. Language is a social institution without which scientific progress is unthinkable, since without it there can be neither science nor a growing and progressive tradition. Writing is a social institution, and so are the organizations for printing and publishing and all the other institutional instruments of scientific method. Scientific method itself has social aspects. Science, and more especially scientific progress, are the results not of isolated efforts but of the *free competition of thought*. For science needs ever more competition between hypotheses and ever more rigorous tests. And the competing hypotheses need personal representation, as it were: they need advocates, they need a jury, and even a public. This personal representation must be institutionally organized if we wish to ensure that it works. And these institutions have to be paid for, and protected by law. Ultimately, progress depends very largely on political factors; on political institutions that safeguard the freedom of thought: on democracy.

It is of some interest that what is usually called '*scientific objectivity*' is based, to some extent, on social institutions. The naïve view that scientific objectivity rests on the mental or psychological attitude of the individual scientist, on his training, care, and scientific detachment, generates as a reaction the sceptical view that scientists can never be objective. On this view their lack of objectivity may be negligible in the natural sciences where their passions are not excited, but for the social sciences where social prejudices, class bias, and personal interests are involved, it may be fatal. This doctrine, developed in detail by the so-called '*sociology of knowledge*' [. . .], entirely overlooks the social or institutional character of scientific knowledge, because it is based on

the naïve view that objectivity depends on the psychology of the individual scientist. It overlooks the fact that neither the dryness nor the remoteness of a topic of natural science prevent partiality and self-interest from interfering with the individual scientist's beliefs, and that if we had to depend on his detachment, science, even natural science, would be quite impossible. *What the 'sociology of knowledge' overlooks is just the sociology of knowledge* – the social or public character of science. It overlooks the fact that it is the public character of science and of its institutions which imposes a mental discipline upon the individual scientist, and which preserves the objectivity of science and its tradition of critically discussing new ideas.

In this connection, I may perhaps touch upon another of the doctrines presented in section 6 [of *The Poverty of Historicism*]. There it was argued that, since scientific research in social problems must itself influence social life, it is impossible for the social scientist who is aware of this influence to retain the proper scientific attitude of disinterested objectivity. But there is nothing peculiar to social science in this situation. A physicist or a physical engineer is in the same position. Without being a social scientist he can realize that the invention of a new aircraft or rocket may have a tremendous influence on society.

I have just sketched some of the institutional conditions on whose realization scientific and industrial progress depends. Now it is important to realize that most of these conditions cannot be called necessary, and that all of them taken together are not sufficient.

The conditions are not necessary, since without these institutions (language perhaps excepted) scientific progress would not be strictly impossible. 'Progress', after all, *has* been made from the spoken to the written word, and even further (although this early development was perhaps not, properly speaking, *scientific* progress).

On the other hand, and this is more important, we must realize that with the best institutional organization in the world, scientific progress may one day stop. There may, for example, be an epidemic of mysticism. This is certainly possible, for since some intellectuals *do* react to scientific progress (or to the demands of an open society) by withdrawing into mysticism, everyone *might* react in this way. Such a possibility may perhaps be counteracted by devising a further set of social institutions, such as educational institutions, to discourage uniformity of outlook and encourage diversity. Also, the idea of progress and its enthusiastic propagation may have some effect. But all this cannot make progress certain. For we cannot exclude the logical possibility, say, of a bacterium or virus that spreads a wish for Nirvana.

We thus find that even the best institutions can never be foolproof. As I have said before, 'Institutions are like fortresses. They must be well designed *and* properly manned'. But we can never make sure that the right man will be attracted by scientific research. Nor can we make sure that there will be men of imagination who have the knack of inventing new hypotheses. And ultimately, much depends on sheer luck, in these matters. For truth is *not manifest*, and it is a mistake to believe – as did Comte and Mill – that once the 'obstacles' (the allusion is to the Church) are removed, truth will be visible to all who genuinely want to see it.

I believe that the result of this analysis can be generalized. The human or personal factor will remain *the* irrational element in most, or all, institutional social theories. The opposite doctrine which teaches the reduction of social theories to psychology, in the same way as we try to reduce chemistry to physics, is, I believe, based on a misunderstanding. It arises from the false belief that this 'methodological psychologism' is a necessary corollary of a methodological individualism – of the quite unassailable doctrine that we must try to understand all collective phenomena as due to the actions, interactions, aims, hopes, and thoughts of individual men, and as due to traditions created and preserved by individual men. But we can be individualists without

accepting psychologism. The 'zero method' of constructing rational models is *not* a psychological but rather a logical method.

In fact, psychology cannot be the basis of social science. First, because it is itself just one of the social sciences: 'human nature' varies considerably with the social institutions, and its study therefore presupposes an understanding of these institutions. Secondly, because the social sciences are largely concerned with the unintended consequences, or repercussions, of human actions. And 'unintended' in this context does not perhaps mean 'not *consciously* intended'; rather it characterizes repercussions which may violate *all* interests of the social agent, whether conscious or unconscious: although some people may claim that a liking for mountains and solitude may be explained psychologically, the fact that, if too many people like the mountains, they cannot enjoy solitude there, is not a psychological fact; but this kind of problem is at the very root of social theory.

With this, we reach a result which contrasts startlingly with the still fashionable method of Comte and Mill. Instead of reducing sociological considerations to the apparently firm basis of the psychology of human nature, we might say that the human factor is *the* ultimately uncertain and wayward element in social life and in all social institutions. Indeed this is the element which ultimately *cannot* be completely controlled by institutions (as Spinoza first saw); for every attempt at controlling it completely must lead to tyranny; which means, to the omnipotence of the human factor – the whims of a few men, or even of one.

But is it not possible to control the human factor by *science* – the opposite of whim? No doubt, biology and psychology can solve, or will soon be able to solve, the 'problem of transforming man'. Yet those who attempt to do this are bound to destroy the objectivity of science, and so science itself, since these are both based upon free competition of thought; that is, upon freedom. If the growth of reason is to continue, and human rationality to survive, then the diversity of individuals and their opinions, aims, and purposes must never be interfered with (expect in extreme cases where political freedom is endangered). Even the emotionally satisfying appeal for a *common purpose*, however excellent, is an appeal to abandon all rival moral opinions and the cross-criticisms and arguments to which they give rise. It is an appeal to abandon rational thought.

The evolutionist who demands the 'scientific' control of human nature does not realize how suicidal this demand is. The mainspring of evolution and progress is the variety of the material which may become subject to selection. So far as human evolution is concerned it is the 'freedom to be odd and unlike one's neighbour' – 'to disagree with the majority, and go one's own way'. Holistic control, which must lead to the equalization not of human rights but of human minds, would mean the end of progress.

Karl R. Popper, *The Poverty of Historicism* (New York: Harper and Row, 1964), pp. 152–9.

Chapter 72

F. A. Hayek, from *The Constitution of Liberty* (1960)

The Socratic maxim that the recognition of our ignorance is the beginning of wisdom has profound significance for our understanding of society. The first requisite for this is that we become aware of men's necessary ignorance of much that helps him to achieve his aims. Most of the advantages of social life, especially in its more advanced forms which we call "civilization," rest on the fact that the individual benefits from more knowledge than he is aware of. It might be said that civilization begins when the individual in the pursuit of his ends can make use of more knowledge than he has himself acquired and when he can transcend the boundaries of his ignorance by profiting from knowledge he does not himself possess.

This fundamental fact of man's unavoidable ignorance of much on which the working of civilization rests has received little attention. Philosophers and students of society have generally glossed it over and treated this ignorance as a minor imperfection which could be more or less disregarded. But, though discussions of moral or social problems based on the assumption of perfect knowledge may occasionally be useful as a preliminary exercise in logic, they are of little use in an attempt to explain the real world. Its problems are dominated by the "practical difficulty" that our knowledge is, in fact, very far from perfect. Perhaps it is only natural that the scientists tend to stress what we do know; but in the social field, where what we do not know is often so much more

important, the effect of this tendency may be very misleading. Many of the utopian constructions are worthless because they follow the lead of the theorists in assuming that we have perfect knowledge.

It must be admitted, however, that our ignorance is a peculiarly difficult subject to discuss. It might at first even seem impossible by definition to talk sense about it. We certainly cannot discuss intelligently something about which we know nothing. We must at least be able to state the questions even if we do not know the answers. This requires some genuine knowledge of the kind of world we are discussing. If we are to understand how society works, we must attempt to define the general nature and range of our ignorance concerning it. Though we cannot see in the dark, we must be able to trace the limits of the dark areas.

The misleading effect of the usual approach stands out clearly if we examine the significance of the assertion that man has created his civilization and that he therefore can also change its institutions as he pleases. This assertion would be justified only if man had deliberately created civilization in full understanding of what he was doing or if he at least clearly knew how it was being maintained. In a sense it is true, of course, that man has made his civilization. It is the product of his actions or, rather, of the action of a few hundred generations. This does not mean, however, that civilization is the product of human design, or even that man knows what its functioning or continued existence depends upon.

The whole conception of man already endowed with a mind capable of conceiving civilization setting out to create it is fundamentally false. Man did not simply impose upon the world a pattern created by his mind. His mind is itself a system that constantly changes as a result of his endeavor to adapt himself to his surroundings. It would be an error to believe that, to achieve a higher civilization, we have merely to put into effect the ideas now guiding us. If we are to advance, we must leave room for a continuous revision of our present conceptions and ideals which will be necessitated by further experience. We are as little able to conceive what civilization will be, or can be, five hundred or even fifty years hence as our medieval forefathers or even our grandparents were able to foresee our manner of life today.

The conception of man deliberately building his civilization stems from an erroneous intellectualism that regards human reason as something standing outside nature and possessed of knowledge and reasoning capacity independent of experience. But the growth of the human mind is part of the growth of civilization; it is the state of civilization at any given moment that determines the scope and the possibilities of human ends and values. The mind can never foresee its own advance. Though we must always strive for the achievement of our present aims, we must also leave room for new experiences and future events to decide which of these aims will be achieved.

It may be an exaggeration to assert, as a modern anthropologist has done, that "it is not man who controls culture but the other way around"; but it is useful to be reminded by him that "it is only our profound and comprehensive ignorance of the nature of culture that makes it possible for us to believe that we direct and control it." He suggests at least an important corrective to the intellectualist conception. His reminder will help us to achieve

a truer image of the incessant interaction between our conscious striving for what our intellect pictures as achievable and the operations of the institutions, traditions, and habits which jointly often produce something very different from what we have aimed at.

There are two important respects in which the conscious knowledge which guides the individual's actions constitutes only part of the conditions which enable him to achieve his ends. There is the fact that man's mind is itself a product of the civilization in which he has grown up and that it is unaware of much of the experience which has shaped it – experience that assists it by being embodied in the habits, conventions, language, and moral beliefs which are part of its makeup. Then there is the further consideration that the knowledge which any individual mind consciously manipulates is only a small part of the knowledge which at any one time contributes to the success of his action. When we reflect how much knowledge possessed by other people is an essential condition for the successful pursuit of our individual aims, the magnitude of our ignorance of the circumstances on which the results of our action depend appears simply staggering. Knowledge exists only as the knowledge of individuals. It is not much better than a metaphor to speak of the knowledge of society as a whole. The sum of the knowledge of all the individuals exists nowhere as an integrated whole. The great problem is how we can all profit from this knowledge, which exists only dispersed as the separate, partial, and sometimes conflicting beliefs of all men.

In other words, it is largely because civilization enables us constantly to profit from knowledge which we individually do not possess and because each individual's use of his particular knowledge may serve to assist others unknown to him in achieving their ends that men as members of civilized society can pursue their individual ends so much more successfully than they could alone. We know little of the particular facts to which the whole of social activity continuously adjusts itself in order to provide what we have learned to expect. We know even less of the forces which bring about this adjustment by appropriately co-ordinating individual activity. And our attitude, when we discover how little we know of what makes us co-operate, is, on the whole, one of resentment rather than of wonder or curiosity. Much of our occasional impetuous desire to smash the whole entangling machinery of civilization is due to this inability of man to understand what he is doing.

[. . .]

We have now reached the point at which the main contention of this chapter will be readily intelligible. It is that the case for individual freedom rests chiefly on the recognition of the inevitable ignorance of all of us concerning a great many of the factors on which the achievement of our ends and welfare depends.

If there were omniscient men, if we could know not only all that affects the attainment of our present wishes but also our future wants and desires, there would be little case for liberty. And, in turn, liberty of the individual would, of course, make complete foresight impossible. Liberty is essential in order to leave room for the unforeseeable and unpredictable; we want it because we have learned to expect from it the opportunity of realizing many of our aims. It is because every individual knows so little and, in particular, because we rarely know which of us knows best that we trust the independent and competitive efforts of many to induce the emergence of what we shall want when we see it.

Humiliating to human pride as it may be, we must recognize that the advance and even the preservation of civilization are dependent upon a maximum of opportunity for accidents to happen. These accidents occur in the combination of knowledge and attitudes, skills and habits, acquired by individual men and also when qualified men are confronted with the particular circumstances which they are equipped to deal with. Our necessary ignorance of so much means that we have to deal largely with probabilities and chances.

Of course, it is true of social as of individual life that favorable accidents usually do not just happen. We must prepare for them. But they still remain chances and do not become certainties. They involve risks deliberately taken, the possible misfortune of individuals and groups who are as meritorious as others who prosper, the possibility of serious failure or relapse even for the majority, and merely a high probability of a net gain on balance. All we can do is to increase the chance that some special constellation of individual endowment and circumstance will result in the shaping of some new tool or the improvement of an old one, and to improve the prospect that such innovations will become rapidly known to those who can take advantage of them.

All political theories assume, of course, that most individuals are very ignorant. Those who plead for liberty differ from the rest in that they include among the ignorant themselves as well as the wisest. Compared with the totality of knowledge which is continually utilized in the evolution of a dynamic civilization, the difference between the knowledge that the wisest and that which the most ignorant individual can deliberately employ is comparatively insignificant.

The classical argument for tolerance formulated by John Milton and John Locke and restated by John Stuart Mill and Walter Bagehot rests, of course, on the recognition of this ignorance of ours. It is a special application of general considerations to which a non-rationalist insight into the working of our mind opens the doors. [. . .] [T]hough we are usually not aware of it, all institutions of freedom are adaptations to this fundamental fact of ignorance, adapted to deal with chances and probabilities, not certainty. Certainty we cannot achieve in human affairs, and it is for this reason that, to make the best use of what knowledge we have, we must adhere to rules which experience has shown to serve best on the whole, though we do not know what will be the consequences of obeying them in the particular instance.

Man learns by the disappointment of expectations. Needless to say, we ought not to increase the unpredictability of events by foolish human institutions. So far as possible, our aim should be to improve human institutions so as to increase the chances of correct foresight. Above all, however, we should provide the maximum of opportunity for unknown individuals to learn of facts that we ourselves are yet unaware of and to make use of this knowledge in their actions.

It is through the mutually adjusted efforts of many people that more knowledge is utilized than any one individual possesses or than it is possible to synthesize intellectually; and it is through such utilization of dispersed knowledge that achievements are made possible greater than any single mind can foresee. It is because freedom means the renunciation of direct control of individual efforts that a free society can make use of so much more knowledge than the mind of the wisest ruler could comprehend.

From this foundation of the argument for liberty it follows that we shall not achieve its ends if we confine liberty to the particular instances where we know it will do good. Freedom granted only when it is known beforehand that its effects will be beneficial is not freedom. If we knew how freedom would be used, the case for it would largely disappear. We shall never get the benefits of freedom, never obtain those unforeseeable new developments for which it provides the opportunity, if it is not also granted where the uses made of it by some do not seem desirable. It is therefore no argument against individual freedom that it is frequently abused. Freedom necessarily means that many things will be done which we do not like. Our faith in freedom does not rest on the foreseeable results in particular circumstances but on the belief that it will, on balance, release more forces for the good than for the bad.

It also follows that the importance of our being free to do a particular thing has nothing to do with the question of whether we or the majority are ever likely to make use of that particular possibility. To grant no more freedom than all can exercise would be to misconceive its function completely. The freedom that will be used by only one man in a million may be more important to society and more beneficial to the majority than any freedom that we all use.

It might even be said that the less likely the opportunity to make use of freedom to do a particular thing, the more precious it will be for society as a whole. The less likely the opportunity, the more serious will it be to miss it when it arises, for the experience that it offers will be nearly unique. It is also probably true that the majority are not directly interested in most of the important things that any one person should be free to do. It is because we do not know how individuals will use their freedom that it is so important. If it were otherwise, the results of freedom could also be achieved by the majority's deciding what should be done by the individuals. But majority action is, of necessity, confined to the already tried and ascertained, to issues on which agreement has already been reached in that process of discussion that must be preceded by different experiences and actions on the part of different individuals.

The benefits I derive from freedom are thus largely the result of the uses of freedom by others, and mostly of those uses of freedom that I could never avail myself of. It is therefore not necessarily freedom that I can exercise myself that is most important for me. It is certainly more important that anything can be tried by somebody than that all can do the same things. It is not because we like to be able to do particular things, not because we regard any particular freedom as essential to our happiness, that we have a claim to freedom. The instinct that makes us revolt against any physical restraint, though a helpful ally, is not always a safe guide for justifying or delimiting freedom. What is important is not what freedom I personally would like to exercise but what freedom some person may need in order to do things beneficial to society. This freedom we can assure to the unknown person only by giving it to all.

The benefits of freedom are therefore not confined to the free – or, at least, a man does not benefit mainly from those aspects of freedom which he himself takes advantage of. There can be no doubt that in history unfree majorities have benefited from the existence of free minorities and that today unfree societies benefit from what they obtain and learn from free societies. Of course the benefits we derive from the freedom of others become greater as the number of those who can exercise freedom increases. The argument for the freedom of some therefore applies to the freedom of all. But it is still better for all that some should be free than none and also that many enjoy full freedom than that all have a restricted freedom. The significant point is that the importance of freedom to do a particular thing has nothing to do with the number of people who want to do it: it might almost be in inverse proportion. One consequence of this is that a society may be hamstrung by controls, although the great majority may not be aware that their freedom has been significantly curtailed. If we proceeded on the assumption that only the exercises of freedom that the majority will practice are important, we would be certain to create a stagnant society with all the characteristic of unfreedom.

[. . .]

When we speak of progress in connection with our individual endeavors or any organized human effort, we mean an advance toward a known goal. It is not in this sense that social evolution can be called progress, for it is not achieved by human reason striving by known means toward a fixed aim. It would be more correct to think of progress as a process of formation and modification of the human intellect, a process of adaptation and learning in which not only the possibilities known to us but also our values and desires continually change. As progress consists in the discovery of the not yet known, its consequences must be unpredictable. It always leads into the unknown, and the most we can expect is to gain an understanding of the kind of forces that bring it about. Yet, though such a general understanding of the character of this process of cumulative growth is indispensable if we are to try to create conditions favorable to it, it can never be knowledge which will enable us to make specific predictions. The claim that we can derive from such insight necessary laws of evolution that we must follow is an absurdity. Human reason can neither predict nor deliberately shape its own future. Its advances consist in finding out where it has been wrong.

Even in the field where the search for new knowledge is most deliberate, i.e., in science, no man can predict what will be the consequences of his work. In fact, there is increasing recognition that even the attempt to make science deliberately aim at useful knowledge – that is, at knowledge whose future uses can be foreseen – is likely to impede progress. Progress by its very nature cannot be planned. We may perhaps legitimately speak of planning progress in a particular field where we aim at the solution of a specific problem and are already on the track of the answer. But we should soon be at the end of our endeavors if we were to confine ourselves to striving for goals now visible and if new problems did not spring up all the time. It is knowing what we have not known before that makes us wiser men.

But often it also makes us sadder men. Though progress consists in part in achieving things we have been striving for, this does not mean that we shall like all its results or that all will be gainers. And since our wishes and aims are also subject to change in the course of the process, it is questionable whether the statement has a clear meaning that the new state of affairs that progress creates is a better one. Progress in the sense of the cumulative growth of knowledge and power over nature is a term that says little about whether the new state will give us more satisfaction than the old. The pleasure may be solely in achieving what we have been striving for, and the assured possession may give us little satisfaction. The question whether, if we had to stop at our present stage of development, we would in any significant sense be better off or happier than if we had stopped a hundred or a thousand years ago is probably unanswerable.

The answer, however, does not matter. What matters is the successful striving for what at each moment seems attainable. It is not the fruits of past success but the living in and for the future in which human intelligence proves itself. Progress is movement for movement's sake, for it is in the process of learning, and in the effects of having learned something new, that man enjoys the gift of his intelligence.

The enjoyment of personal success will be given to large numbers only in a society that, as a whole, progresses fairly rapidly. In a stationary society there will be about as many who will be descending as there will be those rising. In order that the great majority should in their individual lives participate in the advance, it is necessary that it proceed at a considerable speed. There can therefore be little doubt that Adam Smith was right when he said: "It is in the progressive state, while society is advancing to the further acquisition, rather than when it has acquired its full complement of riches, that the condition of the labouring poor, of the great body of people, seems to be happiest and the most comfortable. It is hard in the stationary, and miserable in the declining state. The progressive state is really the cheerful and hearty state of all the different orders of society. The stationary is dull; the declining melancholy."

It is one of the most characteristic facts of a progressive society that in it most things which individuals strive for can be obtained only through further progress. This follows from the necessary character of the process: new knowledge and its benefits can spread only gradually, and the ambitions of the many will always be determined by what is as yet accessible only to the few. It is misleading to think of those new possibilities as if they were, from the beginning, a common possession of society which its members could deliberately share; they become a common possession only through that slow process by which the achievements of the few are made available to the many. This is often obscured by the exaggerated attention usually given to a few conspicuous major steps in the development. But, more often than not, major discoveries merely open new vistas, and long further efforts are necessary before the new knowledge that has sprung up somewhere can be put to general use. It will have to pass through a long course of adaptation, selection, combination, and improvement before full use can be made of it. This means that there will always be people who already benefit from new achievements that have not yet reached others.

The rapid economic advance that we have come to expect seems in a large measure to be the result of this inequality and to be impossible without it. Progress at such a fast rate cannot proceed on a uniform front but must take place in echelon fashion, with some far ahead of the rest. The reason for this is concealed by our habit of regarding economic progress chiefly as an accumulation of ever greater quantities of goods and equipment. But the rise of our standard of life is due at least as much to an increase in knowledge which enables us not merely to consume more of the same things but to use different things, and often things we did not even know before. And though the growth of income depends in part on the accumulation of capital, more probably depends on our learning to use our resources more effectively and for new purposes.

The growth of knowledge is of such special importance because, while the material resources will always remain scarce and will have to be reserved for limited purposes, the uses of new knowledge (where we do not make them artificially scarce by patents of monopoly) are unrestricted. Knowledge, once achieved, becomes gratuitously available for the benefit of all. It is through this free gift of the knowledge acquired by the experiments of some members of society that general progress is made possible, that the achievements of those who have gone before facilitate the advance of those who follow.

At any stage of this process there will always be many things we already know how to produce but which are still too expensive to provide for more than a few. And at an early stage they can be made only through an outlay of resources equal to many times the share of total income that, with an approximately equal distribution, would go to the few who could benefit from them. At first, a new good is commonly "the caprice of the chosen few before it becomes a public need and forms part of the necessities of life. For the luxuries of today are the necessities of tomorrow" [G. Tarde, *Social Laws*]. Furthermore, the new things will often become available to the greater part of the people only *because* for some time they have been the luxuries of the few.

If we, in the wealthier countries, today can provide facilities and conveniences for most which not long ago would have been physically impossible to produce in such quantities, this is in large measure the direct consequence of the fact that they were first made for a few. All the conveniences of a comfortable home, of our means of transportation and communication, of entertainment and enjoyment, we could produce at first only in limited quantities; but it was in doing this that we gradually learned to make them or similar things at a much smaller outlay of resources and thus became able to supply them to the great majority. A large part of the expenditure of the rich, though not intended for that end, thus serves to defray the cost of the experimentation with the new things that, as a result, can later be made available to the poor.

The important point is not merely that we gradually learn to make cheaply on a large scale what we already know how to make expensively in small quantities but that only from an advanced position does the next range of desires and possibilities become visible, so that the selection of new goals and the effort toward their achievement will begin long before the majority can strive for them. If what they will want after their present goals are realized is soon to be made available, it is necessary that the developments that will bear fruit for the masses in twenty or fifty years' time should be guided by the views of people who are already in the position of enjoying them.

If today in the United States or western Europe the relatively poor can have a car or a refrigerator, an airplane trip or a radio, at the cost of a reasonable part of their income, this was made possible because in the past others with larger incomes were able to spend on what was then a luxury. The path of advance is greatly eased by the fact that it has been trodden before. It is because scouts have found the goal that the road can be built for the less lucky or less energetic. What today may seem extravagance or even waste, because it is enjoyed by the few and even undreamed of by the masses, is payment for the experimentation with a style of living that will eventually be available to many. The range of what will be tried and later developed, the fund of experience that will become available to all, is greatly extended by the unequal distribution of present benefits; and the rate of advance will be greatly increased if the first steps are taken long before the majority can profit from them. Many of the improvements would indeed never become a possibility for all if they had not long before been available to some. If all had to wait for better things until they could be provided for all, that day would in many instances never come. Even the poorest today owe their relative material well-being to the results of past inequality.

F. A. Hayek, *The Constitution of Liberty* (London: Routledge and Kegan Paul, 1960), pp. 22–5, 29–32, 40–4.

Chapter 73

Isaiah Berlin, from "Two Concepts of Liberty" (1969)

The One and the Many

One belief, more than any other, is responsible for the slaughter of individuals on the altars of the great historical ideals – justice or progress or the happiness of future generations, or the sacred mission or emancipation of a nation or race or class, or even liberty itself, which demands the sacrifice of individuals for the freedom of society. This is the belief that somewhere, in the past or in the future, in divine revelation or in the mind of an individual thinker, in the pronouncements of history or science, or in the simple heart of an uncorrupted good man, there is a final solution. This ancient faith rests on the conviction that all the positive values in which men have believed must, in the end, be compatible, and perhaps even entail one another. 'Nature binds truth, happiness and virtue together by an indissoluble chain,' said one of the best men who ever lived, and spoke in similar terms of liberty, equality and justice.[1]

But is this true? It is a commonplace that neither political equality nor efficient organisation nor social justice is compatible with more than a modicum of individual liberty, and certainly not with unrestricted *laissez-faire*; that justice and generosity, public and private loyalties, the demands of genius and the claims of society can conflict violently with each other. And it is no great way from that to the generalisation that not all good things are compatible, still less all the ideals of

mankind. But somewhere, we shall be told, and in some way, it must be possible for all these values to live together, for unless this is so, the universe is not a cosmos, not a harmony; unless this is so, conflicts of values may be an intrinsic, irremovable element in human life. To admit that the fulfilment of some of our ideals may in principle make the fulfilment of others impossible is to say that the notion of total human fulfilment is a formal contradiction, a metaphysical chimera. For every rationalist metaphysician, from Plato to the last disciples of Hegel or Marx, this abandonment of the notion of a final harmony in which all riddles are solved, all contradictions reconciled, is a piece of crude empiricism, abdication before brute facts, intolerable bankruptcy of reason before things as they are, failure to explain and to justify, to reduce everything to a system, which 'reason' indignantly rejects.

But if we are not armed with an a priori guarantee of the proposition that a total harmony of true values is somewhere to be found – perhaps in some ideal realm the characteristics of which we can, in our finite state, not so much as conceive – we must fall back on the ordinary resources of empirical observation and ordinary human knowledge. And these certainly give us no warrant for supposing (or even understanding what would be meant by saying) that all good things, or all bad things for that matter, are reconcilable with each other. The world that we encounter in ordinary experience is one in which we are

faced with choices between ends equally ultimate, and claims equally absolute, the realisation of some of which must inevitably involve
the sacrifice of others. Indeed, it is because this
is their situation that men place such immense
value upon the freedom to choose; for if they
had assurance that in some perfect state, realisable by men on earth, no ends pursued by
them would ever be in conflict, the necessity
and agony of choice would disappear, and with
it the central importance of the freedom to
choose. Any method of bringing this final state
nearer would then seem fully justified, no
matter how much freedom were sacrificed to
forward its advance.

It is, I have no doubt, some such dogmatic
certainty that has been responsible for the
deep, serene, unshakeable conviction in the
minds of some of the most merciless tyrants
and persecutors in history that what they did
was fully justified by its purpose. I do not say
that the ideal of self-perfection – whether for
individuals or nations or Churches or classes –
is to be condemned in itself, or that the language which was used in its defence was in all
cases the result of a confused or fraudulent use
of words, or of moral or intellectual perversity.
Indeed, I have tried to show that it is the
notion of freedom in its 'positive' sense that is
at the heart of the demands for national or
social self-direction which animate the most
powerful and morally just public movements
of our time, and that not to recognise this is
to misunderstand the most vital facts and ideas
of our age. But equally it seems to me that the
belief that some single formula can in principle be found whereby all the diverse ends of
men can be harmoniously realised is demon-
strably false. If, as I believe, the ends of men
are many, and not all of them are in principle
compatible with each other, then the possibility of conflict – and of tragedy – can never
wholly be eliminated from human life, either
personal or social. The necessity of choosing
between absolute claims is then an inescapable
characteristic of the human condition. This
gives its value to freedom as Acton conceived
of it – as an end in itself, and not as a temporary need, arising out of our confused notions
and irrational and disordered lives, a predicament which a panacea could one day put right.

I do not wish to say that individual freedom
is, even in the most liberal societies, the sole, or
even the dominant, criterion of social action.
We compel children to be educated, and we
forbid public executions. These are certainly
curbs to freedom. We justify them on the
ground that ignorance, or a barbarian upbringing, or cruel pleasures and excitements are
worse for us than the amount of restraint
needed to repress them. This judgement in
turn depends on how we determine good and
evil, that is to say, on our moral, religious,
intellectual, economic and aesthetic values;
which are, in their turn, bound up with
our conception of man, and of the basic
demands of his nature. In other words, our
solution of such problems is based on our
vision, by which we are consciously or uncon-
sciously guided, of what constitutes a fulfilled
human life, as contrasted with Mill's 'cramped
and dwarfed', 'pinched and hidebound'
natures. To protest against the laws governing
censorship or personal morals as intolerable
infringements of personal liberty presupposes a
belief that the activities which such laws forbid
are fundamental needs of men as men, in a
good (or, indeed, any) society. To defend such
laws is to hold that these needs are not essential, or that they cannot be satisfied without
sacrificing other values which come higher –
satisfy deeper needs – than individual freedom,
determined by some standard that is not
merely subjective, a standard for which some
objective status – empirical or a priori – is
claimed.

The extent of a man's, or a people's, liberty
to choose to live as he or they desire must be
weighed against the claims of many other
values, of which equality, or justice, or happiness, or security, or public order are perhaps
the most obvious examples. For this reason, it
cannot be unlimited. We are rightly reminded
by R. H. Tawney that the liberty of the strong,
whether their strength is physical or economic,
must be restrained. This maxim claims respect,

not as a consequence of some a priori rule, whereby the respect for the liberty of one man logically entails respect for the liberty of others like him; but simply because respect for the principles of justice, or shame at gross inequality of treatment, is as basic in men as the desire for liberty. That we cannot have everything is a necessary, not a contingent, truth. Burke's plea for the constant need to compensate, to reconcile, to balance; Mill's plea for novel 'experiments in living' with their permanent possibility of error – the knowledge that it is not merely in practice but in principle impossible to reach clear-cut and certain answers, even in an ideal world of wholly good and rational men and wholly clear ideas – may madden those who seek for final solutions and single, all-embracing systems, guaranteed to be eternal. Nevertheless, it is a conclusion that cannot be escaped by those who, with Kant, have learnt the truth that 'Out of the crooked timber of humanity no straight thing was ever made.'

There is little need to stress the fact that monism, and faith in a single criterion, has always proved a deep source of satisfaction both to the intellect and to the emotions. Whether the standard of judgement derives from the vision of some future perfection, as in the minds of the *philosophes* in the eighteenth century and their technocratic successors in our own day, or is rooted in the past – *la terre et les morts* – as maintained by German historicists or French theocrats, or neo-Conservatives in English-speaking countries, it is bound, provided it is inflexible enough, to encounter some unforeseen and unforeseeable human development, which it will not fit; and will then be used to justify the a priori barbarities of Procrustes – the vivisection of actual human societies into some fixed pattern dictated by our fallible understanding of a largely imaginary past or a wholly imaginary future. To preserve our absolute categories or ideals at the expense of human lives offends equally against the principles of science and of history; it is an attitude found in equal measure on the right and left wings in our days,

and is not reconcilable with the principles accepted by those who respect the facts.

Pluralism, with the measure of 'negative' liberty that it entails, seems to me a truer and more humane ideal than the goals of those who seek in the great disciplined, authoritarian structures the ideal of 'positive' self-mastery by classes, or peoples, or the whole of mankind. It is truer, because it does, at least, recognise the fact that human goals are many, not all of them commensurable, and in perpetual rivalry with one another. To assume that all values can be graded on one scale, so that it is a mere matter of inspection to determine the highest, seems to me to falsify our knowledge that men are free agents, to represent moral decision as an operation which a slide-rule could, in principle, perform. To say that in some ultimate, all-reconciling yet realisable synthesis duty is interest, or individual freedom is pure democracy or an authoritarian State, is to throw a metaphysical blanket over either self-deceit or deliberate hypocrisy. It is more humane because it does not (as the system-builders do) deprive men, in the name of some remote, or incoherent, ideal, of much that they have found to be indispensable to their life as unpredictably self-transforming human beings.[2] In the end, men choose between ultimate values; they choose as they do because their life and thought are determined by fundamental moral categories and concepts that are, at any rate over large stretches of time and space, and whatever their ultimate origins, a part of their being and thought and sense of their own identity; part of what makes them human.

It may be that the ideal of freedom to choose ends without claiming eternal validity for them, and the pluralism of values connected with this, is only the late fruit of our declining capitalist civilisation: an ideal which remote ages and primitive societies have not recognized, and one which posterity will regard with curiosity, even sympathy, but little comprehension. This may be so; but no sceptical conclusions seem to me to follow. Principles are not less sacred because their duration cannot be guaranteed. Indeed, the very desire for guarantees that our values are eternal and secure in some objective heaven is perhaps only a craving for the certainties of childhood or the absolute values of our primitive past. 'To realise the relative validity of one's convictions', said an admirable writer of our time, 'and yet stand for them unflinchingly is what distinguishes a civilised man from a barbarian.'[3] To demand more than this is perhaps a deep and incurable metaphysical need; but to allow such a need to determine one's practice is a symptom of an equally deep, and more dangerous, moral and political immaturity.

Notes

1 Condorcet, from whose *Esquisse* these words are quoted [. . .], declares that the task of social science is to show 'by what bonds nature has united the progress of enlightenment with that of liberty, virtue and respect for the natural rights of man; how these ideals, which alone are truly good, yet so often separated from each other that they are even believed to be incompatible, should, on the contrary, become inseparable, as soon as enlightenment has reached a certain level simultaneously among a large number of nations'. He goes on to say that 'Men still preserve the errors of their childhood, of their country and of their age long after having recognised all the truths needed for destroying them' [. . .]. Ironically enough, his belief in the need for and possibility of uniting all good things may well be precisely the kind of error he himself so well described.

2 On this also Bentham seems to me to have spoken well: 'Individual interests are the only real interests . . . Can it be conceived that there are men so absurd as to . . . prefer the man who is not, to him who is; to torment the living, under pretence of promoting the happiness of those who are not born, and who may never be born?' [. . .]. This is one of the infrequent occasions when Burke agrees with Bentham; for this passage is at the heart of the empirical, as against the metaphysical, view of politics.

3 Joseph A. Schumpeter, *Capitalism, Socialism, and Democracy* (London, 1943), p. 243.

Isaiah Berlin, "Two Concepts of Liberty," from *Liberty* (Oxford: Oxford University Press, 2002), pp. 212–17.

Chapter 74

John Rawls, from *Justice as Fairness: A Restatement* (2001)

§7 The Idea of Free and Equal Persons

7.1. To this point we have simply used the idea of free and equal persons; we must now explain its meaning and role. Justice as fairness regards citizens as engaged in social cooperation, and hence as fully capable of doing so, and this over a complete life. Persons so regarded have what we may call "the two moral powers," explained as follows:

(i) One such power is the capacity for a sense of justice: it is the capacity to understand, to apply, and to act from (and not merely in accordance with) the principles of political justice that specify the fair terms of social cooperation.

(ii) The other moral power is a capacity for a conception of the good: it is the capacity to have, to revise, and rationally to pursue a conception of the good. Such a conception is an ordered family of final ends and aims which specifies a person's conception of what is of value in human life or, alternatively, of what is regarded as a fully worthwhile life. The elements of such a conception are normally set within, and interpreted by, certain comprehensive religious, philosophical, or moral doctrines in the light of which the various ends and aims are ordered and understood.

[...]

7.4. In what sense are citizens free? Here [...] we must keep in mind that justice as fairness is a political conception of justice for a democratic society. The relevant meaning of free persons is to be drawn from the political culture of such a society and may have little or no connection, for example, with freedom of the will as discussed in the philosophy of mind. Following up this idea, we say that citizens are regarded as free persons in two respects.

First, citizens are free in that they conceive of themselves and of one another as having the moral power to have a conception of the good. This is not to say that, as part of their political conception, they view themselves as inevitably tied to the pursuit of the particular conception of the good which they affirm at any given time. Rather, as citizens, they are seen as capable of revising and changing this conception on reasonable and rational grounds, and they may do this if they so desire. As free persons, citizens claim the right to view their persons as independent from and not identified with any particular conception of the good, or scheme of final ends. Given their moral power to form, to revise, and rationally to pursue a conception of the good, their public or legal identity as free persons is not affected by changes over time in their determinate conception of the good.

For example, when citizens convert from one religion to another, or no longer affirm an established religious faith, they do not cease to be, for questions of political justice, the same persons they were before. There is no loss of what we may call their public, or legal, identity – their identity as a matter of basic law. In general, they still have the same basic rights and duties, they own the same property and can make the same claims as before, except insofar as these claims were connected with their previous religious affiliation. We can imagine a society (indeed history offers numerous examples) in which basic rights and recognized claims depend on religious affiliation and social class. Such a society has a different political conception of the person. It may not have a conception of citizenship at all; for this conception, as we are using it, goes with the conception of society as a fair system of cooperation for reciprocal advantage between free and equal citizens.

[. . .]

7.5. A second respect in which citizens view themselves as free is that they regard themselves as self-authenticating sources of valid claims. That is, they regard themselves as being entitled to make claims on their institutions so as to advance their conceptions of the good (provided these conceptions fall within the range permitted by the public conception of justice). These claims citizens regard as having weight of their own apart from being derived from duties and obligations specified by a political conception of justice, for example, from duties and obligations owed to society. Claims that citizens regard as founded on duties and obligations based on their conception of the good and the moral doctrine they affirm in their own life are also, for our purposes here, to be counted as self-authenticating. Doing this is reasonable in a political conception of justice for a constitutional democracy, for provided the conceptions of the good and the moral doctrine citizens affirm are compatible with the public conception of justice, these duties and obligations are self-authenticating from a political point of view.

When we describe the way in which citizens regard themselves as free, we are relying on how citizens tend to think of themselves in a democratic society when questions of political justice arise. That this aspect belongs to a particular political conception is clear from the contrast with a different political conception in which the members of society are not viewed as self-authenticating sources of valid claims. In this case their claims have no weight except insofar as they can be derived from the duties and obligations owed to society, or from their ascribed roles in a social hierarchy justified by religious or aristocratic values.

To take an extreme case, slaves are human beings who are not counted as sources of claims, not even claims based on social duties or obligations, for slaves are not counted as capable of having duties or obligations. Laws that prohibit the abuse and maltreatment of slaves are not founded on claims made by slaves in their own behalf, but on claims originating either from slaveholders or from the general interests of society (which do not include the interests of slaves). Slaves are, so to speak, socially dead: they are not recognized as persons at all. This contrast with a political conception of justice that allows slavery makes clear why conceiving of citizens as free persons in virtue of their moral powers and their having a conception of the good goes with a particular political conception of justice.

[. . .]

§13 Two Principles of Justice

13.1. To try to answer our question, let us turn to a revised statement of the two principles of justice discussed in *Theory* [Rawls's *A Theory of Justice*], §§11–14. They should now read:

(a) Each person has the same indefeasible claim to a fully adequate scheme of equal basic liberties, which scheme is compatible with the same scheme of liberties for all; and

(b) Social and economic inequalities are to satisfy two conditions: first, they are to be attached to offices and positions open to all under conditions of fair equality of opportunity; and second, they are to be to the greatest benefit of the least-advantaged members of society (the difference principle).

As I explain below, the first principle is prior to the second; also, in the second principle fair equality of opportunity is prior to the difference principle. This priority means that in applying a principle (or checking it against test cases) we assume that the prior principles are fully satisfied. We seek a principle of distribution (in the narrower sense) that holds within the setting of background institutions that secure the basic equal liberties (including the fair value of the political liberties) as well as fair equality of opportunity. How far that principle holds outside that setting is a separate question we shall not consider.

[. . .]

13.3. Consider now the reasons for revising the first principle.[1] One is that the equal basic liberties in this principle are specified by a list as follows: freedom of thought and liberty of conscience; political liberties (for example, the right to vote and to participate in politics) and freedom of association, as well as the rights and liberties specified by the liberty and integrity (physical and psychological) of the person; and finally, the rights and liberties covered by the rule of law. That the basic liberties are specified by a list is quite clear from *Theory*, §11: 61 (1st ed.); but the use of the singular term "basic liberty" in the statement of the principle on *Theory*, §11:60 (1st ed.), obscures this important feature of these liberties.

This revision brings out that no priority is assigned to liberty as such, as if the exercise of something called "liberty" had a preeminent value and were the main, if not the sole, end of political and social justice. While there is a general presumption against imposing legal and other restrictions on conduct without a sufficient reason, this presumption creates no special priority for any particular liberty. Throughout the history of democratic thought the focus has been on achieving certain specific rights and liberties as well as specific constitutional guarantees, as found, for example, in various bills of rights and declarations of the rights of man. Justice as fairness follows this traditional view.

13.4. A list of basic liberties can be drawn up in two ways. One is historical: we survey various democratic regimes and assemble a list of rights and liberties that seem basic and are securely protected in what seem to be historically the more successful regimes. Of course, the veil of ignorance means that this kind of particular information is not available to the parties in the original position, but it is available to you and me in setting up justice as fairness.[2] We are perfectly free to use it to specify the principles of justice we make available to the parties.

A second way of drawing up a list of basic rights and liberties is analytical: we consider what liberties provide the political and social conditions essential for the adequate development and full exercise of the two moral powers of free and equal persons (§7.1). Following this we say: first, that the equal political liberties and freedom of thought enable citizens to develop and to exercise these powers in judging the justice of the basic structure of society and its social policies; and second, that liberty of conscience and freedom of association enable citizens to develop and exercise their moral powers in forming and revising and in rationally pursuing (individually or, more often, in association with others) their conceptions of the good.

Those basic rights and liberties protect and secure the scope required for the exercise of the two moral powers in the two fundamental cases just mentioned: that is to say, the first fundamental case is the exercise of those powers in judging the justice of basic institutions and social policies; while the second fundamental case is the exercise of those powers in pursuing our conception of the good. To exercise our powers in these ways is essential to us as free and equal citizens.

[. . .]

32.1.   As we have said, none of the basic liberties, such as freedom of thought and liberty of conscience, or political liberty and the guarantees of the rule of law, is absolute, as they may be limited when they conflict with one another. Nor is it required that in the finally adjusted scheme each basic liberty is equally provided for (whatever that would mean). Rather, however these liberties are adjusted, that final scheme is to be secured equally for all citizens.

32.2.   In adjusting the basic liberties, we need to distinguish between their restriction and their regulation. The priority of these liberties is not infringed when they are merely regulated, as they must be, in order to be combined into one scheme. So long as what we may call "the central range of application" of each basic liberty is secured, the two principles are fulfilled.

For example, rules of order are essential for regulating free discussion. Not everyone can speak at once, or use the same public facility at the same time for different purposes. Instituting the basic liberties, just like realizing different interests, requires social organization and scheduling as to time and place, and so on. The requisite regulations should not be mistaken for restrictions on the content of speech, for example, prohibitions against publicly arguing for various religious and philosophical, or moral and political doctrines, or against raising questions of general and particular fact about the justice of the basic structure and its social policies.

32.3.   Since the basic liberties have a special status in view of their priority, we should count among them only truly essential liberties. We hope that the liberties that are not counted as basic are satisfactorily allowed for by the general presumption against legal restrictions, once we hold that the burden of

proof against those restrictions is to be decided by the other requirements of the two principles of justice. If there are many basic liberties, their specification into a coherent scheme securing the central range of application of each may prove too cumbersome. This leads us to ask what are the truly fundamental cases and to introduce a criterion of significance of a particular right or liberty. Otherwise we have no way of identifying a fully adequate scheme of basic liberties of the kind we seek.

A serious defect in *Theory* is that its account of the basic liberties proposes two different and conflicting criteria, both unsatisfactory. One is to specify those liberties so as to achieve the most extensive scheme of the liberties (*Theory*, §32: 203, 1st ed.; §37: 201; §39: 220); the other tells us to take up the point of view of the rational representative equal citizen, and then to specify the scheme of liberties in the light of that citizen's rational interests as known at the relevant stage of the four-stage sequence (*Theory*, §32: 179; §39: 217). But (as Hart maintained) the idea of the extent of a basic liberty is useful only in the least important cases, and citizens' rational interests are not sufficiently explained in *Theory* to do the work asked of them. What is a better criterion?

32.4.   The proposed criterion is this: the basic liberties and their priority are to guarantee equally for all citizens the social conditions essential for the adequate development and the full and informed exercise of their two moral powers in what we have referred to as the two fundamental cases (§13.4). These two cases we now specify more fully.

(a)   The first fundamental case is connected with the capacity for a sense of justice and concerns the application of the principles of justice to the basic structure and its social policies. The equal political liberties and freedom of thought are to ensure the opportunity for the free and informed application of the principles of justice to that structure and to its policies by means of the full and effective exercise of citizens' sense of justice. All this is necessary to make possible the free use of public reason.

(b)   The second fundamental case is connected with the capacity for a (complete) conception of the good (normally associated with a comprehensive religious, philosophical, or moral doctrine), and concerns the exercise of citizens' powers of practical reason in forming, revising, and rationally pursuing such a conception over a complete life. Liberty of conscience and freedom of association are to ensure the opportunity for the free and informed exercise of this capacity and its companion powers of practical reason and judgment.

(c)   The remaining and supporting basic liberties – the liberty and integrity (physical and psychological) of the person and the rights and liberties covered by the rule of law – can be connected with the two fundamental cases by noting that they are necessary if the other basic liberties are to be properly guaranteed. What distinguishes the two fundamental cases is, first, their connection with the realization of the fundamental interests of citizens regarded as free and equal as well as reasonable and rational. In addition, there is the broad scope and basic character of the institutions to which the principles of justice are applied in those two cases.

32.5.   Given this division of the basic liberties, the significance of a particular liberty is explained as follows: a liberty is more or less significant depending on whether it is more or less essentially involved in, or is a more or less necessary institutional means to protect, the full and informed exercise of the moral powers in one (or both) of the two fundamental cases. The more significant liberties mark out the central range of application of a particular basic liberty; and in cases of conflict we look for a way to accommodate the more significant liberties within the central range of each.

Consider several illustrative examples. First, the weight of claims to freedom of speech, press, and discussion is to be judged by this criterion. Some kinds of speech are not specially protected, and others may be offenses, for example, libel and defamation of individuals, so-called fighting words (in certain circumstances). Even political speech when it becomes an incitement to the imminent and lawless use of force is no longer protected as a basic liberty.

Why these kinds of speech are offenses may call for careful reflection, and will generally differ from case to case. Libel and defamation of private persons (in contrast with political and other public figures) has no significance at all for the free use of public reason to judge and regulate the basic structure. In addition, those forms of speech are private wrongs. Incitements to imminent and lawless use of force, whatever the significance of the speaker's overall political views, are too disruptive of democratic political procedures to be permitted by the rules of order of public discussion. So long as the advocacy of revolutionary and even seditious doctrines is fully protected, as it should be, there is no restriction on the content of speech, but only regulations as to time and place, and the means used to express it.

Notes

1   This principle may be preceded by a lexically prior principle requiring that basic needs be met, as least insofar as their being met is a necessary condition for citizens to understand and to be able fruitfully to exercise the basic rights and liberties. For a statement of such a principle with further discussion, see R. G. Peffer, *Marxism, Morality, and Social Justice* (Princeton: Princeton University Press, 1990), p. 14.

2   Here I should mention that there are three points of view in justice as fairness that it is essential to distinguish: the point of view of the parties in the original position, the point of view of citizens in a well-ordered society, and the point of view of you and me who are setting up justice as fairness as a

political conception and trying to use it to organize into one coherent view our considered judgments at all levels of generality. Keep in mind that the parties are, as it were, artificial persons who are part of a procedure of construction that we frame for our philosophical purposes. We may know many things that we keep from them. For these three points of view, see *Political Liberalism* [by Rawls], p. 28.

John Rawls, *Justice as Fairness: A Restatement* (Cambridge, MA: Harvard University Press, 2001), pp. 21–4, 42–6, 112–14.

Chapter 75

Joseph Raz, from *The Morality of Freedom* (1986)

[. . .]

Autonomy-based Freedom

The previous section argued that competitive value pluralism of the kind which is required by respect for autonomy generates conflicts between people pursuing valuable but incompatible forms of life. Given the necessity to make those forms of life available in order to secure autonomy there is a need to curb people's actions and their attitudes in those conflicts by principles of toleration. The duty of toleration, and the wider doctrine of freedom of which it is a part, are an aspect of the duty of respect for autonomy. To judge its scope and its limits we need to look at the extent of our autonomy-based duties generally.

Since autonomy is morally valuable there is reason for everyone to make himself and everyone else autonomous. But it is the special character of autonomy that one cannot make another person autonomous. One can bring the horse to the water but one cannot make it drink. One is autonomous if one determines the course of one's life by oneself. This is not to say that others cannot help, but their help is by and large confined to securing the background conditions which enable a person to be autonomous. This is why moral philosophers who regard morality as essentially other-regarding tend to concentrate on autonomy as a capacity for an autonomous life. Our duties towards our fellows are for the most part to secure for them autonomy in its capacity sense. Where some of these writers are wrong is in overlooking the reason for the value of autonomy as a capacity, which is in the use its possessor can make of it, i.e. in the autonomous life it enables him to have.

There is more one can do to help another person have an autonomous life than stand off and refrain from coercing or manipulating him. There are two further categories of autonomy-based duties towards another person. One is to help in creating the inner capacities required for the conduct of an autonomous life. Some of these concern cognitive capacities, such as the power to absorb, remember and use information, reasoning abilities, and the like. Others concern one's emotional and imaginative make-up. Still others concern health, and physical abilities and skills. Finally, there are character traits essential or helpful for a life of autonomy. They include stability, loyalty and the ability to form personal attachments and to maintain intimate relationships. The third type of autonomy-based duty towards another concerns the creation of an adequate range of options for him to choose from.

As anticipated all these duties, though grounded in the value of the autonomous life, are aimed at securing autonomy as a capacity. Apart from cultivating a general awareness of the value of autonomy there is little more one can do. It is not surprising, however, that the principle of autonomy, as I shall call the principle requiring people to secure the conditions of autonomy for all people, yields duties which go far beyond the negative duties of non-interference, which are the only ones recognized by some defenders of autonomy. If the duties of non-interference are autonomy-based then the principle of autonomy provides reasons for holding that there are other autonomy-based duties as well. Every reason of autonomy which leads to the duties of non-interference would lead to other duties as well, unless, of course, it is counteracted by conflicting reasons. Such countervailing reasons are likely to be sometimes present, but they are most unlikely to confine the duties of autonomy to non-interference only.

These reflections clarify the relation between autonomy and freedom. Autonomy is a constituent element of the good life. A person's life is autonomous if it is to a considerable extent his own creation. Naturally the autonomous person has the capacity to control and create his own life. I called this the capacity sense of autonomy, for 'autonomy' is sometimes used to refer to that capacity alone. That capacity, which involves both the possession of certain mental and physical abilities and the availability of an adequate range of options, is sometimes referred to as positive freedom. That notion, like all notions which have become slogans in intellectual battles, is notoriously elusive. I prefer to discuss it in relation to the ideal of personal autonomy because positive freedom derives its value from its contribution to personal autonomy. Positive freedom is intrinsically valuable because it is an essential ingredient and a necessary condition of the autonomous life. It is a capacity whose value derives from its exercise. This provides the clue to its definition.

One's positive freedom is enhanced by whatever enhances one's ability to lead an autonomous life. Disputes concerning the scope and content of positive freedom should be settled by reference to the contribution of the disputed element to autonomy. Since autonomy admits of various degrees so does positive freedom. Since the impact of various courses of action on autonomy is incommensurate so is their impact on positive freedom. This 'imprecision' explains many people's exasperation with such 'woolly' concepts, and their reluctance to use them when engaged in serious theoretical or political arguments. Such reluctance would have been in place had these concepts been blocking our view of something more precise behind them. They do not. They mark features of life which are intrinsically valuable. The imprecision they import is ultimate imprecision. That is it is no imprecision at all but a reflection of the incommensurabilities with which life abounds.

Can negative freedom, i.e. freedom from coercion, be viewed as an aspect of positive freedom, i.e. of autonomy as a capacity? This view is liable to mislead. Autonomy and positive freedom relate primarily to pervasive goals, projects or relationships. The autonomous person freely develops friendships and other ties with people and animals. But that he is not free to talk to Jones now does not diminish his autonomy. The autonomous person chooses his own profession or trade. He may be denied the chance to cut down trees in the next field without any diminution to his autonomy. In other words, autonomy and positive freedom bear directly on relatively pervasive goals and relationships and affect more restricted options only inasmuch as they affect one's ability to pursue the more pervasive ones. Enrolling in a university or standing for Parliament in the general election, are examples of specific actions which affect pervasive choices. Denying one the ability to engage in them curtails to a significant degree one's ability to choose one's career and to feel a full member of a political community. Other specific actions affect one's autonomy not at all. Denying someone a certain choice of ice-cream is generally admitted to be insignificant to the degree of autonomy enjoyed by that person.

Discussions of negative freedom and of coercion usually concentrate on coercing people to perform or avoid specific actions. That is the natural context of coercion. But it may mask its moral significance and has on occasion led to a blind obsession with the avoidance of coercion. Negative freedom, freedom from coercive interferences, is valuable inasmuch as it serves positive freedom and autonomy. It does so in several ways. Coercing another may express contempt, or at any rate disrespect for his autonomy. Secondly, it reduces his options and therefore may be to his disadvantage. It may, in this way, also interfere with his autonomy. It may but it need not: some options one is better off not having. Others are denied one so that one will improve one's options in the future. In judging the value of negative freedom one should never forget that it derives from its contribution to autonomy.

The significance of denial of options to one's autonomy depends on the circumstances one finds oneself in. In some countries the vote does not have the symbolic significance it has in our culture. Its denial to an individual may be a trivial matter. Such factors do not diminish the importance of negative freedom, but they make it more difficult to judge.

The autonomy-based doctrine of freedom is far-reaching in its implications. But it has clear limits to which we must turn.

First, while autonomy requires the availability of an adequate range of options it does not require the presence of any particular option among them. A person or a government can take action eventually to eliminate soccer and substitute for it American football, etc. The degree to which one would wish to tolerate such action will be affected by pragmatic considerations which can normally be expected to favour erring on the side of caution where governmental action or action by big organizations is concerned. But it has to be remembered that social, economic and technological processes are constantly changing the opportunities available in our society. Occupations and careers are being created while others disappear all the time. The acceptable shapes of personal relationships are equally in constant flux, and so is the public culture which colours much of what we can and cannot do. Not everyone would agree that such processes are unobjectionable so long as the government does not take a hand in shaping them. The requirements of autonomy as well as other considerations may well call for governmental intervention in directing or initiating such processes.

It is important in this context to distinguish between the effect of the elimination of an option on those already committed to it, and its effect on others. The longer and the more deeply one is committed to one's projects the less able one is to abandon them (before completion) and pick up some others as substitutes. But even if such a change is possible, denying a person the possibility of carrying on with his projects, commitments and relationships is preventing him from having the life he has chosen. A person who may but has not yet chosen the eliminated option is much less seriously affected. Since all he is entitled to is an adequate range of options the eliminated option can, from his point of view, be replaced by another without loss of autonomy. This accounts for the importance of changes being gradual so that they will not affect committed persons.

The *second* main limitation of autonomy-based freedom has already been mentioned. It does not extend to the morally bad and repugnant. Since autonomy is valuable only if it is directed at the good it supplies no reason to provide, nor any reason to protect, worthless let alone bad options. To be sure autonomy itself is blind to the quality of options chosen. A person is autonomous even if he chooses the bad. Autonomy is even partially blind to the quality of the options available. A person is autonomous, it was argued in the last chapter, only if he pursues the good as he sees it. He can be autonomous only if he believes that he has valuable options to choose from. That is consistent with many of his options being bad ones. But while autonomy is consistent with the presence of bad options, they contribute nothing to its value. Indeed autonomously choosing the bad makes one's life worse than a comparable non-autonomous life is. Since our concern for autonomy is a concern to enable people to have a good life it furnishes us with reason to secure that autonomy which could be valuable. Providing, preserving or protecting bad options does not enable one to enjoy valuable autonomy.

This may sound very rigoristic and paternalistic. It conjures images of the state playing big brother forcing or manipulating people to do what it considers good for them against their will. Nothing could be further from the truth. First, one needs constant reminders that the fact that the state *considers* anything to be valuable or valueless is no reason for anything. Only its being valuable or valueless is a reason.

If it is likely that the government will not judge such matters correctly then it has no authority to judge them at all. Secondly, the autonomy-based doctrine of freedom rests primarily on the importance of autonomy and value-pluralism. Autonomy means that a good life is a life which is a free creation. Value-pluralism means that there will be a multiplicity of valuable options to choose from, and favourable conditions of choice. The resulting doctrine of freedom provides and protects those options and conditions. [. . .]

Joseph Raz, *The Morality of Freedom* (Oxford: Clarendon Press, 1986), pp. 407–12.

Chapter 76

Amartya Sen, from *Inequality Reexamined* (1992)

3.1 Capability Sets

This chapter explores the 'capability' perspective on the assessment of (1) well-being, and (2) the freedom to pursue well-being. The approach has been discussed in some detail elsewhere. Here I shall confine the presentation to only a few elementary aspects of this perspective.

The well-being of a person can be seen in terms of the quality (the 'wellness', as it were) of the person's being. Living may be seen as consisting of a set of interrelated 'functionings', consisting of beings and doings. A person's achievement in this respect can be seen as the vector of his or her functionings. The relevant functionings can vary from such elementary things as being adequately nourished, being in good health, avoiding escapable morbidity and premature mortality, etc., to more complex achievements such as being happy, having self-respect, taking part in the life of the community, and so on. The claim is that functionings are *constitutive* of a person's being, and an evaluation of well-being has to take the form of an assessment of these constituent elements.

Closely related to the notion of functionings is that of the *capability* to function. It represents the various combinations of functionings (beings and doings) that the person can achieve. Capability is, thus, a set of vectors of functionings, reflecting the person's freedom to lead one type of life or another. Just as the so-called 'budget set' in the commodity space represents a person's freedom to buy commodity bundles, the 'capability set' in the functioning space reflects the person's freedom to choose from possible livings.

It is easy to see that the well-being of a person must be thoroughly dependent on the nature of his or her being, i.e. on the functionings achieved. Whether a person is well-nourished, in good health, etc., must be intrinsically important for the wellness of that person's being. But, it may be asked, how do *capabilities* – as opposed to *achieved functionings* – relate to well-being?

The relevance of a person's capability to his or her well-being arises from two distinct but interrelated considerations. First, if the achieved functionings constitute a person's well-being, then the capability to achieve functionings (i.e. all the alternative combinations of functionings a person can choose to have) will constitute the person's freedom – the real opportunities – to have well-being. This 'well-being freedom' may have direct relevance in ethical and political analysis. For example, in forming a view of the goodness of the social state, importance may be attached to the freedoms that different people respectively enjoy to achieve well-being. Alternatively, without taking the route of incorporating well-being freedom in the 'goodness' of the social state, it may be simply taken to be 'right' that individuals should have substantial well-being freedom.

This freedom, reflecting a person's opportunities of well-being, must be valued at least for *instrumental* reasons, e.g. in judging how good a 'deal' a person has in the society. But in addition, as we have been discussing, freedom may be seen as being intrinsically important for a good social structure. A good society, in this view, is also a society of freedom. It is also possible to use the notion of 'rightness' as opposed to 'goodness' of the society to argue for the same substantive arrangements. Those who see that distinction as being very fundamental, and argue for 'the priority of right over ideas of the good' (as Rawls [. . .] puts it), would have to approach this question from that end.

The second connection between well-being and capability takes the direct form of making *achieved* well-being itself depend on the *capability* to function. Choosing may itself be a valuable part of living, and a life of genuine choice with serious options may be seen to be – for that reason – richer. In this view, at least some types of capabilities contribute *directly* to well-being, making one's life richer with the opportunity of reflective choice. But even when freedom in the form of capability is valued only instrumentally (and the level of well-being is not seen as dependent on the extent of freedom of choice as such), capability to function can nevertheless be an important part of social evaluation. The capability set gives us information on the various functioning vectors that are within reach of a person, and this information is important – no matter how exactly well-being is characterized.

In either form, the capability approach clearly differs crucially from the more traditional approaches to individual and social evaluation, based on such variables as *primary goods* (as in Rawlsian evaluative systems), *resources* (as in Dworkin's social analysis), or *real income* (as in the analyses focusing on the GNP, GDP, named-goods vectors). These variables are all concerned with the *instruments* of achieving well-being and other objectives, and can be seen also as the *means* to freedom. In contrast, functionings belong to the constitutive elements of well-being. Capability reflects freedom to pursue these consti-

tutive elements, and may even have – as discussed earlier in this section – a direct role in well-being itself, in so far as deciding and choosing are also parts of living.

[. . .]

3.3 Selection and Weighting

There are always elements of real choice regarding the functionings to be included in the list of relevant functionings and important capabilities. The general format of 'doings' and 'beings' permits additional 'achievements' to be defined and included. Some functionings may be easy to describe, but of no great interest in most contexts (e.g. using a *particular* washing powder – much like other washing powders). There is no escape from the problem of evaluation in selecting a class of functionings – and in the corresponding description of capabilities. The focus has to be related to the underlying concerns and values, in terms of which some definable functionings may be important and others quite trivial and negligible. The need for selection and discrimination is neither an embarrassment, nor a unique difficulty, for the conceptualization of functionings and capabilities.

In the context of some types of welfare analysis, e.g. in dealing with extreme poverty in developing economies, we may be able to go a fairly long distance in terms of a relatively small number of centrally important functionings (and the corresponding basic capabilities, e.g. the ability to be well-nourished and well-sheltered, the capability of escaping avoidable morbidity and premature mortality, and so forth). In other contexts, including more general problems of economic development, the list may have to be much longer and much more diverse.

In his review article of an earlier work of mine, Charles Beitz has illuminatingly discussed various features of the capability approach and has also forcefully raised an important critical issue (one that has been aired in different forms by several other critics as well):

> The chief theoretical difficulty in the capabilities approach to interpersonal comparisons arises from the obvious fact that not all capabilities stand on the same footing. The capacity to move about, for example, has a different significance than the capability to play basketball.[1]

This is a natural worry to face, and it is important that the question be posed and addressed. It is certainly clear that some types of capabilities, broadly conceived, are of little interest or importance, and even the ones that count have to be weighted *vis-à-vis* each other. But these discriminations constitute an integral part of the capability approach, and the need for selection and weighting cannot really be, in any sense, an embarrassment (as 'a theoretical difficulty').

The varying importance of different capabilities is as much a part of the capability framework as the varying value of different commodities is a part of the real-income framework. Equal valuation of all constitutive elements is needed for neither. We cannot criticize the commodity-centred evaluation on the ground that different commodities are weighted differently. Exactly the same applies to functionings and capabilities. The capability approach begins with identifying a relevant space for evaluation, rather than arguing that everything that can be put into the format of that space must, for that reason, be important – not to mention, equally significant.

The primary claim is that in evaluating well-being, the value-objects are the functionings and capabilities. That claim neither entails that all types of capabilities are equally valuable, nor indicates that any capability whatsoever – even if totally remote from the person's life – must have some value in assessing that person's well-being. It is in asserting the need to examine the value of functionings and capabilities as opposed to confining attention to the *means* to these achievements and freedoms (such as resources or primary goods or incomes) that the capability approach has something to offer. The relative valuation of different functionings and capabilities has to be an integral part of the exercise.

Note

1 Charles Beitz, "Amartya Sen's *Resources, Values and Development*," *Economics and Philosophy* 2 (1986), pp. 282–91.

Amartya Sen, *Inequality Reexamined* (Oxford: Oxford University Press, 1992), pp. 39–42, 44–6.

Chapter 77

Thomas Hurka, from "Why Value Autonomy?" (1987)

[...] Autonomy, I assume, involves choice from a wide range of options. And it can seem puzzling that this should have *intrinsic* value. Imagine that there are ten possible actions, which an agent ranks in order of preferability from one to ten. (This is the agent's ranking. We could also use our ranking, or an objective ranking, without fundamentally altering the example.) If all ten are available to her she can choose autonomously among them, or choose more autonomously than if she only had one. But what if that one were the highest-ranked action, the one she prefers to all others? Why would it be worse to lack autonomy if she still had her most-favoured option? Things are different, of course, if we compare having ten options with having only the lowest-ranked among them. Then having more choice is clearly better. But this need have nothing to do with autonomy. We may value the extra options just because they are better, and offer the prospect of better choice. We may, in other words, value the expansion of choice just *instrumentally*, as a means to better results. The important case for the *intrinsic* value of autonomy is the first case, where the extra options are all worse. And this case can seem puzzling. Why should it be better to choose autonomously among ten options than to have only the best among them? Why value extra possibilities when they cannot rationally be chosen?

[...]

This, then, is a challenge to the value of autonomy: if free choice is intrinsically good, it should be better to have one good option and nine bad ones than to have just the good option. And why should this be so? In this paper I will try to meet this challenge, and to vindicate what I take to be our initial intuitions about the value of autonomy.

[...]

One suggestion derives from Mill's claim that an autonomous agent has "a character," while one who is not autonomous has "no character, no more than a steam-engine has a character." Now, if "character" means just "autonomously developed character," Mill's remark is unhelpful. But there is another possibility. A person has a character, we may say, when her choices are unified through time, and reflect some enduring traits and values. She has a character especially when her choices are unified in some distinctive way, so the traits revealed are special to her. And the suggestion then is this. A person who has autonomy can use it to develop her own values, and to express them consistently in action. But someone with no opportunity for choice cannot develop the same way. His acts can only reflect his momentary concerns, without the integration through time that makes for genuine personality.

These points are again serious, and important for a practical discussion of autonomy. But they still treat autonomy as just instrumentally good. The expansion of choice contributes, not to better individual choices, but to a more desirable pattern of choices in one's life as a whole. It is instrumental at a higher level, but still instrumental.

[. . .]

A more promising idea occurs in [a] second passage from Mill, about "perception, judgement, [and] discriminative feeling." Someone with many life-options can deliberate about them, and in so doing exercise his rational powers. He can weigh the merits and defects of his various alternatives, and arrive at a reasoned conclusion about them. The presence of different possibilities calls for reflection upon them, and this reflection is a good.

[. . .]

By giving its citizens varied options a free society encourages the use of their deliberative powers. It encourages a reasoning that would have no practical point if options were closed. But the argument is still instrumental and does not give us what we want, which is deeper values present in the act of free choice itself.

[. . .]

Agency

To locate these values I suggest that we consider an ideal of agency. If one person chooses action *a* from ten options while another has only action *a* available, it may be true of each that she has made *a* the case, and is in that sense responsible for it. But there is an important difference between them. The first or autonomous agent has also made certain alternatives to *a* not the case; if her options included *b*, *c*, and *d*, she is responsible for not-*b*, not-*c*, and not-*d*. The second person did not have this further effect. Since *b*, *c*, and *d* were not possible for her, the responsibility for their non-realization rests with nature, with whoever constrained her – in any case, not with her. It is not in her person that those truths about her action originate. The ideal of agency is one of causal efficacy, of making a causal impact on the world and determining facts about it. And the autonomous agent, just in virtue of her autonomy, more fully realizes this ideal. When she chooses among options she has two effects: realizing some options and

blocking others, and this gives her a larger efficacy than someone whose only effect is the first.

To illustrate, imagine that the first person chooses a career as a teacher from ten available careers, including lawyer, politician, and accountant, while the second becomes a teacher because that is her only option. If we ask why these people are teachers our answer may at one level be the same. But if we ask why they are not lawyers, politicians, or accountants, the answers will be different. In the first case the explanation will point to something inside the agent: to the fact that she chose not to be a lawyer, politician, or accountant. But in the second case it will look outside the agent, to her society or to the people who limited her choice. As the difference in these explanations reveals, the first person is responsible for more facts about her life, and thus is more expansively an agent. To succeed as an agent is to make a difference in what the world does and does not contain, and this is more possible with more numerous options. By letting people decide what they do not do as well as do, autonomy makes them more widely efficacious.

This argument provides a sketch of a justification for autonomy, but to elaborate it we must specify our ideal of agency. To be plausible, this ideal must be one of *intentional* agency, of achieving goals one *intended* to achieve in advance. It is not any causal efficacy that has value, but efficacy that expresses some aim in the mind. And, because of this, autonomy has internal as well as external conditions. It is not sufficient for autonomous action that a person have many options open. He must, most obviously, know about the options, or he cannot intend their non-realization. And he must also make in the fullest sense a choice among them. By this I mean a choice that is for one option *in preference to others*, so his rejection of the others appears in his mind. This does not always occur in intentional action. Someone who is driven by obsession may know that alternatives are available, but his moving intention does not reflect this. It goes blindly for *b*, if *b* is what he does, without preferring *b* to other options. (A strong claim is that the obsessed person intends only *b*, without rejecting anything. A weaker claim is that he rejects only the vague alternative not-*b*. Either way there is not the rejection of individually discriminated alternatives that on my view makes for autonomy.) The same is true of someone who is weak-willed. If a weak-willed agent acted on his best judgement that *a*, he would prefer *a* to other actions. But he does not succumb to temptation in preference to anything; he just succumbs. If autonomy achieves many intensions it requires what I call choice in the fullest sense: a simultaneous realization of some possibilities and rejection of others, so one's knowledge of the others appears in and through what one wills.

[. . .]

Autonomy, then, increases the goals a person achieves, and thereby increases her agency. But it does this even more if her choice follows deliberation. (I now take on Mill's point about "perception" and "judgement.") An agent who deliberates about her options may discover that *a* has the most of some desirable property *F*, that *b* has defect *G*, and so on. When she chooses, then, she intends not only *a* but the-option-with-the-most-*F*; and alongside *b* she rejects the-option-with-*G*. Her deliberative knowledge, if it guides her choice, gives her more intentions in and around her options than if she picked blindly among them. So it increases even further her agency. And there is another effect. If she has deliberated she will choose *a* and reject *b* as means to a single goal, perhaps getting-the-most-*F*-without-*G*. Her various intentions will converge on one aim, and by so doing form a hierarchical means-end structure that realizes sophisticated rationality.

[. . .]

We have, then, two cases: simple autonomy, or any free choice among options, and deliberated autonomy, which follows careful reasoning about them. Of these the second is a greater good. It involves a greater realization of agency, and combines agency with the distinct good of rationality. But in both cases the basic value of choice is the same. An autonomous agent, as autonomous, achieves more ends, whether organized or not, than someone with no choice to make.

Thomas Hurka, "Why Value Autonomy?," *Social Theory and Practice* 13 (1987), pp. 362–8, 370.

Chapter 78

Joel Feinberg, from "The Interest in Liberty on the Scales" (1978)

III

There is a standing presumption against all proposals to criminalize conduct that is derived simply from the interest 'standard persons' are presumed to have in political liberty, but the strength of this presumption varies not only with the type of interest in liberty (welfare, security, or accumulative) but also with the degree to which that interest is actually invaded by the proposed legislation. Invasions of the interest in liberty are as much a matter of degree as invasions of the interest in money, though we lack clear-cut conventional units for measuring them, corresponding to dollars, pounds, and francs. The interest in liberty *as such* – as opposed to the various interests we have in doing the things we may be free or unfree to do – is an interest in having as many *open options* as possible with respect to various kinds of action, omission, and possession. I have an open option with respect to a given act X when I am permitted to do X and I am also permitted to do *not-X* (that is to omit doing X) so that it is up to me entirely whether I do X or not. If I am permitted to do X but not permitted to do *not-X*, I am not in any usual sense at liberty to do X, for if X is the only thing I am permitted to do, it follows that I am compelled to do X, and compulsion, of course, is the plain opposite of liberty. The possession of a liberty is simply the possession of alternative possibilities of action, and the more alternatives, the more liberty. Some criminal statutes reduce our alternatives more than others, though as Isaiah Berlin reminds us, "possibilities of action are not discrete entities like apples which can be exhaustively enumerated," nor like shillings and pence (we might add) which can be accurately counted. Counting and evaluating options, therefore, "can never be more than impressionistic," but there are better and worse ways of gathering one's impressions, and some persons' impressions may be more accurate than others', for all that.

We can think of life as a kind of maze of railroad tracks connected and disjoined, here and there, by switches. Wherever there is an unlocked switch which can be pulled one way or the other, there is an 'open option;' wherever the switch is locked in one position the option is 'closed.' As we chug along our various tracks in the maze, other persons are busily locking and unlocking, opening and closing switches, thereby enlarging and restricting our various possibilities of movement. Some of these switchmen are part of a team of legislators, policemen, and judges; they claim *authority* for their switch positionings. Other switchmen operate illicitly at night, often undoing what was authoritatively arranged in the daylight. This model, of course, is simpler than the real world where the 'tracks' and 'switches' are not so clearly marked; but it does give us a sense for how some closed options can be more restrictive of liberty than others. When a switchman closes and locks a switch, he forces us to continue straight on, or stop, or back up. What we cannot do is move on to a different track heading off in a different direction from the one we are on. Before the switch was locked we had the option of continuing on or else moving to the new track, but now that particular option is closed to us. If the track from which we are barred is only a short line leading to a siding, and coming to a dead end in a country village, then our liberty has not been *much* diminished. We are not at liberty to go to one precise destination, but the whole network of tracks with all its diverse possibilities may yet be open before us. If, on the other hand, the closed switch prevents us from turning on to a trunk line, which itself is connected at a large number of switching points with branch lines heading off in many directions, then our liberty has been severely diminished, since we are debarred not only from turning at this one point, but also from enjoying a vast number of (otherwise) open options at points along the trunk line and its branches. In this case, one locked switch effectively closes dozens of options further up the line. Options that lead to many further options can be called 'fecund;' those that are relatively unfecund can be called 'limited.' The closing of fecund options, then, is more restrictive of liberty, other things being equal, than the closing of limited options, and the more fecund the option closed, the more harm is done to the general interest in liberty.

The railroad model is inadequate in a number of respects. It is an approximate rendering of our idea of liberty of movement, but it is difficult to apply to liberty of expression and opinion, or to 'passive liberties' like the freedom to be let alone, and the like. Moreover, it needs many complications before it can adequately render the full complexity of choices designated by the single word 'options.' Free men are often faced with choices of the form 'to X or not to X': to vote or not to vote, to buy a car or not to buy a car, to travel or to stay at home. Even our more complicated decisions can be crammed into this logical form, but the form in which they present themselves to our minds is often many sided: to vote for candidate A or B or C or D? to buy a Ford or Chevrolet or a Datsun or a Volkswagen or a Renault? to travel to England or France or Holland or Sweden or Spain or Italy? to marry Tom or Dick or Harry or . . . ? Our options in these cases are shaped more like tuning forks than wedges, and a barrier at the base of the fork restricts our liberty more than one at the base of a single prong. Other options disjoin conjunctions of alternatives rather than single possibilities. When the highwayman sticks his gun in one's ribs and says "your money or your life," he allows one the option of giving or not giving one's money, and the option of staying or not staying alive, but he closes the option of keeping *both* one's money *and* one's life – a most fecund option indeed.

The 'open option' theory of liberty is to be preferred, I think, to its main rival, the theory of liberty as the absence of barriers to one's actual desires, whatever they should happen to be. Suppose that Martin Chuzzlewit finds himself on a trunk line with all of its switches closed and locked, and with other 'trains' moving in the same direction on the same track at his rear, so that he has no choice at all but to continue moving straight ahead to destination D. On the 'open option' theory of liberty, this is the clearest example of a total lack of liberty: all of his options are closed, there are not alternative possibilities, he is forced to move to D. But now let us suppose that getting to D is Chuzzlewit's highest ambition in life and his most intensely felt desire. In that case, he is sure to get the thing in life he wants most. Does that affect the way the situation should be described in respect to liberty? According to the theory that one is at liberty to the extent that one can do what one wants, a theory held by the ancient Stoics and Epicureans and many modern writers too, Chuzzlewit enjoys perfect liberty in this situation because he can do what he wants, even though he can do nothing else. But since this theory blurs the distinction between liberty and compulsion, and in this one extreme hypothetical case actually identifies the two, it does not recommend itself to common sense.

Common sense may seem to pose difficulties for the 'open option' theory too. The problem for that analysis of liberty is to explain why we attach so great a value to liberty if it is understood to have no necessary connection to our actual desires. Suppose Tom Pinch's highest ambition in life (again speaking in the terms of the railroad metaphor) is to go to destination *E*, a small siding at a warehouse on a dead end line of a minor branch. Suppose further that the switch enabling trains to move on to that track is unalterably locked in the position barring entry, and is, furthermore, the only locked switch in the entire network of tracks. It may be a small consolation indeed to our frustrated traveler that he is perfectly free to go everywhere except to the one place he wants most to go. The problem for the open-options account is to explain why Chuzzlewit, who *can* do what he wants most to do, but nothing else, *lacks* something of value, and also why Pinch, who *cannot* do what he wants most to do but can do everything else, *possesses* something of value (his liberty).

There are two moves open to a theorist who accepts this challenge. The first is to compromise his open-option theory (as Berlin apparently does) by admitting other elements. Berlin, in a qualifying footnote, suggests that the total amount of liberty enjoyed by a given person at a given time is a function not only of the number and fecundity of his open options, but also "the value [that] not merely the agent, but the general sentiment of the society in which he lives, puts on the various possibilities." If we accept Berlin's suggestion some strange consequences follow. Chuzzlewit, who in our example is compelled to go to *D* whatever he might wish, is not really unfree after all, provided *D* is considered a desirable destination both by Chuzzlewit and "the society in which he lives." I fail to see how the desirability of *D* affects one way or the other the question whether Chuzzlewit has any choice about going there. If Chuzzlewit is allowed no alternative to *D*, it follows that he is forced willy-nilly to go to *D*. His situation

pleases him, no doubt, but that simply shows that persons can do quite willingly what they are compelled to do, that they can be contented in their unfreedom, a fact of experience that has been much observed and long known. As for our poor frustrated traveler Pinch, Berlin's suggestion can take away his last consolation. If his preferred destination is deemed a desirable place to be both by himself and by the 'general sentiment' of his society, then he is not very free after all, even though his options to move through the system of tracks are almost completely open. He may in fact be no freer, or even less free, than Chuzzlewit, although this is hard to determine since Berlin, who accepts both the number and the value of open possibilities as liberty-determining factors, gives us no clue as to their relative importance. If society at large does not agree with Pinch's eccentric estimate of the desirability of his destination (a fact that Pinch might be expected to find irrelevant to the question of how free he is) and thus finds the barriers to his desire not only singular and limited, but also of no great disvalue, it will tell him that he is 'truly free' no matter how frustrated he feels.

A more plausible way of accounting for the value of liberty will make firm but more modest claims on its behalf. As Berlin himself says many times in his main text, liberty is a thing of solid value, but not the only thing that is valuable. In particular, it is implausible to identify liberty with happiness or contentment, other states to which most persons attach high value. Chuzzlewit may be contented with his heart's desire in the absence of alternative possibilities; indeed he may even be better off, on balance, contented and unfree, than he would be free and uncontented. And Pinch might understandably be willing to trade a great amount of unneeded liberty for the one thing that is necessary to his contentment. But what these examples show is not that 'true freedom is contentment' or that compulsion and freedom are compatible (when one is contented with the compulsion), but rather that freedom is one thing and contentment another, that they are both valuable, but sometimes in conflict with one another so that one cannot have both.

IV

What then is the basis of our interest in liberty? Why should it matter that we have few 'open-options' if we have everything else we want and our other interests are flourishing? Our welfare interest in having a tolerable bare minimum of liberty is perhaps the easiest to account for of the various kind of interests persons have in liberty. If human beings had no alternative possibilities at all, if all their actions at all times were the *only* actions permitted them, they might yet be contented provided their desires for alternative possibilities were all thoroughly repressed or extinguished, and they might even achieve things of value, provided that they were wisely programmed to do so. But they could take no credit or blame for any of their achievements, and they could no more be responsible for their lives, in prospect or retrospect, than are robots, or the trains in our fertile metaphor that must run on 'predestined grooves.' They could have dignity neither in their own eyes nor in the eyes of their fellows, and both esteem for others and self-esteem would dwindle. They could not develop and pursue new interests, nor guide the pursuit of old interests into new and congenial channels, for their lack of key to life's important switches would make it impossible for them to maneuver out of their narrow grooves. Only a small number of kinds of ultimate interests would be consistent with what is permitted, and there would be no point in wanting to develop new ones more harmonious with one's temperament or natural propensities. There would be no point, in fact, in thinking of changing in any important way, in changing one's mind, one's purposes, one's ambitions, or one's desires, for without the flexibility that freedom confers, movements in new directions would be defeated by old barriers. The self-monitoring and self-critical capacities, so

essential to human nature, might as well dry up and wither; they would no longer have any function. The contentment with which all of this might still be consistent would not be a recognizably human happiness.

Most of us have fallen into fairly settled grooves by middle life, so the enjoyment of a vast number of open options beyond the requirements of the welfare interest in liberty may not seem very urgent to us. There is no particular comfort in the thought that if I should happen to change my desires or ambitions there will be no externally imposed barrier to my pursuit of the new ones, when the probability of such change seems virtually nil. Still there is something very appealing in the realization that just in case there should be changes in me or my circumstances (contrary to my present expectation), the world will not frustrate and defeat me. The 'breathing space' conferred by alternative possibilities then is an important kind of security.

Another source of the interest in liberty is quite independent of security. Enjoyment of open options is valued by many persons for its own sake, in quite the same way as the enjoyment of a pleasing natural and social environment. There is a kind of symbolic value in possessing a library with more books than one will ever read, or having access to a museum with more exhibits than one can ever see, or eating in a restaurant which offers more dishes than that which one wants most to choose. It is good to have a choice to exercise even when one would be content anyway without it. Alternative options not only secure a person against the possibility of changes of preference, they also permit an appreciation of the richness and diversity of the world's possibilities, and form themselves an environment in which it is pleasant to live.

For young persons whose characters are not fully formed, however, and even for older persons who have not become fixed in their ways, the primary base of the interest in liberty is the necessity to experiment with modes and styles of life, and to search among as large as possible a stock of possible careers for the one that best fits the shape of one's ideals, aptitudes, and preferences. For such persons, open options may be more a vital need that a luxury. But for others, the accumulation of open-options well beyond necessity or security may be itself a kind of ulterior interest, one of those focal aims whose joint advancement constitutes a person's well-being. For some persons an accumulative interest in liberty may have the same status and footing as the interests others may have in the beauty of their surroundings, or in blooming health beyond mere instrumental utility, or in vast wealth or power.

V

Two points about the interest in liberty should be re-emphasized before we conclude. The first is that the interest in liberty is not derived simply from the prior interests we have in things we may or may not be at liberty to do. The motorcyclist's interest in getting to his job quickly and inexpensively is not the same as his interest in having a choice among alternative ways to get to his job, and the suburban scholar's interest in the peace and quiet of his neighborhood is not the same as his interest in having various alternative places where he might study. When we come to 'weigh' and 'balance' the conflicting interests of the motorcyclist and the scholar, their interests in speed, economy, and quiet will go directly and entirely on the scales, but their respective interests in liberty are only fractionally involved. The person against whose interests the legislature or court decides will still have left a great deal of liberty in other respects even though one of his options, in the case at hand, will be authoritatively closed. The weight to be ascribed to the respective interests in liberty, then, will be only part of the total weight of interests each party puts on the scale, and whether it is greater or lesser than the rival's interest in liberty will depend on their respective degrees of fecundity. Criminal proscriptions sometimes infringe our interest in doing the thing prohibited, though this is

not frequently the case, since most of us have no interest in the prohibited conduct to begin with, but the interest in open options is something of quite independent value, and is *always* invaded to some degree by criminalization even when no other actual interest is. That fact has little moral bearing, however, except when the options closed by criminal statues are relatively fecund, in which case it is a fact of high moral importance.

The second point about the interest in liberty derives from the fact that options can effectively be closed by illicit actions of private individuals as well as by the authoritative decrees of legislators as enforced by the police, the courts, and the prisons. Criminal laws are designed to protect interests, including the interest in having open options, from such private incursions. Contemplating criminal legislation, therefore, always involves appraisals of the 'trade-off' between diminished political liberty and enlarged *de facto* freedom. When the statute is clearly justified by the harm principle, most of us *usually* make a gain in *de facto* freedom that more than compensates us for any loss of liberty to engage in the proscribed conduct.

Since legislators normally have interests other than the interest in liberty in mind when they prohibit or discourage certain kinds of conduct, it is difficult to think of clear examples of criminal statutes that enlarge freedom on balance. The clearest cases, of course, are laws prohibiting false imprisonment, kidnapping, high-jacking, forcible detention, and other direct incursions of the liberty of victims to come and go as they wish. When a person is wrongfully locked in a room, for example, it is as if he were an engine on a siding when the only switch connecting to the main track-network is locked against his entry. The option thus closed is therefore an extremely fecund one. On the other side, no matter how circumstances may have brought the 'false imprisoner's' interest in his own liberty into the situation, that interest will surely not sit on the legislative scales with anywhere near so great a weight, since the option closed by the prohibition against false imprisonment, in all but the most exceptional cases, will not be as fecund as the options protected.

Most criminal prohibitions, however, are designed primarily to protect interests in life and limb, health, property, privacy, and the like, and protect liberty only incidentally. Even these statues often find some justification in their net enlargement of liberty, though they would be fully justified by the harm principle in any case because of their protection of other interests. The law forbidding rape, for example, while designed to prevent women from psychological trauma and physical harm, and fully justified on those grounds, also protects the interest in liberty to whatever minor extent that interest sits on the scales. That law closes one relatively unfecund option of most adult males while depriving females of no liberty whatever. At the same time it not only

protects the interest that all females have in the absence of harmful and offensive bodily contacts (an independent merit that looms much larger than liberty in the law's rationale), it protects various of their relatively fecund open options from forcible closure by private individuals. All females, therefore, gain protection of fecund open options with no sacrifice of any other liberty, while most males suffer the closure of one small limited option – a clear net gain for liberty. Criminal legislation, however, is not always and necessarily so good a trade from the point of view of liberty. And in any case, it is the weights of affected interests other than liberty that are likely to be decisive when interests conflict.

Joel Feinberg, "The Interest in Liberty on the Scales," from A. I. Goldman et al. (eds.), *Values and Morals* (Dordrecht: Reidel, 1978), pp. 27–34.

Chapter 79

Ronald Dworkin, from *Taking Rights Seriously* (1977)

[. . .]

Do we have a right to liberty? Thomas Jefferson thought so, and since his day the right to liberty has received more play than the competing rights he mentioned to life and the pursuit of happiness. Liberty gave its name to the most influential political movement of the last century, and many of those who now despise liberals do so on the ground that they are not sufficiently libertarian. Of course, almost everyone concedes that the right to liberty is not the only political right, and that therefore claims to freedom must be limited, for example, by restraints that protect the security or property of others. Nevertheless the consensus in favor of some right to liberty is a vast one, though it is, as I shall argue in this chapter, misguided.

[. . .]

The term 'right' is used in politics and philosophy in many different senses, some of which I have tried to disentangle elsewhere. In order sensibly to ask whether we have a right to liberty in the neutral sense, we must fix on some one meaning of 'right'. It would not be difficult to find a sense of that term in which we could say with some confidence that men have a right to liberty. We might say, for example, that someone has a right to liberty if it is in his interest to have liberty, that is, if he either wants it or if it would be good for him to have it. In this sense, I would be prepared to concede that citizens have a right to liberty. But in this sense I would also have to concede that they have a right, at least generally, to

vanilla ice cream. My concession about liberty, moreover, would have very little value in political debate. I should want to claim, for example, that people have a right to equality in a much stronger sense, that they do not simply want equality but that they are entitled to it, and I would therefore not recognize the claim that some men and women want liberty as requiring any compromise in the efforts that I believe are necessary to give other men and women the equality to which they are entitled.

If the right to liberty is to play the role cut out for it in political debate, therefore, it must be a right in a much stronger sense. In Chapter 7 [of *Taking Rights Seriously*] I defined a strong sense of right that seems to me to capture the claims men mean to make when they appeal to political and moral rights. I do not propose to repeat my analysis here, but only to summarize it in this way. A successful claim of right, in the strong sense I described, has this consequence. If someone has a right to something, then it is wrong for the government to deny it to him even though it would be in the general interest to do so. This sense of a right (which might be called the anti-utilitarian concept of a right) seems to me very close to the sense of right principally used in political and legal writing and argument in recent years. It marks the distinctive concept of an individual right against the State which is the heart, for example, of constitutional theory in the United States.

I do not think that the right to liberty would come to very much, or have much power in political argument, if it relied on any sense of the right any weaker than that. If we settle on this concept of a right, however, then it seems plain that there exists no general right to liberty as such. I have no political right to drive up Lexington Avenue. If the government chooses to make Lexington Avenue one-way down town, it is a sufficient justification that this would be in the general interest, and it would be ridiculous for me to argue that for some reason it would nevertheless be wrong. The vast bulk of the laws which diminish my liberty are justified on utilitarian grounds, as being in the general interest or for the general welfare; if, as Bentham supposes, each of these laws diminishes my liberty, they nevertheless do not take away from me any thing that I have a right to have. It will not do, in the one-way street case, to say that although I have a right to drive up Lexington Avenue, nevertheless the government for special reasons is justified in overriding that right. That seems silly because the government needs no special justification – but only *a* justification – for this sort of legislation. So I can have a political right to liberty, such that every act of constraint diminishes or infringes that right, only in such a weak sense of right that the so called right to liberty is not competitive with strong rights, like the right to equality, at all. In any strong sense of right, which would be competitive with the right to equality, there exists no general right to liberty at all.

It may now be said that I have misunderstood the claim that there is a right to liberty. It does not mean to argue, it will be said, that there is a right to all liberty, but simply to important or basic liberties. Every law is, as Bentham said, an infraction of liberty, but we have a right to be protected against only fundamental or serious infractions. If the constraint on liberty is serious or severe enough, then it is indeed true that the government is not entitled to impose that constraint simply because that would be in the general interest; the government is not entitled to constrain liberty of speech, for example, whenever it thinks that would improve the general welfare.

So there is, after all, a general right to liberty as such, provided that that right is restricted to important liberties or serious deprivations. This qualification does not affect the political arguments I described earlier, it will be said, because the rights to liberty that stand in the way of full equality are rights to basic liberties like, for example, the right to attend a school of one's choice.

But this qualification raises an issue of great importance for liberal theory, which those who argue for a fight to liberty do not face. What does it mean to say that the right to liberty is limited to basic liberties, or that it offers protection only against serious infractions of liberty? That claim might be spelled out in two different ways, with very different theoretical and practical consequences. Let us suppose two cases in which government constrains a citizen from doing what he might want to do: the government prevents him from speaking his mind on political issues; from driving his car uptown on Lexington Avenue. What is the connection between these two cases, and the difference between them, such that though they are both cases in which a citizen is constrained and deprived of liberty, his right to liberty is infringed only in the first, and not in the second?

On the first of the two theories we might consider, the citizen is deprived of the same commodity, namely liberty, in both cases, but the difference is that in the first case the amount of that commodity taken away from him is, for some reason, either greater in amount or greater in its impact than in the second. But that seems bizarre. It is very difficult to think of liberty as a commodity. If we do try to give liberty some operational sense, such that we can measure the relative diminution of liberty occasioned by different sorts of laws or constraints, then the result is unlikely to match our intuitive sense of what are basic liberties and what are not. Suppose, for example, we measure a diminution in liberty by calculating the extent of frustration that it induces. We shall then have to face the fact that laws against theft, and even traffic laws, impose constraints that are felt more keenly by most men than constraints on political speech would be. We might take a different tack, and measure the degree of loss of liberty by the impact that a particular constraint has on future choices. But we should then have to admit that the ordinary criminal code reduces choice for most men more than laws which forbid fringe political activity. So the first theory – that the difference between cases covered and those not covered by our supposed right to liberty is a matter of degree – must fail.

The second theory argues that the difference between the two cases has to do, not with the degree of liberty involved, but with the special character of the liberty involved in the case covered by the right. On this theory, the offense involved in a law that limits free speech is of a different character, and not just different in degree, from a law that prevents a man from driving up Lexington Avenue. That sounds plausible, though as we shall see it is not easy to state what this difference in character comes to, or why it argues for a right in some cases though not in others. My present point, however, is that if the distinction between basic liberties and other liberties is defended in this way, then the notion of a general right to liberty as such has been entirely abandoned. If we have a right to basic liberties not because they are cases in which the commodity of liberty is somehow especially at stake, but because an assault on basic liberties injures us or demeans us in some way that goes beyond its impact on liberty, then what we have a right to is not liberty at all, but to the values or interests or standing that this particular constraint defeats.

This is not simply a question of terminology. The idea of a right to liberty is a misconceived concept that does a disservice to political thought in at least two ways. First, the idea creates a false sense of a necessary conflict between liberty and other values when social regulation, like the busing program, is proposed. Second, the idea provides too easy an answer to the question of why we regard certain kinds of restraints, like the restraint on free speech or the exercise of religion, as especially unjust. The idea of a right to liberty allows us to say that these constraints are unjust because they have a special impact on liberty as such. Once we recognize that this answer is spurious, then we shall have to face the difficult question of what is indeed at stake in these cases.

I should like to turn at once to that question. If there is no general right to liberty, then why do citizens in a democracy have rights to any specific kind of liberty, like freedom of speech or religion or political activity? It is no answer to say that if individuals have these rights, then the community will be better off in the long run as a whole. This idea – that individual rights may lead to overall utility – may or may not be true, but it is irrelevant to the defence of rights as such, because when we say that someone has a right to speak his mind freely, in the relevant political sense, we mean that he is entitled to do so even if this would not be in the general interest. If we want to defend individual rights in the sense in which we claim them, then we must try to discover something beyond utility that argues for these rights.

I mentioned one possibility earlier. We might be able to make out a case that individuals suffer some special damage when the traditional rights are invaded. On this argument, there is something about the liberty to speak out on political issues such that if that liberty is denied the individual suffers a special kind of damage which makes it wrong to inflict that damage upon him even though the community as a whole would benefit. This line of argument will appeal to those who themselves would feel special deprivation at the loss of their political and civil liberties, but it is nevertheless a difficult argument to pursue for two reasons.

First, there are a great many men and women and they undoubtedly form the majority even in democracies like Britain and the United States, who do not exercise political liberties that they have, and who would not count the loss of these liberties as especially grievous. Second, we lack a psychological theory which would justify and explain the idea that the loss of civil liberties, or any particular liberties, involves inevitable or even likely psychological damage. On the contrary, there is now a lively tradition in psychology, led by psychologists like Ronald Laing, who argue that a good deal of mental instability in modern societies may be traced to the demand for too much liberty rather than too little. In their account, the need to choose, which follows from liberty, is an unnecessary source of destructive tension. These theories are not necessarily persuasive, but until we can be confident that they are wrong, we cannot assume that psychology demonstrates the opposite, however appealing that might be on political grounds.

If we want to argue for a right to certain liberties, therefore, we must find another ground. We must argue on grounds of political morality that it is wrong to deprive individuals of these liberties, for some reason, apart from direct psychological damage, in spite of the fact that the common interest would be served by doing so. I put the matter this vaguely because there is no reason to assume, in advance, that only one kind of reason would support that moral position. It might be that a just society would recognize a variety of individual rights, some grounded on very different sorts of moral considerations from others. In what remains of this chapter I shall try to describe only one possible ground for rights. It does not follow that men and women in civil society have only the rights that the argument I shall make would support; but it does follow that they have at least these rights, and that is important enough.

The Right to Liberties

The central concept of my argument will be the concept not of liberty but of equality. I presume that we all accept the following postulates of political morality. Government must

treat those whom it governs with concern, that is, as human beings who are capable of suffering and frustration, and with respect, that is, as human beings who are capable of forming and acting on intelligent conceptions of how their lives should be lived. Government must not only treat people with concern and respect, but with equal concern and respect. It must not distribute goods or opportunities unequally on the ground that some citizens are entitled to more because they are worthy of more concern. It must not constrain liberty on the ground that one citizen's conception of the good life of one group is nobler or superior to another's. These postulates, taken together, state what might be called the liberal conception of equality; but it is a conception of equality, not of liberty as license, that they state.

The sovereign question of political theory, within a state supposed to be governed by the liberal conception of equality, is the question of what inequalities in goods, opportunities and liberties are permitted in such a state, and why. The beginning of an answer lies in the following distinction. Citizens governed by the liberal conception of equality each have a right to equal concern and respect. But there are two different rights that might be comprehended by that abstract right. The first is the right to equal treatment, that is, to the same distribution of goods or opportunities as anyone else has or is given. The Supreme Court, in the Reapportionment Cases, held that citizens have a right to equal treatment in the distribution of voting power; it held that one man must be given one vote in spite of the fact that a different distribution of votes might in fact work for the general benefit. The second is the right to treatment as an equal. This is the right, not to an equal distribution of some good or opportunity, but the right to equal concern and respect in the political decision about how these goods and opportunities are to be distributed. Suppose the question is raised whether an economic policy that injures long-term bondholders is in the general interest. Those who will be injured have a right that their prospective loss be taken into account in deciding whether the general interest is served by the policy. They may not simply be ignored in that calculation. But when their interest is taken into account it may nevertheless be outweighed by the interests of others who will gain from the policy, and in that case their right to equal concern and respect, so defined, would provide no objection. In the case of economic policy, therefore, we might wish to say that those who will be injured if inflation is permitted have a right to treatment as equals in the decision whether that policy would serve the general interest, but no right to equal treatment that would outlaw the policy even if it passed that test.

I propose that the right to treatment as an equal must be taken to be fundamental under the liberal conception of equality, and that the more restrictive right to equal treatment holds only in those special circumstances in which, for some special reason, it follows from the more fundamental right, as perhaps it does in the special circumstance of the Reapportionment Cases. I also propose that individual rights to distinct liberties must be recognized only when the fundamental right to treatment as an equal can be shown to require these rights. If this is correct, then the right to distinct liberties does not conflict with any supposed competing right to equality, but on the contrary follows from a conception of equality conceded to be more fundamental.

Ronald Dworkin, *Taking Rights Seriously* (London: Duckworth, 1977), pp. 266, 268–74.

Chapter 80

Ian Carter, from *A Measure of Freedom* (1999)

The Concept of Overall Freedom

THERE is an important controversy among liberal political philosophers which has yet to be clarified satisfactorily. This chapter [is] aimed at providing such a clarification, as well as defending one side against the other. The division turns on the question, does liberty play a fundamental role in liberal thinking? The initial reaction of many liberals – and I count myself among them – is to say 'yes'. How, indeed, could it not be part of the *essence* of liberalism to see freedom as a fundamental, if not *the* fundamental, component in one's system of values? But is this initial thought borne out by a careful, close analysis of the idea of freedom and of the reasons we have for valuing it? There is a recent tendency among liberal theorists to deny this initial thought, and therefore to deny that freedom is a fundamental good for liberals. There is no such thing as 'freedom' *tout court*, they say; there are only specific *freedoms*, like the freedom to speak one's mind on political matters or the freedom to leave the country or the freedom to practise a certain religion. According to these theorists, liberals stand up for specific freedoms, not freedom as such, and each specific freedom needs to be justified by reference to other goods of a more fundamental nature – goods which do not themselves include freedom. Therefore, freedom is not itself a fundamental good for liberals.

Which side one takes in this disagreement depends on whether one is interested only in specific freedoms, or also in *overall* freedom, where one's overall freedom is the amount of freedom one has in either absolute or relative terms, and represents some kind of an aggregation over one's specific freedoms. The theorists mentioned above, who are sceptical about freedom having value 'as such', are interested only in specific freedoms. They endorse what I shall call the *specific-freedom thesis*.

[...]

At its most extreme, endorsing the specific-freedom thesis means holding the belief that all talk of 'increasing', 'expanding', 'equalizing', or 'maximizing' freedom in some overall sense is simply nonsense. This appears to be the view of Ronald Dworkin. According to Dworkin, liberty cannot be some sort of 'commodity', as if we could say that one restriction of freedom were more undesirable than another on the grounds 'that in the first case the amount of that commodity taken away . . . is, for some reason, either greater in amount or greater in its import than in the second'. That would be 'bizarre'. For liberty is not something which can be taken to be 'even roughly measurable'.

[...]

Dworkin believes that the claim that there is no such thing as overall freedom provides him with ammunition for his polemic against libertarians who assert that there is a general 'right to liberty', as if liberty 'trumped' all other interests *as such*. If there is no such thing as liberty as such, then liberty as such is not something we can have a right to, and so cannot be one of the constitutive ideals of liberalism. Similarly, the specific-freedom thesis undermines the libertarian claim that the policies favoured by egalitarians 'conflict with liberty'. If there is no such thing as liberty as such, then liberty as such is not something with which egalitarian policies can conflict.

[. . .]

Will Kymlicka agrees with Dworkin that freedom as such is not one of the foundational values of liberalism. Again, the emphasis is on giving individuals the freedom to do certain specific things, which, given that we cannot appeal to freedom as such, we must seek to justify by reference to values other than freedom: 'We don't answer [the] question [of how valuable specific liberties are] by determining which liberties contain more or less of a single commodity called "freedom". . . . For the reason it is important to be free in a particular situation is not the amount of freedom it provides, but the importance of the various interests it serves. . . . The idea of freedom as such, and lesser or greater amounts of it, does no work in political argument.'

And the same idea appears also to be present in the work of the later Rawls. Despite Rawls's initial arguments in favour of 'the most extensive liberty', and the rule that 'liberty can be restricted only for the sake of liberty', he has since claimed only to have been interested in defending a list of specific liberties – those which he has all along called the 'basic' liberties. 'No priority is assigned to liberty as such, as if something called "liberty" has a pre-eminent value and is the main if not the sole end of political and social justice.'

[. . .]

The Idea of Non-specific Value

That the love of liberty can be something more than just the love of being free to do certain specific things is initially best made clear by means of an extreme example: think of how a prisoner feels on suddenly being released, or of the sentiment of a people on overthrowing an oppressor. Isaiah Berlin employs this example in an argument directed against MacCallum's explication of freedom as a triadic relation. MacCallum sees any claim about freedom as referring at least implicitly to three elements: an agent, X, who is free from constraints, Y, to do or be a certain thing, Z [. . .]. But, says Berlin, it is quite conceivable for an individual or a people to strive to be free of their oppressor – to desire to be rid of their chains – without aiming towards any particular Z. Berlin has certainly hit on something here. However, I think he is wrong to see this example as creating a problem for MacCallum's explication of freedom. In support of Berlin, John Gray has suggested that 'if a man may wish to be rid of his chains, without having in mind any ulterior end apart from the freedom he gains in attaining this, it seems that freedom must be regarded as basically a dyadic rather than as a triadic concept'. I hold the antecedent in this suggestion to be true, but I reject the consequent, according to which we must abandon the idea of freedom as a triadic relation. I agree with MacCallum and Oppenheim that it does not make sense to talk of an agent (X) being free from constraints (Y) without at least implicit reference to the things (Z) that the agent is free to do or be. However, I believe that there is an alternative way of capturing Berlin's insight without abandoning MacCallum's triadic formula, namely, by interpreting the 'Z' in MacCallum's formula as *non-specific* in nature. The oppressed people in Berlin's example do care about the fact that once they are rid of their chains there will be many new things that they are free to do; the point is that their minds are not focused on any of those things in particular. They value 'being free to do things' in a general, rather than in any specific sense. If they did not value the freedom to do things in at least this general sense, then it would indeed be difficult to explain their dislike for their chains.

In this chapter I intend to show that liberals have good reasons for valuing freedom in exactly this non-specific way. Such reasons identify a quantitative attribute whose measurement depends on our being able to quantify over Zs in the way outlined [above]. They are reasons, that is, for wanting to be able to measure overall freedom.

[. . .]

[. . .] I shall try to show that one of the interests served by the presence of specific freedoms is an interest people have in freedom itself. Thus, while Rawls claims that throughout the history of democratic thought 'the focus has been on achieving certain specific liberties', my point is that this focus has been motivated by, among other things, an interest in freedom *as such*. Again, while Kymlicka states that the value of any set of specific freedoms should be assessed by reference to the various interests it serves, my point is that freedom is *itself* one of our interests. If freedom is itself one of our interests, then when we ask how much a specific set of freedoms contributes to the fulfilment of our interests, *one* of the things we must be asking is *how much that specific set of freedoms contributes to our freedom*. And once we ask this last question, we are assuming an interest in freedom as something of which we can have more or less.

The difference between my view and that of Dworkin and Kymlicka, then, is that their view entails denying that our freedoms have value *independently of the value we attach to the specific things they leave us free to do*. Hence my use of the term 'non-specific value'. The 'non-specific value' of a freedom or set of freedoms is its value in terms of the good 'freedom'. If freedom is 'non-specifically valuable', then we attach value to our freedom not only because of the specific things it allows us to do, but also because of the mere fact of our having freedom. To say that freedom is non-specifically valuable is to say that it is valuable 'as such'.

We may define the non-specific value of a phenomenon (or the value that that phenomenon has 'as such') in the following way:

A phenomenon, *x*, has non-specific value (is valuable as such) iff the value of *x* cannot be described wholly in terms of a good brought about or contributed to by a specific instance of *x* or set of specific instances of *x*.

Perhaps the idea of non-specific value will become clearer if we try applying the above definition to the substance 'gold'. Is gold valuable only in the form of a gold ring or a gold watch or a gold bracelet (certain specific 'instances' of gold)? The answer is clearly 'no'. Gold is also valuable independently of the particular form it takes. We might value having a gold ring more than having a gold nugget, even if the former constitutes a smaller quantity of gold than the latter, but this is not to deny that we also take an interest in 'how much gold' we have. It is not to deny that we take an interest in gold 'as such'. As a matter of fact, we do take such an interest; we do see gold as non-specifically valuable. Similarly, to say that the attribute 'freedom' is non-specifically valuable is to say that its value cannot be described wholly in terms of the valuable phenomena other than freedom which are brought about by or partly constituted by certain specific freedoms, such as the freedom to leave one's country or the freedom to practise Catholicism or the freedom to drive one's car faster than 100 miles per hour.

Dworkin and Kymlicka do not think that freedom has non-specific value. Indeed, they would no doubt say that the analogy I have just drawn with gold is typical of the oversimplistic, 'single commodity' view of freedom that I hold (although this of course caricatures my own position; liberty is only a 'commodity' in the sense – if there is one – in which beauty or well-being are commodities). For Dworkin and Kymlicka, the only kind of value that freedom has is what we may call *specific* value. This means that, in their view, the value, for example, of my being free to play basketball on Tuesday, football on Wednesday, and cricket on Thursday is simply a function of the value of my playing basketball on Tuesday, football on Wednesday, and cricket on Thursday. 'How free' these three specific freedoms make me in comparison with some other set of specific freedoms is a question which, even if intelligible, is of no normative import.

[. . .]

[. . .] [W]e do not need to see freedom as intrinsically valuable in order to see freedom as non-specifically valuable. It is quite coherent to see freedom as having only instrumental value – as being a good thing only because it is a means to some other good – and nevertheless see freedom as being valuable as such. Given the difficulty of arguing that freedom is intrinsically valuable, then, we may just as well [now examine] the arguments for freedom's instrumental value.

Instrumental value can be defined straightforwardly, in terms of the means – ends relation:

> A phenomenon, *x*, has instrumental value iff *x* is a means to some other valuable phenomenon, *y* (and therefore the value of *x* is reducible to the value of *y*).

And, within the concept of instrumental value, we can distinguish the 'non-specific' from the 'specific' variety in the following way:

> A phenomenon, *x*, has non-specific instrumental value iff *x*, without regard to the nature of its specific instances, is a means to some other valuable phenomenon, *y*.

> A phenomenon, *x*, has specific instrumental value iff a certain specific instance (or set of instances) of *x* is a means to some other valuable phenomenon, *y*.

[. . .]

[. . .] What explains the non-specific instrumental value of freedom is the unavoidability of *human ignorance and fallibility*. Put crudely, an important kind of reason for our preferring [a larger choice set to a smaller one] is that we are not *sure* about the values of the various options.

As human beings, we are necessarily uncertain about the instrumental values of specific options. On the other hand, we do know that *some* specific option or set of options (we just do not know which) will serve some specific end – an end the exact nature of which has yet to become clear, or an end which we are aware might change in the future. Now the point here is not just that some freedoms have specific value while others do not, and that we do not yet know which freedoms fall into the first category and which into the second; our lack of knowledge in the present, about which specific freedoms will (with hindsight) turn out to have served our ends, also implies that *at present* freedom is *non*-specifically valuable. To see this, consider an analogy with judgements of probability. Suppose that it is true at time *t* that the probability of event *x* occurring at *t* + 1 is 0.5. And suppose that at *t* + 1 *x* does not in fact occur. We shall then be able to say with hindsight that, at t, *x* was not in fact going to occur. But this does not invalidate the probability judgement originally made at *t*. It remains true that at time *t* the probability of *x* occurring at *t* + 1 was 0.5. Similarly, it might turn out at time *t* + 1 that the freedom we had at time *t* to perform action *a* at *t* + 1 was of no value in pursuing the ends that we in fact turned out (at *t* + 1) to have. But this does not invalidate a judgement made at time *t* according to which the freedom to do *a was* valuable because we could not know at *t* whether or not it would serve our ends. Our ignorance about the future gives value to specific freedoms in the present that otherwise would not have value. Those freedoms have value *in virtue of* our ignorance.

The justifications of freedom's non-specific instrumental value can be usefully categorized under two headings. Freedom may be seen as non-specifically valuable (*a*) as a means to some social goal or (*b*) as a means to individual well-being.

[. . .]

Hayek is an example of a thinker who should in my view be classified as seeing freedom as non-specifically instrumentally valuable as a means to a social goal. For Hayek, the ultimate human value appears to be 'progress', rather than freedom. Progress is the improvement of the 'condition of mankind'. It involves 'a process of adaptation and learning', and 'consists in the discovery of the not yet known'. The best means a society has of attaining progress is, according to Hayek, that of granting freedom to its individual members. And it is our very ignorance of the direction in which progress will lead us that makes this so. Since freedom is only a means to this end, 'if there were omniscient men, if we could know not only all that affects the attainment of our present wishes but also our future wants and desires, there would be little case for liberty'. As it turns out, however, 'the advance and even the preservation of civilization are dependent upon a maximum of opportunity for accidents to happen'. Now, because the concrete nature of our ends is not known to us, it has to be admitted, as Norman Barry puts it, that 'the benefits of liberty are not measurable'. And this means that it is not possible to say of any one particular liberty how valuable it is in terms of the degree of progress to which it is a means. 'We shall not achieve our ends if we confine liberty to the particular instances where we know it will do good . . . If we knew how freedom would be used, the case for it would largely disappear.' Because of our lack of knowledge of future events sand desires (and because of a government's ignorance even of most people's *present* desires), the value of liberty is reducible to that of progress *only in a generalized sense*. All that we know is the truth of the *empirical generalization* that if there is more liberty, greater progress is likely to result.

J. S. Mill appears to be making a similar point to that of Hayek where he defends liberty of thought and expression on the grounds that it is the best means to attaining the truth (since freedom of expression leads to 'the clearer perception and livelier impression of truth, provided by its collision with error'), and where he defends the liberty to

experiment with different ways of living as a means to assessing their worth (since 'the worth of different modes of life should be proved *practically*'). Mill's position appears to be very close to that of Hayek where, in a famous passage in *On Liberty*, he attempts to justify the pursuit of liberty as such by suggesting that one ought to pursue utility in a *general* sense – that is, utility as 'progress': 'it must be utility in the largest sense, grounded on the permanent interests of man as a progressive being.' Given this, it seems to me that the most plausible interpretation of Mill on the value of liberty is that he saw liberty's value as at least including non-specific instrumental value. This interpretation may go some way towards helping to resolve the problem of the oft-noted apparent contradiction in Mill over the question of whether it is liberty or utility that has supreme value. The non-specificity of freedom's value allows the utilitarian consistently to promote certain specific freedoms even where, *as far as we can see*, the exercise of those specific freedoms would lead to an overall reduction in utility. For those specific freedoms will also have value in terms of utility in a more general sense, in virtue of our ignorance and fallibility. Treating freedom as non-specifically valuable as a means to utility may give the false impression that one sees freedom as a value that competes with utility, as another intrinsic good rather than as a good which ultimately reduces to it. Some of Mill's stronger pro-freedom rhetoric might therefore have been wrongly interpreted as implying freedom's intrinsic value when it was only intended to imply freedom's non-specific instrumental value.

[. . .]

[. . .] It is not only as a means to a social goal like progress or collective utility that freedom can have non-specific instrumental value. Individual freedom can also have non-specific instrumental value from the point of view of the individual herself. This will be especially so if individual well-being is seen, as it sometimes is by contemporary utilitarians, as the satisfaction of informed desires. For it is arguable that a rational individual, while valuing freedom as merely instrumental to the satisfaction of certain needs or desires, nevertheless desires as a consequence to have 'as much freedom as possible' (at least *ceteris paribus*). Why should this be so, if freedom is merely instrumentally valuable? The answer to this question can be made clear by reference to [an] analogy [. . .] with money [presented in section 2.1 of *A Measure of Freedom*]). As we saw there, money is not normally considered to be intrinsically valuable; most individuals desire it merely as a means to obtaining other goods (although there is a small minority of 'Scrooges', who come to see money as intrinsically valuable). Nevertheless, because the world is an unpredictable place, and we cannot be sure even of the nature of our own future desires and needs, let alone of the nature of future supply and demand, it is prudent to prefer money to other commodities. Imagine that one wished to present a view of the value of money analogous to the view of freedom implied by the (normative) specific-freedom thesis. Imagine, in other words, an argument aimed at showing that the instrumental value of money is wholly 'specific' in nature. Presumably, such an argument would have to look something like this:

> We don't desire money for its own sake, but as a means to other things that we do value for their own sake. Therefore, there is no need to quantify money. Rather, what people desire is certain specific 'moneys', or specific 'kinds of money', such as food rations, record tokens, and petrol vouchers, according to the ends which they see money as serving.[1]

Clearly, this argument against the need to quantify money fails to deal with the objection outlined above. Because our preferences over 'moneys' are based on less than perfect knowledge of the future, it is rational to desire money in a general sense. Hence money acquires a value which is independent of that of the specific things which it is a means to possessing, and we have not merely record tokens and petrol vouchers, but dollars, pounds, and roubles. This is not to say that money is intrinsically valuable, but merely that it is non-specifically valuable. Scrooges are not the only people in this world interested in money in a non-specific sense, and who are therefore interested in 'how much money' they have. Preferring money to sweet rations does not make one a Scrooge, even if one strongly desires to eat sweets.

A similar case can be made out for the non-specific instrumental value of freedom. Since we cannot be sure of our future desires or needs, we do not value freedom merely as one of the necessary means to our doing *x*, *y*, and *z*, but rather, as one of the means by which we may satisfy whatever our needs and desires may be. Once again, the value of liberty turns out to be reducible *only in a generalized sense* to that of the ends it serves. Once again, we can only be sure (or as sure as possible) of attaining the ends liberty serves by making sure that there is as much liberty as possible (at least *ceteris paribus*). Here, as before, the instrumental value of liberty is of a non-specific kind. The value of liberty lies in that which liberty allows us to do, but (given the lack of certain kinds of knowledge) does not consist in the value of any of the specific things that specific liberties allow us to do.

Note

1 Not a $10 record token or a £10 petrol voucher but, rather, a *one-record* record token or a *six-gallon* petrol voucher.

Ian Carter, *A Measure of Freedom* (Oxford: Oxford University Press, 1999), pp. 11, 18–20, 32–4, 44, 45–7, 50–2.

Part IX

The Measurement
of Freedom

Introduction to Part IX

One way of clarifying the nature of freedom is to specify the necessary and sufficient conditions for an agent to be free or unfree to do some particular thing. This has been the aim of many of the writings contained in the previous sections. But fulfilling such an aim will not yet tell us everything we need to know. It will not explain what it means to be "more or less" free, what we have in mind when we say that a person's freedom has increased or diminished, or how we are able to compare the overall levels of freedom of two or more individuals or societies. The writings in this part of the anthology undertake constructive attempts to say what exactly it would mean to measure freedom in this overall sense.

Some have criticized the idea of measuring overall freedom as a non-starter. Whether or not the project of measuring freedom can succeed, however, there are important reasons for taking it seriously. One such reason may be found in the kind of value we attach to freedom. If, as Ronald Dworkin believes, only certain specific freedoms have value (even prima facie), so that freedom has no value "as such" (even prima facie), then we need not concern ourselves with how free people are. But if, as Ian Carter claims, freedom has "non-specific" value – if the value of our freedom cannot be wholly accounted for in terms of the values of our freedoms to do specific things – then freedom will have value as such (see the contributions by Dworkin and Carter in Part VIII). This will mean that the value of a set of freedoms is in part a function of how large that set is or, more precisely, of how much freedom that set provides.

Another reason for taking an interest in the concept of overall freedom lies in the principles of justice endorsed by political liberals. Many liberals explicitly endorse the principle of "equal freedom" as a principle of justice. Others, especially libertarians, talk of "maximizing" freedom. Others still prescribe "maximal equal" freedom, or a "bare minimum" of freedom for all, or even "maximin" freedom. The meaningfulness of these principles of justice depends on the possibility of gauging degrees of overall freedom, sometimes comparatively, sometimes absolutely. (John Rawls's first major work prescribed the "most extensive liberty" for all, but Rawls later recanted on the implied assumption that we can quantify freedom, favoring instead a list of "basic" liberties to do certain types of thing.)

One of the problems that have motivated a skeptical view of the measurement of overall freedom concerns the individuation of actions. If, as many theorists assume, the freedom of an agent consists in a lack of constraints on the performance of actions (however the relevant constraints are to be characterized), then the extent of an agent's freedom presumably increases with the number of actions he or she is unprevented from performing. But how are these actions to be counted? Are there not innumerable ways of describing and redescribing the things a person can do? How, moreover, should the individual actions be weighted? Should we simply count the sheer number of options, or should we also take account of the degrees to which they are valuable? Does the freedom to commit murder count for the "same amount of freedom" as the freedom to save a life? Some theorists, including Hillel Steiner, have criticized the view that measurements of overall freedom should be a function of such valuational magnitudes. However, their alternative metrics, which involve weighting actions in terms of their physical extensiveness, have in turn been criticized as counterintuitive.

Yet another problem regards the comparability of different ways of constraining freedom. How are we to compare unfreedom created by physical obstacles, say, with unfreedom created by the difficulty or costliness or punishability of actions?

The recent increase in interest in the problem of measuring freedom arises not only from developments in political philosophy but also from the efforts of social choice theorists to find a freedom-based alternative to the standard utilitarian or "welfarist" framework that has tended to dominate their discipline. The work of Robert Sugden, Martin van Hees, and, most influentially, Amartya Sen, has helped to bridge the gap between these two research fields, leading to some fruitful interchange.

The social choice literature on freedom can appear somewhat daunting to those not already familiar with the formal language of rational choice theory. But the basic intuitions behind the axioms and proofs are usually quite readily understandable, and it is interesting to see how similar some of these are to the concerns voiced by the philosophers. In a seminal article reproduced here, Prasanta Pattanaik and Yongsheng Xu deduce a "cardinality approach" from a few apparently uncontroversial axiomatic claims about freedom. Such a "cardinality approach" to measuring freedom partly mirrors the philosophers' concept of the "sheer number" of options. Pattanaik and Xu do not defend this approach, however, but present their deduction as a *reductio ad absurdum*. Since the original publication of their article, there have been a number of attempts – by them and others – to show which of their axioms will, as a consequence, have to be rejected. Many of the alternative metrics proposed, including those of Sen and Sugden, have involved the incorporation of valuational magnitudes in the form of information about the agent's preferences.

Further Reading

Kramer, Matthew H., *The Quality of Freedom* (Oxford: Oxford University Press, 2003), ch. 5 (sympathetic critique of Steiner and Carter and construction of a metric incorporating valuational magnitudes).

O'Neill, Onora, "The Most Extensive Liberty," *Proceedings of the Aristotelian Society* 80 (1980), pp. 45–59 (skeptical assessment of the measurement assumption behind Rawls's first principle of justice as originally formulated).

Oppenheim, Felix E., *Political Concepts: A Reconstruction* (Blackwell: Oxford, 1981), ch. 4 (skeptical assessment of the problem of aggregating various freedom variables).

Pattanaik, Prasanta, and Xu, Yongsheng, "On Preference and Freedom," *Theory and Decision* 44 (1998), pp. 173–98 (formal elaboration of a metric incorporating information about agents' reasonable preferences).

Sen, Amartya, "Welfare, Preference and Freedom," *Journal of Econometrics* 50 (1991), pp. 15–29 (formal elaboration of a metric incorporating information about agents' actual preferences).

Chapter 81

Hillel Steiner, from "How Free: Computing Personal Liberty" (1983)

Judgments about the extent to which an individual is free are easily among the more intractable of the various raw materials which present themselves for philosophical processing. On the one hand, few of us have any qualms about making statements to the effect that Blue is more free than Red. Explicitly or otherwise, such claims are the commonplaces of most history textbooks and of much that passes before us in the news media. And yet, good evidence for the presence of a philosophical puzzle here is to be found in the familiar hesitation we experience when we first reflect on the grounds for such claims. Is it really the case that the average Russian is less free than an Englishman in a dole queue? Are we quite certain that a dirt farmer in the Appalachians enjoys greater personal liberty than the inmate of a well-appointed modern prison? Were citizens of classical Athens more free, or less free, than their counterparts in today's welfare states?

Fashioning a criterion which will yield a set of satisfying answers to these questions is a task traditionally beset by a multitude of difficulties, among which two deserve particular mention. In the first place, there is still widespread disagreement about the meaning of the word 'freedom' of 'liberty'. Nor is this disagreement esoterically confined to the ranks of political philosophers, since ordinary language can readily be seen to sustain many uses of these and related terms, resting on different and opposed conditions for their application. But second, and even where divergent meanings are apparently absent, there is sometimes disagreement – though, more often, embarrassed demurral – over how to measure freedom and unfreedom, that is, how to *count* acknowledged instances of freedom and unfreedom. What I hope to show in this paper is that there is a plausible solution to the second of these difficulties, and that some of the objections levelled at it are misdirected inasmuch as they arise out of differences over the meaning of 'freedom' and not out of any mensural inadequacy in the proposal itself.[1] Duelling with intuitions until a mortal paradox is inflicted is enjoyable but, in the end, unsatisfying – especially when unnecessary.

The solution I have in mind is crude and simple, and runs as follows. Take a list of actions L_1 and discover which of them Red is respectively free and unfree to do. Let F_r and U_r respectively stand for the total numbers of Red's free and unfree actions. To ascertain how free Red is, we need only establish the value of

$$\frac{F_r}{F_r + U_r}.$$

Some objections to this formula are less interesting than others. One might object that had a different list than L_1 been used, say L_2, we might have come up with a different answer to the question of how free Red is. This objection is true, but easily accommodated. For we can simply add all the items appearing only in L_2 to L_1, and perform the same operation. The formula itself remains unimpaired. And it similarly withstands the criticism that the actions which a person is free or unfree to do may be infinitely numerous. For, aside from conceptual differences over what counts as an instance of freedom or unfreedom, there can never be a reason for rejecting any proposed addition to the list. A doctor does not reserve judgment on whether a patient is healthy merely on the grounds that the latter may be afflicted with a disease as yet unknown to medical science. And one is correspondingly unwarranted in refraining from extent-of-freedom judgments because there may be some unknown actions which Red is free or unfree to do. At the very least one is entitled to say that, with respect to those listed actions, Red is free to the computed extent.

A third possible objection to this method of measuring a person's liberty is directed against the structure of the formula itself, rather than the identifiability of its variables. Why, in trying to assess how free Red is, should we take into account those actions which Red is *unfree* to do? Why not confine our calculation of summing those actions which he is free to do? It is an implication of this objection that a modern solitary Robinson Crusoe, equipped with a fair share of current scientific and technological knowledge, would be a great deal more free than Defoe's hero, in the same material circumstances. And more generally, it seems to be a widely held view that members of modern industrial societies are *ipso facto* more free than their counterparts in earlier or more primitive societies. That is, because technological development and increased production have enlarged the number of actions which it is possible for us to do, we must generally be more free than persons lacking these possibilities. Even an inmate of a modern prison – to say nothing of his unimprisoned fellow citizen – may be able unobstructedly to do many more actions than the most free member of a less advanced society.

The problem with this objection is that it confuses liberty with ability. If this is a proper conception of liberty at all, it is certainly not the one which concerns us as political philosophers. Liberty is a social relation, a relation between persons. The restraints imposed upon us by nature, and our struggles and successes in overcoming them, are subjects deserving of our closest attention. But it is not to physicists, doctors or engineers whom we turn in seeking answers to the question of 'How free?' For while it is undoubtedly true that the average member of an advanced society is able to do, and unrestrained from doing, many more actions than his counterparts in less advanced societies, it is equally true that he is able to do, but restrained from doing, many more actions than they. That is, there are many more actions which he is *unfree* to do. Simply to ignore them in estimating the extent of a person's liberty, is to misconstrue the object of such an exercise.

An apparently more interesting objection is sometimes prompted by the familiar problems of act-individuation. As is well enough appreciated, any piece of outward bodily behaviour can be described in a variety of ways, and these variations occur across a number of different dimensions. Since the items entered in the proposed formula's list are definite descriptions of acts, reluctance to accept the formula as an appropriate measure of liberty may be motivated by an apprehension that the compilation of such a list must – because of act-individuation problems – involve either arbitrary omissions or numerous instances of double-counting. Consider the following example, in which a dozen alternative descriptions are offered of a shooting:

1. He tensed his forefinger.
2. He pressed a piece of metal.
3. He released a spring.
4. He pulled the trigger of a gun.
5. He fired a gun.
6. He fired a bullet.

7. He shot a bullet at a man.
8. He shot a bullet towards a man.
9. He shot a man.
10. He killed a man.
11. He committed judicial murder.
12. He saved four lives.

Needless to say, this inventory could be considerably extended. But the question is: should this be a matter for concern and a reason for rejecting the formula? I suggest that what we have here is an objection which is of the same kind as the second one discussed above. There is no reason why *all* these descriptions cannot be entered in our list. The various dimensions in which different act-descriptions subsist – and which discriminate between basic and non-basic acts and between intended and unintended consequences – constitute no effective obstacle in this respect, inasmuch as inclusiveness along these lines at once rules out the possibility of arbitrary omissions and poses no danger of otiose double-counting. Each of the twelve act-descriptions recorded above is only contingently related to the rest and, therefore, each refers to an event which could have occurred even if the others had not. It is consequently perfectly intelligible to ask, in the case of each of them, whether the actor was free to do the action. And there is no reason why the answers to any pair of these twelve questions need have been the same.

Consider, next, the objection that this formula fails to measure the extent to which Red is free because, in simply adding up the numbers of actions he is free and unfree to do, it fails to take account of the extent to which he is free or unfree to do *each* of them. This objection suggests that we can speak, not only of the extent to which a person is free with respect to a list of several actions, but also with respect to a single action. Thus it is sometimes suggested that I am more free to see Walt Disney's film *Sleeping Beauty* than to see Sam Peckinpah's *Straw Dogs*, because the latter is banned in Manchester but not its environs, while the former is not banned at all. This objection fails inasmuch as it is based on an

imprecision of language of a kind that is, admittedly, common enough in our everyday discourse. 'Seeing *Straw Dogs*', or for that matter 'Seeing *Straw Dogs* in Manchester', is not the name of a single action but rather of a *class* of actions. There are many single actions which would count as members of this class. Of course, I am unfree to do any of the single actions which comprise the class of actions called 'Seeing *Straw Dogs* in Manchester'. And I am thus also unfree to do a certain proportion of the single actions comprising the class of actions called 'Seeing *Straw Dogs*'. These classes amount to nothing more than lists of single actions and, as such, constitute sub-lists within the more extensive list which the formula invites us to compile. It is true that, in talking about the extent of a person's liberty, we are often thinking less about single actions than about classes of actions. But we should still wish to be able to distinguish – in terms of differing amounts of freedom – between the position where one is restrained from seeing *Straw Dogs* in Manchester and the position where one is restrained from seeing *Straw Dogs* in Manchester more than once. In the former case one is more unfree than in the latter. And we can only say this if, in making extent-of-freedom judgments, what we are counting are single actions.

Another objection to the formula similarly locates its inadequacy in its neglect of the variable extent to which persons are free or unfree to do the actions they are free or unfree to do. But this variation is held to consist in the variability of the *cost* or *difficulty* of doing an action. A British passport holder, it is said, is less free to enter the United States (at least, through an official entry-point) than a Canadian passport holder, because the former but not the latter requires a visa to do so. It is easy enough to see that this example poses no problem, for the use of the formula as a measure of liberty, if what it alludes to is merely the fact that applications for visas can be rejected. For our list of free and unfree actions can readily include not only entering the United States but also securing a visa to do so. The problem it more perspicaciously attempts to raise resides in the fact that securing a visa is an action which takes time, trouble and resources, even when that action is unthreatened with failure. So the point here is that, for the British passport holder, more actions must be done to do the action of entering the United States than is the case for the Canadian passport holder. And this, it is held, entails that the former is less free than the latter in respect of the action of entering the United States. Again however, the basis of this objection warrants closer scrutiny.

Here we must pause to notice an important distinction. It is often the case that, in order to do an action, a sequence of prior actions must be done: to do E, it may be necessary that one previously do A, B, C, and D, and that they be done in that order. However, the sense in which this prior sequence is necessary can vary. Clearly it is not a *causal* condition of a British passport holder's entering the United States that he secure a visa. It is not impossible for him to enter – even through an official entry-point – without a visa, since it is not impossible for the officials at that entry-point to allow him to enter without a visa. Compare this with the case of an imprisoned person attending the opera. It is a causal condition of his attending the opera that he leave his cell. And it is impossible for his gaoler both to allow him to attend the opera and to restrain him from leaving his cell. Hence, in the first case, we cannot say that it is the visa-issuing officials who make a British passport holder unfree to enter the United States by making him unfree to secure a visa. But we can say that it is the gaoler who makes the prisoner unfree to attend the opera by making him unfree to leave his cell. Where the sequence of actions, required to be done prior to the doing of E, is causally necessary, making a person unfree to do D implies making him unfree to E; and making him unfree to do A implies making him unfree to do B, C, D, and E. But where the relation of necessity between each pair of consecutive actions in the sequence is not a causal relation, making a person unfree to do

an earlier action in the sequence does not imply making him unfree to do any of the subsequent actions. And therefore his unfreedom to do any of them must be due to other restraints. Of course, the actions which must be done in order to do another action need not always be done in a particular sequence. Nor is it the case that, where such previously required actions must be done in a particular sequence, the relation of necessity between every pair of consecutive actions must either be causal throughout the sequence or non-causal throughout the sequence. The relation between submitting a visa application and, say, posting a completed visa application form is one of causal necessity, whereas that between securing a visa and submitting a visa application is not.

The cost or difficulty of doing an action arises from the fact that its performance requires the doing of other actions. If one is free to do each of those other actions, there appear to be no grounds for claiming that one is less than entirely free to do that action itself unless, of course, one is specifically restrained from doing *it* – in which case, one is entirely unfree to do it. And if one is unfree to do one of those prior actions, one is either (still) entirely free to do the action itself (if the relation between those two actions is one of non-causal necessity), or entirely unfree to do the action itself (if the relation between the two actions is one of causal necessity). Since the burden of the present objection is to suggest that the action itself can be one which we are less free to do, without being entirely unfree to do it, this objection fails.

We could perhaps reformulate the objection and say that the British passport holder's allegedly lesser freedom to enter the United States is not a consequence of his being less free to do any of the actions requisitely anterior to entry, but rather is a consequence of there being more such requisitely anterior actions: the greater cost or difficulty of doing an action reduces one's freedom to do it, not because it entails prior actions which one is less free to do, but because it entails a greater number of prior actions. There is an obvious sense in which this is true, but it too fails as an objection to the use of the formula for measuring the extent of a person's liberty. A clear and direct analogy is a hurdle-race. Suppose that the 500-yard track contains five hurdles, and that the action under consideration is crossing the finish-line 60 seconds after the starting-gun. And suppose that I am able to do this action. Now suppose that the organizers of the race add two more hurdles and, as a result, it now takes me 65 seconds to cross the finish-line. The organizers have thus rendered me not merely less free, but entirely unfree, to do the action of crossing the finish-line in 60 seconds. And how have they done this? They have done it by making it impossible for me (making me entirely unfree) to do an action – say, crossing the 450-yard mark in 55 seconds – requisitely anterior to the action of crossing the finish-line in 60 seconds. Increasing the cost or difficulty of doing an action, by increasing the number of requisitely anterior actions – in this case, increasing the number of hurdle-jumps – either leaves one entirely free to do that action or renders one entirely unfree to do it. And it achieves this latter effect by rendering one entirely unfree to do an action anterior to it.

The notion of degrees of freedom to do an action is superfluous, misleading and descriptively imprecise. Why then do we commonly say that British passport holders are less free than their Canadian counterparts (though not unfree) to enter the United States? I suggest that, like much else in ordinary parlance, this locution is an elliptical abbreviation of a probabilistic judgment. Its meaning is more accurately conveyed in saying that British passport holders are less probably free than Canadians to do the action in question. This perfectly sensible statistical judgment reflects the fact that there is a wider range of possible reasons why any British passport holder will be unfree to secure a visa – and hence, will probably be unfree to enter the United States – than is the case for any Canadian passport holder. It is true that more hurdles make success less prob-

able, but only because more hurdles probably make at least one of the actions required for success impossible. A list of actions which have and have not been made impossible for one to do, such as that proposed in the formula, can adequately take account of this truth.

The final objection to be considered is perhaps the most commonsensical of those examined so far, inasmuch as it takes exception to what many would regard as the most counter-intuitive aspect of using the formula to compute personal liberty. Isaiah Berlin suggests an expansive approach to any such computation:

> The extent of my freedom seems to depend on (a) how many possibilities are open to me (although the method of counting these can never be more than impressionistic. Possibilities of action are not discrete entities like apples, which can be exhaustively enumerated); (b) how easy or difficult each of these possibilities is to actualize; (c) how important in my plan of life, given my character and circumstances, these possibilities are when compared with each other; (d) how far they are closed and opened by deliberate human acts; (e) what value not merely the agent, but the general sentiment of the society in which he lives, puts on the various possibilities. All these magnitudes must be 'integrated', and a conclusion, necessarily never precise, or indisputable, drawn from this process.

My argument, as developed above, asserts the computational relevance of (a) while rejecting that of (b) and (d). Should the magnitudes referred to in (c) and (e) – and which I shall conjunctively label 'valuational magnitudes' – figure in our assessment of the extent of a person's liberty?

Evidently, our first reflections on this question strongly incline us to the view that the significance of the actions which we are or are not free to do must enter into our estimations of how free we are.

> When two or more properties or 'respects' are subject to precise mathematical comparison, they will always have some quantitative

element in common. The difficulty in striking resultant totals of 'on balance freedom' derives from the fact that the relation among the various 'areas' in which people are said to be free is not so much like the relation between the height, breadth, and depth of a physical object as it is like the relation between the gasoline economy, styling, and comfort of an automobile. . . . What we more likely mean when we say that one subject is freer on balance than another is that his freedom is greater in the more valuable, important, or significant dimensions, where the 'value' of a dimension is determined by some independent standard.[2]

Can it seriously be maintained that the action of twiddling one's thumbs and the action of casting a ballot in an unrigged election should be accorded equal weight – should each be counted as one action – in measuring an individual's liberty? Charles Taylor attacks the 'crude' and 'tough-minded' negative conception of liberty underlying such a proposal, and suggests that 'it has no place for the notion of significance' and 'will allow only for purely quantitative judgments'. This conception is said to license the 'diabolical defence of Albania' against the charge of being a less free society than Britain, since the presence of severe restraints on religious practice in the former – and their absence in the latter – could thereby be forensically countered by pointing to the considerably fewer traffic restrictions in the former than in the latter.

For the moment, at least, we can leave aside questions like whether the harassed London commuter, diabolical or not, would necessarily be disposed to accept this judgment of relative significance. The question we should first address is whether the use of the formula to compute personal liberty necessarily excludes the integration of valuational magnitudes in performing this computation. Is the formula ineluctably tied to the tough-minded negative conception of liberty? Or can it accommodate the measurement of what Taylor considers to be a more discriminating negative conception of liberty – one which assigns varying degrees

of significance to restrained actions – and which, as he rightly argues, is thus not so readily distinguishable from many positive conceptions of liberty?

Now, in principle, there is no reason why the formula cannot be used to measure the extent of a person's liberty so conceived. Where previously each action was given the numerical value of unity in calculating the sums represented by F_r and U_r, under the proposed dispensation each action would be assigned the numerical value of its significance and the calculation could proceed in the same manner. Clearly the significance of various actions does vary and, although the basis for assigning numerical values to these variations may be unavoidably conventional, such assignability is a necessary condition of comparing the relative amounts of liberty enjoyed by any two persons who – like an Albanian and a Briton – are free or unfree to do different sets of actions. Taylor's previously cited criticism of the crude negative conception is thus somewhat overstated, since even a conception of liberty which *does* give place to the notion of significance must permit the latter's quantification if it is to allow its users to make the kind of comparative judgment he makes. That said, however, it is also the case that computing a person's liberty in this way is not without its logical difficulties, nor is it devoid of strongly counter-intuitive consequences.

Proposals that valuational magnitudes be integrated into the measurement of personal liberty are typically underspecified. On the face of it, we might imagine that the actions which we are free or unfree to do vary not only in their significance, but also that these variations can be either negative or positive. If saving another person's life is a highly significant act, it seems reasonable to think that the act of taking another's life is not perspicuously graded as 'insignificant' but rather (infelicitously) as 'anti-significant', On one interpretation of the integration proposal, then, all acts on our list would be assigned positive or negative numbers representing the valuation of their significance or anti-significance.

Suppose our list thus contains the following six actions and their respective valuations: A (+10), B (+8), C (+6), X (−9), Y (−7), Z (−5). And suppose that Red is free to do A, B, X, and unfree to do C, Y, Z. Applying the formula to compute the extent of Red's liberty, we get the following result:

$$\frac{F_r}{F_r + U_r} = \frac{A + B + X}{(A + B + X) + (C + Y + Z)}$$

$$= \frac{9}{3} = 3.$$

The extent of Red's liberty is 3. But observe that computing Red's liberty in this fashion leads to a contradiction. For suppose that the restraint on his doing Y were removed, and that he was thus free to do Y. The formula gives us the following result for his state of ostensibly increased liberty:

$$\frac{F_r}{F_r + U_r} = \frac{A + B + X + Y}{(A + B + X + Y) + (C + Z)}$$

$$= \frac{2}{3}.$$

That is, Red's newly acquired liberty to do Y would entail a *decrease* in his freedom.

To avoid such contradictions, while still integrating valuational magnitudes into computations of personal liberty, it is thus necessary to exclude the use of negative numbers from our valuational assignments to listed actions. But how can this be done? For as was just noted, whatever positive value we assign to an act of life-saving, it would not make sense that an act of life-taking be assigned merely a lower positive value. If it were, this would have the utterly absurd consequence that a sufficiently large number of life-taking acts would be equal or greater in value than one life-saving act. If any acts have positive value, it is necessarily true that there are acts to which negative values attach.

Hence, to expunge negative valuations from our computation in order to avoid the contradictions they entail, it is necessary to

make a move which is indeed a commonplace in most accounts of the *positive* conception of liberty. That is, we need to remove all negatively valued actions from our list of actions which Red is free or unfree to do. For Red, acts X, Y, Z, being acts which are negatively valued, are ones which he cannot be said to be either free or unfree to do. The boldness of this move deserves attention, for it constitutes a complete shift in the conception of the liberty we are measuring. The fact that Red is unrestrained from doing X and restrained from doing Y and Z no longer implies, as it previously did, that he is free to do X and unfree to do Y and Z. Accordingly, whereas on the crude and tough-minded negative conception, which admits of no valuational weightings in computing personal liberty, the answer to the question 'How free is Red?' is secured thus,

$$\frac{F_r}{F_r + U_r} = \frac{A + B + X}{(A + B + X) + (C + Y + Z)}$$

$$= \frac{3}{6} = \frac{1}{2}.$$

on the positive conception of liberty, the extent of Red's freedom is given thus,

$$\frac{F_r}{F_r + U_r} = \frac{A + B}{(A + B) + C} = \frac{18}{24} = \frac{3}{4}.$$

The difference between these two results does, in fact, reflect the difference commonly found between positive liberty theorists and their negative liberty counterparts, inasmuch as the latter typically charge the former with exaggerating the extent to which individuals are free in some kinds of society where state restraints on action are relatively numerous. Conversely, and as the formula would show, positive theorists find other sorts of society to be ones allowing individuals much less freedom than they are held to enjoy by negative libertarians. Thus, if Red were restrained from doing A and B, and not restrained from doing C, X, Y, Z, the extent of his negative liberty would be represented by $\frac{2}{3}$ while his positive liberty would amount only to $\frac{1}{4}$.

Taylor's argument is therefore correct in its suggestion that the integration of valuational magnitudes into the computation of an individual's liberty shortens the distance alleged to exist between 'more discriminating' negative conceptions and the positive conception of liberty. Indeed, as has been shown, it eliminates that distance altogether. For since no such integration can consistently be performed with respect to negatively valued acts, computations incorporating valuational magnitudes can be computations only of an individual's positive liberty: only positively valued acts can count as ones which we are free and unfree to do. Computations of an individual's negative liberty exclude valuational magni-

tudes, and the numerical weighting assigned to each act which we are negatively free or unfree to do must therefore be unity. The only consistent conception of negative liberty is thus the crude and tough-minded one.

Notes

1 An (imperfect) analogy to this kind of objection is that which takes exception to the capacity of a ruler to measure length, on the grounds that it is scaled in inches rather than centimetres.
2 Joel Feinberg, *Social Philosophy* (Englewood Cliffs: Prentice-Hall, 1973), pp. 18–19.

Hillel Steiner, "How Free: Computing Personal Liberty," from A. Phillips-Griffiths (ed.), *Of Liberty* (Cambridge: Cambridge University Press, 1983), pp. 73–83.

Chapter 82

Ian Carter, from *A Measure of Freedom* (1999)

Individual Freedom: Actions

[...]

As a starting point for a fuller elaboration of the empirical approach [to measuring freedom], it is useful to consider a formula suggested by Hillel Steiner. According to Steiner, the extent of an agent's overall freedom can be represented in the following way. Where 'Red' is an agent, for any given list of actions, Red's freedom is equal to the value of

$$F_r/(F_r + U_r)$$

where F_r and U_r stand for the numbers of actions Red is free and unfree to perform respectively. It is clear that the measurements resulting from this formula will depend on the nature and extent of the 'given list of actions' referred to above. It is equally clear, however, that if we are interested in measuring the *overall* freedom of Red, in the sense implied in Chapters 1 and 2 [of *A Measure of Freedom*], then that 'given list of actions' must be a list of *all* the actions which Red can reasonably be described as either free or unfree to perform.

[...]

Steiner has subsequently expressed dissatisfaction with his formula, and this is presumably because it does not itself provide us with an answer to the objection, neatly expressed by Berlin, that 'possibilities of action are not discrete entities like apples, which can be exhaustively enumerated'. It is certainly not immediately clear what 'counting' available actions amounts to, or whether it is indeed possible. Is the 'number' of actions I might perform not infinite, or at least indeterminate? This consideration constitutes one of the most frequently posed 'epistemic' objections to the idea of measuring freedom [...].

The basic intuition behind Berlin's objection can be unpacked, and so clarified, by pointing to three particular problems to do with the 'counting' of actions. I think that it will be sensible to deal with each of these three problems separately. The first may be called the problem of *indefinite numbers of descriptions*. This is the problem that will first spring to the minds of those philosophers of action who hold that every different description of an action is a description of a different action, and therefore that there are as many actions as there are descriptions of actions. On this view, 'extending my arm' will count for one action, 'signalling for a turn' will count for another, 'following the highway code' will count for yet another, and so on indefinitely. Steiner notes this problem, and the worry that it seems to force us into 'either arbitrary omissions or numerous instances of double counting' in the compilation of our list of actions $(F_r + U_r)$, but suggests, in answer to it, that 'there is no reason why *all* these descriptions cannot be entered in our list'. But this is surely not sufficient to overcome the problem of indefinite numbers of descriptions. After all, if there is an indefinite number of act-descriptions available, and each consitutes a potential entrant on our list of actions, then it will always be possible to reverse a judgement to the effect that A is freer than B by including a sufficient number of descriptions of the actions that A is unfree to perform and B free to perform. As a result, all measurements will appear arbitrary. More recently, Steiner has suggested that the arbitrariness of the number of descriptions we provide will not be a problem as long as we count freedoms and unfreedoms symmetrically, so that if what is intuitively seen as a single freedom (the freedom to do x) were to count for, say, ten (because ten alternative descriptions of x are entered onto the list), the removal of that 'single freedom' (the *un*freedom to do x) would similarly count for ten. But it is not true that the mere symmetrical counting of freedoms and unfreedoms means that the problem of indefinite numbers of descriptions 'poses no danger of deforming our resultant calculation'. For it remains the case that for Steiner an agent's overall freedom is to be calculated in terms of the *proportion* of the actions on our list that she is free to perform. The value of any given fraction expressing that proportion (as well as the ratio of one such fraction to another) will *vary* with the value of a given constant that is added to both the numerator and the denominator.

The second problem is what we might call that of *indefinite subdivision*. Even leaving aside the problem posed by the number of descriptions of actions, if we take any one action, we can see that that action can be subdivided in spatio-temporal terms. For example, should we think of my raising my arm two feet as a single action, or should we think of it as two actions (my raising my arm one foot, and then my raising it another foot)? Or should we think of it as eight actions (my raising my arm three inches, then three more inches . . .)? Similarly, my spending an evening at the theatre 'can be subdivided into my attending Act I, scene i, my attending Act I, scene ii, and so forth, with each of these being further and indefinitely subdivisible'. It seems, as Onora

O'Neill has suggested, that 'it would always be possible to show that any given set of liberties was as numerous as any other merely by listing the component liberties more specifically'.

The third problem may be called the problem of *indefinite causal chains*. I move my arm, I operate a pump, I replenish the water supply, I poison the inhabitants of a house . . . As the events in this causal chain unfold, we feel that the bringing about of each thing that happens is something that I *do*. When should we stop adding to the list of actions that are the bringing about of consequences of my bodily movements? We cannot allow that the addition may go on indefinitely, otherwise we will find ourselves up against the same problem of arbitrary measurements implied by the other two problems. Once again, it seems difficult to fix on a definite number of available actions.

[. . .]

In order to deal with the problem of indefinite numbers of descriptions, we need to be able to make sense of the idea of *re*describing an action. The idea that the problem at hand *is* a problem depends on the idea that we have no non-arbitrary basis on which to stop adding new act-descriptions to our list of all the actions that Red can be described as either free or unfree to perform ($F_r + U_r$). It depends, in other words, on the idea that every distinct act-description is a description of a distinct action. If, on the other hand, we can make sense of the idea of *re*describing an action, then we will have made sense of the idea that a single action can have many descriptions, and it will no longer be true that every different act-description is a description of a different action. This will allow us to fix on one particular description of each possible action, and to enter only that description on our list. It will also allow us both to make sense of, and to avoid, what appears to be the 'double counting' of actions, where to 'double count' an action is, we intuitively feel, to list it twice under alternative descriptions. Just as 'Cary Grant' is a redescription of 'Archie

Leach', so 'signalling for a turn' might simply be a redescription of 'raising one's arm'. If so, seeing these two act-descriptions as describing *two* actions would be akin to counting both Archie Leach and Cary Grant in a head-count of Hollywood actors. Once we have applied the strategy of listing each action under only one description, then we can safely assume that if we are still left with an indefinitely long list, this will not be because of the problem of indefinite numbers of descriptions but, rather, because of one of the other two problems mentioned above – that of indefinite subdivision or that of indefinite causal chains.

The key to being able to redescribe actions lies in conceiving of them, along with Donald Davidson, as spatio-temporally located particulars. This conception of actions provides us with a criterion of act-identity – a criterion which allows us to say when two act-descriptions are descriptions of the *same* action – which fits nicely with the answer provided by the empirical approach to the question of which act-descriptions are relevant to the measurement of freedom. It is an action's physical location (say, raising my arm at the crossroads outside my house at time *t*) which allows us to say that another act-description (say, signalling for a turn) is simply a redescription of that same action (once, that is, we have established that that particular act of signalling takes place outside my house at time *t*). And it is exactly this physical location of an action (which implies, *inter alia*, its physical dimensions) that provides the relevant kind of act-description that we should include in our list.

[. . .]

For two things to be compossible, they must both be members of a single possible world, which is to say that they must be possible in combination. Steiner has already done much to show the importance of the notion of compossibility for political philosophy, above all through his work on the compossibility of rights as a necessary requirement of any acceptable theory of justice. His specification of the conditions under which two or more rights are compossible itself rests on a theory about the conditions under which two or more *actions* (of different people) are compossible. However, he does not appear to take advantage of the applicability of the idea of the compossibility of actions (here, of the same person) to the assessment of degrees of overall freedom.

If a set of actions is compossible, then there is a possible world in which they all occur. For any set of compossible actions, we can ask whether that set of actions is prevented or unprevented for (unavailable or available to) a given individual. We can say that the individual is free to perform that set of compossible actions if she is not restrained by the relevant 'preventing conditions' from bringing it about that the actual world is one of the possible worlds that contains that set. The conditions under which two actions should, for our purposes, be seen as compossible are a matter of debate on which I need not pronounce here. That two actions are compossible might be taken to mean that they are logically compossible, or that they are nomically compossible, or that they are technologically compossible. This will depend on how we interpret the denominator of Steiner's formula [. . .].

To see the relevance of the compossibility of a single agent's available actions to her extent of overall freedom, consider the following three actions: (*a*) walking down the street at time *t*; (*b*) stealing a beer from the shop at *t* + 1, (*c*) walking away from the shop at *t* + 2. Assume that I am free to perform all three of these actions in combination, whereas you are not, because you are being followed by a policeman who would arrest you if you performed (*b*), so preventing you from performing (*c*). Assume, also, that there is nothing stopping you from performing (*c*) if you refrain from performing (*b*). Each of us is free to perform (*a*), free to perform (*b*), and free to perform (*c*). Yet intuitively, it is clear that I am freer than you (in a purely empirical sense) in terms of the availability of these actions. The reason for this is that we feel that freedom judgements should take account not only of the single actions available to an individual agent, but also of the *act combinations* available to her. Some possible act combinations are 'and/or' options; we can perform either one or the other or both (or neither). Others are 'or only' options; we can perform only one or the other (or neither). Others still are 'and only' options; we can only choose to perform both actions (or neither). The way in which we can take account of this fact in our measurements of freedom is by saying that a person's freedom is a function not simply of the number of actions she is constrained and unconstrained from performing, but rather, of the number and size of the *sets of compossible actions* she is constrained and unconstrained from performing. Thus, in the above example, assuming neither of us is free to perform (*b*) or (*c*) without first performing (*a*), I have available the sets of compossible actions (*a*), (*a b*), (*a c*), (*a b c*), whereas you only have available the sets of compossible actions (*a*), (*a b*), (*a c*). Aggregating over sets of compossible actions instead of over single actions allows us to accommodate the basic common-sense comparison according to which, in the above example, *ceteris paribus*, I am freer than you.

This point about compossibility, which is of considerable importance for the analysis of unfreedom proposed [below], suggests that we should revise Steiner's formula as follows. The extent of Red's freedom, we should say, is equal to the value of

$$\sum_{i=1}^{n} F_{r,i} \Bigg/ \left(\sum_{i=1}^{n} F_{r,i} + \sum_{i=1}^{n} U_{r,i} \right)$$

where $F_{r,i}$ stands for the number of sets of compossible actions available to Red of which a specific action, i, is a member, and $U_{r,i}$ stands for the number of sets of compossible actions unavailable to Red, of which i is a member.

[. . .]

We have seen that the problem of adding indefinite numbers of act-descriptions to the list of actions that a person is free and unfree to perform can be overcome in a way that is in tune with the spirit of the empirical approach. This can be done by first of all restricting ourselves to spatio-temporally specified descriptions of actions (and calling all other descriptions of actions *re*descriptions), and then considering the list of actions the agent is free and unfree to perform as a list of sets of compossible actions, so as to produce measurements that are compatible with Davidson's 'unifier thesis' of act-individuation. Solving this first problem is, however, not sufficient to render either Steiner's formula or our revised version of it a feasible model for freedom measurement. We have said that we are to describe actions in terms of the spatio-temporally specified physical movements of which they are the 'bringing about'. But that means that we must now face up to the problem of space and time being indefinitely divisible, which suggests that the set of actions I am free to perform and the set of actions I am unfree to perform are each of an arbitrary size. On one account I might be very free, on another I might be very unfree, and we would seem to be left with no acceptable criterion for judging between these accounts. Steiner says that while the list of actions which a prisoner is prevented from doing is 'indefinitely long', it is also true 'that there is an indefinitely long list . . . of actions which this individual is not prevented from doing', and that this second list is 'not as long as the previous one'. But we do not yet seem to have sufficient grounds for saying that the second list is 'not as long'.

In order to overcome this problem, we need to explore the idea of the 'physical dimensions' of actions [. . .]. In this connection, it is useful to follow Morris Cohen and Ernest Nagel in classifying measurable qualities as either *intensive* or *extensive*. Where a quality is *extensive*, it is possible to *add* one instance of it to another. This possibility of an addition or 'concatenation' operation allows us to say *how much* of a certain quality an object possesses. Thus, for example, if using a balance we have found that object *b* is equal in weight to object *c*, and we also now find that *b* + *c* (*b* concatenated with *c*) is equal in weight to object *a*, then the number we assign to the weight of *a* should be twice that assigned to the weight of *b*. The measurement of an extensive quality involves an *empirical counting procedure*. It is on the basis of the counting of individual units which have been demonstrated to be of equal size (by reference to certain physical dimensions) that we can say that one object possesses 'more of', or 'much more of', a certain extensive quality than another object. An *intensive* quality is one that cannot be measured by means of such an empirical counting procedure. Examples of intensive qualities are the hardness of rocks or the intelligence or pleasure of human beings. The measurement of intensive qualities is generally seen as more complex and problematic than that of extensive qualities, and this partly explains the difficulties involved in attempting to measure utility. Some have indeed suggested that cardinal measurements of intensive qualities are impossible, or even that in the case of intensive qualities one should not talk of 'measurement' at all.

It seems to me that offhand scepticism about the idea of measuring freedom is often motivated by the vague, pre-theoretical belief that overall freedom is an intensive quality. The upshot of the foregoing Steinerian analysis, on the other hand, is that overall freedom is an extensive quality. The basic idea behind the empirical method [. . .] – the basic idea that we are here trying to make sense of – is, after all, that the degree of a person's freedom depends on how 'extensive' the actions available to her are. The measurement of an extensive quality requires, as we have seen, the individuation of units of that quality that can, at least in theory, be concatenated. In order to provide measurements of extents of action, then, we need to divide space and time into equally sized units, and matter into equally sized units that are at least as small as the units of space. Depending on their size, physical objects will then consist in varying numbers of units of matter, and what we shall be interested in measuring is, for any particular unit of matter, the number of space-time units in

which it might be located as a result of hypothetical (prevented or unprevented) actions on the part of the agent. In effect, we shall not be measuring possible motions as such (despite the fact that events are often thought to consist in motions); rather, we shall be counting possible 'occupyings'. Space and time must be thought of as an immobile *grid*, made up of a finite series of spatio-temporal *regions*. A physical object of a standard volume can then be seen as a potential occupant of one or another spatio-temporally fixed region.

This solution to the problem of the actual infinity of movements open to a person has been suggested by Jonathan Bennett, according to whom 'if space and time were *granular*, there would only be finitely many positions that a person's body could occupy'.[1] Bennett says that he would not like to bet on space and time really being granular, and neither should I. What I do mean to suggest is that we need to *think of* space and time *as* granular in order to produce measurements of the 'extensiveness of available action' that reflect our common-sense perceptions of that same phenomenon. In measuring 'extents of available action', we are not interested in getting to the heart of what physical movements 'really' consist in. We are not interested, for example, in the possible movements of protons or electrons. Rather, we are interested in producing mathematical representations of possible movements of matter as we commonly conceive of them.

While it is true that space and time can in theory be divided up indefinitely, then, the division of space and time into equal finite units allows us to represent what we do as a matter of fact see as the possibility of greater or lesser possibilities of movement. The fact that a finite quantity of space can be divided up indefinitely is not something that stops us from saying that it is greater or smaller than another finite quantity of space; if I can move my arm anywhere within a space of a given size, and you can move yours anywhere within a space twice as large (leaving aside the dimension of time), then we will want to say that you have twice as much available action as me in this respect, and the division of space into equal units is something that will allow us to say this.

I should add, in line with the discussion in the previous section, that we shall have to take into account the *compossibility* of the various locations of the various units of matter determinable by the agent's actions. Thus, for example, I may be free to determine the various spatio-temporal locations of a particular unit of matter which forms part of a door that I am free to open or shut, but I am free to determine those locations only in combination with the determining of certain specific locations of the other units of matter which make up the door. If I can only open or shut the door, then the number of combinations will be relatively low. If I am given an axe, with which to chop up the door, then that number will greatly increase. If the door is a Dutch door rather than a standard door, the number will be somewhere in between.

In order to anticipate the objection that I am being wildly optimistic about the feasibility of such intricate measurements and calculations (while also registering my suspicion that physicists and computing technologists will be less impressed by such an objection than the average moral or political philosopher might be), it should also be said that nothing in the foregoing analysis fixes the *size* of the space-time units on the basis of which we are to make our comparisons. Clearly, the smaller the units we are working with, the more accurate our measurements will be in reflecting what is commonly meant by 'the extent of movement available to us'. Ideally, the units will be smaller than any of the distances of the movements (or differences in sizes of objects) that we are interested in measuring. They will be smaller, for instance, than Jones's thumbs in Arneson's Smith–Jones example [see ch. 28 of this anthology], if Jones is to be represented as having any freedom at all. But the only absolute requirement contained in what has been said so far is that the space-time units be of an equal size. This equal size might be increased for practical purposes, as long as one is aware that the measurements one is producing increase in roughness along with increases in the size of the units. An example of a judgement made on the basis of rather larger units than the size of Jones's thumbs is provided by Felix Oppenheim, who, despite his scepticism about the possibility of measuring *overall* freedom, nevertheless suggests that the freedom to visit a museum which is closed on Mondays (and thus open only six days out of seven) can be represented (by means of Steiner's formula) as $6/6 + 1 = 0.857$. If the curator of the museum locks one of the rooms of the museum but leaves people free to visit the other rooms, or if he further limits museum visits to mornings only, then these additional constraints will not be reflected in measurements which assume as their units of time and space, respectively, 'the days' on which one is free to visit 'the museum'. Such additional constraints would, on the other hand, be reflected in measurements which counted 'the hours' in which one is free to visit 'this room' or 'that room' of the museum. So the degree of accuracy of our measurements, even at the level of purely conceptual theory, will clearly depend on the size of the units we adopt.

[. . .]

Finally, there is the problem that action chains might in theory continue for ever. No one lives for ever, but that does not stop an action chain continuing for ever, since [. . .], the time of a causally generated action is the time of the basic action that generates it, and this means that I can be free to perform an action now which is, among other things, the bringing about of a chain of events which in part occurs after my death.

It seems to me that resignation in the face of such a problem rests on a failure to see the acceptability and usefulness of assessing freedom in terms of the *foreseeable* consequences of given possible (or actual) actions, rather than in terms of what *would actually happen* (or does actually happen) as a consequence of the performance of such actions. If we try to look at what *would* happen (or does happen) as a result of our possible (or actual) basic actions, we shall indeed not solve the problem of indefinite causal chains, since it is true that what would happen (or does happen) might consist in never-ending chains of events. Notice, however, that the fact of our not knowing everything about what would happen as a result of the basic actions people are known to be free or unfree to perform does not prevent us from making *common-sense comparisons* of their degrees of overall freedom. And it would surely be bizarre to think that such common-sense comparisons are invalidated by this limitation in our knowledge. After all, as we saw [earlier – ch. 80 of this anthology], this very kind of limitation in our knowledge contributes to making freedom valuable in such a way as to create an interest in making comparisons in the first place. A more sensible way to proceed is by taking a closer look at our common-sense comparisons and seeing why we make them even in the face of the problem of indefinite causal chains. And the answer to this question, it seems to me, is to be found in the fact that in making such comparisons we implicitly limit the list of consequences of possible basic actions to those that we *foresee* as occurring in the event of the basic actions being performed. If this is so, then the presence of indefinitely long causal chains will not be sufficient to invalidate assessments of overall freedom made with respect to a list of *known* available and unavailable actions.

Individual Freedom: Constraints

[. . .] Let us begin by assuming a conception of 'specific freedoms' that admits both physical impossibility and threats as constraint variables. In this case, we shall be assuming that if you threaten me (at least, if you credibly threaten me) with the aim of deterring me from doing *x*, you render me unfree to do *x*. We shall be assuming that when a mafioso says to a shopkeeper, 'give me two million lire or I'll burn your shop down', the shopkeeper suffers a constraint on the freedom not to

hand over the two million lire. The idea is that he has been coerced into handing over his money, and that there is therefore a sense in which he is unfree to keep it. *Ceteris paribus*, his overall freedom has been reduced. But by *how much*? Surely, he is not *as* unfree to keep his money in this case as in one in which the mafioso simply takes his money by force and makes off with it. Surely we should distinguish between these two cases in terms of degrees of freedom, given that there is always the possibility of ignoring a threat, whatever the cost of doing so.

In my view, the problem of seemingly incommensurable constraint variables can be solved by distinguishing more frequently and more precisely between our intuitions about *specific* freedoms and our intuitions about *overall* freedom. Consider the following two propositions:

> When I am subjected to a threat against doing *x*, I remain as free as before.   (P1)

> When I am subjected to a threat against doing *x*, my freedom is restricted.   (P2)

P1 and P2 are usually taken to be incompatible, and most authors on the concept of freedom have therefore denied one or the other. Each side in this debate backs its arguments up by appeal to strong intuitions which are taken to conflict with those of the other side. Hillel Steiner has presented a rigorous defence of P1. He begins by pointing out that the only way in which a threat constrains the range of actions available to its recipient is by altering the relative degrees to which those available actions are desirable. Before you say to me, 'Hand over your money or I'll shoot you', I prefer keeping my money to handing it over, whereas after you have said it (assuming that I find your threat credible), I prefer handing it over to keeping it. Threats simply reverse the preference ordering of the recipient with respect to bringing about and not bringing about the result desired by the threatener. David Miller recognizes that 'we must concede to Steiner that any account of freedom which extends constraint beyond impossibility makes some assumptions about human desires', such that if the agent's desires and aversions were to change radically enough, 'what was formerly a constraint might no longer be so'. But this means that a definition of freedom which includes threats as a form of constraint contradicts a basic, widely supported premiss about the relationship between freedom and desire. This premiss, first argued for explicitly by J. P. Day and Isaiah Berlin, is that the question of whether or not (or the degree to which) I *desire* to do something is *irrelevant* to the question of whether or not (or the degree to which) I am *free* to do it [. . .]. We do not say that a wholly contented slave is wholly free simply on the grounds that she can give full rein to her desires. Neither would we deny that the inmate of a high-security prison is unfree to go to the theatre, even if she does not desire to go to the theatre. Steiner therefore concludes that since it is unacceptable to take an agent's desires into account in assessing her freedom, it cannot be acceptable to see threats as reducing freedom.

[. . .] [M]any have found Steiner's conclusion counter-intuitive. Do we not commonly see threats of punishment as reducing freedom? Does a state which *physically prevents* me from eating green ice cream restrict my freedom more than a state which *threatens life imprisonment* for eating *any* colour of ice cream? Do we not feel, on the contrary, that I am rendered unfree to eat any kind of ice cream in the latter case, whereas in the former I am only rendered unfree to eat green ice cream? It is undeniable that many of us perceive some kind of reduction in the freedom of the recipients of threats. How are we to explain that perception?

An answer can be found if we aim in every possible context to be more precise about whether we are referring to specific freedoms or to overall freedom. For the fact is that our statements about when 'freedom is reduced' are often ambiguous in this respect, and the wording in P1 and P2 is a case in point. A coherent and plausible way of resolving the

ambiguity is surely by interpreting P1 as referring to a specific freedom – the freedom to do *x* – and interpreting P2 as referring to overall freedom. These interpretations make P1 and P2 compatible: those who administer threats generally reduce the *overall* freedom of those whom they threaten, without removing the freedom to perform the specific action they aim to deter. Such interpretations of P1 and P2 also allow us to solve both of the main problems identified so far. First, they allow us to avoid the problem of commensurating degrees of freedom to perform a specific action with the complete freedom or unfreedom to perform an action implied by its physical possibility or impossibility. They do this by removing the need to speak of degrees of freedom to perform a specific action. Second, they allow us to say that a conception of 'specific freedoms' that admits physical impossibility as the only constraint variable can nevertheless accommodate the common-sense comparisons which most strongly motivate people to admit threats as a constraint variable.

In order to see how recipients of threats generally suffer reductions in overall freedom (*without* suffering the removal, on the part of the threatener, of any of their specific freedoms), we need to make use of our earlier analysis of overall freedom in terms of the availability of *sets* of actions.

[. . .]

Goebbels said that 'anybody can write what he likes if he is not afraid of the concentration camp'. There is an element of truth in this. Indeed, he should have gone further, adding that anybody can write what he likes even if he *is* afraid of the concentration camp. On the other hand, we do not supply the whole truth about the freedom of two agents, A and B, if we simply say, 'A in Nazi Germany can write what he likes and B in Britain can write what he likes.' 'Writing what he likes' is an act-type of which A should be seen as being unrestrained from performing a much greater quantity than B, once we look at the spatio-temporal regions within which that act-type can be performed. Unlike B, A is threatened with the concentration camp. As a consequence, *if* A writes what he likes at time *t*, and the threat is both sincere and practicable, he will not be unprevented from doing so at *t* + 1. What is more, there are a great many other actions which A may be restrained from performing *if* he writes what he likes, given that there is not 'much' to be done in a concentration camp. In all likelihood, then, he suffers a great reduction in the number of sets of compossible actions available to him.

[. . .]

In my view, then, the belief that P2 contradicts P1 very often rests on mistaking an intuition about overall freedom for one about specific freedoms. The freedom to do *x* is not a matter of degree; one either is or is not free to do *x*. When we perceive a reduction in the freedom of an agent consequent upon her receiving a threat, what we have really spotted is a likely reduction in the degree of her overall freedom. Those who see a threat against doing *x* as removing the freedom to do *x* may well have wrongly interpreted P2 as arising out of an intuition about *specific* freedom, and consequently as *referring* to a specific freedom. This, in my view, best explains the continued insistence that threats themselves reduce freedom, despite the rigour of Steiner's argument to the contrary. P2 is in fact an *empirical generalization* about the *overall* freedom of the recipients of threats.

Note

1 J. Bennett, *The Act Itself* (Oxford: Clarendon Press, 1995), p. 93, my emphasis.

Ian Carter, *A Measure of Freedom* (Oxford: Oxford University Press, 1999), pp. 171–2, 174–6, 180–6, 188, 226–8.

Chapter 83

Prasanta K. Pattanaik and Yongsheng Xu, "On Ranking Opportunity Sets in Terms of Freedom of Choice" (1990)

1 Introduction

The notion of freedom is one of the most powerful concepts in economic and social philosophy, and it figures prominently in debates about alternative economic systems. In particular, a major defence of the market as an allocative mechanism is often based on an appeal to a certain type of individual freedom that the market mechanism is supposed to guarantee. Despite this, the concept of freedom has not received much attention in the theory of welfare economics and social choice [. . .]. The purpose of this paper is to explore certain aspects of this rich concept. Viewing freedom as the opportunity for choice, we consider the criteria for ranking alternative choice situations in terms of the degrees of freedom that they offer to the agent making choices. We introduce three plausible axioms, and we show that they lead to a rather naive rule for judging the degrees of freedom of choice; under these axioms, judgements about the degree of freedom have to be based exclusively on the number of options available in the choice situation under consideration.

In Section 2, we give the intuitive motivation for our analysis. Section 3 provides the basic notation and axioms, and the main result is proved in Section 4. We conclude in Section 5.

2 Freedom, Utility, and Social Welfare

The conventional theory of welfare economics has tended to view social welfare as being determined exclusively by individual utilities which, in turn, are assumed to be determined by the allocation in the economy. It is clear that this restricted framework cannot possibly accommodate the notion of individual freedom and its significance for social welfare judgments. Consider the competitive equilibrium $((\bar{x}_1, \bar{x}_2), \bar{p})$ in the two person exchange economy shown in Figure 83.1 (w_1, and w_2 are the intial endowments).

Now suppose the market mechanism is replaced by a command system, and the individuals are ordered to consume bundles $\bar{x}_1$, and $\bar{x}_2$ respectively. Then, assuming that the individuals' preferences remain unchanged, their utilities will remain unchanged.

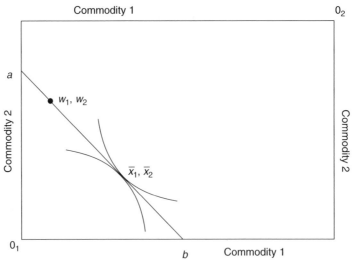

Figure 83.1

Therefore, any ethical system which bases social welfare judgments exclusively on individual utilities will necessarily declare the two situations indistinguishable in terms of social welfare. The fact that the set of options available to 1 has been reduced from the set $a0_1b$ to the singleton $\{\bar{x}_1\}$ where 1 has no choice whatsoever, and that 2 has also faced a similar shrinking of opportunities, will be irrelevant in this framework. Yet, most of us would feel that, in the process of the change, something important has happened which should have a bearing on our judgments about social welfare: in reducing the set of options available to 1 from the set $a0_1b$ to $\{\bar{x}_1\}$, 1's freedom seems to have been curtailed even though he still continues to have the option which he would have chosen in the original situation. The point is that the set of available options has a significance independently of the option that is considered, by the agent concerned, to be best in that set. Its significance arises from the fact that the availability of these options reflects a certain degree of freedom of choice for the agent, and this freedom is impaired when the available set contracts, even when the option judged to be best in the original set of options continues to be available.

This, of course, raises the question as to why freedom of choice may be valued. As Sen points out,[1] it is possible that freedom is considered instrumental in achieving a higher level of individual utilities. Thus, one may believe that the set of available options in the next time period may depend on the degree of freedom that the individuals enjoy in this time period, that if one reduces individual freedom of choice now, then it may stifle innovation and enterprise, and this, through its effect on the feasible set of options in the next time period, may ultimately reduce the individual utilities. There may be other utility-based reasons why an individual may object to a reduction in his freedom of choice even when it would seem that the restriction on his freedom should not have any effect on his utility when utilities are defined in terms of his current preferences. Even if i hates smoking now, he may be worried about a ban on smoking because he cannot be sure that his preferences will never change, in the future, in favour of smoking (see Kreps,[2] for an illuminating discussion of the desire for 'flexibility' when future preferences are uncertain). In contrast to these instrumental justifications for freedom of choice, we have what

Sen calls the *intrinsic value* of freedom: not only do we value freedom for what it can do to increase our utility levels, we also value it for its own sake. It is this intrinsic value of freedom which accounts for our concern about any shrinking of the available set of options even when the best alternative in the original larger set of options continues to be available, and even when any possible effect of the change on the available set of options in the future is ruled out. Clearly, given the intrinsic importance that we attach to freedom of choice, the extent to which the individuals enjoy such freedom should enter into judgements about social welfare independently of the individual utilities. This, of course, immediately raises the problem as to how we rank alternative situations in terms of the freedom of choice that they offer to the agent under consideration. In the following sections, we explore some aspects of this problem, concentrating on the intrinsic value of freedom of choice.

3　The Basic Notation and Definitions

Let X be the universal set of alternatives, assumed to be finite. The alternatives in X can be interpreted in various ways. These alternatives may be conventional consumption bundles; they may be bundles of material characteristics such as calories, amount of warmth in the winter (see Lancaster[3]); they may be vectors of what Sen[4] calls capabilities (*e.g.* the level of well-nourishment, life expectancy, access to friends); alternatively, they may also be interpreted in a wider sense to indicate (mutually exclusive) options which may have "non-economic" dimensions. While, in specific contexts, some of these interpretations may be more fruitful than others, for our purpose, it is not necessary to commit oneself to any particular interpretation.

Let Z be the set of all nonempty subsets of X. The elements of Z are the alternative feasible sets with which the agent may be faced. Let $\geqslant$ be a reflexive and transitive binary rela-

tion defined over Z (note that we do not *assume* connectedness for $\geqslant$). $\forall A, B \in Z$, $(A \geqslant B)$ is to be interpreted as "the degree of freedom offered by the feasible set A is at least as great as the degree of freedom offered by the feasible set B". $>$ and $\sim$ will denote, respectively, the asymmetric and the symmetric factors of $\geqslant$, *i.e.* $>$ denotes the relation of "offering a greater degree of freedom than", and $\sim$ denotes the relation of "offering the same degree of freedom as". We introduce certain properties of $\geqslant$.

3.1　Definition

$\geqslant$ satisfies:

(3.1.1)　*Indifference between No-choice Situations* (INS)
　　　　iff $\forall x, y \in X$, $\{x\} \sim \{y\}$;

(3.1.2)　*Strict Monotonicity* (SM)
　　　　iff for all distinct $x, y \in X$, $\{x, y\} > \{x\}$;

(3.1.3)　*Independence* (IND)
　　　　iff $\forall A, B \in Z$, and $\forall x \in X - (A \cup B)$, $[A \geqslant B$ iff $A \cup \{x\} \geqslant B \cup \{x\}]$.

3.2　Remark

INS requires that if neither of two feasible sets offers the agent any choice in the sense that both the feasible sets are singletons, then the degrees of freedom offered by the two feasible sets are identical (being "zero" from an intuitive point of view). Note that x may be, from the agent's point of view, the most desired alternative in X, while y may be the least desired alternative in X. However, even in that case, it seems to us plausible to say that a feasible set which offers the agent only x does not give him any greater degree of freedom than a feasible set where y is the only available alternative. The agent may love living in London and may hate living in Birmingham. However, a situation where the government tells the agent that he cannot live anywhere excepting London does not seem to offer the agent any more *freedom* (though it offers a lot more *utility*) than the situation where the government tells the agent that he cannot live anywhere excepting Birmingham. Strict monotonicity essentially embodies the principle that, in terms of freedom, a situation where the agent has some choice is better than a situation where the agent has no choice. IND requires that if A and B are two possible available sets and if x does not belong either to A or to B, then the ranking of A and B in terms of freedom corresponds to the ranking of $A \cup \{x\}$ and $B \cup \{x\}$. IND is not as plausible an axiom as INS and SM. Indeed, we shall later present an example to show the type of problem that may arise from an indiscriminate application of IND. However, IND does possess considerable *prima facie* plausibility, and has been widely used in the literature on ranking of sets.

4   Characterization of the Simple Cardinality-based Ordering

In this section, we show that if $\geqslant$ satisfies INS, SM and IND, then it takes a rather naive form in so far as it will rank any two sets only on the basis of the number of elements in each of the two sets, a bigger set being ranked higher than a smaller set.

4.1   *Definition*

$\geqslant$ will be called a *simple cardinality-based ordering* (SCO) iff

(4.1) $\forall A, B \in Z, A \geqslant B$ iff $|A| \geqslant |B|$.

4.2   *Theorem*

$\geqslant$ is the simple cardinality-based ordering iff $\geqslant$ satisfies indifference between no-choice situations, strict monotonicity and independence.

Proof
The necessity part of the theorem is obvious; we prove only sufficiency. Let $\geqslant$ satisfy INS, SM and IND. We first show that

(4.2)   for every positive integer n, if $(|A'| = |B'| = n)$ implies $(A' \sim B')$ for all A', $B' \in Z$, then $(|A| = |B| = n + 1) \Rightarrow (A \sim B)$ for all $A, B \in Z$.

Consider a given positive integer n such that $(|A'| = |B'| = n) \Rightarrow (A' \sim B')$ for all $A', B' \in Z$. Let $A, B \in Z$ be such that $|A| = |B| = n + 1$. Let $C \subseteq A$ such that $|C| = n$, and let $A - C = \{x\}$. Either

(4.3) $x \in B$,

or

(4.4) $x \notin B$.

Suppose (4.3) holds. Then let $D = B - \{x\}$. Since $|C| = |D| = n$ by our assumption, $C \sim D$. Given $C \sim D$, by IND, we have $C \cup \{x\} \sim D \cup \{x\}$, *i.e.* $A \sim B$. Now suppose (4.4) holds. It is clear that if $B - A = \emptyset$, then, given $|A| = |B|$, we would have $A = B$, and hence $A \sim B$. Therefore, consider the case where $B - A \neq \emptyset$. Let $y \in B - A$, and let $E = B - \{y\}$. Then $|C| = |E| = n$, and hence, by our assumption, $C \sim E$ (recall that $C = A - \{x\}$). Given $C \sim E$, by IND, we have $(C \cup \{x\}) \sim (E \cup \{x\})$, *i.e.*

(4.5) $A \sim (E \cup \{x\})$.

Consider $E \cup \{x\}$ and B. Let $z \in E \subset B$. Then, noting that each of the two sets $(E \cup \{x\}) - \{z\}$ and $B - \{z\}$ has exactly n elements, we have $((E \cup \{x\}) - \{z\}) \sim (B - \{z\})$. Hence, by IND, we have

(4.6) $(E \cup \{x\}) \sim B$.

From (4.5) and (4.6), noting that $\geqslant$ is transitive, we have $A \sim B$. This completes the proof of (4.2). Since, by INS, we have $A \sim B$ for all $A, B \in Z$ such $|A| = |B| = 1$, by (4.2) it follows that

(4.7) $A \sim B$ for all $A, B \in Z$ such that $|A| = |B|$.

Now consider $A, B \in Z$ such that $|A| \neq |B|$. Let $|A| > |B|$. Consider $G \subset A$ such that $|G| = |B|$. Then, by (4.7),

(4.8) $G \sim B$.

Let $A = G \cup H$ where $H = \{h_1, \ldots, h_t\}$. Let $G = \{g_1, \ldots, g_r\}$. By SM, $\{g_1, h_1\} > \{g_1\}$. Hence, by the repeated use of IND, we have $G \cup \{h_1\} > G$. Similarly, $[G \cup \{h_1, h_2\} > G \cup \{h_1\}]$, and $[G \cup \{h_1, h_2, h_3\} > G \cup \{h_1, h_2\}]$ and $\ldots$, and $[G \cup H > G \cup H - \{h_t\}]$. By the transitivity of $\geqslant$ it follows that

(4.9) $A > G$.

From (4.8) and (4.9), we have $A > B$. Thus,

(4.10) $\forall A, B \in Z$, if $|A| > |B|$, then $A > B$.

Given (4.7), (4.10) completes the proof.

4.3 Remark

In so far as the simple cardinality-based rule is a rather naive or trivial rule for judging the degree of freedom of choice, Theorem 4.2 shows that axioms INC, SM and IND force on us a rather trivial structure, devoid of richness, in assessing the degree of freedom of choice.

5 Concluding Remarks

As we have seen in the preceding section, INC, SM and IND lead to a trivial cardinality-based rule for assessing the degrees of freedom offered by different opportunity sets. Since INC and SM seem to us to be very plausible properties in this context, we are inclined to put the blame for this triviality result on IND. Indeed, as the following example shows, despite its *prima facie* plausibility, the intuitive appeal of IND may be somewhat doubtful.

Suppose alternative modes of transport are the options under consideration. Then, while we may have {train} ~ {blue car}, we may also have {train, red car} > {blue car, red car}; since the option of travelling by a red car is substantially different from travelling by a train, but is "similar" to the option of travelling by a blue car, one can very plausibly feel that the set {train, red car} represents a greater degree of freedom of choice as compared to the set {blue car, red car}. However, {train} ~ {blue car} and {train, red car} > {blue car, red car} violates IND.

Thus a major failure of IND lies in not taking into account the extents to which the different alternatives are "close" or "similar" to each other. Indeed, our formal structure itself does not contain any information about closeness or similarity of different alternatives. One way of enriching the model will be to introduce, formally and explicitly, a notion of closeness or similarity of options, and to reformulate the Independence axiom to take into account the intuitive difficulty arising in our example. This needs further investigation.

Notes

1   Amartya Sen, "Freedom of Choice: Concept and Content," *European Economic Review* 32 (1988), pp. 269–94.

2   D. M. Kreps, "A Representation Theorem for 'Preference for Flexibility,'" *Econometrica* 47 (1979), pp. 565–77.

3   K. J. Lancaster, "A New Approach to Consumer Theory," *Journal of Political Economy* 74 (1966), pp. 132–57.

4   Amartya Sen, "The Standard of Living," (Lectures I and II), in G. Hawthorn (ed.), *The Standard of Living* (Cambridge: Cambridge University Press, 1987).

Prasanta K. Pattanaik and Yongsheng Xu, "On Ranking Opportunity Sets in Terms of Freedom of Choice," *Recherches Economiques de Louvain* 54 (1990), pp. 383–90.

Chapter 84

Amartya Sen, from "Welfare, Freedom, and Social Choice: a Reply" (1990)

Pattanaik and Xu [Chapter 83, this volume] take up the problem of evaluating the freedom a person enjoys, present some interesting axioms for this purpose, and derive and comment on an important result based on those axioms. The axioms they choose have considerable initial plausibility, and yet the theorem that emerges from them yields a result that seems immediately implausible. Pattanaik and Xu then turn to "what done it", and identify one of their three axioms as ultimately erroneous. Pattanaik and Xu's theorem is elegant, important and, I believe, full of far-reaching significance, even though I will dispute the particular reassessment of the axioms they recommend.

The authors are concerned with ranking "opportunity sets", *i.e.*, sets of alternatives from which the person can choose one alternative. The first of the three axioms, viz, "Indifference between no-choice situations (INS)", indicates that every unit set, such as {x}, {y}, etc., is freedom-wise indifferent to every other. The second axiom, viz, "Strict monotonicity (SM)", insists that any distinct pair {x, y} represents more freedom than a unit set of one of the two alternatives in the pair {x}. The third axiom, "Independence (IND)", argues that if a set A is judged to give at least as much freedom as set B, then that ranking will be unaffected by the addition to each of an alternative x not contained in either A or B. These three axioms – innocuous as they

look – together yield the rather astonishing result that the freedom of any set must be judged only by counting the number of alternatives in it. That is, if set A has at least as many alternatives as B, then A represents at least as much freedom as B.

The result is odd and contrary. If A represents a choice between three alternatives that the person sees as "great", "terrific" and "wonderful", and B stands for three that she finds "bad", "awful" and "dismal", still the latter set B, according to this theorem, gives the person exactly as much freedom as the former set A. Pattanaik and Xu are entirely justified in looking back and asking what went wrong and why. They fix on the property of "Independence", and argue that it is unacceptable because the alternative x that is added to A and B may well be very like another alternative already in one of the sets. Suppose A consists of a solitary alternative of travelling by a blue car and B of another solitary alternative of travelling by train, and the two are judged to be freedomwise indifferent. Now add to each a third alternative, viz travelling by a red car. This addition enriches the second set B (travelling by train) by providing another very different alternative, whereas the first set A is hardly enriched since travelling by a red car is not – for most adults – vastly dissimilar to travelling by a car that is blue. The axiom of Independence insists that the pair (blue car, red car) offers exactly as much freedom as the pair (train, red car), but this, argue Pattanaik and Xu, is quite implausible. Hence they "are inclined to put the blame for this triviality result on IND" [. . .].

Pattanaik and Xu are right to criticize the Independence axiom, for the reason they specify. But does that really explain the contrary result of their theorem? Take a case in which all alternatives are totally different, so that the objection to IND stated earlier would not any longer hold. Surely, we would still have the simple number-counting evaluation of freedom. Three possibilities of travelling by (a stiff tricycle; hopping on one leg; rolling on dust) would still offer, in the Pattanaik–Xu system, exactly as much freedom as travelling by (an efficient bicycle; a smart car; walking on two legs normally). The Independence axiom is criticizable when the alternatives have the type of similarity on which Pattanaik and Xu comment, but the "triviality result" is not dependent on the occurrence of such cases of similarity.

The root of the problem lies, I think, much deeper. The reason the number-counting freedom assessment appears so contrary to us is that we find it absurd to dissociate the extent of our freedom from our preferences over the alternatives. A set of three alternatives that we see as "bad", "awful" and "dismal" cannot, we think, give us as much real freedom as a set of three others that we prefer a great deal more and see as "great", "terrific" and "wonderful". The idea of effective freedom cannot be dissociated from our preferences. Freedom is not just a matter of having a larger number of alternatives; it depends on what kind of alternatives they are.

But given that fact, could we be right in insisting on the axiom INS (Indifference between no-choice situations)? We have to distinguish between (1) our freedom to do (or be) what we would choose to do, and (2) our freedom to have a large number of alternatives to choose from. The latter is not ill-defined as a concept, but rather uninteresting in terms of effective freedom. Suppose I wish to go home from the office by taking a short walk. Con-

sider now two alternatives: (1) I can hop on one leg to home, but I am not permitted to walk, and (2) I can walk normally to home, but I am not permitted to hop on one leg. Given my preferences (in the sense of what I would choose given the choice) it would be absurd to say that I have exactly as much effective freedom in the first case (*i.e.*, hop, not walk) as in the second (*i.e.*, walk, not hop). Of course, my freedom can be seen as being favourably affected if I am permitted to *choose* between walking and hopping, even if I were never to choose hopping, but that is a different matter, and the issue at hand is the comparison of the two unit sets of (hopping on one leg) and (walking). Given the fact that I vastly *prefer* to walk – that I *would choose* to walk given the choice – it would be odd to decide that I have no less freedom when I am forced to hop, which I would never choose given the option of walking, than when I am forced to walk, which I would have chosen anyway. So the problem starts with Pattanaik and Xu's first axiom, viz, INS.

In discussing the paper by Cohen,[1] I made a distinction between the "opportunity" aspect and the "process" aspect of freedom, and argued that *both* aspects are important. In arguing against one of Cohen's claims, I had pointed to the relevance of the "process" aspect. In the present context, in arguing against one of the claims of Pattanaik and Xu, I am trying to point to the relevance of the "opportunity" aspect. As far as the process aspect is concerned, there is indeed much plausibility in Pattanaik and Xu's axiom INS. Both $\{x\}$ and $\{y\}$ offer a "Hobson's choice", and there is a sense in which neither can really offer more freedom than the other. On the other hand, that is not the only aspect of freedom, which relates also to the opportunity that we have to live the way we would like, do the things we would choose to do, achieve the things we would prefer to achieve. And it is because of this "opportunity" aspect of freedom that the "triviality result", as Pattanaik and Xu call it, is so unacceptable, and exactly for the same reason, so is their first axiom INS.

Pattanaik and Xu's paper is important not only because of the interesting and significant theorem they establish, but also because it forcefully raises questions about the nature of freedom and how to assess it. I have pleaded for taking more note, than Pattanaik and Xu do, of *preference* in evaluating freedom. But we can arrive at a "reflective equilibrium" on this subject only through explorations of the relations between axioms and results in the way Pattanaik and Xu have done.

Note

1   G. A. Cohen, "Equality of What? On Welfare, Resources and Capabilities," *Recherches Economiques de Louvain* 56 (1990), pp. 357–82.

Amartya Sen, "Welfare, Freedom, and Social Choice: a Reply," *Recherches Economiques de Louvain* 54 (1990), pp. 469–72.

Chapter 85

Robert Sugden, from "The Metric of Opportunity" (1998)

Why might opportunity be thought to have intrinsic value? One answer is to appeal to what Kenneth Arrow [. . .] calls 'freedom as autonomy' (I shall say *opportunity as autonomy*). A person's actions are autonomous to the extent that they are chosen by him. But one cannot *choose* one action unless there are other actions which one might have chosen instead. The richer the set of opportunities from which a person has chosen his way of life, the more that way of life is *his*. For example, consider two school-leavers: Arthur, who lives in a prosperous city, and Barbara, who lives in a decaying industrial region. Arthur has a wide range of job offers, including some which would provide training for later skilled work; preferring immediate income and leisure, he chooses to be a waiter in a fast-food restaurant. Barbara chooses the same job as the only alternative to unemployment. Arthur's being a waiter is surely the result of a more autonomous choice than is Barbara's being a waiter. Even if the two school-leavers have the same preferences, there is an important difference between their positions: Arthur can look on his occupation as his own choice in a way that Barbara cannot. We might follow Robert Nozick [. . .] in saying that a person who shapes his life according to his own plan is giving meaning to that life; the more a life is self-chosen, the more meaningful it is.

Much of John Stuart Mill's [. . .] famous defence of liberty can be read as an appeal to the value of autonomy in the sense that I have sketched out. However, there is a further important theme in Mill's defence of liberty: the idea that through acts of choosing, an individual cultivates the faculties of observation, reason, judgment, discrimination and self-control. If a person's choices are made for him:

> It is possible that he might be guided in some good path, and kept out of harm's way, without any of these good things [i.e., observation, reason, etc.]. But what will be his comparative worth as a human being? It really is of importance, not only what men do, but what manner of men they are that do it. Among the works of man, which human life is rightly employed in perfecting and beautifying, the first in importance surely is man himself. [. . .]

The idea here seems to be that the faculties that are developed in acts of choosing have intrinsic value. For short, I shall call this idea *opportunity as exercise*: choosing is good for the mental faculties in something like the way that physical exercise is good for the body.

Both of these accounts of the value of opportunity provide reasons for assigning value to an individual's opportunity set, independently of what is chosen from it. The autonomy approach leads to the idea that an opportunity set has value to the extent that it offers the individual a rich array of options; holding constant the option that is actually chosen, it is better that this option has been chosen from a richer rather than from a poorer array. The exercise approach leads to the idea that opportunity sets have value to the extent that they present the individual with decision problems that exercise morally significant faculties.

[. . .]

Measuring Opportunity without Using Preferences

Can opportunity be treated as a physical quantity, to be measured without referring to preferences or values? Ian Carter [. . .] argues that it can: we should think of the size of a person's opportunity set (Carter calls this 'overall freedom') as 'a unidimensional function of the sheer "quantity of action" available to her'.[1] Notice that Carter's idea of 'sheer quantity' goes much further than the separation of measurement and value for which I have been arguing. On my account of measurement, information about preferences might be used in measuring the amount of opportunity offered by a set of options; there is still a separation between measurement and value because there is no presumption that more opportunity is better than less. In this section, I consider some measures of opportunity that do not use preference information at all.

One measure of sheer quantity of opportunity is the *cardinality criterion*. This criterion, which applies only to finite opportunity sets, ranks sets according to the number of options they contain. Prasanta Pattanaik and Yongsheng Xu show how this criterion can be derived from a set of simple axioms, but they do not endorse it as a good measure of opportunity. On the contrary, they now interpret their result as an impossibility theorem which shows that a sheer quantity approach will not work [. . .].

Here I must introduce some notation, which I shall use throughout this paper. Let the finite set X represent the universal set of conceivable *options*; options will be denoted by w, x, y, z. Every non-empty subset of X is interpreted as a possible *opportunity set*; such sets

will be denoted by A, B, C, D. Let $\geq$ be the binary relation 'gives at least as much opportunity as', defined on the set of opportunity sets. The relations $>$, i.e., 'gives more opportunity than', and $\sim$, i.e., 'gives exactly as much opportunity as', are defined from $\geq$ in the usual way. Throughout the paper, I shall assume that $\geq$ is transitive; in general, I shall not assume this relation to be complete.

Now consider the following restrictions which might be imposed on $\geq$:

P1. *Strict Monotonicity*. For all opportunity sets A, B: if B is a strict subset of A, then $A > B$.

P2. *Independence*. For all opportunity sets A, B, and for all options x such that x $\notin$ A, B: $A \geq B \Leftrightarrow A \cup \{x\} \geq B \cup \{x\}$.

P3. *No Choice*. For all options x, y: $\{x\} \sim \{y\}$.

The conjunction of these three axioms is equivalent to the cardinality criterion: this is essentially the result proved by Pattanaik and Xu. To see the intuition behind the proof, consider any distinct options w, x, y, z. By P3, all one-member sets are ranked equally, so $\{x\} \sim \{y\}$. By P2, the equal ranking of those sets is preserved if w is added to both: thus $\{w, x\} \sim \{w, y\}$. By a similar argument, $\{w, y\} \sim \{y, z\}$. Then by transitivity, we have $\{w, x\} \sim \{y, z\}$. Thus, all two-member sets must be ranked equally. Further, since $\{x, y\} > \{x\}$ by P1, two-member sets must be ranked above one-member sets. Extending this argument, it can be shown that all three-member sets are ranked equally, but above two-member sets; and so on.

The cardinality criterion takes no account of the descriptions of the options in an opportunity set: it merely counts options. This has unpalatable implications. Consider the following two opportunity sets. In the case of opportunity set A, a passenger on a plane is offered a choice between three complimentary drinks: a can of Heineken beer, a can of mineral water, or a small bottle of wine. In the case of opportunity set B, she is offered a choice between four drinks; these are four different cans of Heineken beer, distinguishable from one another only by their having different batch numbers printed on them. According to the cardinality criterion, B is larger than A: we might say that the sheer quantity of action is greater in B. But in terms of any of the interpretations of opportunity that I have considered, it would be perverse to claim that B offers more opportunity than A. If we think of opportunity as autonomy, A seems to offer a richer array of options than B. If we think of opportunity as exercise, A seems to present a more challenging decision problem. And if we think of primary-good autonomy, A seems to have a greater tendency to assist a representative individual in the pursuit of his ends. Whichever of these interpretations of opportunity we favour, the cardinality criterion has the same crucial limitation: it does not take account of the *diversity* of options in an opportunity set. We recognize A as offering more opportunity than B because A's options, although fewer in number than B's, are more diverse.

This limitation of the cardinality criterion is a product of the Independence axiom. The abstract appeal of that axiom seems to depend on an intuition that opportunities are additive – that the amount of opportunity offered by the union of two disjoint sets is the sum of the amounts of opportunity offered by those sets separately. But if opportunity is related to diversity, it cannot be additive. Consider another example. Each of a number of room heaters is fitted with a thermostatic control, which has a finite number of settings. For each heater, the set of those temperature settings (in degrees Celsius) can be interpreted as an opportunity set. Consider the opportunity sets A = {15}, B = {19} and the option x = 15.01. Independence implies that if A and B give equal amounts of opportunity, then {15, 15.01} gives just as much opportunity as {15.01, 19}. But it seems clear that the 15.01 option adds more to the diversity of B than it does to that of A: we should not expect the ranking of those two sets to be unaffected when this option is added to each of them.

Although the cardinality criterion itself has found few supporters, the Independence axiom and related principles are often used in characterizing measures of opportunity. That axiom was first used (in a marginally different form) by Patrick Suppes [. . .] as part of a characterization of a measure of opportunity. Suppes's axioms imply the existence of a function v(.) which assigns a positive number to every conceivable option; for any option x we may interpret v(x) as its 'opportunity value'. Then, according to Suppes's measure, the amount of opportunity offered by a set is simply the sum of the opportunity values of its component options. (Notice that the cardinality criterion is the special case of Suppes's measure in which all options have the same opportunity value.) Nicolas Gravel, Jean-François Laslier and Alain Trannoy [. . .] arrive at Suppes's measure by a different route, using an axiom ('Independence of Unanimous Gains from Redistriution') which turns out to be a close relative of Independence.

If we are to find a measure of opportunity which takes account of diversity, it is clear that we need to consider the particular characteristics of options; and we need to consider options in relation to one another (rather than separately, as Independence forces us to do). One possibility might be to look for a measure of opportunity which is sensitive to the *physical* characteristics of options, but which does not make use of any information about preferences. This seems to be what Carter has in mind when he suggests that 'the greater the difference between the spatio-temporal coordinates of a particular event, the greater the "quantity of action" performed by an agent when he brings it about'.[2] Unfortunately, he does not develop this suggestion, merely expressing a hope that there might be approximate intersubjective agreement on a ratio scale for actions. I remain skeptical.

A more concrete proposal of a similar kind is made by Marlies Klemisch-Ahlert [. . .]. This proposal starts from the very general idea that options can be represented by points in an n-dimensional space of real numbers; the dimensions may be interpreted as quantities of different commodities, primary goods, or functionings, depending on the conception of opportunity being used. Klemisch-Ahlert argues that certain 'shape-preserving' transformations of opportunity sets can be regarded as preserving the quantity of opportunity being offered. The simplest of these transformations is a 'shift': every option in a set is transformed by adding to it (or subtracting from it) the same vector.

As an example of the unattractive implications of this principle, consider the following case. Options are to be interpreted as possible prizes in a competition held in London; they are different bundles of airline tickets. An opportunity set is to be interpreted as a choice among alternative prizes. Prize w is a one-way ticket *to* Paris; x is a return ticket to Amsterdam; y is a return ticket to Paris; z is a return ticket to Amsterdam plus a one-way ticket *from* Paris. According to Klemisch-Ahlert's principle, {w, x} and {y, z} offer equal amounts of opportunity, because the latter set is simply the former set, 'shifted' by adding a one-way ticket from Paris to both options. But once we recognize that one half of a return ticket is little use without the other half, it seems natural to say that {w, x}, which effectively offers only a trip to Amsterdam, gives less opportunity than {y, z}, which offers the choice between Amsterdam and Paris. Again, inadequate account is being taken of the nature of the options.

The difficulty for a 'sheer quantity' approach is to find a way of representing concepts such as diversity and complementarity without using any notion of preference or value. So far, no one has come near to solving this problem.

Measures Based on Actual Preferences

Several theorists have argued that a measure of opportunity ought to be defined in relation to a given individual, and should take some account of that individual's preferences over options. In

particular, Pattanaik and Xu's principle of No Choice has been challenged. Consider two distinct opportunity sets, each of which is a singleton, say {x} and {y}. Suppose that x is having a certain dental operation without pain and that y is having the same operation, but with severe pain. And consider a person who (as one would expect) prefers x to y. Do {x} and {y} offer the same amount of opportunity, as the principle of No Choice implies?

Pattanaik and Xu [. . .] argue that the two sets should be ranked equally, on the grounds that what is being measured is freedom of choice and that a singleton set offers no choice at all. All things considered, it may be better to have {x} than {y}; but both sets rank equally in terms of freedom of choice. Against this position, Sen argues that in this kind of case, {x} should be ranked above {y} because 'being forced to [do] what you would have [done] anyway is less restrictive of freedom than being forced to [do] what you wouldn't have [done] anyway'.[3] Each of these arguments seems to have some force, but they contradict one another.

The explanation of this contradiction, I suggest, is that the two arguments appeal to different conceptions of opportunity. If we think of opportunity as exercise, it is hard to deny the principle of No Choice: if there is no choice to be made at all, then there is nothing to exercise the decision-making faculties. The desirability of the options in an opportunity set and the difficulty of the decision problem it presents are two completely different things.

However, if we think of opportunity as autonomy or of primary-good opportunity, then the desirability of options *does* seem to matter. I have argued that opportunity as autonomy increases as an individual's opportunity set becomes richer, and that primary-good opportunity is greater, the greater the degree to which the opportunity set tends to assist a representative individual to achieve his own ends. At least in a case in which (as in the example) almost anyone would prefer x to y, it seems clear that {x} is a richer set than {y}, and does more to assist a representative individual to achieve his ends.

Sen argues that 'any plausible axiomatic structure in the comparison of the extent of freedom would have to take some note of the person's preferences'.[4] Thus, he proposes that the ranking of opportunity sets should depend on the preferences of the relevant individual. It might seem that the obvious way to connect these two relations is to make the ranking of any two opportunity sets the same as the preference ranking of their most-preferred options. This is the *indirect utility ranking*. (The indirect utility of a set is the utility of its most-preferred element.) This is a welfarist measure of the ability of opportunity sets to satisfy the individual's preferences. Sen, however, is not a welfarist; he wants to allow options to contribute to the extent of freedom even if they would not be chosen. Thus, he tries to find a measure of opportunity which takes account both of preference-satisfaction and of the number of options. [. . .]

Here I need to expand the notation. From now on, I shall use P, R and I to denote the relations of strict preference, weak preference and indifference on the set of options. Throughout, I shall assume that preferences are complete (that is, for all x, y in X: xRy or yRx) and transitive. In this section, I shall consider methods for ranking opportunity sets (that is, methods for deriving the relation $\geq$) which use as data the actual preference ordering R of the relevant person.

In place of the No Choice principle, Sen proposes the following principle:

P4. *Extension.* For all options x, y: $\{x\} \geq \{y\} \Leftrightarrow x \, R \, y$.

This makes the relation $\geq$ an 'extension' of the preference R. In this way, Sen requires that his measure of freedom takes some account of preference-satisfaction.

The idea that non-chosen options can contribute to the extent of freedom is contained in Sen's principle of *weak preference dominance*, which is equivalent to the conjunction of the following two principles (Nehring and Puppe[5]):

P5. *Weak Monotonicity.* For all opportunity sets A, B: if B is a strict subset of A, then $A \geq B$.

P6. *Preference-based Independence.* For all opportunity sets A, and for all options x, y $\notin$ A: if x R y, then $A \cup \{x\} \geq A \cup \{y\}$.

Weak Monotonicity says that the addition of options to an opportunity set cannot reduce the extent of freedom. Preference-based Independence seems to depend on two intuitions: that opportunity is additive, and that the 'opportunity value' of an option depends on its position in the preference ordering. Thus, the more preferred an option is, the more it contributes to the extent of freedom.

The principle of Preference-based Independence has the same flaw as the simpler Independence principle P2: it prevents us from taking account of diversity. Consider the example of room heaters, under the assumption that the relevant individual is indifferent between the two options 15 and 19. Then, by Preference-based Independence, we have $\{15, 15.01\} \sim \{15.01, 19\}$. If there is an argument for ranking these two sets equally, as Sen asks us to do, it would seem to be something like the following. Each set has the same number of options, and thus offers the same 'sheer quantity' of choice. Further, since the options in the two sets are either identical (15.01 appears in both sets) or equally preferred (the individual is indifferent between 15 and 19), these sets are equivalent to one another in terms of the individual's preference. Thus (it could be said) the two sets give equal amounts of opportunity. Clearly, what is wrong with this argument is that it fails to compare the extent of diversity in the two sets. The lesson to be learned, I suggest, is that we cannot measure diversity merely by using information about how options are ranked in the individual's preference ordering.

Klaus Nehring and Clemens Puppe [. . .] point out a further problem for Sen's approach. Suppose that the set of conceivable options is not finite, and that options can be located in some continuous space of physical characteristics. Then it seems natural to require that small changes in the physical descriptions of opportunity sets are not associated with discontinuous shifts in the ranking of those sets. But if we add this kind of continuity requirement to Sen's principles, we end up with the indirect utility criterion: the ranking of opportunity sets can take no account of options that would not be chosen, or of the number of options available.

To see how this result comes about, consider again the example of room heaters. Suppose the individual weakly prefers 16 to 18. Now consider the opportunity sets B = {16, 16 + e} and C = {16 + e, 18} where e is any small non-negative number. If e is greater than zero (and less than 2), Preference-based Independence implies B ≥ C. But if e is exactly equal to zero, we have B = {16} and C = {16, 18} and so, by Weak Monotonicity, C ≥ B. If there is not to be a discontinuity in ≥ at e = 0, we must have B ~ C at that point. Thus, given Sen's conditions and a continuity requirement, we can show that a two-option set (i.e., {16, 18}) is ranked equally with the singleton set (i.e., {16}) which contains the more preferred of those two options. Nehring and Puppe's result is a generalization of this conclusion.

The Significance of Potential Preferences

It is a mistake, I suggest, to try to base a measure of opportunity on an individual's *actual* preferences. To make sense of the concept of opportunity, we need to consider *potential preferences* – the range of preferences that the individual might have had in the relevant circumstances. [. . .]

Going back to the complimentary drinks example, I take it that a choice between beer, mineral water and wine (opportunity set A) offers more opportunity than a choice between four barely distinguishable cans of beer (opportunity set B) – even for a person who actually chooses beer. Why is this? If the

answer is that A offers more diversity, what does that mean? I suggest that A offers more diversity because a passenger in the circumstances of the example *might have had* a moderately strong preference for any of the three different drinks over the others, while it is hard to imagine her being other than indifferent between the four cans of beer.

The position for which I am arguing is to be distinguished from the argument that *flexibility* – that is, the current prospect of a wide range of opportunities in the future – has instrumental value to a utility-maximizing individual who is uncertain of her future preferences [. . .]. Proponents of measures of opportunity based on actual preference have rejected the flexibility approach as inappropriate for cases in which preferences are known [. . .]. But my argument is not instrumental in this sense. My claim is that *counterfactual* preferences are relevant for the measurement of opportunity.

Why are counterfactual preferences relevant? The answer to this question depends on what we are trying to achieve by measuring opportunity. One reason for looking for such a measure is that opportunity is seen as contributing to an individual's overall good, either because autonomy is held to have intrinsic value or because the act of choosing tends to cultivate valuable human faculties. On either view, we have to conceive of choice as an autonomous act. That is, we must work within a framework which leaves open what, from the set of options open to her, an individual actually chooses. If preferences are interpreted as dispositions to make specific choices, we cannot also treat them as given data: they must be understood as the product of a process of deliberation in which the agent decides what to choose. Thus, if we wish to measure 'opportunity as autonomy' or 'opportunity as exercise', we must consider the whole range of potential preferences which a person might have held, and not merely the ones on which she finally acts.

Alternatively, we might be trying to achieve a satisfactory theory of justice. Recall that one of the main reasons for defining justice in terms of opportunity rather than welfare is to ensure that an individual's claims of justice are not dependent on her preferences. The whole point of using opportunity in place of welfare would be defeated if each individual's opportunities were measured in terms of her own preferences. Thus, if preference is to be at all relevant to justice, we need to find some conception of preference that applies across individuals and that is independent of each individual's *actual* preferences. Potential preference is one such conception.

Compare Rawls's concept of primary goods. Primary goods are things that normally have a use whatever a person's rational plan of life; in the language of preferences, we might say that they are things that normally have value whatever a person's preferences. In other words, the more primary goods a person has, the better able he is to satisfy his preferences, whatever those preferences may happen to be. Rawls's veil of ignorance provides one way of making sense of potential preferences. The veil of ignorance prevents the contracting parties from using knowledge about the actual preferences they have as individuals: all they are allowed to use is knowledge about the psychology and sociology of preferences in general. Notice that Rawls is not assuming that people really are uncertain about their preferences. His claim is that, when thinking about justice, they should reason *as if* they did not know their preferences. We might think of the contracting parties' general psychological and sociological knowledge as delimiting a set of potential preferences. Using only this knowledge, Rawls thinks, each contracting party can recognize that primary goods are valuable to her. It is a natural extension of this idea to argue that a measure of primary-good opportunity should be based on potential preferences.

If we take any of these approaches, we must be able to identify potential preferences. Although the idea of measuring opportunity in terms of potential preferences has been discussed by a number of writers, little has been said about how such preferences should be

interpreted. There seems to be no way of avoiding appeal to contestable ideas of 'normal', 'reasonable' or 'natural' preferences. For example, I take size 42 shoes. Is my range of opportunity increased if a given style of shoe is available in size 38 as well as size 42? I think not. Given the size of my foot, a preference for size 38 shoes seems too perverse to be taken seriously as a potential preference. But I can remember a time when, among men, a preference for wearing an earring would have seemed just as perverse. Or take the case of the complimentary drinks. I have claimed that the passenger's set of potential preferences does not include strong preferences between different batch numbers on beer cans. But we know that wine connoisseurs set great store by differences between wines that other people would regard as hardly less trivial.

The idea that we can measure opportunity by taking account of potential preferences rests uneasily between two opposing positions. One position is the claim that a person's preferences are fully determined by psychological and social influences, and that no counterfactual preferences can properly be regarded as 'potential'. If we accept this position, a metric based on potential preference collapses to indirect utility. The opposite position is that *all* conceivable preferences are within the range of possibility for an autonomous agent, and that all should count as 'potential'. If we accept this position, the idea of potential preference becomes empty, and we are back to the problem of trying to measure opportunity as some kind of pure quantity.

There is no hiding the seriousness of these difficulties. I can see two alternative ways of getting round them.

One is to appeal to an objective but pluralistic account of the good. This seems to be Sen's strategy. He says that the philosophical basis of his approach is Aristotelian, and that in a capability-based assessment of justice, individual claims are to be assessed 'by the freedoms [persons] actually enjoy to choose lives that they have reason to value'.[6] The idea seems to be that an opportunity set is valuable to the extent that it contains options that might, *with good reason*, be chosen; for a given person, there may be more than one reasonable choice. Translating into the language of this paper, we might say that for a given individual there can be a range of different rankings of options, each of which corresponds with a different but equally valid conception of her good. The set of potential preferences might then be identified with this set of valid rankings in terms of goodness. For example, it might be said that relaxation and achievement are both goods for human beings, but that these two goods can reasonably be weighted in many different ways. A person whose opportunity set includes a beach holiday and a rock-climbing holiday can then be said to have a potential preference for each holiday over the other – irrespective of her actual preferences. But if wearing shoes which are too small for one's feet does not contribute to any dimension of human good, then the corresponding counterfactual preferences do not count as 'potential'.

Those who are sceptical about the existence of objective goodness – even of this pluralist kind – may be more inclined to take the second route round these difficulties. This is to use a sociological interpretation of potential preference. Consider some *reference class* of individuals, defined by characteristics other than their current preferences – for example, the class of middle-aged British men. Each individual in this class has his own actual preferences. We might define the set of potential preferences for each member of a reference class as comprising the actual preferences of all members. The idea here is that if someone who is sufficiently like me in terms of non-preference characteristics has a particular preference ordering, then that preference ordering is to be regarded as one that I might have had.

This second approach is perhaps most defensible if we are looking for a measure of opportunity that can be used in a theory of justice, and if we think of such a theory in contractarian terms. Rawls describes his own strategy of focusing on primary goods as a 'simplifying device', and as representing an agreement on 'the most feasible way to establish a publicly recognized objective measure of people's situations'.[7] Thus, Rawls does not claim that his index of primary goods is the true measure of a person's opportunity to achieve well-being. Rather, he claims that each member of society will be able to agree that this measure should be used within a public conception of justice. Rawls seems to be arguing that the primary-goods metric will command attention as a potential point of agreement for individuals who recognize the need for a public standard of justice, but who lack a common conception of the good. In the same spirit, we might ask what interpretation of 'potential preference' could be agreed on by individuals who recognized the need for a public measure of primary-good opportunity. An interpretation which is to function in this way must be straightforward; it must be operational; and it must be neutral as between different conceptions of the good. A sociological approach, in which a person's potential preferences are defined by reference to the actual preferences of those who are like him in non-preference respects, might meet those requirements.

I hope I have persuaded the reader that, if we are to arrive at a satisfactory measure of opportunity, we need some concept of potential preference. I recognize that I have provided no more than two rough sketches of how such preferences might be interpreted. Much more work needs to be done here. Nevertheless, these sketches may be enough to allow us to make some progress in thinking about the relationship between potential preferences and opportunity.

Range of Opportunity Versus Scope for Significant Choosing

To take account of potential preferences, a further element of notation is needed. Let R_i be a typical relation of potential weak preference, with P_i and I_i denoting the corresponding relations of strict preference and indifference. Each relation R_i is taken to be complete and transitive on X. Recall that I have assumed X to be finite; thus, the set of logically possible preference relations is finite too. The set of all potential preferences is Q: = $\{R_1, \ldots, R_n\}$. Q does not necessarily contain every logically possible ordering of X; it includes only those orderings that are identified as 'potential' by whatever criterion we are using. For a given Q, the problem is to rank opportunity sets in terms of the transitive relation $\geq$ ('gives at least as much opportunity as'). I shall now look at some restrictions that might be imposed on that relation.

Jones and I[8] have considered the following two principles:

P7. *Addition of Eligible Options.* For all opportunity sets S, and for all options $x \notin S$: if there exists some $R_i \in Q$ such that $x \, P_i \, y$ for all $y \in S$, then $S \cup \{x\} > S$.

P8. *Addition of Ineligible Options.* For all opportunity sets S, and for all options $x \notin S$: if there does not exist any $R_i \in Q$ such that $x \, P_i \, y$ for all $y \in S$, then $S \cup \{x\} \sim S$.

An option is *eligible* in relation to a set S if, according to at least one potential preference relation, that option is strictly preferred to every element of S. P7 requires that whenever an eligible option is added to an opportunity set, the expanded set offers more opportunity than does the original set. Notice that, whichever of the potential preference relations is actual, the addition of an option (whether eligible or not) cannot make the chooser worse off. Further, if the additional option is eligible, there is at least one potential preference relation such that the expansion of the opportunity set allows the chooser to become better off. Thus it seems natural to say that the addition of an eligible option expands the range of opportunity.

P8 requires that whenever an ineligible option is added to an opportunity set, the expanded set offers exactly as much opportunity as does the original set. The idea here is

that, whichever of the set of potential preference relations is actual, the addition of an ineligible option does not allow the individual to become any better off than she could be in its absence. In this sense, the addition of an ineligible option adds nothing to the range of opportunity offered by a set.

Notice the following implication of P8. Consider any options x, y such that xI_iy is true for all potential preferences R_i. (Think of the cans of beer that are identical except for their batch numbers.) Then if an opportunity set contains one of these two options, the amount of opportunity it offers is unaffected if the other option is added to or subtracted from the set. Thus, for example, for any third option z we have $\{x, z\} \sim \{x, y, z\} \sim \{y, z\}$. As far as opportunity is concerned, then, it is just as if x and y were not distinct options at all. Indeed, in the spirit of Broome's discussion of 'rational requirements of indifference',[9] we might stipulate that options should not be individuated beyond the point at which there exists a potential strict preference. (In the case of the beer cans, we might define a single option, 'a can of beer', which refers to any one of x and y.)

Jones and I show that the conjunction of these two principles is inconsistent with the principle of No Choice (P3 . . .). To see how this inconsistency arises, consider the case of two options x, y, such that all potential preferences rank x above y (think of the dental operations discussed [above]). In this case, x is eligible in relation to $\{y\}$ while y is ineligible in relation to $\{x\}$. Thus the principle of Addition of Eligible Options implies $\{x, y\} > \{y\}$, while the principle of Addition of Ineligible Options implies $\{x, y\} \sim \{x\}$. Transitivity then implies $\{x\} > \{y\}$, contrary to the principle of No Choice.

This simple impossibility result highlights an inconsistency between two different ways of thinking about the value of opportunity, corresponding with the two sides of the debate over the principle of No Choice, discussed [above]. If we think of opportunity as autonomy, or of primary-good opportunity, we will compare sets by asking which offers the *wider range of opportunity*. Thus, we should reject the principle of No Choice, while accepting the other two principles. In the case in which all potential preferences rank x above y, we should conclude that {x} offers a wider range of opportunity than {y}.

In contrast, if one thinks of opportunity as exercise, one will try to measure the *scope for significant choosing* that is generated by an opportunity set. Then the principle of No Choice should be accepted: a singleton opportunity set provides no scope at all for any kind of choosing. Arguably, the principle of Addition of Ineligible Options is also acceptable. An ineligible option, we might say, is one that the chooser need not deliberate about, since whatever his preferences, there is never a reason to choose it (and it alone). Thus, the addition of an ineligible option does not make the decision problem any more or less challenging. However, the principle of Addition of Eligible Options should certainly be rejected. For example, if all potential preferences rank x above y, then the choice problem {x, y} is just as trivial as the problem {x}: whatever the chooser's preferences, there is only one option in {x, y} that could possibly be worth choosing.

This point can be made more starkly by considering a case in which the addition of an eligible option *reduces* the scope for significant choice. Suppose there are three options v, w, x, such that all potential preferences rank x above both v and w, but some potential preferences rank v above w while others rank w above v. For example, suppose that x is having a dental operation without either pain or later side-effects, v is having the same operation with pain but no side-effects, and w is having the operation with no pain but with an anaesthetic that has unpleasant side-effects. The development of new anaesthetics expands the opportunity set from {v, w} to {v, w, x}. It

seems clear that the larger set offers a wider range of opportunity: it caters more effectively to the range of potential preferences. But does it offer more scope for significant choosing? I suggest that it offers *less*. The smaller set requires the chooser to make a significant decision about his life, while the decision problem presented by the larger set is trivial. No doubt the former decision is one we would all prefer not to have to make, but why should we expect the development of valuable faculties to be pleasurable?

This analysis shows once again that we cannot sensibly discuss the formal properties of a metric of opportunity without first specifying the interpretation of opportunity we are using. [...]

Notes

1 Ian Carter, "The Independent Value of Freedom," *Ethics* 105 (1995), p. 21.
2 Ian Carter, "The Measurement of Pure Negative Freedom," *Political Studies* 40 (1992), p. 46.
3 Amartya Sen, "Welfare, Preference, and Freedom," *Journal of Econometrics* 50 (1991), pp. 15–29.
4 Ibid., p. 22.
5 K. Nehring and C. Puppe, "Continuous Extensions of on Order on a Set to the Power Set," *Journal of Economic Theory* 68 (1996), pp. 456–79.
6 A. Sen, *Inequality Reexamined* (Oxford: Oxford University Press, 1992), pp. 39, 81.
7 John Rawls, *A Theory of Justice* (Cambridge, MA: Harvard University Press, 1971), p. 95.
8 Peter Jones and Robert Sugden. "Evaluating Choice," *International Review of Law and Economics* 2 (1982), pp. 47–65.
9 John Broome, *Weighing Goods* (Oxford: Blackwell, 1991), pp. 104–7.

Robert Sugden, "The Metric of Opportunity," *Economics and Philosophy* 14 (1998), pp. 311–12, 316–29.

Chapter 86

Martin van Hees, from
Legal Reductionism and
Freedom (2000)

Strategies and
Opportunity Sets

In the previous chapter [of *Legal Reductionism and Freedom*] we saw that although the axiomatic-deductive approach has yielded some important new insights, it cannot be concluded that it has led to the final answer to the question of how to determine a person's freedom of choice. First of all, the analysis has been carried out in a rather abstract setting. As we saw, an individual is confronted with a set of alternatives from which it can choose one alternative. The elements of the person's opportunity set, as the set of available choice options was called, is not specified further; they could be actions, goods, commodity bundles, etc. Secondly, the opportunity set is exogenously given and no reference is made to the institutional framework in which individuals usually have to make their choices. Finally, different opinions exist about which conditions to impose on a freedom ranking. A distinction can be drawn between authors who believe that a ranking of freedom should somehow be dependent on the (actual, potential or reasonable) preferences of the individuals involved and those who believe that no such reference to individual preferences is necessary. It was argued that the non-preference-based approaches are more suitable. A preference-based approach conflates the measurement of freedom with the measurement of the *value* of freedom. An important problem

for the non-preference-based approaches is how to take account of the similarity or dissimilarity of the options open for choice. Carter's alternative approach offered an important contribution to the analysis of this problem. However, his approach presupposes a substantial amount of information about the options that are available as well as about the possible states of the world with which they are compatible.

In order to apply the axiomatic-deductive approach to the analysis and measurement of overall legal freedom, I shall first of all reformulate the various definitions and assumptions in the game-theoretic framework, thus giving more institutional 'flesh' to the approach. A set of rights resembles an opportunity set in the sense that it describes the things an individual is allowed to do, but it differs from it in an important sense. In the literature on freedom of choice, the individual opportunity sets consist of specific outcomes, whereas a set of rights consists of *sets* of outcomes. By adopting a particular strategy I ensure that the set of possible outcomes is reduced to a subset of S [where S is the set of all feasible alternatives], but I cannot ensure which one of those possible outcomes eventually will be the actual outcome: usually that will also depend on the strategies adopted by others. In contrast, the notion of opportunity sets suggests that an individual can uniquely determine the final outcome.[1] Since we are interested in legal freedom and are thus interested in the rights individuals have, we should focus on freedom comparisons of sets of rights rather than of opportunity sets consisting of single elements. A rights structure was defined as a specification of a set of rights for each individual, and we can therefore also say that the problem of measuring overall legal freedom comes down to comparing different rights structures in terms of the amount of freedom they provide. Note that we hereby explicitly take account of the possible behaviour of other individuals. After all, in real life we are not confronted with sets of alternatives from which we can choose whatever we like; our range of options will depend on what others do. In other words, rather than measuring freedom in *parametric situations*, we do so in a *strategic situation*, thereby doing more justice to the intuition that freedom is a social concept. By describing opportunity sets in terms of the strategies of a legal-political game we also avoid having to treat opportunity sets necessarily as exogenously given. By analysing hierarchies of game forms we can [. . .] offer an explanation of the existence of specific rights and thus of opportunity sets. We then embed a person's opportunity set in an institutional framework, to wit, in the context of a legal system.

A Measure of
Legal Freedom and
Some Problems

By construing an opportunity set as a set of sets of outcomes, we come closer to the approach adopted by Carter [see Chapter 82 of this volume]. As we saw [previously, in *Legal Reductionism and Freedom*], in his measurement of freedom the notion of compossibility sets plays an important role. The sets of outcomes that an opportunity set forms can be viewed as the sets of states of the world that are compatible with the strategy (i.e., right) in question. A compossibility set was defined as a *set of actions* which are mutually compatible and not as a set of outcomes. However, a strategy itself is a bundle of actions, which by feasibility of the strategy in question are assumed to be mutually compatible. For instance, if I have

a feasible strategy which can be described as the strategy of 'eating Chinese while drinking a beer', then the actions 'eating Chinese' and 'drinking beer' are compossible. In other words, a strategy itself can be seen as describing actions that are compossible. We saw that an application of Carter's freedom measure proceeds by examining, for each possible action, the actions with which it is compossible. Since we refer only to strategies and not to the actions constituting those strategies, one might be inclined to infer that the game-theoretic framework cannot be reconciled with Carter's approach. However, since we describe strategies in terms of the outcomes to which they can lead, there might be a way of circumventing this problem. Suppose, for simplicity's sake, that there are only four possible states of the world: say x 'to eat Chinese while drinking a beer', y 'to eat Chinese and not drink anything', z 'not eating Chinese but drinking a glass of red wine', v 'not eating Chinese and not drinking anything'. Furthermore, assume that the result of my actions is uniquely determined: my first strategy leads to x, my second to y, etc. Each combination of these outcomes describes a possible aspect of the world that might be determined by an action of mine. For instance, the outcomes x and y are characterised by the fact that I will be eating Chinese. If I have a strategy that always leads to either x or y, then I can be said to be able to perform the action of eating Chinese. Similarly, the set of outcomes $\{x,z\}$ describe states of the world in which I will be drinking something. Hence, if I have a strategy that always leads to an element of $\{x,z\}$, then I can perform the act of drinking something. If I have a strategy that always leads to x, then I can perform the act of drinking beer – another possible aspect of the world. The close relationship between actions and outcomes enables us also to say something about the various actions that are feasible. If S denotes the set of possible outcomes, *each* non-empty subset of S denotes a possible aspect of the world which results from the performance of a particular action of mine. This might seem strange: take, for example, the set of outcomes $\{x,v\}$. In x I eat Chinese and drink while in *v* I do neither. To what extent can this set with completely opposing alternatives denote an aspect of the world that I can determine by an action of mine? Well, it can correspond with the action of *not* deciding whether one eats Chinese or drinks something. In the terminology of Chapter 4 [of *Legal Reductionism* . . .], it corresponds with the action of *staying passive* with respect to the issue of eating and drinking. Having such rights to stay passive also contributes to one's freedom and should therefore be reckoned with.

This approach can be used to give a game-theoretic formulation of Carter's measure. A legal-political game describes the strategies of an individual, the outcomes to which those strategies can lead, and the set of all feasible outcomes S. For each non-empty subset *A* of outcomes, one then determines how many strategies of the individual guarantee that the outcome will belong to this set. Ignoring probabilities, this number yields the equivalent of Carter's F_a [i.e. the number of sets of compossible actions of which action *a* is a member]. Denoting this number as F_A we get

$$F_A = \#\{A|A \in [S] \text{ and } A \text{ is a}$$
$$\text{subset of some } B \in R(i)\}$$

where [S] denotes the set of non-empty subsets of S [and R_i denotes the set of rights of individual *i*]. Adding all the numbers for each *A* yields the (non-probabilistic) counterpart of Carter's nominator:

$$F = \sum_{A \in [S]} F_A.$$

Since [. . .] it will be assumed henceforth that the state of technological feasibility remains constant, and hence also the set of technologically feasible outcomes, we can ignore the question of whether the use of a ratio is appropriate or not. The question now is: to what extent can *F* indeed be taken to describe a person's overall legal freedom?

The measure *F* has some clear advantages compared to, for instance, the simple count-ing rule of Pattanaik and Xu. By interpreting an opportunity set as the set of admissible strategies an individual has in a legal-political game, it makes clear that individuals perform actions in strategic rather than parametric situations. Furthermore, the reference to a legal-political game makes clear the extent to which institutional factors determine our freedom.

[. . .]

Strong Monotonicity and Dominance

Given the various problems that we have encountered in trying to find an ideal freedom measure, there are two possible ways of trying to say something about the consequences of having a certain degree of legal freedom. A first route would be to take a freedom measure that somehow approximates best what we feel to be an ideal freedom measure. While acknowledging the non-ideal nature of one's measure, one proceeds with the analysis. Another is to say that although it might be as yet unclear what an ideal measure would be like, we can say that all such measures should satisfy certain conditions and then proceed with the analysis of *all* freedom measures that do indeed satisfy these conditions. I shall adopt this second approach here. In particular, I shall assume that freedom rankings should satisfy at least two conditions: comparisons of a particular person's degree of freedom should satisfy the axiom of strong monotonicity, and comparisons of collective freedom should satisfy an axiom of dominance.

In Section 6.6 [of *Legal Reductionism*] we have already discussed the axiom of strong monotonicity, but it was defined there in terms of ordinary opportunity sets and not in terms of sets of rights. Its formulation in terms of the rights of an individual is as follows:

Strong monotonicity. For all sets of rights $R(i)$ and all rights A not belonging to $R(i)$: the union of $R(i)$ and A offers strictly more freedom than A.

In other words, if an individual obtains an extra right, then his legal freedom will always increase. To apply the axiom, compare examples 1 and 2 [denoted by R_1 and R_2] (where the first and second component of an outcome refer[s] to person i and person j, respectively, taking a bike or the only available car):

$$R(i):\ \{(b,b)\}$$
$$\{(c,b)\}$$

$$R(j):\ \{(b,b),(c,b)\}$$

Rights structure R_1

$$R(i):\ \{(b,b),\ (b,c)\}$$
$$\{(c,b)\}$$

$$R(j):\ \{(b,c),\ (c,b)\}$$
$$\{(b,b),\ (c,b)\}$$

Rights structure R_2

Person j's legal freedom has increased. In the second situation he not only has the unconditional right to take a bike (the right described by the set $\{(b,b),(c,b)\}$) but also the conditional right to take the car ($\{(b,c),\ (c,b)\}$). On the other hand, on the basis of only the axiom of strong monotonicity we cannot infer whether i's legal freedom has increased or decreased. She has lost the right to exclude j from taking the car when she herself takes a bike, viz., the right $\{(b,b)\}$, but has acquired in return the right to enable j to take the car if he takes a bike, viz., the right $\{(b,b),\ (b,c)\}$. Now take the rights structure of example 3:

$$R(i):\ \{(b,b)\}$$
$$\{(b,b),(b,c)\}$$
$$\{(c,b)\}$$

$$R(j):\ \{(b,b),(b,c),(c,b)\}$$
$$\{(b,b),(c,b)\}$$

Rights structure R_3

Applying the axiom of strong monotonicity, we see that this rights structure offers i strictly more freedom than R_1 and R_2. Each of the rights she possesses in the first two rights

structures, she possesses in the third as well. Furthermore, with respect to both of the other situations, she has an extra right. In the first rights structure she does not have the right to enable j to take the car (the right $\{(b,b),\ (b,c)\}$), in the second situation she does not have the right to ensure that they both take a bike (the right $\{(b,b)\}$). As far as the legal freedom of j is concerned, strong monotonicity implies that the third rights structure gives him more legal freedom than the first. On the basis of only the axiom of strong monotonicity, j's freedom in the second and third rights structure cannot be compared. Compared to the second situation, individual j has obtained a new right but has also lost one.

There are several possible objections to imposing the condition of strong monotonicity, most of which have already been touched upon. To recapitulate briefly, one might, first of all, argue that an expansion of one's rights only leads to an increase of that individual's overall legal freedom if at least part of that extra individual freedom is in some sense valuable. Suppose I obtain an extra right that I would never consider exercising, say the right to cut my toes off. As was discussed extensively in the context of preference-based approaches to freedom, the argument conflates the measurement of the degree of freedom an individual enjoys with the measurement of the value of the freedom of that individual. Secondly, it could be maintained that the axiom only makes sense if the extra rights which individuals obtain differ substantially from the rights those individuals already had. Now, although it may be true that the increase of one's freedom in such circumstances may be rather insignificant, there are at least some aspects of the world which you can change and which you hitherto could not. In other words, the increase may be small, but it remains an increase. Another possible objection was based on the view that an expansion of one's rights need not entail an increase of one's freedom if that expansion is also accompanied by an expansion of the things one is not allowed to do. However, this can only be taken to imply a violation of strong monotonicity if these expansions result from a change of the set of technological feasible outcomes.[2] I have assumed, however, that this set stays fixed. We therefore conclude that, as in the case of the measurement of freedom of choice, a measurement of the aggregate level of legal freedom of an individual should always satisfy the axiom of strong monotonicity: if an individual obtains extra legal permissions, his or her legal freedom increases.

Thus far we have spoken about the degree of legal freedom *individuals* can be said to enjoy. The second condition that I shall impose refers to comparisons of *collective* freedom. The notion of freedom is often used in a more general sense. We say, for instance, that there is more freedom in the United States than there is in Libya, that there now is more freedom in Poland than there was twenty years ago, or that the implementation of a certain policy would entail a reduction in the amount of freedom in a society. How can such collective freedom judgements be made, how are they related to individual freedom rankings? Suppose that, despite the difficulties [. . .], we do know for each individual how to rank the various legal systems in terms of the legal freedom he or she enjoys within them. How, on the basis of this information, can we derive a collective freedom judgement, i.e., a ranking of these legal systems in terms of the amount of collective freedom?

Sometimes it seems that that there are no real collective freedom judgements and that they are simply shorthand ways of expressing a large number of individual freedom judgements. To say that there is less freedom in

Libya than in the U.S. could mean, for instance, that the degree of legal freedom of *any* U.S. citizen is larger than that of *any* Libyan citizen. And, indeed, when comparing countries which differ greatly in terms of their respect for individual rights and liberties we often seem to adopt such an interpretation. Yet even in these apparently clear-cut cases such an interpretation is not always justified. It is simply not true that each citizen in a democracy in which basic rights and liberties are respected enjoys more freedom than each citizen in a dictatorship that grossly violates some of those rights and liberties. Although in the latter situation there are obviously many individuals worse off freedom-wise, there is – almost by definition – at least one individual who enjoys a lot of freedom and who is, at least as far as his freedom is concerned, better off than in a democracy: the dictator.

In other words, when we speak about the general level of freedom in a society, and hence also when we speak about the general level of legal freedom offered by a legal system, we are often making genuine collective freedom judgements. The degree of freedom the various individuals enjoy is considered first, and then some sort of balancing and weighing procedure is applied to arrive at a collective freedom judgement. There is thus an aggregation procedure which takes the individual freedom rankings over the set of legal systems as its input and which produces a collective freedom ranking [see Figure 86.1].

In the discussion of the various ways in which an individual freedom ranking can be derived, we did not come up with a defence of a particular procedure but noted that any such procedure should at least satisfy the

Figure 86.1

axiom of strong monotonicity. In a similar vein, I shall not try to defend a particular aggregation procedure for deriving collective freedom rankings, but merely argue that any such procedure should satisfy at least one axiom. This axiom is in the same spirit as the monotonicity axiom:

> Dominance. If A is a legal system in which all individuals enjoy at least as much legal freedom as in legal system B, and if there is at least one individual who enjoys strictly more legal freedom in A, then legal system A offers more legal freedom than legal system B.

Some of the arguments that were raised against the axiom of strong monotonicity could also be raised against the axiom of dominance. For instance, one might claim that the axiom ignores the value of the extra rights obtained by individuals. In this perspective, one might doubt whether increases in individual levels of collective freedom that nobody values really result in an increase in the level of collective freedom. Similarly, it might be argued that no real increase in the level of collective freedom occurs if the increases in the individual level of legal freedom are the result of obtaining permissions that are almost similar to the ones one already had. However, such criticism can be rejected for the very same reasons as it was rejected in the context of individual freedom judgements: it either conflates the measurement of the value of collective freedom with the measurement of collective freedom as such, or it fails to recognise that the increase in the level of overall collective freedom can be very small. In the next section we discuss a different line of criticism, one that is based on the assumption that one can only speak about an increase in the level of collective freedom if extra individual rights and liberties are allocated *equally* among all subjects.

Dominance and Equality

There seems to be an important relationship between the level of collective freedom in a society and the degree of equality or inequality in which the rights and liberties are allocated in society. Consider again the comparison between a dictatorship and a democracy. One of the reasons for saying that there is more legal freedom in a democracy than in a dictatorial regime is the fact that in a democracy individuals are equal before the law. Liberals (and libertarians) might therefore claim that one should maximise *equal freedom*. Such a principle might, for instance, be derived from Rawls whose first principle of justice reads that 'each person is to have an equal right to the most extensive basic liberty compatible with a similar liberty for others'.[3] To argue for a theory of justice in which the notion of maximising equal freedom plays an important role, however, does not imply that collective freedom judgements should depend, in one way or another, on the equal distribution of rights and liberties in a society. On the contrary, to say that one should maximise equal freedom implies that one can maximise freedom in an unequal way, too. If collective freedom can only be said to be maximised if everybody enjoys the same degree of freedom, it would be redundant to speak about a principle of maximal *equal* freedom. Maximal freedom, then, always is maximal equal freedom.

It might, however, also be maintained that collective freedom itself implies a certain degree of equality in the distribution of rights. Philippe van Parijs [. . .] has argued that a free society is a society in which a well-enforced structure of rights ensuring *security* exists, in which each person 'owns herself' under this structure and in which *leximin opportunity* obtains. The latter requirement means that everyone's opportunity is maximised subject to the condition that the maximisation of the opportunities of the persons with least opportunities is lexically prior to the maximisation of the opportunities of those who have more. If these three conditions are satisfied the society is said to provide *leximin freedom* or – as Van Parijs also calls it – *real freedom for all*.

It is not entirely clear whether Van Parijs assumes leximin freedom to be a dichotomous variable – freedom does or does not exist in society – or whether he permits the possibility of different degrees of leximin freedom. If one assumes that it is a dichotomous variable, it follows almost directly that individuals can be given extra rights and liberties without yet realising a society in which freedom is obtained. Consider a rather repressive society in which none of the individuals enjoys freedom of speech and suppose it is transformed into a somewhat less repressive society in which all of the individuals are now free to express any opinion they like, although they still lack a large number of other basic rights and liberties. Since freedom is still not achieved – assuming that the individuals lack security in both situations – and since collective freedom is a dichotomous variable, the transformation is from an unfree society to an unfree society. The allocation of extra rights and liberties has not led to an increase in the level of collective freedom and the axiom of dominance is therefore violated.

This particular counter-example to the axiom of dominance rests crucially on the assumption that collective freedom is a dichotomous variable. This assumption is not very plausible, though. It is simply counterintuitive to maintain that the universal grant of rights would not lead to an increase in collective freedom. For instance, we feel that the abolition of slavery has led to a genuine increase of collective freedom in the United States, that the collapse of communism has led to an increase of freedom in Eastern Europe, that the collapse of the apartheid regime has led to more collective freedom in South Africa, etc. Yet we do not believe that the level of individual freedom of each of the citizens in the respective societies was or has been maximised.

Assume therefore that societies can satisfy leximin freedom in different degrees: the more a society satisfies leximin freedom, the more collective freedom it is said to provide. More precisely, to compare society A with society B we first consider the freedom levels of the persons that are worst off freedom-wise in both societies.[4] If the worst-off person of one of the two societies enjoys more legal freedom than the worst-off person in the other society, then the first society is said to give more collective freedom. If the levels of freedom are the same, we compare the freedom of the second worst-off persons. Again, if one of them enjoys more freedom than the other, the society of that person gives more legal freedom than the other society does. If they enjoy the same amount of freedom we compare the levels of freedom of the third worst off persons, etc. It is not very difficult to see that the resulting collective freedom ordering *does* satisfy the axiom of dominance.[5] In other words, our approach is quite compatible with a conception of collective freedom in which equality considerations play a role. May there not be other conceptions of collective freedom based on equality consideration that do violate dominance? At first sight, it seems that there may very well be. Take, for instance, a totalitarian regime in which only the dictator obtains certain extra rights. Can it really be the case that this leads to an increase in collective freedom? A positive answer to this question is less counter-intuitive then may seem since the axiom of dominance only warrants such an inference if the level of individual freedom of the other individuals has *not* decreased. Usually, this clause will be violated – if a dictator gains extra freedom, it is often at the expense of his subjects' freedom.[6] It is, I believe, precisely because of this fact that we tend to think that an increase in the dictator's freedom cannot possibly be leading to an overall increase in collective freedom, not because of the increase in inequality. Of course, if the freedom of the subjects would also have been increased, e.g. by giving them also extra rights, the resulting increase in collective freedom would have been much larger.

Thus we see no reason to dispute the axiom of dominance on the basis of the fact that it may entail inequalities in the distribution of freedom. Obviously, this is not to say that collective freedom rankings satisfying the condition of dominance always satisfy demands of equality. In fact, as will be shown in the next section, a legal society may be said to give maximal legal freedom in my sense and at the same time violate elementary demands of equality.

Maximal Legal Freedom

The axioms of strong monotonicity and dominance are in themselves insufficient to compare all rights structures freedom-wise. A collective freedom ordering derived on the basis of the axioms of strong monotonicity and dominance only, will be a partial one. Yet there is a way in which can one speak about a legal system *maximising* freedom on the basis of these conditions only. Intuitively, a legal system is said to maximise freedom if one cannot allocate extra rights without violating at least one of the other rights of the individuals. In other words, a rights structure system offers maximal legal freedom if there is no other rights structure which, given the same group of individuals and the same set of feasible alternatives, dominates it freedom-wise. Furthermore, we shall assume that under maximal freedom, acts in which rights are exercised always yield a *unique* outcome if it is the case that all individuals exercise one of their *strong rights*.

We say that a right A is a strong right of an individual i if the individual has no right with respect to a proper subset of A. To illustrate, suppose there are three alternatives x, y, z and that a certain individual has the rights $\{x,y\}$, $\{y,z\}$, $\{z\}$ and $\{x,y,z\}$. The rights $\{x,y\}$ and $\{z\}$ are then strong rights whereas the rights $\{y,z\}$ and $\{x,y,z\}$ are not: the individual does not have the right to realise a proper subset of $\{x,y\}$ and $\{z\}$, whereas he or she does have such a right with respect to some proper subsets of $\{y,z\}$ and $\{x,y,z\}$. In a way, to exercise a strong right means that an individual reduces the set of feasible alternatives as much as possible. Demanding that the set of outcomes is reduced to a unique outcome when each indi-

vidual exercises his or her strong right therefore has a libertarian flavour. It comes down to demanding that acts of exercising rights can in themselves be sufficient to yield a final outcome: the necessity of having a second stage of public decision making is not presupposed.

Maximal Legal Freedom. Given a group of individuals and a set of feasible outcomes, a rights structure provides maximal legal freedom if, and only if, (a) there is no other rights structure which, given that same group of individuals and the same set of feasible alternatives, dominates it, and (b) no stage of public decision making is needed in case each individual exercises one of his or her strong rights.

In other words, a legal system offers maximal freedom if there is no other legal system which gives all individuals at least as much legal freedom while giving at least one individual strictly more, and if acts of exercising rights can in themselves be sufficient to determine the final outcome. Although, as explained above, the definition is rather strong in the sense that it has a libertarian flavour, it is weak in the sense that there will usually be several legal systems, all of which can be said to offer maximal legal freedom. To see how the definition is applied, consider again the rights structure R_3. The rights structure satisfies the second part of the definition. Individual i has two strong rights $\{(b,b)\}$ and $\{(c,b)\}$, which themselves are singleton sets. Hence a combination with j's strong right, which is $\{(b,b),(c,b)\}$, is also a singleton set. However, the first condition of maximal legal freedom is *not* satisfied. To see why, consider all possible rights that have not been allocated to one or both of the individuals and examine whether they can be given to the individual who does not possess it yet. The only constraint we thereby impose is that the allocation of the right should be feasible, given the rights already possessed by others. For instance, j does not have the right described by $\{(b,b)\}$. Can we give it to him without violating the rights of i? No, for it conflicts with i's right $\{(c,b)\}$: the intersection of $\{(b,b)\}$ and $\{(c,b)\}$ is empty. For the same reasons, it follows that we cannot give j the right $\{(b,c)\}$ or the right $\{(c,b)\}$; it conflicts with i's right $\{(b,b)\}$. Similarly, we cannot give j the right $\{(b,c),(b,b)\}$, it conflicts with i's right $\{(c,b)\}$, or the right $\{(c,b),(b,c)\}$, which conflicts with i's right $\{(b,b)\}$. Thus we cannot expand the set of rights of j without violating some of i's rights. Now consider the rights i does not have yet. She lacks the right $\{(b,c)\}$, but it cannot be given to her without violating j's right $\{(b,b),(c,b)\}$. The other rights which she lacks are $\{(b,c),(c,b)\}$, $\{(b,b),(c,b)\}$ and $\{(b,c),(c,b),(b,b)\}$. Now these rights *can* be given to i without having to violate j's rights. The corresponding rights structure is

$$R(i): \quad \{(b,b)\}$$
$$\{(b,b),(b,c)\}$$
$$\{(c,b)\}$$
$$\{(b,c),(c,b)\}$$
$$\{(b,b),(c,b)\}$$
$$\{(b,c),(c,b),(b,b)\}$$

$$R(j): \quad \{(b,c),(c,b),(b,b)\}$$
$$\{(b,b),(c,b)\}$$

Rights structure R_4

and this rights structure *does* give maximal freedom: one cannot give extra rights to one of the individuals without violating at least one of the rights of the other (note also that the second condition still holds).

It is now not so difficult to see that maximal freedom may be at odds with the demand of equality. Individual i has many more rights than j has, and she is therefore better able to determine the final outcome. Furthermore, it should be noticed that whereas the rights structure R_3 already contained the possibility that the acts of exercising rights do not always yield a unique outcome and that therefore a public decision mechanism is needed, the new rights structure contains many other ways in which the individuals can exercise their rights without thereby determining a unique

outcome. The reason is clear: individual i now has many more ways in which she can decide to stay passive.

Rights to stay passive are an essential element of rights structures satisfying maximal freedom. If I have been given the right to settle some issue A, then I can be given the right to stay passive with respect to A without violating the rights of others. Hence, to satisfy maximal freedom I should be given those rights to stay passive as well. It might be argued that this may entail some form of paternalism, which, in the words of Kant, is the worst form of despotism and thus is at odds with liberalism. After all, why should others be enabled to determine such private matters of mine as whether I will smoke or not, drink a glass of milk or not, wear a blue shirt or not, etc.? However, the charge of paternalism is misplaced since it is, after all, the decision of the individual in question to stay passive. If a certain person decides not to exercise one of her rights, then no paternalism is involved; paternalism does not say that one should always exercise the rights one has. However, what the definition of maximal freedom does imply is that, in a legal system maximising legal freedom, there should be some second stage of public decision making by which the individuals can settle the issues about which they remained passive. In other words, in our perspective, maximal legal freedom *entails* the existence of a public decision making mechanism rather than contradicting it. In this sense, the definition is less 'libertarian' than was first suggested.

In the next chapter I shall discuss the possible value of legal systems securing certain degrees of legal freedom. Before turning to this issue, it should be emphasised that I apply the axioms of strong monotonicity and dominance to the first stage of a legal-political game only. Thus when I speak about degrees of freedom, e.g. maximal legal freedom, I do *not* refer to the level of political freedom individuals enjoy, and when I analyse the possible value of legal freedom I thus ignore the possible value of having political rights and liberties.

Notes

1   However, this is merely an interpretation which is commonly made; it does not follow from the definition itself. One could also have interpreted the set S as a set of non-empty sets of outcomes.

2   Take two situations and denote the set of all feasible alternatives in the first by S_1 and in the second by S_2. Furthermore, in the two situations let the two sets of rights of an individual i be $R_1(i)$ and $R_2(i)$, where $R_1(i)$ is a proper subset of $R_2(i)$. By definition of a rights set the set of i's inadmissible strategies in the two situations is $[S_1] - R_1(i)$ and $[S_2] - R_2(i)$, respectively (where $[S_1]$ and $[S_2]$ denote the set of non-empty subsets of set S_1 and S_2, respectively). But then the set of inadmissible strategies in the first situation, $[S_1] - R_1(i)$, can only be a proper subset of the one in the second if S_1 is a proper subset of S_2.

3   John Rawls, *A Theory of Justice* (Cambridge, MA: Harvard University Press, 1971), p. 60.

4   Note that the possibility of interpersonal comparisons of freedom is presupposed.

5   Suppose the sets of rights of some individuals have expanded, whereas the other individuals all have the same rights as before. Since at least one of the individuals' levels of freedom has increased, there must among the individuals whose freedom has been increased be a person who was ranked lowest freedom-wise among them. Hence, the new situation gives more 'leximin' freedom than the old one.

6   This should not be taken as to imply that I conceive of freedom as having a zero-sum nature, i.e., that the gain of one person's freedom always entails the loss of another person's freedom [. . .].

Martin van Hees, *Legal Reductionism and Freedom* (Dordrecht: Kluwer, 2000) pp. 134–7, 141–50.

Additional Writings

The following bibliography contains only works that are neither excerpted in any of the sections of this anthology nor cited in any of the Further Reading lists.

Introductory Works

Carter, I., "Positive and Negative Liberty," *Stanford Encyclopedia of Philosophy*, http://plato.stanford.edu/entries/liberty-positive-negative/, 2003 ⟨brief general introduction to the literature from Berlin onwards⟩.

Feinberg, J., *Social Philosophy* (Englewood Cliffs, NJ: Prentice-Hall, 1979), ch. 1 ⟨brief introduction focused on freedom as a triadic relation⟩.

Gray, T., *Freedom* (London: Macmillan, 1991) ⟨comprehensive general introduction⟩.

Miller, D., *Liberty* (Oxford: Oxford University Press, 1991), 2nd ed., *The Liberty Reader* (Boulder, CO: Paradigm Publishers, 2006) ⟨unabridged reprints of some influential contemporary essays⟩.

Norman, R., *Free and Equal* (Oxford: Oxford University Press, 1987) ⟨introduction focused on the relation between freedom and equality⟩.

Pelczynski, Z. and Gray, J. (eds.), *Conceptions of Liberty in Political Philosophy* (London: Athlone Press, 1984) ⟨collection of essays organized by thinkers rather than themes⟩.

Other Works

Adler, M. J., *The Idea of Freedom* (New York: Doubleday & Co., 1958).

Arendt, H., "What is Freedom?," in H. Arendt, *Between Past and Future: Six Exercises in Political Thought* (London: Faber and Faber, 1961).

Berman, M. N., "The Normative Functions of Coercion Claims," *Legal Theory* 8 (2002), pp. 45–89.

Brenkert, G. G., *Political Freedom* (London: Routledge, 1991).

Carter, I., "Choice, Freedom and Freedom of Choice," *Social Choice and Welfare* 22 (2004), pp. 61–81.

Charvet, J., *A Critique of Freedom and Equality* (Cambridge: Cambridge University Press, 1981).

Christman, J., "Autonomy and Personal History," *Canadian Journal of Philosophy* 20 (1991), pp. 1–24.

Christman, J. and Anderson, J. (eds.), *Autonomy and the Challenges to Liberalism: New Essays* (Cambridge: Cambridge University Press, 2005).

Cohen, G. A., "Freedom and Money," *Revista Argentina de Teoría Jurídica* 2 (2001), http://www.utdt.edu/departamentos/derecho/publicaciones/rtj1/pdf/finalfreedom.PDF

Cranston, M., *Freedom: A New Analysis* (London: Longman, 1953).

Crocker, L., *Positive Liberty* (London: Nijhoff, 1980).

Daniels, N., "Equal Liberty and Unequal Worth of Liberty," in N. Daniels (ed.), *Reading Rawls* (Oxford: Blackwell, 1975).

De Marneffe, P., "Liberalism, Liberty, and Neutrality," *Philosophy and Public Affairs* 19 (1990), pp. 253–74.

Dowding, K. "Choice: Its Increase and Its Value," *British Journal of Political Science* 22 (1992), pp. 301–14.

Dworkin, R., "Do Liberty and Equality Conflict?," in P. Barker (ed.), *Living as Equals* (Oxford: Oxford University Press, 1998).

Frankfurt, H., "Coercion and Moral Responsibility," in H. Frankfurt, *The Importance of What We Care About* (Cambridge: Cambridge University Press, 1988).

Friedrich, C. J. (ed.), *Nomos IV: Liberty* (New York: Atherton Press, 1962).

Gaus, G. F., *Value and Justification. The Foundations of Liberal Theory* (Cambridge: Cambridge University Press, 1990).

Geuss, R. and Hollis, M., "Freedom as an Ideal," *Proceedings of the Aristotelian Society* suppl. vol. 69 (1995), pp. 87–112.

Gibbs, B., *Freedom and Liberation* (London: Chatto and Windus, 1976).

Gray, J., "Against Cohen on Proletarian Unfreedom," *Social Philosophy and Policy* 6 (1988), pp. 77–112.

Griffiths, A. P. (ed.), *Of Liberty* (Cambridge: Cambridge University Press, 1983).

Hart, H. L. A., "Rawls on Liberty and Its Priority," in N. Daniels (ed.), *Reading Rawls* (Oxford: Blackwell, 1975).

Hayek, F. A., *Law, Legislation and Liberty* (London: Routledge and Kegan Paul, 1982).

Hees, M. van, "Freedom of Choice and Diversity of Options: Some Difficulties," *Social Choice and Welfare* 22 (2004), pp. 253–66.

Hees, M. van and Wissenburg, M., "Freedom and Opportunity," *Political Studies* 47 (1999), pp. 67–82.

Hobhouse, L. T., *Liberalism* (London: Greenwood Press, 1911).

Jones, P. and Sugden, R., "Evaluating Choice," *International Review of Law and Economics* 2 (1982), pp. 47–65.

Laborde, C. and Maynor, J. (eds.), *Republicanism and Political Theory* (Oxford: Blackwell, forthcoming).

Laslier, J., Fleurbaey, M., Gravel, N., and Trannoy, A., *Freedom in Economics: New Perspectives in Normative Analysis* (London: Routledge, 1998).

Lindley, R., *Autonomy* (London: Macmillan, 1986).

Lukes, S., "Equality and Liberty: Must They Conflict?," in D. Held (ed.), *Political Theory Today* (Cambridge: Polity Press, 1991).

Mason, A., "Workers' Unfreedom and Women's Unfreedom: Is There a Significant Analogy?," *Political Studies* 44 (1996), pp. 75–87.

Miller, D., *Market, State, and Community. Theoretical Foundations of Market Socialism* (Oxford: Clarendon Press, 1989).

Milne, A. J. M., *Freedom and Rights* (London: Allen and Unwin, 1968).

Nielsen, K., *Equality and Liberty: A Defence of Radical Egalitarianism* (Totowa, NJ: Rowman and Allanheld, 1985).

Norman, W. J., "Taking 'Free Action' Too Seriously," *Ethics* 101 (1991), pp. 505–20.

Oppenheim, F. E., *Dimensions of Freedom* (New York: St. Martin's Press, 1961).

Oppenheim, F. E., "Social Freedom and Its Parameters," *Journal of Theoretical Politics* 7 (1995), pp. 403–20.

Otsuka, M., "Liberty, Equality, Envy, and Abstraction," in J. Burley (ed.), *Dworkin and His Critics* (Oxford and Malden, MA: Blackwell, 2004), pp. 70–8.

Parent, W. A., "Some Recent Work on the Concept of Liberty," *American Philosophical Quarterly* 11 (1974), pp. 149–67.

Pettit, P., "Agency Freedom and Option Freedom," *Journal of Theoretical Politics* 15 (2003), pp. 387–403.

Pogge, T., "Equal Liberty for All?," *Midwest Studies in Philosophy* 28 (2004), pp. 266–81.

Rawls, J., *Political Liberalism* (New York: Columbia University Press, 1993).

Ryan, A., "Freedom," *Philosophy* 40 (1965), pp. 93–112.

Ryan, A. (ed.), *The Idea of Freedom: Essays in Honour of Isaiah Berlin* (Oxford: Oxford University Press, 1979).

Ryan, C. C., "Yours, Mine, and Ours: Property Rights and Individual Liberty," in J. Paul (ed.), *Reading Nozick* (Oxford: Blackwell, 1982).

Scanlon, T. M., "The Significance of Choice," in S. McMurrin (ed.), *The Tanner Lectures on Human Values*, vol. VIII (Cambridge: Cambridge University Press, 1988).

Sen, A., "Freedom of Choice: Concept and Content," *European Economic Review* 32 (1988), pp. 269–94.

Sen, A., *Development as Freedom* (Oxford: Oxford University Press, 1999).

Skinner, Q., "The Paradoxes of Political Liberty," in S. McMurrin (ed.), *The Tanner Lectures on Human Values*, VII (Cambridge: Cambridge University Press, 1986).

Spector, H., *Autonomy and Rights* (Oxford: Clarendon Press, 1992).

Sugden, R., "Opportunity as a Space for Individuality: Its Value and the Impossibility of Measuring It," *Ethics* 113 (2003), pp. 783–809.

Taylor, M., *Community, Anarchy and Liberty* (London: Cambridge University Press, 1982).

Williams, B., "From Freedom to Liberty: The Construction of a Political Value," *Philosophy and Public Affairs* 30 (2001), pp. 3–26.

Wolff, J., "Freedom, Liberty, and Property," *Critical Review* 11 (1997), pp. 345–57.

Index